STUDIES

IN THE HISTORY OF RELIGIONS

(SUPPLEMENTS TO *NUMEN*)

EDITED BY

M. HEERMA VAN VOSS • E. J. SHARPE • R. J. Z. WERBLOWSKY

XLI

THE REDISCOVERY OF GNOSTICISM

VOLUME TWO

LEIDEN
E. J. BRILL
1981

THE REDISCOVERY OF GNOSTICISM

Proceedings of the
International Conference on Gnosticism at Yale
New Haven, Connecticut, March 28-31, 1978

VOLUME TWO

SETHIAN GNOSTICISM

EDITED BY

BENTLEY LAYTON

LEIDEN
E. J. BRILL
1981

ISBN 90 04 06176 2
90 04 06178 9

PRINTED IN BELGIUM

CONTENTS

PART FOUR

SEMINAR ON SETHIAN GNOSTICISM

PART FIVE
RESEARCH PAPERS

PREFACE

This is the second of two volumes containing papers of the International Conference on Gnosticism, held March 28-31, 1978, on the campus of Yale University in New Haven, Connecticut under the sponsorship of the Yale Department of Religious Studies. In the present volume are published papers on Sethian Gnosticism and on related topics including Judaism and Gnosticism and early Manichaeism, as well as a list of conference participants and indexes to the two volumes. Volume 1 contains the plenary addresses; papers on Valentinian Gnosticism, on the Platonic tradition and Gnosticism, and on the question of Gnostic iconography; and a complete program of the conference.

The focal points of the conference were two seminars in which invited specialists discussed research papers that had been written for the occasion and circulated in advance of the meeting. Both the seminar papers and an extensive record of their discussions are included in the present volumes. The seminar themes were Valentinian Gnosticism and Sethian Gnosticism—or as announced, "the so-called Sethian (Ophite, Barbeloite, Gnostikos, etc.) movement"—two ancient Gnostic traditions for which, it seemed, the most extensive and important new evidence now awaited interpretation and synthesis, thanks to the recent availability of the Nag Hammadi library to scholarship. That such a conference could be held only three months after the last codex of that ancient library had been published in facsimile was only possible because provisional transcriptions and translations had long been in circulation, through the characteristic generosity of the Institute for Antiquity and Christianity.

Shorter papers were also solicited from scholars throughout the world—more than 2,000 persons were contacted—to permit the exchange of information on research in progress: fifty-six papers, twenty minutes in length, were accepted for delivery in parallel thematic sections. All told nearly 300 scholars officially participated as speakers, discussants, or auditors, representing twelve countries and four continents.

A broader synthesis of Gnostic studies as they related to the humanities was attempted in a series of public plenary lectures on "Gnosticism and Western Tradition," which brought to bear four different approaches to the problem of Gnosis: ecclesiastical history, psychology, philosophy, and criticism. In addition, coinciding with the conference there was a special exhibition at the Beinecke Rare Book and Manuscript Library of Yale, "Gnosticism in Word and Image," in which most major branches of Gnosticism were represented: Jewish-Christian Gnosticism (the "Pistis Sophia" manuscript, documentary papyri from the Nag Hammadi library, some Greek "Gospel of Thomas" fragments, the leather cover of the Jung Codex, etc.), Mandaeism, Manichaeism, magic, Hermetism, alchemy, Kabbalah, psychoanalysis. Many of the items had been generously loaned by other institutions and scholars, and to them sincere appreciation must be recorded. The exhibition was supported by a Federal Indemnity from the Federal Council on the Arts and the Humanities.

Readers of these volumes will find especially welcome the detail in which the discussion of each of the seminar papers has been reported. Much of the discussion—conducted largely by specialists deeply involved in the study of Gnosticism—goes beyond the substance of the papers into more general, and sometimes even more significant, questions of method and perspective and avenues of future research. Discussions of the seminar on Valentinian Gnosticism have been edited by Kathryn Johnson, and those on Sethian Gnosticism by Ernest Bursey.

All the seminar papers are printed in these two volumes. But it was possible to include only a limited selection (less than half) of the short research papers. Those not published here will, it is hoped, appear in the near future in various learned journals.

While the style of each contribution as printed follows the preference of its author, abbreviations of ancient works in references have been conformed to the familiar Latin abbreviations of Liddell-Scott-Jones, Lampe's *Patristic Greek Lexicon*, Lewis-Short, Souter's *Glossary of Later Latin*; for Philo, *Studia Philonica*; and for Coptic Gnostic works, the series Nag Hammadi Studies. Resolutions of these abbreviations, and such as had to be added to them, may also be found in the indexes at the end of this volume. Citations of the Bible, Pseudepigrapha, Apostolic Fathers, Dead Sea Scrolls, Targums, and Rabbinic literature are cited (except in non-English contributions) as in the *Journal of Biblical Literature*, and in general the form of all references adheres to the style of that journal. In accordance with modern typographical preference no roman numerals have been employed; thus Plotinus *Enn.* 4.8.8,15-16 refers to "*Ennead* 4, tractate 8, chap. 8, at lines 15-16 (in the Henry-Schwyzer edition)."

The indexes cover substantive references to ancient texts (mostly religious) and critical discussions of the views of modern scholars; necessarily, they are selective.

The conference was made possible and supported by a grant from the National Endowment for the Humanities. The Yale Department of Religious Studies gratefully acknowledges the Endowment's interest and support. All opinions expressed in the proceedings are, of course, those of the individual authors, and do not necessarily represent the views of the National Endowment for the Humanities, nor the sponsors of the conference.

The considerable task of planning and administering the conference was shared primarily by members of the staff, who are named in volume 1, and also to a degree by others at the university. To all these persons, both named and unnamed, sincere gratitude must be expressed. In particular we acknowledge the support of President Hanna H. Gray.

My thanks are also due to those who assisted in the preparation of these two volumes: and in particular to David Rensberger for editoral assistance; also to Barbara Greten; to Professors Stanley Insler and Frederik Wisse; to John Fitzgerald (who edited the indexes); and to the A. Whitney Griswold Fund.

In the original call for papers it was hoped that the conference might provide an occasion "to attempt a new integration and synthesis of what has been learned, and to look for the most promising directions of future research on Gnosticism and its place in the Western Tradition." It is appropriate to recall that such an undertaking was only possible thanks to the patient labor of generations of specialists in religion, philosophy, linguistics, literature, and papyrology: a labor now so familiar and fundamentally important to the humanities that their names are known to all.

At the time of the Renaissance, scholars thought they could rediscover a *prisca theologia* from which had sprung the transcendental wisdom of the West. Indeed Plato himself had hinted playfully at its existence; and the Florentine humanists believed they had found it, and published it, in the writings of Mercurius Trismegistus. Only generations later was the Hermetic Corpus unmasked as the work of Gnosticizing Platonists, probably contemporary with Valentinus and the Sethians and themselves engaged in the self-same search that had so fascinated Ficino and his patrons; while the fraudulent Horapollo continued to exert an influence until Champollion's decipherment. Modern historical scholarship, though now critical in the chronology

of its sources, continues to be fascinated by the possibility that earliest
Christianity and therefore Christian culture developed under the influence of a Gnostic competitor or even precursor. At the very least,
it can be said that both Catholic Christianity and Gnosticism shared
and embodied the same intellectual, literary, and social environments;
and that by the mid-second century, if not before, there was a constant
interchange of membership, with each social group claiming to possess
the original teachings of the Christian Savior, or arguing that its *logos*
had informed civilization since before the Flood.

But the coherence and seriousness with which the Gnostics had
argued their case was obscured by a lack of first-hand documentation
and by deliberate, if well-meaning, obfuscation on the part of their
ancient opponents. Not only does the rediscovery, and now complete
publication, of the Gnostic Library of Nag Hammadi go far to fulfill
this lack; it also enables us to move beyond the essentially heresiological inquiry into the alleged priority or origin of Gnosticism, towards
a rediscovery of its actual morphology, its development, its modes of
interaction with other schools, and its place in ancient society. Although the diversity of Gnosticism was perhaps as great as that of its
non-Gnostic counterpart, the evidence of Nag Hammadi strongly
suggests that early Gnosticism appeared in two radically different
species: one a parody or "inversion" of elements from Judaism,
essentially non-Christian in character; the other an allegorical trope
upon Catholicism. These two, Sethianism and Valentinianism, may
have met in the historical figure of Valentinus who, according to an
ancient source, was influenced by one and founded the other. The
exact historical relationship of these two varieties of Gnosticism, and
the dialectic of Gnosticism, Catholicism, the Marcionites, Middle
Platonism, and the religion of Mani, are questions that now lie
before us. The papers of this conference will lay a solid and important
groundwork for that historical inquiry.

ABBREVIATIONS

AA: *Archäologischer Anzeiger*
AB: *The Anchor Bible* (Garden City, N.Y.: Doubleday, 1964-75)
AbhAkBerlin: *Abhandlungen der deutschen (königlichen, preussischen) Akademie der Wissenschaften zu Berlin, philosophisch-historische Klasse*
AbhAkGöttingen: *Abhandlungen der Akademie der Wissenschaften in Göttingen, philologisch-historische Klasse*
AbhAkHeid: *Abhandlungen der heidelberger Akademie der Wissenschaften, philosophisch-historische Klasse*
AbhAkMainz: *Abhandlungen der Akademie der Wissenschaften und der Literatur, Mainz, geistes- und sozialwissenschaftliche Klasse*
AbhAkMün: *Abhandlungen der (königlichen bayerischen) Akademie der Wissenschaften, philosophisch-historische Klasse* (Munich)
AC: *Antike und Christentum*, ed. F.J. Dölger
ADAIK: Abhandlungen des deutschen archäologischen Instituts, Abteilung Kairo
AGJA: Arbeiten zur Geschichte des antiken Judentums und des Urchristentums
AIRF: *Acta Instituti Romani Finlandiae* (Helsinki)
AJP: *American Journal of Philology*.
ANF: The Ante-Nicene Fathers, eds. A. Roberts and J. Donaldson
AO: *Acta Orientalia*
AOHung: *Acta Orientalia Academiae Scientiarum Hungaricae*
APF: *Archiv für Papyrusforschung und verwandte Gebiete*
APOT: R.H. Charles, ed., *The Apocrypha and Pseudepigrapha of the Old Testament in English* (Oxford: Clarendon, 1913)
ArtB: *Art Bulletin*
ARW: *Archiv für Religionswissenschaft*
AttiPARA: *Atti della Pontificia Accademia Romana di Archeologia*
BAG: W. Bauer, W.F. Arndt, & F.W. Gingrich, *Greek-English Lexicon of the New Testament*
BBA: Berliner byzantinistische Arbeiten
BCNH: Bibliothèque copte de Nag Hammadi, section «textes»
BETL: Bibliotheca Ephemeridium Theologicarum Lovaniensium
BEvTh: Beiträge zur evangelischen Theologie
BG: Codex Berolinensis Gnosticus (P. Berol. Copt. 8502)
BHT: Beiträge zur historischen Theologie
BZNW: *ZNW*, Beihefte
CBCR: R. Krautheimer et al., *Corpus Basilicarum Christianarum Romae* (Vatican City: Pontificio Istituto di Archeologia Cristiana, 1937-   )
CBQ: *Catholic Biblical Quarterly*
CCL: Corpus Christianorum, Series Latina
CG: Codex Cairensis Gnosticus (Nag Hammadi Library) = NHC
CIG: *Corpus Inscriptionum Graecarum*, ed. A. Boeckius et al.
CIL: *Corpus Inscriptionum Latinarum* (Berlin)
CivCatt: *La Civiltà Cattolica*
ConNT: *Coniectanea Neotestamentica*
CRAIBL: *Comptes rendus des séances de l'Académie des inscriptions et belles-lettres* (Paris)
CSCO: Corpus Scriptorum Christianorum Orientalium
CSEL: Corpus Scriptorum Ecclesiasticorum Latinorum

DBSup: *Dictionnaire de la Bible, Supplément*
DenkschrAkWien: *Denkschriften der (kaiserlichen, österreichischen) Akademie der Wissenschaften, philologisch-historische Klasse* (Vienna)
DJD: Discoveries in the Judean Desert
EnJud: *Encyclopaedia Judaica* (New York: Macmillan, 1971-72)
ErJb: *Eranos-Jahrbuch*
EvTh: *Evangelische Theologie*
Fondation Hardt, Entretiens: Fondation Hardt pour l'étude de l'antiquité classique, Entretiens
FRLANT: Forschungen zur Religion und Literatur des Alten und Neuen Testaments
GCS: Die griechischen christlichen Schriftsteller der ersten drei Jahrhunderte
GRBS: *Greek, Roman and Byzantine Studies*
HDR: Harvard Dissertations in Religion
Hennecke-Schneemelcher (E.T. ed. Wilson): W. Schneemelcher, ed., *New Testament Apocrypha* (Engl. tr. ed. R.McL. Wilson; Philadelphia: Westminster, 1963-65)
HeyJ: *The Heythrop Journal*
HNT: Handbuch zum Neuen Testament
HTR: *Harvard Theological Review*
HTS: Harvard Theological Studies
HSCP: *Harvard Studies in Classical Philology*
HUCA: *Hebrew Union College Annual*
ICS: *Illinois Classical Studies*
ICUR: *Inscriptiones Christianae Urbis Romae*, ed. G.B. de Rossi
IDBSup: *Interpreter's Dictionary of the Bible, Supplementary Volume*
JA: *Journal asiatique*
JAC: Jahrbuch für Antike und Christentum
JBL: *Journal of Biblical Literature*
JEA: *Journal of Egyptian Archaeology*
JEH: *Journal of Ecclesiastical History*
JHS: *Journal of Hellenic Studies*
JJS: *Journal of Jewish Studies*
JR: *Journal of Religion*
JSJ: *Journal for the Study of Judaism in the Persian, Hellenistic and Roman Period*
JTS: *Journal of Theological Studies*
JWarb: *Journal of the Warburg and Courtauld Institutes*
KuK: *Kunst und Kirche*
LCL: The Loeb Classical Library
LPGP: G.W.H. Lampe, *A Patristic Greek Lexicon* (Oxford: Clarendon, 1961-68)
LSJ: Liddell-Scott-Jones, *Greek-English Lexicon*
LUÅ: Lunds universitets årsskrift
MDAIK: *Mitteilungen des deutschen archäologischen Instituts, Abteilung Kairo;* before 1956, *Mitteilungen des deutschen Instituts für ägyptische Altertumskunde in Kairo*
MDAIR: *Mitteilungen des deutschen archäologischen Instituts, Römische Abteilung*
MGWJ: *Monatsschrift für Geschichte und Wissenschaft des Judentums*
MonAnt: *Monumenti Antichi* (Accademia Nazionale dei Lincei, Rome)
MScRel: *Mélanges de science religieuse*
MUSJ: *Mélanges de l'Université Saint-Joseph* (Beirut)
NachrGesGöttingen: *Nachrichten von der königlichen Gesellschaft der Wissenschaften zu Göttingen, philologisch-historische Klasse*
NHC or NH: Nag Hammadi Codex=CG
NHLibEng: [James M. Robinson, general ed.], *The Nag Hammadi Library in English* (New York, etc.: Harper, 1977)
NHS: Nag Hammadi Studies

NovT: *Novum Testamentum*
NovTSup: *NovT*, Supplements
NTS: *New Testament Studies*
OLZ: *Orientalistische Literaturzeitung*
OrChr: *Oriens Christianus*
PG: J.-P. Migne, ed., *Patrologia Graeca*
PGM: K. Preisendanz, ed., *Papyri Graecae Magicae* (Leipzig: Teubner, 1928-31)
PL: J.-P. Migne, ed., *Patrologia Latina*
PTS: Patristische Texte und Studien
PW: Pauly-Wissowa, *Real-Encyclopädie der classischen Altertumswissenschaft*
PWSup: PW, Supplement
RAC: *Reallexikon für Antike und Christentum*
RB: *Revue biblique*
REAug: *Revue des Études Augustiniennes*
RevQ: *Revue de Qumran*
RevScRel: *Revue des sciences religieuses*
RevThom: *Revue Thomiste*
RGVV: Religionsgeschichtliche Versuche und Vorarbeiten
RhM: *Rheinisches Museum für Philologie*
RHR: *Revue de l'Histoire des Religions*
RivAC: *Rivista di Archeologia Cristiana*
RPh: *Revue de philologie*
RQ: *Römische Quartalschrift für christliche Altertumskunde und für Kirchengeschichte*
RSLR: *Revista di Storia e Letteratura Religiosa*
RSPT: *Revue des sciences philosophiques et théologiques*
RTP: *Revue de théologie et de philosophie*
SBL: Society of Biblical Literature
SBLDS: SBL Dissertation Series
SBLSP: SBL [Annual Meeting], *Seminar Papers*
SBT: Studies in Biblical Theology
SC: Sources chrétiennes
SGKA: Studien zur Geschichte und Kultur des Altertums
SD: Studies and Documents
SitzungsberAkBerlin: *Sitzungsberichte der deutschen (königlichen, preussischen) Akademie der Wissenschaften zu Berlin, philologisch-historische Klasse*
SitzungsberAkHeid: *Sitzungsberichte der heidelberger Akademie der Wissenschaften, philosophisch-historische Klasse*
SJLA: Studies in Judaism in Late Antiquity
SO: *Symbolae Osloenses*
SPB: Studia Post-biblica
SUNT: Studien zur Umwelt des Neuen Testaments
SVF: H. von Arnim, ed., *Stoicorum Veterum Fragmenta* (Leipzig: Teubner, 1903-24)
SymBU: *Symbolae Biblicae Upsalienses*
TAPA: *Transactions of the American Philological Association*
TDNT: G. Kittel and G. Friedrich, eds., *Theological Dictionary of the New Testament* (Grand Rapids, Mich.: Eerdmans, 1964-76)
TextsS: Texts and Studies
TGF: A. Nauck, *Tragicorum Graecorum Fragmenta* (2d ed.; Leipzig: Teubner, 1889)
TLZ: *Theologische Literaturzeitung*
TP: *Theologie und Philosophie*
TRu: *Theologische Rundschau*
TU: Texte und Untersuchungen zur Geschichte der altchristlichen Literatur

TWNT: G. Kittel and G. Friedrich, eds., *Theologisches Wörterbuch zum Neuen Testa-
    ment* (Stuttgart: Kohlhammer, 1933-   )
TZ: *Theologische Zeitschrift*
UALG: Untersuchungen zur antiken Literatur und Geschichte
VC: *Vigiliae Christinae*
Vorsokr.: H. Diels and W. Kranz, eds., *Die Fragmente der Vorsokratiker*
VTSup: *Vetus Testamentum*, Supplements
WF: Wege der Forschung
WMANT: Wissenschaftliche Monographien zum Alten und Neuen Testament
ZAW: *Zeitschrift für die alttestamentliche Wissenschaft*
ZÄS: *Zeitschrift für ägyptische Sprache und Altertumskunde*
ZKG: *Zeitschrift für Kirchengeschichte*
ZNW: *Zeitschrift für die neutestamentliche Wissenschaft und Kunde der älteren Kirche*
ZPE: *Zeitschrift für Papyrologie und Epigraphik*
ZTK: *Zeitschrift für Theologie und Kirche*

PART FOUR

SEMINAR ON SETHIAN GNOSTICISM

DISCUSSANTS

George W. MacRae, chairman
Alexander Böhlig
Henry Chadwick
Carsten Colpe
Robert Kraft
Bentley Layton
George W. E. Nickelsburg
Birger A. Pearson
James M. Robinson
Michael E. Stone
John Strugnell
Frederik Wisse
Kurt Rudolph (in absentia)
Hans-Martin Schenke (in absentia)
Ernest Bursey, secretary

Session One

PHILO ON SETH
Was Philo Aware of Traditions
Which Exalted Seth and His Progeny?

BY

ROBERT KRAFT

MAIN *Philonic Treatments*:

On the Posterity and Exile of Cain—deals at length with Seth in relation to Cain and Abel through expressly nonliteral interpretation of Gen 4:25.

Questions and Answers on Genesis—includes brief comments about Seth based on Gen 4:25 and 5:3.

1. It is clear from Josephus (*Ant.* 1.2.3-3.1 §68-72) that in the first century, Jewish traditions existed which credited virtuous Seth and his virtuous, communally harmonious progeny with astronomical/astrological discoveries which were inscribed on two stelae for preservation through the impending destruction.

2. Philo attributes special significance to Seth and his descendants as symbols, not as historical figures, and seemingly with great restraint. They are not connected with astrological lore or with stelae, nor are they associated with the "angels" (which Philo views as *wicked* spirits) in Gen 6: 1-4.

3. Philo does not mention explicitly interpretations of the Seth materials with which he is in disagreement. (But he does not normally present materials in a polemic context throughout his preserved writings.)

4. Seth represents healing (ἴασις) for Adam's expulsion (= involuntary failure), in contrast to Cain's voluntary flight from God which affords of no cure (*Post.* 10; compare later legends about Seth's quest for the oil of healing, etc.—any relationship?). Seth and Cain both produce some descendants with identical names (parallel genealogies), but Seth's have positive significance while Cain's have negative (ENOCH = χάρις σου, METHUSALEH = ἐξαποστολὴ θανάτου, LAMECH = ταπείνωσις; *Post.* 40-48).

5. Seth represents new beginning (παλιγγενεσία) of Abel, who came from above (so *Quaes. Gen.*) to below and now has returned above

(*Post.* 173); Seth is ἀρχή of another γένεσις (*Quaes. Gen.*), starting from human virtue and "growing" (as a plant that is watered; Seth = ποτισμός) towards the perfect and uncreated (see *Post.* 124, 172-173). Seth is ἀρχηγέτης of those who acknowledge God's gift (ENOCH = "gift") of all good things and who flee a life full of evils so that God translates/removes them (as ENOCH) from corruptible to immortal γένη (*Post.* 42-43).

6. Seth is σπέρμα ἕτερον (Gen 4:25) with regard to Abel, with the the idea of continuity, but explicitly is not σπέρμα ἀλλότριον, with the idea of contrast or disjunction (*Post.* 172; thus he is not ἀλλογενής, at least with respect to Abel—is Philo opposing a current interpretation?). In relation to Cain, Seth is ἐχθρόν, σπέρμα ἕτερον in a contrasting sense.

7. Seth represents a level of ἐπιστήμη that became the basis from which Noah began, and in turn Noah developed παιδεία (?) which became the basis for Abraham, who then developed σοφία which served as the basis for Moses, the one who is πάντα σοφός. Numerologically this sequence is represented in ten generations from Seth (or Adam) to Noah, ten more from Shem to Abra(ha)m, and seven (an even more perfect number!) from Abraham to Moses (*Post.* 173-174; it seems that Philo counts Abram/Abraham as both the end of the group to which he gives his name and the start of the new group; it is less clear that Noah plays a similarly dual role; the precise numbering of the generations from Adam to Enos is problematic—see *Abr.* 12). Elsewhere Philo uses other symbolic arrangements of the early patriarchs—see especially *Abr.* 7-47 (Enos—Enoch—Noah compared with Abraham—Isaac—Jacob).

REPORT ON SETH TRADITIONS
IN THE ARMENIAN ADAM BOOKS

BY

MICHAEL E. STONE

In his publication of the German translation of the Armenian Adam books in 1900, E. Preuschen suggested that these writings may be influenced by Sethian Gnostic views and circles. It is for those more learned in the mysteries of Sethian Gnosticism than the writer to confirm or deny that contention; it may, however, be remarked that Preuschen's views have not always found broad scholarly support.[1] It is true, nonetheless, that the figure of Seth in those Armenian writings is singular in some respects. There is, moreover, a growing awareness of the complexity of the Seth traditions in Jewish, Christian and Gnostic circles and of possible interrelations among them.[2]

Consequently, it seems desirable to present this report. It is designed to convey reliable information about these Armenian Adam books, as far as it is available at the moment, and to set forth some of the chief attributes of Seth as he appears in them. My hope is that some service may thus be rendered to scholars in cognate fields of learning.[3]

---

[1] See Cardona (note 3 below), 646-647 for various views on this subject. Preuschen's position is opposed more or less emphatically by R. Liechtenhan, "Die pseudepigraphische Literatur der Gnostiker," *ZNW* 3 (1902) 222-223; by R. Kabisch, "Die Entstehungszeit der Apokalypse Mose," *ZNW* 6 (1905) 115, 120-124; and by Frey (note 3, below).

[2] So the material assembled by A. F. J. Klijn, *Seth in Jewish, Christian and Gnostic Literature* (Leiden : Brill, 1977).

[3] The information on Armenian sources, as far as it has been published, is found in the following works :

a. *Armenian* texts : S. Yovsēp'ianc', *Ankanon Girk' Hin Ktakaranac'* [*Uncanonical Books of the Old Testament*] (Venice : Mechitarist Press, 1896) 24-26, 307-332.

b. *English translation* : J. Issaverdens, *Uncanonical Writings of the Old Testament* (Venice : Mechitarist Press, 1901 ; 2d ed. 1934) 39-89.

c. *German translation* : E. Preuschen, "Die apokryphen gnostischen Adamschriften aus dem Armenischen übersetzt und untersucht," *Festgruss B. Stade* (ed. W. Diehl et al.; Giessen : Ricker, 1900) 163-252 and *separatim*.

d. *Studies* :

M. R. James, *Apocrypha Anecdota* 2 (TextsS 5/1 ; Cambridge, 1897) 159, 163-164 mentions the works.

J. B. Frey, *DBSup* 1. 125-133.

ARMENIAN SOURCES

1-4. The Cycle of Four Works. 1. *History of the Creation and Transgression of Adam*: Yovsēpʻianc̕, 307-311; Issaverdens, 39-45; from Venice, Mechitarist MS no. 729; Anasyan notes (p. 239) a different form of this in *Zolovacu* published in Constantinople in 1713, pp. 3-9; in *Zolovacu* published in Constantinople in 1730, pp. 3-8; in the same, Constantinople 1747, 3-8; and in the same, Constantinople 1793, 3-9.

2. *History of the Expulsion of Adam from the Garden*: Yovsēpʻianc̕, 312-314; Issaverdens, 47-51; from the same Venice manuscript. Anasyan (p. 239) notes the occurrence of this work in Erevan, Matenadaran no. 682, fols. 96v-97r; and a printing of a different form of this in the same works listed above, ed. 1717, pp. 15-18; ed. 1730, 13-16; ed. 1747, 13-15; ed. 1793, 13-15; and this form in Tiflis, Institute of Manuscripts, no. 47.

3. *History of Cain and Abel, the Sons of Adam*: Yovsēpʻianc̕, 314-319; Issaverdens, 53-61; from the same Venice manuscript. Anasyan (pp. 240-241) notes the occurrence of this work in Venice, Mechitarist no. 262, fols. 163v-167v; Erevan, Matenadaran no. 682, fols. 98r-99r; no. 4618, fols. 138r-140r; no. 2126, fols. 81r-83r; and the printing of a different form of this in the same works listed above, ed. 1717, 23-30; ed. 1730, 20-27; ed. 1747, 19-25; ed. 1793, 19-25; and this form in Tiflis, Institute of Manuscripts, no. 47.

4. *Concerning the Good Tidings of Seth*: Yovsēpʻianc̕, 319-324; Issaverdens, 63-70; from the same Venice manuscript. Anasyan (p. 241) notes the occurrence of this work in Erevan, Matenadaran no. 682, fols 100r-101r; no. 4618, fols. 140r-141v; and the printing of a somewhat different form of it in the same works listed above, ed. 1717, 35-42; ed. 1730, 32-39; ed. 1747, 30-36; ed. 1793, 24-35; cf. Tiflis, Library of Manuscripts, no. 47.

These four writings clearly follow a single narrative line. Each commences with a section designed to overlap with the end of that preceding.

M. E. Stone, "The Death of Adam—An Armenian Adam Book," *HTR* 59 (1966) 283-291.

G. R. Cardona, "Sur le gnosticisme en Arménie: les livres d'Adam," *Le origini dello gnosticismo* (ed. U. Bianchi; Supplements to *Numen* 12; Leiden: Brill, 1967) 645-648.

H. Anasyan, *Haykakan Matenagituṭʻyun* [*Armenian Bibliology*] 1 (Erevan: Academy of Sciences, 1956) 236-250.

e. *Georgian Adam Books*: W. Lüdtke, "Georgische Adam-Bücher," *ZAW* 38 (1919) 155-168.

There is no repetition of incidents beyond this and, taken together, the four writings form a coherent whole. Thus it seems that the *History of the Creation and Transgression of Adam*, the *History of the Expulsion of Adam from the Garden*, the *History of Cain and Abel* and *Concerning the Good Tidings of Seth* are four parts of a single literary work. This is a retelling of the primordial history commencing from the fall of Satan and his hosts before Creation and concluding with the Flood. Henceforth, we call this the *Cycle of Four Works*.

5. *The History of the Repentance of Adam and Eve*, Yovsēp'ianc', 325-330; Issaverdens, 71-80; from an Etchmiadzin manuscript transcribed by F. Conybeare in 1895. Anasyan identifies this as Etchmiadzin no. 914, which is now Erevan, Matenadaran no. 1521, fols. 66r-69r. The *History of the Repentance of Adam and Eve* is another complete retelling of these events, shorter than the *Cycle of Four Works*. It is clearly dependent on the *Book of Adam* (= the *Apocalypse of Moses*) at a number of points.

6. *Adam's Words to Seth*. Yovsēp'ianc', 331-332; Issaverdens, 81-83; from Venice, Mechitarist MS no. 57, fols. 183v-185r. *Adam's Words to Seth* is a quite different document, dealing only with the "quest" of Seth. It is related to the three fragments mentioned below, nos. 9-11.

7. *The Death of Adam*. Yovsēp'ianc', 24-26; Issaverdens, 85-89; from Venice, Mechitarist MS no. 729. Anasyan (p. 321) also notes Jerusalem, Armenian Patriarchate no. 372. The *Death of Adam* is probably an excerpt from a Greek rewritten Bible of which other parts have survived in Armenian.[4] In structure too it is a complete cycle, telling (very briefly to be sure) of the expulsion, the birth of the children and then (in some detail) of visions seen by Eve and Seth and of Adam's death and burial.

8. *The Book of Adam*. In addition to the seven writings listed so far, the collections edited by Yovsēp'ianc' and Issaverdens include the Armenian version of the *Apocalypse of Moses* (= the *Book of Adam*).

It should be observed that each of the writings listed (except the *Apocalypse of Moses*) has been published from a single manuscript.

---

[4] See M. E. Stone, "Some Observations on the Armenian Version of the Paralipomena of Jeremiah," *CBQ* 35 (1973) 56-58; idem, "Armenian Canon Lists III : The Lists of Mechitar of Ayrivank'," *HTR* 69 (1976) 289-300. The "quest" of Seth has been the object of an excellent study by E. C. Quinn, *The Quest of Seth for the Oil of Life* (Chicago : University of Chicago, 1962).

There exist other copies of most of these writings; some were known to Anasyan while others escaped his attention. A new edition of the *Death of Adam* based on five manuscripts is to appear soon and, without doubt, a careful search in manuscript collections will uncover still further copies of the other books.[5] None of the manuscripts known to the writer so far has any particular claim to great antiquity.

The following writings are known to me from manuscripts and are not included in the collection edited by Yovsēpʻianc̣ and translated by Issaverdens.

9-11. Three fragmentàry texts dealing with the Quest of Seth. Two of these texts occur in manuscripts in the library of the Armenian Patriarchate of Jerusalem.[6] One of them is close in wording and general content to *Adam's Words to Seth*; the other differs somewhat and is clearly later in language and form. In both cases Seth brings a branch from the Garden. In the first, he is berated by Adam for bringing a death-dealing and not a vivifying branch. In the second, it is related that the branch was planted on Adam's grave and became a great tree, the wood of which was used eventually in the cross. Thus that which had brought death also brought life. Anasyan (p. 243) mentions another incomplete text, different from the two Jerusalem fragments, which also seems to deal with the same theme (Erevan, Matenadaran no. 3358, fol. 3v).

12. The Penitence of Our Father Adam. This writing is known to survive in three manuscripts, all of the seventeenth century, and a critical edition of it is currently in preparation. The manuscripts are Erevan, Matenadaran no. 3461; Jerusalem, Armenian Patriarchate nos. 1370 and 1458. It is another form of the *Books of Adam and*

---

[5] On the present status of the cataloging of Armenian manuscript collections see M. E. Stone, "The Study of Armenian Manuscripts," *Armenian and Biblical Studies* (ed. M. E. Stone; *Sion,* Supplement 1; Jerusalem : St. James [Armenian Patriarchate], 1976) 283-286. The fact that the catalogue of the largest collection, that in the Matenadaran (Institute of Ancient Manuscripts) in Erevan, Armenia, is only a short list and gives only titles, but no *incipits,* makes the task of identification of additional copies particularly difficult. Concerning the manuscript of the *History of the Repentance of Adam and Eve,* see Issaverdens's note, *Uncanonical Writings,* 71.

[6] These texts and the edition of the *Death of Adam* mentioned above, together with collations of an additional manuscript of the *History of Cain and Abel,* will be published in the writer's forthcoming *Armenian Apocrypha Relating to Patriarchs and Prophets* (Jerusalem : Israel Academy of Sciences, 1981). At the time of writing the present paper, however, copies of these documents were not at my disposal, · for technical reasons.

Eve, making a fourth major type, additional to the well-known Greek, Latin, and Slavonic recensions. In some respects it is close to the Georgian Adam book which has been published in Georgian, but never translated (see no. 16, below). Both contain the story of the protoplasts' penitence, like the Latin *Life of Adam and Eve*, but from the point of the birth of Cain and Abel also exhibit many features similar to the Greek *Apocalypse of Moses*.

13. Concerning Adam, His Sons and Grandsons. This writing has never been published; it is found in Erevan, Matenadaran no. 2245 (fols. 274r-281v) and no. 9220 (fols. 1r-3v). Its *incipit* was printed by Anasyan, whose text we translate:

> And after Adam left the Garden, he was sad and in mourning for thirty years and then, at the commandment of God and the instruction of an angel, he went in to Eve his wife and begat Cain.

Nothing more is known of this writing.[7]

14. Concerning the Contract between Adam and Satan. A brief text, extant in Jerusalem, Armenian Patriarchate no. 840, p. 640, which gives another form of the tradition also found in the *History of the Expulsion of Adam from the Garden* (Issaverdens, p. .49) and in the Slavonic *Life of Adam and Eve* (chapters 33-34). Anasyan mentions a longer text dealing with the same theme. This text is contained in Erevan, Matenadaran no. 9100, fols. 32r-35r. He remarks that its content resembles that of the *History of the Expulsion of Adam from the Garden* but that it is a quite different composition (pp. 242-243).

15. The Letter Sent to Adam by God. A short text exists in Erevan, Matenadaran no. 2111, fol. 229v, which opens:

> This is the letter written by the finger of God and sealed and sent to Adam for the hope of salvation. "In the sixth millennium, on the sixth day, at the beginning of your existence, I shall send the only begotten Son, the Word of God, who came in the body from your seed."

The text goes on to relate the transmission of this document until

> Melkizedek gave it to Cyrus, King of Persia, and he placed it in a room, to be preserved carefully until the Magi (came). The Magi brought it and offered it before Jesus Christ.

---

[7] Anasyan, *Haykakan Matenagitut'yun*, 242. A microfilm copy of it awaits my attention in Jerusalem.

The same tradition recurs in another independent writing in Venice, Mechitarist 240, 10v-11r, and in certain Armenian New Testament apocrypha. As distinct from documents 9-10, 12-14, this writing is known to me only from Anasyan's report (p. 243). There are, moreover, other homiletical and poetical compositions in Armenian which deal with various facets of the Adam cycle. A good deal of information on them may be found in Anasyan, pp. 245-248.

16. Georgian Adam Books. Lüdtke published a report on some Georgian Adam texts which are, apparently, related to some of these Armenian works. One is mentioned by him as analogous to the *Cycle of Four Works* and perhaps translated from Armenian (pp. 155-156). Another is akin to the *Penitence of Our Father Adam* (above, no. 12). There is also a Georgian version of the *Cave of Treasures* and the *Testament of Adam*. His report, however, is the only source of information.

LITERARY RELATIONSHIPS

Thus, there are four published Armenian accounts of the story of the protoplasts: the *Book of Adam* (i.e., the *Apocalypse of Moses*), the *Cycle of Four Works*, the *History of the Repentance of Adam and Eve* and the *Death of Adam*. *Adam's Words to Seth* is also an independent work. This literary analysis is corroborated by the occurrence of the writings in the manuscripts. The *Cycle of Four Works* occurs in a single manuscript, interspersed with fragments of commentary or exegetical material, unfortunately not published by Yovsēp'ianc'.[8] Each of the other writings occurs in a different manuscript.

The question of the literary relationship among these different works is still unresolved. In some preliminary research (carried out at the University of Pennsylvania in 1977-78 under my direction), Mr. L. Lipscomb has compared certain incidents which are related in parallel forms in two or more of these documents. His results suggest the conclusion that the *Cycle of Four Works* and the *History of the Repentance of Adam and Eve* are not directly related to one another. It has been remarked above that the latter does seem to bear a clear

---

[8] See his comments in *Ankanon Girk'*, 307, 311, and 314. Of course, this argument will only be completely persuasive once other manuscripts are studied in detail. The four works were also published together in the eighteenth-century editions of the *Zolovacu* and, according to Anasyan's report, groups of two or three of them occur in other manuscripts (see the discussion of them above). Further information on this point is desirable.

literary relationship to the *Apocalypse of Moses*, and draws as well on many unique traditions.

It may be that further study will enable us to discern various sources and variant traditions in the *Cycle of Four Works*, but as it stands it seems to be a unity. There are other cases in which a retelling of biblical narrative in Armenian is divided into sections, each of which is entitled "The History of So-and-So."[9]

THE FIGURE OF SETH IN THESE TEXTS

An examination of the presentation of Seth by these sources reveals some common themes among them, as well as some interesting variations upon themes known from other Jewish and Christian books. Certain of the details are unique and others are obscure. The chief matters relating to Seth are summarized here.

1. The Cycle of Four Works. In this work five chief elements can be discerned touching on Seth : all occur in the *Good Tidings of Seth*. (i) The annunciation of his birth. This is already outlined at the end of the preceding writing. Seth is to be a consolation; a blessed seed; head of the patriarchs. (ii) The angel foretells the multiplication of Seth's seed and that they will fill the earth. Adam is warned against letting them mix with the Cainites. (iii) After Seth's birth, no more Cainites were born to Adam. The Sethites chased away the Cainites. (iv) Enoch (Seth's son!) is virtuous and eventually assumed to Heaven. Observing this, many of Seth's children retired to the mountains for a life of fasting and purity. (v) The Cainite women increased exceedingly; there were 520 single Sethite men. The Cainite woman went to the mountains and by means of exotic dancing and the use of cosmetics seduced all Sethite men except Noah.

2. The History of the Repentance of Adam and Eve. (i) Following a lacuna is the annunciation by Gabriel of the birth of Seth. The angel brings Adam a branch from the Garden as a sign that a son of consolation will be born to him. (ii) The Quest of Seth occurs later in the text. Seth and Eve set out to seek a branch from the tree that yields oil. The beast Behemoth attacks Seth and is chased away by Eve. At the Garden, the angel comes to tell them that their quest is in vain and that Adam has died in the meanwhile.

---

[9] Such is the *Biblical Paraphrases*, shortly to be published in the volume cited in note 6 above.

3. *Adam's Words to Seth*. (i) Adam relates the story of the expulsion to Seth. (ii) Seth fasts and an 'angel brings him a branch. (iii) Adam recognizes the branch as of the tree that brought death but Seth assures him that it will give life and light. (iv) Adam blesses Seth and Seth repeats Adam's words to Enoch.

4. *The Death of Adam*. (i) Seth, "consoler," is born with a sister Est'era. He obtains blessing of Abel and becomes a shepherd. (ii) Eve reveals to Seth the reason for expulsion from the Garden. She sees a dream intimating Adam's demise. She relates it to Seth and later Seth relates it to Adam's assembled offspring. (iii) Adam instructs Seth and dies. (iv) Seth and Ema, Abel's twin sister, receive dreams with burial instructions.

The following comments make no pretence at being an exhaustive analysis of these interesting texts. Some of the features of the texts are particularly striking, however, and these are noted.

a.) The annunciation of the birth of Seth by an angel is to be found already in *Apocalypse of Moses* 3. It is much more developed in the *Cycle of Four Works*. Of the elements of Seth's antenatal blessing, the idea of Seth as a consolation also occurs in the *History of the Repentance of Adam and Eve*, while "comforter" is said to be the translation of the name in the *Death of Adam*, an etymology not attested elsewhere.[10] The prevalence of this idea in the different cycles in Armenian is notable. The other parts of the blessings relate to Seth's descendants and, indeed, in the *Cycle of Four Works* Seth is chiefly important as the ancestor of the Sethites. The idea that after Seth's birth no more Cainites were born of Adam is perhaps comparable to the rabbinic tradition tied to the exegesis of Gen. 5:3. According to this Adam begat demons and spirits involuntarily during the 130 years between Abel's death and Seth's birth.[11] According to the *History of the Repentance of Adam and Eve* the angel brings Adam a branch as a sign that Seth will be born as a consolation. See below on this unusual

---

[10] L. Lipscomb (in research carried out at the Univ. of Pensylvania in 1977-78 under my direction) points to the Ethiopic *Book of Adam and Eve* 2:1, 17, and Michael Glycas, 235-236 (ed. Bekker) as possible parallels. G.G. Stroumza proposes a solution to this difficulty in a forthcoming note, according to which the etymology is transferred from Noah's name; see below, note 14. Whatever its origin, this exegesis is also to be found in other Armenian Adam works and thus may have been commonly known in Armenia, a factor which bears on this aspect of Stroumza's argument.

[11] See *b.'Erub.* 18b; *Midrash Haggadol* to Gen 5:3; *Midrash Tanḥuma*, ed. S. Buber, 26-27 (1.20).

idea. In this work, it is the angel Gabriel who makes the announcement of Seth's impending birth to Adam, while in *Apocalypse of Moses* 3 it is Michael. The annunciation to Mary, mother of Christ, is made by Gabriel (Luke 1:26). The shift from Michael to Gabriel may be an attempt to bring these two annunciations into a relationship. In this connection, observe that, at the end, the *History of the Repentance of Adam and Eve* relates that Shem buried the bodies of Eve and Adam, Eve's in the cavern in Bethlehem where afterwards Jesus was born and Adam's in Golgotha.[12]

b.) In the form of the Sethite-Cainite tradition found in the *Cycle of Four Works*, its relationship to Gen. 6:1-2 as an explanation of the "sons of God" and the "daughters of men" is only implicit. That the Sethite exegesis of Gen. 6:1-2 is implied is true, however, because the text bothers to explain how there are so many Cainite women to seduce the Sethite men. W. Adler, in a note to the text of George Syncellus (16:6),[13] has traced the development of the Christian interpretation of the "sons of God" (Gen. 6:2) as the Sethites. In it he sees "a convergence of two streams—(1) the impulse to demythologize Gen 6 ..., and (2) the belief that Seth was the first link in a chain of purity, extending down to the Messiah." What is unusual in the *Cycle of Four Works* and in the *Teaching of St. Gregory* (see below) is that in them even the demythologized interpretation of Genesis 6 is suppressed. It is notable that throughout the *Cycle of Four Works* the importance of celibate chastity is stressed. The withdrawal of the Sethites to the mountains is attributed by our text to their desire to emulate Enoch-Enosh's purity. This differs somewhat from the Byzantine tradition found, e.g., in Syncellus 16:6, 16/27:6, where they withdraw to higher ground at Adam's behest.[14]

c.) The "Quest of Seth" theme is not found at all in the *Cycle of Four Works*. It does occur in the *History of the Repentance of Adam and Eve* and in *Adam's Words to Seth*. In the former it is clearly based on

---

[12] Frey compares this with the Ps.-Epiphanian *Homily on Genesis* published by F.C. Conybeare, "The Gospel Commentary of Epiphanius," *ZNW* 7 (1906) 329-330, which knows the same traditions.

[13] "Notes to the Text of George Syncellus and Pseudo-Malalas" (paper circulated privately at the joint Pseudepigrapha/Nag Hammadi special session of the Society of Biblical Literature, held in San Francisco, December, 1977).

[14] W. Adler, "Notes" (on 16:6), adduces many other sources reflecting the same view and variations on it. The suppression of Gen 6:1-2 also occurs in Aphraat, *Demonst.* 13:5 (observation by Adler).

the *Apocalypse of Moses*, and in it Eve's speech in response to the beast's attack on Seth is reflected. What is notable is that Seth's reproach of the beast (in which he stresses that he is the image of God) is omitted by the Armenian writing; his words are preserved by the Latin *Life of Adam and Eve* (37) and the Greek *Apocalypse of Moses* (12). Moreover, in the Armenian text the "quest" is pointless. Seth does not bring back the oil, nor a branch, nor even a message. All that happens is that an angel comes and tells him and Eve that Adam has died in the meanwhile. Two comments are suggested by this bizarre twist to the story. First, it is well to remember that the angel's message to Seth and Eve is surrounded by textual uncertainty in the various recensions of the *Books of Adam and Eve*, perhaps hinting that the oldest form of it was in some way (doctrinally?) objectionable. Second, perhaps the omission of the branch at this point is related in some way to the introduction of a branch into the annunciation story in this same text.

d.) Eve is completely missing from the form of the "quest" tradition in *Adam's Words to Seth*. This document, like the fragments referred to above (nos. 9-11), seems for the most part to be independent of the *Apocalypse of Moses*. Here Seth does receive a branch and it is Seth who interprets the meaning of the branch to Adam, by whom he is blessed. The Garden of Eden is not mentioned either in this document.

e.) In the *Death of Adam*, certain unique features of the Seth figure occur. The interpretation of Seth as the replacement of Abel is very literal—he also receives Abel's blessing and becomes a shepherd. Moreover, he is instructed (the text does not say in what) by Adam before Adam's death. He plays a further role in this tale, but one which is not really exceptional when his position as eldest son is taken into account.

EVALUATION

a.) In the *Cycle of Four Works*, there seems nothing particularly significant associated with the figure of Seth. He is of note chiefly as a son of consolation and father of the Sethites. Once it is realized that *Concerning the Good Tidings of Seth* is to be read as part of a broader literary cycle, then Seth's role falls into perspective.

b.) In the *History of the Repentance of Adam and Eve*, the exact point of the annunciation story is unclear. What is evident, however, is that in its form of the "quest" story, the role played by Seth is minor, when compared with that given him by the Greek and Latin *Books of Adam and Eve*. Again, certain features of this work may indicate that the portrayal of Seth is related to Christ, but the exact nature of the relationship is unclear.

c.) It is in *Adam's Words to Seth* that Seth's peculiar role comes to the fore. In this telling of the story of the "quest" he is the chief actor, he receives the revelation from Adam and the branch from the Garden. More important still, it is he who knows the salvific significance of the branch. He tells Adam that it brings both life and light. He is also blessed by Adam before the latter's demise.

d.) The *Death of Adam* also attributes a somewhat elevated role to Seth, and certain features of this work are notable. G. G. Stroumza has pointed out that the name of Seth's sister given by it, Est'era, occurs as that of a maiden seduced by Shemḥazai according to the *Midrash Shemḥazai and Aza'el*.[15] He goes on to develop important implications of this for the reconstruction of early Jewish legends and their reuse in Gnostic circles. He suggests that the *Death of Adam* ultimately derives this tradition from Sethian Gnostic circles, but is not itself of Sethian Gnostic origin. Cardona pointed to certain features which he considered shared by the Armenian Adam books and the *Apocalypse of Adam* (CG V, 5), which some have termed a Sethian Gnostic writing. Cardona treated the corpus of Armenian Adam books as if they were of common origin, which hypothesis is probably incorrect.[16] Yet, in light of Stroumza's perceptive remarks, it is intriguing that the most striking of these parallels is between the three men who reveal secrets to Adam in the *Apocalypse of Adam* (65:26ff.) and the three heavenly men, one of whom reveals words of comfort to Adam in the *Death of Adam* (vv 17-22).[17] Of particular note too is that Adam

---

[15] Newly edited apud J. T. Milik, *The Books of Enoch* (Oxford, 1976) 321-328. These and the following observations quoted in G. G. Stroumza's name are drawn from his unpublished "The Star and the Angels—A Note on the Genealogy of Seth's Sister". He generously made this available to me in manuscript form and I quote it with his permission.

[16] See the discussion of literary relationships above.

[17] Cardona, "Gnosticisme," 647; so also P. Perkins, "The Genre and Function of the Apocalypse of Adam," *CBQ* 39 (1977) 356. The versification of the *Death of Adam* follows that in Stone, "Death of Adam." A. Götze, *Die Schatzhöhle* (*SitzungsberAkHeid* 1922) 41-44 and 49-50, 59, discusses the relationship between the *Cave of Treasures* and the Armenian Adam Books (all of which he regards as one work). He concludes that "Der erste Teil der Schatzhöhle geht auf ein Sethianisches Adam-Buch zurück, das in einer später Überarbeitung in der armenischen Sammlung zum Teil verliegt" (43). The reevaluation of such views must take at least three factors into account: a) a broader range of themes than Seth traditions alone; b) the results of literary analysis of the Armenian books and a study of associated apocryphal traditions in Armenian literature; and c) the new information which has come to light on Sethian Gnosticism.

instructed Seth before his death. It is only at this point and in
Adam's Words to Seth that the role of revealer or recipient of revelation
is given him in the Armenian Adam literature. In the *Apocalypse of
Adam*, of course, Seth receives secret knowledge from Adam and in
turn reveals it to his seed (85:22).[18]

THE TEACHING OF ST. GREGORY

By way of providing some point of contrast within the Armenian
tradition, we reproduce here some excerpts from a mid-fifth-century
Armenian theological writing. This document, the so-called *Teaching
of St. Gregory*, has been included in the *History* of Agathangelos.
Note that par. 295 (cf. 291), implies that in the eighth generation the
Sethites mixed with the Cainites; i.e., this is another suppressed interpretation of Gen 6:1-2, which verses are not cited explicitly.

> [290] Then another son was established for Adam by God instead of the
> murdered Abel, who was named Seth [Gen 4:25]. ... So the treacherous
> and murderous Cain was cursed. Therefore he was cut off by the command
> of God, for God blessed Seth and gave him a command, that his blessed
> seed should not mingle with the cursed seed of the murderer Cain. Then
> mankind increased generally over both families' regions of the earth.
> [291] The patriarchs of the tribe of Seth were righteous men until the eighth
> generation; the kindness of God was near them, and He was continuously
> close to all men lest they should be forgetful of his confidence. So He
> made the fathers long-lived and granted them long-lived children, that at
> least on account of their desire for sons they might seek God, especially
> because the begetting of offspring is most important in the life of earthly
> creatures. ...   [295] ... The repentance of God [Gen 6:6] is a sign of his
> awesome solicitude, that perhaps thereby He may be able to care for those
> who forgot the power of the Creator, who mingled with the cursed seed
> of Cain in fornication and dissolute lives, to eat carrion [Lev 15:17].[18]

In this text, then, the story of the Sethites and Cainites is so well known
as just to be referred to in passing. As in the *Cycle of Four Works*, Seth
here plays no special role except as son of consolation and ancestor of

---

[18] On this theme, see the remarks of G. W. MacRae, "Seth in Gnostic Texts and
Traditions," *SBLSP 1977* (ed. P. J. Achtemeier; Missoula, Montana : Scholars Press, 1977)
17-19, esp. 18.

[19] Cited from R. W. Thomson, *The Teaching of St. Gregory: An Early Armenian
Catechism* (Cambridge : Harvard University, 1970) 53-54. Note that Thomson refers the
eating of carrion to the prohibition in Leviticus. According to the ancient tradition
in *1 Enoch* 7:5 the giants, the offspring of the union between the angelic sons of God and
the daughters of men, included the drinking of blood among their various sins; cf.
Gen 9:4, etc.

the Sethites. The distinctive Sethian traditions of the other Armenian works are absent.

CONCLUDING OBSERVATIONS

a.) Before serious study of this literature and its affinities can be undertaken, certain basic technical desiderata must be fulfilled: (1) critical editions and accurate translations must be prepared on a broader manuscript base; (2) other unpublished Armenian Adam texts should be edited and translated; (3) cognate Georgian works should be edited and translated; and (4) related traditions in datable Armenian sources should be collected.

b.) Some published works are written in "good" classical Armenian and questions of their date and original language remain open. An exception is the *Death of Adam* which claims to be, and probably is, a translation from Greek.

c.) On the basis of present knowledge, however, we may propose with some confidence that the published Armenian Adam books (apart from the *Apocalypse of Moses*) should be regarded as four disparate compositions: (1) the *Cycle of Four Works*; (2) the *History of the Repentance of Adam and Eve;* (3) *Adam's Words to Seth;* and (4) the *Death of Adam.*

d.) The *Cycle of Four Works* shows the same sort of Seth traditions as the *Teaching of St. Gregory*, which was composed in Armenian in the mid-fifth century. These center on the Sethite-Cainite legend and both writings gloss over its relationship to Gen 6:1-2.

e.) Some features of the *History of the Repentance of Adam and Eve* seem to indicate a minimization of Seth's role (the "quest" story) while others seem to glorify him and bring him into an implicit typological relationship with Christ (the annunciation and burial traditions).

f.) More distinctive traditions about Seth occur in *Adam's Words to Seth* and the *Death of Adam.* There seems to be some basis for detecting the reuse of certain Sethian Gnostic traditions in this latter work (Stroumza, Cardona). The form of the "quest" tradition in the former and its (still unpublished) congeners is unique and merits careful study.

THE FIGURE OF SETH IN GNOSTIC LITERATURE

BY

BIRGER A. PEARSON

I. INTRODUCTION

Gnostic speculation on the figure of Seth, son of Adam, is gaining greater attention among scholars interested in the origins and history of Gnosticism. Studies on this subject have recently multiplied, [1] and the publication of an important monograph on Seth by A. F. J. Klijn, *Seth in Jewish, Christian and Gnostic Literature*, is especially noteworthy. [2] Indeed the ground covered in Klijn's book can be said to pose the question whether it is profitable to presume to carry the investigation any further. It is thus with some hesitation, and perhaps some presumptuousness, that I offer herewith some observations of my own on this subject, though I should perhaps add that I submitted this topic to the Conference Director before I had had a chance to read Klijn's book.

In this paper I shall try to build upon the evidence presented by Klijn and others, as well as upon the research done in connection with my own previous study, [3] in order to show, hopefully with greater

---

[1] See especially the papers presented to a special joint seminar of the Pseudepigrapha Group and the Nag Hammadi Section of the Society of Biblical Literature, at the Society's One Hundred Thirteenth Annual Meeting in San Francisco, December, 1977. The following papers prepared for this seminar are published in the volume of proceedings, *SBLSP 1977* (Missoula, Montana: Scholars Press, 1977): Anitra Bingham Kolenkow, "Trips to the Other World in Antiquity and the Story of Seth in the Life of Adam and Eve," 1-11; William Adler, "Materials Relating to Seth in an Anonymous Chronographer ('Pseudo-Malalas') and in the Chronography of George Syncellus," 13-15 (an introduction to texts and translations); George W. MacRae, "Seth in Gnostic Texts and Traditions," 17-24; and Birger A. Pearson, "Egyptian Seth and Gnostic Seth," 25-43. The following items were presented to the seminar but are as yet unpublished: William Adler et al., "Materials Relating to Seth in an Anonymous Chronographer ('Pseudo Malalas') and in the Chronography of George Syncellus" (texts and translations); William Adler, "Notes to Text of George Syncellus and Pseudo-Malalas"; John T. Townsend, "Seth in Rabbinic Literature: Translations of the Sources"; and Dennis Berman, "Seth in Rabbinic Literature: Translations and Notes." Other studies will be cited below.

[2] Leiden: Brill, 1977.

[3] "Egyptian Seth and Gnostic Seth," Part of the research done for both of these studies was supported by an NEH Senior Stipend for the summer of 1977. I am grateful to the Endowment for its support.

precision than heretofore achieved, the extent to which Gnostic speculation on Seth is based upon scripture interpretation and Jewish traditions
of exegesis. Out of considerations of space, I shall confine my
discussion to the chief patristic sources on Gnosticism and to the
Coptic Gnostic texts, omitting extended treatment of the Manichaean
and Mandaean sources.[4]

II. SURVEY OF THE EVIDENCE

A. *Patristic sources.* Irenaeus, in his description of the doctrines of
a group of Gnostics sometimes called "Sethian-Ophites" (*Haer.* 1. 30),[5]
presents a version of the primeval history based on the opening chapters
of Genesis. The birth of Seth "by the providence of Prunicus (= Sophia)"
and that of his sister Norea[6] are recounted; Seth and Norea are said to
be the progenitors of the rest of mankind (*Haer.* 1.30.9). Nothing further
is said of Seth in this account.

The earliest-known patristic description of the "Sethian" Gnostic sect
(*Sethoitae*) is that of Ps.-Tertullian, *Against All Heresies,*[7] a Latin work
possibly based on Hippolytus's lost *Syntagma.* It is said there (chap. 8)
that two men, Cain and Abel, were created by the angels. After the
death of Abel the "Mother" (= Sophia) intervened and Seth was born.
The chapter concludes with the report that the Sethians identify Christ
with Seth.

Epiphanius's account of the Sethian Gnostics (Σηθιανοί, see *Haer.*
39) is dependent upon Pseudo-Tertullian,[8] though Epiphanius tells
us that he had personal knowledge of the group, presumably in his
travels in Egypt, and had gotten access to some of their books (*Haer.*
39.1.2). He reports that the Sethians trace their race (γένος) from
Seth, son of Adam, and identify him with Christ (39.1.3). Seth was
born at the instigation of the Mother (= Sophia) after Abel's death,

---

[4] For brief surveys of the Mandaean and Manichaean evidence see my paper "Egyptian
Seth and Gnostic Seth," 34-35, and Klijn, *Seth*, 107-111. It might be noted that the
genetic and phenomenological relationships between Mandaean/Manichaean and other
Gnostic speculations on Seth could very profitably be investigated, but this would
require a more extensive study than could be attempted in this paper.

[5] The characterization "Sethian-Ophite" is based on Theodoret of Cyrus's restatement
of Irenaeus's description, *Haer.* 1.14: οἱ δὲ Σηθιανοὶ οὓς Ὀφιανοὺς ἢ Ὀφίτας τινὲς
ὀνομάζουσιν... . Irenaeus's text has only, "alii ..." (1.30.1).

[6] On Norea see Birger A. Pearson, "The Figure of Norea in Gnostic Literature,"
Proceedings of the International Colloquium on Gnosticism, Stockholm, August 20-25, 1973
(ed. Geo Widengren; Kungl. Vitterhets Historie och Antikvitets Akademiens Handlingar,
Filologisk-filosofiska serien 17; Stockholm: Almqvist & Wiksell, 1977) 143-152.

[7] Cf. Klijn, *Seth*, 82-83.

[8] Ibid., 83-86.

and received the spark of divine power (39.2.4, 7). The Mother destroyed Cain's wicked race in the Flood and preserved the righteous race of Seth (39.3.1), though the wicked angels installed Ham into into the ark in order that wickedness might be preserved (39.3.2-3). Jesus Christ, appearing in the world miraculously, is none other than Seth (39.3.5). The Sethians have seven books in the name of Seth, as well as other books (39.5.1). They honor a certain Horaia (= Norea)[9] as the wife of Seth and regard her as a spiritual power in her own right (39.5.2-3).

Two other groups described by Epiphanius, the "Archontics" (Ἀρχοντικοί, *Haer.* 40)[10] and the libertine "Gnostics" (Γνωστικοί, *Haer.* 26)[11] of various stripes, seem clearly to be related to the Sethians (*Haer.* 39). Indeed Michel Tardieu has recently argued that the three sects described by Epiphanius in chaps. 26, 39, and 40 of his opus against heresies are ultimately manifestations of one and the same Gnostic ideology.[12]

Epiphanius locates the Archontics in Palestine. In their system Cain and Abel are the product of a liaison between Eve and the devil (40.5.3), but Seth is the real son of Adam (40.7.1). This Seth, also called "Allogenes," was endowed from on high with spiritual power, and therefore recognized the highest God in distinction from the creator of the world and his archons (40.7.2-3). The Archontics have books in Seth's name and in the name of his seven sons, who are also called "Allogeneis" (40.7.4-5). Of the "Gnostics" Epiphanius reports that they, too, have books in the name of Seth (26.8.1). "Noria" (= Norea)[13] also plays a role in their system (26.1.3-9).

Hippolytus's description of a group he identifies as Sethians (Σηθιανοί)[14] is remarkably different from the accounts of Ps.-Tertullian and Epiphanius on the Sethians; it also differs from Irenaeus's account of the "others," later identified as Sethians (*Haer.* 1.30). Hippolytus's group has an elaborate system based on three principles: Light, Darkness, and intermediate Spirit. Seth is mentioned only once, where

---

[9] Cf. Irenaeus, *Haer.* 1.30.9, and n. 6 above.

[10] Cf. Klijn, *Seth*, 89.

[11] Ibid., 87 n. 21.

[12] Michel Tardieu, "Les livres mis sous le nom de Seth et les Séthiens de l'hérésiologie," *Gnosis and Gnosticism: Papers read at the Seventh International Conference on Patristic Studies, Oxford, September 8th-13th, 1975* (ed. Martin Krause: NHS 8; Leiden: Brill, 1977) 206. He cites Epiphanius, *Haer.* 40.7.5., as an indication that Epiphanius himself was aware of the relationship among the three groups.

[13] Cf. nn. 6 and 9 above.

[14] Cf. note 5. Klijn mentions this group in a footnote; see *Seth*, 89 n. 32.

the three principles (λόγοι) are related allegorically to various biblical triads : Adam, Eve, the serpent; Cain, Abel, Seth; Shem, Ham, Japheth; Abraham, Isaac, Jacob (*Haer*. 5.20). Hippolytus also reports that their system is propounded in a book entitled *Paraphrase of Seth* (5.22).

The Valentinian Gnostics are credited by Irenaeus and other heresiologists with an allegorical interpretation of Cain, Abel, and Seth somewhat comparable to that of Hippolytus's Sethians : the three classes of men, "material" (ὑλικοί), "psychic" (ψυχικοί), and "spiritual" (πνευματικοί), correspond to Cain, Abel and Seth.[15] Seth is therefore the symbolic progenitor and representative of "spiritual" (i.e., Gnostic) mankind, according to the Valentinians.

The aforementioned patristic accounts constitute all that we know of the Gnostic interpretation of Seth from the point of view of the orthodox heresiologists. There are, of course, other patristic accounts and references—e.g., Filaster, Isidore of Seville, Paulus, Honorius, the *Anacephalaiosis* attached to Epiphanius's *Panarion*, John Damascene, Joseppus, Augustine, Praedestinatus, Ps.-Jerome, Didymus the Blind, Serapion of Thmuis, and Origen—but these are all dependent upon the earlier patristic writers.[16]

B. *Coptic Gnostic sources*. The first extensive study of the Nag Hammadi codices was carried out by Jean Doresse, who also propounded the theory that these codices constituted *in toto* a Sethian-Gnostic "library."[17] Further study has dramatically reduced the number of tractates in the Nag Hammadi collection that can properly be labelled as "Sethian." Hans-Martin Schenke, in a very important article, defines the following documents as Sethian : the *Apocryphon of John* (Nag Hammadi Codex II, *1*; III,*1*; IV,*1*; and Berlin Gnostic Codex, *2*) plus parallel in Irenaeus *Haer*. 1.29, the *Hypostasis of the Archons* (NHC II,*4*), *Gospel of the Egyptians* (NHC III,*2*; IV,*2*), *Apocalypse of Adam* (NHC V,*5*), *Three Steles of Seth* (NHC VII,*5*), *Zostrianos* (NHC VIII,*1*), *Melchizedek* (NHC IX,*1*), *Thought of Norea* (NHC IX,*2*), and *Trimorphic Protennoia* (NHC XIII,*1*).[18] In two of these the name

---

[15] Irenaeus, *Haer*. 1.7.5; *Exc. Thdot*. 54.1; Tertullian, *Adv. Val*. 29.

[16] Cf. Klijn, *Seth*, 88.

[17] Jean Doresse, *The Secret Books of the Egyptian Gnostics* (tr. Philip Mairet; London : Hollis & Carter, 1960); see esp. 249-251. For a critique of Doresse's views see Frederick Wisse, "The Sethians and the Nag Hammadi Library," *SBLSP 1972*, 601-607.

[18] Hans-Martin Schenke, "Das sethianische System nach Nag-Hammadi-Handschriften," *Studia Coptica* (ed. Peter Nagel; BBA 45; Berlin : Akademie, 1974) 165-166.

"Seth" does not occur (*Thought of Norea, Trimorphic Protennoia*). In *Melchizedek* the name occurs only in the isolated phrase "the children of Seth" (5:20); other tractates similarly designate the spiritual race (i.e., Gnostics) as the "children," "seed," or "race" of Seth (the *Apocryphon of John, Zostrianos, Three Steles of Seth*, and *Gospel of the Egyptians*). The birth of Seth is given brief mention in the *Hypostasis of the Archons*.

One of the most important of the tractates usually labelled as "Sethian" is the *Apocalypse of Adam*. In this work Adam is represented as giving his son Seth a testamentary revelation. He reveals the future course of the world's history, and also the fact that Seth will be the progenitor of the Gnostic race.

Two of the Nag Hammadi tractates bear titles with Seth's name, the *Second Treatise of the Great Seth* (NHC VII,2) and the *Three Steles of Seth*. No mention is made of Seth in the text of the *Treatise*, though Seth may (perhaps secondarily) be regarded as the putative revealer = "author" of the document. In the *Three Steles of Seth* one Dositheos is represented as interpreting the "steles".

In the *Apocryphon of John* Seth is the (heavenly) son of the perfect Man, Adam, and is placed over the second pleromatic light, Oroiael.

In his article published in this volume he adds *Allogenes (NHC XI,3)* and *Marsanes* (NHC X,1), as well as the untitled tractate from the Bruce Codex. For another list of Gnostic documents implicitly identified as "Sethian" see Alexander Böhlig and Pahor Labib, *Koptisch-Gnostische Apokalypsen aus Codex V von Nag Hammadi* (Sonderband, *Wissenschaftliche Zeitschrift der Martin-Luther Universität Halle-Wittenberg*; Halle/Saale 1963) 87. Böhlig omits the *Hypostasis of the Archons, Melchizedek, Thought of Norea*, and *Trimorphic Protennoia* (probably because he was not familiar with them), and adds *Allogenes*, the *Second Treatise of the Great Seth* and the untitled tractate from the Bruce Codex. Cf. Klijn's discussion of the Nag Hammadi texts, *Seth*, 90-107.

Citations in this paper are according to page and line of the codex. Translations quoted here are taken from *NHLibEng*, as follows: *Allogenes*, translated by John D. Turner and Orval S. Wintermute; the *Apocalypse of Adam*, Douglas M. Parrott; *Apocryphon of John*, Frederik Wisse; *Eugnostos the Blessed*, Parrott; *Gospel of the Egyptians*, Alexander Böhlig and Wisse; *Hypostasis of the Archons*, Bentley Layton; *Mechizedek*, Søren Giversen and myself; *On the Origin of the World*, Hans-Gebhard Bethge and Wintermute; *Paraphrase of Shem*, Wisse; *Three Steles of Seth*, James M. Robinson; *Trimorphic Protennoia*, Turner; *Zostrianus*, John H. Sieber. The Coptic text of all of the Nag Hammadi codices is now available in J.M. Robinson, et al., *The Facsimile Edition of the Nag Hammadi Codices* (10 volumes; Leiden : Brill, 1973-1977). Critical editions of various tractates will be cited below. For bibliography citing publications of, and studies on, the Nag Hammadi tractates and other Gnostic materials see David M. Scholer, *Nag Hammadi Bibliography, 1948-1969* (Leiden: Brill, 1971), annually supplemented in *NovT*.

Translations of ancient texts other than the Nag Hammadi materials appearing in this paper are my own, except where otherwise specified.

The preexistent souls constituting the seed of Seth dwell in the third light, Daveithe. The heavenly Adam and Seth have their earthly counterparts as well, and the birth of Seth is narrated in the text.

The *Gospel of the Egyptians* contains a highly developed doctrine of Seth. This tractate is represented as a book written by the "Great Seth" and placed on a high mountain to be reserved for the elect of the last times. The "Great Seth" is the heavenly son of the incorruptible Man, Adamas. He also plays a savior role, for he is sent into the lower world to rescue the elect, "putting on" Jesus for that purpose.

As we shall see, there is reason to include in our purview documents which have not hitherto been labelled as Sethian, or in which Seth is not named. In two versions of the *Apocryphon of John* Seth is referred to as the "image" of the Son of Man; the latter could, at first glance, be taken as a designation for the heavenly Seth. The "Son of Man" terminology occurs in *Eugnostos the Blessed* (NHC III,*3*; V,*1*) and the *Sophia of Jesus Christ* (NHC III,*4*; BG *3*) and we shall therefore have to consider whether Seth, though unnamed, lies in the background.

Two additional tractates present special problems: the *Paraphrase of Shem* (NHC VII,*1*) and *Allogenes* (NHC XI,*3*). The *Paraphrase of Shem* contains material related to the "Sethian" system described by Hippolytus and supposedly derived by him from a document called "the Paraphrase of Seth." We shall have to consider, therefore, whether the *Paraphrase of Shem* in the Nag Hammadi collection should really be called "the Paraphrase of Seth," even though Seth is never mentioned in the text.[19] *Allogenes* could be regarded as a "Sethian" document on the testimony of Epiphanius that the Sethians possessed books called "Allogenes" (*Haer.* 39.5.1) and that Seth himself was called "Allogenes" (*Haer.* 40.7.7).[20]

As has already been noted in the citations, two of the Nag Hammadi tractates already discussed (the *Apocryphon of John* and the *Sophia of Jesus Christ*) occur also in the Berlin Gnostic Codex (BG).[21] Of the other extant Coptic Gnostic codices, the Askew Codex[22] contains no

---

[19] For discussion of this problem see esp. Frederick Wisse, "The Redeemer Figure in the Paraphrase of Shem," *NovT* 12 (1970) 138; and Tardieu, "Les livres mis sous le nom de Seth," 205.

[20] Böhlig includes *Allogenes* in his list of Sethian books, and Schenke adds it to his list in his most recent treatment. Cf. n. 18.

[21] See Walter C. Till and Hans-Martin Schenke, eds., *Die Gnostische Schriften des koptischen Papyrus Berolinensis 8502* (TU 60[2]; Berlin: Akademie, 1972).

[22] See Carl Schmidt, *Pistis Sophia* (Coptica 2; Copenhagen: Gyldendal, 1925).

reference to Seth; but Seth does occur as a divine being, under the name "Setheus", in the untitled tractate of the Bruce Codex.[23]

In what follows, the sources surveyed above will be utilized to build a typology of the Gnostic figure of Seth,[24] and comparable non-Gnostic materials will be considered in order to achieve some clarity regarding the sources of Gnostic speculation on the figure of Seth, son of Adam.

III. TYPOLOGY OF THE GNOSTIC SETH

Our typology will be arranged according to what the texts tell us of the identity of Seth (A-C) and the function of Seth (D-E). Our procedures will be, under each heading, to consider the primary sources first, and then to bring in the patristic testimonies.

A. *The birth of Seth.*[25] There are several Gnostic accounts of the birth of Seth, and all of them consist of midrashic restatements of the key passages in Genesis 4 (esp. 4:25) and 5 (esp. 5:3). These accounts of the birth of Seth are also designed to counterbalance similar midrashic restatements of the story of Cain and Abel (Gen 4:1-16).

The *Hypostasis of the Archons* (91:11-92:2)[26] contains a midrash on Gen 4:1-15, 25 which is especially important for our purposes. The births of Cain and Abel are narrated as follows:

> Now afterwards (i.e., after the expulsion of Adam and Eve from Paradise) she (Eve) bore Cain, their son; and Cain cultivated the land. Thereupon he (Adam) knew his wife; again becoming pregnant, she bore Abel (91:11-14; parentheses mine).

In this passage, interpreting Gen 4:1-2, Cain is identified as the son of the archons ("their son"). The rape of Eve by the archons had been reported earlier in the text (89:18-30). This idea of the parentage of Cain is based on a widespread Jewish haggadic tradition according to which Cain was the product of a liaison between Eve and the

---

[23] See Carl Schmidt, *Gnostische Schriften in Koptischen Sprache aus dem Codex Brucianus* (TU 8; Leipzig: Hinrichs, 1892); Charlotte A. Baynes, *A Coptic Treatise Contained in the Codex Brucianus* (Cambridge: University Press, 1933). Baynes arranged the leaves of the manuscript in a different order from that of Schmidt's edition; her edition has been used here. Cf. Klijn, *Seth*, 111-112.

[24] A similar procedure is followed by George MacRae, "Seth." MacRae's paper has been of particular help to me in my own treatment of the figure of Seth.

[25] Cf. MacRae, "Seth," 19-20.

[26] The definitive edition is now that of Bentley Layton, "The Hypostasis of the Archons," *HTR* 67 (1974) 351-425 and 69 (1976) 31-101.

angel of death or the devil, Sammael.[27] *Targum Ps.-Jonathan* follows this tradition in its rendering of Gen 4:1-2:

> And Adam was aware that his wife had conceived from Sammael the angel, and she became pregnant and bore Cain, and he was like those on high, not like those below; and she said, "I have acquired a man, the angel of the Lord." And she went on to bear from Adam, her husband, her twin sister and Abel. And Abel was a keeper of sheep, but Cain was a man working in the earth.[28]

The birth of Seth is recounted in the *Hypostasis of the Archons* as follows:

> And Adam [knew] his female counterpart Eve, and she became pregnant, and bore [Seth] to Adam. And she said, "I have borne [another] man through God, in place [of Abel]" (91:30-33).

This passage is an interpretive restatement of Gen 4:25; and the restorations of the names "Seth" and "Abel" in the lacunae are therefore certain. However, it is to be noted that Gen 4:1 is reflected here, too, in the saying attributed to Eve: "I have borne [another] man through God." Cf. Gen 4:1 (LXX): ἐκτησάμην ἄνθρωπον διὰ τοῦ θεοῦ. "Another man" interprets σπέρμα ἕτερον in Gen 4:25. The *Hypostasis of the Archons* does not, therefore, extrapolate from σπέρμα ἕτερον a doctrine of a special "race" or "seed" of Seth, as a number of other Gnostic texts do. Instead, special significance for Gnostic mankind is derived from the birth of the heroine Norea, sister of Seth.

> Again Eve became pregnant, and she bore [Norea]. And she said, "He has begotten on [me a] virgin as an assistance [for] many generations of mankind." She is the virgin whom the Forces did not defile (91:34-92:3).

Norea, sister of Seth, thus renders for mankind the "assistance"

---

[27] Cf. B. Pearson, "The Figure of Norea," 149, 151. On Sammael in Jewish tradition and in Gnosticism see, e.g., Birger A. Pearson, "Jewish Haggadic Traditions in *The Testimony of Truth* from Nag Hammadi (CG IX,3)," *Ex Orbe Religionum: Studia Geo Widengren* (ed. Jan Bergman et al.; Supplements to *Numen* 21; Leiden: Brill, 1972) 467.

[28] Translated by John Bowker, *The Targums and Rabbinic Literature* (Cambridge: University Press, 1969) 132. Cf. Klijn, *Seth*, 3-4. For the text see now David Rieder, *Pseudo-Jonathan: Targum Jonathan Ben Uziel on the Pentateuch* (Jerusalem: Salomon, 1974), an improved collation of the London manuscript used by Ginsburger in his edition. For other testimonies to this tradition of the origin of Cain cf. *Pirqe R. El.* 21; *2 Enoch* 31:6; *b. Yebam.* 103b; *b. 'Abod. Zar.* 22b; *b. Šabb.* 146a; *Zohar* 3.76b; and in the NT John 8:44 and 1 John 3:12.

(βοήθεια; cf. Gen 2:18) requisite for salvation. Her begetting is from God; "he" in Eve's exclamation is clearly a reference to God, the Father of the All.[29] As a virgin she is "undefiled," in contrast to the earthly Eve, whose rape by the archons is narrated earlier in the text.

In view of the notable parallels between the *Hypostasis of the Archons* and *On the Origin of the World* (NHC II,5),[30] one would expect to find in the latter some reference to the birth of Seth. But that is evidently not the case. Eve is described as "the first virgin, not having a husband" (114:4). After giving birth she sings a hymn, the last line of which is, "I have borne a lordly man" (114:15). This appears to refer to Cain, for Gen 4:1 (esp. the Hebrew: קָנִיתִי אִישׁ אֶת־יְהוָה) is in the background.[31] In a later passage the rape of the earthly Eve by the seven archangels is narrated (117:2-15), followed immediately by the birth of Abel and others: "She conceived Abel first from the prime ruler; and she bore the rest of the sons from the seven authorities and their angels" (117:15-18).

Whether Seth was meant to be included in this reference is impossible to say; in any case he is not mentioned in the text. Nothing is said, either, of the birth of Norea. Her name is mentioned only in the title of a book referred to earlier, "The First Book of Noraia" (102:10-11) or "The First Treatise of Oraia" (102:24-25).[32]

We turn to the *Apocryphon of John*. The longer recension (NHC II,1) has the fuller account of the birth of Seth, and I follow that version here.[33] This account is preceded by the story of the birth of Cain and Abel. The seduction of Eve by the chief archon results in the birth of two sons, Eloim called "Cain," and Yawe called "Abel" (24:15-26). The result is the planting of "sexual intercourse" in the world (24:27-31).

That *both* Cain and Abel are the product of Eve's illicit union with

---

[29] So Layton, "Hypostasis," 62. This narrative of the birth of Norea has a parallel in the reference to the birth of Cain's unnamed twin sister in *Tg. Ps.-J.*, quoted above.

[30] See Alexander Böhlig and Pahor Labib, *Die Koptisch-Gnostische Schrift ohne Titel aus Codex II von Nag Hammadi im Koptischen Museum zu Alt-Kairo* (Deutsche Akademie der Wissenschaften zu Berlin, Institut für Orientforschung, 58; Berlin: Akademie, 1962). My references are to the codex pagination, and not to the pagination assigned by Böhlig, following Pahor Labib's publication of plates, *Coptic Gnostic Papyri in the Coptic Museum at Old Cairo* 1 (Cairo, 1956).

[31] MacRae suggests that this passage is a "probable allusion to the birth of Seth"; see "Seth," 19.

[32] Cf. Pearson, "The Figure of Norea," 144.

[33] See Martin Krause and Pahor Labib, *Die Drei Versionen des Apokryphon des Johannes im Koptischen Museum zu Alt-Kairo* (ADAIK, Koptische Reihe 1; Wiesbaden: Harrassowitz, 1962).

the "chief archon" probably reflects a Jewish interpretation of Gen 4:1-2, according to which both Cain and Abel were sons of the devil rather than of Adam.[34]

The birth of Seth is narrated as follows:

> And when Adam recognized the likeness of his own knowledge, he begot the likeness of the son of man. He called him Seth according to the way of the race in the aeons. Likewise the mother also sent down her spirit, which is in her likeness and a copy of those who are in the pleroma, for she will prepare a dwelling place for the aeons which will come down. Thus the seed (σπέρμα) remained for a while assisting (him) in order that, when the Spirit comes forth from the holy aeons, he may raise him up and heal him from the deficiency, that the whole pleroma may (again) become holy and faultless. (24:34-25:16)

In this passage the focal text in Genesis is not 4:25 but 5:3. The key word is "likeness" (ⲉⲓⲘⲉ), rendering both ἰδέα and εἰκών in Gen 5:3 (LXX). The product of Adam's begetting is "the likeness of the son of man," and he is called "Seth," "according to the way of the race in the aeons." The text is here referring back to the "race" or "seed" of the heavenly Seth (cf. 9:11-16). The "Son of Man" in whose "image" Seth is begotten would seem, at first glance, to be a heavenly Seth, but this will have to be tested in another context to be discussed later. In any case we have here an interpretation of Gen 5:1-3:[35] earthly Seth is an "image" of his heavenly prototype, the Son of Man.[36]

It is to be noticed that the "Mother" plays a special providential role in the *Apocryphon of John*, and in that connection we read of the descent of her "spirit" (πνεῦμα) and the "seed" (σπέρμα). The use of the latter term here may reflect interpretation of the key term ἕτερον σπέρμα in Gen 4:25. The heavenly counterpart of the "seed" below is the aforementioned "seed of Seth," dwelling in the third light. The "Mother," of course, is Sophia, who is obliged to intervene in the world below "in order to rectify her deficiency" (cf. 23:20-26).[37]

The patristic reports of Gnostic interpretations of the birth of Seth present ideas similar to those encountered in our primary sources, though

---

[34] Cf. Klijn's discussion of *Gen. Rab.* 24.6; *Pirqe R. El.* 22; *Zohar* 1.55a; *Adam and Eve* 22:3; *1 Enoch* 85:6-8; and the Samaritan *Malef* in *Seth*, 7-10, 16, 21, 28-30.

[35] Cf. MacRae, "Seth," 19.

[36] For discussion of the "birth" of the heavenly Seth see below.

[37] On Gnostic Sophia see above all George MacRae, "The Jewish Background of the Gnostic Sophia Myth," *NovT* 12 (1970) 86-101.

there are some differences in detail. The "others" discussed by
Irenaeus (*Haer.* 1.30), in contrast to the *Hypostasis of the Archons* and
the *Apocryphon of John*, attribute the birth of both Cain and Abel to the
sexual intercourse of Adam and Eve (1.30.9). The birth of Seth is treated
as follows :

> After these they say that Seth was generated by the providence of Prunicus
> (*secundum providentiam Prunici*), then Norea. From these were generated the
> remaining multitude of men (1.30.9).

These Gnostics had a version of the birth of Seth showing points
of similarity both to the *Hypostasis of the Archons* and to the
Apocryphon of John. In common with the former Norea is mentioned;
and in common with the latter the providential role of Sophia
("Prunicus") is stressed. However nothing is said of a special "seed"
of Seth; all mankind is derived from Seth and Norea.

The Sethians described by Ps.-Tertullian attribute the generation of
both Cain and Abel to the angels. Klijn reads Ps.-Tertullian's obviously
garbled account to mean that Cain and Abel were "really the first
creatures,"[38] but probably these Gnostics had a story of the parentage
of Cain and Abel similar to that of the *Apocryphon of John*. It is then
said that the "Mother" (= Sophia) "wanted Seth to be conceived
and born in Abel's place." Here, too, an account similar to the
Apocryphon of John lies in the background, but the phrase "in Abel's
place" shows that their version held closer to the text of Gen 4:25
(ἀντὶ Ἄβελ). The "seed" is mentioned in the following context (cf.
ἕτερον σπέρμα, Gen 4:25). The Mother's purpose is to make the
wicked angels ineffective by means of the "seed."

The Sethians described by Epiphanius evidently attributed the birth
of Cain and Abel to Adam and Eve (δύο ἀνθρώπους, *Haer.* 39.2.1).
The death of Abel was caused by the quarrelling of the angels (39.
2.2). Afterwards the "Mother" caused Seth to be born, "and in him
she placed her power, depositing in him the seed (σπέρμα) of the
power from on high and the spark (σπινθήρ) which is from above,
sent for the first deposit of the seed and the formation" (*Haer.* 39.2.4).
This account of the birth of Seth resembles that of the *Apocryphon
of John*, though it differs from the latter on the origin of Cain and
Abel. Epiphanius later reports that these Sethians also taught that
Seth had a wife named Horaia (39.5.2), a detail which puts us in some

---

[38] Klijn, *Seth*, 82.

contact with the *Hypostasis of the Archons*, according to which Norea is the sister of Seth. "Horaia" and "Norea," of course, are one and the same.[39]

Epiphanius reports of the Archontics that they had a myth according to which Cain and Abel were children of Eve and the devil (*Haer.* 40.5.3). Seth, on the other hand, was the real son of Adam (φύσει ἴδιος αὐτοῦ υἱός). Afterwards the "Power" (δύναμις) from above snatched up Seth and taught him heavenly revelations. The "Power" referred to here may be a reference to Sophia; if so we are again in contact with the account in the *Apocryphon of John*.

As we have seen, all of the various Gnostic accounts of the birth of Seth (and of Cain and Abel) consist of reinterpretations of key passages in scripture; and we have also seen that Jewish exegetical traditions are sometimes to be seen in the background.

B. *Names and titles of Seth.* A number of special names or titles are attached to Seth in Gnostic literature. In this section, which necessarily overlaps other portions of the paper, I shall treat together the various names by which Seth is known.

1. "The Great Seth."[40] In the *Gospel of the Egyptians*[41] the characteristic designation for Seth is "the great Seth" (passim). This title refers not to the earthly Seth, whose birth we have discussed above, but to a Platonic heavenly prototype of the earthly Seth, undoubtedly originating in Gnostic speculation as a projection of the latter onto the transmundane, precosmic plane. The heavenly Seth is then regarded as the "Son" of a heavenly Adam, similarly projected by the Gnostics into the precosmic realm.[42] This can be seen in the following account of the emanation, or "birth," of the great Seth:

> The incorruptible man Adamas asked for them a son out of himself, in order that he (the son) may become father of the immovable, incorruptible race, so that, through it (the race), the silence and the voice may appear, and, through it, the dead aeon may raise itself, so that it may dissolve. And thus there came forth, from above, the power (δύναμις) of the great light, the Manifestation (προφάνεια). She gave birth to the four great lights: Harmozel, Oroiael, Davithe, Eleleth, and the great incorruptible Seth, the son of the incorruptible man Adamas (III 51:5-22).

---

[39] See Pearson, "The Figure of Norea."

[40] Cf. MacRae, "Seth," 20-21.

[41] See Alexander Böhlig and Frederick Wisse, *Nag Hammadi Codices III,2 and IV,2: The Gospel of the Egyptians* (NHS 4; Leiden: Brill, 1975).

[42] Cf. MacRae, "Seth," 20. It should be noted here that the Gnostic Sophia is a similar kind of projection of Eve, the "Mother of the Living." Cf. MacRae, "The Jewish Background", esp. 99-101.

Later on in the text the great Seth is presented as residing in the second light, Oroiael (III 65:16-17) or (anomalously) in the third light, Daveithe (III 56:20; IV 68:3-5). It is the great Seth who initiates the salvation of the elect. The great Seth is also presented as the "author" of the *Gospel of the Egyptians* (III 68:1-2, 11). The great Seth is similarly credited with the authorship of another Nag Hammadi tractate, the *Second Treatise of the Great Seth*.

2. "Emmacha Seth." The heavenly Seth is also designated under names which were probably meant to heighten his transcendent, mysterious character. These names are probably to be understood as *nomina barbara*. In the *Three Steles of Seth*, the heavenly Seth, in blessing his father Geradamas (or "Pigeradamas"), calls himself "Emmacha Seth." The heavenly "son of Adamas" is called "Seth Emmacha Seth" in *Zostrianos* (6:25; 51:14-15). And in the *Gospel of the Egyptians* the heavenly Seth gives praise to yet another, even more exalted, heavenly Seth figure, "the thrice-male child, Telmael Telmael Heli Heli Machar Machar Seth" (III 62:2-4), also called "the incorruptible child Telmael Telmachael Eli Eli Machar Machar Seth" (IV 59:18-21), "the great power Heli Heli Machár Machar Seth" (III 65:8-9), and "the great power Telmachael Telmachael Eli Eli Machar Machar Seth" (IV 77:2-4)!

Klijn has suggested an etymology for "Emmacha," אמה, viz., "servant,"[43] but this does not seem likely. An Egyptian etymology has also been suggested.[44] But in dealing with *nomina barbara* etymological analysis is hazardous at best.

3. "Son of Man"(?) The problem of the Gnostic "Son of Man" is very complex, and certainly cannot be treated here in the detail it deserves.[45] We shall have to satisfy ourselves with a consideration of those texts in which Seth appears to be called "Son of Man," or something similar.

As an example of the complexity of this problem we refer first to the passage from the *Apocryphon of John* quoted earlier in connection with the birth of Seth (II 24:34-25:16). We saw evidence there of an interpretation of Gen 5:1-3, and indicated that at first glance one might tend to identify the "Son of Man" in whose image the earthly Seth is

---

[43] *Seth*, 105 n. 137.

[44] See below for discussion.

[45] For a useful discussion of the evidence see Frederick H. Borsch, *The Christian and Gnostic Son of Man* (SBT, 2d series 14; London : SCM, 1970) esp. 58-121.

begotten as the heavenly Seth. However, a closer look at Gen 5:3 itself, wherein Seth is born as "a son in his own (i.e., Adam's) likeness," will give us greater clarity as to the identity of the "Son of Man" in the *Apocryphon of John*. The title "Son of Man," in fact, applies to a heavenly *Adam* ("Man"), not a heavenly Seth. Earlier in the text of the *Apocryphon of John* a voice comes from heaven as a rebuke to the creator-archon Yaldabaoth: "Man exists and the Son of Man" (II 14:14-15). "Man" in this *bath qol* is none other than the Highest God; the "Son of Man" is another Anthropos figure called "Adamas," "Pigeradamas," etc.[46] His son, in turn, is the heavenly Seth (cf., e.g., *Apocryphon* II 8:28-9:14). The heavenly Seth would then, more consistently, be called "the Son of the Son of Man."

In fact, the designation "the Son of the Son of Man" does occur in another Nag Hammadi tractate, *Eugnostos the Blessed*:

> Now the first aeon is that of Immortal Man. The second aeon is that of Son of Man, the one who is called "First Begetter." ⟨The third is that of the Son of Son of Man,⟩ the one who is called "Savior." (III 85:9-14)[47]

Though the name "Seth" is not found in *Eugnostos the Blessed*, there can be hardly any doubt that "the Son of Son of Man" in this passage is Seth;[48] more specifically he is the heavenly Seth. Curiously, the "third aeon" referred to as "the Son of the Son of Man" is missing from the Christianized parallel text, the *Sophia of Jesus Christ*. The figure of Seth has therefore altogether disappeared from the latter.

Something like a "Son of Man" title is given to the heavenly Seth in some Nag Hammadi tractates. In the *Gospel of the Egyptians* "the great Seth" is also called "the son of the incorruptible man, Adamas" (III 51:20-22; 55:16-18), but in this tractate as in the *Apocryphon of John* the "Son of Man" referred to in the voice from heaven ("the Man exists and the Son of the Man," III 59:1-3) is probably not Seth, but a heavenly Adam/Anthropos, "Son" of the highest Deity ("Man").

---

[46] See esp. Hans-Martin Schenke, *Der Gott "Mensch" in der Gnosis* (Göttingen: Vandenhoeck & Ruprecht, 1962), esp. 34-43. As Schenke has convincingly demonstrated, the Gnostic "Man" speculation consists essentially of interpretation of Gen 1:26b. Cf. also "Das sethianische System."

[47] The material in angular brackets is restored on the basis of the parallel in Codex V. I am quoting here (as noted above) from *NHLibEng*.

[48] See Douglas Parrott, "Evidence of Religious Syncretism in Gnostic Texts from Nag Hammadi," *Religious Syncretism in Antiquity: Essays in Conversation with Geo Widengren* ed. Birger A. Pearson; Missoula, Montana: Scholars Press, 1975) 179-180.

The heavenly Seth is called "the son of Adamas" in *Zostrianos* (6:25-26; 30:9-10; 51:14). And in the first stele of the *Three Steles of Seth* he addresses his father Geradamas (or "Pigeradamas," 118:25-27). But, in fine, it does not appear that Seth is ever given the simple title "Son of Man" either in his heavenly or his earthly manifestation.[49]

4. "Allogenes." The names and titles for Seth already discussed are ultimately tied to speculative interpretation of Gen 5:1-3 (in relation to Gen 1:26-27), but in the case of the name "Allogenes" we have to do with an interpretation of the other key text, Gen 4:25, with its reference to Seth as an ἕτερον σπέρμα ("other seed").

It is in Epiphanius's account of the Archontics that we learn of the name "Allogenes" as applied to Seth (*Haer*. 40.7.1). The same name is given to Seth's seven sons by the Archontics (*Haer*. 40.7.1). In addition, we are told in the same report that the Archontics make use of books called "Allogenes" (καὶ τοῖς ᾿Αλλογένεσι καλουμένοις, 40. 2.2). Epiphanius later adds that the Archontics have written books in Seth's own name, as well as others in his and his seven sons' name (40.7.4).

This coheres well with what we are told of the Sethians. While Epiphanius does not tell us directly that the Sethians call Seth "Allogenes," one can make that assumption nevertheless, for he speaks of seven books in the name of Seth, and "others" called "Allogeneis" (*Haer*. 39.5.1). The seven books of Seth and the "others" are probably the same; Epiphanius has garbled his sources. Perhaps, too, the "many books in the name of Seth" mentioned by Epiphanius in use among the libertine "Gnostics" (*Haer*. 26.8.1) are the same books. Thus we can presume that the epithet "Allogenes" is a Sethian-Gnostic designation for Seth.[50]

Accordingly it is reasonable to regard the Nag Hammadi tractate *Allogenes* as a "Sethian" book, and to assume that the revealer "Allogenes" is to be understood as a manifestation of Seth himself.[51]

---

[49] Unless the term "son of man" in *TriProt* 49:19 is to be understood as referring to a manifestation of Seth. Seth, however, is not named at all in the tractate.

[50] It might be added here that the Sethians, contrary to Klijn (*Seth*, p. 35), did not call Seth ἀνταλλαγή (cf. *Haer*. 39.5.7). This designation is Epiphanius's own interpretation of the name Seth (ὅπερ ἑρμηνεύεται ἀνταλλαγή), based on the phrase ἀντὶ ᾿Αβελ in Gen 4:25.

[51] Cf. the reference to "apocalypses" in the name of Allogenes and others in Porphyry, *Plot*. 16, and the "Apocalypse of the Stranger" (= Allogenes) reported by Theodore bar Konai in use among the Audians. On the latter see esp. Henri-Charles Puech, "Fragments retrouvés de i"Apocalypse d'Allogene'," *Mélanges Franz*

A name similar to Allogenes is used once in *Zostrianos*, "Allogenios" (128:7). Allogenios, together with Eleleth, Kodere, and Epiphanios, constitute "the fourth aeon of the fourth Light." This name is doubtless modelled on "Allogenes," but is not a designation for Seth.

5. "Setheus." This variation on the name Seth—essentially a Graeciza-tion of the Hebrew name— is found in the untitled tractate of the Bruce Codex (passim).[52] In that tractate Setheus is an aspect of the highest God, and has a demiurgic function.[53] As Klijn says, "He has clearly lost all contact with the historical setting in which he was originally placed in the beginning of Genesis."[54] What we see in the Bruce Codex, in fact, is an advanced point along the trajectory of Gnostic speculation on Seth as a heavenly being.

The name "Setheus" occurs also in *Zostrianos* of a figure in the "third light" of the "third aeon" (*Zostrianos* 126:12-16). Here the name seems to be applied to a figure other than Seth, but along the lines of "Allogenios" discussed above.

All of the names and epithets we have discussed refer to the heavenly aspect of Seth, and are to be seen as the product of Gnostic reflection on the transcendent meaning of those key references to Seth in Gen 5:1-3 and 4:25. Thus far, however, we have not discussed the question of gnostic attempts at wordplay or etymology of the name "Seth," such as occurs in the text of Genesis itself: "She bore a son and called his name "Seth' (שֵׁת), for she said, 'God has "set" (שָׁת) for me another offspring instead of Abel.'"[55] A variety of such wordplays on the name "Seth" is displayed in Jewish and Christian literature, and we might therefore expect to find examples of the same kind of thing in Gnostic literature.

Klijn discusses one possible wordplay of this kind, based on Coptic, in the *Apocalypse of Adam* (65:6-9), where Adam says to his son Seth, "I myself have called you by the name of that man who is the seed of the great generation or from whom (it comes)." Klijn,[56] following

---

Cumont (Annuaire de l'Institut de Philologie et d'Histoire Orientales et Slaves de l'Université libre de Bruxelles 4; Brussells, 1936) 955-962.

[52] Cf. n. 23.

[53] This is a very peculiar development in Gnostic speculations on Seth, but the Mandaean Seth, Šitil, plays a similar role in the Mandaean *Book of John*. See, e.g., M. Lidzbarski, *Das Johannesbuch der Mandäer* (Giessen: Töpelmann, 1915) 93, 7; pp. 213, 24-216, 3; cf. Pearson, "Egyptian Seth and Gnostic Seth," 34.

[54] Klijn, *Seth*, 112.

[55] Cf. ibid., 33.

[56] Ibid., 92.

a suggestion made by Rodolphe Kasser,[57] finds a wordplay based
on the similarity of the name Seth (ϲΗΘ) to the Coptic word for "seed"
(ϲΙΤΕ). But this suggestion has to be rejected, not only because the
original language of the *Apocalypse of Adam* was Greek rather than
Coptic, but also because the word for "seed" in this passage is the
Greek word σπορά, not ϲΙΤΕ. Adam is telling his son Seth here that
he is named for the heavenly progenitor (i.e., the heavenly Seth) of
the Gnostic race; the word "seed" reflects a Gnostic interpretation of
Gen 4:25 (ἕτερον σπέρμα).

Another word play suggested by Klijn[58] is more likely. In the
Gospel of the Egyptians it is said that the number of the aeons brought
forth by the great Seth is "the amount of Sodom" (III 60:9-12). The
text goes on to say:

> Some say that Sodom is the place of pasture of the great Seth, which is
> Gomorrah. But others (say) that the great Seth took his plant out of
> Gomorrah and planted it in the second place to which he gave the
> name Sodom. (60:12-18)

The word "plant" (ΤⲰⳠⳐ, both verb and noun) is to be understood as a play on the meaning of the name "Seth" according to
a traditional Jewish explanation, wherein the words שׁת־לי in Gen 4:25
("he has established for me") are related to the word for "plant,"
שׁתיל.[59]

Finally, in another passage not noticed by Klijn, we find an indication
that some Gnostics were aware of the Hebrew wordplay found in
the text of Genesis itself, שֵׁת/שָׁת. Epiphanius reports that, according
to the Sethians, the Mother "placed" (ἔθετο, cf. Gen 4:25 Aquila)[60]
her own power in Seth, "setting down (καταβαλοῦσα) in him the seed
(σπέρμα) of the power from above ..." (*Haer.* 39.2.4). The use of the
words τίθημι and καταβάλλω would possibly indicate a knowledge
of the original Hebrew word play on the name "Seth" in Gen 4:25,

---

[57] "Bibliotheque Gnostique V, Apocalypse d'Adam," in *RTP* 17 (1967) 318 n. 2;
"Textes Gnostiques, Remarques à propos des éditions récentes du Livre Secret de Jean
et des Apocalypses de Paul, Jacques et Adam," in *Muséon* 68 (1965) 93 n. 56.

[58] *Seth*, 102 n. 122.

[59] Cf. Klijn, *Seth*, 34. The source for this tradition is late—Klijn cites the
Syriac *Book of the Bee*—but the wordplay in the *Gospel of the Egyptians* would
seem to indicate that the tradition is at least as old as the latter. For additional
discussion of this passage, see below.

[60] Cf. Frederick Field, *Origenis Hexaplorum quae supersunt sive veterum interpretum
Graecorum in totum Vetus Testamentum Fragmenta* (Oxford, 1875; reprinted, Hildesheim:
Olms, 1964) 1. 20.

שׁת/שֵׁת, for the Hebrew word שִׁית can be rendered with either of these Greek verbs. The LXX rendering of Gen 4:25, on the other hand, uses the word ἐξανίστημι.[61]

C. *Seth as progenitor of the Gnostic race.*[62] Probably the most important feature of Gnostic speculation on Seth is the idea that Gnostics constitute a special "race" of Seth. Indeed this should be seen as "the fixed point of what may be called Sethian Gnosticism."[63]

This idea is fully elaborated in the *Apocalypse of Adam*, wherein Adam reveals the future to his son Seth. In a passage already treated in another context (65:6-9), Adam tells Seth, "I myself have called you by the name of that man who is the seed of the great generation or from whom (it comes)." As we observed, "that man" is the heavenly Seth; he is the "seed" referred to in Gen 4:25 (ἕτερον σπέρμα), and from him there comes the "generation" (γενεά) of Seth, i.e., the Gnostics. Later in the text it is said that the men who came from this seed, who have received the "life of the knowledge," are "strangers" (ϣⲙⲙⲟ) to the Creator (69:12-18), and in this we detect another allusion to the phrase ἕτερον σπέρμα in Gen 4:25.

The revelation to Seth in the *Apocalypse of Adam* consists largely of a "salvation history" of the race of Seth, its origin, its survival of flood and fire, and its final salvation through the coming of a savior, the "Illuminator." This kind of "salvation history" is a regular feature in presumably "Sethian" Gnostic materials. In the *Apocalypse of Adam* we have what seems to be an early stage of this tradition, modelled on Jewish apocalyptic texts and especially on the Jewish apocryphal Adam literature.[64]

The *Gospel of the Egyptians* presents similar features, though more highly developed. In a passage already treated in another context (III 51:5-22) the heavenly Adamas requests a son, "in order that he (the son) may become father of the immovable, incorruptible race" (III 51: 7-9). Thereafter we learn of the birth of "the great incorruptible Seth" (III 51:20) and, in turn, the placing of his seed in the third great light, Davithe (III 56:19-22). After the sowing of the seed of Seth

---

[61] (Non-Gnostic) Christian interpretation of Gen 4:25 capitalized on the apparent reference in Gen 4:25 LXX to the resurrection of Christ; see Klijn, *Seth*, 34-35.

[62] Cf. MacRae, "Seth," 21-22.

[63] MacRae, "Seth," 21.

[64] See, e.g., Pheme Perkins, "Apocalyptic Schematization in the Apocalypse of Adam and the Gospel of the Egyptians," *SBLSP 1972*, 591-595.

into the created aeons (III 60:9-11) the "great incorruptible race" (cf. III
60:25-26) suffers through perils of flood and fire, and is ultimately saved
by Seth himself. The great Seth passes through "three parousias"
(flood, conflagation, and judgement) in order to save his race (III 63:4-8),
"putting on" Jesus for that purpose (III 64:1-3).

In the *Apocryphon of John*, as in the *Gospel of the Egyptians*, we are
told of the precosmic origin of the "seed (σπέρμα) of Seth" which
consists of the preexistent "souls of the saints," and, as in the *Gospel
of the Egyptians*, Seth's seed is located in the third light, Daveithai
(II 9:14-17; cf. BG 36:1-7). However, in the "salvation history" that
is subsequently revealed, the "seed of Seth" is not explicitly mentioned.
We do read of "the immovable race" (ⲧⲅⲉⲛⲉⲁ ⲛ̄ⲁⲧⲕⲓⲙ, II 25:23
et passim) in this connection, and we should probably take this as an
implicit reference to the "seed" or the "race" of Seth.

In the *Three Steles of Seth* the heavenly Seth is designated as "the
Father of the living and unshakeable race" (ⲧⲅⲉⲛⲉⲁ ⲉⲧⲟⲛ̄ϩ ⲁⲩⲱ
ⲛ̄ⲁⲧⲕⲓⲙ, 118:12-13). In praise of his father Geradamas Seth says,
"Thy place is over a race, for thou hast caused all these to increase,
though because of my seed" (120:8-10). Similarly in *Zostrianos* we
read of "the sons of Seth" (7:8-9), the "living seed" that came from
Seth (30:10-14), and "the holy seed of Seth" (130:16-17). On the other
hand, at the beginning of the tractate the heavenly messenger addresses
Zostrianos as "the father of the exalted, my chosen ones," who should
save those who are worthy (4:7-18). Is Zostrianos to be understood
as an incarnation of Seth? A similar question is posed in *Melchizedek*,
where we find the elect referred to both as "the children of Seth" (5:20)
and as "the race of the highpriest," i.e., Melchizedek (6:17). We shall
have to return to his problem.

In patristic sources we find further evidence of Gnostic speculation on
Seth as the father of a special race. Epiphanius begins his description
of the Sethian Gnostics with the observation that they trace their
"race (γένος) back to Seth, son of Adam" (*Haer*. 39.1.3), and to the
action of the "Mother" (Sophia) in depositing in Seth the "seed of
the power from above" (39.2.4-6). A "salvation history" of the race
of Seth is also presented in Epiphanius's account, resembling those we
have encountered in the Coptic sources.

As has already been observed, Hippolytus's account of Sethian
Gnosticism differs remarkably from that of Epiphanius. There we find
no reference to the "seed" or "race" of Seth. Seth merely functions
as an allegorical symbol for the principle of Light, in contrast to

Cain (Darkness) and Abel (Intermediate Spirit; see *Haer.* 5.20). Similarly the Valentinians look upon Seth as an allegorical symbol of the "spiritual" (πνευματικός) class of mankind, i.e., the Gnostics.[65] Finally, in contrast, we should recall that one Gnostic system evidently looked upon Seth as the father of all mankind, not just of the Gnostic "race" (Irenaeus, *Haer.* 1.30.9, discussed above).

The theory of a Gnostic race of Sethian ancestry has important parallels in Jewish speculation on Seth. As an example from Jewish apocalyptic literature, the dream visions of Enoch in *1 Enoch* (chaps. 85-90) could be cited. In that passage a kind of "salvation history" is narrated, telling of the history of the world from creation to the coming of the Messiah. Seth is presented symbolically as a white bull, the people of Israel as a nation of white bulls, and the Messiah as a white bull. The rest of mankind, in contrast, are presented as black oxen. This suggests that Seth is looked upon as the progenitor of the elect race, and finally of the Messiah.[66]

Especially important for our purposes, however, is Philo's treatise *On the Posterity and Exile of Cain*. Commenting on Gen 4:17-25, Philo remarks that all lovers of virtue are descendants of Seth (*Post.* 42), in contrast to the race of Cain. Again, commenting on the term ἕτερον σπέρμα in Gen 4:25, Philo says that Seth is the "seed of human virtue" (*Post.* 173), sown from God (*Post.* 171). For Philo, therefore, all virtuous men are the race of Seth, which means that actual human generation is irrelevant. The Gnostics look upon spiritual or Gnostic mankind in the same way, as symbolic "descendants" of Seth. In both cases this doctrine is read out of Gen 4:25. Indeed it would appear that the Gnostic interpretation of Gen 4:25 is influenced by a Jewish exegetical tradition similar to that encountered in Philo. In any case, no such interpretation of Gen 4:25 is ever found in (non-Gnostic) Christian sources.

D. *Seth as recipient/revealer of gnosis.*[67] A very prominent aspect of Gnostic speculation on Seth is the role that he is thought to play in the transmission of redemptive knowledge, and in that connection Seth is credited with the "authorship" of a number of books. In discussing

---

[65] Cf. discussion above, and the references in n. 15.

[66] Cf. Klijn, *Seth*, 20-23. A number of other texts trace the generations of the righteous back to Seth with a focus on Gen 5:1-3, according to which Seth is the bearer of the "image of God." See, e.g., *Pirqe R. El.* 22 and the Samaritan *Molad Mosheh*; cf. Klijn, *Seth*, 8-10, 29-30.

[67] Cf. MacRae, "Seth," 17-19.

Seth's role in the transmission of revelation, the *Apocalypse of Adam* is the obvious starting point, for this document represents the earliest stage in the development of this idea in Gnostic literature.

The *incipit* of the *Apocalypse of Adam* reads, "The revelation which Adam taught his son Seth in the seven hundredth year, saying ..." (64:2-4). The revelation is to be seen as a "testamentary" revelation, for the "seven hundredth year" is to be understood as the last year of Adam's life.[68] Adam tells his son Seth of his and Eve's experience in paradise, and transmits revelation that he had received from three angelic informants regarding the future adventures of the elect race, the coming destructions by flood and fire, and the coming of a savior. It is specified that special revelation will be written by angels "on a high mountain, upon a rock of truth" (85:10-11). The conclusion to the book informs us that Adam's son, Seth, "taught his seed" about the revelations he had received from Adam (85:19-24).

The *Apocalypse of Adam* is, in a sense, part and parcel of the Jewish apocryphal Adam literature known to have circulated from at least the first century C.E., and shows special affinities with the *Life of Adam and Eve*. In *Adam and Eve* one finds important parallels to the *Apocalypse of Adam*, both in form and content, beginning especially at 25:1. Compare the opening passages of the revelation to Seth in the *Apocalypse of Adam* and *Adam and Eve*:

Apocalypse of Adam: Adam taught his son Seth ... saying, "Listen to my words, my son Seth. When God had created me out of the earth along with Eve your mother ..." (64:2-8)	*Adam and Eve*: And Adam said to Seth, "Hear, my son Seth, that I may relate to thee what I heard and saw after your mother and I had been driven out of paradise ..." (25:1)
	Cf. 32:1: And Adam answered and said, "Hear me, my sons. When God made us, me and your mother ..."[69]

In *Adam and Eve*, as in the *Apocalypse of Adam*, Adam not only tells Seth of his experiences in paradise, but also prophesies the future

---

[68] The "seven hundredth year" indicates the time since the birth of Seth, which (according to the LXX text of Gen 5:3) took place 230 years after Adam's creation. Cf. the parallel in *Adam and Eve*, where however, the 800 years reflects the use of the Hebrew text of Gen 5:3 (130 years). The parallel in *Apoc. Mos.* 5:1-2 specifically states that Adam has lived 930 years (cf. Gen 5:5), and he calls his sons to him to hear his dying words. On the *Apocalypse of Adam* as a "testament," and its relationship to the Jewish Adam literature, see esp. Perkins, "Apocalyptic Schematization," 591-594. Cf. also the paper by George Nickelsburg published in this volume.

[69] The translation used here is that of L. S. A. Wells, in *APOT*, vol. 2.

salvation of the elect (cf. esp. 29 :1-10). At the end of *Adam and Eve*, Eve instructs her children to write what they had heard from Adam and Eve on tables of stone and clay, stone to survive a judgement of flood, and clay to survive a judgement of fire (50:1-2). Seth thereupon makes the tables (51:3).

In this connection we recall the tradition found in Josephus (*Ant.* 1.2.3 §69=71): the progeny of Seth inscribed their (astronomical) discoveries on two steles, one of brick and one of stone, that their lore might survive the destruction by fire and deluge predicted by Adam. The stone stele, Josephus reports, still survives "in the land of Seiris" (κατὰ γῆν τὴν Σειρίδα).

The reference in the *Apocalypse of Adam* to angelic revelations written on stone on a high mountain reflects this tradition found in Josephus and *Adam and Eve*. "The land of Seiris" in Josephus is probably to be understood as the land of Egypt,[70] but other testimonies to the tradition refer to "*Mount* Sir."[71] "Mount Sir" is to be identified as the mountain of the Flood story (cf. the "mountains of Ararat," Gen 8:4)—an identification explicitly made in *Hyp Arch* 92:14—and the name may have been assimilated to the Babylonian name for the mountain of the Flood story, "Nisir."[72]

Seth's role in the transmission of *gnosis* in the *Apocalypse of Adam* consists essentially of handing on to his "seed" the revelations he had heard from Adam. In this respect the *Apocalypse of Adam* adheres to the pattern established in the Jewish Adam books, such as *Adam*

---

[70] Josephus's κατὰ γῆν τὴν Σειρίδα is probably equivalent to ἐν τῇ Σηριαδικῇ γῇ in a Hermetic text ascribed to Manetho and preserved by Syncellus; see W. G. Waddell, tr., *Manetho* (LCL; Cambridge: Harvard University, 1940) 208-209. The σειριὰς γῆ is the home of Isis, who is herself called σειριάς in Graeco-Egyptian texts. For discussion see esp. Richard Reitzenstein, *Poimandres: Studien zur griechisch-ägyptischen und frühchristlichen Literatur* (Leipzig: Teubner, 1904; reprinted, Darmstadt: Wissenschaftliche Buchgesellschaft, 1966) 183.

[71] E.g., the *Chronology* of Ps.-Malalas 6.5: εἰς τὸ Σίριδος ὄρος. See William Adler et al., "Materials Relating to Seth." Cf. also Adler's "Notes to Text of George Syncellus and Pseudo-Malalas"; but Adler overlooks the fact that "the land of Seiris" is probably Egypt. Cf. n. 70, and the excursus below.

[72] Cf. "The Epic of Gilgamesh," *ANET*[2], p. 94 (tablet XI, line 140). Unfortunately the Hellenistic author Berossos does not specify the name of the mountain; he merely reports that the flood hero Xisouthros's boat came to rest ἐν τοῖς Κορδυαίων ὄρεσι τῆς Ἀρμενίας. See fr. 34 in Paul Schnabel, *Berossos und die Babylonisch-Hellenistische Literatur* (Berlin: Teubner, 1923) 266. Alternatively, the name "Mount Sir" may reflect assimilation to the biblical mountain of the Edomites, Mount Seir (Σηιρ), which was also a mountain of divine revelation (cf., e.g., Isa 21:11). This suggestion I owe to John Strugnell of Harvard.

and Eve. The intentionality in the *Apocalypse of Adam*, of course, is
radically different; the Gnostic author is obviously critical of the
Jewish apocryphal Adam tradition,[73] and breathes the Gnostic spirit of
defiance vis-à-vis the Creator.

Seth's role as revealer of *gnosis* is escalated in other Gnostic
documents. The *Gospel of the Egyptians* represents such an escalation
in its treatment, though at numerous points it shares common traditions
with the *Apocalypse of Adam*, including a similar handling of "salvation
history." No mention is made of Adam's role in the transmission of
knowledge in the *Gospel*. At the end of it we are informed that "the great
Seth" (i.e., the heavenly Seth) wrote the book and placed it "in
high mountains" (III 68 : 1-3), "in the mountain that is called Charaxio"
(III 68 : 12-13), that it might be used as revelation for the elect of the end-
time. The *Gospel of the Egyptians* is meant to reveal *gnosis* about
the highest God, and as such is also given the title "The Holy
Book of the Great Invisible Spirit" (III 69 : 16-19; cf. 40 : 12-14).

In the *Three Steles of Seth* the heavenly Seth is credited with
three steles inscribed with praises offered up by Seth to the heavenly
Trinity of Father, Mother, and Son. The reference to "steles" reflects
the Jewish legend of revelatory steles of stone and brick, discussed
above. A certain Dositheos is credited with reading and transmitting
the contents of Seth's steles for the benefit of the elect. The occurrence
of the name "Dositheos" may reflect Samaritan influence.[74]

In this context we should compare *Zostrianos*. At the end of that
document Zostrianos reports, "I wrote three tablets and left them as
knowledge for those who come after me, the living elect" (130 : 1-4).
This seems to reflect the tradition concerning the Sethian "steles"
discussed above, though the word translated "tablets" ($\pi\acute{\nu}\xi o\varsigma$) indicates
a wooden tablet rather than one of stone. The colophon at the end
poses another question: "Zostrianos. Words of truth of Zostrianos.
God of Truth. Words of Zoroaster" (132 : 6-9). Recalling that Zoroaster
may have been identified with Seth in certain circles,[75] and noting
the redemptive role assigned to Zostrianos in the tractate, we are
entitled to wonder whether Zostrianos might not have been regarded
as an incarnation of Seth in the minds of the author and his circle.[76]

---

[73] Cf. Perkins, "Apocalyptic Schematization," 591.

[74] See Schenke, "Das Sethianische System," 171-172.

[75] See esp. Wilhelm Bousset, *Hauptprobleme der Gnosis* (Göttingen: Vandenhoeck &
Ruprecht, 1907) 378-382.

[76] For further discussion of this problem, see below.

The *Second Treatise of the Great Seth* presents an analogous problem, for it is attributed (in a probably secondary title at the end : 70 : 11-12) to the "great Seth." In the body of the text Jesus Christ is the revealer, but it is probable that the *Treatise* was used (if not composed) in circles in which Jesus Christ was venerated as an incarnation of Seth.

This brings us to the testimony of Epiphanius regarding the Sethian Gnostics. As we have already noted, the Sethians known to Epiphanius not only had seven books in the name of Seth (*Haer.* 39.5.1) but also regarded Jesus Christ as a manifestation of Seth himself (39.1.3; 39.3.5). In addition, they had books called "Allogenes" (39.5.1). The Archontics, too, had books called "Allogeneis" (40.2.2), as well as books in Seth's own name (40.7.4). Seth himself, in their system, bore the name "Allogenes" (40.7.1). Books in the name of Seth circulated also among the libertine "Gnostics" (*Haer.* 26.8.1).[77]

The information we have from Epiphanius regarding the use of books called "Allogenes," and the identity of "Allogenes" and Seth, allows us to inquire whether the "Allogenes" who addresses his son "Messos" in the Nag Hammadi tractate *Allogenes* is to be understood as a manifestation of, or incarnation of, Seth. In *Allogenes* the feminine revealer-angel Youel guides Allogenes on a visionary ascent to the heavenly realm; the same kind of revelatory ascent is attributed to Seth-Allogenes by the Archontics, according to Epiphanius (*Haer.* 40.7.1-2).[78] At the end of the tractate Allogenes is commanded to write down the revelations, and to leave the book upon a mountain for the sake of those who are "worthy" (68 : 16-21). These details recall the end of the *Gospel of the Egyptians*, discussed above.[79] At the very end of *Allogenes*, there is a possible reference to other books of Allogenes : "all [the books of] Allo[ge]nes" (69 : 17-19), corroborating Epiphanius's state-

---

[77] In the same passage we read also of "apocalypses of Adam"; it is possible, therefore, that the Nag Hammadi *Apocalypse of Adam* was known to them.

[78] The Cologne Mani Codex (pp. 50-52) quotes from an apocalypse of Seth(el) describing a similar revelatory journey to heaven; see Albert Henrichs and Ludwig Koenen, ed., "Der Kölner Mani-Kodex (P. Colon. inv. nr. 4780) ΠΕΡΙ ΤΗΣ ΓΕΝΝΗΣ ΤΟΥ ΣΩΜΑΤΟΣ ΑΥΤΟΥ, Edition der Seiten 1-72," *ZPE* 10 (1975) 50-52. The parallels between this quotation and the tradition preserved by Epiphanius are such as to suggest that the Manichaeans and the "Archontics" shared a common source.

[79] Perhaps this passage in *Allogenes* might be of help in determining the meaning of the name given to the mountain of revelation in the *Gospel of the Egyptians*, "Charaxio," i.e., "Mountain of the worthy," reflecting a combination of the Hebrew word for "mountain" (הר) and the Greek word for "worthy" (ἄξιος).

ments regarding a plurality of Allogenes books (*Haer.* 39.5.1;
40.2.2).

Hippolytus's information regarding a "*Paraphrase of Seth*" in use
among the Sethians (*Haer.* 5.22), plus the similarity in content between
the *Paraphrase of Shem* and the "Sethian" system described by the
church father, poses the question whether the title given to the Nag
Hammadi tractate is a mistake for the title given by Hippolytus, or *vice
versa.* Alternatively, we might consider the possibility that the names
"Shem" and "Seth" were interchangeable among some Gnostics.[80]
In the *Paraphrase of Shem*, Shem, in a state of ecstasy, receives a
revelation from a redeemer figure called "Derdekeas." At one point in
the text, Derdekeas says to Shem, "I shall reveal to you completely
that you may reveal them to those who will be upon the earth the
second time" (26:21-25). This refers to the postdiluvian world, of which
Shem (son of Noah) is regarded as a representative. It is therefore
possible that Hippolytus's "*Paraphrase of Seth*" was really a secondary,
"Sethianizing" version of a document originally having nothing to do
with Seth.[81] Be that as it may, "Shem" plays a largely passive role in the
text; "Derdekeas" is the revealer-savior.[82]

As we have seen, the earliest stage in the Gnostic treatment of Seth
as a transmitter of *gnosis* is represented by the *Apocalypse of Adam*,
which, in turn, is based upon Jewish apocryphal Adam traditions.
However, it should be added that there are also Jewish
testimonies to the tradition that Seth (and other antediluvian patriarchs)
wrote revelations in his own name.[83] On the other hand, there are no
(non-Gnostic) Christian sources which ascribe any special knowledge
to Seth, apart from Christian adaptations of the traditions found in *Adam
and Eve* and Josephus. Thus Klijn's conclusion regarding the role of
Seth as a transmitter of knowledge in Gnosticism is correct: "The
Gnostics derived their ideas from Jewish sources."[84]

E. *Seth as Savior.*[85] Seth's role as a revealer of knowledge,
described above, is also to be seen as a saving role, for in Gnosticism
the purpose of the Savior's descent is to reveal the salutary knowledge

---

[80] Cf. Frederick Wisse, "The Redeemer Figure," 138; cf. also Klijn, *Seth*, 88.

[81] Cf. Wisse, "The Redeemer Figure."

[82] Cf. Sŭm-Kušta (Sŭm bar Nû) in the Mandaean *Book of John*, chaps. 14-17,
Lidzbarski, *Johannesbuch*, 58-70.

[83] See, e.g., *2 Enoch* 33:10; cf. Klijn, *Seth*, 20.

[84] Klijn, *Seth*, 112.

[85] Cf. MacRae, "Seth," 21; Klijn, *Seth*, 114-115.

to the elect here below. Indeed, from the Gnostic point of view, any proclaimer of saving knowledge is performing the function of a "savior".[86] Thus we have already discussed an aspect of Seth's role as "Savior" in the previous section.

Nevertheless there is more to be said. In the *Apocalypse of Adam*, part of the revelation given to Seth has to do with the coming of a Savior figure called the "Illuminator of Knowledge." The identity of this Savior is not given, but MacRae's suggestion that this figure "is meant to be a (docetic) incarnation of Seth" is very plausible.[87] The role of Seth as Savior is clearer in the *Gospel of the Egyptians*, but there one finds explicit identification of Seth with Jesus Christ: the great Seth is sent from above, passes through "three parousias" (flood, fire, and the judgement of the archons), and "puts on" Jesus in order to save the straying race of Seth (III 63:24-64:9).[88]

In our previous discussion of the use of the epithet "Son of the Son of Man" in *Eug* III 85:9-14, we saw that this is a reference to Seth despite the fact that the name "Seth" does not occur in the document. We also recall that this reference to the heavenly Seth has an additional specification, "the one who is called 'Savior'" (85:13-14). In *Eugnostos the Blessed*, however, there is no explicit reference to an earthly manifestation of the Savior, though "Eugnostos the blessed," writing "to those who are his," may plausibly be assumed to be playing this role (III 70:1-2).

In the previous section we also noted the possibility that Zostrianos, in the tractate that bears his name, might be regarded as an incarnation of Seth, for he plays the role of a revealer of *gnosis*. At the beginning of the tractate Zostrianos is commanded by the heavenly messenger to "preach to a living generation and to save those who are worthy and to strengthen the elect" (4:15-17). At the end, after

---

[86] Cf. Walter Schmithals's discussion of the "apostle" in Gnosticism, in *The Office of Apostle in the Early Church* (tr. John E. Steely; Nashville: Abingdon, 1969) 114-197.

[87] Other scholars see in the passage dealing with the Illuminator evidence of Christian influence. For discussion see, e.g., George MacRae, "The Apocalypse of Adam Reconsidered," *SBLSP 1972*, 575.

[88] Language similar to that employed in the *Gospel of the Egyptians* is found in the *Trimorphic Protennoia*, where the heavenly Protennoia, a Sophia-figure, says, "(As for) me, I put on Jesus ... and my seed, which is mine, I shall [place] into the Holy Light within an intangible Silence" (50:12-20). Cf. *ApocryJn* II 30:11-31:25. In the *Trimorphic Protennoia* the role of Seth has been bypassed; the heavenly Mother ("Protennoia") puts on Jesus herself, without first having become manifest as Seth. Contrast the *Apocryphon of John*, where the heavenly Mother sows (as a father!) her seed in Seth; see *ApocryJn* II 24:34-25:16, quoted above.

Zostrianos's ascent and descent, he addresses the "erring multitude" with these words:

> Release yourselves, and that which has bound you will be dissolved. Save yourselves, in order that it may be saved. The gentle Father has sent you the savior and given you strength. (131:10-16)

We have already noted the numerous references in *Zostrianos* to the heavenly Seth and to the "race of Seth." Given the saving role played by Zostrianos in this tractate, we should probably regard him as an incarnation of the heavenly Seth. Thus in *Zostrianos*—using the terminology of the *Gospel of the Egyptians*—Seth has "put on" Zostrianos in order to awaken his seed to *gnosis*.

This leads us to take another look at the tractate *Melchizedek*, in which we have noted the use of the phrase "the children of Seth." In *Melchizedek* the Savior is the "high priest" Melchizedek himself, who is also envisaged as performing the final work of salvation in the form of the crucified and risen Jesus Christ.[89] But given the reference to the "children of Seth" (5:20), and the parallel reference to the "race of the high priest" (i.e., Melchizedek, 6:17), we should entertain the possibility that in *Melchizedek* the priest-savior Melchizedek is regarded as an earthly incarnation of the heavenly Seth.

As a result of these observations, it might be posited that a constitutive feature of "Sethian" Gnosticism is the notion of Seth as a heavenly redeemer, who can manifest himself in a variety of earthly incarnations, such as Zostrianos, Zoroaster, Melchizedek, Jesus Christ, etc.[90]

The patristic testimonies add little to this picture. It is simply reported of the Sethians that they equate Christ with Seth (Ps.-Tertullian, *Haer.* 8; Epiphanius, *Haer.* 39.1.3; 39.3.5), which means that some (Christian) Sethians regarded Christ as an earthly manifestation of the heavenly Seth. One passage in Epiphanius may be of special interest, however:

---

[89] Cf. Birger A. Pearson, "The Figure of Melchizedek in the First Tractate of the Unpublished Coptic-Gnostic Codex IX from Nag Hammadi," *Proceedings of the XIIth International Congress of the International Association for the History of Religions* (ed. C.J. Bleeker et al.; Supplements to *Numen* 31; Leiden: Brill, 1975) 200-208. It should be noted that greater clarity has been achieved in the understanding of the relationship between Melchizedek and Jesus Christ in *Melchizedek* subsequent to the submission of that article in 1973; see my introduction to *Melchizedek*, *NHLibEng*, p. 399.

[90] As is well known, the same idea is found in Manichaeism. On "Sethel our Savior" in Manichaean literature, see Pearson, "Egyptian Seth and Gnostic Seth," 35, and references cited there.

> But from Seth, according to the seed (κατὰ σπέρμα) and by succession
> of race, came the Christ, Jesus himself, not by human birth but appearing
> in the world miraculously. He is the one who was Seth then and is manifest
> now to the race of men as Christ, having been sent from the Mother
> above. (*Haer.* 39.3.5)

In this passage the identification of "the Christ" (Jesus) with Seth is
tied to an interpretation of the phrase ἕτερον σπέρμα in Gen 4:25.
In the previous context in Epiphanius's account, the usual Sethian
"salvation history" is reported. The manifestation of Seth as "the
Christ" is therefore to be understood as an eschatological event. This,
of course, puts us in contact with the *Apocalypse of Adam* and *Gospel
of the Egyptians*, discussed above, but also raises an additional issue
of considerable interest.

As we have seen, much of the Gnostic speculation on Seth is
derived from Jewish traditions. We are therefore led to inquire into
the possibility that the Gnostic notions of Seth as Savior might
also be based on Jewish traditions. The aforementioned passage from
Epiphanius is of special interest because it may reflect some use of Jewish
messianic speculation on Gen 4:25. As an example of this, the
following passage from *Midrash Genesis Rabbah* is relevant:

> And she called his name Seth, "For God has set me an alien seed," etc.
> Rabbi Tanḥuma in the name of Samuel Kozit said: (She set her eyes on)
> that same seed who will arise from an alien place. And who is this? This
> is the Messianic King.[91]

Although this passage, as indicated especially by its context, refers
to the birth of the Messiah from an alien nation (the Moabitess
Ruth), it is nevertheless notable that the expected Messiah is referred
to in the context of speculation on the story of the birth of Seth. The
association of the Messiah with Seth and his "seed" is made elsewhere
in Jewish literature as well. As we have already noted, the Messiah
and the elect are tied together with Seth by means of apocalyptic
animal symbolism in *1 Enoch* 85-90. And there are Samaritan
parallels for the same basic idea.[92]

It should also be noted that there are numerous Jewish parallels for the
idea that a biblical patriarch such as Seth can appear in another

---

[91] *Gen. Rab.* 23.5; translation by Dennis Berman, "Seth in Rabbinic Literature," 5.
Cf. *Ruth Rab.* 8.1, where the same tradition is credited to R. Ḥuna. Cf. also
Klijn, *Seth*, 7.

[92] See Klijn, *Seth*, 31. The late date of the Samaritan sources used by Klijn,
however, poses a problem.

incarnation. Indeed Melchizedek, according to *2 Enoch*, undergoes several incarnations[93] and in the Dead Sea Scrolls (11QMelch) he emerges as an end-time redeemer.[94] A comparable idea seems to be reflected in those passages in the New Testament where Jesus is identified with one or another of the prophets.[95] The identification of John the Baptist with Elijah reflects the same idea.[96] One can add to this the idea of a preexistent heavenly redeemer who assumes human form—this is what we find in the case of the "Son of Man" in *1 Enoch* 37, 71, implicit in his identification with the patriarch Enoch (chap. 71). There, too, the "Son of Man" (Enoch) is clearly identified as the Messiah of the end-time (esp. chap. 46).

Thus, though no certainty can be achieved on this point, it is reasonable to suppose that the Gnostic view of Seth as eschatological Savior is ultimately based on sectarian Jewish messianic traditions. In any case, the identification of Seth with Jesus Christ seems clearly to be a secondary development of an originally non-Christian, perhaps even pre-Christian, tradition.

IV. EXCURSUS: EGYPTIAN INFLUENCES?

It is often averred that the figure of Seth in Gnosticism is identifiable with, assimilated to, or otherwise related to, the Egyptian god of the same name.[97] Usually no evidence is given for this assertion, for the very good reason that there is none.[98] To be sure, the Egyptian god Seth is ubiquitous in Graeco-Roman magic, in such materials as the magical papyri and curse tablets; and he occurs also in the so-called "Gnostic" gems and amulets.[99] But he is virtually absent from materials that can properly be labelled "Gnostic,"[100] and in any case is never identified with Seth, son of Adam.

[93] Cf. *2 Enoch* 21-23 (ed. Vaillant), on which see esp. M. Delcor, "Melchizedek from Genesis to the Qumran Texts and the Epistle to the Hebrews," *JSJ* 2 (1971) 127-130.

[94] See esp. Ithamar Gruenwald, "The Messianic Image of Melchizedek" (Hebrew), *Mahanayim* 124 (1970) 88-98.

[95] "Elijah ... Jeremiah or one of the prophets," Matt 16:14.

[96] Matt 11:10-14.

[97] See, e.g., Georg Kretschmar, "Sethianer," *RGG*³ 5, 1715; S. G. F. Brandon, "(Egyptian) Set (Seth)" in *Dictionary of Comparative Religion* (London: Weidenfeld and Nicolson, 1970) 570; H. Bonnet, *Reallexikon der ägyptischen Religionsgeschichte* 715; Doresse, *Secret Books*, 104-105; et al.

[98] I have come to this conclusion in a previous study where I examined this question; see "Egyptian Seth and Gnostic Seth."

[99] Cf. Pearson, "Egyptian Seth and Gnostic Seth, " 26-30.

[100] Egyptian Seth occurs in a fragmentary writing in the Bruce Codex and in *Pistis Sophia* under his Greek name "Typhon," and also influences the Gnostic descriptions of Iao. For discussion see Pearson, "Egyptian Seth and Gnostic Seth," 34 and 32.

However, it might be useful to examine here two recent suggestions of possible influences from the Egyptian cult of Seth in the Nag Hammadi library.

In the case of the *Gospel of the Egyptians* A. Böhlig and F. Wisse have suggested that the reason for the use of the title ("Gospel of the Egyptians") is the prominence of Seth in this document, and the association in the minds of Egyptian readers with the Egyptian god of the same name.[101] Such an association is suggested in the document itself, they argue, in a passage where it is said that the number of the seed of Seth is "the amount of Sodom" (ⲡϣⲓ ⲛ̄ⲥⲟⲇⲟⲙⲱⲛ, III 60:11-12).[102] In the same passage, it is also said that Sodom is the "dwelling place" or "place of pasture" (ⲡⲙⲁ ⲙ̄ⲙⲟⲛⲉ) of the great Seth, which is Gomorrah (III 60:13-14). Since the Egyptian Seth had been accused of sodomy (i.e., homosexual intercourse with Horus), and Gnostics can be expected to interpret as good what traditionally is considered evil, we have here an indication of an Egyptian Gnostic attempt to "rehabilitate" the Egyptian god by interpreting him in terms of Seth, son of Adam. Of course, there is nothing in the text of the *Gospel of the Egyptians* which suggests any "sodomite" tendencies on the part of the "great Seth," nor, indeed, does the use of the names "Sodom" and "Gomorrah" indicate any connection with homosexuality, much less a justification of, or denial of, the Egyptian god's rape of his brother! The symbolic use of "Sodom" and "Gomorrah" has biblical precedents (Isa 1:10 and Rev 11:8, meaning Jerusalem!), though, to be sure, "Sodom" and "Gomorrah" are given reverse evaluations in the *Gospel of the Egyptians*, as cities destroyed by the evil Demiurge; this is a typical feature of Gnosticism.[103]

Another suggestion associating the Gnostic Seth with the Egyptian god Seth has been advanced by Konrad Wekel and the Berliner Arbeitskreis für koptisch-gnostische Schriften, in an attempt to arrive at an Egyptian etymology for the name "Emmacha" (cf. "Emmacha Seth,"

Cf. also Wolfgang Fauth, "Seth-Typhon, Onoel und der eselsköpfige Sabaoth: Zur Theriomorphie der ophitisch-barbelognostischen Archonten," *OrChr* 57 (1973) 79-120; this important article was not available to me when I wrote "Egyptian Seth and Gnostic Seth."

[101] In *The Gospel of the Egyptians*, 35.

[102] This passage is quoted above, p. 488.

[103] For Sodom cf. also *ParaShem* 29:1. For additional discussion see Pearson, "Egyptian Seth and Gnostic Seth," 33-34. For the suggestion that Sodom and Gomorrah are meant as purely geographical references (i.e., the Dead Sea region), see Doresse, *Secret Books*, 299.

3StSeth 118:28).[104] It is proposed that "Emmacha" is derived from
an epithet of the Egyptian god Seth attested from the Ptolemaic
period, *ḥm-mȝȝ*.[105] But this is linguistically improbable, for a word
beginning with Eg. *ḥ* would normally come into Greek either with an
initial σ or an initial χ (Coptic ϣ).[106] As has already been noted
in the case of this epithet,[107] it seems fruitless to attempt any etymology at all for such a *nomen barbarum*.

If we are to look for Egyptian influence in the development of
the Gnostic figure of Seth, we might do better to relate the Gnostic
Seth to a god in the Egyptian pantheon other than the wicked Seth-
Typhon, viz., Thoth, the Egyptian Hermes.[108] Manetho is credited by
Syncellus with composing his history of Egypt on the basis of
hieroglyphic inscriptions written by the god Thoth "in the Seriadic
land" (ἐν τῇ Σηριαδικῇ γῇ), i.e., Egypt,[109] and it is probable that
the temples of Egypt had in their archives, from ancient times, hieroglyphic tablets ascribed to Thoth, the divine scribe.[110] In *Discourse
on the Eighth and Ninth* (NHC VI,6) Hermes Trismegistus commands
his "son" to write his revelation in hieroglyphic characters on turquoise
steles for the temple at Diospolis (61:18-30), presumably commanding
the son to follow a venerable precedent established by himself. We
might therefore look to the lore associated with the god Thoth in
Egypt for the origins of the tradition, discussed above, that Seth
wrote revelations on stone steles.

However, it is clear that the Gnostic traditions pertaining to Seth's
steles cannot be derived directly from Egyptian sources, for the Gnostic
traditions reflect details that have no parallel in Egyptian sources.
They are derived, instead, from Jewish sources, such as the apocryphal

---

[104] "Die drei Stelen des Seth," *TLZ* 100 (1975) 572-573.

[105] Citing the Erman-Grapow *Wörterbuch*, 3, 280: *ḥm-mȝȝ* "als Bez. des Seth."

[106] Cf., e.g., Plutarch *Isid.* 79 (383D), where Eg. *ḥry* (Coptic ϣⲁⲗ, "myrrh") is
transliterated into Greek as σαλ; and *Isid.* 37 (365E), where Eg. *ḥt* (Coptic ϣⲉ,
"wood") is reflected in Plutarch's designation for a special ivy sacred to Osiris,
χενόσιρις ("plant of Osiris"). Cf. the notes in J. Gwyn Griffiths, *Plutarch's "De Iside
et Osiride"* (Cambridge: University of Wales, 1970) 568 and 108.

[107] Cf. discussion above, p. 484.

[108] Klijn brings up this possibility in his discussion of the Christian tradition
regarding Seth as the discoverer of letters, but then quickly dismisses it, *Seth*,
50. Cf. on this point Adler, "Notes to Text of George Syncellus and Pseudo-Malalas,"
to Ps.-Malalas, p. 5/6.1-5.

[109] Cf. n. 70,

[110] Cf. A.-J. Festugière, *La Révélation d'Hermès Trismégiste* 1 (Paris: Gabalda,
1950) 74-76.

Adam literature and the tradition preserved by Josephus to the effect that the Sethites had antediluvian revelations on steles of brick and stone.[111] Josephus, possibly our earliest witness to this tradition, probably got his information from a source in which a function of the Egyptian god Thoth-Hermes had been transferred to the pre-Flood patriarch Seth, son of Adam. Be that as it may, the Gnostic tradition is based on *Jewish* sources, and only indirectly—via the Jewish sources—on Egyptian lore pertaining to the god Thoth.

V. CONCLUSIONS

As we have seen, the Gnostic figure of Seth is largely defined on the basis of scripture-interpretation, especially of the key passages Gen 4:25 and 5:1-3. We have also noted that the Hebrew text of Genesis is sometimes utilized as well as the Greek. The Gnostic narratives of the birth of Seth—as well as those of Cain and Abel—are presented in the form of midrashim on the key texts in Genesis, showing parallels in form and content with Jewish haggadic traditions. The notion of a heavenly Seth represents a specifically Gnostic interpretation of the Genesis accounts whereby the earthly figures of Adam and Seth are projected onto the precosmic transmundane plane. The Gnostic traditions pertaining to a special "race" of Seth show clear influence from Jewish traditions regarding the righteous lineage of Seth. The development of the idea of Seth as a transmitter of *gnosis* is based on such Jewish sources as the apocryphal Adam literature. The "salvation history" of the Gnostic (Sethian) "race" is derived from Jewish apocryphal sources, and the notion of Seth as an eschatological savior seems also to reflect Jewish Messianic speculation on the future Messiah as a scion of Seth. In short, virtually every aspect of the typology of Seth discussed above reflects the influence of Jewish scripture and tradition. The sole Christian component of our typology, the identification of Seth with Jesus Christ, is obviously secondary, reflecting a "Christianizing" stage in the development of the Gnostic interpretation of Seth.

I have not attempted here to define the constitutive elements of the "Sethian" Gnostic system,[112] but it does seem clear that the items we have discussed would constitute important elements in the evolution

---

[111] Cf. discussion above, p. 493.
[112] Cf. esp. Schenke, "Das Sethianische System," and his contribution to this volume.

and development of "Sethian" Gnosticism.[113] Inasmuch as the Gnostic traditions pertaining to Seth derive from *Jewish* sources, we are led to posit that the very phenomenon of "Sethian" Gnosticism *per se* is of Jewish, perhaps pre-Christian, origin.[114]

DISCUSSION*

GEORGE MACRAE: AT this first session we shall be discussing contributions to the seminar by Professors Kraft, Stone, and Pearson, all of which deal broadly with the figure of Seth. Because the seminar papers have been distributed in advance to the members of the seminar, I invite each author to draw attention to some particular aspects of his paper prior to our discussion.

ROBERT KRAFT: The context of my paper, "Philo on Seth," is the continuing concern of the SBL Pseudepigrapha Group with Jewish traditions about revered figures of the past, and especially Enoch. For over a year my graduate seminar at the University of Pennsylvania has been looking at materials concerning Seth, ranging from the earliest extant sources to Christian accounts from the Byzantine period. The overall picture resulting from this survey has been diffuse and varied. In returning to Philo, I investigated questions regarding Seth's

---

[113] Although Frederik Wisse has raised some important caveats in his provocative essay in this volume, "Stalking Those Elusive Sethians," I believe it is still useful to speak of a "Sethian" Gnostic system, such as has been isolated by Schenke in his seminal articles. In holding to this terminology we do not need to commit ourselves to any rigid theory of a single Sethian sect. Nor do we have to conclude that the term "Sethian" is a self-designation of one or more Gnostic groups, for, in fact, that particular adjective does not occur in any of our primary texts, and may be an invention of the heresiologists. The heresiologists, nevertheless, would presumably have had some reasons for coming up with this epithet. The material in this paper has hopefully shed some light on their bases for coining the designation "Sethian," if that is what they did.

[114] For all the material he has presented in his book, Klijn seems to me to arrive at very weak conclusions. He notices the Gnostic use of Jewish material but does not want to jump to conclusions about historical relationships; see esp. *Seth*, 119. But what conclusions can we draw, on the basis of the evidence, other than those posited here?

* Discussions of the Seminar on Sethian Gnosticism have been edited by Ernest Bursey, secretary of the Seminar.

exaltation that had been raised by the Gnostic materials. My report summarizes the pertinent evidence regarding Philo's possible awareness of other traditions regarding Seth. I attempted to determine whether Philo was arguing *against* a particular Sethian position in his treatment of Seth. I didn't convince myself that he was. His treatment of Seth is similar to his treatment of other ancient figures. Some of his statements could be interpreted as mildly polemical against a more historical Sethian tradition such as that reported by Josephus. Philo's treatment of Seth is very restrained, though he cannot avoid giving Seth some honorific titles.

MICHAEL STONE: The bulk of the Armenian Adam books remain unpublished, including a unique version of the *Books of Adam and Eve*. I hope we can discuss the views of G. Cardona, G. Stroumsa, etc., on the possible de-Gnosticizing of Sethian Gnostic ideas in the *Death of Adam*. A large literature in Georgian is still unpublished. The Armenian and Georgian literature includes traditions not known in the Syriac-Arabic-Ethiopian tradition nor in the Jewish Adam books. Since not all of the literature was composed in Armenian or Georgian, a third line of tradition must lie behind this material, though the determination of its precise location must await the publication of all the texts. It would help if we all would learn Armenian!

BIRGER PEARSON: My paper includes material presented to the SBL Pseudepigrapha Group at San Francisco in 1977. After examining the magical texts on Seth-Typhon and the Gnostic texts on Seth, I concluded that no relationship existed between Egyptian Seth and Gnostic Seth. In the present paper I have asked what can be said about the Gnostic figure of Seth and its biblical and exegetical backgrounds. My conclusions on the Gnostic figure of Seth do not concern Sethian Gnosticism per se because the figure of Seth appears both in Gnostic contexts which are not Sethian and in Manichaeism and Mandaeism. Though it would be fruitful to produce a typology drawing on the full range of the literature, in this paper I have dealt with only the Gnostic materials, following the model of Professor MacRae's SBL paper, also presented to the 1977 annual meeting, on "Seth in Gnostic Texts and Traditions." I am driven to conclude that the Gnostic Sethian traditions were rooted in Jewish soil, especially those of Scriptural exegesis.

GEORGE NICKELSBURG: Professor Kraft, is Philo's light treatment of Seth due to his attempt to play down another position on Seth? Is he omitting what you might expect him to say in treating the biblical texts?

KRAFT: If one were to assume that Philo is taking a polemical position, the answer to your first question would be "yes." But in the wider perspective of the Sethian tradition in Gnosticism, Philo's treatment of Seth is disappointing. He deals with most of the texts one would expect in his treatment of Seth, but more "lightly" than in the case of comparable figures. His treatment of Seth, unlike his treatment of Cain and others, doesn't even raise the question of history. This is conceivably due to his reaction against a historical treatment of Seth.

JOHN STRUGNELL: Is not any position which Philo counters more likely to be exegetical than sectarian? What we find in Philo is an exegetically motivated discussion : we cannot get behind it to a sectarian life setting.

KRAFT: Elsewhere, Philo does mention sects by name, for example, the Therapeutae, the Essenes, etc.; but here the text gives no reason to suppose that he has in mind a particular group.

JAMES ROBINSON: In Professor Schenke's paper for this seminar he has followed W. Beltz and retained his earlier favoring of a Samaritan origin of Sethianism, though more cautiously than before. Beltz had argued that the Jewish tradition didn't make enough of Seth to provide a launching point while the Samaritan one did. This issue should be brought before us.

STONE: In our discussion at the meeting of the SBL Pseudepigrapha Group in 1977, it became apparent that Seth hardly appears as a revealer figure in non-Gnostic Jewish sources, and that Enoch does not appear as a revealer figure in Gnostic sources. It was noted that these two figures, who have similar functions, seem to occur in complementary distribution. Milik has proposed a Samaritan context for the Enoch tradition, though it is difficult to know what any Samaritan thought before the fourth century C.E.

ROBINSON: When someone doesn't state the chronological framework of literature being used, my rule of thumb is that it must be late!

STONE: If we want to locate possible Jewish contexts there are several possibilities. I find Professor Kraft's Philo passages highly suggestive. Another possibility is the non-Gnostic Adam literature—here I refer to the papers published by W. Adler and Professor MacRae in *SBLSP* 1977. But to explain *obscurum per obscurius* is no way to solve difficult problems.

STRUGNELL: Dositheus, mentioned in the *Three Steles of Seth*, is a possible link to a Samaritan origin of Sethianism. But in all the sources about the Samaritan Dositheus there is almost no mention of Seth.

ROBINSON: I am inclined to consider the mention of Dositheus as secondary in the *Three Steles of Seth*. Both the incipit "the revelation of Dositheus ...," and the explicit, "... and the revelation," were probably not attached to the tractate in its first draft. The body of the text doesn't mention Dositheus or the word "revelation" nor does it substantially contain a revelation. An analogy would be Porphyry's apparent addition of the term "revelation" to the title of works entitled in the Nag Hammadi library simply *Zostrianos* and *Allogenes*. There seems to be also a trend in the Nag Hammadi library to insert, secondarily, canonical nomenclature such as "gospel," "epistle," and "apocalypse" into titles.

STRUGNELL: And would it be the same Dositheus anyway?

ALEXANDER BÖHLIG: With regard to possible Jewish influence on the Nag Hammadi material there are serious chronological and geographical difficulties. But Manichaeism, attested in Egypt, provides an earlier parallel or even link to Jewish influence. We find the figure of the great *strategos*, the great Jacob (James), in the *Gospel of the Egyptians* (thus CG IV 25:28, but misunderstood as "James the Great" in CG III 64:13). A Manichaean text from Central Asia speaks of the angel Jacob, the leader of the angels; I refer you to my article "Jacob as an Angel in Gnosticism and Manichaeism" (*Nag Hammadi and Gnosticism* [R. McL. Wilson, ed.; NHS 14; Leiden: Brill, 1978] 122-30) for a treatment of the lines of evidence leading from the Old Testament to Manichaeism. Mani's use of Jewish materials, including *1 Enoch*, along with allusions to Enoch material and the use of Jewish motifs in tractate CG II,5, argues for a Jewish rather than a Christian origin of these elements.

In the case of James (Jacob) the traditions definitely moved from Judaism to Gnosticism and from there to Manichaeism. We can assume that in Mesopotamia there was general acquaintance with Gnostic material. But to a degree Manichaean ideas could have influenced Gnostic traditions in Egypt since the third century, when the Manichees undertook their mission in Egypt. Not all the Sethian texts from Nag Hammadi are "*ur*-Sethian" nor received their final editorial form before that century. The classification of Iranian names is difficult, e.g., Aphredon (in the *Unbekanntes altgnostisches Werk* of Codex Brucianus). From Iran the way possibly led, via magic, to the Gnostics.

MACRAE: The Cologne Mani Codex provides support for a direct line of Jewish influence because Mani himself speaks of the influence upon himself of various apocalypses of Jewish figures. But in the same context Mani mentions the influence of the Christian Paul. His contact with Jewish apocalyptic seems to have been in a Jewish-Christian context.

BÖHLIG: Mani's roots are in the Elkasaites from whom he learned the Jewish materials and from whom he broke away. His appreciation of Paul came from his later contact with followers of Marcion.

MACRAE: The *Apocalypse of Seth* in the Mani Codex portrays Seth taking a heavenly journey. In traditions about Seth found elsewhere do we see him in this role? I am inclined to doubt it.

PEARSON: Only in Epiphanius's account of the Archontics.

MACRAE: Can we design a typology of roles played by Seth that are restricted to particular circles? Do we know of any Gnostic sources where there is even an allusion to Seth's quest?

PEARSON: No, this occurs only in the Jewish and Christian Adam traditions.

CARSTEN COLPE: Extrapolations have been made from the medieval equation of the tree of life with Christ's cross back to "the quest of Seth for the oil of life" (see the book of that title by E. C. Quinn [Chicago, 1962]) which can be squeezed out of the kernels of the tree of life (= the saving cross).

STONE: I wish to respond briefly to a number of points raised. In the *Prayer of Joseph* an angel of high status named Jacob appears. And I refer you to Sirach 49 for a list of names similar to the names of the revealers in the Mani Codex; Turfan fragments also have names of this sort. But if the mediating source of the Mani Codex is Elkasaite, I don't see how it advances our pursuit of Sethian origins.

The important question concerning the quest of Seth is whether, in any Jewish form of the story Seth went to the garden to get something. There is one Armenian version of that tradition in which Seth brings back a branch from the garden; the branch is not identified with the Cross, but this omission may simply be due to abbreviation. The idea of people going to Paradise and bringing back something that will guarantee life is widespread and early. I don't think the quest tradition can be restricted to medieval Latin manuscripts of the *Vita Adae et Evae*. The same tradition turns up in Armenian and Georgian forms which were translated not from Latin but probably from Greek Christian texts.

NICKELSBURG: The theme does show up in the Greek *Apocalypse of Moses*. The point is that Seth doesn't get what he is seeking, namely, life.

STONE: Whether or not he is successful is secondary. We can still use the quest tradition as a mapping feature, as we can the tradition of Seth as a revealer of heavenly secrets. Correlation of the opposition between the Sethians and the Cainites with the "sons of God" and the "daughters of men" (Gen. 6:1-2) is still another tradition. If we can isolate three or four more we may be able to localize traditions.

BÖHLIG: If Jacob could become an angel, Seth could also. Milik's work on the Enoch fragments gives us another parallel. If Mani knows Seth, that is a possible basis for dating. Also the divinization of Seth under the name Seth-el is known to Mani or his disciples. The

Cologne Mani Codex, with its citation of an *Apocalypse of Seth*, is a substantial reference to the knowledge of Seth literature in Mesopotamia, whose Manichaean reworking had gone back to Egypt with the Manichaean mission and perhaps had influence upon Sethian literature there.

NICKELSBURG: Do we have any non-Gnostic texts depicting Seth as a revealer rather than a recipient of what another has received?

KRAFT: Yes, in the late Byzantine chronographers. But there still remains the possibility that earlier Gnostic traditions influenced them. In response to Professor Robinson's remark on the hypothesis of a Samaritan origin, I would say that the data base for the Samaritan hypothesis is insignificant. A. F. J. Klijn, in his recent work on "Seth in Jewish, Christian, and Gnostic literature" (Leiden, 1977), had to look very hard to find any significance in the Samaritan material.

PEARSON: Only Epiphanius claims that Seth is important to the Samaritans.

COLPE: In a single magical papyrus from Egypt a mistaken identification has been made between Egyptian Seth and Jewish Seth (cf. W. Fauth, *OrChr* 57 [1973] 91-94); but this is evidence only for an individual blending whereas the fact that in general the Jewish name Seth was kept within a surrounding which knew also a demonic Seth may be taken as evidence for an isolated group which rather preserved its Jewish, or even Dosithean, heritage.

PEARSON: Contrary to his earlier good standing, the Egyptian Seth becomes a demonic figure in the late Hellenistic period. It is inconceivable that Egyptian Seth was tied in with a hero of the Gnostic sect. In both Egyptian magic and Gnostic material he gets mixed up with the Jewish Yao.

MACRAE: Although one can conceive of a perverted use of the demonic Seth in Gnostic literature, there is no clear evidence of such an inversion. Can the seminar agree that Egyptian Seth is irrelevant to a discussion of Gnostic Seth, in spite of continual assertions to the contrary?

BÖHLIG: Is it not possible that Gnostics would point to their new Seth as surpassing the Egyptian Seth? For a parallel we need only contrast the evaluation of Sodom and Gomorrah in the Genesis account with that found in subsequent Gnostic literature. We must proceed with caution in assessing the independence of the Gnostic Seth.

BENTLEY LAYTON: From the diachronic perspective of *religionsgeschichte* Professor Pearson's paper on Egyptian Seth has laid to rest the notion that our Gnostic Seth simply developed from Egyptian Seth. But since the Hellenized Isis cult made an important contribution to the shape of Gnostic literature, I find it hard to assert absolutely that the Gnostics had no interest in the Seth of Isis literature. After all, we can detect a significant stylistic influence of Isis literature in certain Gnostic texts. I should like to raise the possibility that there may be present a literary inversion of values in which Egyptian Seth is revalued and thought of as "true" or Gnostic Seth. I am speaking, of course, of a synchronic relationship, and perhaps an incidental one, between the two figures, rather than a diachronic one.

PEARSON: It may be dangerous to suppose that the influence of Isis typology, however clear, carries with it influence, at the level of the details of the myth, as for example adoption of the god Seth. Furthermore, Seth-Typhon does occur in Gnostic literature (for example, in the Bruce Codex and the *Pistis Sophia*) but there he is a demon.

BÖHLIG: The reader of the *Gospel of the Egyptians* would understand the Egyptian Seth to be a demon when at the same time a new Seth was being set forward.

PEARSON: But that is not to say that Egyptian Seth was amalgamated with Gnostic Seth. Further, while a comparison between rivals is conceivable, yet by the time of the Gnostic literature no Egyptians except magicians worshipped Seth. The single contrary text quoted in Kees' article in Pauly-Wissowa, supposedly absolving Seth of killing his brother Osiris, has been misunderstood and should probably be translated, "Seth who did not grieve over his brother ..." (*PGM* 7.963-64; cf. *SBLSP* 1977, 38, n. 28).

MACRAE: The question of whether the Egyptian Seth had any influence on the function of Seth in Gnostic sources has been confused with the question of whether the Gnostics knew anything about the Egyptian Seth. One can answer "no" to the first question and "yes" to the second without self-contradiction. The roles played by Seth in Gnostic literature do seem to be untouched by Egyptian influence. Professor Böhlig's suggestion is easy to imagine, but nowhere is it explicitly supported in the texts.

ROBINSON: Do we exegete the copies of the Nag Hammadi texts found in Egyptian culture or do we exegete some hypothetical original texts which are possibly non-Egyptian in origin? I am increasingly convinced that the most fully attested pagan context at Nag Hammadi is that of Serapis, as the biography of Pachomius and the prayers to Zeus-Serapis in the cave at Jabal al-Ṭarif indicate.

FREDERIK WISSE: I should like to see the implications of Professor Pearson's position on the Jewish backgrounds of Gnosticism clarified. Some of the acknowledged similarities are due to similar though independent interests and exegetical methods. Others should be explained by a Gnostic use of Jewish apocryphal literature. In order to explain the Gnostic texts is one forced to say that in pre-Gnostic Jewish circles these elements were pulled together and cultic inferences drawn from them?

PEARSON: Professor Wisse has asked a difficult question. Klijn leaves the question of a Sethian Jewish sect unresolved. But I am driven to the conclusion that the exegetical methods in Gnostic material presuppose exegetical activity in Jewish Wisdom circles, in which the traditional Wisdom questions were being answered from Scripture.

STRUGNELL: That kind of activity was not restricted to Wisdom circles.

STONE: Professor Pearson's sociological dilemma as he attempts to determine which Jewish circles were antecedent to the Gnostics is paralleled by that of anyone using the Apocrypha and Pseudepigrapha. We have an ample supply both of documents and of names of sects. But matching them to actual developments within Judaism is a problem which may be insoluble unless we revert to Josephus as the criterion. If we take the dating of the Qumran Enoch fragments seriously, we see that the ascent traditions and the technical terminology about the heavenly realm based on Ezekiel 1 were well-developed in Judaism in the third century B.C.E. This ought to warn us against an overly facile description of Jewish groups. There is a vast amount we don't know. Those Enoch books are unlike what we would have guessed the oldest extrabiblical Jewish documents to be like.

WISSE: Can we not avoid complications by using Occam's razor? It seems unnecessary to link our texts to a particular sociological context. The simplest explanation is that the Gnostics were interested in and used Greek copies of Jewish apocryphal works.

PEARSON: We must raise the question of their concrete *Sitz im Leben*. To whom were such works actually available? To whom did this material pose such an interest?

WISSE: Early monastic Hermetic circles.

PEARSON: Then how do we account for the consistent focus of the material when so much else was available in the Hellenistic world?

MACRAE: Before closing this meeting I should like to solicit comment from the auditors.

ITHAMAR GRUENWALD (University of Tel Aviv): I raise a question regarding the old esoteric traditions: Why are similar traditions attributed by one group to one personage and by another group to another? I suggest that the attribution of some of these old traditions to Seth has something to do with the "inversion of values" mentioned by Professor Layton, here in a more heretical manner than with the Enoch tradition. I suggest that maybe Egyptian Seth could have triggered the attribution of esoteric Jewish material into the direction of a figure more appealing to the later Gnostic tradition.

MACRAE: Then is Josephus a Gnostic because he attributes to Seth certain functions which are in a straight line of tradition with the *Apocalypse of Adam* and the *Gospel of the Egyptians*? It would be difficult to attribute the motive of inversion of values to Josephus.

KRAFT: One could try to separate Josephus's remarks on Seth from the Gnostic emphasis on the "other seed" (see Genesis). I was impressed that Philo could not *avoid* this terminology, although he makes a distinction by making Seth "another seed" with respect to Cain, while maintaining Seth's continuity with Abel. This may be Philo's polemic against a tradition of inversion.

Session Two

SOME RELATED TRADITIONS IN THE APOCALYPSE OF ADAM, THE BOOKS OF ADAM AND EVE, AND 1 ENOCH

BY

GEORGE W. E. NICKELSBURG

SINCE the publication of the Gnostic *Apocalypse of Adam* in 1963, scholars have discussed its possible relationships to Jewish literature, traditions, and communities.[1] These discussions have focused on two distinct but related issues. 1) The literary question: How and to what extent have Jewish sources influenced the *Apocalypse of Adam?* 2) The historical question: Did the author know these sources in Jewish or christianized form; i.e., was the *Apocalypse of Adam* composed in Jewish (or judaized) or Christian (or christianized) Gnostic circles? In this paper I shall limit myself almost exclusively to the former question.

Most commentators agree that the *Apocalypse of Adam* (hereafter *ApocAd*) stands in a special relationship to the "Jewish" Adam books, particularly the Latin *Life of Adam and Eve* (hereafter *Adam and Eve*).[2] This work, in turn, stands in a close, but complex, relationship to the *Apocalypse of Moses* (hereafter *Apoc. Moses*). Our task in this

---

[1] The initial publication is A. Böhlig and P. Labib, *Koptisch-gnostische Apokalypsen aus Codex V von Nag Hammadi im Koptischen Museum zu Alt-Kairo* (Sonderband, *Wissenschaftliche Zeitschrift der Martin-Luther Universität Halle-Wittenberg*; Halle/Saale, 1963). Since this volume was not available to me, I cite its contents as they are summarized by G. W. MacRae, "The Coptic Gnostic Apocalypse of Adam," *HeyJ* 6 (1965) 31-34. Subsequent literature arguing a Jewish context in various ways includes: MacRae, *ibid*, 32-33; A. Böhlig, "Jüdisches und Iranisches in der Adamapokalypse des Codex V von Nag Hammadi," *Mysterion und Wahrheit* (AGJU 6; Leiden: Brill, 1968)149-61, esp. 154; W. Beltz, "Die Adam-Apokalypse aus Codex V von Nag Hammadi: Jüdische Bausteine in gnostischen Systemen" (Habilitationsschrift, Humboldt-Universität [Berlin], 1970); G. MacRae, "The Apocalypse of Adam Reconsidered," *SBLSP* 1972, 2, 573-77; P. Perkins, "Apocalypse of Adam: The Genre and Function of a Gnostic Apocalypse," *CBQ* 39 (1977) 382-95; A. F. J. Klijn, *Seth in Jewish, Christian, and Gnostic Literature* (NovTSup 47; Leiden: Brill, 1977).

[2] I leave open the question whether these books were originally Jewish or Jewish-Christian. A study of the Armenian *Penitence of Our Father Adam* may shed light on this question. See below, n. 7.

paper is twofold. Part I will look at aspects of the interrelationships of *Apoc. Moses* and *Adam and Eve*. Part II will discuss *ApocAd* in light of the findings of Part I. In neither case is it possible to be exhaustive. The treatment of the Jewish Adam books will be limited to matters that may help to elucidate the task in Part II. In the latter the possible relationships to the Jewish works will be in focus. However, even in this respect, the exposition is intended to be suggestive of further investigation rather than exhaustive.

I. Jewish Literature on Adam and Eve

THE APOCALYPSE OF MOSES

The *Apocalypse of Moses* and *Adam and Eve* are two recensions of a single work.[3] The *Apocalypse of Moses* is the shorter and simpler of the two recensions and is primarily an account of Adam's death, its cause and its cure. Chaps. 1-4 are an expansion and recasting of Genesis 4 and serve as a preface to the work. Their primary function is to introduce Seth, who is the recipient of important traditions and, in other ways, an important figure in the book.

When Seth has appeared, the narrator turns at once to Adam's terminal illness (5:1-2), which is the subject matter of all but the very end of the book. Most of the elements of the testament genre are present in chaps. 6-41, although the plot and the balance of the narrative are governed by the author's theological viewpoint.

When Adam sees that he is going to die, he summons his children (5:2; cf. *T. Levi* 1:2; *1 Enoch* 91:1-2; *T. Job* 1:1, etc.). Their query about the meaning of his predicament (5:4-6:3) leads Adam to recount briefly the story of the temptation, the fall, and the first parents' punishment (chaps. 7-8). This narrative differs in function from the biographical introduction of the typical testament, which recounts events from the patriarch's life as examples to be emulated or avoided (cf. *T. 12 Patr.* passim). Adam's narrative explains the reason

---

[3] My analysis here is based on my forthcoming article on Jewish narrative literature in *Compendia Rerum Judaicarum ad Novum Testamentum*. Not available to me was M. Nagel, *La Vie grecque d'Adam et d'Eve (Apocalypse de Möise)* (Dissertation, Strasbourg, 1972). For the Greek text of the *Apocalypse of Moses*, see K. von Tischendorf, *Apocalypses Apocryphae* (Leipzig: Mendelssohn, 1866; reprinted, Hildesheim: Olms, 1966) 1-23. For the Latin text of *Adam and Eve*, see W. Meyer, "Vita Adae et Evae," *AbhAkMün* 14/3 (1878) 187-250; and J. H. Mozley, "Documents: The 'Vita Adae'," *JTS* 30 (1929) 121-49. Versification follows L. S. A. Wells, *APOT* 2, 134 ff.

for his present plight and recalls for the reader those events which led to the sentence of death. This is essential to the author's message, the first part of which asserts the necessity of Adam's death.

In the narrative sequence that follows (9:3-13:6), the author breaks with the testamentary form in the interest of this message. Wishing to avoid the inevitable, Adam dispatches Eve and Seth to paradise in search of the oil of mercy that will bring him relief (9:3). On the way, Seth is attacked by a beast (chaps. 10-12)—evidence that God's word in Gen 3:15 is in effect (cf. 24:4). Adam's request is denied, and we hear for the first time what might be called the "kerygma" of *Apoc. Mos.*.

> (The oil of mercy) will *not* be yours *now, but at the ends of the times*. Then will arise all flesh from Adam to that great day .... Then all the joy of paradise will be given to them. ... (13:2-4)

For the present, however, Seth and Eve must return to Adam and announce that he has three days until his death. Thus, this digression from the testamentary form is a narrative embodiment of the first part of the author's message: Adam must bear the ultimate consequence of his sin; he must die.[4]

The author returns to the testamentary form, recapitulating the situation in 5:1-2. Adam knows that he is going to die, and he bids Eve to gather the children and to recount to them the circumstances of their sin (14:1-3). Eve's narrative (chaps. 15-29) is a lengthy and imaginative elaboration of Genesis 3. Of importance for us is its latter part (chaps. 22-29). God appears in paradise on his chariot and accompanied by his angels. His throne is fixed, and he indicts and sentences his creatures. The consequences of the fall are spelled out in detail (chaps. 24-26). As Adam and Eve are being expelled from paradise, Adam seeks mercy (27:2; cf. his request for the oil of mercy). God commands the angels to get on with the expulsion (27:4-28:1). Again Adam pleads, this time for access to the Tree of Life (28:2). God's response recapitulates the situation in chap. 13.

> You shall *not* take from it *now* ... if you keep yourself from all evil, as one about to die, when again the resurrection comes to pass, *I shall raise you up*. And then there shall be given to you from the tree of life. (28:3-4)

---

[4] At a number of points, *Apoc. Mos.* is reminiscent of the *Testament of Abraham*. There, the entire plot is structured around Abraham's repeated attempts to put off the day of his death, and God's repeated refusal; see G. W. E. Nickelsburg, "Structure and Message in the Testament of Abraham," *Studies on the Testament of Abraham* (ed. G. W. E. Nickelsburg; SBLSCS 6; Missoula, Montana: Scholars Press, 1976) 85-93.

Yet another time Adam pleads with God for herbs from paradise to offer incense and seeds to grow food. This request God grants before Adam and Eve are expelled from the garden (chap. 29).

Eve's narrative creates something of a literary problem. In its immediate context, the narrative is governed by testamentary protocol relating to *Adam's death*. In keeping with the testament genre, we should expect Adam to narrate the story of the fall—as he has done earlier:

Adam's imminent death and gathering of the children	5:1-3	14:1b-3
Query as to why	5:4-6:3	....
Narrative explanation	7-8	15-29

In point of fact, much of Eve's narrative attributes to *Adam* a prominent role which exceeds the scriptural text. The first half of the narrative (chaps. 15-21) follows the cue of Gen 3:1-7 and emphasizes Eve's role in the fall. In chaps. 22-29, however, Adam is the central figure. God appears in the garden to judge Adam (22:2). It is he who is addressed and judged first (chap. 24, *contra* Gen 3:17-19). He alone bargains with God as they are being expelled, a remarkable change from the prominent role of Eve's dialog in the Bible. Moreover, Eve concludes the narrative with a typical testamentary admonition (chap. 30; cf., e.g., *T. Judah* 13:1-2; 14:1; *T. Gad* 6:; etc.), which again recalls Adam's deathbed situation in chap. 14. These data may indicate that at some point in the tradition behind the second part of Eve's narrative there may have been an Adamic narrative more extensive than chaps. 7-8. The possibility must be borne in mind, because, as we shall see, *Adam and Eve* 25:1-29:1 (the counterpart to *Apoc. Mos.* 22-29) is placed on Adam's lips. In the present context, however, chaps. 15-21 fit well with the viewpoint expressed elsewhere in *Apoc. Mos.* that Eve is primarily responsible for the fall.[5] Similarly, the section about Adam's bargaining with God is a vehicle for the author's "not yet ... but at the resurrection" formulation.

After Eve's admonition (chap. 30), the narrative focuses again on Adam's imminent death. At Adam's request, Eve intercedes for him, for he is uncertain of his salvation (31-32:2). Adam dies, and in response to Eve's prayer, she is granted a vision (for which Seth serves as *angelus interpres*) of the salvation of Adam's soul (32:3-37:6). The whole

---

[5] See *Apoc. Mos.* 14:2, "O Eve (B), what have you done to us;" cf. *2 Apoc. Bar.* 48:42; 4 Ezra 7:118, "O Adam, what have you done!" Both passages deal with the consequences of sin for humankind, whereas Gen 3:13 ("What is this that you have done") has different connotations. For Eve's culpability, cf. also *Apoc. Mos.* 32:1-2.

sequence serves once again to carry forward the author's message. Yes, Adam must die; but he is not damned. The section contains a brief prediction of the ultimate destruction of Satan and the future exaltation of Adam (39:2-3), which may be compared with apocalyptic predictions in other testaments, but which carries the author's message.

The major part of the book concludes in good testamentary fashion with a description of Adam's burial (38:1-42:2). This section ends with a final reprise of the book's central message, formulated here as an expansion on Gen 3:19.

> I told you that you are dust, and *to dust you will return*. Again I promise you the resurrection. *I shall raise you up on the last day*, in the resurrection, with every man who is of your seed. (41:2-3)

The concluding portion of the book describes Eve's death and her burial by Seth, who is commanded to bury in this fashion everyone who dies until the day of the resurrection (43:3ff.).

Our analysis of *Apoc. Mos.* indicates that the heart of this work is structured roughly in the form of a testament of Adam. The sections that break this form, or throw it out of balance, are bearers of the book's central message: the fruitless trip to paradise; to some extent Adam's bargaining with God; the lengthy scene that is prolog to Adam's burial. This evidence may be read in at least two ways. Either *Apoc. Mos.* is an expansion of Genesis 3-4, influenced by elements of the testament form, or it is a redacted version of a testament of Adam, revised in line with the redactor's theological concerns. Two factors may favor the latter alternative. 1) Literary tensions in the work, particularly in Eve's narrative, seem to suggest a previous stage of composition. 2) One might expect that a work which is as influenced by the testament form as *Apoc. Mos.* is would begin and end like a testament.

THE LIFE OF ADAM AND EVE

Approximately one half of the Latin *Life of Adam and Eve* overlaps (table 1) with a similar proportion of *Apoc. Mos.* The material found in Adam and Eve, but not in *Apoc. Mos.*, occurs in three blocks (1, 3, 7). Conversely, Eve's narrative in *Apoc. Mos.* is missing in *Adam and Eve.*

In this version, the narrative material that precedes the testamentary situation (2) is prefaced by yet another narrative, which picks up immediately after the expulsion from the garden (i.e., between Gen 3:24 and 4:1). Two intertwined threads bind together the

TABLE 1

CONTENTS OF ADAM AND EVE AND APOC. MOSES

		Life of Adam and Eve	Apocalypse of Moses
1	Penitence, devil's narrative, Cain's birth	1:1-22:2	....
2	Birth of (Cain), Abel, Seth, et al.	22:3-24:2	1:1-5:1a
3	Adam's revelations to Seth	25-29	....
4	Adam's sickness, journey to paradise, testamentary situation	30-44	5:1b-14:3
5	Eve's narrative, admonition	....	15-30
6	Adam's death, Eve's vision, Adam's burial	45-48	31:1-42:2
7	Eve's testament	49:1-50:2	....
8	Eve's death, burial	50:3-51:3	42:3-43:4

narrative in *Adam and Eve* 1-22: the quest for food and the penitence of Adam and Eve. Driven from paradise (without any seeds), Adam and Eve find the earth devoid of food (1:1-4:2). Adam proposes that they stand for an extended period of time in the Jordan and Tigris Rivers respectively, in the hope that these acts of penitence will incur divine favor (4:3-6:2). The devil tricks Eve into coming out of the water and brings her to Adam (chaps. 9-11). In chaps. 12-17, the tempter explains the reasons for his actions. After Cain's birth (chaps. 18-21), which illustrates Gen 3:16 (cf. *Adam and Eve* 19:1 and *Apoc. Mos.* 25:3), God provides Adam with seeds and agricultural know-how (22:1-2). *Adam and Eve* 22:3-24:2 and *Apoc. Mos.* 1:1-5:1a parallel one another in content with some occasional correspondence in wording.

In chaps. 25-29, Adam transmits two pieces of secret information to Seth, which we shall analyze in detail later. In the first, Adam describes his vision of God after his expulsion from the garden (25:1-29:1). The second is an historical apocalypse, containing information that Adam had learned after eating from the Tree of Knowledge (29:2-10). The placement of the material here is strange. While it has overtones of a testamentary revelation, it is introduced before Adam's death is announced. In fact, it lacks any situational introduction. Adam is suddenly talking to Seth.

Following this instruction, the narrative line of *Adam and Eve* again begins to parallel that of *Apoc. Mos.*:[6] Adam is dying; he assembles his

---

[6] Here, as in other places, L.S.A. Wells's synoptic treatment of the two recensions is confusing (*APOT* 2, 139). *Apoc. Mos.* 5:1b-2 does not belong on p. 139, but on p. 141 opposite *Adam and Eve* 30:1.

sons and explains the reasons for the situation in a testamentary narrative; he sends Eve and Seth after the oil of life; they meet and overcome the beast; they are refused the oil and are sent home to announce Adam's death (*Adam and Eve* 30-44; cf. *Apoc. Mos.* 5:1b-14:3). Again there are occasional correspondences in wording. In the place of the formulaic "not now, but at the ends of the times" (*Apoc. Mos.* 13:2-5) is a patent reference to Jesus, his baptism in the Jordan, and the opening of paradise (*Adam and Eve* 42:2-5).[7] With the omission of Eve's narrative, *Adam and Eve* 45 continues with the deathbed scene and with Adam's death, with vv 1-3a paralleling *Apoc. Mos.* 31. The story of Eve's vision and of Adam's burial is told in significantly shorter form in *Adam and Eve* 46-48 than in *Apoc. Mos.* 35-42:2.

Eve's death is prefaced by a testamentary situation (chaps. 49-50), which parallels that of Adam. Knowing that she is going to die, she assembles her children and transmits to them a brief revelation which she has received from Michael. Because of their transgression, God will judge the human race twice, once by water and once by fire. She instructs her children to inscribe their parents' life on columns of clay and stone that will withstand these judgments. Thereafter the narrative presents the story of Eve's death and burial in brief form, paralleling *Apoc. Mos.* With Seth fulfilling his mother's command to inscribe the story, the book ends.[8]

The central part of *Adam and Eve* is a testamentary account of Adam's death. Of the major elements in *Apoc. Mos.*, only Eve's narrative is missing. Nonetheless, it has its counterparts in sections 1, 3, and 7.

Adam's search for food and receipt of the seeds (*Adam and Eve* 1:1-22:2) corresponds to the final episode in the expulsion in *Apoc. Mos.* 29. Both passages evidence the same pattern: request for mercy/ answer (*Apoc. Mos.* 29:1-4/5-6; *Adam and Eve* 4:3/22:1-2). An

---

[7] This passage has been interpolated from the *Gospel of Nicodemus* 19, Meyer, "Vita," 204-5. In the Arm. *Penitence* (see below, with n. 10), the passage corresponding to this passage describes how Christ will baptize Adam in the river Jordan. Thus the interpolation from the *Gospel of Nicodemus* appears to have replaced a patent Christian reference already in the Adam book. Whether this reference is a Christian expansion of a text like *Apoc. Mos.* 13:2-5, or whether the latter is a de-christianized form of the text in the Arm. *Penitence* is a question that must await publication of the text. Prof. Michael Stone believes the Christian form is more original.

[8] It is not accidental that a command to write the story occurs at the end of the book. Cf., e.g., Dan 12:9; *1 Enoch* 104:11-13; *4 Ezra* 14; Rev 22:10.

important theological difference between the two versions is evident, however. In *Apoc. Mos.*, Adam's request is simply granted. In *Adam and Eve*, they do an act of penitence.

The first part of Adam's instructions to Seth, the description of his ascent to paradise (*Adam and Eve* 25:1-29:1), corresponds to the last part of Eve's narrative, God's appearance in paradise, the judgment and expulsion (*Apoc. Mos.* 22-29). Both take place in "paradise" (*Adam and Eve* 25:3; *Apoc. Mos.* 22:3). Adam sees God, on his chariot throne, accompanied by his angels (*Adam and Eve* 25:3; *Apoc. Mos.* 22:3-4). A word of judgment is spoken to Adam, which paraphrases Gen 3:17 (and 19) (*Adam and Eve* 26:2; *Apoc. Mos.* 24:1). Adam pleads for mercy and receives a concession from God that refers to the future (*Adam and Eve* 27; *Apoc. Mos.* 27-28). There is some similarity in wording in the descriptions of Adam's and the angels' prostration before God in this scene (*Adam and Eve* 26:1; 27:1; 28:1; *Apoc. Mos.* 27:5). Both sections end with Adam's expulsion from paradise and return to earth (*Adam and Eve* 28:3-29:1; *Apoc. Mos.* 29:6b-7). In view of these parallels, there can be little doubt that these passages are related traditions. We shall discuss other aspects of their relationship below.

The remaining two sections (3b and 7) are unique to *Adam and Eve* in terms of their content. There is no historical apocalypse in *Apoc. Mos.* On the other hand, there is a formal similarity between *Adam and Eve* 49-50 and Eve's narrative in *Apoc. Mos.* 15-29. Both are attributed to Eve. As we noted above, *Apoc. Mos.* 15-29 is modelled on biographical sections of testaments and has the typical admonitory conclusion. *Adam and Eve* 49-50 is explicitly testamentary instruction. With respect to Eve's testament, it is curious that Josephus preserves the same tradition, but attributes it to Adam (*Ant.* 1.2.3 § 70-71). Thus, the same ambiguity pertains to this passage in *Adam and Eve* as pertains in Eve's narrative in *Apoc. Mos.*

A recension that stands midway between *Apoc. Mos.* and *Adam and Eve* is found in the as yet unpublished Armenian *Penitence of our Father Adam.* My summary and comments here are based on a partial translation of the work which Prof. Michael E. Stone kindly made available to me and discussed with me.[9] The book begins with an account of the

---

[9] I wish to thank Prof. Stone for calling to my attention (during the seminar session) the relevance of this document for the present discussion and for permitting me to discuss its contents here before he publishes it in his volume *Armenian Apocryphal Writings Relating to the Patriarchs and Prophets.* All opinions expressed here are my

penitence of Adam and Eve and the birth of Cain which corresponds section by section with *Adam and Eve* 1:1-22:2, albeit with many variations in wording. Thereafter, the *Penitence* agrees in its structure with *Apoc. Mos.* against *Adam and Eve*. That is, it lacks Adam's revelations to Seth and Eve's testament (sections 3, 7 in table 1), and it contains Eve's narrative (section 5). In the account of the expulsion (cf. *Apoc. Mos.* 29:4-6), however, it omits mention of the seeds for food. Thus the first chapters describe how Adam and Eve obtain the food which, according to Eve's narrative, they did not take out of Paradise with them.[10]

A related form of the story occurs in the so-called Slavonic *Life of Adam and Eve*.[11] This work is, for the most part, a short version of *Apoc. Mos.*, which follows the story line of *Apoc. Mos.*, presenting all its pericopes in order and generally in considerably shorter form. Where *Apoc. Mos.* and the Latin *Adam and Eve* parallel one another, the wording of the Slavonic book is generally closer to *Apoc. Mos.* than to *Adam and Eve*. Its one divergence from *Apoc. Mos.* is in the expulsion scene (Slav. *Adam and Eve* 25-27). The plea for mercy is very brief. Adam then requests food, but the angels drive him out. He asks for incense for sacrifice, and they give him this.[12] The narrative then continues with the search for food and Adam and Eve's penitence (chaps. 28-39).[13] The devil's narrative, the story of Cain's birth, and Adam's actual receipt of the seeds (= Lat. *Adam and Eve* 11-22:2) are missing, and the narrative continues with chap. 40 paralleling *Apoc. Mos.* 31.

The evidence of the Slav. *Adam and Eve* raises two different but related questions, to which we can give only brief attention here. 1) In both the Slav. *Adam and Eve* and the Arm. *Penitence*, the story of the quest for food and the penitence is the counterpart to the request for seeds in *Apoc. Mos.* 29:4-6. Is the longer story an expansion of the latter

---

own unless otherwise indicated. On the corpus of Armenian Adam Books, see M. E. Stone, "Report on Seth Traditions in the Armenian Adam Books," pp. 459-471 in this volume.

[10] Evidently closely related to the Arm. *Penitence* is the Georgian version of *Adam and Eve*, on which see W. Lüdtke, "Georgische Adam-Bücher," *ZAW* 38/39 (1919-21) 155-68. It, too, lacks sections 3 and 7, but begins with the penitence and also contains Eve's narrative.

[11] For a text and translation, see V. Jagić, "Slavische Beiträge zu den biblischen Apocryphen: I, Die altkirchenslavischen Texte des Adambuches," *DenkschrAkWien* 42 (1893) 1-103.

[12] For a similar pattern, cf. *Adam and Eve* 42-43. Adam is refused the oil of mercy, but Seth and Eve bring back herbs.

[13] Note that Wells (*APOT* 2. 134) places material from Slav. *Adam and Eve* 28 ff. in a column parallel to *Adam and Eve* 1 ff.

incident, or are the relevant elements in *Apoc. Mos.* 29:4-6 a compression of the longer story? 2) Does the Slav. *Adam and Eve* or the Arm. *Penitence* (and the Lat. *Adam and Eve*) preserve the original placement of this episode?

THE RELATIONSHIP AMONG THE ADAM AND EVE BOOKS

As will be evident by now, the relationship among *Apoc. Mos., Adam and Eve*, and the Arm. *Penitence* is a highly complex matter. Our conclusions here must remain tentative. Any attempt at a definitive statement on the relationship among these recensions must be based on a careful sifting of all the textual and exegetical material, which is far beyond the scope of this paper and must, in any event, await the publication of the Armenian and a study of the related Georgian version.[14]

Central and essential to *Apoc. Mos., Adam and Eve*, and the Arm. *Penitence* is a common core of material (sections 2, 4, 6, 8 in table 1) with the same sequence of elements and some considerable correspondence in wording. This is sufficient to warrant an hypothesis of substantial (literary?) interdependence.

This common core of material is basically a testamentary account of Adam's death and burial with a brief narrative preface and epilog describing Eve's death and burial. In all three versions, this story is interwoven with a concern for Adam's salvation.[15] This focus may have been a constituent part of an original Adam book represented now by this common material. More likely, I believe, it was the central theological tendency of an author who rewrote an earlier Adamic testament.

This rewritten testament corresponds either to *Apoc. Mos.* or the Arm. *Penitence* (or alternatively, the order represented by the Slav. *Adam and Eve*). If *Apoc. Mos.* is the prior form, the request for seeds has been expanded, for theological reasons, into the story of the quest for food and the penitence. If the Arm. *Penitence* is the prior form, the penitence has been excised, and the quest for food has been replaced by a request for seeds, which has been fitted neatly into the already existent pattern in the end of Eve's narrative. It is not evident

---

[14] See above, n. 10.

[15] By extension, the author is also concerned about the descendents of Adam. See, e.g., *Apoc. Mos.* 43:2. The prescriptions for Adam's burial apply to every man who waits for the resurrection. Cf. also 13:3, "the holy people." On this subject, see J. Sharpe, "The Second Adam in the Apocalypse of Moses," *CBQ* 35 (1973) 35-46.

why the motif would have been retained since it serves no function in the narrative. *Apoc. Mos.* seems to be the prior form.

The Lat. *Adam and Eve* represents yet another stage in the development of the book beyond the Arm. *Penitence*. In *Apoc. Mos.* 14:3 and its counterpart in the Arm. *Penitence*, Eve's narrative is introduced by Adam's command that she tell their children the story of the fall. In the corresponding part of *Adam and Eve* (44:2), Adam commands Eve to tell the story "after my death." Six days after Adam's death, Eve gathers her children and transmits her testament (chaps. 49-50). Of course, it is not the story of the fall, but what Michael revealed to Adam and Eve after the fall.

These data suggest the following explanation. At some point in the tradition, Eve's narrative was moved to the end of the book (thus the *wording* of 44:3), probably to provide Eve with a proper testament. This narrative was subsequently removed. Part of it was rewritten in the form of Adam's narrative (*Adam and Eve* 25:1-29:1), to which was added an historical apocalypse. Related apocalyptic material now provided the contents for Eve's testament at the end of the book.

Although Adam's first revelation to Seth is secondary to the version in Eve's narrative (see the next section), the other two sections unique to *Adam and Eve*—the historical apocalypse and Eve's testament—may represent independent traditions that derived from an Adamic testament, albeit not the same testament that was, putatively, the source of the material common to *Apoc. Mos.*, the Arm. *Penitence*, and *Adam and Eve*. The historical apocalypse in 29:2-10 is a form typical of testamental literature (cf., e.g., *T. Levi* 16-18; *T. Judah* 21-25; *1 Enoch* 85-93).[16] *Adam and Eve* 49-50 are also predictive, and they have an explicit testamentary setting—before Eve's death. The fact that Josephus attributes this same tradition to Adam (*Ant.* 1.2.3 § 70-71) may indicate that the author of *Adam and Eve* has derived it from an Adamic tradition.

The hypothesis of the last part of this paper will be that *Adam and Eve* 29:2-10 + 49-50 and the Gnostic *Apocalypse of Adam* (hereafter *ApocAd*) derive from a testament of Adam that was influenced by traditions found in *1 Enoch*, which are reflected in both *Adam and Eve* and *ApocAd*. Before turning to *ApocAd.*, we shall look at possible connections between *Adam and Eve* 25-29 and *1 Enoch*.

---

[16] Although the Arm. *Penitence* does not contain the historical apocalypse, it may know such an Adamic tradition. According to chap. 20, God taught Adam sowing and also what was coming upon him and his descendents.

ADAM AND EVE 25-29; 49-50 AND THEIR PARALLELS IN 1 ENOCH

Adam and Eve 25-29:1 and 1 Enoch 14. We have noted the many similarities between *Adam and Eve* 25-29:1 and *Apoc. Mos.* 22-29. The major differences between these two corresponding sections relate to the different loci in which the theophanies take place. In *Apoc. Mos.*, God appears in paradise, the home of Adam and Eve, and this appearance and the word of condemnation against Adam are parts of an extensive elaboration of Genesis 3. In *Adam and Eve*, after the first parents' expulsion from their home (25:1), Adam is taken to "the paradise of righteousness" for a vision of God.[17] The narrative has many parallels with biblical and postbiblical accounts of epiphanies. However, as a whole, and at most of the points which are unique to it with reference to *Apoc. Mos.*, it parallels most closely the account of Enoch's ascent in *1 Enoch* 13:7-16:4. Adam and Eve are praying (25:2); Enoch is interceding for the fallen watchers (13:7).[18] Adam is taken to the paradise of righteousness on a windlike chariot (25:3); Enoch is carried to heaven by the winds (14:8).[19] Both Adam and Enoch see the Lord seated on his chariot throne, surrounded by many thousands of angels (*Adam and Eve* 25:3, *1 Enoch* 14:20-22).[20] For Adam, God's face is a flaming fire that cannot be endured (25:3); in *1 Enoch*, God is surrounded by a series of impenetrable fire barriers, and from beneath his throne issue flames that fill his presence. Even the angels cannot behold his face (14:9-22). The descriptions of the violent physical and emotional reactions of Adam and Enoch are very similar (cf. *Adam and Eve* 26:1 and *1 Enoch* 14:13-14, 24).

All the aforementioned elements are at home in *1 Enoch* 14, where they constitute integral parts of a classical commissioning scene with especially close parallels to Ezekiel 1-2.[21] The major variant from the form of Ezekiel's vision, the *ascent* to meet God, marks a transition

---

[17] The term "paradise of righteousness" occurs in *1 Enoch* 32:3. It is located in the northeast by J. T. Milik, *The Books of Enoch: Aramaic Fragments of Qumran Cave 4* (Oxford: Clarendon, 1976) 37. "Paradise" is a common term for the third heaven, where the blessed reside.

[18] Cf. also *1 Enoch* 12:3-4.

[19] This is reminiscent also of 2 Kgs 2:1; however, the Enoch story may also reflect the Elijah story, cf. *1 Enoch* 70:2.

[20] Different from *Apoc. Mos.* 22:3; *Adam and Eve* 25:3 and *1 Enoch* 14:22 speak of *thousands* of angels.

[21] This was first noted in detail by H. L. Jansen, *Die Henochgestalt* (Oslo: Dybwad, 1939) 115-17.

from the prophetic tradition toward mystical traditions, in which the righteous one ascends to heaven for a vision of God.[22]

In view of these parallels, it is striking and unexpected that Adam should be caught up to paradise in order to hear the sentence of death spoken against himself. This is at complete odds with the tradition that a prophet or righteous man was given special access to 'God's presence.

This anomaly is one of several instances in which parallels between *Adam and Eve* 25-29:1 and *Apoc. Mos.* 22-28 appear to have their more primitive form in the latter. 1) The sentence of death, with its paraphrase of Gen 3:17, is to be expected in *Apoc. Mos.* 22 ff., which is a rewritten form of Genesis 3. Interestingly it occurs in *Apoc. Mos.* 24:1 in a paraphrase of Gen 3:17-19a, rather than as a conflation of Gen 3:17a + 19b (or v 3). 2) *Apoc. Mos.* 22ff. is properly set in the earthly paradise and ends with expulsion from it. *Adam and Eve* 25-29:1 violates both the Genesis and the Enochic setting in this case. The original Genesis setting leads the author to describe an ascent to the paradise of righteousness, rather than to the heavenly temple as in *1 Enoch* 14. On the other hand, the ascent to this paradise diverges from Genesis where *Apoc. Mos.* follows it. 3) The *Apocalypse of Moses* has the more primitive form of the plea for mercy and its answer. In *Apoc. Mos.* 28:4, God's answer is an expression of the typical "not now, but later" formulation of that book. In *Adam and Eve* 27:3, the word of future grace relates to Adam's progeny, a motif that is paralleled in another context in *1 Enoch*, as we shall indicate below.

Two elements common to *Adam and Eve* and *Apoc. Mos.* appear to be in more primitive form in *Adam and Eve* than in *Apoc. Mos.* and may be a secondary reflex of the *Adam and Eve* tradition on the final form of *Apoc. Mos.* God's appearance with chariot throne and angels better fits the visionary context of *Adam and Eve* than the setting in the garden. The prostration to the ground is an essential part of the vision, but there is no biblical warrant for it in the paraphrase of Genesis 3 in *Apoc. Mos.*, much less for the *angels* to be prostrating themselves.

Although there are ambiguities in any hypothesis of the relationship of these two obviously related paraphrases of Genesis 3, the weight of probability supports the primitivity of the form in *Apoc. Mos.*

---

[22] The parallel with mystical literature is noted by Gershom Scholem, *Major Trends in Jewish Mysticism* (New York : Schocken, 1961) 44.

22-29. For the author of *Adam and Eve* 25-29:1, two factors may have been at work in his radical rewriting of his tradition. First, a theology of a transcendent God may have led him to place the theophany in the heavenly paradise, rather than to depict God coming to earth à la Genesis 3.[23] God's chariot throne is a fixed piece of furniture in heaven, as it is for Enoch, rather than a vehicle by which he comes to earth, as it is, e.g., in Ezekiel 1-2 and *Apoc. Mos.* Secondly, *1 Enoch* 14 was a reasonable text in which to find a model for a rewriting of the tradition about Adam's condemnation for his part in the primordial sin. Enoch ascends to heaven in order to hear the sentence of condemnation against the watchers, whose intercourse with women has incarnated a host of evil demons on earth.

Adam and Eve 25-29 *and 1 Enoch* 83-90. In chaps. 25-29, Adam transmits to his son Seth two very different revelations, each distinguished by its own formal chronological introduction (25:1-2; 29:2-3). Moreover, this revelation is given only to Seth, apart from more general testamentary instruction to all of Adam's sons. This same set of circumstances obtains in *1 Enoch* 83-84; 85-90. Although Enoch will later gather all his children and instruct them (see 91:1 ff.), here he addresses Methuselah alone, transmitting to him two dream visions, each with its own chronological introduction (83:1-2; 85:1-3). Thus, in these parallel instances, Seth and Methuselah have similar roles as recipients and guarantors of revelation.

In addition to these formal parallels, there are similarities in the contents of the two sets of revelation. *1 Enoch* 83-84 centers around an oracle of doom. Enoch forsees the flood, and he fears that he will be left without offspring (83:8; 84:5-6). He prays that this will not be so (chap. 84). He receives divine assurance that his prayer has been answered, and he praises God for this (83:11).[24] Adam hears the sentence of death (*Adam and Eve* 26:2). He prays that his name will not be blotted out (27:1). He is assured that his seed will continue to serve God (27:3), and he praises God for his mercy (28:1-2).[25] With

---

[23] This explanation was suggested to me by my colleague Helen Goldstein.

[24] The prayer recorded in chap. 84 is the one that is prayed at 83:10, so that the events recorded in 83:11 belong *chronologically* after chap. 84. For a similar device, cf. *1 Enoch* 13-14, where the vision which Enoch saw is told (in two parts) in chap. 14, though it has been referred to in the narrative in 13:8, where it is followed by other events.

[25] For another parallel, cf. the negative expressions in both *Adam and Eve* 27:2 and *1 Enoch* 84:6c.

respect to this prayer—answer sequence, *Adam and Eve* is closer to
1 Enoch than it is to its counterpart in *Apoc. Mos.* 27-29. There is,
secondly, a similarity between the second of the two visions in
Adam and Eve and *1 Enoch*. Both are historical apocalypses. However,
while there are numerous similarities in the contents of these two
apocalypses, *Adam and Eve* 29:2-10 is more closely related to yet
another Enochic tradition, viz., the Apocalypse of Weeks.

Adam and Eve 29:2-10 and 49-50+51:3 and 1 Enoch 93:1-10; 91:11-
17. In *Adam and Eve* 29:2-10 Adam transmits to Seth eschatological
information he had learned after eating from the Tree of Knowledge.[26]
It takes the form of an historical apocalypse that describes events
from the giving of the Torah to the eschaton. Two thought-complexes
structure the contents of the apocalypse. The first (indicated in the
middle two columns of table 2) relates to the character of human conduct
and its judgment by God. The second (the last column in table 2)
centers on the sanctuary in its various forms. In the text, attitudes
toward the sanctuary and its fate overlap with the first complex of
thought.

It is not by accident that the apocalypse begins with the giving of
"commandments and statutes" on Mount Sinai, for the Torah is basic
to all that follows. Israel's first obedience is seen in their worship
of God in the tabernacle (verse 4). When they enter the land, their
obedience is further shown in the construction of the temple. However,
they begin to transgress "his statutes." In consequence the temple is
burnt, and the people are dispersed. A new time begins with their return.
Their righteousness is shown in the rebuilding of the temple. (A
proleptic view of the future glory of the temple appears here out of
place [6].) Again there will be a time characterized by iniquity (7).
This is followed by the theophany, which marks the beginning of the
judgment and eschaton (7). This will be a time of righteousness (7).
Naturally, the house of God will be honored (7; cf. 6). The righteous,
here defined by their faith, will be protected from their enemies. In
parallel clauses, the author notes that God will stir up a faithful people,
whom he will save; and that he will punish the impious, defined as

---

[26] A. F. J. Klijn (*Seth*, 17n. 56) cites three rabbinic references to Adam's
knowledge of the future (*b. Sanh.* 38b; *b. 'Abod. Zar.* 5a; *'Abot R. Nat.* 31). These
are an *ad hoc* interpretation of Gen 5:1, which may well presume an interpretation
like the present one, but in none of these passages is this knowledge tied to
his eating from the tree. See also above, n. 16.

TABLE 2

THEMATIC ANALYSIS OF ADAM AND EVE 29:2-10

VERSE	HUMAN CONDUCT	GOD'S JUDGMENT	REFERENCES TO SANCTUARY
4	Israel will sanctify God	....	....
	....	....	* The tabernacle
5			* They will build the Temple
	* They will transgress his statutes	....	
	....	* The Temple will be burnt	....
	....	* The people will be dispersed	....
6	....	The people will return	....
	....	....	The Temple will be rebuilt and exalted
7	* Iniquity will exceed righteousness	....	....
	....	God will dwell with men	....
	* Righteousness will begin to shine	....	....
	....	....	* The Temple will be honored
	....	Believers' enemies will not hurt them	....
	....	* The impious will be punished	....
8	* All creation and creatures will obey God and be changed from forsaking the law	....	....
9		* God will repel the wicked; the just will shine	
	....		....
	Some will be purified by water	....	....
10	Others will not be purified	....	....
	....	Those not purified by water will be condemned	....
	....	In the judgment happy will be the one who rules his soul	....

* Elements with parallels in the Apocalypse of Weeks.

those who refused to love his law. In verse 8, the apocalypse assumes a universalistic tone. All of creation—heaven and earth, nights and days, and all creatures—will not "transgress his commandments." This means a conversion from "forsaking the law of the Lord." Then we hear of the final separation, in two sets of parallel clauses: he will repel the wicked, and the just will shine (9); men will be purified by water, and those who are unwilling will be condemned (9-10). The final verse comments on the blessed eschatological condition of the one who is prepared for the judgment (10).

The comparison of this apocalypse with any given Jewish historical apocalypse has its problems. Claims of dependence must deal with the fact that all historical apocalypses have the same set of events in biblical history to record. Moreover, in comparing this apocalypse with the Apocalypse of Weeks, we must note this major difference: the latter begins with Enoch and refers to the flood and Abraham before moving on to Sinai. We shall return to this difficulty presently.

Similarities between this apocalypse and the Apocalypse of Weeks include the following items (marked in table 2 by an asterisk). Both apocalypses are very sketchy, describing long periods of history by brief references to typical events. In both apocalypses, the structure of history is seen solely in the righteousness or unrighteousness of the people and in God's judgment of this behavior.[27] In both apocalypses, there are fairly exhaustive references to the sanctuary in its various phases: the tabernacle; the Solomonic temple; its being burnt; (the temple of Zerubbabel may be meant in *Adam and Eve* 29:6, for which there is no counterpart in *1 Enoch* 93:9; however, the formulation of the sentence and its reference to "the last time" suggests the analogy of *1 Enoch* 91:13); the glory of the eschatological temple (verse 7 and perhaps 6bc). In the eschatological section (7b-10), there is, of course, the typical judgment. The conversion of humankind (8) suggests *1 Enoch* 91:14b, and reference to the elements is reminiscent of *1 Enoch* 91:16.

The omission of events in the first three weeks (whether or not the author knows the Apocalypse of Weeks) is probably due to the author's theological emphasis. He is not sketching the history of the people of God from Abraham to the eschaton.[28] Rather he emphasizes righteousness

---

[27] See my discussion of the Apocalypse of Weeks in "The Apocalyptic Message of *1 Enoch* 92-105," *CBQ* 39 (1977) 313-15.

[28] For this aspect of the Apocalypse of Weeks, see the discussion below on the *ApocAd.*

as it relates to the law given on Sinai. Thus, Sinai is a proper place to begin.

Although the Flood is not mentioned in this apocalypse, it is central to Eve's apocalypse in *Adam and Eve* 49-50. Formally, this section is a piece of testamentary instruction, in which Eve transmits to her children information conveyed to her by Michael. Its contents are the revelation that God will destroy the world by two acts of judgment, one by water (the deluge), the other by fire (presumably the last judgment). In view of this, Eve's children are to record their parents' lives on columns that can withstand these destructions. The command is carried out by Seth.

A number of factors tie chaps. 49-50 to chaps. 25-29. Like 25-29:1, chaps. 49-50 are a revelation mediated by Michael.[29] Both 29:2-10 and 49:3 contain revelations of eschatological import. The latter supplements the former by informing us that the final judgment will be by fire and that it will have a prototype in the Flood. In 25-29, Seth is the recipient of tradition; in chap. 51, he is its guarantor by virtue of his recording the tradition. Although in chap. 49 Eve addresses all her children, in effect Seth is the special son in focus. Finally, we may note again that Josephus refers to this tradition as Adamic: Adam predicted the two catastrophes, one by fire, the other by a deluge (*sic*!). In view of this the children of Seth inscribed esoteric information on two pillars (*Ant.* 1.2.3. § 70-71).

The typology of two judgments—the flood and the final judgment—is so central to the Enochic corpus that its existence there need not be defended here.[30] We need only note that in the case of the Apocalypse of Weeks, the deluge is called "the first end" (93:4). As in the case of the final judgment, it is preceded by "violence and deceit" (cf. 91:11 in 4QHen[g] 1 iv 14). While there may well be other sources for the idea of double judgment by water and fire,[31] it is noteworthy that in the Apocalypse of Weeks, the burning of the temple and dispersion of the people are construed as judgment (93:8).

Our investigation indicates that the two traditions completely unique

---

[29] Perkins, "Apocalypse of Adam," 386.

[30] Ibid., 387 n. 19, citing *1 Enoch* 54:7-55:2. Cf. also *1 Enoch* 10, where a description of judgment by the Flood flows into a description of the end-time; see G. W. E. Nickelsburg, "Apocalyptic and Myth in *1 Enoch* 6-11," *JBL* 96 (1977) 387-89.

[31] See the discussion in Perkins, "Apocalypse of Adam," 387-89, and Klijn, *Seth*, 121-24.

to *Adam and Eve*, chaps. 29:2-10 and 49-50+51:3, have enough in common that they should probably the considered to be one piece. The appearance of the tradition of the two judgments in chap. 49:3 strengthens the case for seeing in 29:2-10 a reflection of the Apocalypse of Weeks.

In summary: the core of *Adam and Eve* derives from a tradition common to *Apoc. Mos.*, and perhaps ultimately from *Apoc. Mos.* itself. Of the sections of *Adam and Eve* that in their present form are unique to that book (sections 1, 3, 7), chaps. 1-22:2, perhaps, and 25-29:1 are elaborations or developments of traditions in Eve's narrative in *Apoc. Mos.* Chaps. 25-29:1 parallel the account of Enoch's ascent in *1 Enoch* 13-16. Chaps. 29:2-10 and 49-50+51:3 may well have come from a separate tradition which was influenced by material in *1 Enoch*. While arguments regarding literary dependency are tricky, the combined parallels to three separate sections in *1 Enoch* may well speak for such a literary relationship.

II. The Gnostic Apocalypse of Adam

The *Apocalypse of Adam (ApocAd)* is a testament of Adam.[32] As such it records Adam's deathbed instruction to his son, Seth. In comparison with Jewish testamentary literature in general, however, its components are considerably out of balance. The narrative framework (CG V 64:2-4; 85:19-32) is atypically short and lacks the usual (more or less) detailed information about the circumstances of the patriarch's death and burial. The nature of the testamentary instruction is also atypical. A relatively short biographical section (64:5-68:14) is not followed by an ethical exhortation based on it, but rather by an abnormally extensive historical apocalypse (68:14-85:18), which is the heart of the document. Indeed, the apocalypse is so long that the title on the codex is not at all inappropriate. The relative lengths of the narrative introduction and of the apocalypse are more typical of works generally classified as apocalypses than of testaments.

P. Perkins has drawn attention to the testamentary characteristics of *Adam and Eve*, has noted some parallels with *ApocAd*, and has suggested that the latter and Eve's testament in *Adam and Eve* 49-50 are related to a common Adamic testamentary tradition.[33] In our

---

[32] Perkins, "Apocalypse of Adam," 384-85.
[33] Ibid., 384-87.

investigation above, we have argued that the material common to *Apoc. Mos.* and *Adam and Eve* constitutes a testament of Adam. This testament has in common with *ApocAd* a dearth of ethical and parenetic material,[34] even with the addition of Eve's narrative in *Apoc. Mos.*, we have only two sentences (chap. 30). A major formal difference between *ApocAd* and *Apoc. Mos.* is the latter's total lack of a formal apocalypse.[35]

Comparison with *Adam and Eve* produces very different results. While it is true that this work is primarily narrative in form, and the largest part of its testamentary section is narrative, two of its three unique sections are said to be revelations. Moreover, as Perkins has noted, these revelations have formal and material parallels with *ApocAd*. Like the apocalypse in *ApocAd*, Adam's vision of God and the revelation about the two judgments are angelically mediated.[36] Three men appear to Adam (65:25-27). Michael is the mediator in *Adam and Eve* 25:2; 49:2. As in *Adam and Eve* 49:3, we hear of judgment by water and fire in *Apoc.Ad* (67:19 ff.; 75:9 ff.).[37]

We may press the similarities between *Adam and Eve* and *ApocAd* another step. *Adam and Eve* 29:2-10 is an historical apocalypse with a number of similarities in detail to *ApocAd*.[38] In both cases, Adam transmits to Seth an account of future events which culminates in the judgment and end-time. Both make reference at the end to water rituals, *Adam and Eve* 29:10 to purification of sins by water, *ApocAd* 83:5 ff. to baptism. Both contain similar macarisms immediately thereafter:

> Happy (*felix*) is every man who corrects his soul,
>> when the day of the great judgment comes to pass among mortals
>>> (*Adam and Eve* 29:10)
> Blessed (*naiats*) is the soul of those men,
>> because they have known God with a knowledge of truth
>>> (*ApocAd* 83:11-14)

Adam and Eve 29:2-10 makes no reference to the events before Sinai

---

[34] Ibid., 386.

[35] There is a brief prediction of the future exaltation of Adam in *Apoc. Mos.* 39:2-3 and the occasional references to the resurrection. These *presume* apocalyptic descriptions, but are not formal apocalypse.

[36] Perkins, "Apocalypse of Adam," 386.

[37] Ibid., 387.

[38] Perkins ("Apocalypse of Adam," 386) mentions this section only briefly without suggesting any substantial parallels to *ApocAd*.

and thus differs in content from a substantial portion of the apocalypse in *ApocAd*. However, if we see chaps. 29 and 49-50 as complementary traditions, part of the gap is filled. Put another way, the consideration of similarities between *ApocAd* and *Adam and Eve* 29:2-10 supports and complements Perkins's suggestion that *ApocAd* and *Adam and Eve* 49-50 have descended from a common Adamic testamentary tradition. In this respect, it is noteworthy that the major part of *ApocAd* corresponds to those parts of *Adam and Eve* for which there are no material parallels in *Apoc. Mos.*[39] This strengthens our suspicion that *Adam and Eve* 29:2-10; 49-50 may have derived from a testament of Adam.

We have noted the parallels between *1 Enoch* and *Adam and Eve*, and we have suggested that *Adam and Eve* 29:2-10 evidences some notable similarities with the Apocalypse of Weeks. Substantial similarities with the Apocalypse of Weeks are evident in the apocalypse in *ApocAd*. In fact, the former provides the closest Jewish analogy to the latter. In the comparison that follows, we are taking account of the Gnostic irony in *ApocAd*, which leads the author to reverse the identities of the righteous and the wicked.[40]

Both apocalypses speak of three judgments.[41] The first is by water, in both cases, the Deluge. The second is by fire, or in connection with fire. *ApocAd* 75:9-10 employs imagery reminiscent of the story of Sodom and Gomorrah.[42] In *1 Enoch* 93:8 (as well as in *Adam and Eve* 29:5), God judges his people by dispersing them and burning the temple. The third judgment is the final judgment, in *1 Enoch* 91:11-15 construed as a threefold judgment: against the wicked oppressors, against all humankind, and against the angels.[43]

Both apocalypses focus on the fate of the elect community. In

---

[39] One might also compare the devil's narrative (*Adam and Eve* 12-17) and *ApocAd* 64:14ff. The latter is, of course, part of a whole Gnostic complex of thought. However, the particular explanation for the devil's envy in *Adam and Eve* 13-15 is peculiarly close to the Gnostic idea. I am presupposing the Gnostic equation of the devil with the God of creation, so that the image of the creator God in *Adam and Eve* is transformed into the glory of the invisible God.

[40] For a substantive discussion of these ironies, see Perkins, "Apocalypse of Adam," 391-394.

[41] On these judgments, see ibid., 387-89.

[42] Ibid., 387.

[43] The judgment against the oppressors and the judgment of the angels may have counterparts in *ApocAd*. However, the former can be accounted for in the use of the story of the persecuted righteous one (see below), and the latter is too obvious an eventuality in a Gnostic document.

ApocAd these are the children of Seth and those children of Ham and Japheth who join their community. At the Flood, they are delivered from the wrath of the Creator, and later they are protected from the judgment by fire. After much harrassment, they are vindicated at the final judgment. They are the Gnostics, who are blessed because "they have known God in a pure knowledge of truth" (83:11-14). In at least one place, the author uses an agricultural image to designate them as a remnant (76:11-15). According to *1 Enoch* 93:1, the Apocalypse of Weeks is written concerning "the sons of righteousness, the elect of eternity, and the plant of truth." When deceit and violence "spring up," Noah, the righteous plant, is saved.[44] Abraham is chosen as the plant of righteousness (or "truth"), and his descendents will become that plant (93:5) for eternity. After the return from the Exile, in an age of iniquity, the elect are chosen from that plant (93:10). To them is given "sevenfold wisdom and knowledge." They will execute judgment against their enemies (91:11-12). Thus this apocalypse traces the history of a chosen community, purified through and preserved from judgment, which will come to fruition at the final judgment, when they will have full knowledge and will participate in that judgment. In their essential focus and thrust, these two apocalypses are alike.

Of special concern to both apocalypses is the theme of the preservation of the elect. According to the Apocalypse of Weeks, Noah is saved from the Flood, Elijah ascends in the midst of a wicked generation, and before the final judgment the elect are chosen from the midst of a wicked Israel.[45] In *ApocAd*, once again at the Flood, the children of Seth are taken by angels to a special land (69:19 ff.), where they are later joined by some of the descendents of Ham and Japheth. At the time of the fire judgment, they are again taken by angels (75:22-76:7). This motif is similar not only to the aforementioned passages in the Apocalypse of Weeks, but to others in Enochic and Enoch-related literature. While the Apocalypse of Weeks sees Enoch living in a righteous generation (93:3), other passages see his removal from earth as protection from evil (see Wis 4:10-15, an interpretation of Isa 57:1). In *2 Enoch*, in the Melchizedek appendix 4, Michael spirits the young Melchizedek to heaven before the Flood. In the

---

[44] In view of the other plant imagery, we are doubtless justified in citing the parallel of *1 Enoch* 10:3 (according to the text of Syncellus).

[45] On this motif as an essential part of the apocalypse, see Nickelsburg, "Apocalyptic Message," 313-15.

chronology of George Syncellus (17:2 ff.; cf. 27:1 ff.), an Enochic tradition is transformed into one about the children of Seth. The watchers who descended on Mount Hermon were in fact the children of Seth, who dwelt with the angels in the elevated land of paradise to protect them from the children of Cain, whose daughters finally seduced the Sethites.

Our investigation of *ApocAd* has revealed substantial similarities between the apocalypse in *ApocAd* and the Apocalypse of Weeks. In view of our previous conclusions, I suggest the following as an hypothesis. Both *Adam and Eve* 29:2-10; 49-50 and the apocalypse in *ApocAd* stem from a common tradition, an apocalyptic testament of Adam which was influenced by the Apocalypse of Weeks and perhaps other Enochic traditions. In *Adam and Eve*, this tradition is bifurcated. One part is assigned to Adam. Because of its emphasis on law rather than community, the historical account begins with the giving of the Torah. A remnant of the flood story appears in chap. 49, where it is part of a testament of Eve, which at some point replaced Eve's biographical narrative. The Enochic influence on the Adamic testament continued to pervade and has influenced other traditions in *Adam and Eve*.

We may note a final connection with the Enochic tradition in *ApocAd*. Perkins has shown, correctly, I believe, the influence upon *ApocAd* of an Isaianic tradition about the persecution and exaltation of the righteous one.[46] This tradition finds classical expression in Wisdom of Solomon 2; 4-5. However, as I have argued in my exposition of this tradition, the exaltation scene of this tradition is also to be found in *1 Enoch* 62-63, where the elect one/son of man functions as judge.[47] As is well known, *1 Enoch* 71 identifies the son of man with Enoch himself. This may have some relevance for the text in Wisdom of Solomon, because the author of that work denotes Enoch as the righteous man par excellence.[48] It requires no stretch of the exegetical imagination to identify the exalted righteous one in Wisdom of Solomon 5 with Enoch. Another contact with

---

[46] "Apocalypse of Adam," 390-391. It is noteworthy that some of the wording in *ApocAd* 83:10ff. corresponds to that in Wisdom of Solomon 5. Cf. 83:14-15 with Wis 5:15; 84:2-3 with Wis 5:9ff.; 83:23-25 with Wis 5:4-8 (cf. 4:17), etc.

[47] G. W. E. Nickelsburg, *Resurrection, Immortality, and Eternal Life in Intertestamental Judaism* (HTS 26; Cambridge: Harvard, 1972) 70-74.

[48] Wis 4:10-15 (he is deleted from the list of heroes in chaps. 10-11). In order to see the paradigmatic function of Enoch, one must compare the wording of 4:15 with 4:17 and then with 2:21-22; 3:2-4; and 5:4-7.

1 Enoch is evident in the structure of the argument in Wisdom of Solomon 2-5, which has numerous parallels with the same structure in *1 Enoch* 102-103.[49] To what extent any of these Enochic sources or overtones might have been known to the author of *ApocAd* or its prototype is a matter of conjecture; however, in view of other Enochic parallels, they are mentioned for completeness.

In this paper, I have not dealt with questions of historical setting, provenance, *Sitz im Leben*, and the like. Here I draw attention to only one possible point for consideration. George MacRae, following the cue of A. Böhlig, suggested that *ApocAd* may have emanated from a Gnostic group whose roots were in the Jewish baptist circles from which Mani came.[50] As we noted, water purification of sins is mentioned in *Adam and Eve* 29:10, at a place corresponding to a reference to baptism in *ApocAd*. However, this is not the only mention of ablution in *Adam and Eve*. Following their expulsion from paradise, the first parents carry out an act of penitence by standing at length in the Rivers Tigris and Jordan (chaps. 1 ff.) In an explicitly Christian reference, *Adam and Eve* 42:2-5 speaks of Jesus' baptism in the Jordan.[51] Perhaps the description of the seraphim washing Adam's body in the Acherusian Lake also reflects the practice of ritual ablution (*Apoc. Mos.* 37:3). In any event, reference to ablutions of various kinds for sin(ners) and of Jesus' baptism may indicate that this writing, and its traditions in various stages of its growth, circulated in circles for whom ritual immersion of one kind or another was an important rite.[52]

Postcript: Several additional observations are pertinent within the context of the seminar discussion. The Books of Adam and Eve are Adamic rather than Sethian. Their principal concern centers on Adam's death and its implications. They enshrine an Adamic testament. Seth's roles are secondary. He journeys to the garden for the oil of mercy *together with Eve*. This narrative functions to demonstrate the *failure* of the quest. Thus Seth is not a savior figure here. We can only speculate whether the present narrative reflects an earlier tradition about a successful quest. What would be the function of such a narrative? After all, according to biblical tradition, Adam does die. In

---

[49] Nickelsburg, *Resurrection*, 128-29.

[50] MacRae, "The Apocalypse of Adam Reconsidered," 577.

[51] The passage in the Arm. *Penitence* is closer to *Adam and Eve* 2 ff., for both describe Adam's immersion in the Jordan.

[52] This paper was written during a research leave made possible by a Fellowship from the John Simon Guggenheim Foundation, whose support I gratefully acknowledge.

any event, the existence of such a tradition is indemonstrable from the present text.

In the *Life of Adam and Eve*, Seth is not the primary recipient or transmitter of revelation (he may approach this function in *Apoc. Mos.* 35-36), but the secondary recipient and transmitter of revelations received by Adam (and Eve). He serves the same role in *ApocAd*. In this secondary role, Seth inscribes the columns mentioned in *Adam and Eve* 50; 51:3. In the Gnostic tractate *Three Steles of Seth*, however, Seth's role as revealer is primary, and there is no indication that the contents of the steles were first revealed to Adam or Eve.

SETHIAN AND ZOROASTRIAN AGES OF THE WORLD

BY

CARSTEN COLPE

THIS paper* elaborates hypotheses which H.-M. Schenke[1] and A. Böhlig[2] advanced about the four great aeons and the three illuminators, and which I myself advanced about the combination of history and cosmology in the *Paraphrase of Shem*.[3] The following grouping of source references is in some instances arbitrary and allows for some overlap between the various categories.

I. Sethian Evidence
  A. Distinction of patterns of fourfold cosmological and historical time and threefold eschatological time
    1. Cosmic ages of the universe (speculation about Harmozel, Oroiael, Daveithe, and Eleleth in *ApocryJn* cod. II 7:30-8:28; *GEgypt* cod. III 51:14-53:12; *Zost* 29:1-20; *Zost* 127:15-128:7; *TriProt* 38:30-39:27)
    2. Stages of terrestrial salvation history (*ApocryJn* II 8:33-9:24; *GEgypt* III 60:19-61:1; *GEgypt* III 64:4-8; *ParaShem* 25:8-45:31)
    3. Threefold advent of the savior (*ApocryJn* II 30:11-31:25; *HypArch* 96:27-35; *ApocAd* 76:8-17 or 77:27; *TriProt* 37:21-38:4; *TriProt* 47:4-15)
  B. Fusion of the patterns
    1. Cosmic and terrestrial salvation history (aeons of the primeval Sethians and the historical Sethians in *GEgypt* III 56:13-57:11; of the Adamites before them and the resting souls after them in *ApocryJn* II 8:28-9:24 and *GEgypt* III 64:9-65:26)
    2. Cosmic and eschatological history (Adam-Christ typology [?]

---

* Translated from the German by Anne M. McGuire.

[1] "Das sethianische System nach Nag-Hammadi-Handschriften," *Studia Coptica* (P. Nagel, ed.; Berlin [D.D.R.], 1974) 165-72, and his paper for this seminar, below, pp. 588-616.

[2] *Koptisch-gnostische Apokalypsen aus Codex V von Nag Hammadi im koptischen Museum zu Alt-Kairo* (Halle-Wittenberg, 1963) 90 f.

[3] JAC 16 (1973) 109-116.

within the aeon speculation, *Melch* 5:24-6:11; judgment upon the Sethians, *ApocAd* 74:27-75:4; *ApocAd* 75:17-27)

3. Terrestrial salvation and eschatological history (Eleleth's decisive bringing of gnosis in *HypArch* 93:7-94:8 and *TriProt* 39:14-40:4; dialogue about the completion of the three periods in *Pistis Sophia* chap. 76, tr. Schmidt-Till 108,34-110,12)

II. Iranian and Zoroastrian Evidence

A. Distinction of patterns of fourfold cosmological and historical time and threefold or fourfold eschatological time

1. Periods of the world year (description and short analysis of the 12,000-year universe and its four 3,000-year periods)

2. Scheme of the three or four kingdoms (genesis of the sequence of Assyrians or Neobabylonians, Medes, Persians, and Macedonians)

3. Eschatological epochs according to the Pahlavi literature (description and short analysis of the sequence Ušētar bāmīk, Ušētarmāh, Sōšāns including and excluding Zarathustra)

B. Fusion of the patterns

1. Universal and terrestrial history (combination of the sequence of kingdoms of Vištāspa, Ardašīr, Xosrau Anōšarwān, and the demons with the four branches of the world tree symbolizing four world ages in *Bahman Yašt* 3.23-29 Anklesaria = 2.16-22 West and 1.1-11 = 1.1-5)

2. World year and eschatology (combination of the millennia of the saviors Zarathustra, Ušētar, a Kai and Pišyōtan with the world ages in *Bahman Yašt* 7.2-9.23 = 3.13-61)

3. Terrestrial and eschatological history (identification of the first world age with Zarathustra's tenth millennium in *Bahman Yašt* 3.20-6.13 = 2.15-3.11)

III. Conclusions

The substantive difference between the two doctrines of time or ages is great enough to exclude direct influence in either direction. But the formal patterns and especially their fusions, which render the conceptions of time or ages in both the Sethian texts and the *Bahman Yašt* indistinct, are so similar that the two developments of doctrine must be interrelated. It is precisely in the fusion of time patterns that this remarkable resemblance can be seen. This, along with the similarity of the doctrines of cosmic mixture in the *Paraphrase of Shem* and in the *Bundahišns*, perhaps gives as a terminus post quem the systematization of the Zoroastrian concept of time in the second or third century A.D. in Arsacid Mesopotamia. The reason for the Sethians' adoption of the Iranian principle of time fusion and for their providing it with its own contents (including its own astrology) may have been a periodization of history that was either genuinely Jewish (Seth, Noah, Abraham, and Moses), or else one that was Judaeo-Christian (the true prophet coming in different forms in subsequent epochs).

II A 1. The Iranian doctrine of world ages occurs in various systems. It is probably not yet found in Xanthus the Lydian or Eudoxus of Cnidus, but is first attested in Theopompus. It is then amplified in the two *Bundahišns*, in *Mēnōīk Xrat* (*MX*), in *Artā Wīrāz Nāmak* (*AWN*), in *Dātastān i Dēnīk* (*DD*), in *Wičītakīhā i Zātspram* (*WZs*), in the *ʿUlemā-ye Islām*, according to Šahrastānī, Bīrūnī, Theodore bar Konai, and Eznik of Kolb. The systems include probably not two ages of the world, but rather three world ages, a rounding up of the latter to 10,000 years, and four world ages. Each of the systems is often so vaguely presupposed that we must assume there has been strong influence of interpretations that correspond more closely to another system. The following reconstruction of the development of the doctrine of world ages is hypothetical. It attempts to report on the summings up of world ages and on their inner structure in such a way that the systems of world ages can also be placed in other relationships to one another.

In both *Bundahišns* (*GrBd* 1.14-28 = *IndBd* 1.8-20) it is apparently the unity of the four world ages that is primary, because the resultant total of 12,000 years presupposes the Babylonian zodiac and the related notion of a twelve-month year. In the latter each of the twelve constellations represents a millennium (the coordination is found, e.g., in *GrBd* 36 = *IndBd* 34). Since the division of the zodiac into twelve parts could hardly have occurred in Babylonia before the beginning of the fourth century B.C., this is the terminus post quem. To this division there also corresponds the time which the Magi may have used after the Persian conquest of Babylonia (538 B.C.) in an effort to become more closely acquainted with the astrology of the Chaldaeans and to provide it with Iranian interpretations.

In this system the first age is "Creation" (literally, "given condition") of Ohrmazd in the *mēnōk* (= spiritual) state (years 1-2,999). The second is the transformation of this enduring *mēnōk* world into a *gētīk* (= earthly-material) world (years 3,000-5,999) in which Gayōmart and the Primeval Ox reign. Sin does not yet exist. Over against the latter Ahriman first generates a "Counter-Creation." The third age (years 6,000-8,999) is the mixture, accompanied by struggle, of Good and Evil under Yima in the first millennium of this age; Aži Dahāka ¸in the second; other kings in the third. The fourth (years 9,000-12,000) is the eschatological age that goes up to the Fraškart (often translated "Glorification," better "the Making Useful").

A historical sketch of the 6,000 years since the mixture that results from Ahriman's invasion of the spiritual and material "Creation" of Ohrmazd is found in *GrBd* 33 with many historical details (it is missing from *IndBd*). This is also the view presupposed in *Pahlavi-Vendidad* 2, *'Ulemā-ye Islām* 8-37, *Wičitakīhā i Zātspram* 1.1-24, and Bīrūnī *Chronol.* p. 14. The origin of the division into four world ages remains unknown. That it derives from Babylonian astronomy—the tentative hypothesis of H.-M. Schenke (using A. Jeremias)—cannot be accepted, as the investigations of B. Landsberger, E. Weidner, A. Sachs, and O. Neugebauer ˑhave indicated, unless one should consider the Iranian world year itself to be secondary evidence that as in the earthly year a division according to the two solstice points and the two equinox points had been adopted. Whatever epochs may at that time have been known to the Babylonians were not governed each by its own planet. The attempt to account for the fourfold division on the basis of the fourfold form of the Zurvan Akarana, or on the basis of the Indian doctrine of the four Yugas, only transfers the difficulty to a new location.

After the establishment of the fourfold schema, it may have been possible to give up its connection with Babylonian astronomy or astrology, which would have provided the indispensible impetus for the original formulation of such a system. A classification more appropriate to the Iranian division into three periods may have been adopted : World Creation (of the spiritual and material world together), Mixture of Good and Evil, Dissolution (corresponding to the eschatology)—in all, 9,000 years (*Artā Wīrāz Nāmak* 18.57; 54.11; *Mēnōik Xrat* 8.9-11; 28.2, 9; 57.31; *Dātastān i Dēnīk* 36.9; Theopompus in Plutarch, *Isid.* 47; Eznik *De Deo* 2.78 f.; Theodore bar Konai, p. 111 ff. Pognon). It is disputed whether 9000 (the duration of the conflict between Ohrmazd and Ahriman, according to *IndBd* 1.18 and *GrBd* 1.26), 10,000 (Šahrastānī 1.2.2.2.; p. 183 Cureton, p. 277 Haarbrücker), or 12,000 years is the number in Zurvanism. A total of 6,000 years would result depending on whether the most important aspect of the world year as a whole lies in the theogony and divine conflict that endures from the beginning to the end or in a period that actually only begins with the Primeval Man and ends with the Saošyant. This number is, however, hypothetical at best; it is inferred from Xanthus the Lydian, according to whom Zoroaster lived 600 (sic) years before Xerxes' campaign (D. L., prooem. 2, with the possible implication that the original reading 6,000 referred to the time between an archetypal primeval event and a historical culmination), and from Eudoxus of Cnidus, according to whom Zarathustra lived 6,000 years before Plato (Plin. *H.N.* 30.1.3, with a similar possible implication: this could be the period between the first savior and the reincarnated savior who perfects this aeon). Since, however, both authors lived before the time in which the zodiac system could have been completed, and since it seems very forced to maintain that Zarathustra became a representative of the beginning of the world and Xerxes and Plato representatives of the end of the world, the hypothesis of 6,000 years has hardly any greater scientific value than the ancient assertions upon which it is based. The 6,000-year period of the *Oracles of Hystaspes* is of different origin.

II A 2. Even before Daniel (2:31-45; 7:3-8, 17-25), the schema of world kingdoms occurs in Aemilius Sura, writing before 171 B.C. (according to Velleius Paterculus 1.6: Assyrians, Medes, Persians, Macedonians). Indeed, one can infer the sequence Assyrians, Medes, and Persians already from the structure of Herodotus's presentation (cf. also 1.95, 130) of history (cf. also Ctesias in D. S. 2.1-34). Since the Neobabylonians and Medes shared in the reign after the end of the Assyrian kingdom in 612 B.C. and since the Neobabylonians are not named in these schemata the sequence of world kingdoms could only have come into use in the realm of the erstwhile Medean dominion (M. Noth). As revealed by a new join in the cuneiform cylinder of Cyrus made by D. Metzler, Cyrus II the Great (559-529 B.C.) consciously incorporated himself into this schema, since he eluded the Babylonian royal legitimacy and took the Assyrian king Ashurbanipal (669-626 B.C.) as his political model. The Book of Daniel was the first to erroneously put the Neobabylonians in the place of the Assyrians. The Iranians, like the Jews, had similar good reason for extending the sequence to include the Macedonians.

II A 3. Zarathustra had described the perfection of his activity in symbols that mediated not only between this world and the yonder, but also between the present and the future. An eschatological tension is thus built up by Zarathustra himself through the prophetic components of his activity—hardly, as many think, through implicit reference to a presupposed system like that of the Pahlavi texts. This eschatological tension was capable of being expanded and made into a fundamental principle by following generations. The later Avesta already attests to this systematization. It appears that national Iranian political hopes for a savior also entered in this way. These hopes make it possible to conclude that there was a further development of the eschatology in connection with an expansion of Zoroastrianism over Xwārezm at least as far as Sīstān and into other East Iranian regions.

The locus classicus (Yašt 19.92-96) for the true Saošyant Astvaṭ.ərəta ("the one who makes Aša, or truth, boney [i.e., corporeal]") has him equipped with the club that has slain previous historical enemies of the Iranian people (only mythicized in the case of Aži Dahāka). This deliverance is considered to be at one with the more universal deliverance in which Aša, Vohu Manah, Haurvatāt and Amərətāt (who have now become distinguished companions of the Astvaṭ.ərəta by means of the Zoroastrian virtues) each defeat their specific enemies, and all together defeat Aēšma and Aŋra Mainyu. That the resurrection precedes this (Yašt 19.89) may here still rest upon literary composition. Also through the latter Astvaṭ.ərəta can become the Saošyant proper (Yašt 13.129; probably also meant in Yasna 59.28; 26.10), even though this title is otherwise generally reserved for those who continue the work of Zarathustra, probably meaning priests (Yasna 12.7; 17.2; 13.3; 14.1; 20.3; Visprat 11.3) and worldly helpers, perhaps even princes ("Saošyants of the lands": Yasna 70.4 and Visprat 11.3; warriors: probably Yasna 13.38). Uxšyaṭ.ərəta ("he who makes Aša grow") and Uxšyaṭ.nəmah ("he who makes devotion increase")—both invoked only in Yašt 13.128—apparently do not yet belong here; such beings are remote also in the case of the four other figures that are invoked before Astvaṭ.ərəta in Yasna 13.110 and 117. Astvaṭ.ərəta has a mother, who is called Vispa.taurvairī ("sole conqueror") or Ǝrətaṭ.fədrī ("she who creates prosperity for the father," cf. Yašt 13.142; 19.92), and he comes out of the Lake Kạsaoya in Sīstān. The invocations of the twenty-six women who believe in Aša, beginning with the legendary wife of Zarathustra, precede the invocation of the mother in Yašt 13.139-142. The antepenultimate and penultimate ones are Srūtaṯ.fədrī ("she who has a renowned father"), and Vaŋhu.fədrī ("she who has a good father"), who are also perhaps led up to the mother of the last Saošyant, to judge from their place in the liturgical list. In any case, a place in the finite time is staked out, until whose end the ideas of the national unity of the Iranian people and the liturgical correctness of public worship can be extended.

It appears that this place could still be filled with a completely heterogeneous conception, namely that of the unlimited duration of the activity of the Fravašis in the finite time. The natural duration of Lake Vourukaša and of the stars join with it; and the resuscitatable body of Kərəsāspa (who is not among those who use the club of *Yašt* 19.92f.) and the seminal fluid of Zarathustra that has not dried up, thereby gain eschatological significance. All that which remains is guarded by 99,999 Fravašis (*Yašt* 13.59-62).

The Pahlavi books attest to the integration of all of these conceptions, which now appear to be homogeneous; in each specific case, new elements are adopted. While historical details, recognizable as such, frequently yield a terminus post quem for the dating of the text in question or its redaction, the origin of the fundamental concept is obscured in utter darkness. Perhaps in both tendencies there were endogenous impulses to suspend the sequence of individual redemptions after death within a simultaneous and final consummation, and · to arrange the final, eschatological parts of litanies to accord with the last world ages of the world year (see *II A 1*). National Iranian color never disappears, and this compels one to seek other, fundamental impulses in the history of Iranian society. In particular the following can be sketchily distinguished:

a) The Millennium of Zarathustra, 9,000-9,999 of the world year. Cf. *GrBd* 33.12-28; *WZs* 4.1-28.7 Anklesaria = 12.1-24.19 + 0.1-9 West; *Dēnkart (Dk)* 7.8.1, 44-61; 8.14.3-11; *Ayātkār i Jāmāspīk (AJ)* 16.2-54 = *Jāmāsp Nāmak (JN)*; Pahlavi Rivayat to *Dātastān i Dēnīk* (PRDD) 48.1 = p. 141 Dhabhar (contradictory duration of 1,500 years—textual error?); *Bahman Yašt* 1.6-2.1; 3.20-7.2 Anklesaria = 1.3-6; 2.15-3.13 West.

At the beginning Zarathustra is thirty years old. There are struggles between Iranians and non-Iranians in almost every generation. Alexander destroys the religion and burns the Avesta, but Ardašīr restores it. The enemies in question allowed the dead bodies to be buried and washed and eaten, which are outright sins against the Zoroastrian purity regulations. Kai Wahrām and Pišyōtan bring these violations to an end (*GrBd*). When thirty winters are still left in the tenth century, the fifteen-year old virgin Nāmīk-pit (translation of Srūtaṯ.fədrī) comes to "the water" (no name of a lake is mentioned). She drinks (sic) the seed floating in it which Zarathustra had poured over his wife Hwōw on the next-to-last occasion he tried to couple with her. She thereby conceives the Wahšēnītār-ahrāyīh (translation of Uxšyaṯ.ərəta, also corrupted to the form Ušētar, and often occurring with the epithet bāmīk, "brilliant"). When he is thirty years old, the sun returns to the place to which it had been appointed at the creation, and remains there for ten days and ten nights (*Dēnkart*). Perjury, vengeance, Arab invasions, lawlessness, and anarchy are the order of the day. Non-Iranians rule. In the social order, the lowest becomes the highest; even childlessness appears desirable to people (*ǰN*). In the *Bahman Yašt* the enemies become concrete and their number is augmented: Arabs, Romans, Turks. There is a struggle of Mithra against Hēšm = Aēšma, Bēwarasp = Aži Dahāka and a female demon. Another pretender invades Iranian territory from Zawul and fights the last battle together with the King of Patašxwargār before the arrival of Pišyōtan and of Ušētar. The hateful Mazdak comes (mentioned also in *GrBd*), but Xosrau holds him back. Demons with parted hair from the race of Hēšm (male members of East Iranian orgiastic leagues? Greeks?) burn down house and land in Iran and do not observe treaties. The years, months, and days become shorter as mankind becomes smaller and more wicked; rites and festivals are prevented or have no effect. There are unseasonable winds and rains. Livestock of all sorts becomes smaller and weaker. Kingship, dominion, and property fall to foreigners from the East and West. Metals break forth from the earth, the sun becomes dark, and the moon grows pale. There are mists, earthquakes, and storms. A few observe the rites and thus preserve the quality of the age of Vištāspa (i.e., of Zarathustra) through three eschatological battles up to the arrival of Ušētar, for whom three different birthplaces are mentioned, one being Lake Kạsaoya (*Bahman Yašt*).

b) The Millennium of Ušētar, 10,000-10,999 of the world year. Cf. *GrBd* 33.29-31; *Dk* 7.9.1-23; 8.4.12; *Aǰ* 17.2f.; PR*DD* 48.2-22 = p. 141-145; *Bahman Yašt* 7.3-9.10 A. = 3.14-51 W.

Ušētar brings revelation. Robbery disappears, peace returns, trees become green, and waters flow again. The power of medicinal plants is concentrated. One dies only of old age or murder, no longer of illness. The species of wolves disappear. Towards the end of the millennium a three-year Mahrkūša rain falls. Mankind endures this rainfall in a secretly built Yama fortress (*GrBd*, the latter also in *Dk* and in PR*DD*). The description of the conception and birth of Waxšēnītār-nyāyišn (translation of Uxšyaṯ.nəmah, instead of the usual corruption Ušētarmāh) by Wēh-pit (translation of Vaŋhu.fədrī), is like that of the preceding redeemer, and occurs also thirty years before the end of the millennium. This time the sun remains standing twenty days and nights. The livestock population increases. The relationship of the pious to the wicked goes out of balance in favor of the former, two to one. The depraved beings of the world unite to form a gianť wolf, a Drug, which Ušētar cannot defeat. Animals are no longer slaughtered at the command of Artwahišt = Aša vahišta, but are eaten when they are old (PR*DD*). Eighteen rulers govern in this millennium (*AǓ*). A Kai is born, variously identified; his coming is ascribed to many places (a falling star announces it); and he strikes down his enemies (detailed description). Yazatas (= divinities) and demons participate in the struggle. Pišyōtan continues his work; the world becomes again as Ohrmazd wanted it (*Bahman Yašt*).

c) *The Millennium of Ušētarmāh, 11,000-11,970 or 12,000.* Cf. *GrBd* 33.32; 34.2-5 = *IndBd* 30 West = 31 Justi, 2-6; *Dk* 7.10.1-14; 8.14.13; *AǓ* 17.3-8; PR*DD* 48.23-37 = p. 145-47; *Bahman Yašt* 9.11-23 A. = 3.52-61 W.

Ušētarmāh also brings the revelation of Zarathustra. Serpents and other noxious animals disappear. Aži Dahāka unbinds himself and Frētōn is unable to vanquish him. Krišasp = Kərəsāspa is raised from the dead (according to *AǓ*, his father Sām) and kills him (*GrBd*, *Dk*, *Bahman Yašt*, PR*DD*). All the serpents unite to form a giant snake, which Ušētarmāh cannot defeat (PR*DD*). The conception and birth of Sūtomand Pērōžkār ("victorious redeemer" as the rendering of Astvaṯ.ərəta instead of the usual generalization as Sōšāns = simply Saošyant; also called Tan-Kartār, "body maker") through Gōbāk-pit (translation of Ǝrətaṯ.fədrī) is described as coming thirty years before the end of this millennium as with the preceding redeemers. The sun now remains standing in the sky thirty days and nights. Kai Xosrau appears with helpers who will assist the Sōšāns in the achievement of the Fraškart (*Dk*). At first, people eat less, then they become vegetarian, and then eat nothing more. The transition to Fraškart is constituted by resurrection of the dead. In *GrBd* this transition is given a rationalistic explanation.

d) *Fraškart.* Cf. *GrBd* 34.6-33 = *IndBd* 30 West = 31 Justi, 7-33;

Dk 7.11.1-9; 8.14.14f.; 9.8.1-6; 32.25; 41.8; 42.1; 53 passim; 58.10f.; *WZs* 34.1-35.47 Anklesaria (didactic reflection); Plutarch, *Isid.* 47 (only 370bc); *AĴ* 17.9 (there and *MX* 2.95, it is inconsistently designated as "Millennium of the Sōšāns") to 17.16; Lact., *Inst.* 7.16 (parallels to *Bahman Yašt* and *Bd*); Justin, *1 Apol.* 20; *Bahman Yašt* 9.24 A. = 3.62 W.; *MX* 57.7; PR*DD* 48.38-107 = p. 147-159 (the most detailed description).

In the Pahlavi books the imperishable world without old age, disintegration, or decomposition, which all three Sōšāns bring about, can be designated as Fraškart, "Making Useful" (*Dk* 7.8.50). Yet the Fraškart is almost always the work of the last Sōšāns. Understood pedantically, it includes the fifty-seven years of his activity, and therefore endures at the end of the world year from 11,970 until 12,027 (*GrBd* 34.7 = *IndBd* 30 [31].7). Yet the beginning, i.e., the resurrection and the time immediately thereafter (*GrBd* 34.16 = *IndBd* 30 [31].17), as well as the end of those fifty-seven years (*Dk* 7.11.7), can be designated as Fraškart, too. According to *DD* 2.10; 36.5; *MX* 27.63; *Dk* 9.58.10, the last and true Sōšāns frequently assists in the resurrection as the initiator. With the decline and disappearance of the need for nourishment, it is preceded by a gradual transition of the living to immortality. Therewith they cancel out the fall of the first human beings, Mašyak and Mašyānak, which inter alia consisted in eating more food than was needed (cf. *GrBd* 34 = *IndBd* 30 [31].1-3 with *GrBd* 14.16-20 = *IndBd* 15.9-12). Sōšāns makes the dead to arise in the course of his fifty-seven years, starting with the prototype Gayōmart and the two protoplasts, Mašyak and Mašyānak (*GrBd* 34.6-9 = *IndBd* 30 [31].7-9). After an ordeal by fire with molten metal, by which means evildoers are purified (*GrBd* 34.18f. = *IndBd* 30 [31].19f.), he sacrifices the bull Haδayaos and mixes its fat with the perfect white Haoma, in order to prepare a potion of immortality for all of mankind (*GrBd* 34.23 = *IndBd* 30 [31].25). Finally, Sōšāns and his helpers reward persons on the basis of their deeds. This reward consists essentially in their introduction into "paradise," Garōdmān (literally "house of the hymn of praise"). The Yazatas and Aməša Spəntas triumph over the Dēws and the Drugs (*GrBd* 34.25-27 = *IndBd* 30 [31].27-29). The new state of the world, which then is finally ascribed to Ohrmazd, is also called *tan i pasēn*, "the future body" (*Dk* 7.1.54; 7.3.30). It falls outside of the world year; depending on how it is calculated, and on the duration of Fraškart, its beginning coincides either with the date of the latter and thus with the whole Fraškart itself, or else with the end of the Fraškart. That which is brought about in the Fraškart endures in the future body; no further work of creation is to be done. Those who died in immaturity live like fifteen-year olds and those who died in adulthood live like forty-year olds forever on. In them *tan* (body), *ruwān*, and *jān* (perhaps free soul and spiritual soul) are united. Ohrmazd himself officiates as high priest. The substance of darkness is purged from the world and burns together with the Lie (Drug) in molten metal, which is probably the same that had already served at the final ordeal in the separation of good from evil and in the purification of the latter. The place reserved until that time for hell is henceforth at the disposal of the "good creation," in which bliss reigns (*Dk* 7.11.7). The mountains are level (*GrBd* 34.22-33 = *IndBd* 30 [31].24-33). The Good Religion has until now lasted down through the succession of generations (*Dk* 7.1.41f.)—the restorers of the world are ultimately descended from the body of Gayōmart (*MX* 27.17). The temples of idols are destroyed (*Dk* 7.1.39f.). Sins for which penalties had previously been exacted can now be expiated (e.g., *AWN* 64.13; 87.9: the adoption of a child who was expelled or not nursed with mother's milk).

The Sōšāns takes only spiritual nourishment. His body is like the sun—with six eyes he sees in all directions. He has the Xvarənah (royal charisma) of Frētōn, Kai Xosrau, Fraŋrasyan, and Kai Wištasp. Under his rule sickness, old age, death, grief, false belief, and despotism disappear (additional information in *Dk*, see references above).

Variants to this picture, which has been put together from *Bd* and *Dk* and which can perhaps be further analyzed in terms of tradition history, are found above all in PR*DD* (reproduced here in a somewhat different sequence). Here the earth in the future body is twice its present length and width. In it Kai Xosrau reigns for fifty-seven years over the seven Karšvars (parts of the earth), and Sōšāns is the High Mōbed. Through Sōšāns the resurrection takes place in five Yašt performances, one-fifth of mankind at a time, as well as the destruction of the evil by molten metal, which Šahrēwar pours into a hole into which they—the so-called "Drug of apostasy"—along with, probably, the giant wolf and the giant snake of the preceding millennia, had been pushed by an army before the resurrection. There is a thousand times the present nourishment, yet human beings no longer need to eat meat, since they have a lingering taste of meat in their mouths: thus both sexes of livestock are transformed back into the androgynous Primeval Ox. Everyone receives a marital partner and has sexual intercourse, but no one begets offspring. Those who had sawed Yima to pieces, and other evildoers, die again and are raised once more from the dead to be punished. All creatures, even the sun and fire, assume a human forty-year-old and immortal form and worship Ohrmazd in majesty.

II B 1. The concept of a sequence of world kingdoms described above under *II A 2* permitted Cyrus the Great, who adopted it, to vindicate his reign over against non-Iranian subjects. It brought the ethnic dissimilarity of ruler and ruled, which had arisen long before, into a schema of legitimation that later became independent as a symbol. Once this independence had been realized, the schema could be transposed to the purely Iranian history and filled out in various manners. In *Bahman Yašt* 1.1-11 A. = 1.1-5 W, the world kingdoms are symbolized as golden, silver, steel, and iron branches on the world tree; they are defined as the dominion of Vištāspa (patron of Zara-thustra between the tenth and sixth centuries B.C.), of Ardašīr I (Sassanian precursor, ca. 225-240 A.D.), of Xosrau Anōšarwān (for the author ob-viously an equally important originator of a new epoch in the promotion of Good Religion, 531-579 A.D.), and of the demons. In the *Bahman Yašt* 3.20 or 23-29 A. = 2.15 or 16-22 W. is found an expansion of the schema to seven reigns by inserting, between the second and third reigns of chap. 1, Šāhpur (probably the First, 240-272, rather than Šāhpur II, 309-379, or Šāhpur III, 383-388), an Arsacid king (chronologically impossible), and Bahram Gōr (421-439). They are now represented by seven branches on the world tree. But both schemas, which are at once universalized and cosmologized through their symbolization as world tree branches, belong rather in the millennium of Zarathustra, therefore only in 9,000-9,999 of the world year. According to the count of *GrBd* 33.12-28 (lacking in *IndBd*) this is the fourth millennium, which is followed by a fifth millennium—that of Ušētar (33.29-31)—and a sixth—that of Ušētarmāh (33.32). The schema of world kingdoms is here broken down through many additional details; the Fraškart is sketched only briefly in 33.33-35.

II B 2 and 3. Here it may suffice to refer to material in English transla-tion in Behramgore Tehmuras Anklesaria, *Zand-i Vohuman Yasn*, and *Two Pahlavi Fragments with Text, Transliteration, and Translation in English* (Bombay, 1957); in E. W. West, *Pahlavi Texts I* (The Sacred Books of the East 5; Oxford, 1880; reprinted Delhi, 1965)

191-235; and in Samuel K. Eddy, *The King is Dead* (Lincoln, Nebraska, 1961) 343-349 (abstract of the parts which, according to Eddy, belong already to the Hellenistic period). The interpretation results from the superscriptions and references named above on p. 541, sub *II B 2* and *3*. Insofar as the chronological divisions can be detached from the fusions adopted there, their contents are taken into consideration under *II A 3 a-d*.

DISCUSSION

GEORGE MacRAE: OUR last session ended with the question of how to account for the Jewish elements in the various treatments of Seth and Sethianism. Is it by the use of similar but independent exegetical methods or by the use of ideas already joined at the pre-Gnostic level? Some of the points made in the papers of Professors Nickelsburg and Colpe deal with this question.

GEORGE NICKELSBURG: My paper grows out of my interest in the development of Enochic traditions. It is primarily an analysis of literary relationships between *Adam and Eve*, *1 Enoch*, and the *Apocalypse of Adam*. The core of the recensions of the *Apocalypse of Moses* and *Adam and Eve* is not Sethian but Adamic. I argued for the existence of a testament of Adam which served as a common source in these text. Seth appears as a secondary figure, and on two levels. First, Seth is recipient and transmitter of the revelation of Adam, who is the primary revealer figure. Second, the pattern of "not yet, but later on" is worked out when Seth is unsuccessful in getting the oil of mercy from Paradise for the dying Adam. At the end of *Adam and Eve* Seth records certain revelations on steles—a tradition in continuity with Josephus and Gnostic texts. But in the parallel Gnostic material the focus is on the episode with Seth and his steles (this is the point at which *Adam and Eve* ends).

The material in *Adam and Eve* which differs from *Apocalypse of Moses* appears to have been affected by Enochic tradition. Adam's confrontation with God takes place in an ascent to a heavenly paradise similar to that of Enoch in *1 Enoch* 14. The historical apocalypse and Eve's brief testament in chaps. 49-50 have some relationship with the Apocalypse of Weeks in *1 Enoch*. Precisely these unique traditions constitute the core of the Gnostic *Apocalypse of Adam*. In *Adam and*

Eve and the *Apocalypse of Adam* there is the testamentary revelation from Adam to Seth. Seth becomes the counterpart of Methuselah as a mediating figure.

MICHAEL STONE: Can you expatiate on the contacts of *Adam and Eve* with the Enoch literature?

NICKELSBURG: Yes, at three points. First, the confrontation with God in the ascent to heaven is expressed in language similar to that of *1 Enoch* 14. In both accounts the ascent results in receiving bad news—an inversion of the usual ascent pattern. Second, there is a historical apocalypse in both. Third, there is the formal relationship of two revelations given by father to elder son, the first being simply a brief message of doom.

STONE: You need to show clearly that the ascent materials in *1 Enoch* 14 and *Adam and Eve* 25:29 contain specific terminological similarities which are at the same time different from the rest of the ascent traditions. Otherwise you are simply saying that both use terminology of which *1 Enoch* 14 is the oldest of a number of witnesses, without there being any necessary relationship between *1 Enoch* and *Adam and Eve*. Second, brief apocalyptic rehearsals of biblical history as in the Apocalypse of Weeks and *Adam and Eve* will have much in common, as you already noted. The strongest, most interesting part of your paper concerns the primacy of the testamentary form. Do you consider the Adam books and the *Apocalypse of Moses* to be Jewish documents?

NICKELSBURG: In my paper that is a secondary issue. *Adam and Eve* in its present form has Christian elements, for example, the baptism of Jesus.

STONE: But the reference to Jesus' baptism in chapter 41 of the Latin *Vita Adam et Evae* is due to a literary borrowing from the *Gospel of Nicodemus*.

NICKELSBURG: My own feeling is that these works are Jewish literature. The tradition of the steles of Seth was known by Josephus. The central soteriological concern doesn't find any expression in specific Christian terminology or content; for example, there is no mention of Jesus' resurrection. Yet the documents are late, probably taken over and owned by Christians.

BIRGER PEARSON: Do you see any necessarily Christian elements in the Gnostic *Apocalypse of Adam?*

NICKELSBURG: Not having read it recently with this question in mind, I can only think of the language of baptism as conceivably a Christian element. Otherwise, no.

ROBERT KRAFT: Let's assume for argument's sake that at some stage, in a Jewish setting, Seth had played a primary role, and that some scholar put forward evidence of a Christian subordination of Seth to Jesus, such as Seth's failure to bring the oil of mercy. Could you refute this hypothesis and show that Seth was already secondary in the Jewish background?

NICKELSBURG: It is interesting that Josephus picked out Seth as a mediator of revelation. But I have only the documents to work with, and they give no evidence for your assumption.

KRAFT: But those documents did pass through Christian hands. Granted, what I have set forth is methodologically dubious. But how strong a case can we make for Seth being a primary figure in the early stages of these documents?

NICKELSBURG: The documents center around Adam, yet Seth is a necessary figure. Every testament must have a recipient. I don't see how to get behind Seth's necessary function as a recipient of the testament from Adam, the central figure, to some other role for Seth.

KRAFT: One could argue that certain *Jewish* circles were interested in elevating Moses or another figure, and that this resulted in the subordination of Seth. I only point out that there is an alternative to the assumption that in all stages of this literature Seth played only a secondary role.

NICKELSBURG: I prefer to approach the issue with a literary argument —the testament is a genre known elsewhere at this time in Jewish literature. Given the standard features of the genre and the interest here in the problem of death and salvation, the choice of the figure of Adam is natural and the role of Seth follows naturally from this. The failure of Seth, and the resurrection are also derived from the focus on mortality and salvation. For a parallel we can turn to the *Testament of Abraham*, where Abraham does not want to die. I see no evidence in the document that we should imagine any other role being played by Seth.

STONE: The unique Sethian material is Seth's quest. Observe two things: first, that Michael's answer to Seth, the climax after Seth's fasting in the garden, suffers from textual problems in all known versions. In the Latin versions these chapters have been lost and are supplied from the Latin *Gospel of Nicodemus*. The message in the Greek *Apocalypse of Moses* seems oddly short and contextually difficult. The Greek *Gospel of Nicodemus* is also difficult. Why is there such a sensitivity in the textual tradition at the climax of this episode? The text has either been made "orthodox" or been Christianized—I am not sure which. Second, that in the Latin text the incident of Seth with the beast contains a play on Seth's being in the image of God; and that in some manuscripts the beast is the serpent. So once more we get the attempt of the serpent to attack man, now as Seth. One recalls Professor Pearson's treatment of Aramaic word-play in his article on the *Testimony of Truth*. The beast is unable to attack Seth, the true image. There may be richer Sethian material behind the way Seth is presented in that incident.

NICKELSBURG: But do any of the manuscripts lack the almost kerygmatic formula in the angel's response of "not now, but later"?

STONE: Isn't it a question of what he doesn't get now and what later?

NICKELSBURG: The point is that Adam is dying with a "sickness unto death" that he wants to forestall. The story of Seth is a dramatization of the author's point that there is no forestalling death and that the resurrection is the future cure.

MACRAE: In the *Apocalypse of Adam* several important features of the Adamic tradition are either missing or nonfunctional—the issue of

Adam's death and the question of mortality, and Seth's quest. The *Apocalypse of Adam* is a testament of Adam. Is its relationship to the Adam literature restricted to this form?

NICKELSBURG: No, it is really a periodized apocalypse of the history of the elect and of various judgments, including that of fire and water, that parallels material in *Adam and Eve* and the Apocalypse of Weeks in *1 Enoch*. The literary problem of the Adam literature is slippery. Probably the Adamic traditions were loosely transmitted. The special material in the *Vita* may have been part of a Jewish Adam testament which also lies behind *Apocalypse of Adam*.

MACRAE: Yes, you have drawn both back to a common ancestor. But are the detailed elements you have pointed out so unique as to require postulating a hypothetical testament of Adam?

STONE: Until the Georgian and Armenian forms are translated and sorted out properly I don't think that question can be answered. These two crystallizations must be studied alongside the Latin, Greek, and Slavonic forms.

NICKELSBURG: Seth as a savior figure is not found anywhere in the Adam literature except in *Apocalypse of Adam*.

MACRAE: The periodization of history is a widespread phenomenon as Professor Colpe's paper shows. Nothing Seth does in *Apocalypse of Adam* fits into the Adam literature. I am forced to conclude that if a hypothetical testament of Adam underlies both, it contains either nothing or everything! Even without access to the Georgian and Armenian materials, it is important to get behind *Apocalypse of Adam*. I agree with Professor Böhlig's point, expressed fourteen years ago, that the *Apocalypse of Adam* is pivotal in any discussion of Sethian Gnosticism.

PEARSON: One group of unnoted parallels may advance our discussion of the relationships. In *Vita* 32 ff. the Paradise scene lays out the problem of man's sin, accounting for the present reality of death. The *Apocalypse of Adam* opens with a similar narrative drawn from a similar source, yet with quite a different evaluation, which is deliberately polemical—it is not our sin but that wretched god who made us which accounts for our present misery.

KRAFT: By rewriting this hypothetical testament of Adam I am going to try an experiment that is methodologically thin but that illustrates my difficulties in reading behind documents like that of Philo. In my hypothetical testament a rejected Adam would be dying. The angel Michael indicates that Seth marks the beginning of the salvific line. Through Seth, Adam will be healed. The "other seed", which is both continuous and discontinuous with the other Adamic descendants, crystallizes in Seth and the line he begins. Why couldn't the Adam literature we now have represent an "orthodox" rescuing of such a tradition by downplaying this hypothetical role of Seth?

NICKELSBURG: The problem of getting behind the text remains. (To MacRae) There are typical Sethian Gnostic elements in the Apocalypse of Adam that are not found in the sources underlying the books of Adam and Eve. But I am especially impressed by the resemblance between the Enochic Apocalypse of Weeks and Gnostic Apocalypse of Adam: somehow we must decide, Is this purely coincidental, or is there a tradition of "Adam testaments"?

MACRAE: The existence of yet another testament of Adam and apocalypse of Adam is demonstrated by a quotation in the Cologne Mani Codex which does not correspond to any of our literature and yet is referred to as an apocalypse of Adam.

JAMES ROBINSON: One thing the Nag Hammadi materials indicate by their poor correlation with patristic and other sources is the vast quantity of lost literature. The number of known gaps has increased.

ALEXANDER BÖHLIG: In the case of an apocalypse the name is given of the one who received it. Thus the Apocalypse of Adam is the revelation which Adam received and handed on to Seth. The Jewish elements in this Nag Hammadi tractate are particularly obvious in the first part. The statement about baptism near the end of the tractate (CG V 84:4ff.), which is generally taken to be negative, changes to positive if we translate the Coptic differently. (But one need not advance an emendation as Schenke does: it suffices to understand the quotation as being introduced by the second *je* [84:8] of the passage. I can corroborate this suggestion [made by U. Luz] by understanding the first *je* [84:5] as equivalent to *nči*, as it already is once in 67:18.) This would agree with what Professor Schenke has written about baptism among the Sethians.

CARSTEN COLPE: In my paper I am elaborating two hypotheses independently laid down by Professors Schenke and Böhlig. I have regrouped their references and added to them from both the Iranian and the Nag Hammadi literature. A thorough exegesis of the passages cited could not be carried out in the scope of this paper. The contribution of this paper is to have grouped references so as to distinguish three time patterns and then to have pointed out in the Iranian and Gnostic texts themselves amalgamations of these patterns which are often misunderstood by scholarly exegetes. The paper does not attempt to revive the old Iranian hypothesis on the origin of Gnosticism but deals with a limited doctrinal range. The paper depends on the validity of the grouping of the passages—for example, Schenke's view of Harmozel, Oroiael, Daveithe, and Eleleth as representing cosmic ages of the universe. Finally, the distinction of time patterns has value apart from our study of Nag Hammadi—as, for example, in correcting mistaken associations of the Iranian patterns with the four kingdoms of Daniel 2.

MACRAE: Aside from inconsistent use of terms, if the four names correspond to the cosmic ages one might expect the Sethians to have known in what ages they and Seth belonged. But in the *Gospel of the Egyptians* the two statements about who belongs to which age do not coincide.

COLPE: This inconsistency can be accounted for by a history of redaction and interpretation and by an early amalgamation which made these schemes indistinct for the readers. In parallel fashion, the *Bahman Yašt* text also suffered from new exegesis incorporated into the text.

MACRAE: Almost symptomatic of Gnostic literature is the mingling of temporal and spatial imagery. Is this characteristic of the Iranian sources?

COLPE: Only of the Zoroastrian ones. But even in Judaism, time as the coming aeon is so hypostatized that it can be conceived as a state of the world that includes the sense of space.

FREDERIK WISSE: I want to be able to picture the development from what is alive and basic to what Professor Schenke can call dead building blocks (*tote Bausteine*).

COLPE: You have only to see how Lactantius has altered the periods of time in his use of the New Testament Apocalypse and the Oracle of Hystaspes.

WISSE: But we are dealing with the Sethians' own books. How could the amalgamation of time patterns be one of their basic principles?

COLPE: I don't think it was one of their basic principles. The number of texts cited is limited and difficult. At an earlier time, when the sect arose, it could have been central.

JOHN STRUGNELL: The phenomenon of blending various patterns of historiography was common in the Mediterranean world, as in the Jewish amalgamation (in Daniel 2, *2 Baruch*, and the *Sibylline Oracles*) of the sequence of four metals with Yahwistic eschatology. Is the Iranian temporal amalgamation taken over by the Sethians in some sense distinct from that of Judaism?

COLPE: In Daniel and the Sibyllines just two patterns are blended. But here we have three patterns which are paired in the three possible combinations. The difference is a matter of increased complexity both in the Sethian texts and the *Bahman Yašt*. The Judaeo-Christian concept of the four ages of Seth, Noah, Abraham, and Moses, and the Sethian concept of salvation may account for the differences between the Sethian and the Iranian texts. I would also stress the resemblance of the doctrine of cosmic mixture in the *Paraphrase of Shem* with that in Manichaeism and in the *Great* and the *Indian Bundahišn*, which allows us to hypothesize a common locality of interacting traditions. Cumulatively, the arguments advanced support one another.

ROBINSON: Could you expand on the suggestion that the lines of transmission were through Mesopotamian Jews?

COLPE: Assuming the existence of Sethianism, there could have been a Jewish group in Arsacid Mesopotamia which reflected a syncretistic cosmology stressing amalgamation; Manichaeism and Zoroastrianism will have drawn upon it as well. Sethians moving to Palestine and merging with likeminded sapiential groups, and then perhaps to Egypt, could have brought with them traditions which would have been successively overlaid with subsequent tradition. H. C. Puech's view that the Archontics were Palestinian Sethians fits with this scheme.

ROBINSON: Is Sethianism Gnostic at this stage?

COLPE: No, because it is not dualistic, only sapiential.

ROBINSON: How do you respond to the "alchemy of ideas" criticism? How is it that isolated and independent, but likeminded, groups existed and emerged by migration?

COLPE: I refer you to Professor Schenke's paper where he advances a new argument for the resemblance of at least ten Nag Hammadi texts termed Sethian. I am clearly aware that labeling these texts "Sethian" is on our initiative. To posit real groups behind them is hypothetical. Perhaps there were several successive but different processes in the movement from Mesopotamia to Egypt within a span of two or three centuries.

ROBINSON: In getting at the cause of Gnosticization, you have suggested a prophetic figure like Mani or Simon Magus. But in the Sethian tradition, which has no known founder, what led to the Gnosticization of the sapiential tradition?

COLPE: I don't know. Perhaps dualistic speculation.

ROBINSON: You don't see the Gnosticization and the Christianization coinciding with the figure of Jesus?

COLPE: No, the Christian traces are too small.

ROBINSON: So we have pre-Gnostic Jewish Sethianism, then Gnostic Jewish Sethianism, then Gnostic Christian Sethianism?

COLPE: Yes, or a Christianized Sethianism. And if you could have read the proofs of my sixth report on Nag Hammadi, concerning *Zostrianos*, you could have quoted from it here!

MACRAE: A. Adam argued years ago that Wisdom schools could have been the origins of Gnosticism. Were you in any conscious dialogue with Adam's suggestion?

COLPE: Yes. I don't dare, however, speak of Sethian "schools" ˌ in this case. But to speak of "schools" makes some things more probable than to speak of a circumscribed "sect." Unbeknownst to Adam his suggestion had been demonstrated much earlier by Max Weber, who spoke of "schools" composed of intellectuals who had lost their administrative power. Kurt Rudolph used the same argument. The same inferences support the hypothesis of a "school" as support the hypothesis of a "sect." Nothing is proved. If you are attracted to the sociological question it is sometimes better to infer the existence of a "school."

BÖHLIG: How do you evaluate the Western influences on Iranian sources?

COLPE: That is a complex question. Bailey demonstrated the presence of Western astronomy in the *Indian Bundahišn*. I would say the doctrine of cosmic mixture is per se of Western origin and more Empedoclean than Zoroastrian. But by the time of our evidence it has been "Iranianized". The doctrines of the ages are Iranian.

BÖHLIG: Of course, the texts are complex, and we cannot explain them in terms of Western or Eastern influences alone.

GEDALIAHU STROUMSA (auditor from Harvard University): Professor Colpe, what is the relationship between Professor Böhlig's earlier treatment of the three partitions of history and your position?

COLPE: It is secondary relationship. I see a partition of eschatological history which is additional to the partitions of of cosmic and terrestrial history.

BöHLIG : We must distinguish between the heavenly world of the aeons and the cosmic world. The four aeons are not the same as the four time periods.

COLPE: But secondarily they were probably blended, as the second group of texts in my paper suggests.

Session Three

STALKING THOSE ELUSIVE SETHIANS

BY

FREDERIK WISSE

In the discussion of the gnostic schools and sects the Sethians have long had a secure though unspectacular place. Thanks to the discovery of the Nag Hammadi codices and the claim that they constituted a Sethian library, they have suddenly come to stand in the center of interest of gnostic studies.[1] At the same time doubts have arisen about the way the terms Sethian and Sethians have been used in ancient as well as in modern literature.[2] It is the purpose of this paper to test whether it is historically legitimate to speak of a Sethian sect and Sethian teaching.

In the discussion not too much attention should be paid to the name "Sethian" itself. Clement of Alexandria indicates that the names used by the heresiologists did not originate with the sects, but were supplied by their opponents on the basis of the alleged founder of the sect, or the author of their holy books, or a prominent figure in their mythology.[3] For example, Hippolytus reports that the Naassenes call themselves Gnostics, but he seems to think that they do not deserve this still respectable name.[4] For him only the orthodox have the right to be called Christians and Gnostics. Names such as Valentinians or Sethians were necessary not only for easy reference, but also to distinguish between truth and falsehood. This fact is not necessarily an argument against the use of the names of the sects supplied by the Church Fathers. Insofar as we are dealing with a group with a clear identity over against other groups inside or outside the Church, there is a practical need for a name, if possible

---

[1] This goes back to Jean Doresse's early assessment based on a hasty survey of the collection in *The Secret Books of the Egyptian Gnostics* (New York, 1960) 249 ff. His premature conclusions have been widely quoted and long remained unquestioned since no one could check them.

[2] Cf. F. Wisse, "The Sethians and the Nag Hammadi Library," *SBLSP 1972*, 601-607; and M. Tardieu, "Les livres mis sous le nom de Seth et les Séthiens de l'hérésiologie," *Gnosis and Gnosticism* (ed. M. Krause; NHS 8; Leiden, 1977) 204-210.

[3] *Str.* 7.108.1-2.

[4] *Haer.* 5,11.

an apt one. Thus to the name "Sethian" we should add the qualification "properly or improperly so called." We should not expect this name to appear in a gnostic book. As a matter of fact, the traditional names of the gnostic sects are conspicuously absent in the Nag Hammadi tractates, except in a curious excerpt in the *Testimony of Truth* (IX,3), which may well have been taken over from an orthodox heresiological writing and in any case was written by an opponent of the heresiarchs mentioned.[5]

If the proof does not lie in the name Sethian, it needs to be made clear what criteria are used to determine whether there ever existed a gnostic sect properly or improperly called the Sethians. We must have some idea what we are looking for, otherwise we might call Sethian what is not Sethian, or solid evidence about the sect might escape our notice. In any case we are looking for a definite group of people who shared certain practices and beliefs, and who were distinguishable from other, similar groups. This standard of some internal cohesion and external distinctiveness must be maintained if our venture is not to be doomed from the outset. Our starting definition must be restricted even further. The potential evidence we are dealing with lies almost exclusively in the area of the beliefs and literature of the sect. Information about social makeup and religious practices is lacking. Since the ancient reports about other sects occasionally include such information[6] we may assume that our informants did not possess evidence of this kind. This would be a serious handicap if these same reports did not claim that the differences between the groups or sects lay primarily in their teachings, while presumably their practices were similar.[7] It is therefore justified to look for a distinctive Sethian teaching to prove the existence of the sect.

The evidence which is potentially relevant to the search for the Sethians is fairly obvious and manageable in quantity. With the completion of the *Facsimile Edition of the Nag Hammadi Codices*[8] and the availability of

---

[5] IX 55-60: 4. See F. Wisse, "The Nag Hammadi Library and the Heresiologists," *VC* 25 (1971) 208; and K. Koschorke, *Die Polemik der Gnostiker gegen das Kirchliche Christentum* (NHS 12; Leiden: Brill, 1978) 152-160. The excerpt mentions the names of Valentinus and Isidore the son of Basilides.

[6] E.g., Irenaeus, *Haer.* 1.13, the account of the Marcosians; and Epiphanius, *Haer.* 26, "Against the Gnostics, also called Borborites."

[7] Cf. Irenaeus, *Haer.* 1.11.1, which claims that it would be impossible to find two or three Gnostics who agree on an issue (see also *Haer.* 1.9.5).

[8] Published under the auspices of the Department of Antiquities of the Arab Republic of Egypt in conjunction with UNESCO (Leiden: Brill, 1962-1978).

translations of all the tractates[9] the new evidence can now be brought to bear on the issue. The ancient secondary sources have long been known but can now be reexamined in light of the newly discovered primary materials. Another fortunate circumstance is the recent appearance of A. F. J. Klijn's monograph *Seth in Jewish, Christian and Gnostic Literature*, which provides a wealth of background material.[10] Expectations are justified that some old questions will finally be answered. But beyond that we now have the opportunity and duty to start afresh, and leave no assumption unquestioned or unexposed. For the time being only the basic questions are allowed. Other issues about the Sethian "system", such as its origin and relationship to other sects must be postponed. First the relevant evidence must be surveyed for the kind of conclusions it is capable of supplying. The internal limitations of the evidence must be exposed so that the expectations can be set accordingly. We must be open not just to positive results but also to negative ones and to remaining uncertainties which lie in the nature of the evidence.

In order to see the question and the range of potential answers clearly it is useful to spell out at some length a similar problem from the history of zoology. The problem we face with the Sethians runs largely parallel to that of the unicorn. In both cases there is similarity in the evidence as well as in the resulting predicament for the scholar to prove or disprove the historicity of the object in question. Of course, the example of the unicorn is meant to function only as a model of the problem and the line of argument and not to suggest parallel conclusions.

For an inquiry about the historicity of the unicorn the starting point is ancient reports going back to Ctesias, a Greek physician and historian of the fourth century B.C.E., who collected a great deal of lore about the Near East and India in his books *Persica* and *Indica*. Of these books only abridgements or quotations by later authors remain, yet it is clear that Ctesias did not present an eyewitness report of the unicorn but only transmitted what he had heard or read in Persian sources of which we do not know the character or quality. Notwithstanding the obscure origins of the reports little doubt was expressed until modern times that there existed or had existed in India strange one-horned animals whose horn was a powerful antidote against

---

[9] *NHLibEng.*
[10] Leiden, 1977.

poison. About the description of the beast there were some disagreements among the ancients, but most commonly they mentioned or drew, apart from the long twisted horn set in the middle of the forehead, a body of a horse or ass, the hindlegs of an antelope, the tail of a lion, and the beard of a goat.[11] In this way it is depicted in the royal arms of England and Scotland.

Since an animal approximating this description does not at present exist in India or elsewhere, the only way to test the accuracy of the ancient reports are animal fossils from the time in which the reports originated. No doubt there have been found in India skeletons or bones of animals which lived in the first millennium B.C.E. Let us take for granted for the sake of argument that among these animal remains there are some from animals which are now extinct, but that none of these confirms the existence of the unicorn, though some show similarities to the features mentioned in the traditional description. We can now survey the options open to the zoologist as to the historicity of the unicorn. There are basically four :

1) The zoologist can judge the ancient reports to be trustworthy and explain the absence of fossil confirmation as a historical accident which might be remedied by future finds. This option is only open if the ancient reports can be proven to be basically correct in other instances. Needless to say this is not the case, for the ancient bestiaries abound with fabulous animals and true wisdom in the Hellenistic period had become for many people knowledge about fantastic customs and animals in far-off lands.[12] No zoologist today would trust the bestiaries without unambiguous outside support.

2) If then the first option is closed, the zoologist can consider whether the ancient reports may not have a historical basis while being inaccurate, incomplete, or confused in the details. To allow for this option there must be, in spite of the obvious discrepancies, some significant correspondence between the fossils of an extinct animal and the ancient descriptions of the unicorn. Such correspondence should not be incidental and should not be open to other kinds of interpretation. For example, the skull of a horned animal can not be used as proof of the existence of the unicorn if there are no further and clearer agreements with the ancient reports. It must be certain that it cannot belong

---

[11] See "Einhorn," *RAC* 4. 840-862.

[12] A good example of this is the wisdom of Apollonius of Tyana described by Philostratus in the *Vita*; but also the wisdom of Solomon as portrayed in 1 Kgs 4:33.

to a rhinoceros, oryx, or another living or extinct animal which is known to have lived in that area. The emphasis in the search has here shifted from the reports to the fossils, and the latter are used, if the conditions have been met, to correct the former.

3) If the preceding options are closed, we can already draw the conclusion that there never was a unicorn as the ancients described it, even if their reports are allowed a large margin of error. The search could stop here, but there are still the reports and the fossils which beg for some kind of explanation. We may still want to know about the animal world of that time which gave rise to such incredible reports. Thus it is possible that the fossils alone furnish proof of the existence of an animal now extinct. The ancient reports on the unicorn would correspond only incidentally with this animal, and it is uncertain whether the newly discovered extinct animal gave rise to the reports.

4) In the last option there is no longer any question about an extinct animal, related or unrelated to the unicorn, which deserves to be taken into account in zoology. The ancient reports about the unicorn can be shown to be a conflation of reports of a number of exotic animals mixed with fantasy and superstition, and the fossils which showed some correspondence with the description of the fabulous unicorn can be explained in terms of known animals.

Let us now return to the question of the Sethians and try out in turn the options developed with reference to the unicorn. It will be useful to keep the example of the unicorn in mind in order to follow the line of argument. As with the unicorn, we have two very different sets of data which need to be matched. There are, first of all, the ancient reports, the heresiological "bestiaries" about the gnostic schools and sects. Similarly to the bestiaries, such as the Physiologos, the Church Fathers were not only interested in presenting the whole array of exotic heresies, but also included a pious moral for the intended readers.[13] The other set of data is the gnostic treatises, mainly those contained in the Nag Hammadi codices. Like fossils they have no name written on them linking them to one sect or another. How typical or descriptive they are of the teaching of a particular sect is completely unclear. It is not known how they were used and what relationship they bear to the beliefs of the Gnostics who produced or

---

[13] The refutations written by the Church Fathers were not meant to convert the heretics but to confirm the faith of the orthodox Church members, who might be swayed by gnostic propaganda.

used them. There is no obvious correspondence between these two sets of data to prove on the one hand the accuracy of the heresiological reports of the Sethians or, on the other hand, to identify one or more of the gnostic books as being clearly Sethian. This being the situation, we must explore the options to determine what conclusions can be made about the historicity of the Sethians.

The first step will be to test whether the ancient reports on the Sethians might not be trustworthy and whether the absence of clearly corroborating material among the gnostic books must not be considered a historical accident. The situation is here somewhat more complicated than with the unicorn, but the basic work about the interrelationship of the heresiological reports was done a century ago already by R. A. Lipsius, A. Harnack, and A. Hilgenfeld.[14] Thus it appears that all ancient and modern references to the Sethians go back to no more than two variant reports, which curiously enough may well be from the hand of the same author, Hippolytus of Rome, who lived from about 160-235 C.E. The earliest of the two accounts, in the *Syntagma*, is actually lost, but Lipsius has shown that the *Syntagma* was preserved in outline in Pseudo-Tertullian's *Adversus omnes haereses*, and that it forms the basis of the reports by Epiphanius and Philaster.[15] On the basis of these witnesses the *Syntagma* of Hippolytus can be reconstructed to have contained 32 heresies running from Dositheus to Noetus.

About the sources used by Hippolytus in his *Syntagma* we know much less. It is fairly clear and to be expected that he used the antiheretical work of his revered teacher Irenaeus, but whether he drew also upon other heresiological works is uncertain. Important for us is that Hippolytus's treatment of the Ophites, Cainites, and Sethians is clearly related to Irenaeus's *Haer.* 1.29-31,[16] in which the teachings of some unnamed "Gnostics" are summed up. Actually *Haer.* 1.29 does not appear to be the teaching of a sect but rather the summary of an early version of what we know as the *Apocryphon of John*,[17] and *Haer.* 1.30 is most likely a condensation of another gnostic book which

---

[14] R. A. Lipsius, *Zur Quellenkritik des Epiphanios* (Vienna, 1865); A. Harnack, *Zur Quellenkritik der Geschichte des Gnosticismus* (Leipzig, 1873); A. Hilgenfeld, *Die Ketzergeschichte des Urchristentums* (Leipzig, 1884; reprinted, Darmstadt, 1966).

[15] Lipsius, *Quellenkritik*, 33 ff.

[16] Hilgenfeld, *Ketzergeschichte*, 250 f.

[17] See Carl Schmidt, "Irenaeus und seine Quelle in *adv. haer.* I, 29," *Philotesia Paul Kleinert zum LXX Geburtstag dargebracht* (Berlin, 1907) 315-336.

has not survived but which bears similarities to a number of Nag Hammadi tractates.[18] In *Haer.* 1.31 Irenaeus or his source had lost interest in quoting or summarizing extensively from gnostic writings, and instead mentions one by name, the *Gospel of Judas*, and refers to a "collection of their writings in which they advocate doing away with the works of Hystera." Later heresiologists, beginning with Hippolytus, did not want to leave the Gnostics of *Haer.* 1.29-31 unnamed, and thus supplied the names Barbelo-Gnostics (1.29), Ophites or Sethians (1.30), and Cainites (1.31). It is clear that these names were not derived from new information about Irenaeus's Gnostics, but simply were coined on the basis of a prominent theme or name mentioned in Irenaeus's account.

In reworking *Haer.* 1.29-31, Hippolytus does not present anything basically new in his account of the Ophites and Cainites. For the Sethians, however, he adds some information not mentioned by Irenaeus. The new source, which was most likely a literary piece, filled in more detail about the creation of Cain and Abel, the birth of Seth, and the fate of the race of Seth. The account as preserved in Pseudo-Tertullian[19] is rather sketchy and confused compared with the treatment of the Sethians by Epiphanius.[20] One is tempted to think that Epiphanius had new and better information, but that would probably be a mistake. He mentions that he may have encountered this heresy in Egypt[21]—he is not even sure about the country—but there is no evidence that this added anything of substance to his report. The uncertainty in his mind is apparently not whether or not he met sectarians but whether these sectarians he had met in the past were actually Sethians. More significant is his claim that the Cainites and Sethians had more or less disappeared in this time. This means that he based their existence on heresiological reports and supposed literary remains. As in other cases, Epiphanius boasts that he bases his account partly on "face to face inquiry."[22] If this was true in the case of the Sethians it had no noticeable effect on his account.

When one compares the reports on the teaching of the Sethians by Pseudo-Tertullian and Epiphanius it becomes clear that the only

---

[18] E.g., the *Hypostasis of the Archons* (II,4) and the *Gospel of the Egyptians* (III,2 and IV,2).

[19] *Haer.* 8.

[20] *Haer.* 39.

[21] *Haer.* 39.1.2.

[22] Ibid.

difference is that Epiphanius tried to improve on his source. This was a common tendency among the heresiologists and still is a temptation to the modern scholar. The gnostic tractates, particularly those representing mythological gnosis, are frustratingly abstruse. A summary of the content made by a trained theologian is usually forced into the mold of a more or less coherent system which can be evaluated and compared with other theological systems. The question should be asked whether or not this Procrustean bed does violence to the gnostic writing. Thus we can observe that Epiphanius makes connections and draws implications which his sources had left unstated.[23] His account has been made to look like the teachings of a sect which competes with the teaching of the Church. The gnostic writing used by Hippolytus or his source has receded more and more into the background.

The second account of the Sethians is found in a later and much more ambitious heresiological writing by Hippolytus, the *Refutatio omnium haeresium*.[24] It bears no relationship in content to the treatment of the Sethians in the *Syntagma*. Hippolytus bases his new account on the *Paraphrase of Seth*, a book which he believes to contain the complete teachings of the sect. Strangely enough, there is no mention here of the beginnings of the race of Seth, the key feature in the earlier account in the *Syntagma*. No reason presents itself for connecting this work to the Sethians except the name in the title. In a similar way Epiphanius took it for granted that the seven books in the name of Seth he had heard about had originated with the Sethian sect.[25] This erroneous procedure of the Church Fathers of assigning sects to books and vice versa is here particularly apparent. Chance has it that the Nag Hammadi library has provided us with a book which, though not identical with the *Paraphrase of Seth*, is closely related to it; but it bears the name *Paraphrase of Shem*.[26] Had Hippolytus known the work by its Nag Hammadi title he would most likely have created a new sect called the Shemites.

All other references to the Sethians in Patristic literature are basically dependent on Hippolytus. These later authors had no direct knowledge of the Sethians nor new information.[27] The account

---

[23] E.g., the relationship between Seth and Christ in 39.3.5.

[24] *Haer.* 5.19-22.

[25] *Haer.* 39.5.1.

[26] On this relationship see Doresse, *The Secret Books*, 150; F. Wisse, "The Redeemer Figure in the Paraphrase of Shem," *NovT* 12 (1970) 138; M. Krause, "Die Paraphrase des Sêem und der Bericht Hippolyts," *Proceedings of the International Colloquium on Gnosticism, Stockholm, August* 20-25, 1973 (Stockholm, 1977) 101-110.

[27] See Klijn, *Seth*, 87 f.

of Sethian teaching in the *Refutatio* tells us something about the false assumptions of the author rather than something about the sect. The report in the *Syntagma* as it survives in later writings tells us only that Hippolytus knew of a gnostic book or books which described the origin of the race of Seth and their survival until after the flood. No existence of a Sethian sect can be inferred from this. The reports of the Church Fathers are not trustworthy on this point, and the first option must be considered closed.

To test the second option, our attention must shift to the gnostic fossils, the Nag Hammadi tractates which may be of relevance to the question of the Sethians. The possibility must be explored whether some of these works may not have sufficient points of contact with the description of Sethian teaching in the *Syntagma* to function as control and possibly as independent proof of the existence of a distinctly Sethian teaching. The tractates in question are now sufficiently known that we can dispense here with a description, and limit ourselves to some observations and conclusions.[28]

1) A number of the tractates in question refer to Seth as recipient and transmitter of divine revelation. This is the way he functions in the *Gospel of the Egyptians* (III,2; IV,2), the *Apocalypse of Adam* (V,5), the *Second Treatise of the Great Seth* (VII,2), and the *Three Steles of Seth* (VII,5). Klijn has drawn together the Jewish background of this function of Seth.[29] It was a fairly common theme in esoteric Jewish and Christian literature, and so it is not surprising to find it in Gnosticism. Epiphanius mentions of several sects that they possessed books of Seth.[30] To these one could add books attributed to Allogenes,[31] a title of Seth based on Gen 4:25. This function of Seth is found in a variety of writings and cannot be considered characteristic of one sect.

2) Seth is also put forward as the progenitor of the pure and indestructible race which lived before the flood. This theme was already developed in Jewish literature and was eagerly picked up by a variety of Gnostics. It is present in Valentinian literature, where Seth is the prototype of the pneumatics.[32] Epiphanius attributes this theme not only to the Sethians but also to the Archontics.[33] There is an incidental

---

[28] See Birger A. Pearson, "The Figure of Seth in Gnostic Literature," in this volume.

[29] *Seth*, 48-60; see also Pearson, "The Figure of Seth."

[30] *Haer.* 26.8.1; 39.5.1; 40.7.4.

[31] *Haer.* 39.5.1; 40.7.4-5.

[32] Irenaeus, *Haer.* 1.7.5.

[33] *Haer.* 40.7.1-3.

reference to the pure offspring of Seth in the *Apocryphon of John* (II,*1*; III,*1*; IV,*1*).[34] They play a more prominent role in the *Gospel of the Egyptians* and the *Apocalypse of Adam*.[35] However, there is significant difference in detail in these writings, and it appears that the idea of a pure race of Seth was developed independently by a number of gnostic authors. Thus, according to Epiphanius the flood was caused by the Mother (Sophia) to destroy the evil race and save Noah who belonged to the race of Seth,[36] while in the *Apocalypse of Adam* the flood is caused by the evil Demiurge who wants to destroy the race of Seth and save Noah who belongs to him.[37] Again it must be concluded that we are dealing here with a well-known and popular mythologumenon and not the distinct teaching of a sect.

3) A third theme is Seth as savior figure. It is much less common than the preceding two, and it is mentioned in the account of the Sethians by Pseudo-Tertullian and Epiphanius. Here Seth is identified with Christ. A similar identification is made in the *Gospel of the Egyptians*, though the two references are somewhat obscure and probably secondary.[38] There are two factors which may have given rise to such speculations. On the basis of a forced reading of the Greek text of Gen 4:26 it could be inferred that Seth was called "God".[39] More important was the tendency already visible in the New Testament to identify types or preexistent forms of Christ in the Old Testament. In the *Testimony of Truth* the bronze serpent which Moses lifted up is identified with Christ, no doubt on the basis of John 3:14.[40] In a similar way the heavenly Seth could have become connected with Christ. The few existing references to the identification of Seth with Christ may well go back to a common source, but an independent development cannot be excluded. The brevity and relative obscurity of the references suggest that the issue was not considered very important. It is difficult to conceive of it as a basic feature of the teaching of a sect.

The main themes in the heresiological descriptions of Sethian teaching

---

[34] II 9:14-17.

[35] See Klijn, *Seth*, 90-104, and Pearson, "The Figure of Seth."

[36] *Haer.* 39.3.1.

[37] V 69:2-71:7.

[38] III 64:1-3 and 65:17.

[39] See Klein, *Seth*, 40.

[40] IX 48:27-49:10. In the *Concept of our Great Power* it is prophesied of the savior that "he will speak in parables; he will proclaim the aeon that is to come, just as he spoke to Noah in the first aeon of the flesh" (VI 40:30-41:2).

which are also found in gnostic literature proved to be of no help in locating tractates which might contain the teaching of a sect properly or improperly called the Sethians. Either the themes in question were so common that they could not be the distinctive teaching of a sect, or they were too incidental to be given much weight. This means that neither the heresiological reports nor the gnostic books nor a combination of these can substantiate the existence of a Sethian sect. The heresiological references to the Sethians appear to be due to a wrongheaded approach and false assumptions. We are forced to the conclusion that there never was a sect properly or improperly called Sethian. The name should be eliminated from the lists of gnostic schools and sects. The views and books which until now have been called Sethian will need another and better-founded explanation.

In the third option it is taken for granted that there never was a Sethian sect. The task which remains is to account for the considerable number of gnostic writings which were called Sethian in the past, or which were thought to be related to Sethian teaching. Among this body of material there are also the reports on the Sethians which were based on Hippolytus's *Syntagma*, which in turn was most likely based on some piece of gnostic literature. A serious attempt has already been made to explain the interrelationships of this diverse body of literature, though this was done in the context of locating the essence of Sethian teaching. I am referring to Hans-Martin Schenke's article "Das sethianische System nach Nag-Hammadi-Handschriften."[41] It will be evaluated here not as an attempt to understand the Sethian "system"—an illegitimate venture if the argument as I have presented it thus far has been correct—but as an attempt to find a unified theological system behind a number of related gnostic tractates.[42] If Schenke has been successful, he may have located the teaching of a distinct school or sect. What name this teaching gets is a matter of secondary importance.

Schenke identifies the following themes which he thinks all belonged to one gnostic system:

1) the self-understanding of the Gnostics that they are the pneumatic seed of Seth;

2) Seth as the heavenly-earthly savior of his seed;

3) the four lights of the Autogenes (Harmozel, Oroiael, Daveithe, and Eleleth), who constitute the heavenly dwelling places of Adam,

---

[41] Published in *Studia Coptica* (ed. Peter Nagel; Berlin, 1974) 165-173.
[42] Schenke, "Sethianische System," 166.

Seth, and the seed of Seth;

   4) the heavenly trinity of the Father, the Mother (Barbelo), and the Son (the Autogenes or Anthropos);

   5) the evil Demiurge Yaldabaoth who tried to destroy the seed of Seth;

   6) the division of history into three ages and the appearance of the savior in each age.

As Schenke knows, the gnostic tractates in question only seldom contain all these themes; generally they have only a few of them. This may, of course, be due to a difference in scope or subject matter. More disconcerting is the fact that the same theme may appear in different forms, in different contexts, and with different applications from tractate to tractate.[43] The exact meaning or role of the theme is often so obscure in its present context that it is a hazardous venture to say what place it had in the original system. For example, the expected connection between the seed of Seth before the flood and the gnostic readers of the tractate is generally not made. The savior function of Seth is often obscured by the role of his "father" Adamas. The same function can also be taken by Shem and, according to one of Irenaeus's sources, even by Cain.[44] The four lights are, indeed, frequently mentioned, but their place and role in the "system" remain far from clear, and are certainly not uniform. Also, that which one would expect to be a central feature, the heavenly trinity, is developed in a variety of ways with a baffling variety of detail.[45] The description of the Demiurge Yaldabaoth is far from uniform and it is also found outside the group of tractates which Schenke considers Sethian. The same is true for the three ages and the three appearances of the savior.[46]

If the themes isolated by Schenke all go back to one system, it needs to be explained what caused the present diversity among the tractates. One could suggest contamination from other systems, but that would be an admission that the system as a whole had little significance for the authors of the tractates. If the uncorrupted form has not survived and a reconstruction of it leaves many puzzles and questions, then it is legitimate to ask if there ever was a unified system.

---

   [43] A good example of this is the treatment of the four lights.
   [44] *Haer.* 1.31.1.
   [45] See A. Böhlig, | "Triade und Trinität in den Schriften von Nag Hammadi," in this volume.
   [46] E.g., in the *Concept of our Great Power* (VI,4).

That a system undergoes development, that some details are dropped or added, and that new applications are found is to be expected, but how the unified system which Schenke tries to reconstruct could have become so muddled, deformed, and corrupted as the gnostic tractates portray is beyond comprehension. It appears that Schenke makes the same false assumption as the heresiologists. He mistakes the gnostic authors for sect theologians and their books for compendia of gnostic doctrine. Obscurity must then be due to inept translators and copyists, and the modern student has the task of reconstructing the theology of the author and the "system" of the sect.

The dilemma Schenke faces is that the more clearly he draws the interrelationship among his themes the farther he gets away from the occurrences of these themes in the gnostic books. The system he wants to recover makes the tractates in question more puzzling instead of less. He has no evidence that his reconstructed system ever functioned as the teaching of a sect. The tractates he needs as evidence seem to prove the opposite. His "Sethian" books are the best proof that there never was a "Sethian" theological system.

It is left to the last option to provide an adequate explanation for the unity and diversity among the gnostic tractates which until now have been considered Sethian. If they are not variants or emanations of one gnostic system, what can explain the similarities among them? An attempt at an answer will be made in the form of a number of theses. They should be seen more as hypotheses which need further testing than as final conclusions.

1) The gnostic tractates in question must not be seen as the teaching of a sect or sects, but as the inspired creations of individuals who did not feel bound by the opinions of a religious community.

2) Recurring themes such as those Schenke isolated were not part of a particular gnostic system but "free-floating" theologumena and mythologumena which one could use as one saw fit. As Klijn and others have shown, quite a number of these can be traced back to esoteric Jewish circles, and they can be shown to have been available to persons of diverse religious backgrounds. Even if a definite meaning was attached to these theologumena the gnostic author felt free to change the meaning and original context.

3) This group of writings should be evaluated and interpreted differently from theological treatises in the orthodox tradition. They do not adhere to the expected pattern of systematic thinking and argumentation. Conflicting thoughts do not appear to offend the

author; often obvious implications are not drawn or taken into account; necessary transitions are omitted and a comprehensive preunderstanding seems to be demanded from the reader, though most likely not intentionally. A penetrating analysis of the structure of such writings would be improper, disappointing, or the occasion of unwarranted speculation.

4) The original purpose of these writings must be sought in private meditation. The intended readers would have been the esoteric group of "like-minded" Gnostics, not in the sense of members of a sect but as individuals with a similar attitude towards this world, other-worldly vision, and ascetic lifestyle. These books helped them to understand themselves in their estrangement from this world and oneness with their heavenly home to which they longed to return.

DIE "SETHIANISCHE" GNOSIS—EINE HÄRESIOLOGISCHE FIKTION?

VON

KURT RUDOLPH

[Vorläufiges Arbeitsresümee vom 16. Januar 1978:]

ERST Hippolyt (3. Jh.), Pseudotertullian (*Haer.* 2) und vor allem Epiphanius (4. Jh.) sprechen von „Sethianern" als einer eigenen gnostischen Sekte, die sich auf den Adamiten Seth zurückführt, eigene Schriften (u.a. die „Paraphrase des Seth", sieben Bücher namens „Allogeneis" nach den gleichnamigen sieben Söhnen Seths) und (so nur nach Hippolyt) eine "Dreiprinzipienlehre" (Licht, Geist, Finsternis) besitzt. Irenäus (2. Jh.) und Clemens Alex. (um 200) sprechen nur davon, daß die Valentinianer, Seth als Ursprung des pneumatischen (bei Irenäus fälschlich psychischen) Geschlechts ansehen (Exc. Thdot. 54,1,3; Haer. 1 7,5 = Epiphanius Haer. 31,23,1). Ähnliches schreibt Irenäus (1 30,9) auch den Ophiten zu, die dann später von Theodoret (5. Jh.) zu Sethianern gemacht werden.

Zieht man die Originalquellen heran, so gibt es kein eindeutiges Indiz für die Existenz einer geschlossenen gnostischen Gemeinschaft, die sich als „Sethianer" titulieren und ein eigenes „System" besaßen. Mehrere Schriften kennen Seth als Inhaber einer Äons (unbekanntes altgnostisches Werk Cod. Brucianus; ApkrJoh [ApocryJn]), als Offenbarungsmittler (ApkrJoh, ÄgEv [GEgypt], 3 StelSeth [3StSeth], 2 LogSeth [GrSeth]), als Apostel und Erlöser (ÄgEv; 2LogSeth; ApkrJoh[?], Manichäer, Mandäer), als Christus AgEv; 2LogSeth; bestätigt von Epiphanius 39,1,3; 3,5), als Ahn des pneumatischen Geschlechts (ApkrJoh; ÄgEv; 3StelSeth; Zostr.), als reinste Seele im Seelengericht (Mandäer). Ferner finden sich Züge des ägyptischen "Gottesfeindes" Seth aus dem Osirismythos: Eselsgesicht, Onoēl, Typhon, Emmacha.

Die Verbindung der Originalangaben mit denen der Häresiologen läßt nur den Schluß zu, daß Seth für viele gnostische Überlieferungen (auch der mandäischen und manichäischen) eine auf der biblischen (Gen 4,24f.; 5,3f.) und nachbiblischen Tradition beruhende ausgezeichnete Gestalt der Urzeit war, der sich die Gnostiker als

„auserwähltes", „lebendiges" Geschlecht verbunden glaubten. Die These eines angeblich „sethianischen Systems" arbeitet mit zwei unsicheren Voraussetzungen : dem Dreiprinzipiensystem Hippolyts und der nicht beweisbaren Identität der "Paraphrasis Seths" mit der "Paraphrasis Sems" [ParaShem] (NHC VII,1). Man sollte die häresiologischen Klassifizierungen nicht ungeprüft übernehmen, da sie vielfach nur den Zugang zu den Originalen erschweren.

DISCUSSION

GEORGE MACRAE: I WANT to begin by offering a provisional review and assessment of our previous two sessions. We generally agreed that the Egyptian Seth did not directly influence the figure of Seth in the Gnostic sources. We found remarkably little support for a Samaritan origin for Sethianism. We reached agreement that some legendary accretions about Seth's role in ancient and medieval literature do not belong to either Gnostic or Jewish-Christian traditions. We acknowledged that the neglected oriental Christian sources deserve scholarly examination. We considered the possibility that Philo consciously avoided a "heretical" view of Seth. We noted that the roles of certain figures in literature of Jewish background functioned independently of the personages to whom they are attributed—for example, we saw the similarity between Enoch's role in literature leading to Jewish mysticism and that of Seth in literature leading to Gnosticism (although we did not deal with the implications of this). We looked at the possibility that there existed a Jewish tradition of a testament and/or apocalypse of Adam which was modified by giving increasing prominence to Seth. Finally we looked at an intriguing theory of Iranian influence on Gnosticism mediated through Jewish Wisdom circles. We did not give any profile to the Gnostic Seth. While our initial assesment of Seth and the Sethian traditions in Judaism as providing the basis of the Gnostic myth fell short of general consensus, I don't despair of that emerging later.

We now turn to the question of the existence of Sethianism. Professor Wisse has reminded us that it is important to distinguish between the sociological entity of "sect" and a cast of thought preserved only in literary evidence. Professor Rudolph's abstract indicates a similar caution; in the last paragraph he stresses the difficulties of the hypothesis of a Sethian system. As roadblocks to the utilization of patristic sources Rudolph points to the teaching of the three principles mentioned by Hippolytus and to the impossibility of firmly identifying the *Paraphrase of Seth* with the *Paraphrase of Shem*. We shall begin our present discussion by asking Professor Wisse to introduce his paper.

FREDERIK WISSE: The issue divides into two parts. First, there is the evaluation of the heresiological material on the Sethians and its coordination with the Nag Hammadi tractates—here Professor Rudolph's conclusions are more cautious than mine. The heresiologists beginning with Hippolytus believed in the existence of a Sethian sect through a misunderstanding. Because they found differences among books that they were reading they· concluded that a different sect lay behind each difference. Second, I object to postulating, as Schenke has done, the existence of a sect possessing a coherent system on the basis of the evidence of literary texts we now possess. I see Gnostics collecting interesting literary traditions much like the amateur collector picking up pottery sherds for his shelves. Like Elaine Pagels (in her paper on presbyters and bishops), I see the various theological systems described by the heresiologists in detail as artificial constructs used by an "orthodox" hierarchy to show the error of their rivals. The Gnostics were not system builders. So we should not expect to find a system in their literature. Even the so-called contradictions within any Gnostic tractate are the result of our drawing them into a system.

JAMES ROBINSON: Professor Wisse, you work inductively as a positivist. The clear methodological distinction between you and Professor Schenke's school has significance for more than Sethianism alone. The whole scholarly community can be aligned along an axis between these two kinds of approach. The danger of your approach to the Sethian tractates lies in the "alchemy of ideas." How do we get to the system of a Valentinus or Basilides from this casual picking of the literary sherds? Were the four luminaries included in several different tractates by mere coincidence? Some of Schenke's evidence calls for an explanation that acknowledges a continuity of tradition. Schenke's approach has a weakness like that of assuming that *behind* the New Testament writers lay the Apostles' Creed. But even though primitive Christianity didn't have a single coherent system, Christianity

nevertheless did exist. And there is no more variation among the
Sethian tractates than there is variation in the literary remains from
the first three centuries of Christianity.

I am seeking a middle position between positivism and the
dogmatic system, one that avoids the problems of both. Like Hans
Jonas, I read the Gnostic texts as attempts to understand existence.
To illustrate, in the Gnostic texts there are a number of different
descriptions of the chain of beings between the high God and us. But
in every version there is a twist in that line. Every author senses
the human dilemma.

WISSE: I am in agreement with what Jonas has set forth on the
Gnostic views of the world, evil, etc. Yes, the Gnostics had more
than praxis in common. But we have to conceive of a group which
was not concerned about the way these common concerns were
expressed—for example, vitually anything that supports celibacy is
included. This kind of standard is foreign to us. Nor does it fit the pattern
of the church congregation. I find the most likely social setting
to be a monasticism in which speculation was tolerated in at least the
early stages.

ALEXANDER BÖHLIG: I believe that we must distinguish between
the contents and the forms (I refer you to my "Zur Struktur
gnostischen Denkens," *NTS* 24 [1978] 469-509). Variation in content
must have been possible within a group. We must remember that
Gnostics used a mythological mode of thought and expression which
is different from the one we are accustomed to in the Platonic
tradition. This allows for much more variation. I would agree
that the differentiation between Gnostic groups was mainly the work of
outsiders. Yet the term "Sethian" is useful in that it helps us to
group together a number of common elements found in different
writings.

WISSE: Professor Böhlig, I can accept your usage of the term "Sethian."
But I am not sure the term can be rescued without false sociological
categories being imported.

BÖHLIG: The sociological situation is hardly visible in these writings,
since they did not function as the "rule of faith" of a group.

MacRae: I have two questions for discussion. We assume that in some cases the church fathers encountered Gnosticism in a literary form. Would they not have naturally concluded from their own experience as members in a church that the different points of view in the literary texts must speak for the existence of different groups? And would not the problem be compunded by their attempt to confront mythological thought with logical thought as Professor Böhlig has noted? Second, can we assume that the situation remained the same during three to four hundred years? I find Epiphanius sometimes impressively specific in his information about groups of people. Was Gnosticism the same phenomenon in the second century that it was in the fourth century? Such questions seem particularly relevant to the issue of the relationship between Nag Hammadi and the patristic evidence.

Henry Chadwick: Epiphanius is not the earliest extant writer to regard the Gnostics as a number of coherent groups. Celsus thought there were groups identified by name who were not friendly to each other and who were opposed to the *megalē ekklēsia*.

Robert Kraft: The question of the reliability of the early heresiologists must be kept separate from the question of whether the Nag Hammadi materials represent groups mentioned by the heresiologists. Conceivably a Sethian group may have existed which is not represented at all by the Nag Hammadi texts. It would be dangerous to take Nag Hammadi as providing a complete profile of Sethian groups so as to establish that Hippolytus and the subsequent heresiologists are wrong.

Michael Stone: In attempting to correlate the heresiologists and the Nag Hammadi texts we have a clear analogy in scholars' attempts to align Josephus's reports of the Essenes with the disparate Qumran documents. There are the same problems of trying to match even a portion of the documents with the reports and of deciding what to do with the contradictions.

Böhlig: We also know of instances in which outsiders assigned different names to Christians with which they did not agree. It is true that the long span of time complicates matters of identification. How much had Marcionism changed from the beginning until the time that Mani had contacts with it?

GEORGE NICKELSBURG : Professor MacRae's question about the church fathers' literary encounters with Gnosticism is complicated because we cannot even make an intelligent guess as to what the church fathers knew about the documents in their possession.

ROBINSON: Let us consider leaders of movements. We are not challenging the existence of Valentinianism as we are Sethianism because there was a Valentinus. Though it would be wrong to speak of a sect of "Origenites," major figures like Origen tended to produce disruptive groups within the larger church body. These groups could be identified and excommunicated. The problem here is that we are dealing with groups of people linked with nonhuman characters—Barbelo, Seth, etc. The question is whether these groups go back to some person whose name wasn't attached to them, like the Methodists' Wesley, or whether there were amorphous kinds of Gnosticism that were mistakenly fitted into the analogy of a school or sect by the church fathers. This is a more complicated way of posing our alternatives.

MACRAE: Our alternatives become further confounded by recalling the irreconcilability of what Irenaeus and Hippolytus reported of Basilides. Doubtless they had the same Basilides in mind.

ROBINSON: Professor Rudolph's questioning of the patristic evidence is misleading. We have agreed to bracket Hippolytus's discussion of Sethianism as a separate and limited problem.

BIRGER PEARSON: A number of questions arise over the heresiologists' identification and description of sects. None of us disputes the existence of certain groups named after sect founders, although it is doubtful the identifications were self-designations. Clement states that sects are named after their founders. Epiphanius tells us about the Ebionites whom he derives from a nonexistent founder. Yet there were Ebionites whose designation was probably self-chosen. The Ebionites and the Ophites provide a closer analogy to the Sethians than the Valentinians. Did the heresiologists identify some sects according to key names and figures in the literary works they read? Perhaps the church fathers noticed the prominence of the serpent in certain texts and identified these as "Ophite." But in the case of the Sethians we are justified in suggesting that the designation of "Sethian" was self-chosen as with the Ebionites. Could it be that the phrases "the generation of Seth," "the children of Seth," and "the seed of Seth" were the result of individual musings? These seem to call for an identifiable group who traced their own spiritual lineage back to the figure of Seth. Once we acknowledge this we can do as Schenke has done in looking for similarities in certain mythologumena of the literature to aid us in delineating the group's profile. I am not. satisfied with Professor Wisse's explanation that leaves us with only isolated individuals without any sectarian identification producing the literature we possess.

WISSE: Do we assume the existence of a special group behind every document of the Apocrypha? Each succeeding generation of heresiologists borrowed from the previous ones and added new names to the roster of heresies. The Nicolaitans are a prime example of their capacity to create a full-blown sect from mere literary references. Of course there is solid evidence for the existence of a number of groups. But in the case of Hippolytus who knew of a *Paraphrase of Seth* it is likely that he rather casually made a connection between the Sethians and this writing in his *Syntagma*. Furthermore, individuals probably produced holy books without the backing of a sect.

PEARSON: But books are intended to be read.

WISSE: And, as important revelations from heaven, these books were intended for a public readership as wide as possible, including Christians and non-Christians.

PEARSON: Then you grant the possibility of the grouping of like-minded individuals who are attracted to this kind of literature?

WISSE: They may be hermits.

JOHN STRUGNELL: Granted that not every book in antiquity was written by a committee, the question is whether there are internal evidences of sectarian elements in the books. By analogy, the relationship between the *Book of Jubilees and* Qumran seems close. Both share the peculiar astrological and calendaric interests. But we are forced to read *Jubilees* itself carefully to determine its relationship with the Qumran sect since we cannot know its date of composition. Likewise we are obliged to read the Nag Hammadi texts for sectarian information.

A couple of questions can help. First, does the document refer to the readers in sectarian terms? In addition to the designations Professor Pearson pointed out in the Sethian literature, the peculiar designation of "the unshakeable people" sounds like a terminus technicus. The documents appear to have been written by individuals who were at least in agreement about communal identifications!

Second, I would look for questions of halachah. Baptism is surely communal in nature. In the case of the "Sethian" tractates we appear to find communal practices associated with sectarian self-designations. I find this approach more productive than the collecting of similar mythic homologumena in determining if there was actually a community that was guided by this literature or if a number of likeminded but unrelated individuals wrote analogous literature.

WISSE: The term "race of Seth" in the Nag Hammadi texts refers to ancient Sethites who are more like types than spiritual ancestors. Regarding the reference to baptism—I picture individuals leaving the church and, like the desert fathers, trying to spiritualize the sacraments to remove any dependence on the church. A number of tractates even polemicize against baptism.

ROBINSON: I see a logical fallacy in what Professor Pearson said. While the term "seed of Seth" implies an *ekklēsia*, it may be a self-designation used to cover all Gnostics, not just a Gnostic sect. This does not mean every Gnostic would describe himself and other Gnostics with this designation.

Regarding Professor Wisse's reference to the mythological Sethites, some kind of succession is understood by the authors and users of the literature referring to the "Sethites." Otherwise, why is reference made to the hiding of truth to the end of time? Speaking to a larger issue, I assume the heresiologist was annoyed by some walking version of those books inside the congregation or at least at close enough range for him to decide to refute them. We cannot avoid supposing a sociological setting that included the author and/or the reader that triggered the heresiologist's refutation.

WISSE: There was also a delight in presenting the whole array of exotic animals and sometimes the attempt to defame contemporary opponents by associating them with the incredible cast of strange groups. We cannot assume a confrontation behind every mention of a sect.

MacRae: Though I have infinite faith in the range of Epiphanius's imagination, I find it hard to dismiss his comparison of the Sethians and Archontics. He certainly was comparing groups here about which he knew a considerable amount of specific information.

Robinson: Epiphanius lists three sects who possessed books attributed to Seth. But only one of them, the Sethians, fits Professor Wisse's theory that the heresiologists inferred the existence of sects from the titles of tractates. Why are not the other two, the Archontics and the Gnostics, collapsed into one designation, "Sethians"?

Wisse: Many names were transmitted to Epiphanius in fixed traditions. Perhaps he was only able to fill in the gaps.

Carsten Colpe: We need to distinguish between two types of groups—those possessing a rite of initiation, a creed, and a constitution, and those which were, like the present-day Bultmannians, only loose collections of likeminded people even separated by space, but still easily distinguishable from everyone else. The groups we are dealing with fall into the latter category.

Robinson: The experience of excommunication can create groups and might serve as an unintended initiation ceremony. At least some members of an excommunicated portion of the *Grosskirche* will continue to worship together. The subsequent organization will be tighter than their association together before excommunication.

Colpe: Whether the result of excommunication is diffusion or organization depends on a number of variables.

Stone: The degree of difference in opinion that an organization can tolerate before throwing out the dissidents is also a function of a number of variables. These factors get involved in our discussion of sects and orthodoxy. The elasticity of the Church of England and that of Seventh-Day Adventists differ considerably.

MacRae: Dean Chadwick's picture in his address last evening of a Pachomian monk who buried his private library when his livelihood in the monastery was threatened is plausible to me. How does this scenario align with our discussion of Gnosticism as sectarian group versus intellectual pursuit? Perhaps, Dean Chadwick, you were suggesting that Gnosticism became an intellectual pursuit?

CHADWICK: We really don't know, do we? Perhaps any time after the middle of the second century, Gnosticism existed in time and space. The circulation of large amounts of apocryphal literature especially among the monks seems most probable, due to an encratic interest. Witness the enormous amount of apocryphal material transmitted by Irish monks. The circulation of apocryphal Gnostic documents especially of an encratic nature does not imply the existence of independent coherent groups. Though I would expect something quite different from Professor Schenke's dogmatic coherence in the Sethian literature, I entertain the possibility of underground groups who thought Seth's role had been generally underestimated and who invited others to join them in seeing the truth.

MACRAE: I am not sure whether we have dismissed the Sethians as an identifiable group or not. In keeping with our practice of inviting comment from auditors, perhaps Professor Werblowsky would respond.

R. J. ZWI WERBLOWSKY (the Hebrew University, Jerusalem): Perhaps an outsider's summing up will be helpful in looking at what was discussed. First, it is difficult to know whether we are dealing with a self-designation or an imposed designation. We do know that the church fathers' obsession to catalog led to an impossibly large list of Gnostic sects. In deciding we must remember that the moment of self-designation by a group also starts the process of deciding who is outside the group. Second, the heresiologists named groups either after founders or teachers or according to a main feature. Third, it is important to distinguish between tightly structured groups and those composed of free-floating individuals—an analogy is provided by comparison of the early Freudian school and later Freudians, and even the universal employment of technical terms generated by the early Freudians. Finally, I wish to suggest the possibility of binary opposition in understanding spiritual lineage. I cannot think of the Sethites without thinking of those who called themselves "Cainites." Assuming a derivation from Adam, you must derive yourself from one son or the other. So there is a polemical edge to the term "Sethites." Even without an organized school or sect there would be a tendency to claim a spiritual lineage from Seth.

BÖHLIG: There was an obvious need from the side of the church to distinguish itself from other views. This lies behind the names assigned to the Gnostics by the church fathers. Most likely these Gnostics belonged to *haereses* in the old meaning of "schools" without separate or distinctive "church" organization.

Session Four

THE PHENOMENON AND SIGNIFICANCE OF GNOSTIC SETHIANISM

BY

HANS-MARTIN SCHENKE

ONE of the most important insights bestowed upon us by the Nag Hammadi Library comes in the form of the discovery, or rather the elucidation, of a variety of Gnosticism that may be well compared to Valentinianism in both extent and historical importance.* In the Nag Hammadi codices there exists a constellation of texts that clearly stand apart as a relatively close-knit group (however much they may also be related to other Nag Hammadi writings). Clear membership in the group is enjoyed not only by the texts that are central to it, but also by those that are peripheral. This text group includes:

The *Apocryphon of John* (CG II,*1*; III,*1*; IV,*1*; plus the BG version and the parallel in Irenaeus *Haer.* 1.29)

The *Hypostasis of the Archons* (II,*4*)

The *Gospel of the Egyptians* (III,*2*; IV,*2*)

The *Apocalypse of Adam* (V,*5*)

The *Three Steles of Seth* (VII,*5*)

Zostrianus (VIII,*1*)

Melchizedek (IX,*1*)

The *Thought of Norea* (IX,*2*)

Marsanes (X)

Allogenes (XI,*3*)

The *Trimorphic Protennoia* (XIII)

In the light of the above-mentioned text group, still other writings can be seen to belong to this variety of Gnosticism. These are, of original Gnostic writings (besides the aforementioned BG,*2*), the *Untitled Treatise* of the Codex Brucianus; and from the domain of antiheretical literature (besides the aforementioned system of Irenaeus

---

* Heartfelt thanks are due to my colleague and friend Bentley Layton for translating this paper into English.

Haer. 1.29), the doctrines of the so-called Gnostics, Sethians, and Archontics of Epiphanius (*Haer.* 26.39.40).

The texts of this group shed light upon one another if compared synoptically; and the proportion and relationship of common, shared material to special, unique material permits a process of deduction that leads to considerable insight not only into the development of the teaching they contain, but also into the history of the community that transmitted them.

One instance of how these texts illuminate one another is the way certain shadowy figures suddenly spring to life. Thus the lightgiver Eleleth, who in most texts of our group looks like a long-dead component of the system, unexpectedly encounters us in the *Hypostasis of the Archons* as a surprisingly lively savior and revealer (93:2 ff.), and in the *Gospel of the Egyptians* and the *Trimorphic Protennoia* is even the luminous being who gives rise to the origin of the lower world (CG III 56:22 ff. = IV 68:5 ff.; XIII 39:13 ff.). Thus, too, in *Allogenes* Youel, "the one pertaining to all the glories,"[1] who according to the *Gospel of the Egyptians* is merely the consort of the thrice-male child[2] (= divine Autogenes = celestial Adamas),[3] plays a leading role as giver of revelation (CG XI 50:20; 52:14; 55:18, 34; 57:25).

An outline of my view of this phenomenon, based on a lecture delivered in 1971,[4] has already been published. It is not my intention to bring up what was said before, to the extent that it still seems correct. Rather, I should like to make certain additions, to shift the emphasis somewhat, and to stress certain points that have become important in the interim, generally approaching the same topic from a slightly different perspective and in a more fundamental way. Although in our text group both major and minor issues are interesting and important, and there are problems of both general and very specific import, I would stress that its special significance lies largely in the fact that it is also limited, and therefore constitutes a readily

---

[1] The strange stereotyped epithet ⲧⲁⲛⲓⲉⲟⲟⲩ ⲧⲏⲣⲟⲩ probably renders only a single Greek adjective, perhaps something like πανένδοξος.

[2] I no longer hold to my former understanding of ⲱⲟⲙⲛ̄ⲧ ⲛ̄ϩⲟⲟⲩⲧ ⲛ̄ⲁⲗⲟⲩ (and the like) as "*Dreimännerkind*" (*NTS* 16 [1969] 197 n. 1; *Studia Coptica*, [below, n. 4], 170). This was an exegetical exaggeration.

[3] Cf. further the *Untitled Treatise* from Codex Brucianus (ed. Baynes) 18.29, 48.3; *Zost* 53:14; 54:17; 63:11; 125:14.

[4] "Das sethianische System nach Nag-Hammadi-Handschriften," *Studia Coptica* (P. Nagel, ed.; BBA 45; Berlin, 1974) 165-73.

surveyable field of observation, which we can use as an ideal model
for studying fundamental problems of the overall phenomenon of
Gnosticism.

1. THE DESIGNATION OF THE TEXT GROUP AS "SETHIAN" AND ITS IMPLICATIONS

As a kind of shorthand, one could designate our text group by any
neutral convention, such as *X*-group, *Apocryphon of John* group,
etc. On the other hand, the label of a thing can be legitimately
expected to say something about its nature. Moreover, it can hardly
be ignored that there are already designations for the texts of our group,
which attempt to say something about their essential nature. And in this
connection the term Sethianism, which is borrowed from the church
fathers, has played a leading role ever since the Nag Hammadi
codices have become known. According to G. MacRae, for example,
the *Apocalypse of Adam* is a literary product of Sethian Gnostics.[5]
A. Böhlig and F. Wisse define the content of the *Gospel of the
Egyptians* as a combination of Barbelo-Gnosticism and Sethianism.[6]
Y. Janssens calls the Gnostics from whom the main witnesses of our
text group derive "Barbélognostiques-séthiens" and the like.[7] Nevertheless, to use the terms "Barbelo-Gnostic" and "Sethian" as alternatives
and in combination with one another seems suspect to me since
the terms come from different sources: the first originates from
Irenaeus (*Haer.* 1.29.1), who for his part does not use the term
"Sethians" at all; the second derives from the so-called "Sethians" of
Hippolytus, Epiphanius, and Theodoret, Theodoret being the first to
attribute the system of Irenaeus *Haer.* 1.30 to the Sethians. With the two
formally distinct terms one could unintentionally refer to one and
the same object. And if we are permitted to consider our text
group as being essentially Sethian, this will actually turn out to be
the case.

In the literature, of course, other texts not in fact belonging to
our group have also been designated as Sethian. Here it becomes
apparent, as F. Wisse has well emphasized, that what the antiheretical
writers of the church said about Sethianism and Sethians is entirely

---

[5] "Adam, Apocalypse of," *IDBSup* 10.

[6] *Nag Hammadi Codices III,2 and IV,2: The Gospel of the Egyptians* (NHS 4; Leiden, 1975) 32, 36.

[7] "Le codex XIII de Nag Hammadi," *Le Muséon* 78 (1974) 348 etc.

inadequate for distinguishing meaningfully and unambiguously, which Gnostic texts are Sethian.[8] Yet this does not necessarily preclude the opposite procedure, viz., of starting out from certain texts in which Seth has a key function and in the light of them examining, testing, and confirming or rejecting the church fathers' accounts of Sethianism. In such a procedure what counts is not ·the fact that Seth appears in a writing (or that he is its reputed author), but the way in which he appears. I must confess that I do not feel that the criticisms advanced at the end of M. Tardieu's recent article[9] really apply to me, all the less so since in his paper on the *Three Steles of Seth* Tardieu without reservation considers the latter text to be Sethian.[10] The question is not one of old or new artificial names of heresies. Rather, presupposing (as the church fathers seem to have done) that Gnostic Sethianism, viz., Gnostics who designated and understood themselves as Sethians, really did exist, it is a question of using primary sources to bring order into the pertinent statements of the church fathers and to inquire after the essence of real Sethianism.

The occurrence of the figure and name of Seth (along with his equivalents such as "child of the child" or "Allogenes") in our text group seems to me essential and basic. For instance, the mythic concept of the four lightgivers and their aeons, so typical of these texts, is directly connected with the idea of Seth, for they are the celestial home of Seth and his offspring. But all of this need not be pointed out for a second time! Especially characteristic are the self-designation and self-understanding of our Gnostics as the "seed of Seth," which runs throughout these texts, either verbatim or in the form of synonyms ("the unshakable race," "great race," etc.). In my opinion the most fitting way to express the essence of the texts in our group is to designate them as "Sethian." And then, I believe, on the basis of the texts in our group, it will be possible also to determine what Sethian or Sethianism does and does not mean, and also where the statements of the church fathers are right and where they are wrong.

The question of names immediately gives rise to a further question,

---

[8] Cf. F. Wisse, "The Sethians and the Nag Hammadi Library," *SBLSP 1972*, 601-607.

[9] "Les livres mis sous le nom de Seth et les Séthiens de l'hérésiologie," *Gnosis and Gnosticism* (NHS 8; Leiden, 1977) 204-10.

[10] "Les Trois stèles de Seth—Un écrit gnostique retrouvé à Nag Hammadi, Introduit et traduit," *RSPhTh* 57 (1973) 545-75.

the answer to which is much more difficult: it concerns the actual persons (quite apart from dramatis personae) who held the ideas expressed in the texts of our group. The phenomenon and structure of our text group, its extent, the unity behind its variety, the varying density of what is essential, all this gives the impression that we have before us the genuine product of one and the same human community of no small dimensions, but one that is in the process of natural development and movement. That is, I cannot think of our documents as having no basis in a group of human beings, nor do I think of this basis as being artificial and short-lived. Now if, from this perspective, we can conclude from the relevant terms of the texts that it is precisely this group of human beings who understood themselves to be the seed and offspring of Seth, the obvious question about the origins of this social group and about its traditions is brought into focus. Does this connection with Seth give evidence of a non-Gnostic prehistory of these Sethian Gnostics?

I consider this question to be important, even more important, of course, than my own first attempts to answer it! In view of the tradition that we find integrated (and partly Gnosticized) in the writings of the group in question, the problem of its origins has quite rightly played a considerable role in research. But in any case it would seem to be an oversimplification of the problem if, a priori, only Judaism were to be taken into account as a possible background or source or field of origin. For my old idea of a link between Gnostic Sethianism and the Samaritans the only obvious point of connection is the reference to Dositheus as the (fictious) guarantor of the content of the three steles of Seth (in the prefatory frame of that text, but without further mention; cf. CG VII 118:10f.). Thrilling as may be the appearance of this famous name in a Gnostic primary source, I must concede that for our present problem its value is open to question. Since this name does not reappear in any other text of our group it may, in terms of tradition history, be either genuine or fictitious. Hence, the name can as well be seen on the same level as "Zostrianus" in the book which bears that name (CG VIII,*1*). That is, the Sethians could have borrowed the name Dositheus from elsewhere on account of its legendary fame.[11] Nevertheless, I would think it incorrect to assume that the problem is laid to rest simply because there exists an alternative

---

[11] The matter is seen to be ambiguous in just this way by K. Wekel, "Die drei Stelen des Seth (NHC VII,5), Text—Übersetzung—Kommentar" (Th.D. diss., Humboldt Universität, Berlin [DDR], 1977) 75-77.

solution. The supposed indifference of Judaism towards the figure of Seth as compared with the great esteem for Seth among the Samaritans, arguments which I once adduced,[12] is problematic on both scores, just as my reference to J. Bowman offers me no real support. Here I am indebted to U. Luz and O. Hofius[13] for valuable criticisms. But I am not yet ready to lay down arms. Rather, I should prefer to keep the question open and for my part to pursue the Samaritan track a little longer, just as Luz and Hofius especially prefer to do with the Jewish one. If thereby it emerges that there really were Jewish groups seeing themselves in a special connection with Seth and that, consequently, it would be more suitable to consider them as the ancestors of Gnostic Sethianism, I should be content with that outcome as well.

2. THE IDENTITY OF THE SETHIAN TEXT GROUP AND ITS MUTUAL RELATIONSHIPS

The group of Sethian documents is held together not simply by the role that Seth plays in them, but rather by the role of Seth plus the fundamental identity of the system. Accordingly, it is possible to identify a given writing as Sethian, even if Seth (for whatever reason) does not appear in it at all, whether under his own name or as one of its equivalents.

Besides those things that connect all writings of the group with one another, there is an extremely interesting network of special relations between individual members of the group. The connections include:

A special prayer: *3StSeth* 125:23-126:16, and *Allog* 54:11-37[14]

A specific deployment of negative theology: *Apocryphon of John* and *Allogenes*[15]

A division of the Autogenēs into the triad of Kalyptos, Protophanēs, Autogenēs: *Three Steles of Seth, Zostrianus, Allogenes*[16]

A specific philosophical terminology: *Three Steles of Seth, Zostrianus, Marsanes, Allogenes*

---

[12] "Das sethianische System," 171.
[13] Letters of January 30, 1975, from each of these scholars.
[14] See below p. 601.
[15] Cf. A. Werner, "Das Apokryphon des Johannes in seinen vier Versionen synoptisch betrachtet und unter besonderer Berücksichtigung anderer Nag-Hammadi-Schriften in Auswahl erläutert" (Th.D. diss., Humboldt Universität, Berlin [DDR], 1977) 19; J. M. Robinson, "The Three Steles of Seth and the Gnostics of Plotinus," *Proceedings of the International Colloquium on Gnosticism, Stockholm, August 20-25, 1973* (Stockholm, 1977) 136; *NHLibEng* 443.
[16] Cf. *ZÄS* 102 (1975) 137.

Obvious (secondary) Christianization: *Apocryphon of John, Hypostasis of the Archons, Melchizedek*

The presupposition of a second tetrad (Gamaliel, Gabriel, Samblo, Abrasax [or the like]) alongside the four lightgivers: *Gospel of the Egyptians, Apocalypse of Adam, Zostrianus, Melchizedek, Marsanes, Trimorphic Protennoia*

The designation (in Coptic) "Pigeradamas"[17] for Adamas: *Apocryphon of John* (CG II), *Three Steles of Seth, Zostrianus, Melchizedek*

The concept of Eleleth as cause of the terrestrial world: *Gospel of the Egyptians, Trimorphic Protennoia*[18]

The name and figure of Mirothea/Mirotheos (or the like): *Gospel of the Egyptians, Three Steles of Seth, Zostrianus, Trimorphic Protennoia*

By referring to mythological and magical names, the network of connecting lines could be given even more complexity.

The texts of our group are different in length and quite varied in degree of preservation. Consequently, the shorter ones (such as the *Thought of Norea*, so-called) and the fragmentary ones (such as *Melchizedek* and *Marsanes*) have relatively less chance of displaying their Sethian character. Herein lies the problem of the identifiability of Sethian writings. This problem is weighty and deserves our interest, even if it is raised and discussed here only belatedly. In my opinion, the Sethian system, or that which is Sethian within the system, is sufficiently characteristic that we can proceed in this matter like the specialist in ancient ceramics, who is able to reconstruct the original form of a vessel without difficulty from a surviving handle or fragment of a rim.

The identification depends on a number of distinctive features or on the quality of those features. A single "Sethian" feature is not sufficient

---

[17] In my opinion a fully satisfactory explanation of this epithet is still awaited. Every attempt thus far has its weak points: my "Sethianische(s) System," 170; *TLZ* 100 (1975) 573; F. Wisse, communication of April 5, 1974; A. Böhlig, "Zum 'Pluralismus' in den Schriften von Nag Hammadi: Die Behandlung des Adamas in den Drei Stelen des Seth und im Ägypterevangelium," *Essays on the Nag Hammadi Texts* (NHS 6; Leiden, 1975) 25f.; Tardieu, "Les trois stèles de Seth," 567 [he translates: "O vénérable (γέρας) Adamas (Ἀδαμας)"]; K. Wekel, "Drei Stelen," 87f. I think it must be considered striking that until now neither the form *гєрλλⲁⲙⲁⲥ (without the supposed demonstrative article) nor the form *ⲡгєрλλⲁⲙⲁⲥ (with normal article) is attested. Incidentally, if in the first half the Greek stem γερ- is involved, I think one would have to assume that something like ὁ γεραρὸς Ἀδαμᾶς (with an adjective) were the basis of the Coptic expression.

[18] See below p. 615 and above p. 589.

as an indicator of Sethianism. I should like to illustrate both the problem and the possibility of identification in the case of the short text without title, CG IX,2 (called by the American Coptic Gnostic Library Project "The Thought of Norea," but by our Berliner Arbeitskreis "Ode on Norea"). Now, the distinctive features of that text are "the divine Autogenes" (28:6f.) and "the four holy helpers" (28:27f.), who can hardly be anyone else but the four lightgivers Harmozel, Oroiael, Daveithe, and Eleleth, or their four messengers Gamaliel, Gabriel, Samblo, and Abrasax. Add to this the figure of Norea herself, not so much the figure in general as the specific manner in which she appears, namely, as the female equivalent of Seth. This is especially displayed by the concept of her "assumption" (27:24f.). The role that Norea plays here and the presupposed situation connect our text with the second part of the *Hypostasis of the Archons*. Finally, it is of importance that the features mentioned, both those that are unambiguous and those that are not, do not enter into competition with distinctive features from any other system. (Incidentally, now as before, it is not the content and its identification that is the main problem of this text in my view, but its peculiar form. Indeed, that is the sole reason why we resist so obstinately the temptation of simply taking the expression *noēsis n-Norea* ["thought of Norea"], which occurs in the body of the text [29:3], as its title.[19])

Similar problems appear when we make the border or periphery of Sethianism the object of our practical and theoretic reflections. First of all, it must be maintained theoretically that the Sethian scriptures, though spiritual products of the Gnostic group of Sethians, did not remain only in the hands of the Sethians, but circulated and were used also in other Gnostic circles and even in non-Gnostic communities. Indeed, in the case of the Sethian writings of Nag Hammadi, it is probable that the last link in the chain of tradition was a foreign one, not only non-Sethian, but even non-Gnostic.[20] What is true of whole documents is naturally true also of single mythic concepts and single ideas. Sethian mythic concepts and ideas could easily spread beyond the limits of the group and thus, for example, gain entry into writings of quite a different origin, into the scriptures of other Gnostic communities as well as into writings which came into being only as isolated literary works of single individuals.

---

[19] On the figure of Norea and its background cf. B. Pearson, "The Figure of Norea in Gnostic Literature," *Proceedings of the International Colloquium, Stockholm*, 143-52.

[20] F. Wisse, "Gnosticism and Early Monasticism in Egypt," *Gnosis, Festschrift für Hans Jonas* (Göttingen, 1978) 431-40.

That in this sense the outer contours of Sethianism have to be thought
of as a bit soft must not, of course, be taken conversely as a reason
to doubt the existence of a hard inner core. Here, too, I should like to
make use of an image: that of the Coptic dialects, which do not
lack an identity simply because in areas near the dialect boundaries there
are overlapping features shared with other dialects; nor is it possible
to recognize a dialect from a single feature.

Now, the whole matter becomes quite practical as soon as one
takes up the question of whether an entire, well-preserved writing
that seems near to being Sethian or that contains Sethian elements
is really and truly Sethian. Such a decision would seem to depend
essentially upon the proportion of the Sethian or Sethianlike material
to the non-Sethian. For, Sethianism itself could just as well take in
material from outside. In the case of *Eugnostus the Blessed* and the
Sophia of Jesus Christ it is possible to state with confidence that they
are not Sethian (pace R. McL. Wilson, who sees *Eugnostus* and the
Sophia of Jesus Christ as comparable to the *Apocryphon of John*,
the *Apocalypse of Adam*, and the *Hypostasis of the Archons*[21]). The
connection of the *Gospel of the Egyptians* and *Eugnostus* through the
mere name "Eugnostus" is of no relevance. So faint are the signs of
connection that are discernible between the texts of our group and the
Pistis Sophia (Codex Askewianus) and even the two *Books of Jeû*,
that one can only characterize these writings as slightly influenced
by Sethianism.

But the question becomes really serious in the case of the *Hypostasis
of the Archons* and the treatise *On the Origin of the World* (CG II,5). I
would suggest that the *Hypostasis of the Archons* be treated as
belonging to Sethianism (as I have been presupposing above), but
not so *On the Origin of the World*. To arrive at this conclusion is by no
means simple, because of the obviously close relationship between
the two texts (from which must be explained, incidentally, the very
curious fact that both writings are silent on the celestial world, the
sphere of the ogdoad). Probably the two texts are both dependent upon
a third; it can be hypothesized that this was an *Apocalypse of Norea*,
in which the topic of the ogdoad had already been omitted from
discussion.[22] Significant for determining the particular character of
Gnosticism that marks the *Hypostasis of the Archons* is the figure of the

---

[21] "The Gospel of the Egyptians," *Studia Patristica* 14 (TU 117; Berlin, 1976) 249.
[22] Cf. *OLZ* 72 (1977) 379-81.

angel Eleleth, and all that is said about him; especially, that he is one of the four lightgivers who stand in the presence of the Great Invisible Spirit (93:20-22);[23] and his stereotyped designation as "Understanding" (*tmntrmnhēt* 93:19; 94:3f.; or *tmntsabe* 93:3).[24] To this may be added Norea as an equivalent of Seth; the motif of the threefold coming of the savior (96:27-31); and the figure of Pistis Sophia (assuming that in the non-Sethian writing *Pistis Sophia* her status as daughter of Barbelo preserves a genuinely Sethian theologoumenon).[25] Now, while nothing speaks against the assumption that the hypothetical source (*Apocalypse of Norea*) was already Sethian in character, the constellation of elements in the second offshoot of this source, *On the Origin of the World*, is quite different. Since the angel Eleleth does not appear, it lacks the only unambiguous Sethian element. For the author of *On the Origin of the World*, the hypothetical *Apocalypse of Norea* is only one source among many, even if it is perhaps the most important one. The parallels to the *Hypostasis of the Archons* have, because of their context in the *Origin of the World*, quite a different function. The latter treatise has not only no Sethian aspect, but in general no communitarian one, nothing that proves it to be the product of a community. It is a treatise through which a single Gnostic writer intends to publicly propagandize on behalf of the Gnostic world view.[26] If the author was in fact a Sethian, he seems nevertheless to have made no use of his sectarian affiliation in this work.

3. The Interdependence of Content and Form In the Sethian Texts

During the earlier phase of publication and research on Nag Hammadi (when typical premature conclusions were being drawn as to the age of the new texts, their grouping, their Christian or non-Christian character, etc.), one got the impression that judgments as to the relationship of the texts (including some from our group), either to one another or to other works of literature, were being formed only on the basis of their content, without regard to their external form.

---

[23] "The Great Invisible Spirit" is the terminus technicus for the highest deity in Sethianism.

[24] The two Coptic expressions correspond to Greek ἡ φρόνησις; for its systematic correspondence to Eleleth see, e.g., *GEgypt* CG III 52:13; 69:9.

[25] C. Schmidt-W. Till, *Koptisch-Gnostische Schriften* 1 (GCS 45; 2d ed.; Berlin, 1954) 234.40; C. Schmidt, *Pistis Sophia* (Coptica 2; Copenhagen, 1925) 356.25.

[26] Cf. *NHLibEng* 161.

Such an undertaking is dubious in many respects. In writings like ours the content is, almost as a m̄atter of course, no longer displayed within its original framework. Rather, in various ways during the history of its usage, the content has been reframed, and as a result has not been able to remain what it once was.

Just how helpful the analytical consideration of our writings can be for understanding their content has been shown by C. W. Hedrick, in the case of the *Apocalypse of Adam*.[27] Now, as to whether the two threads of text that he has extracted (his source A and source B) were ever real sources and actual, independent texts, I have not yet been able to decide. But the two threads as such really do exist. Even more surely, Hedrick has made clear the existence of the textual cruces on which his theory is based. It is not entirely clear to me whether in constructing his "bold" literary analysis Hedrick really is obliged to exclude our own text critical hypothesis on 84:5-8, a hypothesis that is limited and much more moderate in boldness.[28] Indeed, literary criticism and textual criticism need not be mutually exclusive. Moreover, close study of the Nag Hammadi texts, especially from the linguistic point of view, shows that many passages of the text are not in good order. In principle, I should wish to concede a methodological pride of place to textual criticism. Here, in *ApocAd* 84:5-8, the understanding of the text greatly depends on whether one is prepared to see the words M̄ΙΧΕΥ M̄N M̄ΙΧΑΡ M̄N M̄NHCINOYC· NH ΕΤϨΙΧ͟N ΠΙΧⲰΚⲘ ΕΤΟΥΑΑΒ M̄N ΠΙⲘΟΟΥ Ε̣ΤΟΝϨ {ΧΕ} as being a foreign body in the text. For myself, in principle I do not see the matter any differently than I did in 1966. Rather, in the meantime I have become more confident of my position, especially since the broader context of overall Sethianism (which was not yet known to me at the time) seems to completely exclude the possibility that the guardians of the holy baptismal water Micheus, Michar, and Mnesinous are *fallen* angels. The celestial scolding in 84:4ff. can only be directed at human beings, namely those who have been hostile to Gnostics and Gnosticism.

Actually, in speaking of "form," I should like to turn to something higher than the linguistic and material intactness of a text or its composite nature. I mean "form" in the sense proper to form criticism

---

[27] "The Apocalypse of Adam: A Literary and Source Analysis," *SBLSP 1972*, 581-90.

[28] "Apocalypse of Adam," 586. F. Morard regards our hypothesis as possible but not necessary; cf. "L'Apocalypse d'Adam de Nag Hammadi: Un essai d'interpretation," *Gnosis and Gnosticism* (NHS 8; Leiden, 1977) 37.

(*Formgeschichte*)—though not of the scholastic kind still widely practised in the field of New Testament scholarship, rather, a kind of form criticism that seeks once again a connection with modern linguistics. The question is to comprehend and describe the genre (*Textsorte*) to which a given text belongs, and to determine the degree of dependence thereupon displayed by its content. Incidentally, investigation of genre is necessary and promising not only for the Sethian text group but also for the rest of the Nag Hammadi Library. Thus, for example, in the *Hypostasis of the Archons*, it is not only the character of the hypothetical source (*Apocalypse of Norea*) that causes the upper world to be completely left out of consideration, but also the aim of this writing, which sets out to include only what a Gnostic needs to know about the evil and dangerous archons. It would therefore be erroneous to suppose that the absence of certain of Sethian characteristics which belong to the upper world mean that this writing is non-Sethian in character.

In the case of *Allogenes* we have, in a way, the opposite extreme. The theme here is exclusively the doctrine of God. The terrestrial world and the entire upper world, except for its summit, are thematically excluded. The content of the text is divided into two parts. Seth (here "Allogenes"), while on earth in bodily form, is taught by Youel about the highest deity and its proper being and life. After a period of one hundred years of life in this state of Gnosis Seth is also permitted, during what amounts to a celestial journey, to see that which up to this point he had merely heard. But since such a vision cannot be communicated, the second part of the theology of this text appears again in words. And as speakers, there are now introduced the (four) lightgivers or their powers. The whole complex is not told purely and simply, but is cast in the frame of tidings of these events which Seth himself gives. As the recipient of these tidings there is introduced a member of the offspring of Seth, a certain Messus, who, after an intervening period with the usual catastrophes, is supposed to find the book containing these tidings; it will be in the form of the steles of Seth, completely intact, on the top of a high mountain. Again, we should not conclude anything, at least not directly, from things that are not present in the writing and which indeed cannot be, given its purpose.

The *Hypostasis of the Archons* and *Allogenes* are simply two examples of how the content of a text depends upon its form. But with the *Gospel of the Egyptians* and the *Three Steles of Seth* the question of genre becomes really difficult and crucial. In Böhlig and Wisse's edition of the two versions of the *Gospel of the Egyptians*, a masterful edition that provides at long last a reliable basis for investigating this important Sethian writing, the question of genre, if I understand rightly, has neither been asked nor in any sense (not even implicitly) answered. This is sorely missed in their edition, for without taking up the remarkable form of the text, a satisfactory overall evaluation of the *Gospel of the Egyptians* is unfeasible. The writing is not simply to be understood as the development of a mythological (Sethian) system, and therefore cannot be directly compared with writings that are. I should like to stress now as before that we must start from the fact that the main and most consistent subject of this writing is prayer, rather than emanation or action. And this trait makes sense only if the main issue is prayer, that is, if the writing aims to demonstrate and teach how to invoke the supercelestial powers correctly and efficaciously, and which powers to invoke. After all, the emphasis of the text lies upon the final part, that is, the mystical prayer of baptism and regeneration, which apparently represents the climax of the whole work.[29] Accordingly the *Gospel of the Egyptians* has to be understood as the mythological justification of a well-defined ritual of baptism including the invocations that must be performed therein. Incidentally, despite the edition of Böhlig and Wisse, I must hold to my old idea concerning the title at the beginning. For, various objections must be raised against the reconstruction of the title by these editors. Their attempt to demonstrate that the content has a specifically Egyptian character is not successful. The way in which they postulate a connection between Seth son of Adam and the Graeco-Egyptian deity of that name is unacceptable.[30] Above all, their reconstruction seems to contradict their own fundamental insights according to which the colophon as a whole is secondary and the designation of the book as "according to the *Egyptians*" has been given from the outside. In short, still nothing prevents the search for a Greek feminine nomen actionis which can take as its genetivus objectivus

---

[29] Cf. *NTS* 16 (1969) 196.

[30] Cf. B. A. Pearson, "Egyptian Seth and Gnostic Seth," *SBLSP 1977*, 33-34 with nn. 75-78. In this essay Pearson finally lays to rest the old idea, still held over from the "prehistoric" days of research in Gnosticism, that there was a connection between Gnostic Sethianism and the Egyptian god Seth. For the figure of Seth son of Adam in general, see recently A. F. J. Klijn, *Seth in Jewish, Christian and Gnostic Literature* (Leiden, 1977).

the Invisible Spirit. And I still consider ἐπίκλησις, "invocation," to be the best candidate. For the rest, the amount of agreement and disagreement between the two versions in the incipit would be in no way greater than within the book, if we read :

III πχωωμε ν̄τ2̣[ιε]ρ[ᴀ ν̄επικᴀнсιс] etc.

IV [πχωωμε ετογᴀ]ᴀ̣в ν̄τε νι[επικᴀнсιс] etc.

III "The Book of the H[ol]y [Invocation]" etc.

IV "[The Ho]ly [Book] of the [Invocation]s" etc.

That the *Three Steles of Seth* is relevant in terms of form, criticism can easily be seen. Incidentally, the form critical approach has received special attention from K. Wekel in his commentary on the text.[31] And it is likely from the outset that the peculiarities of the content (e.g., the simplicity of the system, the absence of dualistic traits) are in the first instance related to the form of the text. Now, J. M. Robinson, in an analysis of *Allogenes* and its connections with the *Three Steles of Seth*,[32] has noted the parallelism of two very specific doxologies in the two works, a parallel that is significant in terms of form criticism (*Allog* 54:11-37, paralleled by *3StSeth* 125:23-126:16). This striking connection was also discovered independently by K. Wekel, and discussed in his commentary.[33] I should like, incidentally, to question Robinson's idea that in *Allogenes* it is Youel who has to be seen as the speaker of that doxology.[34] Hypostatized knowledge ("Gnosis") seems to me a more likely candidate. Now, in the same context Robinson also assigns considerable weight to *3StSeth* 127:6-21;[35] this passage, in my opinion, is the key to an overall form critical understanding of this text. But Robinson concludes from it that the *Three Steles of Seth*, just like *Allogenes*, presupposes a celestial journey and that accordingly the three invocations of the *Three Steles of Seth* have their place in the course of such a celestial journey. Though to a degree this is right, it seems to me that the further deductions made by him run exactly in the wrong direction. If we were only interested in the relationship of the documents, all would be in order. But there is reason, I think, not to treat the *Three Steles of Seth* and *Allogenes* alike. That the one celestial journey is not

---

[31] "Die Drei Stelen des Seth."
[32] "The Three Steles of Seth and Plotinus," 133-36.
[33] "Die Drei Stelen des Seth," 181-91.
[34] P. 134.
[35] P. 136; see also *NHLibEng* 362 f.

equivalent to the other is already made clear by the emphasis laid upon "we" in the *Three Steles of Seth*. *Allogenes* commemorates the exceptional experiences of a single individual. Here the role of Allogenes-Seth is that of a mediator of a revelation. The *Three Steles of Seth*, however, deals with progressive invocations of the deity by Seth, functioning as prototype—invocations which effect an ascension and which the community can and must reproduce. In short, I cannot help seeing the *Three Steles of Seth* as a typical liturgical text. And the passage 127:6-21 mentioned above is something like a rubric, in which is expressed how the three prayer formulas are to be used and what results from performance of the ritual. Our text does not represent the pure formula, as it were, but has been stylized and framed as an etiology of the ritual. The *Three Steles of Seth* is the etiology of a mystery of ascension of the Sethian community.

4. Cultic Practice in Sethianism

Should our form critical evaluation of the *Three Steles of Seth* be correct, this would have an importance reaching far beyond the confines of Sethianism. For while we are well and extensively informed about the Gnostic thought world, information about Gnostic practice is hard to come by: every new source, whether discovered or reconstructed, is of exceptional value.

If we remain within the corpus of Sethian writings, we can ascertain that the Sethians, or at least some Sethians, had two sacraments, two mysteries. First, there is a more commonplace sacrament, baptism, to which quite frequent and varied reference is made in our text group; this fact has been repeatedly stressed in the literature on the various tractates. The second sacrament, higher in degree and repeatable, is the mystery of cultic ascension, discussed above. Because of the diversity of its attestation, the Sethian mystery of baptism is perhaps the more problematic rite; and perhaps it is also the more important one.

The importance that baptism has for the Sethians is displayed not least, and perhaps even most conspicuously, by a distinct ideology or mythology of baptism. In their view there is a baptism not only on earth but also in heaven. During his celestial journey Zostrianus can enter the celestial spheres only if he becomes like their inhabitants. And he achieves this by first undergoing a (celestial) baptism. According to the *Trimorphic Protennoia* the ascension after death of each Gnostic is tied up with a celestial baptism (CG XIII 45:17f.; 48:18-21).

The water used for baptism on earth is thought of as being of celestial quality and has its source in heaven, where above all the two (or three) guardians Micheus and Michar (and also Mnesinous) watch over it (cf. *GEgypt* III 64:14-16, 19f. and parallels in IV 76:2-4, 8-10; *ApocAd* 84:5-8;[36] *TriProt* 48:19f.; *Zost* 6:9f., 15f.; *Untitled Treatise* from Codex Brucianus [ed. Baynes] 61.15-21). Another triad of persons or names, Jesseus Mazareus Jessedekeus (or the like) seems to embody the celestial water of baptism itself. At any rate, I do not know what else the stereotyped apposition ⲡ(ⲓ)ⲙⲟⲟⲩ ⲉⲧⲟⲛⲍ could mean (cf. *ApocAd* 85:30f.; *GEgypt* III 64:10-12; 66:19f., parr. IV 75:25-27; 78:12f.; *Zost* 47:5f.; 57:5f.).

In the domain of baptismal ideology probably belongs also the curious concept of the five seals, especially since baptism and sealing refer to one and the same act, or designate only different procedures within one and the same act (cf., e.g., *Zost* 6:13-17). The expression "the five seals" occurs in: *TriProt* 48:31; 49:27f., 29; 50:9f.: ⲁⲩⲱ ⲁⲉⲓⲧⲁϣⲉ ⲟⲉⲓϣ ⲛⲁⲩ ⲛ̄ⲧ[ⲙⲉⲍ†ⲉ ⲛ̄]|[ⲛⲓⲥⲫⲣ]ⲁ̣ⲅⲓⲥ ⲛ̄ⲁⲧϣⲁⲭⲉ ⲙ̄ⲙⲟⲟⲩ;[37] *ApocryJn* II 31:24 parr. IV 49:4 (hymn of Pronoia at the end of the long version); *GEgypt* IV 56:25; 58:6, 27f.; 59:27f.; III 55:12 parr. IV 66:25f.; III 63:3 parr. IV 74:16; III 66:3 parr. IV 78:4f.; *Untitled Treatise* from Codex Brucianus (ed. Baynes) 18.21f. Possibly the conclusion of *Allogenes* belongs here as well, if we read: [. . . ⲧⲁϣⲉ | ⲟ]ⲉⲓϣ ⲙ̣[ⲙⲟⲟⲩ ⲱ̄ ⲡⲁ]|ϣⲏⲣⲉ ⲙⲉ̣[ⲥⲥ]ⲟ̣ⲥ [†ⲧⲉ ⲛ̄]|ⲥⲫⲣⲁ̣ⲅ̣ⲓ̣ⲥ [ⲛ̄]ⲧⲉ [ⲛⲓⲭⲱ]|ⲱⲙⲉ ⲧⲏⲣⲟⲩ ⲛ̄[ⲧⲉ] | ⲡⲁⲗⲗⲟ[ⲅⲉ]ⲛ̣ⲏⲥ̣ (XI 69:14-19). If this reconstruction is correct, the five seals are designated, by an actual Sethian, as typically Sethian in character.[38] The meaning and implication of the five seals, what they are, what they consist of, is in the first instance an enigma, which gives rise to all sorts of speculation.[39] We should now like to speculate that it is the designation of a divine "Quinity" of the Sethians (that is, five divine persons in one essence, parallel to the Christian Trinity). The reason for this designation would be that, probably, every time one of the five names is invoked in the rite of baptism

---

[36] As I said above (p. 598) I cannot believe that in the *Apocalypse of Adam* it is presupposed that Micheus, Michar, and Mnesinous have deserted their charge.

[37] Text established by G. Schenke, "Die dreigestaltige Protennoia" (Th.D. diss., Rostock, 1977) 45, 138.

[38] This is by and large the Claremont project's reconstruction, only with a change of the unsyntactic [ⲛ̄ⲣ̄ⲡ̄] (line 16) before ⲥⲫⲣⲁⲅⲓⲥ, which was to mean: "[and make] (the) seal [of] all [the books of] Allo[ge]nes"; see *NHLibEng* 452.

[39] Cf. Böhlig-Wisse, *Gospel of the Egyptians*, 27, 50, 174.

the person being baptized is provided with a σφραγίς.[40] The clearest evidence for this interpretation is a pair of sentences (*TriProt* 49:26-34), especially the genetivus epexegeticus in ⲧ̄ⲧⲉ ⲛ̄ⲥ̄ⲫⲣⲁⲅⲓⲥ ⲛ̄ⲧⲉ ⲛ̣̄ⲉⲉⲓⲣⲁⲛ ⲉⲧⲉ ⲛⲁⲓ̈ ⲛⲉ (line 29f.). Thus the concept of the five seals would seem to provide a direct connection between baptismal ideology and the execution of baptism.

Likewise the soteriological relevance of Sethian baptism finds expression precisely in the *Trimorphic Protennoia*; cf. further, besides the immediate context of the "five seals", (41:20-24): "It is I that descended first on account of my portion that is left behind, that is, the spirit that (now) dwells in the soul, < in order > that it might come into being ⟨again⟩ by the water of life and by the baptism of mysteries." Baptism brings Gnosis and total salvation. As for the connection of celestial baptism with that performed on earth, it probably lies essentially in the fact that the two baptisms are cultically identical. In the act of baptism there is already performed the putting off of darkness and the putting on of light (CG XIII 47:34-48:14; 49:28-34).

The first half of this process is given especially interesting and striking expression in the baptismal doctrine of the *Gospel of the Egyptians*. According to what was said above the *Gospel of the Egyptians* is in any case our main witness for Sethian baptism. And the most conspicuous trait of the understanding of baptism developed or presupposed in this tractate is that, in striking analogy to Col 2:11-15 and its background,[41] baptism is comprehended as ἀπέκδυσις τοῦ σώματος τῆς σαρκός, "putting off the body of flesh." This ἀπέκδυσις is seen to be rooted in the savior's having left behind his carnal body on the cross in order to return to his celestial home; the Gnostic now mysteriously repeats this event during baptism. Incidentally, this can scarcely be explained as the influence of Colossians upon the *Gospel of the Egyptians*; rather, both works seem to have drawn independently upon the same conceptual field.

Incidentally, this interpretation of the text is in no small way dependent on a matter of philological detail. It is a matter of a single letter: *pi* or *beta*. The question is this: in CG III 63:9, 16f. and its parallel IV 74:24; 75:3f., is the actual reading of the text ϩⲱⲧⲡ or ϩⲱⲧⲃ? Codex III reads ϩⲱⲧⲡ, Codex IV reads ϩⲱⲧⲃ (75:3; in 74:24 the verb is not preserved). The contrast between the *signifiants*

---

[40] Cf. G. Schenke, "Protennoia," 125-27, 134f.

[41] Cf. K.-W. Tröger, ed., *Gnosis und Neues Testament* (Berlin, 1973) 222f.

is minimal, but the difference of the *signifiés* is immense : salvation at baptism consists either in the *reconciliation* (ϩⲱⲧⲡ) of the world (*with* the world), or in the *killing* (ϩⲱⲧⲃ) of the world (*by* the world). As long as only the Codex III version was available, it was understandable that scholars translated the text as "reconciliation" and then tried to make the best of it.[42] But now, given a choice of variants that must be made primarily on the basis of context, I cannot understand why Böhlig and Wisse nevertheless retain a reading that stands in contradiction to the context.[43] Our Berlin *Arbeitskreis* had already for some time suspected that ϩⲱⲧⲡ in Codex III was an error of transmission and now finds this to be confirmed by the reading of Codex IV.

Also quite typical of the concept of ἀπέκδυσις τοῦ σώματος τῆς σαρκός is an immediately curious statement about crucifixion of the aeons :

III ⲁⲩⲱ ⲁϥⲱϥⲧ ⲛⲛⲁⲩⲛⲁⲙⲓⲥ ⲙ̄- ⲡⲙⲛ̄ⲧϣⲟⲙⲧⲉ ⲛⲁⲓⲱⲛ

IV ⲁ[ⲩ]ⲱ ⲁϥ†ⲉⲓϭⲧ̄ ⲛ̄ⲛⲓϭⲟⲙ ⲛ̄ⲧⲉ ⲡⲓⲙⲛ̄ⲧϣⲟⲙⲧⲉ ⲛ̄ⲛⲉⲱⲛ

III ⲁⲩⲱ ⲁϥⲕⲩⲣⲟⲩ ⲉⲃⲟⲗ ϩⲓⲧⲟⲟⲧϥ̄ (p. 64:3-5)

IV ⲁⲩⲱ ⲁϥⲟⲩⲟⲥϥⲟⲩ ⲉⲃⲟⲗ ϩ̄ⲓⲧⲟⲟⲧϥ̄ (p. 75:17-20)

The phrase ⲉⲃⲟⲗ ϩⲓⲧⲟⲟⲧϥ̄ corresponds strikingly to ἐν αὐτῷ of Col 2:15. Therefore I hardly think it refers to Jesus (as the passive agent of Seth); rather it must refer either to the fact of the crucifixion of the powers of the aeons (Seth in the form of Jesus lets his earthly body be nailed to the cross by the archons and delivers it to destruction, but in reality it is the archons who are crucified and destroyed) or else to the cross (which, however, is not explicitly mentioned in the text, merely presupposed). Furthermore, the obscure expression ⲕⲩⲣⲟⲩ has to be interpreted in the light of the clear parallel ⲟⲩⲟⲥϥⲟⲩ. That is, ⲕⲩⲣⲟⲩ in this passage can no longer be taken to be a Greek verb. Rather it seems likely that the -ⲟⲩ of ⲕⲩⲣⲟⲩ is a suffix, and the rest accordingly a corrupt form of a Coptic status pronominalis (e.g., from ⲕⲱⲣϥ or ⲕⲱⲱⲣⲉ). Therefore our sentence means "he nailed the powers of the thirteen aeons to the cross and thereby (or : by it, viz., the cross) brought them to naught."

The special meaning that baptism had for the Sethians is reflected also in the fragments of *Melchizedek*. Here we find a long baptismal prayer, which in its overall structure is very reminiscent of the baptismal

---

[42] Thus already J. Doresse, *JA* 254 (1966) 405 and my own earlier article, *NTS* 16 (1969) 205.

[43] *Gospel of the Egyptians*, 30, 144 f.; cf. now also *NHLibEng* 203.

prayer at the end of the *Gospel of the Egyptians*. On p. 16 it is already under way and extends to p. 18:6. In a sense it is a highpriestly prayer, spoken (by Melchizedek) or meant to be spoken precisely on the occasion of baptism. The best preserved passage reads: "I have offered up myself to you as a sacrifice, together with those that are mine, to you yourself, (O) Father of the All, and (to) those things which you love, which have come forth from you who are holy (and) [living]. And ⟨according to⟩ the [perfect] laws, I shall pronounce my name as I receive baptism [now] (and) for ever among the living (and) holy [names], and in the [waters], Amen" (16:7-16; trans. S. Giversen and B. Pearson, *NHLibEng* [slightly modified]).

Now, many statements on earthly baptism in the Sethian texts are phrased such that it could be asked whether this baptism was actually performed, in real water, i.e., whether the passages in question do not rather point to a spiritualized cultic act. Such a hypothesis does indeed play a role in the literature on various tractates of our corpus. We cannot actually exclude the possibility that there were also groups of Gnostic Sethians who had completely sublimated their sacrament of baptism, for we must not suppose the entire Sethian community to have been completely homogeneous and fixed. But even the clearest statements in this regard do not compel us to such a conclusion. Epiphanius's statement that the so-called Archontics repudiated baptism (*Haer.* 40.2.6; ed. Holl 2. 82.27f.) possibly refers only to the baptism of the Great Church. Moreover, talk of the defilement of the water of life by non-Gnostics (CG V 84:17-23) might run along the same lines as the polemic of the Mandaeans against Christian baptism.[44]

But above all, the whole of Sethian statements on baptism, including the most sublimated and speculative ones, can conversely only be understood, I think, on the basis of a strong, deep-rooted, and obviously already traditional practice of water baptism. And so we find once again a perspective similar to the Sethians' self-understanding as offspring of Seth, a perspective that permits us to look behind the domain of Gnosticism to the possibility of a pre-Gnostic phase of Gnostic Sethianism. If the practice of baptism is really as deep-rooted in Sethianism as it seems, then one could draw a parallel between the Sethians and the Mandaeans, both being Gnosticized baptist sects, and accordingly look for the ultimate origin of Gnostic Sethianism in the

---

[44] Cf. M. Lidzbarski, *Ginzā* (Göttingen, 1925) 51.12-17.

baptist circles of Palestine. Such a conjecture has already been suggested by G. MacRae (after A. Böhlig) in the light of the *Apocalypse of Adam*.[45]

5. The Interaction of Sethianism With Christianity

Originally and essentially Gnostic Sethianism, or Sethian Gnosis, is non-Christian and even pre-Christian: pre-Christian at least in substance; even if not in chronology, about which nothing can be said. This in my opinion is incontestable; it has justly been stressed by experts again and again in the literature on the various Sethian tractates. It is plainly visible in that: most writings of our text group contain no Christian elements at all (*Three Steles of Seth, Allogenes, Marsanes, Thought of Norea*); others contain barely Christian motifs (*Zostrianus, Apocalypse of Adam*) or display only here and there a Christian veneer (*Trimorphic Protennoia, Gospel of the Egyptians*); while only a few (*Hypostasis of the Archons, Melchizedek, Apocryphon of John*) come near to being what is called Christian Gnosis. Incidentally, I should like to take this opportunity to formally retract my earlier objection to Böhlig's evaluation of the *Apocalypse of Adam* as a product of pre-Christian Gnosis. I must also retract my counter-hypothesis that the *Apocalypse of Adam* should be regarded as a late product of Gnosis;[46] this former view of mine, which now seems unjustified in the broader perspective, is still occasionally attributed to me in the literature, to my regret.

But it is not the essentially non-Christian character of Sethianism that we wish to make the object of our consideration here, but rather the phenomenon of its secondary Christianization; our intention is to utilize the Sethian text group as an attestation, an illustration, and a model of the interaction of Gnosis with Christianity. This, it is true, will give us only a onesided view of the meeting of these two world views, which are at once so similar and yet so different. For we shall only see how Sethianism reacted to Christianity. Nevertheless such a utilization of the Sethian texts may make an important contribution to the vast and complex set of problems concerning the Christianness of Gnosis: what Christian Gnosis properly is; in which spectrum of possibilities it occurs; who are the representatives of such combinations of Gnosis and Christianity or of Gnostic and Christian elements; and

---

[45] "The Apocalypse of Adam Reconsidered," *SBLSP 1972*, 577; "Adam, Apocalypse of," 10.

[46] *OLZ* 61 (1966) 31 f.

when and how it is legitimate to call their products (writings of various text types) "Christian-Gnostic."[47]

To determine the Christianness or non-Christianness of texts can be more difficult than it seems at first glance: this has been forcefully argued by R. McL. Wilson, with reference to certain texts of our group.[48] I must admit that Wilson's noncommittal handling of the problem is foreign to my own position; furthermore he exaggerates the value of the occurrence in our texts of single words of the New Testament as being an indication of Christian influence. Yet I do not want to toss the voice of his admonition to the winds. The problem to which he points truly does exist, even though for me it seems important in other places and other ways.

In the first instance I am concerned with such passages as:

Zost 48:26-28: "In that place there was also that one who suffers although he is unable to suffer."

ApocAd 76:28-77:3: "[Then there will co]me [the great] lightgiver [of Gnosis] ... and will perform signs and wonders in order to bring to naught these powers and their ruler."

ApocAd 77:16-18: "Then they will punish the flesh of that man (with death) upon whom the holy spirit has come."

The last-quoted passage, for example, occasioned G. MacRae, because of the non-Christian character that the document as a whole displays, to undertake a forced and, I believe, unsatisfactory search for parallels and possible conceptual models in the Jewish domain.[49] In my opinion, such a procedure and the approach that it presupposes is no longer adequate to the complicated textual relationships. Comprehension of the deep-rooted non-Christian character of Sethian Gnosis as a whole frees us also to objectively examine and deal with the individual passages that are not in accord with the overall conclusion, and if it seems correct, to decide that secondary Christian influence is present.[50] On the other hand one may not infringe upon the sovereignty of the individual texts, but rather one must guarantee equal

---

[47] An important aspect of this problem has been recently treated by K.-W. Tröger, "Die Passion Jesu Christi in der Gnosis nach den Schriften von Nag Hammadi" (Th.D. diss., Humboldt Universität, Berlin [DDR], 1978); this area of research has also been of particular interest to K. Koschorke.

[48] "Gospel of the Egyptians," 243-50; "The Trimorphic Protennoia," *Gnosis and Gnosticism* (NHS 8; Leiden, 1977) 50-54.

[49] "Apocalypse of Adam Reconsidered," 575.

[50] Cf. for example Tröger, "Passion Jesu Christi," 192, 290.

rights for all of them! By this I mean that it is not fair to assert, e.g., that 1 Cor 2:8 and the well-known passages from Colossians, Ephesians, and the fourth gospel are best understood against a background of Gnosis, and then to deny that Christianity may be the best perspective for understanding Gnostic passages like the ones quoted above from *Zostrianus* and the *Apocalypse of Adam*. At least, I could not do so in good conscience.

In my earlier paper I noted two points in the Sethian system, with two associated modalities, where Sethianism can be—indeed was—most easily combined with Christian concepts.[51] Not long ago, our Berlin *Arbeitskreis* was investigating the first of these, a propos of the secondary Christianization of the *Trimorphic Protennoia*, whereby the divine Autogenes (properly and originally the celestial Adam, for Sethians) is combined with the Christian concept of the preexistence of Christ. Specifically, it was asked whether the anointing, before the beginning of time, of the Autogenes with the father's ⲘⲚⲦⲬⲢⲤ (goodness, *khrēstotēs*) was already a feature of the pre-Christian stage or whether it owed its existence (or at least its elaboration) within the Sethian system to Christian influence alone. (The motif in question occurs in *TriProt* 37:30-33; *ApocryJn* BG 30:14-31:1 and parallels; Irenaeus *Haer.* 1.29.1 ["et videntem Patrem lumen hoc unxisse illud sua benignitate, ut perfectum fieret. Hunc autem dicunt esse Christum"]; *GEgypt* (CG III 44:22-24 = IV 55:11-14.) The matter is difficult and it is still an open question. At this point I think that the most obvious answer, and the one that accords best with the texts, is to say that in the Sethian system the pre-Christian form of this motif was the transfer of the goodness (*khrēstotēs*) of the Invisible Spirit to the divine Autogenes, enabling the latter to discharge his office of ruler of the universe and redeemer of those who belong to him (cf. *Allog* 58:6-15; *Zost* 131:14f.); and that this served as the connecting link with the motif of annointing, which from the way it occurs in the above-mentioned passages of the *Trimorphic Protennoia*, *Apocryphon of John*, and *Gospel of the Egyptians* must represent Christian influence. The mere word *sōtēr*, "savior," on the other hand, which occurs in the two passages from *Allogenes* and *Zostrianus*, does not seem to me to require in itself a Christian background for those passages.

Despite one's first impression that the *Trimorphic Protennoia* only

---

[51] Cf. my "Sethianische(s) System," 169-71.

displays quite superficial and occasional Christianization[52] our work
on this tractate has shown that the entire passage 48:35-49:22 must be
seen in this perspective. This passage seems to have the aim of describing
for a second time the descent of the Logos as redeemer through the
spheres of the archons and his accommodation to the inhabitants
of those spheres. But closer investigation shows that this repetition has
the additional aim of giving an etiological account of certain well-
known honorific titles that Christianity had conferred upon Jesus, viz.,
"Christ," "Son of God," "Son of Man," and possibly "Angel";
and of shedding critical light upon them from the viewpoint of
Sethian Gnosis. At any rate, it is only as a polemic against ordinary
Christianity that this difficult text in all its nuances becomes fully understandable to exegesis. Thus here it is already presupposed that the
Logos has "put on" Jesus, a view that is explicitly stated only
later (50:12-15). Only the Gnostics recognized Jesus to be the garment
worn by their beloved brother who had descended to them; the archons,
and Christians dominated by them, were completely wrong in their
understanding of the descent.[53]

That the relationship of Sethianism to Christianity is not limited to
the possibility of direct confrontation (i.e., rejection or acceptance) but
can have had a deeper dimension is also clear in the *Trimorphic
Protennoia*, just as it was in our discussion of baptismal ideology in the
Gospel of the Egyptians. For, the understanding of baptism in the
Gospel of the Egyptians as ἀπέκδυσις τοῦ σώματος τῆς σαρκός "putting
off the body of flesh," has its real parallel not in Col 2:11-15, but in
the source of this passage, that is, the hymn that is quoted there.
Similarly the numerous parallels (noted by Gesine Schenke in her
dissertation) of the *Trimorphic Protennoia* with Col 1:15ff. on the
one hand and with the fourth gospel on the other hand suggest a
relationship of our Sethian text not to these writings, but to their
respective Gnostic sources—at any rate, this aspect is the more
important one. J. M. Robinson has called attention to a similar deep-
level connection between the coming of the savior in the *Apocalypse
of Adam* and, above all, the beginning of the gospel of Mark.[54]

Sethian concepts and texts receive their most "Christian" appearance
when they are provided with a Christian framework. In the case of

---

[52] Cf. Tröger, ed., *Gnosis und NT*, 75 f.; *TLZ* 99 (1974) 733.

[53] Cf. G. Schenke, "Protennoia," 128 f.

[54] "On the Gattung of Mark (and John)," *Jesus and Man's Hope* 1 (Pittsburgh, 1970)
118-26.

the *Hypostasis of the Archons* the Christian framework is very thin (at the beginning there is a quotation from Paul [Eph 6:12], and at the end, the term "son"), and it functions in a very forced and unnatural way. This framework stands in distinct contrast to the few, light Christian accents that have been imposed upon the relatively extensive contents; practically, these accents consist only of the preference given to the term "*Holy* Spirit"[55] and the presupposition that the predicted entry of the "perfect" or "true" man (also "that seed," cf. Gen 3:15) into a human body will be unique.

The same discrepancy between framework and contents appears even more clearly in the most "Christian" of all Sethian writings, the *Apocryphon of John*. By means of the framework, in which John the son of Zebedee receives instructions from the ascended Jesus, the ancient editor gives the writing a New Testament coloring. Thus the framework is scarcely Gnostic in its tendency. Reminiscences of Christian, and especially of Jewish Christian, traditions can be detected. But the framework, which is so distinctly Christian, has no clearly discernible continuation in the interior of the writing, except in the simple addresses to the revealer in the dialogue passages. But in themselves these dialogue passages of the second half of the text must be kept separate literarily from the events of the frame story. Rather, what is found is a fictitious conversation, with no specifically Christian traits, between a revealer and an ideal recipient of revelation. Though in the eyes of the ancient editor Jesus speaks also in the interior of the *Apocryphon of John* and it is John whose questions he answers, in terms of the history of tradition the revealer who speaks in the interior of the writing, especially in the paraphrase and parody of Genesis, has first of all to be distinguished from Jesus who speaks in the frame story. And it is not redaction history but the history of tradition that is fruitful in the exegesis of the *Apocryphon of John*. This has been worked out convincingly by A. Werner in his dissertation on the *Apocryphon of John*.[56] Werner also makes us raise the question of whether the speaker in the interior of the document is actually male. This is a fascinating question, for the possibility that the speaker was originally a female persona sheds light upon some features that are still obscure, especially in the context of the other Sethian writings. In particular we would

---

[55] Applied to three different personae: (1) the spirit of truth that dwells within the Gnostics; (2) Barbelo; (3) the highest deity, the Invisible Spirit.

[56] See above note 15.

have here an important connection with the *Hypostasis of the Archons.*
For the first half of the *Apocryphon of John* there is also evidence of the
artificiality of the Christian framework in the parallel of Irenaeus
Haer. 1.29. This chapter of Irenaeus excerpts from a Sethian writing
that did not yet have such a framework, and displays only a weak sign
of contact with Christianity when it endows (typically) the Sethian
son figure with the name of "Christ." This alone constitutes the
Christianness of the content of the revelation that "Jesus" transmits
in the *Apocryphon of John.*

From all these facts, one could arrive at an impression which I
should now like to formulate as a working hypothesis: Gnostic
Sethianism not only is in substance pre-Christian, but also in its essence
is so autonomous and non-Christian that when it encountered and
coexisted with Christianity, despite the attraction that Christianity
exerted here and there, a genuine combination with Christianity did not
result, and indeed it could not. In the domain of Sethianism there is no
Christian Gnosis worthy of the name.

6. THE ENCOUNTER OF SETHIANISM WITH PHILOSOPHY

It is interesting that our group of Sethian texts not only shows the
reaction of Sethianism to the religious challenge of Christianity, but
also, just as distinctly, its reaction to late-antique philosophy. This
took place in the form of an effort towards conciliation, or even
affiliation, with that philosophy. The specific phenomenon of Gnostic
Sethianism ranges from one extreme limit of Gnosis to the other.
The most exciting aspect of this perspective is that even the
Gnostics in Rome who were members or visitors of the school of
Plotinus, and who became the occasion for the only polemical
work that Plotinus ever wrote (*Ennead* 2.9 [= 33]), were apparently none
other than Sethians, or more exactly, a particular branch of Sethians.
Now, the tendency of Gnosis towards philosophy as such is well
known.[57] But that also Sethianism, which is so deeply rooted in
mythology and even devoted to magic in no small measure, was
caught up by this tendency, and that it was just this of all
branches of Gnosis that could challenge Neoplatonism, is fairly a
matter of astonishment.

The first grounds for this view are about as old as the Nag
Hammadi find itself. The two writings *Zostrianus* and *Allogenes,*

---

[57] See recently B. Aland, "Gnosis und Philosophie," *Proceedings of the International
Colloquium on Gnosticism, Stockholm, 1973,* 34-73.

or more precisely, what was formerly known of them, immediately called forth comparisons with Porphyry's *Life of Plotinus*, chap. 16,[58] and identification of the two new writings with those mentioned by Porphyry.[59] But the word "and" occurred not only between the names Zoroaster and Zostrianus, but also between Allogenes and Mesus, and seemed to cause no small difficulty; also there certainly once existed many writings under the names of Allogenes (cf. Epiphanius *Haer*. 39.5.1; 40.2.2)—and accordingly perhaps also under the unfamiliar name of Zostrianus; and therefore it was possible to remain sceptical and disinterested in the face of these identifications. To this moment the effort to establish such direct external interconnections, even if now based on accurate knowledge of the new material, seems doubtful to me. I have in mind the attempts of J. M. Robinson and B. A. Pearson to show that also the *Three Steles of Seth* (as an apocalypse of Dositheus) and *Marsanes* were in the hands of Plotinus's Gnostic adversaries in Rome, and that these writings are included in Porphyry's reference to ἀποκαλύψεις ... ἄλλων τοιού-των.[60]

These external considerations would be important only if it were possible to show that the complete anti-Gnostic writing of Plotinus, that is, the original treatise consisting of *Enneads* 3.8, 5.8, 5.5, and 2.9 (= 30-33), were clearly directed against distinct positions that are represented in the pertinent Nag Hammadi writings (*Zostrianus, Allogenes, Three Steles of Seth, Marsanes*). To our surprise, in fact, it suddenly became clear to us that this is actually the case as we undertook the critical evaluation of a book by C. Elsas on this topic: it is the newest and actually the most important treatment of the identity of the Gnostics opposed by Plotinus, a book in which the author himself, however, comes to a different result, which if correct would be devastating for the above-mentioned attempts at identifying

---

[58] γεγόνασι δὲ κατ' αὐτὸν τῶν Χριστιανῶν πολλοὶ μὲν καὶ ἄλλοι, αἱρετικοὶ δὲ ἐκ τῆς παλαιᾶς φιλοσοφίας ἀνηγμένοι οἱ περὶ 'Αδέλφιον καὶ 'Ακυλῖνον, οἳ τὰ 'Αλεξάνδρου τοῦ Λίβυος καὶ Φιλοκώμου καὶ Δημοστράτου τοῦ Λυδοῦ συγγράμματα πλεῖστα κεκτημένοι ἀποκαλύψεις τε προφέροντες Ζωροάστρου καὶ Ζωστριανοῦ καὶ Νικοθέου καὶ 'Αλλογενοῦς καὶ Μέσου καὶ ἄλλων τοιούτων πολλοὺς ἐξηπάτων καὶ αὐτοὶ ἠπατημένοι, ὡς δὴ τοῦ Πλάτωνος εἰς τὸ βάθος τῆς νοητῆς οὐσίας οὐ πελάσαν-τος.

[59] Cf. above all, J. Doresse, "Les apocalypses de Zoroastre, de Zostrien, de Nicothée," *Coptic Studies in Honor of W. E. Crum* (Boston, 1950) 255-63.

[60] Robinson, "The Three Steles of Seth and Plotinus," 132 f.; B. A. Pearson, "The Tractate Marsanes (NHC X) and the Platonic Tradition," *Gnosis, Festschrift für Hans Jonas* (Göttingen, 1978) 375.

those four Nag Hammadi documents.[61] Elsas first gives an immediately plausible and instructive elaboration of the opponents' position(s) against which Plotinus directs himself. Then follows a comparison of the individual motifs of the opponents' position(s) with a selected field of concepts from the intellectual and spiritual environment. As a grid, Elsas uses a catalogue of graded single motifs; this grid would be very useful in recording the Gnostic world view as a whole, but used as a means of identifying a particular variety of Gnosis or Gnostic system, where only the distinctive features are in fact relevant, it is a source of problems. And this is not without bearing upon the results. The utilization of motif analysis for the total assessment of Plotinus's adversaries is in principle carried out by reversing the direction of analysis, i.e., by synthesis. Just as analysis traces the single motifs back to various areas, so by synthesis the total phenomenon under investigation is held to have grown together out of those different areas. Thus Elsas himself comes to the syncretistic—and therefore indefinable—character of the Gnosis of Plotinus's opponents. If, however, on the basis of the same material the distinctive features of the opponents' teaching are taken as clues to the identity of Plotinus's Gnostic opponents, one arrives at precisely the Sethianism that we see represented in the group of texts under discussion.[62] In this connection also particular terms gain a considerable importance, especially the triad παροικήσεις, ἀντίτυποι, μετάνοιαι (cf. *Ennead* 2.9.6.2;[63] and the appearance of these terms in *Zostrianus* [e.g., on p. 8][64]). This is, by the way, only the "second edition"—though with a new look—of an older hypothesis, held especially by C. Schmidt, of the essentially Sethian character of the Gnostics opposed by Plotinus.[65]

In this perspective many things, both general and specific, in certain writings of our text group can be seen in a new light. In the *Three Steles of Seth*, for example, it can be discovered that dualism, considered so typical of Gnosticism, is curiously missing. Now, surely this is first of all a function of the liturgical character of the

---

[61] *Neuplatonische und gnostische Weltablehnung in der Schule Plotins* (RGVV 34; Berlin, 1975).

[62] Cf. *TLZ* 102 (1977) 644-46.

[63] Elsas, *Weltablehnung*, 74.

[64] Cf. J. H. Sieber, "An Introduction to the Tractate Zostrianus from Nag Hammadi," *NovT* 15 (1973) 238; Tröger, "Passion Jesu Christi," 191.

[65] Cf. C. Schmidt, *Plotins Stellung zum Gnostizismus und kirchlichen Christentum* (TU N.F. 5/4; Leipzig, 1901); Schmidt/Till, *Koptisch-Gnostische Schriften* 1, XXXIII f.

text. In a Gnostic liturgy of ascension it is quite understandable that the orientation towards a destination above could result in silence about dualism, even if dualism were presupposed. On the other hand, already the one-sided emphasis upon "whither," while leaving out of consideration "whence," can be suspected to be an attempt to move *away from* properly dualistic Gnosis and *towards* a more strongly monistic, philosophic world view. B. A. Pearson has noted a similar subsiding of dualism in *Marsanes* and *Allogenes* and draws in fact the same conclusion.[66] It could perhaps even be conjectured that to this tendency is also related a transformation in the domain of mythology, as in the attribution of the origin of the lower world to no less a being than the lightgiver Eleleth (*Gospel of the Egyptians, Trimorphic Protennoia*). Without intending to contest the relevance of these phenomena in our present context, it must be noted that as regards dualism there is another way to handle the question once we look beyond the borders of Sethianism to the whole complex of Gnosis. The Nag Hammadi Library has bestowed upon us so many Gnostic writings in which dualism plays no special role that there is reason to ask whether our usual premises are really correct: is dualism actually so essential to Gnosis as one has always said, and if so, which kind?

Not least, there is a considerable gain of importance for the terminology (already striking) of the Sethian writings in question. In a high degree, *Zostrianus, Allogenes*, the *Three Steles of Seth*, and *Marsanes* speak the same language as the philosophy of that day. J. M. Robinson has emphasized the especially interesting "trinity" of Being, Intelligence, and Life (ὕπαρξις, νοῦς, ζωή and equivalents) and interpreted it as being such a connecting link.[67] It is the striking term of Nonbeing (ἀνούσιος/ⲀⲧⲞⲨⲤⲒⲀ etc.) and its relevance within the present perspective to which B. A. Pearson has devoted particular attention.[68] M. Tardieu has investigated the whole, extensive philosophical concept system of the *Three Steles of Seth*, isolated it, and brought it into order. Now, when he claims that this philosophical system *underlies* the *Three Steles of Seth* (it is a "structure métaphysique sous-jacente"), this accords well with our way of seeing things, provided one understands Tardieu or uses his results in such a way that in the *Three Steles of Seth*, within the framework of a liturgy of ascension,

---

[66] "The Tractate Marsanes," 383 f.
[67] "The Three Steles of Seth and Plotinus," 140-42.
[68] "The Tractate Marsanes," 381-84.

it is still Sethian Gnosis that is seen to be articulated in this striking use of a coherent philosophical concept system.[69]

For, however philosophic our texts may give themselves out to be, however much they may have been able to seduce students of philosophy and to challenge philosophical masters, they nevertheless remain Sethian Gnosis. On this score, too, both in its encounter and in its coexistence with philosophy, Sethianism did not overstep the categorical boundary line distinguishing it from the neighboring phenomenon in the history of mind.

---

[69] "Trois Stèles de Seth," 560-67.

TRIADE UND TRINITÄT IN DEN SCHRIFTEN VON NAG HAMMADI

VON

ALEXANDER BÖHLIG

Die Erfassung der Welt in der Zahl ist eine der großartigsten Erfindungen des Griechentums, wie gerade die moderne Physik bestätigt. In der Zeit der Klassiker ist von Platon im Timaios in dieser Hinsicht ganz Bedeutendes geleistet worden. Doch hat die hellenistische Zeit die Kenntnis der allgemeinen Bildung auf dem Gebiet der Mathematik sehr absinken lassen, so daß ein Werk wie das des Theon von Smyrna[1] nötig wurde, in dem die Anfangsgründe der Arithmetik, Musik und Astronomie, soweit man sie zum Verständnis Platons brauchte, geboten wurden. Auch in der mythologischen Form gnostischer Literatur findet sich Arithmologie, allerdings in einer schlagwortartig und spielerisch wirkenden Weise. Immerhin wird an gewissen Stellen auch das Problem der Zahl angesprochen. Man ist sich klar, daß die Zahl "Eins" nur dann Zahl ist, wenn "Zwei" oder "Drei" folgen. Diese Zahlen artikuliert auch die Sprache durch ihre Formenbildung. Sie besitzt in gewissen Idiomen, nicht nur in semitischen, mit der Dualform eine Möglichkeit, die Zweiheit auszudrücken. Damit beginnt, wie in den "Stelen des Seth" [3StSeth] von der Barbelo gesagt wird, das eigentliche Zählen.[2] Die Dreiheit dient als schlechthinniges Mittel zur Formulierung der Mehrzahl, was z.B. die Bezeichnung des Plurals durch drei Striche im Ägyptischen klar erkennen läßt. Der Plural, oder besser die Dreiheit, ist der Ausdruck für die kleinste Form einer produktiven Familie: Vater—Mutter—Kind. Damit kann man auch die Teilung Maskulinum—Femininum—Neutrum verbinden. Maskulinum und Femininum treten als handelnde Personen dem Neutrum gegenüber, wobei ursprünglich belebt und leblos nebeneinander stehen (man denke an die zweiendigen Adiectiva im Griechischen!), danach das Belebte in Maskulinum und Femininum geteilt wird. Auch die Zeit wird als

---

[1] Autor des 2. Jh's n. Chr. Ausgaben: E. Hiller (Leipzig, 1878); J. Dupuis (Paris, 1892, mit französischer Übersetzung).
[2] NH VII 123, 7 ff.

eine pluralische oder, genauer gesagt, triadische Größe dargestellt. Von der Gegenwart aus schaut der sich seiner Existenz bewußt gewordene Mensch zurück in die Vergangenheit und voraus in die Zukunft.

Ist die Drei auf diese Weise als eine in die Breite und die Länge führende Größe aufgefaßt, so kann sie durch die Steigerung auch als Form der Intensivierung dienen. So zeigt beim Adjektiv der Komparativ an, daß etwas qualitativ besser oder schlechter ist als das im Positiv Genannte. Der Superlativ als Form oder ein ihm entsprechender Ausdruck heben eine oder mehrere Größen aus einer pluralischen Gruppe heraus. Eine ähnliche Qualifizierung bedeutet die Kennzeichnung eines Adjektivs durch die Vorsilbe τρισ- „dreifach". Unter Umständen wird sie noch dadurch verdeutlicht, daß die drei Bezeichnungen dieser besonders gearteten Größe aufgeführt werden; so z.B. im Ägypterevangelium [GEgypt], wenn das dreifachmännliche Kind mit den drei Namen seiner Bestandteile und einem zusammenfassenden Namen (Seth) benannt wird.[3] So drückt Dreifachheit besondere Qualität durch Dreiheit in Einheit, also Dreifaltigkeit, aus.[4]

Dort, wo nach der Einheit Gottes, sei es im Sinne der Immanenz, sei es der Transzendenz, gestrebt wird, liegt es nahe, eine Triade zur Trinität zu machen. So steht es gerade im Christentum, das vom Monotheismus beherrscht ist, während das mythologische Denken des Gnostizismus eher einen zum Monotheismus strebenden organisierten Polytheismus bietet, der zwar die mythologische Ausdrucksform deutlich hervorhebt, aber das trinitarische Element als tieferen Inhalt doch durchaus erkennen läßt.[5]

Das Christentum besitzt die Trinität Vater—Sohn—Geist als charakteristisches Merkmal,[6] der Gnosticismus bietet sehr häufig die Dreiheit Vater— Mutter— Sohn. Die religionsgeschichtliche Forschung möchte nun nachweisen, daß die christliche Trinität aus der vorderorientalischen, speziell aber aus der ägyptischen Triade entstanden ist.[7]

---

[3] Vgl. A. Böhlig und F. Wisse, eds., *The Gospel of the Egyptians* (Leiden, 1975) 43 ff.

[4] So ist die Vierheit der Namen zu erklären. Zugleich wird Seth der Platz des Sohnes Gottes eingeräumt. Es ist fraglich, ob Seth eine sekundäre Hinzufügung zu diesem Traditionsstück ist. Auf jeden Fall wurde er nachgetragen, als diese Schrift als Sethevangelium redigiert wurde.

[5] Das Christentum mußte sich vor der Gefahr hüten, sich in Mythologumena zu verlieren. Der Gnostizismus akzeptierte zwar diese, war aber doch auf ihre Überwindung angelegt.

[6] Vgl. die Regula fidei.

[7] S. Morenz, *Die Begegnung Europas mit Ägypten* (Zürich, 1969) 89; ders., *Ägyptische Religion* (Stuttgart, 1960) 150 ff., 270 ff.; W. Westendorf, "Zweiheit, Dreiheit und Einheit in der altägyptischen Theologie", *ZÄS* 100 (1974) 136-141.

Das würde voraussetzen, bereits auf die Vorstellung vom Sohne Gottes und des Heiligen Geistes hätten die in der Formel Vater-Mutter-Sohn zusammengefaßten Gedanken maßgeblichen Einfluß gehabt. Wo aber im Gnostizismus die christliche und die pagane Formel begegnen, machen sie sich gegenseitig Schwierigkeiten.[8] Sie treten in Gegensatz zueinander und müssen ausgeglichen werden. Es kann deshalb kaum angenommen werden, daß eine Entstehung der christlichen aus der paganen Formel vorliegt. Das Umgekehrte scheidet sowieso aus, infolge des älteren Vorkommens der paganen Vorstellung: man denke nur an den Tempelbezirk von Baalbek (Jupiter, Venus, Merkur)[9] oder an Osiris, Isis und Horus in Ägypten.[10] Religionsgeschichtliche Abhängigkeiten, die etwa im Marienkult den Isiskult als Wurzel erkennen lassen, dürfen nicht für die Entwicklung des Trinitätsglaubens in Anspruch genommen werden. Denn Maria wird ja zusätzlich zur Trinität hinzugefügt.[11] Ist die christliche Formel aber als abhängig festzustellen, so muß erst einmal gefragt werden, ob sie nicht auch anders erklärt werden kann. Und mindestens muß untersucht werden, ob die trinitarische Formel der Alten Kirche die gleiche wie die der Urkirche war.

Die Formel der Urkirche ist kein festes Theologumenon oder auch Mythologumenon wie die Vorstellung von Vater-Mutter-Sohn in Paganismus und Gnostizismus. Vielmehr ist die Stellung des Geistes noch nicht so in ein Schema gefügt wie in der späteren katholischen Kirche. Immerhin dürfte aber ein besonders wichtiges Factum sein, daß Jesus nicht von einer göttlichen Mutter erzeugt ist, sondern, wie M. Hengel gezeigt hat, als Sohn Gottes angesehen wird:[12] Röm 1,3f. "der geworden ist aus dem Samen Davids dem Fleische nach, der eingesetzt ist zum Sohne Gottes in Macht dem Geist der Heiligkeit nach auf Grund der Auferstehung der Toten". Diesen Glauben konnte die Gemeinde der heiligen Schrift des Alten Testamentes entnehmen. Jesus als der leidende Gerechte konnte als Gottessohn angesehen werden. Wenn man die Weiterentwicklung hin zu den Vorstellungen von

---

[8] Das zeigt sich darin, daß in manchen gnostischen Schriften vom Heiligen Geist kaum die Rede ist. Das Auftauchen des Heiligen Geistes ist ein Indiz dafür, wie christlich die jeweilige Schrift ist.

[9] Vgl. H. Gese, *Die Religionen Altsyriens* (Stuttgart, 1970) 222 ff.

[10] H. Bonnet, *Reallexikon der ägyptischen Religionsgeschichte* (2. Aufl.; Berlin, 1971) 326 ff.

[11] So steht die Mutter Maria in Gebeten erst nach den Erzengeln. Vgl. W. E. Crum und H. I. Bell, *Wadi Sarga* (Kopenhagen, 1922) 59 ff.

[12] M. Hengel, *Der Sohn Gottes* (Tübingen, 1975).

Präexistenz, Schöpfungsmittlerschaft und Sendung in die Welt als theologische Leistung des griechischsprechenden Judenchristentums betrachten kann, so benötigt man keine hellenistische These vom Ursprung der Sohn-Gottes-Lehre, soweit nicht sowieso hellenistische Gedanken in Palästina kursierten.[13] Dem griechischsprechenden Judenchristentum verdankt dann aber Paulus und die Urkirche überhaupt die Vorstellung vom Pneuma. Wie die Septuaginta das aramäische rūḥā in griechisches πνεῦμα übersetzt hat, so haben auch diese Judenchristen in πνεῦμα kaum noch ein Femininum gesehen. Dieser Geist ist für sie und dann für Paulus eine Größe, in der sich Gott offenbart, so daß er sogar parallel zu Christus stehen kann. Ja, er kann bei Johannes gewissermaßen an die Stelle des kommenden Christus treten, wenn er als Paraklet, der Geist der Wahrheit, erscheint.[14] Doch das Neue Testament weist auch bereits Stellen auf, an denen Vater, Sohn und Geist zusammen als Dreiheit zu finden sind, so in der Tauformel „und taufet sie im Namen des Vaters und des Sohnes und des Heiligen Geistes"[15] oder im Briefschluß „die Gnade unseres Herrn Jesu Christi und die Liebe Gottes und die Gemeinschaft des Heiligen Geistes sei mit euch allen".[16]

Um die Triadenvorstellung bei den Sethianern und ein etwaiges Trinitätsdenken zu erarbeiten, muß man Sethianer und Barbelognostiker zusammenfassen, da ja die Schriften, in denen Seth begegnet, auch weitgehend die göttliche Mutter, die Barbelo, kennen. Es ist überhaupt die Frage, ob jede Schrift, die den Namen Seth enthält, auch als wirklich sethianisch bezeichnet werden kann. Somit können barbelognostische und sethianische Schriften schwer gegeneinander abgegrenzt werden.[17]

Den Schriften, die eine oder mehrere Triaden von Vater, Mutter und Sohn enthalten, sind solche gegenüberzustellen, in denen eine

---

[13] Vgl. M. Hengel, a.a.O. 104 ff.; ders., "Zwischen Jesus und Paulus. Die "Hellenisten", die "Sieben" und Stephanus", *ZTK* 72 (1975) 151-206.

[14] Joh 14,16. 26; 15,26; 16,7.

[15] Mt 28,19.

[16] 2 Kor 13,13.

[17] Das hängt auch mit der Entstehung der Sammlung von Nag Hammadi zusammen. Man kann sie ja schon lange nicht mehr wie J. Doresse als sethianische Bibliothek betrachten. Aber immerhin liegen starke sethianische Einflüsse vor. Doch scheinen in diesen Kreisen sowohl diese als auch barbelognostische Strömungen neben valentinianischen und hermetischen wirksam gewesen zu sein. Vielleicht hat sogar der Manichäismus bei der Entstehung der späteren Schriften Pate gestanden. Darüber ausführlicher an anderer Stelle! Aber es geht nicht allein darum, daß die Sammlung aus verschiedenartigen Büchern besteht, sondern es fällt auf, daß innerhalb der einzelnen Schriften verschiedenartige Strömungen zu finden sind.

Kombination von Vater-Mutter-Sohn mit dem christlichen Schema Vater-Sohn-Geist vorhanden ist, so daß sich Vater-Geist-Sohn ergibt. Wenn dann ein Text von der Jungfrau des heiligen Geistes spricht, sieht man hier deutlich, wie weit der Übergang fortgeschritten ist.[18]

Neben solchen triadischen Spekulationen ist zu erwägen, wie weit trinitarische Vorstellungen auf dieser Ebene zu beobachten sind. In solchen Fällen ist die Mutter mit Vater und Sohn identisch.

Voll verstehen kann man das Material aber nur, wenn man auch einen Blick auf die Schriften von Nag Hammadi wirft, die nicht sethianisch, barbelognostisch oder ophitisch sind, sondern von christlicher Sicht her auf gnostische Weise zu denken versuchen. Hier geht es besonders um Schriften, die dem Valentinianismus nahestehen oder direkt angehören.

Wie kann nun der religionsgeschichtliche Vorgang vom Zusammenhang Ursache — Wirkung aus beurteilt werden? Es gibt folgende Möglichkeiten:

1. Dem Christentum mit seiner Lehre von einer Trinität Vater-Sohn-Geist steht ein Gnostizismus gegenüber, der das Mythologumenon Vater-Mutter-Sohn als ein Theologumenon seiner Metaphysik verwendet. Dieser Gnostizismus bezieht die Figur des präexistenten Christus in sein System auf mehr oder weniger geschickte oder intensive Weise ein. Auch die Lehre vom Heiligen Geist ist in verschiedenem Grad wirksam. Man möchte annehmen, daß ein gnostisches Denken, das sich parasitär[19] zunächst dem Heidentum angelagert hatte, nun dem Christentum gegenübertritt, um es ganz in seinem Geiste umzugestalten. Insbesondere zeigen die gnostischen Schriften, die noch deutlich eine pagane Formel als ursprüngliche Denkform des Textes erkennen lassen, wie man versucht, sowohl Jesus als auch Christus oder auch Jesus Christus zu usurpieren.

2. Daneben gibt es christliche Theologen, die von dem gnostischen Denken stark beeinflußt waren, so daß ihr Zentrum zwar Jesus Christus ist, dieser Heiland aber mit dem gnostischen Belehrer der Menschen identifiziert wurde und sie selbst in der Form und Ausgestaltung ihrer Werke zu Gnostikern wurden, zumal unterschwellig mythologische Elemente bei ihnen auch zu erkennen sind.[20]

3. Wollte man einen Weg ohne die vorherige Existenz eines gnostischen Denkens annehmen, wäre der christliche Glaube auf die heidni-

---

[18] Dies ist der Fall in der Schrift NH II,5 [OnOrgWld]; s.u.

[19] Vgl. A. Böhlig, "Zur Struktur gnostischen Denkens", *NTS* 24 (1978) 496-509.

[20] Besonders am Evangelium Veritatis [GTr] zu sehen.

sche Formel gestoßen und die Auseinandersetzung zwischen Christentum und Paganismus geführt worden. Das würde aber schlecht die Notwendigkeit christianisierter gnostischer Schriften erklären.[21] Woher käme dann das spezifisch Gnostische? Aus dem Christentum doch wohl nicht, wenn es sich so gegensätzlich zu ihm stellt. Sondern doch wohl aus einem Untergrund gnostischen Denkens, der sich die paganen Vorstellungen zur Darstellung seiner Modelle dienstbar gemacht hat.

Bei der Behandlung der Triade Vater-Mutter-Sohn ist es zweckmäßig, zunächst die Stellen zu interpretieren, in denen diese Formel eindeutig begegnet. Die Fälle mythologischer Ausmalung, die nicht nur exzessive Darstellung ist, sondern manchmal auch durch den Versuch bedingt scheint, die Vorstellungen vom höchsten Gott und dem Sohne Gottes schärfer herauszuarbeiten, können erst danach erfolgreich behandelt werden.

Bereits zuvor soll aber vermerkt werden, daß oft auch für die einzelnen Figuren der Triade die Dreifachheit ausgesprochen wird. Man kann vielleicht annehmen, daß Triade — Dreifachheit — Trinität in einem kausalen Verhältnis zueinander stehen. Die Dreifachheit der einzelnen göttlichen Figur stellt ihre superlativische Steigerung dar. Es kann sogar vorkommen, daß ihr drei Namen beigelegt werden und sie somit in drei weitere Figuren zerlegt wird, worauf oben schon hingewiesen wurde. Das gilt z.B. im Ägypterevangelium für das dreifachmännliche Kind, das die Namen Telmäel, Eli, Machar erhält und dann als Einheit durch einen vierten Namen, Seth, zusammengefaßt wird. Damit ist bereits das Zusammenfallen von Steigerung und Trinität gegeben. Lag es nicht nahe, mit Hilfe einer mythologischen Vorstellung, die eine Triade bot, die Dreifachheit der Gottheit und die darin liegende Steigerung vom Gesichtspunkt der Familie und der in ihr vorhandenen Geschlossenheit von Vater-Mutter-Sohn aus allseitig zu beleuchten, zumal diese Triade ja von der orientalischen Religion her allgemein bekannt war?

Die heidnische mythologische Formel für die Trias unterliegt in der Zeit des Gnostizismus einer Interpretatio graeca. Der Vater ist der große unsichtbare Geist. Die Mutter ist ἔννοια oder πρόνοια. Der Sohn ist der Logos. Schon in der Bezeichnung „großer unsichtbarer Geist" kommt dessen Transzendierung zum Ausdruck. Daß man

---

[21] Die Christianisierung von Schriften wie der titellosen Schrift des Codex II (II,5), des Ägypterevangeliums, des Johannesapokryphons [ApocryJh], der dreifachen Protennoia [TriProt] erscheint mir sicher. Freilich darf man nicht die letzte Redaktion für die eigentliche Schrift halten.

TRIADE UND TRINITÄT 623

diesen Geist πνεῦμα nennt, geht wohl auf die Stoa zurück, die in seiner Einheit von Stoff, Kraft, Leben, Form und Geist das πρῶτον αἴτιον sieht.[22] Dieses πνεῦμα, das alles von ihm Gewollte durchweht, hat keine eigene Gestalt. Somit ist es nicht schwer, bei einer Transzendierung in ihm den negativ beschriebenen fernen Gott zu sehen. Denn bei aller Transzendierung steht doch das πνεῦμα immer noch mit den πνεύματα, den Geistern in der Welt, in engster Verbindung.[23] Pneumatiker zu sein, ist die Voraussetzung des Heiles. Aber auch die Auffassung des πνεῦμα als Mittlerwesen, die ebenfalls in gnostizistischer Kosmologie begegnet,[24] ist eine Vorstellung, die auf den Gebrauch des Wortes in der griechischen Medizin, Philosophie und Religion zurückgeht.[25]

Der höchste Gott lebt in einer Lichtwelt. Die dritte "Stele des Seth" faßt die diesbezüglichen Vorstellungen stark gräzisierend zusammen:[26] "Du Ungeborener! Aus dir stammen die Ewigen und die Äonen, die Vollkommenen als Gesamtheit und die einzelnen Vollkommenen. Wir preisen dich, der du keine οὐσία hast, dich Existenz, die vor den Existenzen ist, dich erstes Wesen, das vor den Wesen ist, dich Vater der Göttlichkeit und Lebendigkeit, dich Erschaffer des Nus, dich Spender von Gutem, dich Spender von Seligkeit."

Der hierbei erwähnten Erschaffung des Nus entspricht in der Mythologie die Erschaffung der weiblichen Größe, der Mutter. Sie wird in den verschiedenen gnostischen Schriften bzw. Systemen verschieden benannt. So heißt sie im Manichäismus "der große Geist, die Mutter des Lebens (bzw. der Lebendigen)".[27] Daß hier Mutter und Geist identifiziert wird, darf auf die Schöpfungsgeschichte zurückgeführt werden: "Der Geist Gottes schwebte über den Wassern".[28] Ganz abgesehen von der Auffassung des Verfassers der Genesisstelle im

---

[22] H. Kleinknecht in *Theol. Wörterb. zum NT* 6, 353.
[23] Man denke an die "guten und unschuldigen Geister" NH II 107, 13f., die aus der Welt Sabaoths und seiner guten Kräfte stammen. Ebenso ist von ihnen 124, 10. 34 die Rede. Sie sind vom unsterblichen Vater gesandt, damit sie ein Gegenstück zu den Kreaturen bilden. Die "unschuldigen Geister" sind die Ebenbilder der Gnostiker. Der Erlöser hat die Geister in ihrer Erwähltheit und Seligkeit offenkundig gemacht.
[24] Vgl. NH VII 1, 26 und Hippolyt, Haer. 5, 19, 1 ff.
[25] Vgl. *Theol. Wörterb. zum NT* 6, 351 ff.
[26] NH VII 124, 21-33. Vgl. A. Böhlig, "Der Name Gottes in Gnostizismus und Manichäismus", *Der Name Gottes*, hrsg. H. von Stietencron (Düsseldorf 1975) 131-55, hier besonders 140 ff.
[27] Vgl. H. J. Polotsky, "Manichäismus", PWSup 6, Sp. 251.
[28] Gen 1,2. Die Stelle wird allerdings von Gnostikern auf ganz verschiedene Weise gedeutet.

einzelnen ist der Geist Gottes ein physisch belebendes Prinzip. Da "Geist" im Hebräischen bzw. Aramäischen Femininum ist, lag es für eine mythologische Ausdeutung der Stelle nahe, im Geist die aus Gott hervortretende schaffende Mutter zu sehen. Wie wir aus aramäischen Wortspielen in gnostischen Texten wissen, sind hier jüdische Traditionen verwendet worden.[29] Man kann wahrscheinlich mit einem außerchristlichen jüdischen Einfluß auf den Gnostizismus rechnen. So kann es geschehen, daß im Philippusevangelium [GPh] der kirchlichen Meinung, Maria sei vom Geist befruchtet worden, der Widerspruch entgegengestellt wird, eine Frau könne ja nicht von einer Frau befruchtet werden.[30] In den Texten, die uns in unserem Seminar besonders angehen, wird die weibliche Muttergröße meist als "Barbelo" bezeichnet. Die Deutung dieses Namens ist problematisch. Man hat ihn aus dem Hebräischen erklärt: b'arba' 'lōh "in Vier ist Gott". Dann wäre der Name ein Satz, wie wir es von den ägyptischen Königsnamen kennen. Kann man für diese Zeit und die gnostischen Kreise annehmen, daß eine Verbindung der Mutter zur griechischen Tetraktys hergestellt wurde? Oder spielte der mannweibliche Charakter der Gottheit eine bestimmende Rolle, so daß man von einer Gottheit sprach, die mit vier (nämlich Brüsten) versehen sei, wie im Ägypterevangelium eine vorkommt?[31] Oder kann es sich angesichts des Hebräischen um eine Deutung des Tetragramms handeln, — Ihwh ist eben der geheime Name? Barbelo, die Muttergottheit, stammt ja aus dem unsichtbaren Geist. Sie ist seine Transformation, die, wie wir das in der Schrift von der dreifachen Protennoia [TriProt] finden,[32] zur Offenbarung dienen soll.

Wie man die Frage des Namens auch beantworten mag, mit dieser Größe tritt die "Zwei" aus der "Eins", die Dyas aus dem Hen, hervor. Das war für die Gnostiker, selbst wenn es sich dabei um die Entstehung der himmlischen Welt handelte, doch ein Abstieg.[33] Sie war gegenüber der Ferne und Einsamkeit des Vaters, der sie entstammt, eine Erscheinungsform, der erste Äon, besitzt aber doch

---

[29] Vgl. den Rückgriff auf Gen. Rab. 20,11 zur Erklärung der Eva.
[30] NH II 55, 23 ff.
[31] NH III 56, 4-13 (die Version in IV ist hier zerstört).
[32] NH XIII 35, 1-50, 24.
[33] Das bezeugen die Stellen, die auf die Notwendigkeit einer Rückbildung von der Zweiheit zur Einheit hinweisen. Vgl. die erste Jakobusapokalypse [1 ApocJas] von Nag Hammadi NH V 41, 15 ff.; dazu auch Clem. Alex., Str. 3, 8, 63; 13, 92, wo aus dem Ägypterevangelium (nicht dem von Nag Hammadi!) zitiert wird; vgl. auch 2 Clem. 12,2.

echten Einblick über das Denkbare hinaus. Von ihr und ihrer Zwischenstellung heißt es in den "Stelen des Seth":[34] "Du hast gesehen, daß die Ewigen von einem Schatten kommen, und du hast gezählt. Du hast zwar gefunden, daß du *eine* bliebst. Wenn du aber zählst, um zu teilen, bist du dreifaltig. Du bist wirklich dreifach gefaltet. Du bist *eine* aus dem Einen und du bist Schatten von ihm, dem Verborgenen. Du bist ein Kosmos des Wissens. Du weißt, daß die Angehörigen dieses Einen vom Schatten stammen. Und diese hast du im Herzen. Deshalb hast du den Ewigen Kraft gegeben durch die Existentialität, du hast der Göttlichkeit Kraft gegeben in der Lebendigkeit." Durch die Emanation in der Gestalt der Barbelo schafft sich der höchste Gott eine wahrhaft existierende Welt. Die Barbelo braucht allerdings nicht nur als eine mythologische Paargenossin des höchsten Gottes verstanden zu werden; sie ist vielmehr nach der Interpretatio graeca der Nus, der den himmlischen Größen Existenz verleiht und vom potentiell Vorhandenen zum Seienden, von der Einheit zur Vielheit führt. Insofern kann die Zweiheit sowohl Einheit als auch Dreiheit = Vielheit bedeuten. Man fühlt sich auf Plotins Auffassung vom Nus hingewiesen, der bei der Hinwendung nach innen zugleich bei "sich" wie beim "Hen" ist.[35] Die Betrachtung der Barbelo als eines "Kosmos des Wissens" und die Aussage, daß sie die vom Vater stammenden himmlischen Größen im Herzen trägt, entspricht der philosophischen Vorstellung von den Ideen im Nus.[36] Eine Vielheit ist die Barbelo, wenn sie als "zuerst erschienener großer männlicher Nus, der väterliche Nus, das göttliche Kind" angerufen[37] und ihr dabei die besondere Eigenart, "die Hervorbringerin der Zahl, entsprechend der Aufteilung aller wirklich Existierenden"[38] zu sein, zugesprochen wird.

Neben der mythologischen Bezeichnung Barbelo wird die Muttergöttin auch ἀρχή, πρόνοια, ἔννοια und σοφία genannt. Das Bild von einer himmlischen Gefährtin Gottes kann man wohl auf das hellenistische Judentum zurückführen. Dort ist sie ein Geschöpf Gottes und bei ihm wie ein Kind.[39] Im Gnostizismus kann sie wie die Barbelo

---

[34] NH VII 122, 6-21.

[35] H.J. Krämer, *Der Ursprung der Geistmetaphysik* (2. Aufl.; Amsterdam, 1967) 317f.

[36] H.J. Krämer, "Grundfragen der aristotelischen Theologie, 2. Teil: Xenokrates und die Ideen im Geiste Gottes", *TP* 44 (1969) 481-505.

[37] NH VII 123, 4ff.

[38] NH VII 123, 7ff.

[39] Vgl. Prov 8 und Sap Salom 7, sowie Jesus Sir 24.

im Vater ihren Sitz haben.⁴⁰ Eine Triade bildet sie in der „Sophia Jesu Christi" [SJC] als Partnerin des Menschensohnes und Mutter sowohl des Alls als auch Christi.⁴¹

Die dritte Größe der Trinität, der Sohn, wird mit philosophischer Terminologie als Logos⁴² oder der Abkunft nach als Sohn bezeichnet.⁴³ Gewisse Systeme kennen den "Ersten" bzw. den "wahren Menschen". Auch der Lichtadamas kann, wie in den "Stelen des Seth", als dritte Größe der Trias verwendet werden.⁴⁴ Den Ausdruck "Urmensch" möchte ich vermeiden, weil er durch die Konstruktionen der Religions-geschichtlichen Schule mit zuviel Thesen belastet ist, und hoffen, daß die wörtliche Übersetzung "der Erste Mensch" eindeutiger ist; immer muß man sich allerdings darüber klar sein, daß es sich bei ihm um eine himmlische Größe, nicht um den choïschen Adam handelt. Von diesem Ersten Menschen wissen wir schon lange aus den manichäischen Texten; wir kennen ihn aus der titellosen Schrift [OnOrgWld] des Codex II von Nag Hammadi ebenso wie aus dem Ägypterevangelium.⁴⁵ Er zieht in den Kampf oder bringt die Anmaßung des Ober-archon bzw. den Mangel zu Fall. Es sei hier noch einmal darauf hingewiesen, daß in den sethianischen Schriften der theologische Inhalt durch die mythologische Darstellung auch gerade deshalb nicht klarer gemacht wird, weil verschiedene Mythologumena untereinander und mit philosophischen Funktionsbeschreibungen konkurrieren und gegebenenfalls ausgeglichen werden. So wird z.B. im Ägypterevangelium der Logos mit dem Adamas kombiniert, so daß die Version im Codex III sogar lauten kann:⁴⁶ "Dann wurde der große von selbst

---

⁴⁰ Z.B. NH V 35, 7f.
⁴¹ Nach BG 98, 15ff.; 102, 15ff.; vgl. auch 93, 17.
⁴² Im Ägypterevangelium NH IV 60, 1-11 (s.u.).
⁴³ Vgl. Ägypterevangelium NH III 44, 22f. ~ IV 55, 11f.
⁴⁴ NH VII 118, 26; vgl. auch IX 6, 6; II 8, 34. Der Artikel ⲡⲓ in ⲡⲓⲅⲉⲣⲁⲁⲙⲁ(ⲥ) zeigt, daß die Bezeichnung sich von einem Appellativum zu einem Nomen proprium entwickelt hat; denn der supralineare Strich über dem Namen schließt ⲡⲓ mit ein. ⲅⲉⲣ- kann von γέρων genommen sein. Es wird sich wohl um eine volksetymologische Bildung handeln, weil das Wort sonst nicht begegnet. Vgl. dagegen ⲅⲉⲣⲁⲁⲙⲁⲥ NH VIII 6, 23; 13, 6; 51, 7.
⁴⁵ Der Erste Mensch ist im Manichäismus Sohn Gottes. Der wahre Mensch in NH II 103, 19 ähnelt diesem manichäischen Ersten Menschen sehr, da auch er hinab-steigt und bei seinem Wiederaufstieg zunächst gehemmt ist (112, 10ff.) wegen des Mangels, der sich mit ihm vermischt hat. Im Ägypterevangelium wird der Lichtadamas als Inkarnation des Ersten Menschen (Gott) betrachtet; so jedenfalls NH III 49, 8-16: "Der unfaßbare und unerkennbare Vater kam hervor und kam heraus von oben nach unten zur Vernichtung des Mangels." Bei seiner Erschaffung ist die Moirothea am Werk.
⁴⁶ NH III 49, 16-22.

entstandene göttliche Logos und der unverderbliche Mensch Adamas zu einer Verbindung, die der Mensch ist. Und der Mensch entstand durch ein Wort." Der stoische Begriff des Logos ist hier mit der jüdischen Vorstellung vom Schöpfungswort gekoppelt. Der Logos spricht ja als dritter Bestandteil einer Triade, die man aus dem unsichtbaren Geist, der Pronoia und dem Logos herstellen kann.[47] Im gnostischen Mythos ist er der Gestalter des Pleromas der Lichtwelt. Man kann dabei Züge aus dem Platonismus und seiner Vorstellung vom Demiurgen erkennen. Im Gnostizismus geht es aber bei seinem Werk nicht um die Schöpfung der Welt, sondern um die Gestaltung der Lichtwelt. Das Material, aus dem gestaltet wird, ist nicht Hyle, sondern Licht. Seine Herkunft wird allerdings nicht mit einer Geburt aus der göttlichen Mutter beschrieben. So steht im Ägypterevangelium im Brennpunkt der Betrachtung die Herkunft des Logos vom unsichtbaren Geist:[48] "der von selbst entstandene lebendige Logos, der wahre Gott, die ungeborene Natur ($\varphi\acute{u}\sigma\iota\varsigma$), dessen Namen ich mit Worten ausspreche (es folgt eine willkürliche Buchstabengruppe), d.i. der Sohn des großen Christus, d.i. der Sohn des unaussprechlichen Schweigens, der aus dem großen unsichtbaren und unverderblichen Geist hervorgekommen ist". Die doppelte Interpretation des Logos durch erklärende Sätze, die mit „d.i." eingeleitet sind, läßt darauf schließen, daß einer der beiden Sätze sekundär hinzugefügt worden ist. Man kann annehmen, daß dies für die Bezeichnung als „Sohn des großen Christus" gilt (ebenso wie für alle übrigen Stellen, an denen im Ägypterevangelium der große Christus vorkommt).[49] Auf diese Frage ist im Zusammenhang mit dem Johannesapokryphon [ApocryJn] nochmals einzugehen.

Im Gegensatz zu den "Stelen des Seth" bietet das Ägypterevangelium eine recht komplexe Darstellung von Trias und Trinität. Ließ sich die oben erwähnte Trias nur ableiten und ist nicht als solche gekennzeichnet, so ist von einer konkreten Dreiheit gleich zu Beginn der Schrift die Rede.[50] Sie wird aber nicht so dargestellt, daß die Mutter aus dem Vater und danach der Sohn entsteht, sondern sie erscheint auf einmal aus dem großen unsichtbaren Geist, der auch als Vater

---

[47] Die Pronoia kommt aus dem unsichtbaren Geist hervor im Ägypterevangelium NH IV 58, 23 ff. Darauf folgt der Logos: NH IV 59, 29 ff.

[48] NH IV 60, 1-11.

[49] NH IV [55, 6]; III 44, 22 f. ~ IV 55, 12; IV 56, 27; IV 59, 17; IV 60, 8; III 54, 20 ~ IV 66, 8.

[50] NH III 41, 7 ff. ~ IV 50, 23 ff.

bezeichnet wird. Es ist, als ob der Vater, der in einsamer Höhe schwebt und der ja im Gnostizismus so gern via negationis beschrieben wird, sich in einer Zwischenform als Trias von Vater, Mutter und Sohn entfaltet. Eine solche Zwischenform des Vaters begegnet auch im Eugnostosbrief [Eug], wo dem προπάτωρ der αὐτοπάτωρ entstammt.[51] Daß die Pronoia aber doch auch als Partnerin des unsichtbaren Geistes betrachtet werden kann, wird aus folgendem Satz ersichtlich: „Von jenem Ort kamen die drei Kräfte hervor, die drei Ogdoaden, die der Vater schweigend mit seiner Pronoia aus seinem Schoße hervorbringt: Vater, Mutter, Sohn."[52] Diese werden dann wieder in Gestalt von Ogdoaden geschildert. Deren zweite wird dabei übrigens als Barbelo bezeichnet. Neben diese Triade tritt noch eine weitere. Denn aus dem Vater kommt auf Bitten dieser Trinität noch ein Emanation hervor, das dreifachmännliche Kind.[53] Dieses wiederum läßt sich durch die Juël ergänzen[54] und hat selbst ein Kind, das deshalb auch „das Kind des Kindes" genannt wird, Esephech bzw. Ephesech,[55] der Splenditenens. Es scheint, als ob mythologische Figuren, die in anderen Texten frei im Raum stehen, hier im Ägypterevangelium im Sinne unseres Problemes systematisiert sind.

Vergleicht man mit der Metaphysik des Ägypterevangeliums die des Johannesapokryphons, so wird man beachtliche Übereinstimmungen finden. Doch ist hier der mythologische Stoff nicht erst sekundär christianisiert wie im Ägypterevangelium, sondern bei der Gestaltung des Werkes dürfte schon die Tradition tiefergehend in Richtung auf die christliche Umformung des gnostischen Mythos gebildet worden sein. Das Vorkommen Jesu im Ägypterevangelium widerspricht dem in keinerlei Weise. Denn die Geburt des Seth durch eine Jungfrau in der Gestalt Jesu gehört zu den festen Dogmen des Sethianismus.[56] Jesus residiert ja auch in der himmlischen Welt auf dem Leuchter Orojaël zusammen mit Seth, dessen Inkarnation er ist.[57] Der große Christus ist dagegen eine ganz andere Größe. Erst beim Jesus Christus des Kolophons zum Ägypterevangelium handelt es sich um die volle Einordnung in die christliche Terminologie.[58]

---

[51] NH III 74, 20 ff.
[52] NH III 42, 1 ff. (Ägypterevangelium).
[53] NH III 44, 14 ff. ~ IV 54, 21 ff.
[54] NH IV 56, 11 ff.
[55] NH IV 56, 20 ff.
[56] Epiphan., Haer. 39, 1, 3; 3, 5.
[57] NH III 65, 16 f. ~ IV 77, 12 ff.
[58] NH III 69, 6-17.

Im Johannesapokryphon ist zwar infolge der noch radikaleren Verwendung der via negationis für die Beschreibung Gottes einerseits die Ferne Gottes noch stärker betont, doch findet sich andererseits seine Einbeziehung in die Trinität. Ein trinitarischer Zug ist bereits in der Rahmenerzählung vorhanden, in der Jesus bei seiner Begegnung mit Johannes sich als Vater, Mutter und Sohn zugleich bezeichnet.[59] Die Trias bildet sich durch Emanation. Aus dem unsichtbaren Geist geht die Barbelo hervor.[60] Sie wird mannigfaltig qualifiziert, um ihren Charakter der Ursprünglichkeit hervorzuheben. Sie ist ja auch wie in anderen gnostischen Schriften ("Stelen", Allogenes [Allog]) die erste Erscheinung; das bezeugt ihr Alter. Darum heißt sie auch "Großvater" und "Erster Mensch".[61] Dieser Name steht hier in Konkurrenz zum Sohn, der in dieser Schrift nicht diesen Namen trägt. Von Interesse ist ihre Identifikation mit dem Heiligen Geist.[62] Ihre Bedeutung wird durch die Betonung ihrer Dreifachheit gesteigert: sie ist dreifachmännlich, die dreifach kräftige, die mannweibliche mit den drei Namen. Sie ist von Ewigkeit und bleibt auf ihre Bitte in Ewigkeit. Sie wird zwar vielfältig ausgestaltet, aber ihr wichtigstes Werk ist die Geburt eines seligen Lichtfunkens. Er ist der μονογενής, ein αὐτογένητος und erstgeborener Sohn des Alls. Er wird gesalbt, er wird Christus. Nus und Logos sind seine Helfer. „Denn durch den Logos hat Christus alle Dinge geschaffen."[63] So wie im Ägypterevangelium der Logos für die Entstehung der vier großen Leuchter sorgt, so übernimmt das Christus im Johannesapokryphon. Man merkt beim Bericht über die Entstehung Christi aber deutlich noch das Durchklingen der vorchristlichen Vorstellungen.

Die konsequente Durchführung des Schemas Vater-Mutter-Sohn ergibt bei einer Deutung des Sohnes auf Christus im Vergleich mit dem urchristlichen Schema Vater-Sohn-Geist, daß Geist und Mutter sich gegenüberstehen, wenn auch die Plätze vertauscht sind. So kann die Mutter also, wie wir gesehen haben, auch mit dem Geist identifiziert

---

[59] Nach BG 21, 3-13.

[60] BG 27, 5 ff.

[61] "Erster Mensch, das ist der jungfräuliche Geist, der dreifach Männliche, der mit den drei Kräften, den drei Namen und den drei Zeugungen, der Äon, der nicht altert, der männlich-weibliche, der aus seiner πρόνοια hervorging" BG 27, 19-28, 4 ~ NH III 7, 23-8, 5. NH II 5, 5-7, lautet: „Sie wurde der Mutterschoß des Alls, denn sie ist früher als sie alle: der Großvater, der Erste Mensch, der Heilige Geist. ..."

[62] In der Version in NH II; s. voranstehende Anm.

[63] BG 31, 16 ff. ~ NH III 10, 21 f. ~ NH II 7, 10 f.

werden. Sie ist ja die ἔννοια Gottes, die ἐπίνοια, die Mutter der Lebendigen. Man kann den Heiligen Geist durchaus ähnlich dem des Christentums wiederfinden, wenn man den Geist als den Geist Gottes ansieht.[64] So entspricht es durchaus neutestamentlicher Auffassung, wenn der Heilige Geist zur Erweckung kommt,[65] wenn er von Gott über die Sophia ausgegossen wird,[66] wenn das Lästern gegen ihn als Sünde bewertet wird.[67]

Eine ähnliche, aber noch viel weitergehende Entwicklung ist im Philippusevangelium zu erkennen. Den typisch allgemeinchristlichen Vorstellungen stehen Sätze gegenüber, die im mythologischen Schema gedacht sind. Ganz christlich ist die Verleihung des Geistes bei den Sakramenten (Ölung, Taufe, Abendmahl),[68] ebenso der Gedanke vom Geist als Beschützer.[69] Die Verbindung von Licht und Geist,[70] seine Allanwesenheit[71] und seine Herrschaft[72] brauchen nicht ins Mythologische zu gehören, können aber zu den offenkundigen Belegen dafür vielleicht eine Brücke bilden. Bei diesen handelt es sich um die schon erwähnte Betonung, daß der "Geist" ein Femininum[73] und Heiliger Geist ein zweiteiliger Name[74] sei. Zweiteilige Dinge sind aber im Semitischen Feminina.[75] Wenn dieser Text auch valentinianisch ist, so muß er doch als Typ eines Zusammenstoßes der Modelle auch in unserem Zusammenhang erwähnt werden.

Auch im Evangelium Veritatis [GTr] scheint mir ein Anklang an mythisches Denken bezüglich unserer Fragestellung vorzuliegen. "Der Vater offenbart seinen Busen. Sein Busen aber ist der Heilige Geist, der sein Verborgenes offenbart. Sein Verborgenes ist sein Sohn."[76] Wohl kann man diese Stelle auch auf 1 Kor 2 zurückführen. Aber die

---

[64] NH II 8, 27-28.
[65] In der Adamapokalypse [ApocAd] NH V 77, 18.
[66] Im Johannesapokryphon NH II 14, 5 f.
[67] Im Thomasevangelium [GTh] NH II 40, 29.
[68] Ölung NH II 74, 21; Taufe 69, 5; 77, 14; Abendmahl 75, 18.
[69] NH II 66, 2 ff.
[70] NH II 58, 12.
[71] NH II 59, 16.
[72] NH II 60, 28.
[73] NH II 55, 24.
[74] NH II 59, 12.
[75] Vgl. C. Brockelmann, *Grundriß der vergleichenden Grammatik der semitischen Sprachen* 1 (Berlin, 1908) 422: "Als Feminina werden ferner vielfach Körperteile, namentlich die paarweise vorkommenden, als dienende Werkzeuge behandelt."
[76] NH I 24, 11 ff.

Linie Vater-Geist-Sohn kann gleichfalls auf die Vorstellung von Gott-Muttergöttin-Sohn zurückgehen.

Einen deutlichen Übergang vom paganen zum christlichen Modell weist die titellose Schrift des Codex II auf.[77] Hier wird geschildert, daß neben Sabaoth als Untergott zu seiner Rechten Jesus Christus, zu seiner Linken die Jungfrau des heiligen Geisten sitzt. Die Rangfolge ist Mitte-Rechts-Links, also Sabaoth–Jesus–Jungfrau des heiligen Geistes. Das ist die urchristliche Reihenfolge; aber der Geist wird noch als Femininum empfunden.

Gewiß war in den bisher genannten Beispielen schon manches vorhanden, was von der Triade zur Trinität führte. Man denke insbesondere an‘ die Stellung der Barbelo in- und außerhalb des Vaters und ihre Verbindung mit dem Sohn. Ein besonders gewichtiges Dokument für diese Problematik einer wirklichen Trinität ist die drei-gestaltige Protennoia aus Codex XIII. Sie tritt in drei großen Offenbarungsreden hervor. In der ersten spricht sie im Namen des Vaters. Sie ist sein Ruf und kann als die Größe, die im unerreichbaren Vater wohnt, aber auch aus ihm heraustritt, zu den Gnostikern sprechen und tiefste Geheimnisse kundtun, gerade in dieser ersten Rede.[78] Sie wird dabei bereits als Trinität bezeichnet: "genannt mit drei Namen, aber allein vollkommen".[79] Die besteht aus drei μοναί, d.i. himmlischen Wohnungen; diese sind der Vater, die Mutter, der Sohn.[80] So wie im Johannesapokryphon[81] die Barbelo hat hier die Protennoia[82] drei Männlichkeiten, drei Kräfte und drei Namen, „die auf diese Weise die drei viereckigen Räume[83] bilden". Diese drei Namen sind eben Vater, Mutter und Sohn, die latent im unsichtbaren und unaussprechbaren Vater ruhen. Sie läßt die Protennoia als der Ruf mittels ihres Auftretens als Vater, Mutter und Sohn zur Erscheinung kommen. Zugleich kann sie aber auch an dem Sohn die Salbung vornehmen.[84]

---

[77] NH II 105, 20 ff.
[78] NH XIII 35, 1-42, 3.
[79] NH XIII 35, 6 f.
[80] NH XIII 37, 20 ff.
[81] NH II 5, 7 ff.; s.o.
[82] Sie wird NH XIII 38, 8 f. mit der Barbelo gleichgesetzt.
[83] Die drei Quadrate sollen wohl die μοναί darstellen. Eine Umstellung des Satz-abschnittes ⲉⲩϣⲟⲟⲡ ... ⲕⲟⲟϩ (37, 27-29) nach Z. 22 (hinter ⲙⲟⲛⲏ), wie sie G. Schenke vorschlägt, halte ich nicht für nötig. Vgl. G. Schenke, „Die dreigestaltige Protennoia (Nag-Hammadi-Codex XIII) herausgegeben und kommentiert" (Theol. Diss., Rostock, 1977) zur Stelle.
[84] NH XIII 37, 30 ff.

In der zweiten Rede tritt schon gleich zu Beginn der Charakter der Mutter hervor. Wichtig ist die Betonung, daß die Protennoia zum zweiten Mal in der Gestalt einer Frau kommt; zugleich wird aber auch die bei der Gottespartnerin ja bekannte Doppelgeschlechtlichkeit hervorgehoben. Wenn sie ausspricht, daß sie Mutter und Vater ist, zugleich auch die Schöpfergottheit Moirothea, so schildert sie ihr Wirken in der Welt mit dem Ausblick auf die himmlische Heimkehr.[85] In einer dritten Rede gibt sie sich als den Logos.[86] Sie ist also ganz modalistisch gezeichnet. Warum ist aber gerade die Barbelo bzw. die ihr entsprechende Größe die, die redet und verkündet? Daß nicht der höchste Gott in dieser Rolle auftritt, dürfte verständlich sein. Aber warum nicht der Logos? Auch hierin zeigt sich ein Unterschied zu der urchristlichen Auffassung. Wie in den „Stelen des Seth" wird sie als Vermittlerin zwischen Gott und Welt dargestellt. Als zweite Größe, die Frau und Mutter ist, kann sie als Teil der ersten sprechen, dann ihre spezielle Aufgabe schildern und schließlich den Sohn, der ja aus ihr wie aus dem Vater stammt, verkörpern und in ihm erscheinen. Bei der Christianisierung des Textes kann sie in den letzten, wohl christlich-sethianischen, später hinzugefügten Worten sagen:[87] „Ich habe Jesus angezogen, ich trug ihn weg von dem verfluchten Holz und versetzte ihn in die Wohnungen seines Vaters. Und nicht erkannten mich die, die da wachen über ihre Wohnungen. Denn ich bin unangreifbar samt meinem Samen. Und meinen Samen werde ich überantworten dem lauteren Licht."

In anderen mythologischen Schriften von Nag Hammadi ist die Betonung der Mutter zu finden. Man beachte die Bedeutung, die ihr im "Allogenes" oder im "Zostrianos" [Zost] geschenkt wird. Berücksichtigt man das, so versteht man auch die Schrift vom "Donner" [Thund] als gnostischen Text.[88] Der Donner ist dem Blitz gegenüber etwas Sekundäres. Insofern kann sich die Muttergöttin als Nus betrachten lassen, da der Nus ja oft als die zweite aus dem höchsten Gott entsandte Größe angesehen wird. Die Complexio oppositorum, wie sie in dieser letzteren Schrift zum Ausdruck kommt, soll ihren allumfassenden Charakter beschreiben. Wenn sie sich als σιγή, ἐπίνοια und λόγος bezeichnet, so steht sie der Denkart von Codex XIII sehr nahe. Als eine Parallele ist das kleine Lied in der titellosen Schrift

---

[85] NH XIII 42, 4-46, 3.
[86] NH XIII 46, 5-50, 21.
[87] NH XIII 50, 12-20.
[88] NH VI 13, 1-21, 32: "Der Donner, der vollkommene Nus".

von Codex II anzusehen, in dem der mannweibliche zweite Mensch
sich als Gattin und Mutter und zugleich als Gatten, also als Vater,
Mutter und Kind, betrachtet.[89]

Gerade die letzten Beispiele machten deutlich, daß hinter den
mannigfaltigen mythischen Figuren sich ein monotheistisches Denken
verbirgt, das letztlich die Gestalten des Mythos als Mittel zur
Differenzierung gebrauchte. Und das war besonders deshalb nötig, weil
so in der Welt verborgene Diskrepanzen (Licht—Finsternis, Gut— Böse
etc.) am besten konkret vor Augen geführt werden konnten. Am
schwierigsten für den antiken Leser — und auch für uns — ist es, die
Schwelle zu überschreiten, wo man nur noch via negationis beschreiben
konnte. Ein Text, der hierum sehr bemüht ist und bereits im Sinne
christlicher Theologie eine Lösung sucht, ist ein nichtsethianischer, den
Valentinianern zumindest nahestehender, der Tractatus tripartitus
[TriTrac]. Er kann hier nicht übergangen werden. In ihm ist das
Schema Vater-Mutter-Sohn zugunsten eines dem urchristlichen nahen
Schemas Vater-Sohn-Kirche aufgegeben. Wenn Tertullian dieses Modell
dem Gnostiker Herakleon zuweist, so kann man noch weitergehen und
den Apostolus haereticorum spüren, wie er in den Deuteropaulinen
die Anregungen solchen Denkens gegeben haben mag. Zugleich
wird auch in dieser Schrift mit unendlicher Mühe und viel Dialektik
versucht, die Gleichewigkeit von Vater und Sohn herauszuarbeiten.

---

[89] NH II 114, 7-15:

1. ⲁⲛⲟⲕ ⲡⲉ ⲡⲙⲉⲣⲟⲥ ⲛⲧⲁⲙⲁⲁⲩ	Ich bin der Teil meiner Mutter
ⲁⲩⲱ ⲁⲛⲟⲕ ⲧⲉ ⲧⲙⲁⲁⲩ	und ich bin die Mutter.
ⲁⲛⲟⲕ ⲧⲉ ⲧϩⲓⲙⲉ	Ich bin das Weib.
ⲁⲛⲟⲕ ⲧⲉ ⲧⲡⲁⲣⲑⲉⲛⲟⲥ	Ich bin die Jungfrau.
ⲁⲛⲟⲕ ⲧⲉⲧⲉⲉⲧ	Ich bin die Schwangere.
ⲁⲛⲟⲕ ⲧⲉ ⲧⲥⲟⲉⲓⲛ	Ich bin die Ärztin.
ⲁⲛⲟⲕ ⲧⲉ ⲧⲣⲉϥⲥⲟⲗⲥⲗ ⲛⲛⲁⲕⲉ.	Ich bin die Trösterin der Wehen.
2. ⲡⲁϩⲁⲉⲓ ⲡⲉⲛⲧⲁϩϫⲡⲟⲉⲓ	Mein Gatte hat mich erzeugt
ⲁⲩⲱ ⲁⲛⲟⲕ ⲧⲉ ⲧⲉϥⲙⲁⲁⲩ	und ich bin seine Mutter
ⲁⲩⲱ ⲛⲧⲟϥ ⲡⲉ ⲡⲁⲉⲓⲱⲧ	und er ist mein Vater
ⲁⲩⲱ ⲡⲁϫⲟⲉⲓⲥ	und mein Herr.
ⲛⲧⲟϥ ⲡⲉ ⲧⲁϭⲟⲙ	Er ist meine Kraft.
ⲡⲉⲧϥⲟⲩⲁϣϥ ϥϫⲱ ⲙⲙⲟϥ	Was er will, sagt er.
ⲉⲩⲗⲟⲅⲱⲥ ϯϣⲱⲡⲉ	Auf richtige Weise werde ich geschaffen.
ⲁⲗⲗⲁ ⲁϩⲓϫⲡⲉ ⲟⲩⲣⲱⲙⲉ	Darum habe ich einen Menschen
ⲛϫⲟⲉⲓⲥ	im Vollsinn hervorgebracht.

Zu ἀλλά in der letzten Zeile vgl. W. Bauer, *Wörterbuch zum NT*, s.v. Zur Interpretation von ⲛϫⲟⲉⲓⲥ als adjektivisches κύριος vgl. A. Böhlig, „Zum Gottesbegriff
des Tractatus tripartitus", *Kerygma und Logos. Festschrift f. C. Andresen* (Göttingen
1979) 49-67. Vgl. auch A. Böhlig, „Zur Stellung des adjektivischen Attributs im
Koptischen", *Festschrift f. E. Edel* (Bamberg 1979) 42-53.

Der Sohn ist der Erstgeborene, weil es keinen vor ihm gibt, und er ist der Einziggeborene, weil es keinen nach ihm gibt. Die Kirche aber ist der bei den zwischen Vater und Sohn ausgetauschten Küssen entstehende Überschuß.

Es wurde in der Darlegung versucht, urchristliche und gnostische Trinitätslehre in ihrem Zusammenstoß zu schildern. Eine ausführliche Untersuchung darüber wird in meiner in Arbeit befindlichen Studie über den hellenistischen Einfluß auf die Metaphysik der Texte von Nag Hammadi vorgelegt werden.

DISCUSSION

GEORGE MacRAE: WHILE there is an unavoidable awkwardness in discussing Professor Schenke's paper in his absence, he has given us much to work with. We shall begin by asking Professor Colpe to report on Schenke's introductory remarks to his own paper transmitted to him by telephone prior to this session.*

CARSTEN COLPE: I have the English version of Professor Schenke's paper. I will use it in attempting to answer your questions in his absence since it is a revised version of the German text that members of this seminar have already received. Professor Schenke asked me to start by conveying several responses he made to material presented thus far in the seminar. First, regarding the non-Gnostic Jewish background of the Sethians, he views the identification of the Sethians with the "sons of the gods" on the mountain of Paradise in Genesis 6 as very important. Second, he singled out several passages in Professor Pearson's paper, "The Figure of Seth in Gnostic Literature." The use of the terms "Sodom" and "Gomorrah" in the *Gospel of the Egyptians* does not require a Jewish *Vorlage* in which these terms were understood symbolically, as Professor Pearson has proposed. Schenke favors a Sethian reinterpretation of traditions that were connected with the actual geographical area by the Dead Sea.

BIRGER PEARSON: Jean Doresse held a similar position, to which I refer in footnote 17 of my paper.

---

* See also Professor Schenke's postscript below, pp. 683-86.

COLPE: Regarding Professor Pearson's treatment of the birth of Seth, Schenke reminds us that Seth had no mother, lending him a special nature different from that of Cain and Abel. Schenke finds Pearson's hypothesis that Zostrianos was an incarnation of Seth very useful in supporting his own views.

Third, Professor Schenke asked me to laugh for him here in front of all of you over Professor Wisse's unicorn—a request which I am constitutionally unable to carry out though I practiced this morning in front of the mirror!

Fourth, he wished to withdraw the harshness of his paper where he speaks of the connection made by Professors Böhlig and Wisse between the Egyptian god Seth and the Gnostic Seth. While he cannot follow them in this connection for reasons he finds compelling (for example, the accusation of sodomy made against the Egyptian Seth was impossible for the Jewish Seth) he acknowledges the positive contribution they have made in their critical edition of the text of the *Gospel of the Egyptians*. The forthcoming English version of Schenke's paper contains a lengthy addition [above, p. 600] to the German version that you have read, in which he develops more fully his assessment of the strengths and limitations of their edition and in which he proposes that the *Gospel of the Egyptians* served to initiate the Sethian catechumen into the ritual and invocations of baptism.

I asked Professor Schenke to comment on my paper which as you know relies on both his and Professor Böhlig's earlier work, though attempting to refine it. He indicated his approval of what I had done. After our conversation yesterday I told him I was particularly convinced by what he wrote in his paper about the identity of the ten "Sethian" texts and their mutual relationships. He agreed with our opinion here that these relationships are on several different levels and that the "Sethian" texts could point to a loosely constructed "school" with distinctive doctrines but rather indistinct boundaries.

MACRAE: To open the discussion we could ask ourselves if we are in general agreement with Professor Schenke's grouping of the "Sethian" texts. Are there additions or deletions that you want to make?

ROBERT KRAFT: In light of yesterday's discussion [sessions 1-3] we have to pay attention to the presuppositions underlying any particular grouping of "Sethian" texts, as for example our commitment to the

Gnostics' consistency or lack of it, our postulation of their social context as being "school" or "sect", etc.

PEARSON: Given the disparate nature of the texts in Professor Schenke's catalog, he might have included the *Untitled Tractate* from the Bruce Codex with its mention of the important figures of the heavenly world.

MACRAE: This document also uses series of magical nomina barbara such as Abrasax, Sablo, and Gamaliel. A number of the "Sethian" texts do also—the *Apocalypse of Adam, Gospel of the Egyptians, Zostrianos*, etc. And these are texts with which the *Untitled Tractate* shares additional common features. The magical names were not a matter of indifference to the writers but were treated with great respect. That certain groupings of names appear in certain documents and only in them must be significant.

JAMES ROBINSON: Professor Schenke's catalog of Sethian texts listed at the beginning of his paper was apparently reached inductively in a manner similar to Professor MacRae's treatment of the *nomina barbara*. Notice Schenke's list of common characteristics in the second section of his paper. Whether one moves as far as he does or whether we agree on the Sethian identity of the documents on the fringes is beside the point. One must produce some historical accounting for the inter-relationships he has pointed out. In working with this data one holding a position like that of Professor Wisse seems compelled to acknowledge some traditional connections between the authors of these texts.

FREDERIK WISSE: The standards for inclusion and exclusion are not clear to me. Both the *Letter of Peter to Philip*, in spite of its connection with the *Apocryphon of John*, and the *Concept of Our Great Power*, with its three ages, were probably excluded from the list because they were too Christian, But if one follows Professor Schenke in excluding them, the fact that they share common themes with others on the list ends up in support of my position that these themes were readily available in a variety of environments.

GEORGE NICKELSBURG: Do we find evidence in these "Sethian" texts of any large theological or mythical structure shared uniquely by them, aside from a mere carrying over of traditional terms? Think of the way we treat Jewish apocryphal texts on a purely literary level. We don't assume a sociological connection between one text and another with a similar tradition. Perhaps we can account for those Gnostic texts that are on the outer edges of the circle of the "Sethian" texts by assuming purely literary relationships in these instance.

ROBINSON : In my article on "The Three Steles of Seth and the Gnostics of Plotinus" (*Proceedings of the International Colloquium on Gnosticism, Stockholm: August 20-25, 1973* [Leiden: Brill, 1977], 132-42) I pointed out a common hymnic tradition shared by the three tractates. If the hymnic ingredients reflect a cultic practice, then these three would share a sociological relationship.

JOHN STRUGNELL: Three items on Professor Schenke's list of common characteristics puzzle me. First, how specific must the unfolding of negative theology be for it to qualify as an indication of a Sethian tendency? The phenomenon is so widespread. Likewise, how closely must philosophical terminology be knitted to the Sethian mythical system for us to include "eine spezifisch philosophische Terminologie"? Almost by definition philosophical terminology is borrowed from the outside. And the criterion of "offenkundige Verchristlichung" puzzles me. How does this distinguish this list of "Sethian" documents from any others in the Nag Hammadi library?

COLPE: Of course I cannot answer authoritatively for Professor Schenke. But I could guess that while each individual argument doesn't account for the identification of the group, the items taken collectively have a persuasive force in establishing the "Sethian" texts. For example, a specific unfolding of negative theology is generally not found together with a "Verchristlichung."

ALEXANDER BÖHLIG: But we have this in the *Tripartite Tractate*. It attempts to express Christian concepts in philosophical terms.

COLPE: Perhaps my guess is wrong.

STRUGNELL: We still are not able to get back to a Sethian sect on the basis of this list. What we have is the evidence for the history of the traditions.

MacRae: Perhaps as many of the individual items in this list could be found in the excluded *Eugnostos* and *Sophia Jesu Christi* as could be found in any single document Schenke has labeled as "Sethian."

Böhlig: The second list involves tractates which seem to belong together for reasons other than stated here, but which have certain incidental points in common such as a philosophical emphasis. These are in themselves not distinctive characteristics.

Wisse: A number of the items on the list of characteristics could be used to support the idea of diversity among the "Sethian" texts. If just two or three agree, what are we to make of the divergence of the others? For example, Eleleth's role in the creation of the world, as found in a few tractates, is performed in other "Sethian" tractates by other beings.

Pearson: The matter of interrelationships is complicated by observing a number of interlocking connections between texts on this list and others not on it. For example, the figure of Norea occurs in a number of texts including the *Hypostasis of the Archons*. And the *Hypostasis of the Archons* is itself significantly paralleled by the treatise *On the Origin of the World* [CG II,5], which is "non-Sethian" by its omission of virtually all of the characteristics on Schenke's list. Some "Sethian" texts, such as *Allogenes*, *Zostrianos*, and *Marsanes*, have a Platonic ring about them. The myth of the *Apocryphon of John* parallels the Valentinian myth, etc.

Robinson: Pertinent to a decision as to whether literary relationships or the interactions of a "sect" were primary, a number of the differences among the "Sethian" texts in their use of motifs may actually point towards the sociological explanation. To me the varied treatment of the Eleleth motif among the documents is harder to account for by literary borrowing or commentary than by imagining it to be the result of continuing historical tradition in which Eleleth is described in a number of settings.

Strugnell: The use of names must be assessed carefully. The tradition that Noah's wife was named Norea was more widespread than the tradition about the specific acts she and her husband perform in the "Sethian" texts. It is only when encountering names that were invented in the course of articulating the specific mythology that we can be sure we won't find these outside the group.

BöHLIG: Of course, not every writing which mentions Seth is Sethian. When, however, a number of similar elements occur in different writings we must assume the existence of a group for whom these elements meant something special. Eleleth was a likely candidâte to be connected with creation for he was the lowest of the great lights. We have here pieces of tradition known to the members of a group, which could be used to make some theological point.

NICKELSBURG: I find certain analogies between mythology and narrative; for example, myths move from point to point with their own logic. Speaking as a nonspecialist in Gnostic literature, I wonder what attempts are being made to "unpack" the structure of the various Gnostic myths so that we could make typological comparisons between them and determine in what way one myth might be dependent upon another one. We have been talking of the various interlocking relationships among the "Sethian" texts. With the Nag Hammadi documents now accessible, I wonder if it isn't time for the Gnostic specialists to try this approach.

COLPE: I'm trying all the time to develop typologies. I can tell you how difficult this approach is. Though I present my findings in lectures and seminars, I have not yet felt able to put them into print. One can easily distinguish between carefully constructed systems and those that range widely and loosely in their speculations. The Manichaean system has provided the main example of the former type. The Central Asian novelistic literature which is connected with Manichaeism demonstrates how tales could be attached to the system with very slender points of reference. It is even possible in every case to say where the points of reference to the constructed system lie and even why one particular Buddhist story or legend was adopted and not some other one. Also, the excellent tables prepared by Professor Böhlig at the beginning of his edition of the *Kephalaia* allow one to see at once the original mythological kernel in spite of the accumulated tales surrounding it. In the case of Manichaeism we know Mani himself must have constructed the system. Similarly, the coherent and self-contained character of the earliest Valentinian system about the Pleroma points to its construction by Valentinus.

But in the case of the Sethian texts I don't find this kind of careful mythological construction. Instead, floating pieces of tradition appear to be held together by certain principles or points of association. We are still far from constructing a definitive typology of Gnostic myths, though I think the task is possible. In the looser type of mythological construction which is characteristic of the "Sethian" material we have not even determined the primary element—is it the folk tale material or the mythological construction? Likewise, in the case of the Mandaean material it has been impossible to decide whether the very basis of the Mandaean doctrines was a collection of folk tales which were subsequently systematized or whether the folk materials were attached to a constructed system.

We must also distinguish between "myth" and "system." Unlike the Manichaean myth, there are myths which are not systems. There are myths which develop into tales or narratives. The criterion for defining a myth is its ability to make the past event a present reality. According to Eliade this phenomenon can only occur in a cultic environment in which the myth is made a present reality. But we know next to nothing about the cultic life of the Gnostic sects.

BÖHLIG: Does Schenke still believe that there was at one time a unified Sethian system?

COLPE: Thirteen years ago Professor Schenke contributed the section on Gnosticism in a work by J. Leipoldt and W. Grundmann entitled *Umwelt des Urchristentums* (Berlin, 1967; 2. 350-418) in which he proposed an original Gnostic myth and a euhemeristic explanation of the numerous extant varieties. I don't think he has repeated this view since that time. And he wouldn't propose anything like it about the Sethians. In earlier articles he spoke about a "Sethian system." But I don't find any clear indications that he still refers to a Sethian "system."

MACRAE: May I suggest that we now move to the discussion of Professor Böhlig's paper.

ROBINSON: (*To Colpe*) In my paper I quoted your statement that the occurence of the trinity Father-Mother-Son in the *Trimorphic Protennoia* led you to concede the tractate was under Christian influence, on the grounds that this particular trinitarian form was

Syrian Christian in origin. But Professor Böhlig suggests that this form of the trinity was a non-Christian Gnostic theologumenon.

COLPE: There is no real contradiction. Many phenomena including this one can be read as either Christian or non-Christian. Drijvers's work on Bardesanes points out that the Syrian trinity Father-Spirit-Son lies close to the non-Christian form Father-Mother-Son, since "spirit" is feminine in Syriac. The Christian element is the change of "Mother" to "Spirit."

BÖHLIG: This trinity of Father-Mother-Son is very familar in Near Eastern paganism.

COLPE: Gnostics could have made the same substitution as Syrian Christianity, so that from the trinitarian formula alone one cannot determine whether the setting is Gnostic. In the case of the *Trimorphic Protennoia* there are other indications of Christian influence so that the presence of "Mother" must be viewed as a "re-Semitization."

BÖHLIG: There was not one unified Christian concept of the trinity in the early church. The Logos theology of the Apologists has little in common with the *Urgemeinde*. There is a danger of either reading Gnostic influences into all kinds of Christian statements on the trinity or of treating Gnosticism simply as a Christian sect. We are still caught in the vicious circle typified by the articles of W. Schmithals and O. Betz in *Verkündigung und Forschung: Neues Testament* (BEvTh 21; 1976) 22-80. I have spoken to this issue in my *NTS* article "Zur Struktur gnostischen Denkens." Gnostic references to the Father-Mother-Son trinity are understandable only against a pagan background. The texts do often show awareness of the Christian concept. But we should also note the intertwining of the concepts in the *Gospel of Philip*: here the concepts are in competition.

ROBINSON: (*To Böhlig*) Your paper supports Schenke's argument to the extent that the trinity of Father-Mother-Son could have been an essential ingredient of a non-Christian Gnosticism.

BÖHLIG: Yes, it does.

STRUGNELL: Let us pay some attention to "Son" in this trinity.

The "Sophia" figure had long before appeared in Judaism as cocreator of the world with God. But the presence of the "Son" as a third heavenly figure might show a connection between Gnostic and early Christian trinitarian doctrine.

BöHLIG: In his book on the Son of God, Professor Hengel has shown the Jewish background of this concept. The circles which speak of the "Mother" in the trinity have a Gnostic background.

PEARSON: There is another point of differentiation between "orthodox" Christianity and Gnosticism—the Jewish figure of Wisdom lies behind Christ as the Logos while in Gnostic circles Wisdom becomes the Mother.

BöHLIG: In the *Tripartite Tractate* we can observe the transition from the Gnostic to the Christian usage. In general, this writing helps us to see which issues were important in early Catholicism.

Session Five

SETHIANS AND JOHANNINE THOUGHT
The Trimorphic Protennoia *and the Prologue of the Gospel of John*

BY

JAMES M. ROBINSON

THE question of Sethianism opens the basic question of the relation of the heresiological sources to the Nag Hammadi texts. It has become apparent that the former do not simply present what one might think of as a rather normal kind of inexactitude, the inaccuracy, contradictions and tendentiousness that one might postulate a priori. For when confronted by the Nag Hammadi texts the heresiological reports display a further problem : the heresiologists' sects at times do not correlate well with the new texts, in that the new texts often do not clearly fit the previously assumed sects, or fit several, but not one to the exclusion of others. This has led to various working hypotheses : perhaps the heresiologists knew primarily texts, and inferred from some prominent term in a text, such as Gnostic, Barbelo, Archon, Snake or Seth, that behind the text there was a distinctive sect and that this sect either bore that prominent term as its title or could be branded with that term as a fitting title. Or one could conversely postulate that the Nag Hammadi texts are secondary, reflecting a contamination, conflation or merging of traditions originally emanating from or distinctive of a single sect, traditions that were then contributed to a more ecumenical Gnostic theology reflected in the Nag Hammadi texts. Or one can with Frederik Wisse suspect that the area of unity was falsely identified by the heresiologists and subsequent scholars as theology, where in fact heterogeneity always prevailed, rather than conduct, where in fact there was something like a shared Gnostic-ascetic-elitist ethos.[1]

Depending on the position one takes among such alternatives one would mean different things by the term Sethian : Sethian refers not to

---

[1] Frederik Wisse, "The Nag Hammadi Library and the Heresiologists," *VC* 25 (1971) 205-223. See also his paper in the present volume, "Stalking those Elusive Sethians."

a sect, but to a tradition or text in which Seth figures in the title or is prominent in the text, etc. Or Sethian could mean the name of a sect, be it Christian Gnostic, Jewish Gnostic, or pre-Gnostic (or a trajectory moving from one to the other). There are of course other nuances and alternatives. Presumably the Seminar on Sethian Gnosticism will be grappling with these problems.

The present paper, with its focus on the *Trimorphic Protennoia* (Nag Hammadi Codex XIII,*1*) and the prologue of John, is caught up in the problematic of Sethianism in a particularly acute way: Seth is not named in the text. Whereas Jean Doresse pointed to Sethian, Hermetic and especially Simonian possibilities,[2] Janssens called it Barbelo-Gnostic.[3] Yet an important group of scholars has classified it as Sethian. Thus the present paper presents two topics for discussion by the Seminar, the Sethianism of *Trimorphic Protennoia*, as an aspect of the problem of defining Sethianism, and the relation of *Trimorphic Protennoia* to the prologue of John, an important issue irrespective of whether the former be "Sethian" or not.

1. The Debate over the Non-Christian "Sethianism" of the Trimorphic Protennoia

The ambiguities with regard to the term Sethian have been resolved in one way by Hans-Martin Schenke.[4] Impressed by the potentially

---

[2] Jean Doresse, *The Secret Books of the Egyptian Gnostics: An Introduction to the Gnostic Coptic Manuscripts Discovered at Chenoboskion* (London: Hollis & Carter, 1960), appendix 1, "The Teaching of Simon Magus in the Chenoboskion Manuscripts," pp. 329, 331, 332: "All this, it is true, differs hardly at all from what we are told by most of the Sethian revelations restored to us by the Chenoboskion library.... Must we then suppose that ... [the *Trimorphic Protennoia*] drew freely from the source of standard Hermetism? ... A third solution, however, ought to be considered. Let us refer back to the expositions of the teaching of Simon Magus, such as that presented in the *Philosophumena* ... and in particular to the summary of the *Great Revelation* or *Revelation of the Voice and of the Name proceeding from the Great Power* which are attributed to Simon. We shall be struck by the strange likeness that is apparent between the ideas that are developed in the Simonian doctrine on the one hand, and, on the other, in our treatises [the *Trimorphic Protennoia* and *Great Power*]. We even find—and this especially in the case of [the *Trimorphic Protennoia*]—a good many expressions that are identical."

[3] Yvonne Janssens, "Le codex XIII de Nag Hammadi," *Le Muséon* 78 (1974) 342. This "first reading" of the Coptic text has been considerably improved and the commentary augmented in a second edition, *La prôtennoia trimorphe (NH XIII,1)* (Bibliothèque copte de Nag Hammadi, Section "Textes" 4; Québec: Université Laval, 1978). The reference is on p. 2 of the latter.

[4] Hans-Martin Schenke, "Das sethianische System nach Nag-Hammadi-Handschriften," *Studia Coptica* (ed. Peter Nagel; Berliner Byzantinische Arbeiten 45; Berlin: Akademie, 1974) 165-173. See also his paper in the present volume, "The Phenomenon and Significance of Gnostic Sethianism" (above, pp. 588-616).

misleading role of the term Seth in titles (*Second Treatise of the Great Seth* and Epiphanius's source the *Paraphrase of Seth*), he prefers to work inductively toward a definition of Sethianism, though presupposing that there was such as sect as reported in Epiphanius, *Haer.* 39. He seeks the common denominator among the Nag Hammadi tractates he considers "with certainty" "more or less[!] Sethian": the *Apocryphon of John, Hypostasis of the Archons, Gospel of the Egyptians, Apocalypse of Adam, Three Steles of Seth, Zostrianos, Melchizedek, Thought of Norea, Trimorphic Protennoia*. In his essay in the present volume he adds *Marsanes* and *Allogenes* to this list. A text is considered Sethian if it includes the following ingredients: Seth, who is the redeemer (*Gospel of the Egyptians*) or is mediator for the redeemer Adamas (*Three Steles of Seth*), has descendents who are the members of the sect. Adam, Seth, and the mythological and historical descendants live in four aeons designated Harmozel, Oroiael, Daveithe and Eleleth (which names, however, are missing from the *Apocalypse of Adam, Three Steles of Seth, Thought of Norea, Marsanes* and *Allogenes*). These four are luminaries of Autogenes, who is the Son in a Father-Mother-Son trinity, which is thus inherently Sethian. Yaldabaoth is present in Sethianism, but not only here, and hence is not a specific characteristic of Sethianism. (Of course the fact that Barbelo is the female in the trinity in the *Apocalypse of John, Three Steles of Seth, Zostrianos, Melchizedek, Thought of Norea* and *Trimorphic Protennoia* could lead to a similar inference, but does not, since the Barbeloite section of Irenaeus, *Haer.* 1.29, is, like these tractates, classed as Sethian; nor does the fact that the term Luminary occurs in the *Letter of Peter to Philip* prevent this term from being classed as distinctively Sethian.) Finally, a periodizing in terms of Yaldabaoth's attack on the Sethians through the flood on the one hand and through fire and brimstone at Sodom and Gomorrah on the other is distinctively Sethian. In non-Christian Sethianism the Son, Autogenes, is Adamas (*Three Steles of Seth, Zostrianos*), but in Christian Sethianism is Christ (*Apocryphon of John, Gospel of the Egyptians*). Similarly Seth is Christianized as Jesus. Sethianism is traced back to the pre-Gnostic Samaritan Dosithean sect (rather than, e.g., to Judaism); support for this view is derived from the Three Steles of Seth (Dositheus).[5]

---

[5] On the Samaritan connection see (in addition to Doresse, note 2 above) Walter Beltz, "Samaritanertum und Gnosis," *Gnosis und Neues Testament: Studien aus Religionswissenschaft und Theologie* (ed. Karl-Wolfgang Tröger; Berlin: Evangelische Verlagsanstalt, 1973) 89-95. In his contribution to the present volume Schenke, following K. Wekel, U. Luz, and O. Hofius, withdraws his support for a Samaritan origin of

Michel Tardieu concedes that Schenke has

> ... disengaged with considerable thoroughness some of the possible solutions
> for the investigation of a "non-Christian" type of Gnosticism. But why
> characterize it still as "Sethian"? Leave to the heresiologists their categories,
> and let us return to the texts of the Gnostics themselves, to appreciate
> the dosage of the sources, the continuity of the parallels, the diversity of the
> forms of thought, logical or not, and their constants.[6]

Tardieu has quoted with approval R. A. Lipsius:

> The name Gnostic originally was no general designation, but rather a self-
> designation of the heretical parties brought together usually under the name
> "Ophites," i.e., the oldest Syrian common Gnosticism.[7]

Tardieu himself notes:

> The remark of Epiphanius 40.7.5 shows well that Sethians, Archontics
> and Gnostics do not constitute three distinct groups, but rather one and
> the same ideology to be subsumed under the tag "Gnostic" in the
> restricted sense of this term noted by Lipsius.[8]

Thus by transmuting Schenke's "Sethians" into "non-Christian
Gnostics" Tardieu does not seem fully to have left behind the
heresiologists' terminology, but to have opted for Epiphanius's
designation "Gnostic" (*Haer*. 26) as including also what Epiphanius
usually treats as separate groups, "Sethians" (*Haer*. 39) and
"Archontics" (*Haer*. 40).[9]

Even though it is thus not beyond dispute that Schenke's definition of
Sethianism is actually a description of a Sethian sect, or even of any

---

Sethianism. See also A.F.J. Klijn, *Seth in Jewish, Christian and Gnostic Literature*
(Leiden: Brill, 1977). With regard to a Samaritan background to John see Oscar
Cullmann, *Der Johanneische Kreis: Zum Ursprung des Johannesevangeliums* (Tübingen:
Mohr [Siebeck], 1975).

[6] Michel Tardieu, "Les livres mis sous le nom de Seth et les Séthiens de
l'hérésiologie," *Gnosis and Gnosticism: Papers read at the Seventh International Conference
on Patristic Studies*, Oxford, September 8th-13th, 1975 (ed. Martin Krause; NHS 8;
Leiden: Brill, 1977) 204-210, esp. p. 210.

[7] Ibid., 206 n. 8.

[8] Ibid., 206 n. 11.

[9] Norbert Brox, "Gnostikoi als häresiologischer Terminus," *ZNW* 57 (1966) 105-114,
esp. p. 113, argues that a small group in the early period designated itself as
"Gnostikoi in a specific sense," and then that members of other sects used the term
less as the name of a sect than as a self-designation for their individual self-understanding, much as they would use such terms as "pneumatic" or "elect." It was
first Irenaeus who used the term in the broad sense current in modern scholarship
as a designation for the whole movement as consisting of "Gnostics."

given sect, the definition does function as the typology in terms of which the Berliner Arbeitskreis für koptisch-gnostische Schriften has designated the *Trimorphic Protennoia* (hereafter *TriProt*) as Sethian:

> Incidentally, most probably Seth, the Father of the true humanity, i.e., of the Gnostics, is to be understood by the "Father" who is said to have written these three discourses in a book [XIII 50:23]. The material presupposed in the whole is the Sethian system: the God who came into being by himself (Autogenes) (38:22f.), the four Luminaries (38:33-39:5; 48:29), Meirothea (38:15; 45:9f.), the fallen (guileless) Sophia (39:29; 40:15; 47:33f.); Epinoia of light (39:19, 30f., 32f.), the Demiurge Yaltabaoth = Saklas = Samael (39:27f.), etc. This is present in a formulation that has contact especially with that of the *Gospel of the Egyptians* (NHC III,2), compare especially 39:13ff. with *GEgypt* III,2 56:22ff. The form that dominates the whole is found in the "I am" statements of Protennoia....[10]

This same view is repeated in the introduction to the translation of this text by the Berliner Arbeitskreis für koptisch-gnostische Schriften prepared by Gesine Schenke. This introduction is however a considerably more detailed presentation:

> According to the mythological material *Protennoia* is a clearly Sethian writing, immersed in the Gnosticized female version of the pantheistic concept, even though it only presupposes the Sethian cosmology and does not develop it... Furthermore the framework is considerably enlarged by means of cosmological, eschatological and soteriological material that in its concrete formation corresponds especially to the variant of the Sethian system that is at the basis of the *Gospel of the Egyptians* III,2....
>
> On a closer look the material and temporal location of our writing within the whole framework of Gnosticism also proves to be problematical. On the one hand the striking tension between dualism and monism and the pantheistic concept overarching the dualism suggests a relatively late composition of our writing. On the other hand with regard to the situation of man that it presupposes it seems instead archaic, as an early form, in which the anthropology is conceived only from the Gnostic understanding of the world and of existence. The view of man is thus completely non-Christian, purely Gnostic. The only thing that is clearly "Christian" is a single sentence at the end of the third discourse (50:12-15) and the fact that the mere name of Christ is added or attributed to the divine Autogenes (38:22; 39:6f.; 49:8). Measured by the context, on first glance one can really see in this hardly more than a very weak secondary "Christianizing" of the Gnostic text....[11]

---

[10] Berliner Arbeitskreis für koptisch-gnostische Schriften, "Die Bedeutung der Texte von Nag Hammadi für die moderne Gnosisforschung," *Gnosis und Neues Testament*, 75.

[11] "'Die dreigestaltige Protennoia': Eine gnostische Offenbarungsrede in koptischer Sprache aus dem Fund von Nag Hammadi," *TLZ* 99 (1974) 731-746, esp. col. 732.

Wolf-Peter Funk of the Berlin group designates *TriProt* "the 'most literary' among the Sethian texts":

> Whereas in the other texts liturgical completeness or speculative calculation dominates, there really seems to be here something like a poetic power of imagination.[12]

Carsten Colpe concurs with the Berliner Arbeitskreis, with which he is in contact, in regarding *TriProt* as a "classic within the Sethian corpus."[13] Furthermore, Kurt Rudolph, at times a commuting member from Leipzig, follows the view of the Berliner Arbeitskreis as to the secondary Christianization of *TriProt*,[14] though he agrees with Frederik Wisse in contesting the existence of a sect of "Sethians."[15]

The dissertation on *TriProt* by Schenke carries through in considerable detail the Berlin thesis, with a significant modification, namely an increase in the amount of text held to reflect Christianity.

> *48:35-49:22:* This section seems to seek to portray once again the descent of the Redeemer through the spheres of the Archons by assimilation to the inhabitants of each sphere. Yet a closer examination shows that this repetition apparently has a quite specific further goal. For the modification in the formulation of the description of the descent seems to serve the purpose of explaining aetiologically or illuminating in a Gnostic way certain christological titles and concepts. In any case one gets the impression that this passage is first intelligible and in every nuance transparent only if one would be prepared to see and interpret it on the background of an already presupposed Christian christology.
>
> Especially the text seems to reinterpret the predications of Jesus as "Christ," "Son of God," and "Son of Man" in terms of the myth of the descending Redeemer. In this view it could even seem as if an early Christian angel christology is involved.
>
> The interpretation given on the basis of this myth holds that Jesus wrongly bears all these titles. For the Archons have seen him thus only because for a time he became similar to them or seemed to fit into their categories. On the other hand he is rightly called "the Beloved"; the false identification of the Archons in regard to this (traditional) title consists only in that the Demiurge had taken the descending redeemer for *his* Beloved (Son), whereas in reality he is the Beloved (Brother?) of the Gnostics....

---

[12] In his review of the *Facsimile Edition of the Nag Hammadi Codices, Codices XI, XII, and XIII,* in *OLZ* 73 (1978) 154.

[13] Carsten Colpe, "Heidnische, jüdische und christliche Überlieferung in den Schriften aus Nag Hammadi III," JAC 17 (1974) 122.

[14] Kurt Rudolph, *Die Gnosis: Wesen und Geschichte einer spätantiken Religion* (Leipzig: Koehler & Amelang, 1977) 153-157.

[15] In the abstract "Die 'sethianische' Gnosis—eine häresiologische Fiktion?" communicated to the Seminar on Sethian Gnosticism at the International Conference on Gnosticism at Yale, above, pp. 577-578.

The exegeted topos of the change of form explains how the error of the Archontic powers took place at all. One could also interpret this whole presentation as non-Christian, in the normal Gnostic mythological meaning of this topos (see above to 47:34 ff.). But the individual statements become plastic and pregnant only when one recognizes in them a reinterpretation of early Christian christology. The first statement could be paraphrased as follows: "In my descent I deceived the Demiurge in such a way that he held me to be his Son. And in his eyes I maintained this role consistently until the death on the cross, i.e., until, by letting Jesus rise and by mediating gnosis to those who recognized my true being, I put an end to Chaos's ignorance about me and thus disgraced the Demiurge and his followers."

Although the text is non-Christian, indeed in this part even anti-Christian, there seems to be presupposed the form most normal in Christian Gnosticism of the idea that the communication of gnosis takes place only after the resurrection (and only through the Resurrected). The cross is the break between ignorance and knowledge among humans too. These at first took him also for the Son of "God"; only after the triumphal resurrection is there for some the possibility of recognition.

In the course of the descent scheme the concept of Jesus as an angel or like an angel, which apparently was at home in certain groups of early Christianity and appears, e.g., as a foil in the Letter to the Hebrews, is also distorted in the typically Gnostic way: the Redeemer was of course like an angel, but only in his appearance, so as to deceive the angels.

The formulation of the concept among humans becomes especially transparent if one understands it as an explanation for how one arrived at the title Son of Man for Jesus: through the error of the Archons and humans, who mistook him and had falsely taken him really for a human! This explanation already presupposes a concept in terms of which the title Son of Man as a christological predication balancing the title Son of God describes the twofold nature of Jesus: true God and true man, a concept which the Gnostic author here distorts.[16]

This newly identified area of secondary Christianization is then associated with the main such passage previously identified:

To all appearances there is already presupposed here the statement "I put on Jesus" (50:12-15) and the author intends to make clear how one is to understand correctly this statement...

One could perhaps explain the fact that in this statement [50:12-15] in a certain sense the docetism of Seth incarnate in Jesus comes through, in that this inserted christological topos, which is still part of the camouflage scene of 48:35 ff. (see the commentary on this passage) and perhaps even formed together with it a distinct unit of tradition, has in the course

---

[16] Gesine Schenke, "Die dreigestaltige Protennoia (Nag-Hammadi-Codex XIII) herausgegeben und kommentiert" (Dr. theol. dissertation, Rostock, 1977) 2. 128, 130-132.

of the Christianizing of Gnosticism, (secondarily?) gained entrance into our
text and hence effected, as it were, an overlay of the threads of tradition.[17]

In her summary statements Schenke clearly retains the concept of
non-Christian Gnosticism secondarily Christianized, although she is less
precise as to whether this is in the case of *TriProt* to be explained in
terms of a secondary redaction or in terms of Christian Gnostic traditions
impinging upon a basically non-Christian Gnostic author.

> In Sethianism however a genuine fusion [with Christianity] is not even
> attained. With regard to our text one can doubtless only say that in its
> basic substance it presents itself as a document of non-Christian Gnosticism,
> but the individual Christian motifs and elements that have flowed into it attest
> already the discussions of the variegated religious streams in the early
> period of Christianity. Typical is the passage in the third discourse that
> reinterprets Christian traditions (titles of Christ) and finds its high point in a
> docetic statement. Only an extensive redaction-historical analysis could
> show whether this passage, which hardly fits well in the context, first got into
> the text secondarily, or was no longer sensed by the author as Christian
> and was taken over already as "Gnostic" tradition, just as generally the
> degree of "Christianness" is to be assessed only after detailed examination
> of the history of its origin.
>
> In its basic substance the text is non-Christian, but nonetheless contains
> —along with weak Christianization by appending the mere name "Christ"
> to the divine Autogenes—a negatively reinterpreted and clearly Christian
> part within the explanations about the appearance of Protennoia in the
> Logos, which seems to presuppose already thought-out Christian Gnosti-
> cism.[18]

2. THE TRIMORPHIC PROTENNOIA AND THE PROLOGUE OF THE
GOSPEL OF JOHN

Gesine Schenke published for the Berliner Arbeitskreis für die
koptisch-gnostische Schriften the following claim for *TriProt*:

> For the question of the scholarly value of our new text, especially
> interesting and perhaps of great significance is the third revelatory discourse
> of *Protennoia* [*TriProt*], which—and not only it—in large part presents actually
> a material parallel to the prologue of the Fourth Gospel. Quite unusually close
> is the affinity of many thoughts and expressions of this third discourse, and
> of corresponding parts of the two others, to those of the Johannine prologue.
> Both texts interpret each other, but it seems at first glance that the light
> falls more from *Protennoia* onto the Johannine prologue than the reverse.
> Now for a person who thinks of the prologue in terms of source
> criticism and the history of religions, basically in the way generally

---

[17] Ibid., 2. 129, 141.
[18] Ibid., 1. xxvi-xxvii; 2. 146.

practiced in the sphere of influence of R. Bultmann's Johannine interpretation, our text will be a brilliant confirmation of the long-known
hypothesis. He will see the substance of the third discourse of *Protennoia* as
on the same plane as the Gnostic Logos hymn assumed as the source of the
Johannine prologue. But since, in spite of the doubtless widespread
unanimity concerning the necessity for source criticism in the case of the
Johannine prologue, there is not such unity of individual results, it is
advisable, in order not to narrow in advance the perspectives, to grasp
the phenomenon of the similarity of the two texts also, or at least initially,
without taking into consideration source theories on the Johannine prologue.
In this perspective one has the impression that the relevant statements of
Protennoia stand in their natural context, whereas their parallels in the
Johannine prologue, as we find it in the Fourth Gospel, seem to have
been artificially made serviceable to a purpose really alien to them.[19]

This position was spelled out in more detail by Carsten Colpe, who
itemized "the stupendous 'parallels' to the prologue of the Gospel of
John."

One need not go back behind the discussion that has meanwhile been
terminated with some consensus as to what a parallel is and is not,
what can be explained thus and what not. Quite to the contrary! Also
this is not to forget what has been produced by way of materials in the
impressive number of Johannine commentaries to every word and every
sentence of the prologue. [A footnote refers to the lists of parallels
to wisdom literature and Philo in C. H. Dodd, *The Interpretation of the
Fourth Gospel* (1954) 274-277.] But what is disparate there, stands together
here, even though not in the sequence of the prologue. This would seem to
be unique up to the present: perhaps exact stylistic investigations of the
Coptic wording will some day show that these "parallels" even stand
formally nearer to the text of the Johannine prologue than do others.
In terms of content this impression already presses itself on us, when one
leaves out the Sethian terms. What follows is only a selection of the most
striking instances:
    John 1:1-2, cf. XIII 35:1, 4-6: "[I] am ... [the first-]born among those
who [came to be, she who exists] before the All."
    John 1:3, cf. XIII 38:12-13: "It is through me that the All took shape."
    John 1:4, cf. XIII 35:12-13: "I am the life of my Epinoia."
    John 1:5, cf. XIII 36:5: "I shone down [upon the darkness]."
    John 1:7, cf. XIII 37:3-6, 8-9: "Then the Son ...—that is, the Word
who originated through that Voice ...—(this Son) revealed the everlasting
things and all the unknowns were known."
    John 1:9, cf. XIII 47:28-29: "[I] am the Light that illumines the All."
    John 1:10, cf. XIII 38:16-18; 50:15-16: "Then the Perfect Son revealed
himself to his Aeons who originated through him.... And those who
watch over their dwelling places did not recognize me."

[19] *TLZ* 99 (1974) 733.

John 1:11, cf. XIII 41:15-16; 47:22-25: "Indeed all these I explained to those who are mine, who are the Sons of the Light, ... And I hid myself within them until I revealed myself to my [brethren]. And none of them (the Powers) knew me, [although] it is I who work in them."

John 1:12, cf. XIII 37:18-20: "And he taught irreproducible doctrines to all those who became Sons of the Light."

John 1:13, cf. XIII 49:25-28: "... to the Sons of the Light alone, that is, the ordinances of the Father. These are the glories that are higher than every glory, ... complete by virtue of Intellect."

John 1:14, cf. XIII 47:13-15, 16-17; 38:20-22. "The third time I revealed myself to them [in] their tents as the Word.... And I wore everyone's (sc. the Powers') garment.... and (he) stood in the glory with which he glorified himself. They blessed the Perfect Son, the Christ...."

John 1:16, cf. XIII 46:16-19: "It (the Word?) is a hidden Light, ... pouring forth ... from the ... immeasurable spring."

John 1:18, cf. XIII 36:30; 36:17-22: "It is invisible.... I am the Thought of the Father and through me proceeded [the] Voice, that is, the knowledge of the everlasting things.... I am joined to the unknowable and intangible Thought."

Hopefully no one will now say: "So the Evangelist John" (or whoever) "demythologized, Christianized, historicized a Gnostic hymn after all." Of course this remains still possible. But now that *TriProt* is accessible, the historical question should be put more precisely. The text itself implicitly offers indications of its age—of course only relative to the history of traditions, not in terms of an absolute chronology—in that there remains still clearly recognizable the basic sapiential speculation out of which Gnostic mythology could have developed and into which it can also return again.... Also the "parallels" drawn to the Johannine prologue are an indication of this, since they, as they stand thus isolated, can be fitted into sapiential as well as into Gnostic contexts. The question to be posed is then as follows: in order to find the reference points for the creation of the theology of the Johannine prologue, does one henceforth need no longer to search as in the past with a divining rod through the very diffuse sapiential streams of the first century A.D. in the eastern Mediterranean; rather are such reference points now more specifically to be expected in that sapiential speculation that would become one among many other bases of Sethian mythology? Such a question may also be justified on the grounds that there are indications of Sethianism having wandered from Mesopotamia to Egypt via Syria/Palestine—after all, the Archontics were perhaps a branch of it in that area. To be sure, it still remains to be clarified whether the Sethian or Archontic mythology was also partially developed in Syria or Palestine, or whether it, coming from the syncretistic neighborhood of the magi in Mesopotamia, could find a new home especially easily there, since the milieu was prepared by ideas which were widely sensed as related to the sapiential bases of Sethianism.[20]

---

[20] Carsten Colpe, "Heidnische, jüdische und christliche Überlieferung ... III," 122-124. I quote throughout from John Turner's translation of *TriProt* published in *NHLibEng*, 461-70.

In the same year Yvonne Janssens published her edition,[21] in which she approached *TriProt* as a Barbeloite text and hence as Christian Gnostic. Since she was at the time unaware of the position of the Berliner Arbeitskreis, the question of secondary Christianization was not explicitly a topic for discussion. It is thus first with R. McL. Wilson's paper at the patristic conference at Oxford in 1975 that the implications of Janssens's presentation are presented as a clear alternative to the position of the Berliner Arbeitskreis, even though Colpe's itemization had not yet come to his attention nor had the subsequent literature on the topic yet become available.[22] Wilson's essay none-theless presents a point of departure for itemizing some of the alternatives and investigating their methodological presuppositions. It is hoped that the International Conference on Gnosticism will provide a forum in which the principals can engage each other so as to advance the discussion, which is thus far only at a very tentative and preliminary stage, on into a more advanced clarification, where some results of a methodological and substantive kind can be attained. (It is greatly to be regretted that the invited members of the Berliner Arbeits-kreis für koptisch-gnostische Schriften from the German Democratic Republic, Hans-Martin Schenke and Kurt Rudolph, were not able to attend the International Conference on Gnosticism at Yale.)

Wilson confronts the thesis of secondary Christianization with a counterproposal of secondary de-Christianization:

> ... one possibility not always taken into consideration is that there may also in some cases have been *de*-Christianization. It must be remembered that the *only* form accessible is the Christianized version—any non-Christian form has to be reconstructed by elimination of the Christian elements. How can we distinguish a de-Christianized text from one that is purely Gnostic in origin? It is well-nigh certain that if we had a Christian-Gnostic text and also a de-Christianized version, the latter would be claimed as the basis of the former.[23]

Usually in such instances there is a whole series of minor indications of priority and secondariness, which are often not doctrinal at all, but provide all the better objective criteria of the direction of the flow. This is no doubt most demonstrable when both editions

---

[21] See note 3 above.

[22] R. McL. Wilson, "The *Trimorphic Protennoia*," *Gnosis and Gnosticism* (NHS 8; Leiden: Brill, 1977), 50-54.

[23] Ibid. Unless otherwise indicated, references below to Wilson's views are found in this article.

are extant, as in the case of *Eugnostos the Blessed* and the *Sophia of Jesus Christ*. One need merely think of such a classic case study as the Synoptic problem, where the mass of minor improvements of Matthew and Luke over Mark, from Greek style and taste to weightier matters such as christology, present a rather insurmountable barrier to the perennial attempt to exploit the weaknesses of the classical two-document hypothesis in such a way as to overthrow it.

Wilson argues that since (in the forms so far accessible to us) "the Sethian and Barbelognostic systems show at least some degree of Christian influence," "there is therefore some probability that a document from this milieu in which the Christian element is weaker may be the result of de-Christianization." Such reasoning that results in an a priori probability for the traditional view seems far from compelling. It is well known that our sources have been nearly exclusively the citations of Christian heresiologists so narrowly concerned with purifying the Church of error that they normally limited themselves to Christian Gnosticism, thus leading to the traditional view of Gnosticism as an inner-Christian aberration, the view challenged by the History of Religions School. Since the Nag Hammadi library apparently emanated from Christian monastic circles, one might also expect scribal glossing of a Christianizing kind, suggested in such minor details as the use of *nomina sacra*, but also evident, e.g., in the Christianizing of the title of the *Gospel of the Egyptians*.

Yet even when both editions are not extant, a decision need not always be either dependent on such general assumptions or as arbitrary as Wilson suggests, if one may apply effectively, e.g., the methodological criterion of "natural" vs. "artificial" suggested by the Berliner Arbeitskreis. This may be illustrated in terms of an analogous case proposed by Wilson in a written response to the present paper: *GTh* 79 "combines two logia from Luke, which fit so well that without Luke one would never think of a combination. *Has* Thomas combined, or did Luke break up an original unity?" This is in effect an appeal to the criterion of "naturalness," in that they "fit so well." But the two logia are only externally similar, in that they share the phrase "blessed is the womb." There is no substantive unity between a rejected beatitude referring to Mary and an approved beatitude referring to the barren. Thus even if one were unaware that the two logia are separate in Luke one would opt in favor of the alternative that Thomas combined them secondarily, on the basis that their union is external, "artificial," more like a catchword connection than a continuous train of thought. Thus even when both editions are not present one may at times establish priority in terms of naturalness vs. artificiality. Wilson himself concedes there is secondary Christianization in some cases even when both editions are not extant, e.g., the *Gospel of Mary*[24] and the *Apocryphon of John*.[25]

Wilson rightly points out that since de-Christianization "would not necessarily eliminate each and every Christian element," one should expect "words and phrases current in Christian usage which may betray some legacy from Christian influence." However, such words and phrases may also be part of non-Christian Gnosticism (or apocalypticism, etc.), whose influence on Christianity is the implication of the view opposed by Wilson. For example, both Colpe and Janssens point to XIII 47:14 as parallel to John 1:14, and to XIII 50:15-16 as parallel to John 1:10, with opposing assumptions as to the directionality of the influence. In order to move beyond such an impasse, one would need to ask whether the words and phrases, though current in Christian usage, are distinctive of Christianity in comparison with other Hellenistic religions.

At this point it is important to draw attention to a logical fallacy latent in our culture, which one could characterize as the transferring of an epistemological fact of life into an ontological claim. Our greater familiarity and empathy with the early Christian literature over against the non-Christian literature of that period may suggest to us that the former is basic and prior, whereas the latter, since subsequently learned as part of our mature erudition, is secondary. This would merely be an instance of our prejudice, not a valid working hypothesis for reconstructing the reality of the Hellenistic world. There is of course, as Wilson points out, the possibility of the reverse prejudice. In any case, such "Christian" words and phrases should not merely be listed. They should be investigated, their profile established from the secondary literature of scholarship and the Hellenistic sources on which it is based. Are the words and phrases that seem to suggest the originally Christian nature of the texts so widespread in Hellenistic religiosity as to be irrelevant, or perhaps even long since suspect in scholarly circles as indicative of a Gnostic influence on Christian texts, and thus

---

[24] R. McL. Wilson, "The New Testament in the Gnostic Gospel of Mary," *NTS* 3 (1956) 236-243.

[25] Wilson refers to Willem Cornelis van Unnik; see the latter's *Evangelien aus dem Nilsand* (Frankfurt: Scheffler, [1959]) 81-92, especially the conclusion drawn on p. 92 of a non-Christian origin of the *Apocryphon of John*.

more naturally to be taken as supporting documentation for the alternate view? One may recall by way of analogy the assumed Paulinism of John, which on closer examination proved to be simply the dependence of John on Hellenistic Christianity, not specifically on Paul, in that the terminology distinctive of Paul was missing. The fact that Paul was the only Hellenistic Christian literature available prior to the Gospels had misled scholarship until a distinction was made among words and phrases in Paul as to whether they were common Christian (or Hellenistic) terms, or whether they were distinctively Pauline.

Wilson's critical awareness leads him to dismiss as in most cases "at best remote parallels" five New Testament references Janssens mentions in her footnotes[26]—he does not even itemize them. But those in Janssens's commentary he considers "more promising." One having to do with John is the following:

> 37:20-22: "Now the Voice that originated from my Thought exists as three *permanences*: the Father, the Mother, the Son." (Janssens also mentions 46:28-31: "It is the eye of the three *permanences*, which exist as a Voice by virtue of Thought. And it is a Word by virtue of the Sound.")
>
> John 14:2: "There are many *dwelling-places* in my Father's house."

Here the shared term μονή "might conceivably echo" the New Testament passage. Anything is possible, but the historian's task is to find methodologically discussable ways to weigh degrees of possibility and probability. The three permanences seem to be something like the modes in a modal monarchianism, or perhaps a more substantive doctrine of the trinity. The mythological presupposition may be that divine personages are also places (i.e., Aeons, spatially parts of the Pleroma).[27] But such a mythological background of the use of μονή

---

[26] Janssens, in her second edition, *La prôtennoia trimorphe*, includes all but the second instance within her commentary.

[27] Gesine Schenke in her dissertation (2. 36 n. 2) conjectures that one has to do with an inexact formulation whose intention is to designate one μονή as belonging to each member of the trinity, in which case μονή retains its purely spatial significance. She also conjectures (2. 37) that 37:27-29 is out of place, either having been a gloss on μονή that was introduced into the text at the wrong position, or that the text originally lacked the term μονή but had only the drawing of the three quadrangles, which was secondarily glossed with the comment "μονή written as three quadrangles." These efforts to render the text more intelligible are quite speculative, and hence can hardly receive widespread acceptance, although one must keep in mind that the conjectural emendation of a Nag Hammadi text of which there is only one manuscript, and that in a version, is a much more reasonable and indeed necessary methodological tool than, e.g., in the case of the Bible, where the quantity of manuscripts in the original language makes conjectural emendation much less appropriate.

does not come to expression in John. If a Gnostic exegete was familiar with that background, he might (as might a historian of religion) recognize John 14:2 as an outgrowth of such a background. But an early Christian unfamiliar with that background (as has been traditional Christian exegesis) would not be led to engender it as a creative development from Johannine thought. But if John 14:2 at most could have "triggered" a Gnostic already familiar with that background to give expression to it, that is to say, if John 14:2 is at best the occasion, not the cause, then the absence of the Johannine point and the causal presence of the background in the thinking of the author of *TriProt* make the recourse to John 14:2 superfluous. The author of *TriProt* writes fluently from his own world of thought and does not need John to provide him an occasion to think in terms of his own thought patterns. Even if one knew he was familiar with John 14:2, one would have to conclude that he nonetheless was explicating not John but his own world of thought. Is this not a good instance of what the Berliner Arbeitskreis means when it says (in terms of the Johannine prologue) that in *TriProt* such concepts are in their natural context, whereas in John they seem artificial?

If one wants to see how a Gnostic would interpret John 14:2, one may turn to the passage the Berliner Arbeitskreis considers clearly Christian and a secondary Christianization, to which Wilson refers in this contect only to suggest that μονή is here translated into Coptic: 50:12-16: "(As for) me, I put on Jesus. I bore him from the cursed wood, and established him in the *dwelling-places* of his Father. And those who watch over their *dwelling-places* did not recognize me." Here (in sharp distinction to the two other passages where μονή occurs) the scope of the Johannine verse, namely that Christ is ascending to prepare the abode for the believers, comes to expression, as well as the mythological presupposition of the concept, namely that every heavenly being, the evil Archons as well as the good divine personnages above, has its abode. Here the Johannine verse (or some equivalent Christian tradition) is reimbedded in its mythological background, a quite intelligible Gnostic exegesis. Thus 50:12-16 illustrates one prerequisite for arguing convincingly that a Gnostic text echoes Christian material, namely, that both ingredients, the Christian as well as the Gnostic, are clearly attested. Hence in 50:12-16 it is possible that the influence of John 14:2 has led to a new Christian Gnostic usage of that mythological background. Such a textual situation is perhaps easiest to explain —especially in view of the quite different situation at 37:20-22; 46:28-

31—in terms of a Christian Gnostic interpolation into a non-Christian Gnostic text, which is the solution offered by the Berliner Arbeitskreis.

Janssens has subsequently made explicit her opposition to her over-simplification of the view of the Berliner Arbeitskreis (though apparently unaware of Colpe's article).[28]

> Is it necessary to conclude from this that John borrows these terms from *TriProt*? Let us say right away that for us it is rather the reverse that took place.

She lists the parallels to the prologue of John as follows:

> John 1:1, cf. XIII 46:5, 14; 47:14-15: "I am [the Word].... I alone am the Word.... I revealed myself to them [in] their tents as the Word."
> John 1:3, cf. XIII 35:3-4; 36:7-8: "[She in whom the] All takes its stand.... It is I who have produced the All" [or: "... I am the one who gradually dawns on the All."]
> John 1:4, cf. XIII 35:12: "I am the life...."
> John 1:4-5, 9, cf. XIII 38:13; 47:28-31: "(I am) the Mother (as well as) the Light which she appointed.... I] am the Light that illumines the All. I am the Light that rejoices [in my] brethren."
> John 1:5, cf. XIII 37:5, 14; 46:30-32: "The Word... revealed himself to those who dwell in darkness.... And it is a Word by virtue of the Sound; it was sent to illumine those who dwell in the [darkness]."
> John 1:9b, cf. XIII 47:31-32: "For I came down to the world [of] mortals."
> John 1:10, cf. XIII 47:18-19, 24; 50:15-16: "And [they] did not know the one who empowers me.... And none of them (the Powers) knew me.... And those who watch over their dwelling-places did not recognize me."
> John 1:11, cf. XIII 40:31, 36; 41:15-16, 27-28; 45:28-29: "I was [with] my own.... to those who [are mine ...] Indeed all these I explained to those who are mine.... I spoke my mysteries to my own.... It is I who put the breath within my own."
> John 1:12, cf. XIII 37:19-20; 42:15-16; 49:25: "Those who became Sons of the Light.... Those who have known me, that is, the Sons of the Light.... The Sons of the Light."
> John 1:14, cf. XIII 47:13-15: "The third time I revealed myself to them [in] their tents as the Word."
> John 1:18, cf. XIII 35:7-9; 36:30-32: "I am invisible within the Thought of the Invisible One.... It is invisible [to all those who are] visible in the All."
> John 1:18b, cf. XIII 41:2-3, 27-28; 36:9-10; 35:21-22: "I shall tell you an ineffable and indivulgeable mystery... I spoke my mysteries to my own—a hidden mystery.... It is through me that knowledge comes forth.... Those who sleep I [awaken]."

[28] "Une source gnostique du Prologue?" *L'Évangile de Jean: Sources, rédaction, théologie* (BETL 44; Gembloux: Louvain University Press, 1977) 355-358.

Janssens accentuates somewhat overly simply the divergence in meaning, in that John is oriented to faith and *TriProt* to knowledge. She does concede one point to the Berliner Arbeitskreis.

> With regard to the "natural" context, it is true that in Codex XIII the "Word" follows logically the Thought and Voice as an expression of the divine.

But she takes recourse to the familiar derivation of the New Testament from the Old Testament in abstraction from the question of which exegetical context mediated the Old Testament, thus ignoring the possibility that the Old Testament background might have been mediated to John through Gnostic, or, as Colpe would argue, Gnosticizing sapiential hermeneutical traditions.

> In brief, it seems to us easy enough to establish a parallel between the first five verses of the prologue .of John and those of Genesis (and others have done this prior to us). If the same terms are found in Codex XIII, they are not there in the same order and the meaning is, by the way, not at all the same.... John would find adequately elements in the Old Testament not to have to look for them elsewhere.

In view of the extensive use of the Old Testament, especially the early chapters of Genesis, both in Nag Hammadi tractates and in other Gnostic literature, such an either-or choice between "Gnostic" or "Old Testament" should be recognized as a logical fallacy.

One parallel has been noted by all commentators:

> 47:13-16: "The third time I revealed myself to them [in] their *tents* as the Word and I revealed myself in the likeness of their shape."
>
> John 1:14: "So the Word became flesh; he came to *dwell* among us, and we saw his glory...."

The terms σκηνή in *TriProt* and ἐσκήνωσεν in John are indeed a striking parallel. No doubt it was this that led Wilson to say this "looks like an interpretation of John" and Colpe to list it as an instance of *TriProt* providing the background of John. Jan Heldermann has devoted a lengthy article to this parallel, in support of Janssens's view.[29] His conclusion is as follows:

> The Logos manifests/reveals himself to his own in human form. As necessary for salvation he bears the human body of every pneumatic and also works, just as he had before, in a hidden way in them. The manifestation takes place in the world of the chosen persons: in their environ-

---

[29] "'In ihren Zelten...': Bemerkungen zu Codex XIII Nag Hammadi p. 47:14-18 im Hinblick auf Joh. i 14," *Miscellanea Neotestamentica* (ed. T. Baarda, A. F. J. Klijn, W. C. van Unnik; Leiden: Brill, 1978) 1. 181-211. The quotation is from pp. 206-208.

ment. Hence in my opinion "their tents ..." points to the human dwelling-world, which has to serve as the stage for this manifestation, in brief, the necessary scenario (derived from σκηνή in the meaning of stage!) in which the call sounds out!

Thus in *TriProt* 47:14-15 the point of John 1:14 is intentionally reinterpreted. In the latter, a real dwelling of the person Jesus as a residence among and with humans for a long period of time is indicated, but in the former it is suggested that the Revealer (Barbelo/Protennoia) does not himself dwell among and with humans in the same nature, but rather only uses their environment as the scenario and their bodies as camouflage, in order that his word may be heard like a person, even though in a manifestation of short duration. Here we encounter pure docetism. The loanword σκηνή (tent, not body), which, in any case as far as I can see, occurs only here in the Nag Hammadi texts, was chosen as a common loanword precisely in view of John 1:14, yet not in the verbal form found there, but rather as a substantive, so that now in the strict sense this word could emphasize that the scenario of the human world is present only briefly, indeed that it would soon be dismantled, as is customary with a stage setting. The reinterpretation of John 1:14 seems clear to us: "Dwelling" is reserved only for the world of light, existence in the Invisible Spirit (*TriProt* 37:21; 46:29; *ApocryJn*, Papyrus Berolinensis 8502, 26:13)... The *TriProt* then in my opinion also does not have [merely] a "hair-thin Christian veneer"; the reinterpretation is too consciously *polemic* toward John 1:14 for that!

However, this conclusion results from detailed analysis of the Coptic usage, and hence at best would refer to the understanding of the Coptic translator. But since the Sahidic and Bohairic translations of John 1:14 do not use the loanword, the Coptic translator of *TriProt.* may well not have had John 1:14 in mind. With regard to the Greek original, Heldermann points out[30] that a loanword in the Coptic translation may not be the same word as in the Greek original, and that if σκηνή were in the Greek original, it is a term meaning both "tent" and "abode," with "the latter meaning to be emphasized," so that the dichotomy between "dwelling" above and "camping" below could hardly be derived from the term. Thus there seems no clear evidence of a polemic against John 1:14 on the part of the original Greek author of *TriProt*.

Klaus Koschorke[31] has identified a section of the *Letter of Peter to Philip* that he considers a Gnostic interpretation of the prologue of John (VIII 136:16-137:4):

---

[30] *Ibid.*, 189.

[31] "Eine gnostische Paraphrase des johanneischen Prologs: Zur Interpretation von 'Epistula Petri ad Philippum' (NHC VIII,2) 136,16-137,4," *VC*, 33 (1979) 383-392.

Next concerning the Pleroma, it is I. [And] I was sent down in the body [John 1:14a] because of the seed which had fallen away [John 1:9b]. And I came down to their dead product. But they did not recognize me [John 1:10c]; they were thinking of me that I was a mortal man. And I spoke [John 1:1, 14] with him who belongs to me [John 1:11-12]. And he hearkened in order that he might enter into the inheritance of his fatherhood [John 1:12b]. And I took [...(Koschorke: him up into the aeons)] they were filled [...] in his salvation. And since he was a deficiency, for this reason he became a Pleroma [John 1:16].

Marvin W. Meyer points out that this passage is so typical of the tractate, points out that this passage is such a typical instance of the Gnostic myth that a specific dependence on the prologue of John (in distinction from a dependence of this tractate in general upon Luke-Acts) is hard to demonstrate.[32] In any case it is striking how similar it is specifically to XIII 50:12-16, which is generally agreed to be Christian and perhaps reflecting the prologue of John, but not in any distinctive way to the rest of *TriProt*.

Elaine Pagels has analyzed the Gnostic exegesis of the prologue of John by the Naassenes, Peratae and Valentinians.[33] She has shown both how divergent Gnostic exegeses of a given passage can be, and yet how each such exegesis can be understood in terms of the theology or mythology of the Gnostic position from which the exegesis comes. Any discussion of Gnostic exegesis of the prologue of John in Nag Hammadi texts should at least survey these heresiological sources and her analysis of them.

One could in conclusion draw attention to the Pronoia hymn appended to the long version of the *Apocryphon of John* (II 30:11-31:25), whose striking parallels to *TriProt* are noted by Janssens.[34] For its parallels to *TriProt* are in large part also parallels to the prologue of John, although the Pronoia hymn, narrating three descents of the Redeemer, is not explicitly Christian. Is one to classify it as a de-Christianized re-mythologized Gnostic interpretation of the prologue, or is it not more reasonable to see here something like the "natural" context in which this material existed prior to its

[32] Marvin W. Meyer, "The Letter of Peter to Philip (NHC VIII,2): Text, Translation and Commentary" (Ph.D. diss., Claremont, 1979) 233-37. See also Klaus Koschorke, "Eine gnostische Pfingstpredigt: Zur Auseinandersetzung zwischen gnostischem und kirchlichem Christentum am Beispiel der 'Epistula Petri ad Philippum' (NHC VIII,2)," *ZTK* 74 (1977) 323-343.

[33] *The Johannine Gospel in Gnostic Exegesis: Heracleon's Commentary on John* (SBLMS 17; Nashville and New York: Abingdon, 1973) 20-50.

[34] *La prôtennoia trimorphe*, 11-12.

Christianization? The traces in the prologue of John of periodization, namely the Logos being in the primordial period, in the pre-Christian "spermatic" period, and in the incarnate period, would then become intelligible as the way in which that non-Christian tradition was adapted to and unified in Christ, in a way that at times seems a bit "artificial," when compared with *TriProt*.

DISCUSSION

GEORGE MACRAE: PROFESSOR Robinson has proposed that we discuss whether the *Trimorphic Protennoia* is a witness to the same development of thought as found in the prologue to the Fourth Gospel. I have invited Professor Robert McL. Wilson, a member of the Valentinian seminar, to join us for this session since he has written on this topic.

JAMES ROBINSON: My purpose in writing my paper was to prepare a workbook culled from the published works of two opposing viewpoints represented at this conference that would allow us to look at specific texts and discuss the methodological presuppositions involved in what may be an important aspect of Gnostic studies in the future. The unexpected absence of Professor Schenke undercuts to some extent the momentum of our discussion here.

Apart from the *Gospel of Thomas*, no greater claim has been made for the relevance of the Nag Hammadi texts to the New Testament than that made by the Berliner Arbeitskreis regarding the *Trimorphic Protennoia*. The debate over that claim may permit us to compare the cogency of the explanations of "de-Christianization" and "secondary Christianization" to explain certain phenomena in Gnostic literature. Although Professor Wilson would charge me with hiding my light under a bushel if I claimed neutrality, I have not taken a final position on the debate.

To speak of non-Christian Gnosticism one must presume a Gnosticism which arose without the benefit of Christianity. At this stage we have not found any Gnostic texts that clearly antedate the origin of Christianity. But neither is everything in the Nag Hammadi texts obviously post-Christian so as to carry the day for those who would describe Gnosticism as a post-Christian phenomenon. A careful attention to methodology is required to move us beyond the present impasse. With this in mind I have included in my paper the discussion on the word, *monē*, which appears in John 14:2 and *Trimorphic Protennoia* 37:20-22 and 46:28-31. When a Gnostic parallel includes a Christian addition to a general Hellenistic concept the dependence on Christianity is clear. But why suggest a borrowing from Christianity when only a general Hellenistic concept is paralleled?

My second illustration deals with the triad and the three comings of the redeemer. Perhaps the triad in the *Trimorphic Protennoia* provides the missing link in explaining the development from the female Sophia of the Jewish Wisdom literature to the male Logos of the Johannine prologue, as well as accounting for the prominence of the Logos in the prologue.

We need to remember that we are talking about the traditions behind the two documents and not the documents themselves. The Berlin School's position is that the present text of *Trimorphic Protennoia* attests to an older tradition sufficiently ancient to have influenced the prologue, enabling us to pinpoint a stream of tradition that is the closest matrix of the prologue of John yet to have been identified.

MacRae: Professor Colpe, would you care to make any preliminary remarks?

Carsten Colpe: I should add to Professor Robinson's remarks that there is no Gnostic parallel to the phrase, *ho logos sarks egeneto*, nor to the comparison with Moses in John 1:17. Wherever one finds the phrase, *ho logos sarks egeneto*, one is certainly not dealing with a Gnostic text! As to the alternatives of "Christianization" versus "de-Christianization" in the case of the prologue to John and *Trimorphic Protennoia*, we can proceed by assuming that both shared a similar sapiential background. The non-docetic Christianization of the sapiential tradition could have been accomplished by adding the phrase, *ho logos sarks egeneto*. At this point I am unable to determine whether for the *Trimorphic Protennoia* the probability is in favor of a docetic Christianization of the sapiential tradition or whether the phrase was excluded, making the Coptic assertions sapiential and even Gnostic in character.

MacRae: Professor Wilson, would you care to make any preliminary remarks?

ROBERT McL. WILSON: My paper to which Professor Robinson has made vigorous and repeated reference was a five-page communication intended to look at the *Trimorphic Protennoia* in a preliminary fashion. He does me too much credit by erecting my brief discussion into a countertheory—something I never intended. At the outset I was struck by the more than twenty differences between Janssens's French translation and the translation of the Berlin group on just the first page, due to the number of conjectural reconstructions by the Berlin group. The paper simply raised the possibility of de-Christianization—a possibility not even considered by some. In noting this bias I do not have the Berlin group specifically in mind. The possibility of de-Christianization did not occur to me alone. I refer to p. 120 of Professor Colpe's paper which Professor Robinson provided me. I am willing to consider that the movement might have been towards Christianization, as in the *Apocryphon of John* and the *Gospel of Mary*. The important issue is whether it is possible to find criteria for determining which way the process has gone in the case of the Johannine prologue and *Trimorphic Protennoia*. My paper left the question open pending the opportunity to see Dr. Gesine Schenke's case in full.

Professor Colpe argues for a sapiential tradition at a stage earlier than the Gospel of John. I do not see anything wrong with his argument and am inclined to see sapiential traditions behind both the prologue and *Trimorphic Protennoia*.

On the more general question of Christianization, we need to distinguish different kinds of evidence. First, the clear use of quotation establishes literary dependence. Second, literary allusions can only confirm a literary dependence already established by the use of quotation. Given only allusions one must be tentative in drawing conclusions. For example, in my paper I suggested that the shared term *monē* "might conceivably echo" the New Testament passage. We cannot say more than that. Third, there are parallels in thought which may indicate only a common background.

COLPE: We must be careful about the order of sequence in the triadic formulas. The filioque controversy in the ancient church makes sense only if the "Son" is in the second position and not in the third. The Christian trinity is "Father, Son, Spirit", while the old Semitic trinity is "Father, Mother, Son." My argument for de-Christianization would have been stronger if the *Trimorphic Protennoia* formula had been "Father, Son, Mother." What is needed is a careful examination of the order of sequence in all the triadic formulas. I spoke of "de-Christianization" because of other apparent Christian allusions in the tractate. If literary criticism shows these to be the result of secondary Christianization, then my argument for de-Christianization fails.

MACRAE: In his article Professor Colpe organized the list of parallels between the prologue and *Trimorphic Protennoia* in the order of the verses of the prologue, i.e. starting with verse 1. The parallels in the *Trimorphic Protennoia* are scattered throughout the tractate without any apparent sequence. The significance of this scattering might have been more apparent to us if the list of parallels had been in the sequence in which they appeared in *Trimorphic Protennoia*. To what extent does the particular literary genre of the two works being compared provide us with criteria for determining dependence or borrowing?

ROBINSON : I would pose a slightly different question. I cannot conceive of someone distributing a hymnic description of a single personage, the Logos, among the three personages of a triad, the last of which is called "Logos." To hold such a position is to imply the pre-Jonas view of Gnostics as senseless people who would do anything. But it is historically intelligible to see the author of the prologue focusing the different concepts of a mythological thought world into the one Christ, just as the evangelist has ascribed "way", "light", "door", etc. solely to Jesus.

ALEXANDER BÖHLIG: That makes sense. In the Gospel of John we do not have the "Logos" but the "Word" from the Old Testament. On the one hand it is possible that Gnosticism as a parasitic movement associated these characteristics with Christ under influence of Christianity. On the other hand we have the question of the gospel genre. There is a development from the Synoptics to the Gospel of John which has added a cosmic dimension to the prologue. This development need not be Gnostic. Hengel believes that it can be explained within Judaism. Yet I would not want to exclude the possibility of a Gnostic influence at this point.

ROBINSON: Professors Colpe and Böhlig both have vacillated in deciding whether the background of the two texts is already Gnostic or still Jewish Wisdom. Admittedly one can't use the *Trimorphic Protennoia* to establish the Gnostic origin of the Johannine prologue. But Professor Wilson is understating the evidence when he speaks of both texts as simply going back to Jewish Wisdom literature. Given the mass of Jewish literature available, why do we find the only concentrated cluster of parallels to the prologue in one text, *Trimorphic Protennoia*? We must try to use this fact in a more pointed fashion. I agree that the background is Jewish Wisdom literature. But these two texts shared in the same converging force that drew out from Jewish Wisdom a unique concentration. At this point I would speak of a "trajectory." We may never solve the question of whether the Wisdom tradition behind the prologue or the *Trimorphic Protennoia* was Gnostic. But to pose the question that way may result in blocking out the insight that the development of the Jewish Wisdom tradition towards Gnosticism was already at work in the background of the two documents. Otherwise one is unable to account for these two crystallizations. The historian's task is not to decide whether or not a given text is Gnostic but to locate the text within the development or trajectory from non-Gnostic Jewish literature to Gnosticism. The shadow land between Jewish Wisdom and Gnosticism must be accorded the status of an historical reality.

WILSON: I agree with Professor Robinson that we cannot pin down the fluid development of an emerging Gnosticism. But as a golfer I object to his term "trajectory." What is needed is a term conveying the notion of accretion. A golf ball does not take on anything in flight except perhaps some mud upon landing.

ROBERT KRAFT: It seems hasty to assert that no one in the ancient world would think of scattering the attributes of the Logos among a triad. One should try to locate available parallels in literature which could provide a control for testing this assertion, though I don't know of anyone who has yet done this. I wouldn't be surprised to find Philo dealing with a scriptural text in a Platonizing fashion similar to the process Professor Robinson has ruled out. Do we have enough of Heracleon to see what he does with the Gospel of John? One could also look at the Platonizing interpreters of Homer to see whether the terminology was scattered.

ROBINSON: Your approach would be a logical one if we were

talking of the Logos becoming triple. For example, to speak in the superlative fashion of a "Trishagion" permits a subsequent interpreter to believe that there were three beings. So if Jewish Wisdom is in the background of *Trimorphic Protennoia*, Sophia could conceivably become three beings. But where in Christian Gnostic texts does Jesus develop into a trinity?

BIRGER PEARSON: At the beginning of the *Apocryphon of John* Jesus says, "I am the Father, the Mother, and the Son."

ROBINSON: That might be an analogy. But it might be more analogous to the Johannine prologue claiming non-Christian titles for Jesus, especially if the *Apocryphon of John*, as has been rather widely assumed, is secondarily Christianized by the addition of such things as the opening framework of a resurrection appearance from which the quotation comes. For it would then not be a matter of Jesus being developed into a trinity, but rather of already developed mythological personages (as in CG II, 9:10-11) being claimed for the Christian savior. The second reservation I have to Professor Kraft's suggestion involves the flood of mythological language in the *Trimorphic Protennoia*. We haven't discussed the other cosmogonic elements in the tractate which are not paralleled in the prologue but which still fit naturally together with them into a unified whole. It is more reasonable to assume the Johannine author took a sampling of the whole range of cosmogonic speculation in the thought environment behind the *Trimorphic Protennoia* than to think that less than half a dozen terms in the prologue could be exploded to produce the whole cosmogonic vocabulary of the *Trimorphic Protennoia*.

KRAFT: Philo can take the words from a Greek text considered scriptural and scatter them about in a highly Platonized form that doesn't seem artifical to the context.

JOHN STRUGNELL: I grant that the prologue to John may contain a variant of the mythic structure seen in the *Trimorphic Protennoia*. However it does seem significant that the prologue takes up one page compared with five or six pages for the tractate. In dealing with literary phenomena one usually says the shorter reading is preferred, i.e., earlier. Second, is it not possible that only verbal parallels and not the mythic structure were drawn from the Fourth Gospel? The issue seems to be one of textual criticism. With the exception of the argument on the term *monē*, to which I think I have an answer, Professor Robinson, you seem to have given up on finding criteria by which one could determine in which of the two contexts a particular element makes better sense. Are there literary seams in the one or the other? Have you concluded that the Founth Gospel turns out to be a "seamless robe"?

ROBINSON: The Baptist passages are often held to be interpolations.

STRUGNELL: Granted.

ROBINSON: Besides the Christianized conclusion, there are a few scattered allusions to Christ that are considered secondary in the *Trimorphic Protennoia*. The two references to *monē* can be compared to each other since one of them is in the Christianized portion and hence dependent on the New Testament. Admittedly, if one knows Christianization occurred in one instance it is impossible to prove it didn't occur in another instance. Anything is possible; let us talk about what is probable. The word *monogenēs* is at home in an atmosphere that plays on prefixes for the first concept. Given a community possessing a wealth of mythological language, why assume that here and there one would insert a word from the Johannine vocabulary to refer to Barbelo?

PEARSON: Professor Wilson is not the only one to speak of "de-Christianization." Professor Schenke originally thought the *Sophia Jesu Christi* was prior to *Eugnostos*. It has recently been argued that a de-Christianization has been going on in the *Tripartite Tractate*. It may be profitable to ask how one spots de-Christianization.

COLPE: One can also speak of "repaganization." At the outset of the *Gospel of Truth* one gets the impression that the text is Christian. But by the end the reader knows that impression was wrong. The initial disguise of the essentially non-Christian viewpoint seems to have been intentional. One could compare the Gnostic texts with contemporary literature which could not have been conceived without the precedent of Christian doctrine but which is nevertheless not Christian but post-Christian. Excluding the genuine Christian Gnostics

like Clement of Alexandria, the Gnostics were the first post-Christians
of history.

PEARSON: One must avoid posing the question of de-Christianization
as though an idealized Christian doctrinal system was changed into
a pagan system. The history of Christianity itself is the history of
the paganization of a Jewish Messianic sect as it spread throughout
the Graeco-Roman world. But in quite a different sense one can speak
of "de-Christianization" to refer to the appropriation and modification
of a Christian text by a completely non-Christian group for its own
ethical or religious uses.

FREDERIK WISSE: The *Concept of Our Great Power* certainly exhibits
a kind of de-Christianization if only to cast the life of Jesus into
prophetic speech. At the same time a generalizing aspect aided the
Gnostic interpretation.

MICHAEL STONE: In Jewish literature there was the appropriation
of Egyptian wisdom sayings in the Jewish book of Proverbs along
with a neutralization of the pagan elements.

MACRAE: To highlight Professor Pearson's question, can we think
of any work in the ancient world that was so fully de-Christianized
that its Christian origin was completely suppressed?

STONE: Then how could you know it had been de-Christianized?

ROBINSON: The *Sentences of Sextus*, if Professor Chadwick is right.

HENRY CHADWICK: A considerable number of texts over a very wide
area were used for exactly the opposite purpose than the one for which
they had been originally intended. Iconoclast saints were turned into
iconophiles, etc.

MACRAE: But aren't these all in a Christian context?

CHADWICK: Granted, but that doesn't bear against my point. May
I insert a comment at this point on the relation between the Johannine
prologue and the *Trimorphic Protennoia*? I feel sure the *Trimorphic*

Protennoia could not have simply been a de-Christianized version of the prologue. The antithesis between *phōnē* and *logos* is of cardinal importance in the structure of the prologue. But in the *Protennoia* there is no subordination of *phōnē*. This distinction seems to me to have bearing on the possible literary relationship between the two documents. I confess I am not quite persuaded that such a literary relationship exists.

MACRAE: A number of us have indicated a willingness to eliminate the dependence of *Trimorphic Protennoia* on the Gospel prologue. There are other options. To say they have a common background raises the question of how they are related to that background. Professor Robinson's earlier remarks would suggest that the Wisdom background was not inert, but that out of its directional development these two documents have a common dependence. I find that kind of analysis attractive. The presence of references to Jesus in the *Trimorphic Protennoia* does not disturb me. I can envision the common background of the two documents to be already moving into Christianity, but not in the sense that the people involved are reading the New Testament.

Session Six

CONCLUDING DISCUSSION

GEORGE MACRAE : FOR our last session together we can address some general questions in light of what we have read and discussed during our two days together. As I pointed out yesterday [session 3] we have come to some agreement on certain points. For our present discussion I suggest we operate on the basic assumption that something exists that we would call "Sethian." This assumption is held by most of us as our previous discussions have shown. I further suggest we avoid at the outset the issue of whether that Sethian entity would best be described as a school or sect or exegetical tradition, etc. For our discussion I propose three basic questions that will traverse the ground we have covered in roughly reverse order. First what are the essential characteristics of this entity we call "Sethian"? Perhaps we will be content to affirm or deny Professor Schenke's description of the Sethian system written in his 1974 article which has been presumed in much of our discussion together. Second, what was the origin of this Sethian phenomenon? We have already looked at a number of suggestions and agree that the major contribution was Jewish. But how should we define the setting of this Jewish element? Third, what was the nature of the group we are discussing? What hypothetical choices would we rule out?

Though time may not permit, two additional but less pressing questions might be pursued. First, what particular literature belongs to or even reflects this Sethian entity? My own feeling is that Schenke's list is too restrictive. Second, was this movement or phenomenon originally, and possibly perpetually, non-Christian? As we know, Schenke's definition of "Sethian" remains essentially non-Christian even when it stands in a syncretistic contact with Christianity.

FREDERIK WISSE: To ask for essential characteristics is to place oneself in a dilemma. On the one hand, a precise description of Sethianism may remain elusive even if we think we know what it is. But if we conceive of it as just a vague way of pursuing mythological speculation, we will have difficulty in excluding the unquestionably non-Sethian elements.

MacRae: (*To Wisse*) You yourself said some years ago that the irreducible minimum of anything "Sethian" was that its adherents regard themselves as the spiritual descendants of Seth in a way that set them apart from the rest of humanity.

Wisse: This is a bit too tight. It is conceivable that in a number of "Sethian" tractates Seth plays no role because the issue didn't arise. And we have heard of possible reincarnations of Seth under a different name.

Macrae: In Irenaeus *Haer*. 1.30, a group is described that Irenaeus calls "the others." Seth is explicitly mentioned as being considered by them as the common parent of all humanity. Whatever Irenaeus is describing, I would not want to call it "Sethian." While it is ironic that Theodoret inserts the name "Sethian" in describing the same group as Irenaeus, we would not be willing to omit from the characteristics of the "Sethian" phenomenon the concept of an exclusive race of people descended from Seth.

Birger Pearson: Can't we broaden the scope of our question to include some implicit questions about the existence of other sects of an analogous character? The Sethites had their counterpart in the Cainites, as we were reminded yesterday. The heresiologists speak of Cainites, Ophites, and Sethites together. Are the Sethites a special case that deserves to be examined alone?

Macrae: No one has suggested that any of the documents among the Nag Hammadi collection were Cainite.

Pearson: Some of the tractates were preliminarily labeled "Ophite."

Macrae: Solely on the grounds of Irenaeus *Haer*. 1.30, where the term "Ophite" is secondary.

Robert Kraft: Just how we conceive of the origin and early beginning of a group is crucial in determining the methodology we should follow in attempting to describe it. If the group began with an individual as in the case of Valentinus, we can examine the literature for thematic consistency as Schenke has done in inductively creating the "Sethian system." But other groups, including those without the names of founders, appear to have begun in a less organized fashion. Imagine the Nag Hammadi library as composed solely of the New Testament documents. If we tried to sort out the collection of writings without any knowledge of mainstream Christianity we would erroneously develop several different groups because we would have overlooked the nonhomogeneous character of early mainstream Christianity. In the case of the Sethians, are we treading on a historical development that doesn't allow us to proceed as Schenke did? To answer that question we are unfortunately driven to choosing between the heresiologists and the literature as sources of information.

MACRAE: If in your hypothetical illustration using the New Testament we had concluded that there were a number of separate groups we would have been right, according to the prevailing orthodoxy of New Testament scholarship!

KRAFT: It does seem strange that the Paulinists and the Mattheans ever got together in one group.

MACRAE: As far as we know that only happened in an anachronistic fashion when our present New Testament was put together as scripture, quite some time later.

MICHAEL STONE: Speaking as one not intimately acquainted with the entire Nag Hammadi corpus, I see the issue here as analogous in two ways to problems I have long wrestled with in Jewish literature. I have stopped wrestling with one of them—the relationship of Josephus's description of the Essenes to the Qumran documents. This problem presumes a prior division of the Qumran documents into those which are truly "Qumranian," those which are peripherally "Qumranian," and those only copied or preserved by the community. The present position of scholarship, namely, that the documents from Qumran must provide the criteria for judging Josephus and not vice verse, is doubtless correct. The implications for our discussion here are clear enough.

The second problem involves deciding what documents could have been produced by the same group and determining what measure of difference must exist between documents to indicate that they were produced by different groups. The answers to these questions cannot be formulated abstractly, but depend on a host of historical and sociological factors. If among the Nag Hammadi library you find documents which conceptually cohere, then it is important that you hang them together. Your knowledge of the Sethians will inevitably continue to be largely drawn from the texts. It really doesn't matter whether you use the heresiologists' label and call them "Sethian." The name we call them is not what distinguishes them from other groups.

The rush to compare the heresiologists' report to the insiders' self-description is useless. The two will never be the same. Look at the conflict between what one group says about itself and how another group sees them in our present society of Jew and Christian, Roman Catholic and Lutheran, etc. Why should we expect antiquity to be otherwise?

MacRae: Your point is methodologically sound.

Pearson: And well taken, except that at one place the analogy breaks down. The excavations at Faw Qibli (Pbou) failed to produce a community that could serve as a locus for the Nag Hammadi library. The collection turns out to be only an ad hoc collection copied in a Pachomian Christian community. We don't have the same sociological and archaeological evidence with which to proceed as we can with the Qumran materials.

Stone: I don't think this makes any difference for the exegesis of the texts.

John Strugnell: Qumran did give us a communal setting which overlaps with Josephus's description. Some documents gave practical counsel on the peculiar communal life. One could move out from the *Manual of Discipline* and trace in other texts the Qumranian vocabulary. Earlier biblical and nonbiblical works would be excluded, for example, Tobit and possibly *Jubilees*. The lack of all this in the Nag Hammadi materials is crucial.

MacRae: I'm not persuaded on that point. One problem of scholarship is the failure to even consider using the accepted methods of scholarship of one's primary area of investigation when dealing with another area. On the basis of an analogous situation, we who are New Testament scholars ought to remember when we deal with the Nag Hammadi material that Pauline theology is derived from the

Pauline letters and not from Acts. And we further distinguish between authentically Pauline documents and those that most of us exclude from the pale of Pauline theology. I personally follow Professor Stone's suggestion that in the present state of Nag Hammadi scholarship the analogy with Qumran is valid. It is more fruitful to study the documents themselves to determine whether they represent a coherent mythological picture. Why should we falter at the lack of social control? The lack of social control in the case of the New Testament documents has not prevented us from making extraordinary claims merely on the basis of those documents.

STRUGNELL: But we do have social information inside those New Testament documents.

GEORGE NICKELSBURG: Professor Stone's analogy is a bit more complicated. Who doubts that there were Pharisees, Sadducees, and Essenes? But there are people in this room who question whether the Sethians existed. Futhermore, Josephus speaks of three sects while the scholars of Judaica suspect there were many more. But in the case of the heresiologists' bestiaries, the number of sects stretches beyond the probable. In determining whether the Nag Hammadi documents reveal the existence of groups that consciously set themselves off from others, perhaps the pseudepigraphical material could serve as a helpful parallel, as for example the reference in the book of Enoch to preserving a revelation for the spiritual descendants of Enoch's son.

JAMES ROBINSON: Perhaps we would sense that the New Testament is analogous to Nag Hammadi if we had names for the sects of Luke, Paul, and Matthew. Perhaps they were isolated and just as definable as "sects" as the Sethians. If the heresiological references to the Sethians didn't exist and we just had the texts, our response would be Schenke's method of grouping them by common characteristics. Then we would work up from these parallels in the "Sethian" texts to decide whether the Sethian phenomenon was a disembodied tradition or sect or school, etc.

KRAFT: Though I agree that methodologically the Nag Hammadi literature must be given priority, there remains the possibility that what we isolate from the "Sethian" tractates might be quite different

from the various elements which coalesced in the literature at the stage
we have it. Paul was embedded in a particular interpretation by the
Marcionites. Furthermore, from one perspective Sethianism may be a
pulling together of sources quite different in origin and use from each
other.

WISSE: By raising our expectations the church fathers have led us
astray. If we viewed the Nag Hammadi literature as we do the apocryphal literature we would not assume social control but would rather
assume a setting in which individuals were able to present their
visionary interests to broad sections of the church.

MACRAE: That's too loose a model.

ROBINSON: A parallel case may be Jewish apocalypticism where
we have a body of literature but no sect as the bearer of it. The Qumran
sect produced only a portion of the extant apocalyptic literature.
In spite of the continuity we trace in Jewish apocalypticism we do not
assume a school or sect but rather a tradition. Jewish wisdom literature
likewise was not produced by a sect, though we speak of "Wisdom
circles." Conceivably the Sethian literature could be categorized
similarly.

STONE: When we have drawn together a group of documents that
share a pattern of ideas our findings still may not reflect a social
reality. And even if they did, there are the possibilities that a pattern
of ideas was shared by a number of distinctive groups or that a given
social group held several patterns in tension. At least ten or more
different streams of religious thought are reflected in the Qumran
library. The Pachomian monastery doesn't seem to be so different.
Maybe the available patristic descriptions of Gnosticism include a
richer delineation of sectarian differences than what we have of the
Jewish sects. But the heresiologists' descriptions do seem to be
schematized like Josephus.

MACRAE: Although I'm old enough to know I won't get an answer,
I would be curious to know how many of us are content with Schenke's
description of what could plausibly be called "Sethian" from an analysis
of these documents.

CARSTEN COLPE: I am.

MACRAE: So am I.

KRAFT: Doesn't the answer to your question depend on what you mean by "Sethian"?

MACRAE: No, I view the effort to formulate a definition as a retrograde step. The question stands: Is Schenke describing a reality, regardless of what we call it?

KRAFT: Were you actually asking if the documents Professor Schenke identifies are homogeneous and distinct from other documents?

MACRAE: Yes, in terms of those points he isolates as significant. I would myself cast his net somewhat wider.

ROBINSON: You would presumably also be going a step further by accounting for that homogeneity on the basis of a historical or sociological entity?

MACRAE: Yes, I think there has to be a bearer though I am not sure I could describe it.

STRUGNELL: In looking for essential characteristics I suggest going through Professor Schenke's list to decide which characteristics are constitutive either of the myth or of a social entity and which ones are not. Some of the characteristics are constitutive for the very existence of the myth. Those that are found in only two or three documents could have formed part of a secondary development in Sethianism. There could have been various churches of Sethians, each with a different specification of the Sethian myth. It would be interesting to ask for the bare minimum we need from Schenke's list in order to talk about Sethianism.

ROBINSON: In Professor Schenke's earlier article where he outlines the essential characteristics of Sethian Gnosticism he does attempt to show how these characteristics are bound up with each other. On the basis of his attempt I could imagine a process of development beginning with "proto-Sethians" who viewed themselves as "the seed of Seth." Within this context the mythological and cosmogonic system could develop, resulting in the periodization of the aeons and the stratification of the hierarchy. Hypothetically we would call the resulting development at this stage the indispensable essence of Sethian Gnosticism. Subsequent development and mythological attachment to the system would have taken place. Incidentally, the article Schenke gave to us for this seminar was an attempt to see how those Sethian documents, which were already selected on the basis of the definition of Sethianism given in the earlier article, mutually illuminate each other.

ALEXANDER BÖHLIG: We must not look at these texts as timeless entities, but we must try to arrive at a *Sitz im Leben* for each one. In an article which will appear in *Aufstieg und Niedergang der römischen Welt*, I have asked the question how the different misunderstandings and mistakes have arisen in our Coptic copies. It appears that only a limited understanding of the text is reflected in the last copies. Furthermore, we have to direct our attention to the Greek *Vorlage* and possible Armaic influences. I have studied the instances in which an Aramaic *Vorlage* is assumed by some scholars and found that generally it was not necessary to posit an Aramaic or Syriac original. For mythological texts it is to be expected that they are compilations. In this way we can reach some conclusions about the earlier stages, though we have no arguments to propose as to the beginning. Also the church fathers are not much help here. For the time being we must concentrate on the differences and agreements between certain texts.

ROBINSON: Because the Valentinian seminar has drawn the more philosophically oriented participants, one dimension of our discussion has been largely overlooked. In this seminar we have been exploring the frontier of Jewish traditions leading into Christianity and Sethianism. But our Sethian corpus stretches from Adam to Plotinus! We are talking about a movement that eventually developed into a Neoplatonic school. I found that the three tractates, *Allogenes, Zostrianos*, and the *Three Steles of Seth*, were being pulled into the Neoplatonic orbit with the closest Neoplatonic parallels dated in the fourth century—a century later than the presumed date of these Nag Hammadi tractates. Essentially they were moving towards a philosophical Gnosis.

MacRae: In this regard Pheme Perkins's remarkable and insightful paper read at the San Francisco SBL meeting in 1977 dealt with the translation of philosophical *topoi* into mythological language in the tractate *On the Origin of the World* (II,5). The *topoi*, which were very specific, were located in particular places and times in both the Middle Platonic and Stoic traditions. Professor Robinson is right in reminding us of this movement towards philosophizing, which Jonas himself saw. I have had difficulty in recognizing the similarities between *Allogenes* and the *Apocalypse of Adam*. Perhaps they belong together a couple of centuries apart!

Böhlig: We must remember that the middle class in Egypt was educated in the Greek schools. I have argued in *Zum Hellenismus in den Schriften von Nag Hammadi* (Wiesbaden, 1975) that many texts reflect a level of education such as was available in these schools. This tells us something about the people behind the texts. It does not tell us yet what kind of people the Sethians were, but the texts give some indications.

MacRae: The second question I put before this group concerned the essentially Jewish origin of Sethianism. Professor Colpe has offered us a specific suggestion to account for certain Iranian influences which he suggests were mediated through Jewish circles. Without attempting to reconstruct a scenario, are there other remarks to be made on the extent of the Jewish elements? We have spent considerable time on the relationships between the Jewish and Gnostic literature.

Pearson: One could argue for a Jewish background for each of the descriptions of Seth I noted in my paper.

MacRae: Your paper argued that what was at stake was a Jewish exegetical tradition that at some point became recognizably Gnostic. But has this position found general agreement among us? May I ask Professor Colpe if he envisions that the fundamental activity of the Jewish Wisdom tradition was exegesis?

Colpe: Yes. Many things can be developed from exegesis. For instance, the Jewish-Christian interest in legitimate succession led to an exegetical activity dealing with the whole of the Old Testament.

Jewish Christianity could have asserted its legitimacy in two ways—either by extending the lines of Prophetic succession to Jesus or by going back from a new Torah to the earlier one. This method of exegesis by systematizing and collecting of scriptural material on the same topic was also done in midrash. One topic of Jewish exegesis could have been the shaping of salvation history. Of course the result was completely Jewish. And by Jewish I insist on a developing Judaism, not the romantic fiction of an unchanging Judaism.

STONE: A.F.J. Klijn's book is a flawed yet brave beginning of the urgent task of mapping out the broad range of Sethian traditions. The amount of definitely attested Jewish material about Seth is tiny. Beyond the odds and ends in the Bible and what is in Philo and Josephus, the other Jewish material is either peripheral or chronologically contemporary with Gnosticism. Methodologically we must begin with what we have. A particularly acute question is whether there is more lurking behind Philo's remarks about Seth. Philo is the one source that is full of pregnant but ambiguous material that could have developed in the way Gnostic tradition took up Seth. I would like to see some study of other themes that Philo treated ambigously. On the basis of what Jewish sources we now possess I find myself hard pressed to speak of "Sethian exegesis." Even the rabbinic material is ambiguous. In the present status of our knowledge Professor MacRae's question is extremely difficult to answer. At this point we need to gather the whole range of material from Jewish, Christian, and Moslem contemplations on the figure of Seth and to map out the broad outlines, keeping an eye on the dates of our sources. I would not want to argue back to Jewish Wisdom schools in Mesopotamia unless I had other evidence.

COLPE: Sometimes we can proceed better with a hypothesis built on a weak inference than with no hypothesis at all. The reservations of Professor Stone are correct. But there is nothing that speaks directly against this hypothesis. So let us work with it for a while.

STONE: I wouldn't argue against a Jewish context, but it would be strengthened by looking at the wider range of literature.

MACRAE: You are not advocating that meanwhile we just mark time?

STONE: No, let us get on with the task.

MACRAE: But it will be a century before all the material is available.

NICKELSBURG: I am still meditating on Professor MacRae's comment about the hypothetical testament of Adam containing either everything or nothing. The Jewish Adam books dealt with the problem of death and resurrection. What was carried over into the Gnostic materials was only a formal structure of Seth as a recipient and mediator of revelation. Much of what was in the container of the formal structure was dumped out, with other material replacing it in the 'Gnostic literature. The question of why the Gnostics emphasized Seth 'and not Enoch has a similar force.

Another overlooked contribution from the San Francisco SBL meeting is the wealth of Christian material in Syncellus that William Adler collected. This material might serve as a control in our reading of the Nag Hammadi materials by demonstrating parallel development in a non-Gnostic context.

WISSE: In reference to Professor Colpe's suggestion, I do not understand how explaining facts A, B, and C, about which we know a little, by X, Y, and Z, about which we know nothing, can be anything but regression.

MACRAE: How do you you understand a hypothesis to work?

WISSE: A hypothesis is an explanation that accounts for the relation of certain facts to the whole picture and to each other. It can be tested so that a new fact can lead to its modification or abandonment. But here we are speaking of unknown factors.

COLPE: Every author of an introduction to the New Testament offers a hypothesis as to where Matthew was written. But a hypothesis that is offered about the geographical locus of Matthew is not given to explain the book itself.

WISSE: You were trying to explain certain phenomena in Sethianism by your hypothesis.

COLPE: No, not in Sethianism. For any historical explanation of Sethianism we would need external data which we don't have here.

WISSE: Then what was the purpose of the hypothesis?

COLPE: To establish a hypothetical temporal and geographical basis for Sethianism for the purpose of comparison and combination with other hypotheses or data. While at some later date this hypothesis may be useful in answering historical questions about Sethianism, it was not proposed to explain anything in those documents on which it was based.

PEARSON: In my research on the figure of Seth I was struck by how the specifically Christian tradition about Seth was absent in Gnosticism. We are pushed to another setting for the antecedent to the Gnostic tradition. And if not Jewish, what could it be? Once we establish the Jewish character of the building blocks of the Gnostic system and then note the attitude of Gnosticism towards Judaism, i.e., the Torah and the people of the Torah, the resulting Gnostic hermeneutics should take us to the heart of Gnosticism.

KRAFT: Perhaps Seth was of little interest to the emerging mainstream of Christianity, at least after Julius Africanus, until the time of the Byzantine chronographers because a portion of the rival Gnostics were forcefully using the Sethian traditions. When the emerging church established its boundaries and its canon, Seth was safely reintroduced into the tradition. Professor Pearson, what did you mean by "specifically Christian tradition about Seth"?

PEARSON: For instance, the interpretation of the sons of God in Genesis 6 as the sons of Seth.

KRAFT: That's not specifically Christian.

PEARSON: It turns up throughout the Christian literature almost without exception. It doesn't occur in the Gnostic materials and very weakly in the Jewish sources, if at all.

KRAFT: Virtually everything of this sort attested in the Jewish sources is "very weakly attested".

MACRAE: Doubtless most of us will continue to write with reference to "Sethianism." What are we going to write about? A Sethian "sect" or "tradition" or "way of mythologizing" or what?

COLPE: I would speak of "Sethianism" and avoid "school," "sect," etc.

KRAFT: I would speak of "Sethian themes" used among people who want to talk about Seth.

MACRAE: In recent years in my department's weekly discussions we have been identifying each other as "minimalists" and "maximalists" in interpretation. When there is an issue over which both a maximal position and a minimal position are possible, there is usually a decided difference of opinion. I suspect that in our methodological pre-occupations in this seminar we have each identified some maximalists and some minimalists. But I assure you I will not point them out!

Two final words of appreciation are appropriate. First, to the participants of this seminar and this conference from whom I, for one, have learned a great deal. Second, we all owe an enormous debt of gratitude to the initiative, industry, and scholarly acumen of our colleague who invited us to this meeting.

[*Professor Schenke was unexpectedly absent from the meetings of the seminar. After the conference he kindly contributed the following postscript*:

HANS-MARTIN SCHENKE: Just as unusual as the nonattendance of a firmly committed seminar member must be reckoned, I think, the subsequent possibility for such a person still to contribute to the seminar discussion. In my view, though, it would be a misuse of this chance if I let myself be carried away and made an evaluation of all the seminar proceedings. For, immediately after the end of the conference, in Princeton and New Haven, I conversed with active and passive seminar participants and was brought face to face with their overall impressions; also, once I had returned home, thanks to the tape recordings that Professor Layton had sent along with me I could let the seminar discussions run through my mind calmly and in their entirety. Rather, I have in mind something like an "inter-polation": belatedly, I should like to try and add my voice here and there to the duets and polyphony of my colleagues and friends as they conduct their discussion. Actually, I must admit that it is hardly necessary. For my case was represented by excellent counsel at the conference.

Most exciting of all I found to be the fifth session, because there things became very concrete: in turn, its highpoint was for me Professor Robinson's exclamation, "Anything is possible; let us talk about what is probable" (above, p. 668). Those words expressed my heartfelt thoughts at this point—and they are also applicable at other points of the discussion. For my own part, I would also gladly have added, "The matter at hand has many aspects; let us talk of what is essential."

As regards specific details, which it is possible though not terribly essential to note, I felt no slight dismay to learn that I had apparently constructed my paper so maladroitly that Professors Pearson and MacRae both could overlook (above, p. 636) the fact that the *Untitled Tractate* from the Bruce Codex should be naturally included in the complex of Sethian writings. In response to Professor Wisse's objection concerning the standards for including or not including writings in the text group (above, p. 636) I should like to confess that the grounds which he imputes to me for not including the *Letter of Peter to Philip* and the *Concept of Our Great Power* had not come into my conscious mind anyhow. In the end, each of the Gnostic texts is connected with the next in some way. But it is a matter of the interpretation and evaluation of the lines of connection, namely, which are to be seen as "solid lines" and which as "tenuous" ones. I am also a bit sceptical about the wish, expressed especially by Professor MacRae, of seeing the "net" somewhat enlarged (above, p. 677). It seems to me that then all too quickly and quite unintentionally we shall have caught all available "fish."

In terms of methodology Professor Robinson sees my kind of endeavor as being in direct opposition to that of Professor Wisse (above, p. 579); this I gladly accept. And I admit that I should be glad to know how to avoid the weakness of which he complains in my position. Since in principle I see the history of early Christianity in the same "unorthodox" way as he (and Koester—as adherents of W. Bauer), I certainly cannot see the movement that produced the Sethian texts as being any less lively and varied than Christianity. I hope the fact that once in the beginning as the contours of the common element in these writings began to emerge before my astonished eyes, in the first joy of discovery and still completely innocent, I described it with the concept of "system" will not be unalterably detrimental to what I meant to express. Professor Colpe's information concerning me (above, p. 640) is correct. And if in my present paper (as I notice after the fact) the word "system" is often used, it is by no means meant in the strictest sense, but rather serves as a shorthand for something like "complex of interconnected basic beliefs and basic concepts."

Of relevance in understanding the opposition between Wisse's position and my own is perhaps, apart from our different methods of textual investigation, our different presuppositions as to a *concept of Gnosis* as a whole phenomenon. While I feel that I am in the following of Hans Jonas, it seems to me that Wisse not only doubts the existence of a specifically Sethian Gnosis, but likewise actually questions the existence of Gnosis in general, that is, Gnosis as a major religious movement of Late Antiquity that can, despite its manifoldness, be recognized as one thing. In any case up to now I have been able to interpret many of Wisse's statements only in such a way, and this would have been my basic question for him.

Finally, I also suppose that I would have tried, here and there, to somewhat change the *overall direction* that the discussion took. Indeed, it is no accident that Professor Robinson—representing Jonas, as it were—thought many times that he perceived the reappearance of the ghost of an "alchemy of ideas" and attempted to exorcize it. For my taste the search has been made too long and too often for a path that would lead as it were directly from a Jewish Seth tradition to Sethian Gnosis. It is precisely the opposite mental process, analytical investigation, that I recognize as alone being legitimate and fruitful—an investigation that proceeds from the given Gnostic texts *as Gnostic* and on this solid basis looks retrospectively, and indeed *only among other projects*, for possibly pre-Gnostic, Jewish (or even "half-Jewish") elements; or under certain circumstances, enquires about how they seem to be present here in the "Sethian" text group; or even enquires after a cohering non-Gnostic substrate. Gnostic Sethianism, or Sethian Gnosis, too, is primarily Gnosis: only secondarily is it Sethian.]

PART FIVE

RESEARCH PAPERS

THE ARROGANT ARCHON AND THE LEWD SOPHIA:

Jewish Traditions in Gnostic Revolt

BY

NILS A. DAHL

THE presence of Jewish traditions in gnosticism is generally recognized. Scholars also agree that at least in some branches of gnosticism there is an element of revolt. The question is how to explain this combination of traditional and revolutionary, Jewish and anti-Jewish components. What, exactly, were the early gnostics revolting against? The most impressive answer to such questions is that of Hans Jonas: the target of the gnostic revolt was the world itself. Gnostic anti-Judaism is an aspect of an anticosmic attitude.[1] Jonas is certainly right that the theory of Jewish origins does not in itself explain what made gnosticism gnostic. But against Jonas's own explanation it must be objected that the target of the gnostic revolt is the Creator of the world rather than the world itself. According to widespread gnostic opinion, the world is indeed better than its Creator. The Demiurge thought that he had created the world by his own power but, without knowing it, he had been inspired by his mother, Wisdom; he modelled his work after the pattern of higher realms.

The difference between gnostics and more orthodox Jews and Christians is not to be located in the degree of evil and misery ascribed to human existence in the world so much as in the explanation given for the regrettable state of affairs. According to the orthodox explanation the one God, who is both good and just, subjected the world to futility as a punishment for the transgressions of angelic and human beings. The misery of life on earth is evidence of God's punishment and of his pedagogical discipline. The gnostics, in contrast, traced evils and misery back to the inferiority of the god who created the world, and to his subordinate powers. Both parts in the conflict thought

---

[1] See esp. H. Jonas, "Delimitation of the Gnostic Phenomenon," in *Le Origini dello Gnosticismo: Colloquio de Messina* (ed. U. Bianchi; Supplements to *Numen* 12; Leiden: Brill, 1967) 90-104. This volume contains several contributions to the theme Gnosticism and Judaism. See also the collection *Gnosis und Gnostizismus*, ed. K. Rudolph (WF 262; Darmstadt: Wissenschaftliche Buchgesellschaft, 1975), esp. articles by Kretschmar, van Unnik, Rudolph, Nock, Pokorný, and Drijvers.

their opponents to be guilty of blasphemy. Representatives of biblical orthodoxy thought that the gnostics were guilty of blaspheming the one God, the Creator and Father. Radical gnostics thought that their monotheistic opponents committed blasphemy by attributing passions like jealousy and wrath to the Supreme Being, making his judgement and punishment causes of evil.

The god against whom the radical gnostics revolted was, obviously, the God of exclusivist, biblical monotheism. The radicalism of the revolt presupposes both a close contact and a situation of conflict. We can therefore restate the problem of the Jewish origins of gnosticism by asking: Was the gnostic identification of the inferior Demiurge with the God of "psychic," orthodox Christians preceded by an earlier stage, at which some gnostics revolted against the God of strictly monotheistic Jews?[2] Not only the presence of Jewish components in gnosticism but also some rabbinic texts favor a positive answer to this question.

In his investigation of rabbinic polemics against those who say that "there are two powers in heaven," Alan Segal has made it seem likely that at its earliest stage this polemic was directed against speculations about a secondary divine being, the agent or vice-regent of God. It matters relatively little whether this being was called the Angel, Archangel, Logos, Eikon, *deuteros theos,* "lesser YHWH," or something else. Only at a later stage, "two powers in heaven" became a catchall phrase which included Christians, gnostics, and others who deviated from strict monotheism.[3]

In their defense of monotheism, second-century rabbis appealed to passages like Deut 32:39, "I, even I, am He, and there is no other god beside me." In a number of gnostic texts, similar passages, mostly drawn from Isaiah 44-46, are attributed to the Creator of this world, the Demiurge. Within a gnostic context, the formula of divine self-revelation has become a vain claim made by an Archon ignorant of the powers above himself. The close correspondence between rabbinic and gnostic texts is best explained on the assumption that some "two

---

[2] For the conflict between Valentinian gnostic and orthodox Christians, see esp. Elaine H. Pagels, "'The Demiurge and His Archons'—A Gnostic View of the Bishop and Presbyters?" *HTR* 69 (1976) 301-24. Pagels raises the question "how the doctrine of God actually functions in each type of literature" (303). In cooperation with Alan Segal, I have for some years tried to approach the early stage of the gnostic controversy with a similar question.

[3] See A. E. Segal, *Two Powers in Heaven: Early Rabbinic Reports about Christianity and Gnosticism* (SJLA 25; Leiden: Brill, 1977). The book is a revised version of a Yale dissertation, 1975.

powers heretics" responded to the rabbinic polemic by portraying the god of their intransigent monotheistic opponents as an inferior deity, an ignorant and arrogant Archon. In the situation of conflict, the doctrine of two powers was radicalized. The secondary element in the deity was degraded and no longer simply seen as a manifestation and agent of the supreme God.[4] As a result of the polarization, "two powers heretics" who became gnostics made a separation between the agent of creation and giver of the law on the one hand and the agent of true revelation and redemption on the other. This explanation of the gnostic split in the deity accounts for the presence of Jewish traditions in the gnostic revolt, while at the same time providing reasons for the great ambivalence with which these traditions are used.

The theory set forth by Segal and myself assumes that at least one main branch of radical gnosticism originated in some syncretistic Jewish fringe group, in opposition to the strict monotheism of emerging "normative Judaism." The theory explains a number of data better than any current explanation.[5] The question is whether the theory will stand closer scrutiny. It might be objected that the correspondence between rabbinic polemic and gnostic response is less than complete.[6] But this hardly means more than that both parts in the controversy

---

[4] The most important text occurs in *Mek. R. Ishmael*, Shirta 4 (on Exod 15:3) and Baḥodesh 5 (on Exod 20:2), with a somewhat divergent version in *Mek. R. Shimeon*, Beshallaḥ 15. See Segal, *Two Powers*, 33-57, for text and commentary, and esp. 251-59 for the correlation of rabbinic and gnostic evidence. In his conclusions, p. 265, Segal formulates the hypothesis "that the radicalization of gnosticism was a product of the battle between the rabbis, the Christians and various other two powers sectarians who inhabited the outskirts of Judaism."

[5] I have myself discussed the correlation of rabbinic and gnostic texts in papers presented at a Harvard-Yale New Testament colloquium, spring 1977, and at the SBL Annual Meeting in St. Louis, fall 1977. It is of special interest to observe that *Mek. R. Ishmael*, Baḥodesh 5, contains a comment of R. Nathan which is not found in the parallels (see note 4). This comment seems to presuppose a form of the heresy which considered the "two powers" to be antagonistic, rather than correlated; see Segal, *Two Powers*, 57-59. Arguing that Exod 20:2 could be used to refute the heretics, R. Nathan is reported to have said, "For when the Holy One, Blessed be He, stood up and exclaimed, 'I am the Lord thy God,' was there any one who stood up to protest against him?" A similar argument would seem to be presupposed by gnostic texts which report that the Archon was indeed rebuked for his claim to be the only God; see p. 694 below.

[6] The rabbis mainly draw upon Deut 32:39 or 6:4 and relate these passages to the Sinai revelation, while gnostic exegetes more often use passages from Second Isaiah. Cf. G. W. MacRae, "The Ego-Proclamation in Gnostic Sources," *The Trial of Jesus* (ed. E. Bammel; SBT, 2d ser. 13, London: SCM, 1970), esp. 123-29.

stressed the aspect which was most important to them. The rabbis were mainly interested in demonstrating that the God of Israel, who gave the Torah at Mount Sinai, was the only God, beside whom there is no other. He is both YHWH and Elohim, at the same time just and full of mercy.[7] It is, therefore, quite natural that early rabbinic polemic against the two powers heresy is contained in a midrash on Exod 20:2.[8] The interests of the early gnostics were different. They placed the claim of the Archon, that he is God and there is no other, within the context of the creation story, because paraphrase and reinterpretation of the early chapters of Genesis made it possible to argue that they themselves possessed a higher wisdom than did the creator of the world and that their inner self was of a higher nature than he. In practice, this meant that they were not subject to the Creator-Archon nor to the authority of the interpreters of his law.

The purpose of the present paper is to show that a closer investigation of gnostic sources is likely to support the theory that controversy with representatives of strict Jewish monotheism is one factor in the gnostic revolt. I can only make suggestions and shall concentrate my remarks on three points: (1) the setting of the "vain claim" within the context of gnostic exegesis—or alteration—of the creation story in Genesis; (2) the relationship of the gnostic myth to the widespread theme of a ruler (god, angel, or man), who in his hybris claims to be God or like God; (3) the interrelations between the arrogant Archon and his mother, Sophia or Achamoth, who is sometimes called Prunikos, the Lewd One.

THE VAIN CLAIM AND GNOSTIC GENESIS INTERPRETATION

The idea that the Power who created the world, or some other intermediary being, assumed that he or she existed alone, or claimed to be divine, occurs in a number of texts, many of which report the claim in some oblique form.[9] In several texts, including Irenaeus's and Hippo-

---

[7] In addition to Segal, *Two Powers*, 53-57, see N. A. Dahl and A. Segal, "Philo and the Rabbis on the Names of God," *JSJ* 9 (1978) 1-28.

[8] See the preceding notes, 4-7. *Mek. R. Ishmael*, Baḥodesh 5, however, contains also prooftexts from Isa 46:4; 44:6; 41:4; and, in the saying of R. Nathan, Isa 45:19, a passage which the rabbis read as a reference to the revelation at Sinai, where the Torah was offered to all nations. Other rabbinic texts make it clear that the early chapters of Genesis were of key importance for "two powers" heretics; see Segal, *Two Powers*, 74-83, 108-20, 121-34, 135-39, 148-51.

[9] See examples in note 12. Oblique forms of the claim occur also in *ApocryJn*, CG II 12:4-9 and BG 42:19-43:6; *OnOrgWld*, CG II 100:29-33; *SJC*, CG III 107:9-12;

lytus's versions of Valentinian cosmogonies, the claim of the Demiurge, that he is the only God, is reported in direct speech and in words which in the Bible are attributed to God himself.[10] I shall here concentrate on a special group of texts which have several features in common : the *Hypostasis of the Archons* (CG II,*4*); the work without title, now called *On the Origin of the World* (CG II,*5*); the *Apocryphon of John* (CG II,*1* and BG,*2*); the *Gospel of the Egyptians* (CG III,*2*); and Irenaeus, *Adversus haereses* 1.29 and 30.[11] From these texts, it is possible to abstract a pattern which in its complete, but nonexistent, form includes the following items:

1. *Setting*, at some point in the story of creation.

2. *Introduction*, several times with introductory comments. E.g., *HypArch* 86: 27-30: "Their chief is blind; [because of his] Power and his ignorance [and his] arrogance, he said, with his [Power]: ..."; *ApocryJn*, BG 44: 9-13: "He looked at the creation that was with him, and the multitude of angels that was with him ... and said to them: ..." See also *HypArch* 94: 19-21; *OnOrgWld* 103: 8-10; *ApocryJn*, BG 11: 18-19; 13: 5-8; *GEgypt* 58: 23-24; Irenaeus, *Haer.* 1.29.4; 30.6.

3. *Vain claim*, in words derived from Isa 45:5, 6, 18, 21; 46:9 (or sim.). E.g., *HypArch* 86: 30-31: "It is I who am God; there is none [apart from me]." Cf. *HypArch* 94: 21f. (95: 5); *OnOrgWld* 103: 11-13 (107: 30f., 112: 28f.); *ApocryJn*, CG II 11: 20f.; Irenaeus, *Haer.* 1.30.6. *ApocryJn*, BG 44: 14f.: "I am a jealous God; apart from me there is none" (Exod 20:5; Isa 46:9, or sim.). Cf. CG II 13: 8f.; *GEgypt* 58: 25f.; Irenaeus, *Haer.* 1.29.4.

4. *Comment*. E.g., *HypArch* 86: 31f., 94: 22f.: "When he said this,

---

BG 118:19-22. I am indebted to Anne McGuire, who has prepared a comprehensive chart of the many variants of the vain claim, checking the Coptic texts. For the purpose of the present paper I have mostly relied upon, and quoted from, *NHLibEng*. I have also made use of translations in W. Foerster, ed., *Gnosis* (tr. R. McL. Wilson; 2 vols.; Cambridge: University Press, 1972). References to Irenaeus, *Adversus haereses*, follow the traditional system of enumeration (Mangey, Stieren, et al.), which is also reproduced in the edition of Harvey.

[10] According to Irenaeus, *Haer.* 1.5.4, it was through the prophets that the Demiurge made his claim, "I am God and there is no other." This could, possibly, be an early form, as argued by H.-M. Schenke, *Der Gott "Mensch" in der Gnosis* (Göttingen: Vandenhoeck & Ruprecht, 1962) 88. More likely, the reference to the prophets is a Valentinian modification of more mythological versions. The parallel passage in Clement, *Excerpta ex Theodoto*, does not mention the "vain claim" but only the ignorance of the Demiurge (49.1, cf. 53.4). See also, however, *Haer.* 2.9.2 and Hippolytus, *Haer.* 6.33.

[11] Some of the same items, but not the claim itself, were already part of the teaching of Satornilos (or Saturninus), as summarized by Irenaeus, *Haer.* 1.24.1-2. Both the claim and related items recur in Epiphanius, *Haer.* 25, on libertine Gnostics.

he sinned against the Entirety." Cf. *OnOrgWld* 103: 13f. Other comments, *ApocryJn*, CG II 11: 21f.; *GEgypt* 58: 26-59.1. *ApocryJn*, BG 44: 15ff.: "Already showing the angels with him that another god existed," etc.; cf. CG II 13: 9-13.

5. *Rebuke*, by a voice from above (from Incorruptibility, from the Mother, or sim.). E.g., *HypArch* 86: 32-87: 4: "You are mistaken, Samael." Cf. *HypArch* 94: 24-26; 95: 5-7; *OnOrgWld* 103: 15-18. Irenaeus, *Haer.* 1.30.6: "Do not lie, Yaldabaoth."

6. *Disclosure*, combined with the rebuke or as an alternative to it. *ApocryJn*, BG 47: 15-18; CG II 14: 13-15: "The Man exists and the son of Man." Cf. *GEgypt* 59: 1-3; Irenaeus, *Haer.* 1.30.6. *OnOrgWld* 103: 19-28: "An enlightened, immortal man [or: an immortal Light-Man] exists before you," etc.

7. *Challenge*; the Archon calls for a revelation. *HypArch* 94: 27f.: "If any other thing exists before me, let it become visible to me!" *OnOrgWld* 107: 36-108: 2: "If someone exists before me, let him appear so that we may see his light."

8. *Appearance* of an image (in the water) and/or of light. *HypArch* 87: 11-16: "As Incorruptibility looked down into the region of the Waters, her Image appeared in the Waters," etc. Cf. *OnOrgWld* 103: 28-31; 107: 18f. (Gen 1:2b?). *HypArch* 94: 28-31: "And immediately Sophia stretched forth her finger and introduced Light into Matter." Cf. *OnOrgWld* 108: 2-14; 111: 29-31; 112: 25f. (Gen 1:3). *ApocryJn*, BG 48: 1-9; CG II 14: 18-34; *GEgypt* 59: 4-9 (Gen 1:2b-3?).

9. *Proposal* to create man, made by the Archon or his Powers (Gen 1:26). *HypArch* 87: 23-26; *OnOrgWld* 112: 32-113: 4; *ApocryJn*, CG II 15: 1-4; BG 48: 10-14; Irenaeus, *Haer.* 1.30.6.

10. *Formation* of man from the earth (Gen 1:27 + 2:7). *HypArch* 87: 27ff.; *OnOrgWld* 113: 9ff.; *ApocryJn*, BG 48: 14ff.; CG II 15: 5ff.; *GEgypt* 59: 9; Irenaeus, *Haer.* 1.30.6.

Only *On the Origin of the World* contains all items in this "pattern," but here the sequence is interrupted by other items, by repeated appearances, and also by back references to the "vain claim." Both in the *Hypostasis of the Archons* and in the long recension of the *Apocryphon of John* elements of the pattern recur several times. The abstract pattern does not pretend to reproduce the literary composition of the texts as we have them, nor did it ever have an independent existence of its own. Differences of outline and in details make it unlikely that the similarities are due to dependence upon any one written source. Yet, it is not only the individual items that recur;

even the order of the items remains remarkably constant wherever key elements of the pattern occur. This indicates that the various writings and reports in which we find traces of the "pattern" all draw upon some common tradition.

The three last items in the pattern are all directly related to the creation story in Genesis, the "appearance" to Gen 1:2b or 1:3, the "proposal" to Gen 1:26, and the "formation" of man to Gen 1:27 and 2:7. Some other texts suggest that it was satisfaction with his work of creation that made the Demiurge think that he was divine.[12] But in the group of texts on which we have concentrated our attention, the "vain claim" always precedes the proposal to create man in Gen 1:26. So do the items which are most closely related to the claim: the introduction, comment, rebuke, and also the disclosure and challenge wherever these elements occur (items 2-5 and 6 and 7). Occasionally, the vain claim is placed right at the beginning of the story of creation: the Archon made his arrogant claim when he opened his eyes and saw a vast quantity of matter without limit (Gen 1:2a; see *HypArch* 94: 19-22).[13] More often, he is reported to have made his claim after he had generated offspring or created powers, angels, etc.[14] But even so the claim is placed before the Spirit moved upon the waters (Gen 1:2b), as well as before there was light (Gen 1:3).[15] The

---

[12] *TriTrac*, CG I 100: 36-101: 5 clearly alludes to the refrain "God saw that it was good" (Gen 1:10, 25, 31, etc.); cf. 100: 19-25 and 101: 20, 25. "Oblique claims" after the creation of the world are also attested by *Ps.-Clem. Rec.* 2.57 (Simon); and by Hippolytus, *Haer.* 5.25.3 (cf. 23.4-5, [Pseudo-] Basilides) and 26.15 (Justin's *Baruch*).

[13] At this point, *OnOrgWld* 100: 29-33 only reports that the Archon, when he only saw water and darkness, thought that he alone existed. A similar illusion is attributed to "Darkness" in *ParaShem*, CG VII 2: 15-16; 3: 3-4, and to the "Pleromas" and the "Powers" in *TriTrac* 79: 12-18 and 84: 3-7.

[14] See *HypArch* 94: 34-95: 5; *ApocryJn*, CG II 11: 18-22 (cf. 12: 4-9; BG 42: 18-43: 4); Irenaeus, *Haer.* 1.29.4. According to *ApocryJn*, CG II 13: 5-9; BG 44: 9-15, and *OnOrgWld* 103: 2-13 the Archon addressed his boasting claim to the angels which he had created. All of these texts presuppose that the angels (or powers) were created on the first day, in accordance with ancient Jewish tradition attested by *Jub.* 2:2; see R. H. Charles, *The Book of Jubilees* (London: Black, 1902) 10-13. Thus also *The Cave of Treasures* 1:3 (C. Bezold, ed., *Die Schatzhöhle* [Leipzig, 1883] 1; P. Riessler, *Altjüdisches Schrifttum* [Augsburg: Filser, 1928] 942). In agreement with *Jub.* 2:3, *OnOrgWld* 103: 5-8 also reports that the angels praised their Creator. The standard rabbinic opinion, that the angels and spirits were not created until the second (or fifth) day, betrays an antiheretical tendency.

[15] Thus also *HypArch* 86: 27-31 and *GEgypt* 58: 23-59: 1. Only Irenaeus, *Haer.* 1.30, allows for a later setting of the claim. Here there is no "appearance," and reminiscences of Gen 1:2-6 occur before the birth of the Archon, within the Sophia myth. But since similar events recur at various stages in gnostic cosmogonies, this does not tell us where the vain claim should be located in Gen 1:1-25. The Valentinian

696 NILS A. DAHL

appearance of the image (or likeness) according to which the Archon and his powers wanted to create man (item 8) can be associated either with the Spirit upon the waters or with the light of the first day. As both the Spirit and the Light (of Wisdom) could be interpreted as manifestations of the Mother, some texts seem to conflate Gen 1:2b and 1:3. Only *On the Origin of the World* has retained a clear distinction between the revelation of "the likeness of her [Pistis's] greatness in the waters" and the appearance of the light, in which a human likeness was revealed.[16]

In general, *On the Origin of the World* has incorporated larger portions of the creation story in Genesis than have the other writings with which we are concerned. This treatise alludes to all the seven days of creation, even though the biblical Hexaëmeron (or Heptaëmeron) has been rearranged into an Octaëmeron which has a different order of days.[17] The other texts of the group do not follow the whole

---

cosmogonies in Irenaeus, *Haer.* 1.1-8, and Hippolytus, *Haer.* 6.29-36, do not contain items 4-8 of the "pattern," but even here the creation of man follows upon the "vain claim." A setting within the creation story is probably also presupposed in references to the claim which the Archon once made, in *GrSeth*, CG VII 53: 27-54: 4 and 64: 18-65: 1, and *TriProt*, CG XIII 43: 27-44: 4, as well as in *OnOrgWld* 107: 31-34 and 112: 25-31 and Irenaeus, *Haer.* 1.30.7.

[16] The appearance of the likeness of Pistis in the waters (Gen 1:2b) made the Archon grieve (*OnOrgWld* 103: 28-34; 107: 18-34; see also 108: 28-32). Then the coming of the light, in which a human likeness appeared (Gen 1:3), made him ashamed and made the Authorities laugh at him (*OnOrgWld* 108: 2-24; 111: 29-34; 112: 10-113: 5). Apparent complications are mainly caused by the intervening sections on Sabaoth (103: 32-106: 18, with another allusion to Gen 1:3 in 104:3-9) and on Eros (109: 1-25). The long recension of the *Apocryphon of John* ingeniously combines Gen 1:2b and 1:3: the Image of the Father was, in a human form, revealed in the waters above, whose underside was illuminated so that the Authorities, through the light, could see the form of the image in the water (CG II 14: 18-34). Even *ApocryJn*, BG 48: 1-9 and *GEgypt* 54: 4-9 presuppose a conflation of Gen 1:2b and 3 into one appearance of the image.

[17] Events of the first day of Genesis (1:1-5) are reported both in *OnOrgWld* 94: 30-101: 2 and in 102: 35-103: 2 and 107: 18-109: 1. The events of the second and third days (Gen 1:6-10) have been condensed (*OnOrgWld* 101:2-9). The creation of plants on the third day is combined with the trees of Paradise (Gen 1:11-12; 2:8-9; *OnOrgWld* 109:25-111:24). The creation of the animals on the fifth, and part of the sixth, day (Gen 1:20-23, 24-25) has been placed before the creation of the luminaries on the fourth (Gen 1:14-19; *OnOrgWld* 111:24-28; 112:1-10). For the creation of man on the sixth day (Gen 1:26-31 and 2:7), see 112: 29-113: 13 and 114: 18-115: 3, with an insertion about how Sophia Zoe anticipated the Authorities and created her man first, the androgynous "Eve of Life," *OnOrgWld* 113: 13-114: 15 (cf. Gen 1:3; 2:21). For the rest on the seventh day (Gen 2:1-3), see *OnOrgWld* 115: 23-27. Finally, the third, earthly Adam, the "man of the law," is said to have appeared on the eighth day (*OnOrgWld* 117: 28-118: 2), apparently a reference to *OnOrgWld* 115: 31-116: 8 (Gen 2:23, cf. 2:7).

The transposition of the fourth and fifth days has obscured the meaning of the

text of Genesis 1 but move directly from Gen 1:1-3 to Gen 1:26-27 and from there to Gen 2:7ff. In the *Hypostasis of the Archons* both the first part (86: 20-93: 2) and the revelation of Eleleth to Norea (93: 2-97: 22) follow this abbreviated outline of Genesis 1-2, and the *Apocryphon of John* and the relevant section of the *Gospel of the Egyptians* do the same. The report of Irenaeus in *Haer.* 1.29 breaks off with the vain claim, but the continuation is likely to have been more or less similar to what we read in the *Apocryphon of John*.

The omission of large portions of Genesis 1 in these texts is all the more remarkable because most of them follow the biblical account more closely from the creation of man onward, in several cases up to the Flood story. The concentration upon Gen 1:1-3, 1:26-27, and 2:7 makes it clear that the origin of mankind, not the origin of the world, is in the focus of interest. The main point of the plot is that human beings, enlightened by revealed wisdom, have a knowledge that the Creator did not have, and therefore realize that they are his superiors. The general theme may have been the origin and preservation of the seed of Seth. In the treatise *On the Origin of the World*, traditions similar to those preserved in the *Hypostasis of the Archons* and the *Apocryphon of John* seem to have been incorporated, together with heterogenous elements, into a more complete retelling of the creation story.[18]

The various texts with which we have dealt have in common both the "vain claim," the surrounding "pattern," and the basis in the biblical story of creation. Yet they differ not only in wording, in details, and in exegesis, but also in the way in which the plot works, exposing the foolishness of the Creator and his associates, with the

---

statement that the Light-Adam, who appeared on the first day, remained upon the earth for two days. It goes back to the Jewish tradition that after the third day the original light of Gen 1:3 was withdrawn and reserved for the age to come, and then the luminaries were created on the fourth day (e.g., *Gen. Rab.* 3.6; *b. Ḥag.* 12a). This has been overlooked both by A. Böhlig in Böhlig and P. Labib, *Die koptisch-gnostische Schrift ohne Titel* (Berlin: Akademie, 1962) 68f., and by M. Tardieu, *Trois mythes gnostiques* (Paris: Etudes Augustiennes, 1974) 94. Tardieu, pp. 85-139, esp. 131-35, has made a learned and interesting attempt to interpret the eight-day scheme of the present text. His construction, however, would collapse if only two letters (co) are to be restored in the lacuna in CG II 117: 32, as presupposed by the translation "on the sixth day" adopted by Bethge and Wintermute, *NHLibEng*, 173. Tardieu follows Böhlig in reading "on the fourth day." "Sixth" seems preferable, even though a lacuna in the Coptic text makes both readings possible, as Anne McGuire informs me.

[18] In spite of close parallels between *On the Origin of the World* and the *Hypostasis of the Archons*, it is unlikely that one of these works was a literary source for the other.

result that their plans fail and the divine element in mankind is preserved and eventually redeemed. The differences extend through the stories of Adam and Eve, Paradise and transgression, up to the Flood story. Some disagreements are quite substantial, but even so they are variations of common themes and patterns of thought, as distinct from the surface pattern of items listed above.

In some respects, the differences within our group of gnostic texts are like disagreements between exegetes who belong to the same religious community or the same theological school. They disagree in their exegesis but approach the texts with the same general presuppositions. I am even reminded of the difference between individual rabbis, apparent, e.g., in the early chapters of *Genesis Rabbah*. The gnostics, of course, did not edit their texts as midrashim, recording the opinions of various teachers. But I have the impression that behind our group of texts there is some sort of an esoteric, yet flexible, exegetical school tradition. The gnostics read their own ideas into the texts, but so have exegetes done at all times. Sometimes they interpreted what the biblical authors ought to have said rather than what they actually said. But even that phenomenon is neither exclusively ancient nor exclusively gnostic. But the gnostics went even further. They consciously turned the texts upside down. The illuminated understanding and the esoteric tradition became more normative than the written text. The *Apocryphon of John* can explicitly say that Moses was wrong (BG 45: 8ff.; 58: 16ff.; 59: 17ff.; CG II 13: 18ff.; 22: 21ff.; 23: 3f.).

A conflict between theologies, in which interpretation and reinterpretation of Scripture, and even biblical criticism, provide the weapons, is nothing unusual.[19] But the radical gnostics with whom we are dealing did not merely fight the false theology of their opponents, they maintained that this theology referred to a false God. The character of the gnostic interpretation of the early chapters of Genesis indicates that originally these opponents were Jews and not Christians.

All the gnostic texts which have the "vain claim" and the surrounding pattern include some Christian elements. But in the *Hypostasis of*

---

[19] Thus, there are both major differences and striking analogies between the controversy between the gnostics and their Jewish and Christian opponents and Paul's conflict with non-Christian and Christian Jews. Even in Paul's case, both the understanding of God and the social identity of his elect ones are at stake. See "The One God of Jews and Gentiles," in my *Studies in Paul* (Minneapolis: Augsburg, 1977), and the unpublished Oslo dissertation (1978) by Halvor Moxnes, "Theology in Conflict: Studies in Paul's understanding of God in Romans" (forthcoming in the series NovTSup).

the Archons the overtly Christian component is minimal, mainly to be found in the introduction (86: 20-27) and in the conclusion (96: 20ff.). It is considerably stronger in other texts, at least in the *Apocryphon of John, On the Origin of the World,* and Irenaeus, *Haer.* 1.30.[20] But the Christian elements in these texts vary a great deal and they are incorporated into the literary compositions at different points. What our texts have in common is due to their basis in the early chapters of Genesis, into which the pattern for the vain claim has been inserted. There is no evidence of Christian influence upon the main elements of this esoteric Genesis interpretation. The New Testament authors and other early Christian writers had an interest in the first chapters of Genesis that centered on christology and eschatology. Christ was the mediator of creation as well as of redemption, the Logos or the Image of God; there was an analogy between the first creation and the new creation in Christ, etc.[21] The points of contact between this Christian use and the early gnostic interpretation of Genesis are few and do not require the assumption of any direct contact one way or the other.[22]

If we turn to Jewish sources, however, it is obvious and generally recognized that the gnostic texts include a number of features which are also known from Jewish exegesis, mostly either from Philo of from targumim and rabbinic midrashim. The clearest example may be the understanding of the creation of Adam, including the theme of the

---

[20] Christian elements are less prominent in the source used by Irenaeus, *Haer.* 1.29, than in the preserved versions of the *Apocryphon of John.* The *Gospel of the Egyptians* raises special problems, since Seth is depicted as a heavenly redeemer who manifested himself in Jesus (e.g., 63: 4-64: 9). The *Apocalypse of Adam* may be a non-Christian gnostic work, but the conjecture that a form of the "vain claim" should be read in CG V 66: 26f. is hardly tenable. Mandaean texts contain some analogies to the boast of the Demiurge, e.g., *Ginza* R III, Petermann 93 (ET, after Rudolph, in Foerster, *Gnosis,* 2, 170f.). It might be interesting to investigate how far they too reflect a conflict situation.

[21] See, e.g., John 1:1-18; Rom 5:12-19; 8:18-30; 1 Cor 8:6; 11:3-11; 15:21-22, 44-49; 2 Cor 4:6; 5:17; 11:3; Gal 3:27-28; Eph 5:30-32; Col 1:15-20; Heb 1:2-4; 4:3-11; Rev 21:1; 22:1-5. On the correlation of the first and the last things, see my essay "Christ, Creation, and the Church" (1956), reprinted in *Jesus in the Memory of the Early Church* (Minneapolis: Augsburg, 1976) 120-40.

[22] I see no evidence that New Testament authors presuppose or combat a split within the deity or a separation between the mediator of redemption and the agent of creation. Cf., e.g., H. Hegermann, *Die Vorstellung von Schöpfungsmittler im hellenistischen Judentum und Urchristentum* (Berlin: Akademie, 1961). This, however, does not mean that gnostic parallels to the New Testament are irrelevant. The rabbis considered both gnostics and "orthodox" Christians two powers heretics and both groups are likely to have reinterpreted similar traditions, e.g., about the divine Eikon or Logos, each in its own way.

"golem" (Gen 2:7).[23] Other examples include the understanding of the light of the first day as a heavenly light (Gen 1:3) and of the image in Gen 1:26 as an hypostatized manifestation of the supreme God.[24] It even happens that two divergent interpretations of the same verse, e.g., Gen 4:1, are attested both in gnostic and in rabbinic sources.[25]

It is unnecessary to add further details, but some more general features should be mentioned. Hebrew or Aramaic names and etymologies are so common in our gnostic sources that at least some elements of the gnostic Genesis interpretation must go back to exegetes who were more familiar with the original languages of the Jewish Scriptures than was Philo. We also find traces of speculations about the names of God in the Hebrew Bible.[26] The anthropomorphic and anthropopathic language used about God in Genesis 2-3 or 6:6-7 was offensive to the gnostic exegetes. We know that it also caused problems to Philo and, to some extent, to the rabbis, while the early Christians hardly addressed such problems. An influence of Platonic traditions, especially from the *Timaeus*, upon gnostic

---

[23] See esp. Birger A. Pearson, *The Psychikos-Pneumatikos Terminology* (SBLDS 12; Missoula, Montana: Scholars Press, 1973) 17-23, 51-81.

[24] On Jewish traditions about the original light, see S. Aalen, *Die Begriffe "Licht" und "Finsternis" im Alten Testament, im Spätjudentum, und Rabbinismus* (Oslo: Norske Videnskaps-Akademi, 1951) 163-70, 262-69. On the "Image" in Gen. 1:26f., see J. Jervell, *Imago Dei: Gen. 1:26f. im Spätjudentum, in der Gnosis und in den paulinischen Briefen* (FRLANT 76; Göttingen: Vandenhoeck & Ruprecht, 1960), esp. 52-69, 76-86, 96-107, 136-40; H.-M. Schenke, *Der Gott "Mensch"*, esp. 69-71, 120-43.

[25] According to Irenaeus, *Haer.* 1.30.9, Cain and Abel were sons of Adam and Eve, but *HypArch* 89: 28-31; 91: 12 makes Cain the son of the Archons; see B. Layton in *HTR* 70 (1977) 60-61, notes 84 and 85. *GEgypt* 117: 15-18 and *ApocryJn*, CG II 24: 15-25; BG 62: 7-63: 5, have other variants of an exegesis which took Gen 4:1 to mean that an angelic prince, called Yahweh, had seduced Eve and begotten Cain and Abel. Outside gnosticism, this angel was identified with Satan, as already John 8:44; 1 John 3:12; and 2 Cor 11:3, 14. See my article "Der Erstgeborene Satans und der Vater des Teufels," *Apophoreta: Festschrift ... Haenchen* (ed. W. Eltester; BZNW 30; Berlin: Töpelmann, 1964) 70-84.

[26] See, e.g., *ApocryJn*, CG II 24:15-25; IV 38: 1-4; BG 62: 7-63: 5, where "Yave" and "Eloim" are identified with Cain and Abel, or vice versa. One can even wonder if the notion that the angelic agent of creation claimed to be God has something to do with the use of divine names in Genesis 1 ff. To a gnostic, as to a skeptical reader, the YHWH Elohim of Genesis 2-3 could not be the true God, as he was ignorant and envious (see, e.g., *TestimTr*, CG IX 45: 23-48: 15). Yet in Gen 1:1-2:4 the Creator is called Elohim. If the agent of creation was identical with the giver of the Law, he would himself have claimed to be God. Only Justin's book *Baruch* differs from other gnostic texts in considering Elohim, the Creator, to be the second god, who in his vanity thought that he was Kyrios, the Good One (Hippolytus, *Haer.* 5.26.15f.). In several gnostic texts Hebrew names of God reappear as names of some of the seven powers, e.g., Irenaeus, *Haer.* 1.30.5; *ApocryJn*, CG II 11:26-12: 25.

Genesis interpretation is present, e.g., in the notion that earthly realities are imitations of heavenly models. Like Philo, the gnostic exegetes also assimilate elements of hellenistic astronomy, physics, physiology, etc., with the biblical story of creation. Only from the late second century onward did Christian theologians like Theophilus of Antioch begin to incorporate the type of learned Jewish Genesis exegesis which the gnostic texts presuppose and transform.

All of this points to some fringe group of hellenized Judaism, not towards early Christianity, as the original setting for the type of Genesis interpretation which has been preserved in the *Hypostasis of the Archons*, the *Apocryphon of John*, and related writings. Both the variability of gnostic exegesis and its affinity, in points of detail, to diverse Jewish sources indicate that the contact between "proto-gnostic" and more "orthodox" Jewish exegetes extended over some period of time. This is just what we should expect if the assumption is correct that the gnostic portrayal of the biblical Creator-God as an ignorant and arrogant Archon reflects a sharpening of the controversy, on both sides. Under the attack of strict Jewish monotheism, some early form of gnosticism was radicalized, and speculative, probably esoteric, Genesis interpretation was turned into a gnostic myth.[27]

The Myth of the Arrogant Ruler

What I have here called the "vain claim," i.e., the attribution of proof texts for an exclusive monotheism, e.g., Isa 45:5 or 46:9, to a

---

[27] I must leave open the question when and where this radicalization occurred. The known evidence suggests that the rabbinic polemic against "two powers" sectarians goes back to the period 70-135 C.E. This is also likely to be the time in which adherents of the doctrine of "two powers" revolted and turned radical gnostics. Excluded from the synagogues, some of them found a temporary refuge in the Christian church. It should be added, however, that not all branches of the gnostic movement were equally revolutionary. The "vain claim" and related features are not attested for the earliest Samaritan and Syriac gnostics (Simon Magus, Dositheus, Menander, Saturninus) nor does it occur in writings like *Poimandres*, the *Naassene Sermon*, the *Apophasis Megale*, *Eugnostos the Blessed*, or the *Gospel of Truth*. The interest in esoteric knowledge of cosmological secrets, more or less dependent upon Genesis, must also have continued outside what we call gnosticism, see, e.g., *2 Enoch* 24-33 and *Sefer Yeṣirah*. More syncretistic examples occur in K. Preisendanz, ed., *Papyri Graecae Magicae* 1-2 (2d ed.; Stuttgart: Teubner, 1973-74). The "Leiden Cosmogony" in *PGM* 13, 138-206, with a parallel in 443-564, can even be considered to be gnostic in a wider sense of the term. We hear, e.g., about rivalry between the seven gods who were created when God laughed seven times (177-86, 191-206, and, with additional details, 494-563). But even apart from its magical use, this text is an example of cosmological, perhaps esoteric, gnosis, but not of saving, dualistic, or revolutionary gnosticism.

subordinate Demiurge or Archon, is generally seen as a classical example of gnostic radicalism. Relatively few scholars seem to have discussed the claim in any detail, however. The notion that the world was created by one or several agents or angels[28] does not in itself explain the polarization which makes the agent a counterfeit of the supreme God. H.-M. Schenke has taken the "vain claim" to illustrate the development from allegory to myth.[29] But the attribution of sayings of the God of the Bible to an inferior deity can hardly be considered an example of allegorical interpretation, and the notion of a process of development does not explain the revolutionary character of the gnostic use of Scripture.

As an example of a different approach, I quote R. A. Bullard: "The account of the blasphemy of the Demiurge is probably not so much a creation of Gnostic exegesis as a result of a myth of the haughty Demiurge coming into contact with Jewish monotheism."[30] But Bullard's explanation is not the only alternative to that of Schenke. On the one hand, gnostic interpretation is itself mythopoetic. On the other hand, in religions that recognize sacred scriptures as in some sense normative, interpretation of the scriptures provides the chief means for incorporating scientific knowledge, philosophical insights, or even myths. The outcome of such efforts may well be something that is new, not only in comparison with more traditional interpretations of the sacred texts but also in comparison with the ideas that informed the reading of the texts. That happens even when the reinterpretation is less radical than in gnosticism.

Where the Creator is portrayed as an arrogant Archon, he is indeed cast into a mythical role. But I do not see evidence that the gnostic myth of the haughty Demiurge preceded the contact with biblical monotheism. What happened in this case, as in others, was much more that some gnostics in their mythopoetic exegesis made use of already existing mythological, though not gnostic, motifs. The motif of a god, angel, prince, or man who wanted to be like God, or who in his

---

[28] Cf. G. Quispel, "The Origin of the Gnostic Demiurge," *Gnostic Studies* 1 (Istanbul: Nederlands Historisch-Archaeologisch Instituut, 1974) 213-20 (reprinted from *Kyriakon: Festschrift J. Quasten* [1970] 271-76). According to Jarl Fossum, who at the Yale Conference read a paper on "The Origin of the Concept of the Demiurge," there is also some Samaritan evidence for the notion that the world was created by an angel.

[29] *Der Gott "Mensch,"* 87-93. Schenke's other examples are much more to the point (pp. 72-84 and 69-71).

[30] *The Hypostasis of the Archons* (PTS 10; Berlin: De Gruyter, 1970) 51.

vanity and hybris claimed that he was himself God, occurs in many variations, both in ancient myths and in fairy tales.[31] For our purpose, it is not necessary to discusses whether we have to do with one myth in several variations or with several myths with a common theme. The Old Testament has preserved two classical variants of the theme, in Isaiah 14 and Ezekiel 28. Perhaps the story of the fall in Genesis 3 should be added as a third, modified variant (see esp. Gen 3:5).

Isaiah 14 is an ironical lamentation for the king of Babylon, the Day Star, son of Dawn, who would ascend above the heights of the clouds and make himself like the Most High but who is brought down to the depths of the Pit (see esp. Isa 14:12-15). The oracle in Ezekiel 28 is directed against the prince (*nāgîd*, ἄρχων) of Tyre, who said, "I am a god" (Ezek 28:2, 9) and considered himself wise as a god (Ezek 28:6). Moreover, in Ezek 28:11ff. he is depicted with features of the first man who, full of wisdom, was placed in Eden but later cast away so that he, like the king of Babylon in Isaiah 14, became an object of mockery. The Archon of our gnostic texts has been cast in the role of such haughty rulers. It is possible to detect some allusions to the biblical texts, especially Isaiah 14, and it is quite probable that the designation of the Archon as an "aborted fetus" goes back to an understanding of Isa 14:19 which is attested both by the targum and by Symmachus.[32]

---

[31] See, e.g., J. Morgenstern, "The Mythological Background of Psalm 82," *HUCA* 14 (1939) 29-126, esp. 101-14; M. Pope, *El in the Ugaritic Texts* (*VT*Sup 2, Leiden: Brill, 1955) 27-32, 97-103; A. Yarbro Collins, *The Combat Myth in the Book of Revelation* (HDR 9; Missoula, Montana: Scholars Press, 1976) 81 with notes 130-34 and 162 with note 27. More or less distant analogies to the gnostic myths of the Demiurge have been collected by U. Bianchi, "Le problème des origines du gnosticisme et l'histoire des religions," *Numen* 12 (1965), esp. 166-68 with notes. For the ongoing discussion about the mythological background of Isaiah 14, see also B. S. Childs, *Myth and Reality in the Old Testament* (SBT 27; London: SCM, 1960) 61-71; and articles by P. Grelot, *RHR* 149 (1956) 18-48; V. Oldenburg, *ZAW* 82 (1970) 187-208; J. W. McKay, *VT* 20 (1970) 451-64; P. C. Craigie, *ZAW* 85 (1973) 223-25. On Ezekiel 28 see, e.g., H. G. May, "The King of the Garden of Eden," *Israel's Prophetic Heritage: Essays in Honor of James Muilenburg* (ed. B. W. Anderson and W. Harrelson; London: SCM, 1962) 166-76.

[32] For *kĕnēṣer nit'āb* in Isa 14:19 the Septuagint has ὡς νεκρὸς ἐβδελυγμένος, Symmachus ὡς ἔκτρωμα (ἐβδελυγμένος), and targum *kĕyahaṭ ṭĕmîr*. See J. Ziegler, ed., *Isaiah* (Göttingen Septuaginta 14; 1939) and L. Lütkemann and A. Rahlfs, "Hexaplarische Randnoten zu Is. 1-16," in *Mitteilungen des Septuaginta-Unternehmens* 2 (*NachrGesGöttingen*, 1915, Beiheft) 328-29. For the Archon as an ἔκτρωμα, see *HypArch* 94: 15; *ApocryJn*, BG 46: 9-14 (CG II 13: 33-36, "the cover of darkness" [?]); Hippolytus, *Haer.* 6.31.1-5 (Valent.). Cf. *OnOrgWld* 99: 1-100: 6. The term ἔκτρωμα can

It would require detailed investigations to find out how far the gnostic myth of the arrogant Archon draws upon Isaiah 14 and Ezekiel 28, and how far it is influenced by other variants of the mythical theme. In any case, already the biblical oracles apply ancient mythological motifs to enemies of the people of God. Later on, various adversaries were depicted as haughty rulers who claimed to be divine or were acclaimed as gods: Nebuchadnezzar in Judith (3:8; 6:12); Antiochus Epiphanes in Daniel (11:36f.); Pompey in the *Psalms of Solomon* (2:28f.); Caligula in Philo (*Gaium* 22, 74-80, 93-97, 118, 162); Herod Agrippa in Acts (12:21-23) and Josephus (*Ant.* 19.8.2 § 344-50); Nero in the *Sibylline Oracles* (5.33-35, 137-54, 214-21) and in the *Ascension of Isaiah* (4:6-8). In 2 Thessalonians (2:4) the "man of lawlessness" is said to proclaim himself to be God. Traces of the theme recur in Rev 13:1, 5-6. Later it became part of the Antichrist tradition.[33] Not only the general theme but also allusions to Isaiah 14 are also used in Christian polemic against Simon Magus and, possibly, in Jewish polemic against Jesus.[34]

In some cases, the polemic against political or religious adversaries was clearly occasioned by claims that were actually made by them or on their behalf. Yet there is no clear distinction between historical persons, symbolic representatives, and eschatological figures, but rather

---

also be applied to the lower Sophia: Irenaeus, *Haer.* 1.4.1; 8.2 (with reference to 1 Cor 15:8); Hippolytus, *Haer.* 6.36.3; or to other entities: *OnOrgWld* 99: 8-10 (Envy); Hippolytus, *Haer.* 5.25.6 (the Sonship left without form, according to Ps.-Basilides). For anthropological applications, see Clement, *Exc. Thdot.* 68, and Hippolytus, *Haer.* 5.17.6 (Perates). Tardieu, *Trois mythes*, 59 n. 60, compares with the Harpocrates myth in Plutarch, *Isid.* 19 and 65 (358D-E, 377B-C). A combination of a biblical passage with current hellenistic ideas is just what we should expect. For the connotations of the term ἔκτρωμα, see esp. J. Munck, "Paulus tanquam abortivus (I Cor. 15:8)," *New Testament Essays: Studies in Memory of T.W. Manson* (ed. A.J.B. Higgins; Manchester: University Press, 1959) 180-94, with references to earlier studies by A. Fridrichsen in *Symbolae Philologicae O.A. Danielsson* (Uppsala, 1932) and G. Björck in *ConNT* 3 (1939).

[33] For the theme in general, see also Sir 36:10 and the midrash on rulers who considered themselves divine in *Mek. R. Ishmael*, Shirta 8 (on Exod 15:11); cf. *b. Ḥul.* 89a; *Tanḥ. B. Wa'era* 7-8 (11b). See further E. Haag, *Studien zum Buche Judith* (Trier Theological Studies 16; Trier: Paulinus, 1963) 22-25, 33-35, 68-78; J.J. Collins, *The Sibylline Oracles of Egyptian Judaism* (SBLDS 13; Missoula, Montana: Scholars Press, 1974) 84-85; Yarbro Collins, *The Combat Myth*, 162-63, 166-68, 178-83; R.A. Aus, "God's Plan and God's Power," *JBL* 96 (1977), esp. 542 on 2 Thess 2:4 and Ezek 28:2.

[34] For legends about Simon, see *A. Petr.* (Verc.) 4, 10, 31f. (= *Mart.* 2-3); *Ps.-Clem. Rec.* 2.9.5-7, cf. 10.2; 3.47; Arnobius, *Adv. nat,* 2.12. For Jewish polemic, possibly against Jesus, *y. Ta'an.* 2.1 (65b, 59f.).

an interplay between history and myth and between claims made and polemical response. We should keep in mind that even the great adversary, the devil, was depicted as the Lucifer of Isaiah 14.[35] The name Samael makes it likely that some features have been transferred from the fallen prince of angels to the arrogant Archon of the gnostics.[36] But the gnostic Archon is not a satanic figure. On the whole, the Lucifer myth and the gnostic myth of the Creator-Archon are most likely to be analogous examples of mythopoetic exegesis and reinterpretations of ancient mythologoumena.[37]

The gnostics followed a fairly common practice in making polemical use of a mythological theme. What is unique is that they cast the Creator of the world himself into the role of the arrogant ruler who claims that he is God and that there is no other. We can say that the theme was remythologized. The mythopoetic polemic is not directed against an earthly ruler, against the symbolic or eschatological adversary of the people of God, or against the religious hero of a heretical

---

[35] E.g., *Life of Adam and Eve* 15; *2 Enoch*, recension A, 29:4f.; (apocryphal) 3 Cor. 3:11; cf. *Asc. Isa.* 10:13. Morgenstern, *HUCA* 14 99-106; K. L. Schmidt, "Lucifer als gefallene Engelmacht," *TZ* 7 (1951) 161-79.

[36] On Sam(m)ael as a name of the devil, see *3 Apoc. Bar.* 4:8; 9:7; *Asc. Isa.* 2:1, etc.; G. Scholem, *EncJud* 14. 719-22. Scholem has explained the obscure name Yaldabaoth as meaning "begetter of *abaoth*," wherein *abaoth* was an equivalent of Sabaoth, as in magical papyri. See Scholem, "Jaldabaoth Reconsidered," in *Mélanges d'histoire des religions offerts à Henri-Charles Puech* (Paris: Presses Universitaires, 1974) 405-21; cf. Layton, *HTR* 70, 72-74 n. 67. Yaldabaoth is indeed depicted both as the father of Sabaoth and as the begetter of the heavenly forces (*ṣabaoth*), identical with the Archigenetor who claimed, "I am God [and I am] your Father and it is I who [begot] you and there is no [other] beside me" (*TriProt*, CG XIII 43: 35-44: 2, cf. Deut 32:6, 18). Explanations offered in *OnOrgWld* 100: 10-14 and, possibly, 103: 23f. are secondary, but Scholem's explanation hardly excludes the possibility that the name Yaldabaoth was understood as a persiflage of *Yah(weh)* ʾēl(ōhê) ṣabaōth. The differentiation between Yaldabaoth and his son Sabaoth illustrates the ambiguous attitude to the God of the Bible; see esp. *HypArch* 95: 1-96: 14; *OnOrgWld* 103: 2-107: 14. One might guess that this differentiation corresponds to a distinction between the zealous opponents of the gnostics and other Jews or, at a later stage, Christians for whom there was a hope of repentance. See now Francis T. Fallon, *The Enthronement of Sabaoth* (NHS 10; Leiden: Brill, 1978).

[37] It is highly unlikely that the mythical motif was "degnosticized" and transferred from the Demiurge to the devil, as Schenke argued in *Der Gott "Mensch"*, 92f. There is even less reason to assume a gnostic background for the motif in late versions of legends about Yima, the primordial king (or man); see A. Christensen, *Le premier homme et le premier roi dans l'histoire légendaire des Iraniens* 2 (Leiden: Brill, 1934) 69, 103; cf. 86, 91, 116. We have much more to do with variations of a common theme, as recognized by O. Wintermute, "Gnostic Exegesis of the Old Testament," *Interpretation of the Old Testament in the New: Studies in Honor of W.F. Stinespring* (ed. J. M. Efird; Durham, North Carolina: Duke University Press, 1972), esp. 256-60.

group, but against the God of monotheistic opponents. The early
Christians applied the same mythical theme to an Antichrist figure.
But Yaldabaoth, Samael, or whatever he is called, is not an Antichrist
but a counterfeit God. This confirms that, originally, the gnostic revolt
was directed against the jealous God of exclusivist Jewish monotheism
and his zealous representatives on earth. Only later was the polemic
redirected to aim at the God of the Christians and against the
hierarchical authorities who acted as his representatives. But, at least
in Valentinianism, the revolutionary element was modified.[38]

THE LEWD SOPHIA

It is still necessary to add some remarks about the relationship
between the Archon-Creator and his mother, Sophia or Achamoth. In
some texts she is called Prunikos, the Lewd One, and thereby distinguished from a higher Sophia. In many respects, she is a gnosticized
variant of the hypostasized Ḥokmah of Jewish Wisdom literature (e.g.,
Proverbs 8, Job 28, Sirach 24).[39] But to a higher degree than her
Jewish antecedent, the gnostic Sophia has also features of a female
deity. For our purpose, it does not matter whether these features
have been taken over from Isis or from some other goddess. In any
case, the gnostic Sophia is a mother figure, the universal Mother
as well as the mother of the Archon, her aborted fetus. She is identified
with the heavenly Eve, the "mother of the living," and with the
Spirit (*rûaḥ*), which is female. Thus, she is the Spirit of God that
moved upon the water (Gen 1:2b).[40] In many gnostic texts, the

---

[38] See Pagels, "The Demiurge and his Archons," esp. 323 f., and cf. her *The Gnostic
Paul* (Philadelphia: Fortress, 1975). The opposite trend is clear in the *Second Treatise
of the Great Seth,* where the polemic against the God and the hierarchy of the church
is very sharp. See esp. CG VII 59: 19-61: 14 and 64: 18-65: 17; J. A. Gibbons, "The
Second Logos of the Great Seth: Considerations and Questions," in *SBLSP 1973*
(ed. G. MacRae) 2. 242-61. The data do not allow for the construction of any single
trajectory, whether the line of development is supposed to lead from a strictly dualistic
gnosis toward modified, more monistic systems, or from esoteric knowledge over
pre-gnostic and proto-gnostic ideas toward dualistic "gnosticism." In order to account
for the complex realities, one would have to take account of both trends and to pay
special attention to the relationship between gnostic groups and the larger religious
communities upon which they depend like parasites upon the host.

[39] See G. C. Stead, "The Valentinian Myth of Sophia," *JTS* 20 (1969) 75-104;
G. MacRae, "The Jewish Background of the Gnostic Sophia Myth," *NovT* 12 (1970)
86-101.

[40] See esp. A. Orbe, "Spiritus Domini ferebatur super aquas," *Gregorianum* 44 (1963)
691-731. On Wisdom as the daughter or consort of God and mother of all things, see

Mother not only has many names and aspects, she is also split up into several separate figures.

The distinction between a lower, earthly, and a higher, heavenly, wisdom is ancient, but the gnostic duplication, or multiplication, of "the Mother" cannot simply be understood as a mythologized version of this distinction. Nor is the combination of various components in the gnostic Sophia figure likely to provide a sufficient explanation. The gnostic Sophia myths are highly complex. They may contain reinterpretation of earlier mythologoumena as well as mythopoetic exegesis. Be that as it may, the gnostic Sophia myth, in most of its manifold variants, provides an etiology for the origin of the arrogant Archon and his vanity.[41] This suggests that we may find a clue in the notion of Sophia as the mother of the Logos. Philo attests not only this notion but also a divine triad of God the Father, the Mother, Sophia, and the Logos (or the world).[42] The triad of Father, Mother, and Son (the supreme deity, the female aspect of the deity, and the divine agent) reappears again and again in gnostic texts.[43] But whereas the Philonic Logos was the agent of revelation and salvation as well as the agent of creation, gnostics made a separation between the agent of creation, the Archon, on the one hand, and the divine agent of revelation and redemption on the other. This duality of of agents implied the assumption of two "Son" figures and necessitated a duplication of the Mother, e.g., a distinction between the female

---

B. L. Mack, *Logos und Sophia* (SUNT 10; Göttingen: Vandenhoeck & Ruprecht, 1973) 13f., 67-70, 155-58, etc. On the Holy Spirit as mother of Jesus, see the *Gospel of the Hebrews*, fragments 2 and 3 in Hennecke-Schneemelcher (E.T. ed. Wilson) 1. 163f. Cf. also the invocations of the Mother Holy Spirit in *A. Thom.* 27 and 50 and the devaluation of Ruḥa in Mandaic texts.

[41] See *HypArch* 84: 2-19; *OnOrgWld* 98: 11-100: 29; *ApocryJn*, CG II 9: 25-10: 19; BG 26: 15-38: 17; Irenaeus, *Haer.* 1. 29.2-4; 30.1-3. The accounts of the origin and fall of the Mothers contain mythopoetic Genesis exegesis, mostly based upon Gen 1:1-3, 26f.; 2:7; 3:20. The principle of successive series of models and copies allowed for projections of elements from Genesis 1-5 into the supramundane realms. But because of its premundane setting, the Sophia myth could not be patterned after the narrative sequence in Genesis. That may be one reason why the gnostic Sophia myth is open to much more variation than the myth of the arrogant Archon.

[42] *Fuga* 108-9; *Ebr.* 30-33; *Leg. All.* 2.49. In Philo's doctrine, Logos is much more important than Sophia; see Mack, *Logos und Sophia*. The triad God, Sophia, and Logos is therefore likely to have been current in some branch of hellenized Judaism. Cf. the christianized version of the triad in Theophilus, *Autol.* 1.7; 2.15.

[43] E.g., *ApocryJn*, CG II 2: 13; 9: 9-11; BG 21: 19-20; 35: 18-20; *GEgypt* 41: 7-9; 42: 4, etc.; Irenaeus, *Haer.* 1.29.3; 30.2. Cf. *OnOrgWld* 105: 23-31; *TriProt* 37: 20-22 and passim. See also A. Böhlig's paper in this volume, 617-634.

consort of the Supreme Being, mother of the Redeemer-Son, and the lower Sophia who produced the arrogant Archon. In most of our texts, the system of divine emanations or aeons is even more complicated, as the origin of the lower Sophia is preceded by several male-female couples.[44]

The function of the gnostic Sophia myth as an etiology of the origin of the Creator-Archon provides a key factor that explains the duplication or multiplication of Mother Wisdom. It does not, however, explain why the lower Sophia in some texts is called Prunikos, the Lewd One. Antecedents for the idea suggested by this name may be found in Jewish Wisdom traditions as well as in the character of female deities. Figurative language in Proverbs 1-9 depicts wisdom as a lady who, like her counterpart, the seductive "alien woman" (or "Lady Foolishness"), invites men to her house.[45] Several Jewish texts use sexual imagery to describe love for wisdom and her pleasures.[46] Gnostic texts are pervaded with sexual imagery, most often in the form of references to heavenly syzygies. The term Prunikos is well attested by the heresiologists,[47] and the *Second Treatise of the Great*

---

[44] Even in this connection, Gen 1:26-27 served either as a point of departure or as a point of contact or, most likely, as both. The passage not only provided a biblical warrant for a Platonic doctrine of models and copies but suggested also that, like the first created man, even the higher "images" were "male and female," i.e., either androgynous or couples. Already Philo, *Fuga* 51, made the comment that Wisdom, the daughter of God, could be said to be a father, since her nature is male; see Layton, *HTR* 70, 47-48 n. 15.

[45] See Prov 9:1-18; cf. 2:16-19; 4:6-7; 7:1-27; G. Boström, *Proverbia-Studien: Die Weisheit und das fremde Weib in Spr. 1-9* (LUÅ, N.S. 1, 30/1; Lund: Gleerup, 1935), esp. 156-74.

[46] See, e.g., Sir 15:2; Wis 6:12, 17f.; 7:7-10, 28; 8:2; and esp. 11QPs^a 21.11ff. (= Sir 51:13-30), ed. J. A. Sanders, *The Dead Sea Psalms Scroll* (Ithaca, N.Y.: Cornell University, 1967) 113-17; *DJD* 4 (1965) 79-85. For ancient themes and later interpretations, see M. Pope, *The Song of Songs* (AB 7C; New York: Doubleday, 1977), esp. 110f., 153-79. Cf. also the materials collected by H. Schlier, *Der Brief an die Epheser* (Düsseldorf: Patmos, 1958) 159-66, 264-76.

[47] The name Προύνικος is attested by Celsus (Origen, *Cels.* 6.34). See further Irenaeus, *Haer.* 1.29.4; 30.3, 7, 9, 11, 12; Epiphanius, *Haer.* 21.2.4.5 (Simonians), 25.3.2 (libertine Gnostics); (37.3.2; 4.2 (Ophites). According to Origen, *Cels.* 6.35, even Valentinians used the name. See also Epiphanius, *Haer.* 31.5.8-9; 6.9, on Valentinian aeons as androgyne *prunikoi*. Epiphanius also attests the verb προυνικεύω, *Haer.* 25.4.1 and 37.6.2, and the abstract noun προυνικία, 31.5.7. Outside gnostic writings, the adjective is used with sexual connotations in *Anthologia Palatina* 12.209 (προύνικα φιλήματα). Elsewhere, the unusual noun προύνικος (from προ-ενεικω ?) could designate a (hired) porter or, as a term of abuse, a low fellow. The semantic development has, apparently, a partial analogy in that of the English word "lewd," which earlier meant vulgar, rude, base, etc. In the gnostic usage, προύνικος has clearly sexual connotations (lewd, unchaste, lascivious, voluptuous or sim.) but it is not a term for a prostitute or a promiscuous woman.

Seth explicitly speaks of "our sister Sophia who is a whore" (CG VII 50: 25-28). But harlotry is not a prominent feature in the versions of the Sophia myth attested by the writings with which we have mainly been concerned, the *Hypostasis of the Archons, Apocryphon of John*, etc.[48]

The lewdness of the lower Sophia may be suggested by reports that in her libidinous passion she conceived and gave birth, or rather aborted, without a consort, or without the consent of her consort.[49] An enigmatic passage in Irenaeus, *Haer.* 1.30.7, may be especially relevant in this connection. Here we learn that, according to some Ophite gnostics, Prunikos rejoiced because she saw that Yaldabaoth and his powers were overcome by their own creation, since Adam and Eve, after they had eaten from the tree of knowledge, recognized the Power who is above all and separated themselves from their makers. She is said to have exclaimed, once again, that since the Incorruptible Father existed, he who once called himself father (i.e., Yaldabaoth) lied, and since the Father and the First Female existed, even she had sinned by her adultery ("et haec adulterans peccavit"). It is not quite clear whether *haec* refers to Prunikos herself or to the "Female from the Female," who originated from the body which Prunikos put off and who became the mother of Yaldabaoth.[50] There is nothing in the context to suggest adultery in the sense of illicit sexual intercourse.

---

[48] In some other texts, the main female figure is described as promiscuous. The statement "I am the whore and the holy one" is an example of unity in contrasts (*Thund*, CG VI 13: 18; not in the similar words of Eve, "the instructor," as reported in *OnOrgWld* 114: 8-15). In Justin's book *Baruch*, the virgin Israel-Edem is identified with Leda, Danae, and Hosea's harlot wife (Hippolytus, *Haer*. 5.26.34, 35 and 27.4; Hos 1:2). She is the mythological representative of the soul (5.26.8, 25, 36). The *Exegesis on the Soul* (CG II,6) describes the soul as a prostitute, but provides at best a distant parallel to the Sophia myth. The figure of Ennoia-Helena provides a closer analogy to the lewd Sophia; see G. Lüdemann, *Untersuchungen zur simonianischen Gnosis* (Göttinger Theologische Arbeiten 1; Göttingen: Vandenhoeck & Ruprecht, 1975) 55-78. Lüdemann suggests that the story of Simon and the harlot Helena is a Christian counter-legend, but that there was some warrant for it in genuine Simon Magus traditions. According to Epiphanius, *Haer*. 25.2 and 3, some "Gnostics" taught that the Powers were robbed of their "seed" through intercourse with Barbelo or Prunikos, who appeared to them in beauty. Some even reenacted the myth sacramentally, collecting semen and menstrual blood. Apparently, the legend of the seduction of Eve has been transformed into gnostic myth and ritual. See note 25 and, for another gnostic use of the motif, *HypArch* 89: 14-33; *OnOrgWld* 116: 32-117: 15.

[49] See, e.g., Irenaeus, *Haer*. 1.29.4 (without consort); *HypArch* 94: 5-8; *ApocryJn*, CG II 9: 25-32; BG 36: 16-37: 16; *SJC*, CG III 114: 13-18.

[50] Foerster, *Gnosis* (ET) 1. 90, takes *haec* to be the object of *peccavit* and *adulterans* to have the general sense of falsifying, but adds a parenthetical question mark.

The participle *adulterans* may refer either to the fall of Prunikos, who descended into the water and took on a body, or to the action of the Female from the Female which caused the birth of the Archon. In any case, the connotation seems to be the passion and lust of an adventurous woman, in contrast to the integrity of the Incorruptible Father and his consort the First Female. Such an understanding would also fit the description of Prunikos in Irenaeus, *Haer.* 1.29.3, and of Sophia in the *Apocryphon of John* and the *Hypostasis of the Archons.*[51]

The term "a Female from a Female" is also attested in a password to be used by the ascending soul when it arrives at the place of the "detainers" who steal souls: "Achamoth had no father nor male consort, but she is a female from a female. She produced you (pl.) without a male, since she was alone and in ignorance as to what [lives through] her mother because she thought that she alone existed. But [I] shall cry out to her mother" (*1ApocJas*, CG V 35: 10-19, with a close parallel in Irenaeus's report about the Marcosians, *Haer.* 1. 21.5). The double attestation of the formula makes it likely that it is ancient. One part of it has a partial parallel in the *Apocryphon of John*, where the ignorant Archon is said to have thought that there existed no other but his mother alone (CG II 13: 28-30; BG 46: 4f.). I would guess that this is a later variation of the theme that the Mother herself had the illusion that she alone existed. The idea is clearly reminiscent of the words of the virgin daughter of Babylon: "I am, and there is no one besides me" (Isa 47: 8, 10). Since the "vain claim" of the Archon is derived from passages in Isaiah 44-46, there can hardly be any doubt that the analogous claim of his mother goes back to Isaiah 47. If so, the name προύνικος might be an otherwise unattested translation of the equally unusual Hebrew word *'ădînâ*, ("you lover of pleasures," RSV), which in Isa 47:8 is used as a designation of the virgin daughter of Babylon.[52]

---

[51] *ApocryJn*, BG 37: 10f., explicitly says that Sophia brought her product forth "because of the lewd element (προύνικος) within her" (CG II 10: 1 has "because of the invisible power that is in her.") According to Irenaeus, *Haer.* 1.29.4, Prunikos looked down into the lower regions in the hope of finding a consort there. In 1.30.3 the agitation of Prunikos is associated with the "moving" of Gen 1:2b. Reports about Valentinian cosmogonies stress the passion of Sophia (Irenaeus, *Haer.* 1.2.2, especially her search for the Father). Another version of the theme occurs in *OnOrgWld* 108: 14-19, where Pronoia, the consort of the Archon, is said to have become enamored of Light-Adam.

[52] For *'ădînâ* in Isa 47:8 the targum has *mĕpannaqtā'*; LXX has τρυφερά. The text of Symmachus and other later Greek versions does not seem to have been preserved.

As the arrogant Archon was cast into the role of the king of Babylon in Isaiah 14, so his mother would seem to have been cast into the role of Babylon herself. The two analogous examples of mythopoetic exegesis with a polemical scope are likely to have been interrelated, even if the interconnection is no longer clearly visible in our sources. This suggestion receives some indirect confirmation from the analogy with apocalyptic use of Isaiah 14 and 47. As features from the king of Babylon in Isaiah 14 were transferred to the eschatological adversary, so were features from Isaiah 47 transferred to the great harlot, Babylon/Rome; see esp. Revelation 17-18. A Sibylline oracle announces that Rome shall sit as a widow because she said, "I alone am (μόνη εἰμὶ), and none shall bring ruin on me" (*Sib. Or.* 5.168-77, cf. Isa 47:8-10).[53] Thus, there is some similarity between the gnostic Archon and the eschatological adversary and between the lower wisdom in gnosticism and the world city in apocalyptic. But this similarity does not favor the theory of a development from apocalypticism to gnosticism, once suggested by Robert M. Grant.[54] What happened was, much more, that similar, in part biblical, in part mythological, imagery could be applied to counter-entities, in apocalyptic to the last adversary and to the world city in contrast to the heavenly Jerusalem, in gnosticism to the Creator-Archon and to his mother the lower Sophia in contrast to the higher Wisdom that had been revealed to the gnostics.

Philo can depict Wisdom or Virtue, represented by Sarah, as a heavenly city, whereas Hagar, "sojourning," is a symbol of encyclical education.[55] Some gnostic, mainly Valentinian, texts identify the lower, psychic Wisdom with the heavenly Jerusalem.[56] It might be too bold to suggest that this identification goes back to the same circle of early gnostic exegetes who also depicted the lower Sophia with features of the lewd virgin daughter of Babylon.[57] Even without this conjecture,

---

[53] See J. J. Collins, *Sibylline Oracles*, 79; cf. 66-71 on *Sib. Or.* 3.75-92 and 11.243-60, 271-314. Collins refers to Isa 47:8-9 on p. 67f. but, strangely enough, not on p. 79.

[54] *Gnosticism and Early Christianity* (1959; 2d ed., New York: Harper & Row, 1966).

[55] See, e.g., *Leg. All.* 3.1, 3, 244, and cf. the allusion to Isa 54:1 in *Praem.* 158. For the Hagar-Sarah allegory in general, see, e.g., *Cher.* 3-10; *Mut.* 137-41, 253-62. In Gal 4:21-31 Paul draws upon a variant of the allegory; cf. J. B. Lightfoot, *St Paul's Epistle to the Galatians* (London: Macmillan, 1876) 198-200. The Pauline version suggests that the identification of the Mother (Sarah, Wisdom) with the heavenly city (Jerusalem) may have been more important in the tradition than in Philo's use of it.

[56] See Irenaeus, *Haer.* 1.5.3; Hippolytus, *Haer.* 6.34.3-4; cf. 30.3. The Naassene use of the notion is somewhat different: Hippolytus, *Haer.* 5.8.7.

[57] In the book *Baruch*, Babylon is one of the angels of Israel-Edem and identified with Aphrodite and Omphale; see Hippolytus, *Haer.* 5.26.4, 20, 28. Thus, an identi-

the gnostic Sophia myth, like the myth of the arrogant and ignorant Creator, is an example of Jewish traditions in gnostic revolt.

On the whole, the lewd Sophia comes off much better in the gnostic texts than does her son, the arrogant Archon. This confirms that the real target of the gnostic revolt was not the wisdom of the dissenters' strictly monotheistic opponents, but their god, the God in whose name some early rabbis condemned the forerunners of the gnostics as "two powers heretics" who violated the one basic doctrine of Judaism: the Lord our God, the Lord is one.

---

fication of the heavenly Jerusalem with Babylon, the virgin daughter and the harlot, is quite conceivable as part of the gnostic revolt, but the evidence is slim.

ASPECTS OF THE JEWISH-GNOSTIC CONTROVERSY

BY

ITHAMAR GRUENWALD

THE scholarly discussion of the relation between Judaism and Gnosticism
has taken various directions. The chief problems discussed by scholars
are: (a) the amount, form and nature of the contribution of Judaism
to the formation of Gnosticism; (b) the extent and nature of the
Jewish polemic against Gnosticism; (c) the assumed influence of Gnosticism on Judaism; and (d) the possible existence of a Jewish heterodox
Gnosis that paved the way for Christian and heretical Gnosticism.
In the present paper we shall concentrate on several aspects relating
mainly to the first and fourth points, namely the Jewish contribution
to the formation of Gnosticism and the possible existence of a Jewish
heterodox Gnosis.[1]

As has been variously recognized, the Gnostic texts which were
discovered at Nag Hammadi show many points of connection with
Jewish ideas and literary sources. The same holds true concerning
certain points in the polemical accounts given by the Church Fathers
about the Gnostic systems which they set out to refute. However,
with the Jewish influence on Gnosticism taken for granted, there is
still no consensus as to the source and the means by which the Jewish
material came to the knowledge of the Gnostic writers. Obviously, no
generalizations can be made concerning those particularly complex
problems, since the sources and the channels through which the Jewish
material could have reached the Gnostic writers need not have been
the same in all cases. Furthermore, it has elsewhere been shown by
the present writer that upon close examination of certain details in two
of the Gnostic writings discovered at Nag Hammadi one is led to the
conclusion that not everything that on first sight appears to be an
idea which was directly borrowed from Jewish sources really is so.[2]
It has been shown that the dependence of the Gnostic writers on
Jewish sources is not as simple as one could have assumed if the

---

[1] A first version of this paper was read and discussed at the Seventh World
Congress of Jewish Studies in Jerusalem, August 1977.
[2] "Jewish Sources for the Gnostic Texts from Nag Hammadi?" in *Proceedings
of the Sixth World Congress of Jewish Studies*, vol. 3 (Jerusalem, 1977) 45-56.

major points of difference between the alleged Jewish sources and the Gnostic manner of using them were overlooked. The manner in which the Gnostic writers used the Jewish material which they allegedly knew is so idiosyncratic that a question mark had to be put against the phrase "Jewish Sources for the Gnostic Texts from Nag Hammadi." Indeed, it is difficult to tell in what manner the Jewish material reached the Gnostic writers: was it in the form of literary documents such as Targum and Midrash, or as general ideas that were just in the air in the syncretistic cultural atmosphere of the first centuries of the Christian era?

It is said in *Yerushalmi Sanhedrin* (10.6; ed. Venice 29c) in the name of Rabbi Yoḥanan that the people of Israel did not go into exile before they had become twenty-four sects of heretics (in Hebrew: *kittot shel minim*). Sayings of this kind have been taken by scholars to indicate the existence of Jewish sects of a heretical nature, possibly Jewish Gnostics. If this were true, the conclusion could be drawn that beside the general inventory of Talmudic, Midrashic, and Targumic sources which eventually stood at the disposal of the Gnostic writers there were Jews who pulled the Jewish heretical strings together for those writers. In fact, several attempts have been made to identify those Jews, as if the existence of a Jewish type of a heterodox Gnosis was an established historical fact. Thus, we may find H. Grätz speaking about a "jüdische Gnosis,"[3] M. Friedländer strongly defending his case for the existence of a "vorchristliche jüdische Gnosticismus,"[4] and G. Quispel advocating in our day the idea of a Jewish heterodox origin of Gnosis.[5] We may, of course, add the names of other scholars who went along similar lines of speculation, but it appears that in our case the *vox populi* cannot be accepted as *vox dei*. It may be argued that the theory of the existence of a Jewish Gnosis became possible only because people were reading backwards, from Gnosticism to Judaism. However, reading the Jewish texts themselves without knowing what happened to some of them in the course of the development of Gnosticism, one can hardly find any explicit indications in them for

---

[3] H. Grätz, *Gnosticismus und Judenthum* (Krotischin, 1846; Gregg reprint, 1971).

[4] M. Friedländer, *Der vorchristliche jüdische Gnosticismus* (Göttingen, 1898; Gregg reprint, 1972). See also B. A. Pearson, "Friedländer Revisited," *Studia Philonica* 2 (1973) 23-39.

[5] G. Quispel, *Gnostic Studies* (Istanbul: Nederlands historisch-archaeologisch instituut, 1974) 1. 195: "Es wurde wahrscheinlich, dass es eine vielleicht vorchristliche, judaisierende Gnosis gegeben hat ..."; ibid. 26: "And in so far as Gnosis is pre-Christian, it goes back to heterodox Jewish conceptions."

the existence of such a heterodox kind of Jewish Gnosis. Furthermore, even when the Gnostic texts are read with the intention of throwing light on Jewish texts in order to discover in them an articulate kind of Jewish Gnosis that was previously unnoticed, scholars usually reach conclusions that are based on misinterpretations and speculations. There are many stones scattered all over the Jewish field, and when the mason gathers them he will be able to build any house he likes; but there is almost nothing in those single stones that can be taken as a sign that they had previously been part of a house the like of which the mason now intends to construct.

Speaking about the Jewish sources of Gnosticism one has to notice that the Gnostic writers themselves were reluctant to acknowledge their indebtedness to Jewish writings and ideas. On the contrary, as is well known, their attitude towards Judaism was unsympathetic and even hostile. In fact, Gnosticism crystallized in an atmosphere of a total rejection of Judaism. It seems likely that the Gnostic attitude towards Judaism owes a lot to the manner in which some Christian writers treated the Jewish writings and ideas which they used or criticized in their own writings. The letters of Paul were but a first, though significant, step in establishing a style of anti-Jewish propaganda the tones of which are later on echoed in some of the other writings of the New Testament and in such Apostolic writings as the *Epistle of Barnabas*. Both the letters of Paul and the *Epistle* attributed to Barnabas set out to attack Judaism in its own terms of reference and on its own territory. It is bitter irony of fate that the religious ideas preached by those Christian writers were so deeply rooted in the religious system which they set out to refute. They used the old foundations, sometimes even the old building materials, in order to erect a new shrine that proclaimed the inefficiency and uselessness of the old one. Naturally, in this process of adapting Jewish ideas for the new religion these ideas lost much of their original identity. However, one thing remains clear: although certain Christian ideas are imbedded in Judaism, we cannot draw the conclusion that some kind of "Pauline" Ur-Christianity existed in Judaism.

Before we proceed to the Gnostic writings and the attitude maintained therein towards Judaism, we have to cast another glance at the New Testament and at remarks that it contains concerning the Jewish Law. It is thrice claimed in the New Testament that the Law was given by the angels. First, we find Stephen accusing the Jews of disobeying the Law which, as he put it, was "delivered by the angels" (Acts

7:53). Then, Paul in Gal 3:19 argues that the Law "was ordained by angels." Finally, the writer of the letter to the Hebrews referred to the same idea when he mentioned the "message which was declared by the angels" (Heb 2:2). It is conceivable that statements of this kind prepared the way for more radical positions such as those expressed in the *Epistle of Barnabas* which maintain that the Jewish people were wrong in the manner they interpreted Scripture and observed its laws, such as the sacrifices and circumcision. According to the *Epistle of Barnabas*, the correct way of understanding Scripture was to be gained by an allegorical reading of Scripture; only in this manner could the spiritual sense of Scripture come through. However, the *Epistle of Barnabas* claims, the Jews did not follow that spiritual mode of reading the Scriptures. They "erred because an evil angel was misleading them" (9:4). Accordingly, if the Jewish Scriptures are still to keep their relevance, they have to be reinterpreted in a manner that will enable the Christian light to shine through them.

It is in these respects that we may consider the kind of writings mentioned here as preparing the way for the attitude maintained by some Gnostic writers towards the Jewish Scriptures. It is a well-known fact that the Gnostic writers leaned heavily on the Genesis story in explicating their idiosyncratic cosmology. But, in contradistinction to the allegation made by the writer of the *Epistle of Barnabas*, to the effect that the Jews were misled by an evil angel, the Gnostic writers desired to show that Scripture had to be understood in an inverted manner: what the Jews considered as good was in fact evil. Scripture had to be rephrased so as to expose the information which the Archons desired to implant in mankind in order to misguide it from the way to salvation. The Gnostic writers retold the story of Genesis in a manner that aimed at making clear to their readers the activities of the evil God. In fact, Jewish prophecy derived from the Archons. Thus, for instance, we find Irenaeus reporting that according to the Gnostics "Moses was the prophet of Yaldabaoth, as were Joshua, Amos, and Habakkuk; Samuel, Nathan, Jonah, and Micah (the son of Imlah) were prophets of Jao; Elijah, Joel, and Zechariah were prophets of Sabaoth; Isaiah, Ezekiel, Jeremiah, and Daniel were prophets of Adonai; Tobias and Haggai were prophets of Eloi; Micah and Nahum were prophets of Oreus; and Ezra and Zephaniah were prophets of Astanfeus" (*Haer.* 1.30.11). The seven Archons mentioned in this passage as being those who inspired the Jewish prophets are also known from several Gnostic texts discovered at Nag Hammadi, such as the *Apocryphon of John*, the *Hypostasis of the Archons*, and the so-called "Untitled Work on the Creation of the World" [*OnOrgWld*]. In addition, we find in the *Apocryphon of John*, which inter alia contains an extensive cosmological section, that things happened not as they were reported in Scripture. It is repeatedly stated in the *Apocryphon of John* that Moses did not give a correct account of what happened: "Do not think it was as Moses said"; "not such as Moses wrote as you have heard"; "not as Moses said"; and "not such as Moses said." In other words, according to that text, certain details in the Biblical story as it was told to and by Moses are lies. This allegation is reminiscent of what Apelles, one of Marcion's disciples, said regarding Scripture. According to Hippolytus, on whose account we rely, Apelles criticised Scripture for containing lies (*Haer.* 7.38.2).

It is obviously remarkable that the Gnostic writers who were so opposed to the Jews and their Scriptures still found it necessary, or possible, to incorporate into their writings material that belonged to the very heart of the false revelation. In addition, the Jewish material was introduced into some of the most important theological passages in those Gnostic writings, and it is in place to ask: Why did the Gnostic writers incorporate the Jewish lore into their writings? What made them reveal their indebtedness to the rejected religion? The answer to that question is by no means an easy one, and one may argue that in doing so the Gnostic writers imitated the Christian practice. One may even say that from the point of view of religious propaganda, the Gnostic procedure could have had a strong impact on the Gnostic audience. The Scriptures of your enemy are rewritten in such a manner that they are made to declare not only their own falsity, but also the truth of the Gnostics. Obviously, this is a shrewd method, and it certainly had its overwhelming success in inverting Jewish values into Gnosticism.

But one may go a step further and ask: For whom were these writings written? Or: Who could be able to see the point made by these Gnostic writings? Obviously, the first answer brings up the names of the Jews. Only Jews could see the full relevance of the Gnostic argument made through the Jewish Scriptures. In other words, it stands to reason to say that the Gnostic writings which contain the Jewish material were written for Jews, or ex-Jews, who had to be convinced of both the falsity of their understanding of Scripture and of the truth latently maintained in their Scriptures; non-Jews, that is heathen believers, could not see the point made by such a shrewd procedure. Thus, it is conceivable that the Gnostic writings under discussion were mainly addressed to Jews, or to people who had previously been Jewish believers, apparently Christians.

In the account given by Irenaeus (*Haer.* 1.24.6) about the system of Basilides it is said that the disciples of Basilides are "no longer Jews and not yet Christians." Although the context of this saying makes it clear that Irenaeus is concerned with a comparative gradation of the disciples of Basilides, that is, that in spite of the fact that they are no longer Jews they have not yet reached the status of true Christians, it is also possible to see in his statement an historical affiliation. If so, Irenaeus admits the Jewish origin of Basilides' disciples. This concurs with another statement made in the Gnostic *GPh* 6 which distinguishes between the Jews, who are like orphans without a father, and the Christians who have both a father and a mother. In other words, the *Gospel of Philip* thinks more highly of the Christians than of the Jews. Both in Irenaeus and in the *Gospel of Philip* the Jews are considered to be the bottom of the scale. The difference between Irenaeus and the *Gospel of Philip* lies in the relative estimation of the Christian and the Gnostics. The Christian bishop of Lyons sees the Christians at the top of the scale, while the Gnostic author of the *Gospel of Philip* places the Gnostics at the top and the Christians in the middle. The *Gospel of Philip* also maintains that those who have not received the Lord are still Jews (*GPh* 46). Thus the Jews are a typological representation of the nonbelievers, and this according to Christians and Gnostics alike. In other words, both Christians and Gnostics seem to agree that Judaism was their respective point of departure, but not before it had been turned into the negative pole.

Admittedly, not all Gnostic writings postulated a negative attitude towards the Jewish Scriptures. In an article discussing the Gnostic relation to the Jewish Scriptures, M. Krause rightly pointed out the fact that one can discover an "unterschiedliche Bewertung des alten Testaments" in the Gnostic writings.[6] However, even if one notices a lack of negative tones in relation to the Jewish Scriptures in some of the Gnostic writings, the general truth still remains that Gnosticism as such maintained a negative attitude towards Judaism and its Scriptures. The question then again arises: Why did the Gnostic

---

[6] M. Krause, "Aussagen über das alte Testament in z.T. bisher unveröffentlichen gnostischen Texten aus Nag Hammadi," *Ex Orbe Religionum: Studia Geo Widengren* (Leiden: Brill, 1972) 449-56.

writers bother so much about the Scriptures of a rejected religion? The answer to that question can, I believe, come from the answer to a different question, already asked before, namely, for whom were these writings written? Or: What was the audience to which these writings were addressed?

It may be argued that the introduction of Jewish material into the Gnostic writings and the direct reference to the Jewish Scriptures therein may be attributed to the syncretistic practices adopted by the Gnostic writers. True, the Gnostic writers lived in an age when the borders between cultures and religions were not as markedly outlined as they were in other ages. But this is not to say that whenever we find one religion or culture borrowing from its neighbors and distant companions, we can always dismiss the case as a mere syncretistic fashion. Syncretism is a term that is sometimes too loosely used and it is liable to cause us to overlook the operation of deeper motivations and purposes. In the case of the writings from Nag Hammadi one is too easily able to dismiss the Jewish material as either a mere syncretistic fashion or as a formal imitation of Christian exegetical techniques. By doing so, one is likely to overlook the inherent problems that are posed by that material and which are so important to a full evaluation of these texts. It appears that the people to whom these writings, which, among other things, rewrote the story of the creation of the world as told in the Jewish Scriptures, could have made any sense were people familiar with those Scriptures and their Targumic and Midrashic exegetical tradition. Those people could be either Jews or ex-Jews. It is also conceivable that they were Christians who were familiar with Christian methods of biblical interpretation. As for the first class, Jews, or ex-Jews, it seems that by addressing them in their own terms the Gnostic writers wanted to achieve two things at the same time: first, they wanted to show those Jews that their own way of reading the Scriptures was wrongly oriented and, second, to show them the right way to redemption by pointing out to them the *via negativa* and the *via positiva* side by side. However, the second class, namely certain early Christians, could also be viewed as being addressed by these writings: for them a line of propaganda that undermined the Scriptural foundations of Christianity could have led to what the Gnostic writers considered a more truthful understanding of Christianity. One should always bear in mind that the Gnostic idea of the Savior owes a lot to Christianity, even more than it does to Jewish messianism. Thus, the Gnostic debt to Christianity should always weigh heavily in any attempt to identify the early Gnostic believers. One may, of course, suggest that even the Christians who were addressed by the Gnostic writings had previously been Jews, but the question still remains: If it is true that Jews were addressed by, or even wrote, the Gnostic writings under discussion, then who are those Jews and what was there in their belief that prepared their way to Gnosticism?

As already pointed out before, it has often been argued that there existed an early Jewish heresy in which one can discover the foundations of Gnosticism. However, it has been argued by the present writer that although Judaism contributed in many ways to the formation of Gnosticism, this was not in a conscious and planned manner but rather as an inventory of contributing historical and ideological factors.[7] There is nothing in the Jewish writings of the pre-Christian era and in Talmudic times that can point to the existence of a well-defined Jewish heresy. The term *minut*, and its equivalents in Jewish writings of the Talmudic period, is very loosely used and can stand for all kinds of beliefs and views which existed at the periphery of Judaism. Indeed, the rabbis, and even Philo of Alexandria before them, argued against all kinds of apostasy, but it is nowhere stated in so many words that there was a Jewish heresy within Judaism. Thus the views which hold that there was a Jewish Gnosis from which Gnosticism arose, or that Gnosticism arose from within Judaism, appear to me to infer too much from too little. It can be shown that many of the sayings in the rabbinic corpus of writings that are quoted to sustain the belief in the alleged existence of a Jewish heretical Gnosis say much less than they are believed to contain. We cannot analyze here all the cases in question, but we may briefly refer to one or two examples. M. Friedländer, who spoke about the existence of a pre-Christian Jewish Gnosticism, argued that the prohibition maintained in *Mishnah Hagigah* against cosmogonic and theosophical speculations (*maʿaseh bereshit* and *maʿaseh merkabah*, as they are called in Hebrew) can be explained by the heretical turn these speculations took. However, we now know more about these speculations than did Friedländer, and we may say that there were quite different reasons for that prohibition than the assumed clash with certain circles within Judaism that allegedly held heretical views. Speaking of *merkabah* speculations, we also know of the apostasy of Elisha ben Avuyah, who was nicknamed *Aḥer*, that is,

---

[7] See I. Gruenwald, "Knowledge and Vision," *Israel Oriental Studies* 3 (1973) 63 ff.

apostate. It is told in *b. Ḥag.* 15a that his apostasy was caused by the fact that he saw Metatron sitting in heaven. Knowing that only God and not the angels sits, he was led into the conclusion that there were Two Powers in heaven. Now, the belief in Two Powers in heaven was considered heretical by the Jews in Talmudic times.[8] However, it is doubtful whether this was an inner Jewish heresy or an outer heresy. It seems more likely to think that the Jewish polemic against Two Powers in heaven was directed towards a non-Jewish heresy. Thus, one of the key proof texts in the case for the existence of a Jewish heretical Gnosis is not a definite proof but rather a doubtful example. What is more, this particular explanation of the apostasy of Elisha the son of Avuyah is only one in a series of such explanations given in rabbinic sources and, for that matter, not the oldest one. Finally, we may mention the *sifrei minim* often mentioned in rabbinic writings. These *sifrei minim* are very often interpreted as Jewish heretical books, and thus assumed to prove the case for the Jewish Gnosis. But, as we know, a very early Jewish explanation says that the *sifrei minim* are Jewish Scriptures written by apostates.[9]

We may now add a general remark about the application of Jewish sources in the study of the Gnostic writings. It is a well known fact that the dating of rabbinic material is an extremely difficult job. A saying attributed to a rabbi living in the third century C.E. could well reflect a view originating in the first century C.E. And an idea found in a Midrashic compilation from the Middle Ages could well go back to the early centuries of the Christian era. However, one should be careful not to apply this possibility of predating rabbinic material in a careless manner. It is very easy to point out a great many cases in which a later idea is attributed to an early sage; and one is easily tempted to follow a line of argumentation according to which the existence of a certain idea in a Gnostic text written in the early centuries of the Christran era is sufficient indication for the early existence of the parallel Jewish idea found in a Medieval Jewish text. The fact, for instance, that something is said in *Perkei de-Rabbi Eliezer*, a Jewish Midrashic compilation composed in the Land of Israel in the eighth century C.E., and in the *Zohar*, the major Kabbalistic text which was

---

[8] See A. F. Segal, *Two Powers in Heaven* (Leiden: Brill, 1977).

[9] See B. Lewin, *Otzar ha-Geonim*; *Tractate Shabbat* (Haifa, 1930) 102 (in the name of Haj Gaon). There is, however, another explanation, quoted in Joseph Alphasi's Commentary to *b. Sanh.* 100b: books in which explanations are given to Scripture not on the basis of the sayings of the sages.

composed in Spain in the thirteenth century, is no indication whatever of the exact date of that particular saying or idea. Thus, reference books as Strack-Billerbeck and *The Legends of the Jews* should be used with the utmost caution. One note in *The Legends of the Jews* may sometimes require a careful study of all the references it contains, before the material is quoted and applied in the exegetical work done on the Gnostic texts. In any event, it is here suggested that the exegetical work done on the Gnostic texts from Nag Hammadi should be done by a joint effort of experts from the different branches of knowledge that are required in order to produce serious and solid results.

In conclusion it may be said that the position maintained in some of the Gnostic texts found at Nag Hammadi in relation to Judaism in general and to the Jewish Scriptures in particular is by no means easy to define. The mere reference in those writings to material incorporated in the Jewish Scriptures and in the Rabbinic writings may induce the impression that after all the Gnostic writers were not as directly opposed to the Jewish religion as is sometimes assumed. Indeed, when one penetrates more deeply into the Gnostic writings, one can notice a certain degree of ambivalence in the Gnostic attitude towards Judaism: on the one hand, the Gnostic writers used Jewish material, and on the other, they used that material in order to reject the traditional authority of the God of the Jews and His revelation. However, many Gnostic writings actually contain an outright proclamation against the Jewish Scriptures. One may, of course, argue that the preoccupation of the Gnostic writers with Jewish sources actually reveals the attempt made on the part of the Gnostic writers to fight Judaism on its own territory and with its own weapons. Such tactics, it was suggested here, could have made sense only if they were directed against those people who could feel the point of the dagger. Those people were either Jews, ex-Jews, or Christians. There was no point in arguing against the Jewish Scriptures and the Jewish tradition that went along with them if those Gnostic writings had been addressed to people who knew nothing about those Scriptures and tradition. The Gnostic controversy against the Jewish lore had to have some sense; and it could have had it only in the eyes of people who saw the relevance of the Gnostic line of argumentation against the Jewish tradition. In other words, the Gnostic writings under discussion were written not only against Jews but also for them. We may even assume that some Jews or ex-Jews had an important role in transmitting the Jewish material into Gnostic hands.[10] Did these Jews also have a share in the very writing of those texts? The answer to this question is not clear. However, a close study of the Jewish material incorporated in the Gnostic writings shows at least that basically these writings depend on Jewish material which is known to us from Palestinian sources, and one may consequently conclude that those writings were addressed to people who came from that milieu. As a matter of principle, this does not exclude the possibility that the Gnostic heresy developed somewhere in the Diaspora. But the Jews who shared in and were addressed by the Gnostic heresy were familiar with Palestinian, sometimes Alexandrian, traditions. It still remains to further investigation to show how much Christianity, if at all, was needed for the Gnostic heresy to develop. Although many of the Gnostic texts discovered at Nag Hammadi do not reveal direct dependence on Christian writings or concepts, it still appears that Gnosticism made its first steps in the footsteps of concepts and occurrences that developed alongside, or as a consequence of, the rise of Christianity. In any event, this is the picture which the Church Fathers wanted us to gain. Whether this picture was tendentious in this respect or not is still an open question.

---

[10] Scholem assumes that Jews transmitted the Jewish lore to the Gnostics; see "Jaldabaoth Reconsidered," *Mélanges d'histoire des religions offerts à Henri-Charles Puech* (1974) 405-21.

LITERARY CRITICISM OF THE COLOGNE MANI CODEX

BY

ALBERT HENRICHS

T HE Cologne Mani Codex (henceforth CMC) requires no lengthy introduction. Its existence and general content have been known for eight
years;[1] the first seventy-two of the one hundred and ninety-two pages,
or roughly half of the surviving text, were published in 1975;[2] and,
at long last, publication of the next instalment is imminent : pp. 72-99,
which contain important new evidence for the Jewish-Christian background of Mani's baptists and their alleged affiliation with Elchasai,
will become available shortly.[3]

It is safe to predict that once published in full the CMC will be
more widely read by students of Gnosticism and Christianity than most
other Manichaean texts. The CMC was designed to serve as a basic
introduction to Mani's life and doctrine for the ancient believer, and it
is likely to render a similar service for the modern scholar regardless
of his different interests and critical attitude. Compared to the lofty
theology, poetic beauty, and slow pace of the Coptic Manichaean library, the CMC is unpretentious, prosaic, and straightforward. Such
simple virtues make it an extremely convenient source, especially since
its merits by far outweigh the faults which are generally inherent in
a text of this nature. No other Manichaean document of comparable
importance is written in a language so widely accessible as Greek, or
covers such varied aspects of Manichaean tradition within the limited
space of what will eventually amount to some fifty printed pages of
Greek. The few hours which it takes to peruse the extant text in its
entirety will be time well spent for anyone who wishes to find out
about the historical origins of Manichaeism, about Mani's view of
himself, or about the central role of books, and of Mani's own words,
in the propagation of his religion.

---

[1] A. Henrichs and L. Koenen, "Ein griechischer Mani-Codex," *ZPE* 5 (1970) 97-216,
reviewed by K. Rudolph in *Mélanges d'Histoire des Religions offerts à Henri-Charles
Puech* (1974) 471-486.

[2] A. Henrichs and L. Koenen, "Der Kölner Mani-Kodex. Edition der Seiten 1-72,"
ZPE 19 (1975) 1-85.

[3] Now published in *ZPE* 32 (1978) 87-199.

But the CMC is more than a convenient source which has filled a gap in the uneven documentation of Mani's early life. It is also a unique specimen of religious writing that ought to be studied and appreciated in its own right and not only for its value as a source. Not even the most casual reader of the text published so far can fail to notice the frequent change and colorful variety of narrative forms throughout which include such well-known types as aretalogies,[4] revelation discourse,[5] homily,[6] apocalypse,[7] epistle,[8] and gospel.[9] The CMC confirms that Manichaean literature, and especially its more popular and propagandistic examples, adopted every available literary mechanism from Jewish, Christian, and Gnostic tradition. Eclecticism was the hallmark not only of Manichaean religion but also of Manichaean journalism. The CMC enables us to study this process of literary syncretism in unprecedented detail, on various levels of accomplishment, and through the written remains of different authors including Mani himself. The language of the Christian gospels, the phraseology of Pauline letters, and the conventional narrative patterns of conversion stories are often echoed and occasionally taken over verbatim in appropriate parts of the CMC. Passages from Jewish apocalypses and tales from the repertory of baptist storytellers are carefully worked into Manichaean arguments and quoted with an implied or explicit Manichaean twist. The apocryphal acts of the apostles, with their emphasis on travel, adventures, miracles, and paradoxography, provided the narrative framework and the highlights for the long account of Mani's first missionary journeys which occupies the fragmentary last third of the CMC. In short, then, almost every page of the new text reverberates with literary reminiscences which connect it with earlier religious literature. It would be impossible within the limits of this

---

[4] Used here in the nontechnical sense of "Wundererzählungen" which lead up to a conversion or to a state of utter surprise (in the words of Apuleius, *Met.* 11.13, *populi mirantur, religiosi venerantur tam evidentem maximi numinis potentiam*). See below on the two miracle stories of CMC 6.7-8.14 and 9.1-10.15.

[5] This literary form which is predominant in parts II and IV of the codex (CMC pp. 14-72 and 99-116, respectively), is of course a stock-in-trade of Gnostic literature.

[6] CMC 45.1-72.7 and 72.9-74.5.

[7] CMC 48.16-60.12 (new texts of Jewish origin).

[8] CMC 64.8-65.22 (from Mani's letter to Edessa).

[9] CMC 66.4-69.8, presumably continued in 69.9-70.10. Mani's Euangelion, which is quoted on these pages, was *sui generis* and does not seem to have shared any of the main features of either the synoptic gospels or the Gnostic gospels in the Nag Hammadi corpus. The new fragments tend to confirm Puech's suggestion that Mani's Gospel was a doctrinal work. See Henrichs, *HSCP* 77 (1973) 30 n. 28.

short presentation to follow each echo to its distant source. But as long as some portions of the codex remain unpublished, it may be of interest to illustrate its unparalleled wealth of narrative forms by a brief analysis of its content and composition.

Though biographical in content and even autobiographical in appearance, the CMC is formally an anthology. Its narrative is not continuous, nor is it the work of a single author. It consists of excerpts from the writings of Mani's immediate disciples, and occasionally from Mani's own works, which an unknown editor collected and arranged so as to give a roughly chronological sequence. In the language of synoptic criticism, the CMC resembles a proto-gospel, except that the Lord is Mani, not Jesus. From a strictly literary point of view, the CMC is biography in a raw state, still waiting for the finishing touch of the master stylist. But the Manichees consciously sacrificed formal perfection to authenticity of content. Unlike Jesus, Mani himself wrote about his own life. He thus became his own witness, and his oral and written utterances remained the recognized canon of doctrinal and biographical authenticity.[10] Ideally, therefore, Mani himself should have been his one and only biographer. In practice, however, the story of his life had to be reconstructed from his scattered autobiographical statements and from the reports of his disciples, who in turn claimed him as their source.[11] With few exceptions, the CMC maintains the "I"-narrative of autobiography, and it is not always possible to distinguish plausibly between genuine autobiographical excerpts and literary fiction.

Each excerpt in the CMC must be presumed to reflect three separate and successive stages of redaction. At the first stage, Mani himself will have narrated an event in his life, perhaps on more than one occasion and presumably not always in exactly the same form. The paucity of authentic autobiographical quotations from Mani's own writings makes it extremely difficult if not impossible to recover this

---

[10] *Keph.* 6.16-25; 7.18-9.10; F. C. Andreas and W. Henning, *SitzungsberAkBerlin*, 1933, 295 f.; *ZPE* 5 (1970) 113 n. 36 and *HSCP* 77 (1973) 28 f.; the Chinese Manichaean MS Stein 3969 on the tradition of Mani's sayings: "As to the authorized teachings stated during the remainder of (Mani's) sixty years, the disciples noted them down according to opportunity" (tr. G. Haloun and W. B. Henning, *Asia Major* 3 [1953] 195).

[11] Islam knows a similar method of authentication by which *obiter dicta* are traced back to the Prophet himself or to one of his "Companions" through a chain of corroborating witnesses called "support" (*isnād*); cf. W. A. Graham, *Divine Word and Prophetic Word in Early Islam* (1977) 9-24, esp. 18. This seems to be another instance of Manichaean influence on early Islam.

first stage and to differentiate it from the second. But it can be shown, for instance, that Mani's own descriptions of his major revelations were fairly consistent, whereas later Manichaean tradition tried to obscure the distinction between an earlier and later revelation on which Mani himself insisted.[12]

At the second stage, Mani's disciples will have recorded their own recollections of his autobiographical statements which they circulated under their own names but still in the form of "I"-narratives ascribed to Mani. The same event in Mani's life was sometimes reported by more than one witness, which explains the occasional appearance of two names rather than one in the captions of the CMC.[13] Apart from their contributions to the codex, next to nothing is known about the Manichaean authorities whose works were excerpted by the compiler of the CMC. Reasonable guesses about their method of composition or their personal bias can only be ventured in those rare cases in which we have several excerpts by the same authority for comparison.[14] But Baraies is the only authority quoted in the codex who emerges from this comparison with a recognizable literary identity: excerpts ascribed to him are more ambitious, more intelligent, and demonstrably more authentic than the others.[15]

The third and final redaction is due to the anonymous editor who tends to hide behind the authority of his sources. Far from being a purely mechanical collector, he had a mind of his own which left its imprint on the organization of the anthology as a whole. But the editor did not always confine himself to his principal role as literary executor. Occasionally he went further and meddled with the very text of his sources in order to facilitate transition from one excerpt to the next. Such transitions are usually very abrupt and leave chronological and thematic gaps which the editor could not or would not close.[16] But on pages 94 and 99 he tried unsuccessfully to impose a uniform style on disparate sources. In both instances, he interpolated brief connective passages which create the formal illusion of a continuous speech by Mani that extends over three successive excerpts.[17] But whereas both

---

[12] Below, n. 18.

[13] CMC 74.6-7, and apparently the fragmentary caption CMC 140.7-9.

[14] Baraies, CMC 14.4-26.5; 45.1-72.7 (assigned); 72.8-74.5; 79.13-93.23; Timotheos, CMC 33.8-44.18; 77.4-79.12; 99.11-114.5; 116.14-123.13; and perhaps 123.14-124.14.

[15] ZPE 19 (1975) 80 n. 80.

[16] For instance CMC 14.2-4; 44.18-45.1; 72.7-9; 74.5-8; 79.12-14.

[17] A discussion of the two interpolations, at CMC 94.1-8 and 99.11-100.4, respectively, will be found in our forthcoming edition.

interpolations are clumsily executed and easy to detect, they are not entirely without merit or interest. They both occur in the middle of Mani's final confrontation with the baptists and at the dramatic climax of the extant biography. The fact that the editor indulged in such conspicuous interpolation only here and apparently nowhere else is in itself significant: at the decisive turning point of his life, Mani had to be allowed to speak for himself, and against the baptists, to the greatest extent possible, even at the price of bad writing and possible distortion of the historical record. Though a clumsy redactor in his treatment of literary from, the compiler thus proved himself a true master of religious persuasion by the very way in which he selected and arranged his source material here and elsewhere.

Many different authors, including Mani himself, contributed to the astonishing variety of narrative forms in the CMC. Wherever possible, their individual styles and the religious literatures which inspired them will have to be dealt with separately in the context of each excerpt. At the same time, however, the overall design of the editor has to be kept in mind. He interpreted Mani's life as a chronological succession of different religious experiences and activities or, in other words, as successive stages of spiritual growth and self-realization. It follows that literary criticism of the CMC must always be two-dimensional in order to do equal justice both to the compilation as a whole and to its separate components.

A rapid survey of the preserved content of the CMC will show that the compiler treated the first twenty-four years of Mani's life as five thematic units, each of which is marked by a special religious experience and documented by a self-contained set of source material that follows a consistent stylistic pattern. The five parts can be tabulated as follows:

I (pp. 2-14) Mani's childhood, with emphasis on miracle stories

II (pp. 14-72) Mani's first, and second, major revelation, with emphasis on revelation discourse[18]

III (pp. 72-99) Mani's break with the baptists, with emphasis on controversy dialogue

---

[18] In the excerpt from Baraies on pp. 14.4-26.5, at least one description of Mani's second major revelation (received at the age of twenty-four) precedes several other autobiographical quotations which describe his first major revelation (received when he was only twelve years old). By quoting Mani's own elaborate dating of the later event but leaving his descriptions of the earlier revelation undated and thus unidentified, Baraies palpably tried to conceal Mani's claim that he had been the recipient of an important divine message while still a child. See *ZPE* 19 (1975) 77-78.

IV (pp. 99-116) Mani's second major revelation and separation from
   the baptists, with emphasis on revelation discourse
V (pp. 116-192) Mani's first missionary activities, with emphasis
   on miracle stories

The first thematic unit, on pages 2-14, covers years four through
twelve of Mani's childhood and describes his first contacts with the
supernatural and his growing alienation from the baptists. One could
call it Mani's initiation into the lesser, or preliminary, mysteries.[19]
Emphasis throughout is on the miraculous: Mani had visitations by
angels, saw divine visions, heard mysterious voices, and met water per-
sonified. At least three different sources have been used in this part.
Brief descriptions of miracles which affected only Mani himself frame
two full-fledged conversion stories in the second source in which talking
trees[20] and bleeding plants[21] convince some of the baptists of Mani's
supernatural powers. The narrative technique of these two stories can
be paralleled from numerous Jewish and Christian texts:[22] the miracle
happens, the human witness (in this case, a baptist) is alarmed, pros-
trates himself before the divine agent (here, young Mani), and finally
makes a brief speech which implies his awareness or recognition of the
agent's religious identity. Not only the form but also the content of
the two miracles is conventional: talking trees are known from Jewish
tradition, and bleeding plants occur in paradoxographical literature.
But they are given a new Manichaean interpretation in the CMC.
Perhaps not much of interest was known about Mani's early life, and
divine providence in its traditional manifestations conveniently filled
the gap. But again the compiler put his meager sources to effective use:
in his arrangement, the impact of the supernatural on Mani's life is
first gradual and gentle, then sudden and massive as Mani confronts
individual baptists, and finally stable and permanent once we reach the
heavenly voice on page 13 ("a voice, like that of the Twin, spoke to

[19] Cf. CMC 3.7-12.
[20] Talking trees are an important leitmotif of miracle stories whose history can be
traced to pagan paradoxography on the one hand and Jewish apocryphal literature
on the other (*ZPE* 19 [1975] 8 ff. nn. 14, 18, and 21). Of considerable interest in this
connection are the verbal echoes of the *Testament of Abraham* (A 3 p. 79.88 ff. James)
in CMC 7.2-8.14 and 10.8-10. See now *Bull. Amer. Soc. Pap.* 16 (1979) 85-108.
[21] On the Manichaean doctrine of the Living Soul and of *Jesus patibilis* as illustrated
by these stories see *ZPE* 5 (1970) 145-155; L. Koenen, *ICS* 3 (1978) 176 ff.
[22] Typical examples include 2 Macc 3:24-36; *Testament of Abraham* 3 (p. 79.16 ff.
James); *Joseph and Aseneth* 14.1-10; Luke 17:11-16; Acts 9:3-8; *A. Phil.* 42 (p. 19
Bonnet) and 74-76 (p. 29 Bonnet); *A. Thom.* 54 (pp. 170 f. Bonnet).

me out of the air ...") which prepares us for the major revelations described in the second part.

Similar preoccupation with miracles characterized the fifth and last extant part of the codex, on pages 116-192, which can be best described as *Acta Manichaei*, or a very fragmentary itinerary of Mani's first missionary journeys in which numerous conversion stories follow in quick succession.[23] Converts to Manichaeism include such stock characters of missionary legend as the man with a sick daughter,[24] the hairy anchorite,[25] and the local shah with his court.[26]

It is not immediately clear whether this close correspondence between the first and the fifth part of the extant codex is intentional and the result of conscious selection by the compiler, or whether it is simply a matter of thematic coincidence. In any case, the first twelve and the last seventy-seven pages of the CMC are more monotonous, less informative, and more concerned with legendary material than any other part of the codex, at least from the point of view of the modern scholar. Ancient reader, who expected fantastic and edifying tales in a work like this, will have been more tolerant.

The second thematic unit, on pages 14-72, is the most emphatically Gnostic section in the entire codex. The central figure is Mani as recipient of gnosis through the mediation of his celestial alter ego, the so-called *syzygos* or Twin. In the course of three unconnected excerpts, more than half a dozen statements by Mani are quoted in which he describes the cosmological, anthropological, and soteriological content of his revelations. Many fundamental Gnostic concepts are referred to in passing, but with the exception of the concept of one's meeting with one's own self not a single Gnostic idea is treated in an exhaustive or innovative fashion. Four typical narrative forms of Gnostic revelation

---

[23] Emphasis throughout is on travel, miracles, and conversion. The apocryphal acts of the apostles provided the model for the description of Mani's missionary journeys. Cf. P. Nagel, "Die apokryphen Apostelakten des 2. und 3. Jahrhunderts in der manichäischen Literatur," *Gnosis und Neues Testament* (ed. K.-W. Tröger; 1973) 149-182; R. Söder, *Die apokryphen Apostelgeschichten und die romanhafte Literatur der Antike* (1932; reprinted, 1969).

[24] CMC pp. 122-123. Cf. Mark 5:21 ff. par.; *A. Phil* 37-44.

[25] Who becomes a convert to Manichaeism on pp. 126-129 of the CMC. Cf. C. A. Williams, "Oriental Affinities of the Legend of the Hairy Anchorite," *University of Illinois Studies in Language and Literature* 10 (1925) no. 2, 11 (1926) no. 4.

[26] CMC pp. 130-134. This conversion story is similar to, but not identical with, the conversion of various local shahs reported in Iranian translations of Mani's "Missionary History." See W. Sundermann, "Iranische Lebensbeschreibungen Manis," *AO* 36 (1974) 125-149, and "Weiteres zur frühen missionarischen Wirksamkeit Manis," *AOHung* 24 (1971) 371-379. Cf. *A. Thom.* 17-27.

literature are used in this part of the codex: plain descriptions of the epiphany of the divine messenger[27] alternate with a catalogue of existential questions,[28] with a highly rhetorical declaration of Mani's identity with his Twin,[29] and with revelation discourse, or dialogue, between the two.[30] At this point, the framework of autobiographical narrative is temporarily abandoned in order to make room for a fourth excerpt which continues the theme of revelation but which is formally a homily on Mani's predecessors.[31] Long passages from Jewish apocalypses under the names of Adam and various Adamites, and two letters of St. Paul, are quoted in support of Mani's own revelations, which are once again illustrated by quotations from Mani's letter to Edessa and from his Gospel. Nowhere else in the CMC are quotations within excerpts thus identified by their exact provenance. The apologetic tone and the didactic stance of this excerpt are also unique in the codex, and its inclusion by the compiler is somewhat of a surprise: only eight of the twenty-seven pages of this excerpt are biographical. Of special interest of course are the valuable quotations of Jewish, Christian, and Manichaean texts which exemplify the Manichaean doctrine of successive incarnations of savior figures, of whom Mani was the last. This is an instructive demonstration of Manichaean eclecticism as it applied to earlier religious literature: almost anything religious that could be given a Manichaean interpretation was likely to be included in their reading list, and reflected in their writings.

Again, this second section has a thematic pendant further on in part IV of the codex, or pages 99-116, which describes Mani's physical separation from the baptists and his divine call to become a missionary. Throughout this latter part, Mani's Twin makes his appearances. But this time his message is less metaphysical and more pragmatic: he brings encouragement and instructions for the foundation of Manichaeism as a world religion. The narrative mode throughout is the dialogue.

The third thematic unit on pages 72-99 in the very center of the extant volume is far and away the most informative and exciting part of the biography. Nowhere else do we find a comparable concentration of detail both innovative and historically relevant. A dramatic sequence

---

[27] CMC pp. 17-19, 32, 69-70.
[28] CMC pp. 21-23, 65.
[29] CMC p. 24.
[30] CMC pp. 36-42.
[31] CMC pp. 45-72.

of events which culminates in Mani's break with the baptists is described
in a series of five separate excerpts, two of which were artificially
connected by the compiler, as we have mentioned earlier. After the
long apologetic digression on pages 45-72, we are reminded of Mani's
mission, and of his alienation from the baptists, in a brief biographical
excerpt from Baraies (pages 72-74) which summarizes the spiritual
essence of Mani's early life. The two excerpts which follow on pages
74-79 establish in vivid metaphors that Sita, the baptist leader, is a
materialist and a lost soul: Mani withstands the temptation to accept
Sita's wordly treasures whereas Sita perishes in the dark waters of
this world. We are now ready for the climax and final separation. In
the course of a long doctrinal dispute between Mani and the baptists
on pages 79-99, Mani demolishes their ritualistic religion and replaces
it with his own dualistic spiritualism. Right has prevailed over wrong,
at least in this symptomatic clash of opposite opinions. Henceforth the
battle of salvation will be fought on a more prominent battlefield as
Mani leaves the baptists and confronts the world at large. This is
religious drama at its most effective, and our compiler deserves credit
for his impressive scenario.

Among the various narrative forms in this third part, parable and
controversy dialogue are the most conspicuous. The description of this
controversy follows similar literary conventions found in the Gospel
of John and in Acts.[32] The intellectual level of Mani's arguments in
his dispute with the baptists is never reached again elsewhere in the
codex. Both in content and form, this central piece is the highlight
of the extant volume, and was clearly intended as such by the editor.

It is time to conclude. The CMC is a rich repertory of Manichaean
history, beliefs, and literary skill. Most of the credit for its unique
content, and for its presentation, is obviously due to the authors of
the individual excerpts and to Mani himself. But as I have tried to
show in this brief analysis, the unknown editor too deserves attention,
and perhaps a small share of our appreciation. The end product as we
have it is the work of his industry, and both the selection and careful
arrangement of the source material are entirely his own. As religious
biography, the CMC merits comparison with the Christian gospels

---

[32] Compare CMC 85.13-88.15 with John 7:40-44; Acts 17:32-34; *Ps.-Clem. Hom.*
1.13.1; *A. Phil.* 37 (p. 18.10-17 Bonnet).

and with Philostratus's *Life of Apollonius*, although it cannot rival their literary pretensions. But as a religious anthology of multiple authorship, it has no parallel outside Manichaean literature.[33]

---

[33] The Manichaean *Psalm-Book* and *Kephalaia* are formally comparable, even though their content is very different.

FROM BAPTISM TO THE GNOSIS OF MANICHAEISM

BY

LUDWIG KOENEN

ACCORDING to the Cologne Mani Codex (hereafter CMC),[1] in the year 240, after Mani had reached the age of twenty-four in a community of Babylonian baptists who believed in the commandments of the Lord and had emerged from Judaeo-Christian traditions, he tried to reform the religious beliefs and rites of this community.[2] He first talked to single baptists and, in the manner of Socrates, questioned their beliefs (79.14-80.5);[3] then he addressed a larger crowd and attacked their rites for purifying food (80.22).[4] What he was thought to have said on this occasion is reported in an excerpt from Baraies, one of the authors quoted in the Cologne Mani Codex. To some extent, Mani's speech imitates Jesus' disputes with the Pharisees about their purificatory rites,[5] just as the literary form of the extant part[6] of the codex resembles, *mutatis mutandis*, Tatian's Diatessaron.[7] Mani's speech is also full of

---

[1] This lecture is based on the forthcoming edition of, and commentary on, the Cologne Mani Codex (CMC) pp. 72-99 by A. Henrichs and myself (see now *ZPE* 32 [1978] 87-199). My friends R. W. Daniel and Bruce Frier and my daughter-in-law Mary Koenen have improved the English of successive drafts of this paper.

[2] *ZPE* 5 (1970) 133 ff.; *ICS* 3 (1978) 154 ff.; A. Henrichs, *HSCP* 77 (1973) 23 ff.; K. Rudolph in *Mélanges d'histoire des religions offerts à H.-Ch. Puech* (Paris, 1974) 475 ff.; idem, *Die Gnosis* (Leipzig, 1977) 351 ff.; B. Aland in *Synkretismus im syrisch-persischen Kulturgebiet* (ed. A. Dietrich; Göttingen, 1975) 123 ff.

[3] Socrates had become the example for philosophers and theologians. Cf. H. D. Betz (*Der Apostel Paulus und die sokratische Tradition* [BHT 45; Tübingen, 1972]) on 2 Corinthians 10-13. It is difficult to separate the literary forms in which this imitation is reported from the actual imitation in life and patterns of behavior.

[4] For Mani's rejection of baptism see the evidence collected in our commentary (on CMC 84.11), and cf. below n. 86.

[5] Cf. A. Henrichs, "Literary Criticism," above, 732; commentary, nn. 189, 186, cf. 147, 183, 216, and 223.

[6] The CMC is part of a work entitled "On the Birth of His Body" (περὶ τῆς γέννης τοῦ σώματος αὐτοῦ). The entire work covered, probably, early Manichaean church history in addition to Mani's vita; alternatively a separate work on the early history of the Manichaean church was organized and structured in the same way as Mani's vita. See *ZPE* 8 (1971) 250; *ICS* 3 (1978) 164 ff. On the literary form of the CMC see A. Henrichs, "Literary Criticism."

[7] There are differences, in part due to the different nature of the sources used. The literary form differs too, since the compiler of Mani's vita records as the heading for each subsequent section the name or names of authors excerpted by him. This design gives the impression of documentary exactness. The Diatessaron was in all

gnostic ideas and Middle Platonic phrases and thoughts.[8] Whether any
of the speech is authentic, and if so, how much of it, is hard to say.
The imitation of Jesus and the literary form do not discredit it. For
Mani perceived himself as an embodiment of the "Apostle of Light,"
which is how he thought of Jesus.[9] He performed the same function that
Jesus had for previous men. This *imitatio Jesu* grew out of Mani's
understanding of his own identity and may have been reflected already
in his early speeches. In any case, the account of Mani's attack on the

---

likelihood the form in which the gospels were known to Mani; see *ICS* 3 (1978) 171 f.
and 193 f., and compare the use of the Diatessaron in the *Odes of Solomon*, as
H. J. W. Drijvers will show in a forthcoming article on *Ode* 19. Whereas, on the whole,
the compiler's work resembles the Diatessaron, the underlying autobiographical narratives
(A. Henrichs, "Literary Criticism," 726 ff.) belong to the generic history of autobiography
which was, in origin, closely connected with aretalogy (cf. Achilleus Tatius; *Ps.-
Clementines*; Augustine). This needs further investigation. Cf. also *ZPE* 32 (1978) 175
n. 264.

[8] See *ZPE* 19 (1975) 73-75; A. Henrichs, *HSCP* 77 (1973) 58; also the commentary
in the edition of the text, nn. 187 f., 191, 194; and below nn. 33, 57, 62, 83, and
p. 742 f. on self-recognition. In patristic polemics, there was admittedly a tendency to
cast suspicion on heretics by labeling their ideas Greek and pagan (see, for example,
K. Koschorke, *Hippolyt's Ketzerbekämpfung und Polemik gegen die Gnostiker* [Göttinger
Orientforschungen, 6. Reihe, Bd. 4; Wiesbaden, 1975] 10 ff.; cf. also the baptists of
the CMC who accuse Mani of "going to the Greeks" [see A. Henrichs, *HSCP* 77, 51]).
Yet Platonism was in fact a decisive element in the philosophical structure of the
syncretistic system of gnosticism (cf. A. Böhlig's preface to Koschorke's book). Though
one also has to reckon with some influence of gnosticism on the later development
of the Platonic school (particularly via Numenius), in most instances it can be assumed
that thoughts and phrases which appear in early Manichaean writings and are characteristic
of Neoplatonists belong to the common Platonic tradition (late Plato, Old Academy,
or Middle Platonism); similarly the occurrence of Neoplatonic thoughts and phrases
in Origen or Philo indicates that they date back to, at least, Middle Platonism.
To Mani those words and ideas were, of course, transmitted by earlier gnostics,
particularly by Bardesanes. On the whole question see H. J. Krämer, *Der Ursprung
der Geistmetaphysik* (Amsterdam, 1964) 223 ff. and (on Philo) 264 ff.; cf. H. Jonas,
Gnosis und spätantiker Geist (Göttingen, ³1964), index; Ch. Elsas, *Neuplatonische und
gnostische Weltablehnung in der Schule Plotins* (RGVV 34; Berlin and New York, 1975);
J. Dillon, *The Middle Platonists* (Ithaca, N.Y., 1977) 384 ff. The Platonic influence
is now clearly recognizable in the Nag Hammadi texts, though further investigation
is needed; cf., e.g., A. Böhlig, *Zum Hellenismus in den Schriften von Nag Hammadi*
(with F. Wisse; Göttinger Orientforschungen, 6. Reihe, Bd. 2; Wiesbaden, 1975)
34 ff.; J. Leipoldt, *Das Evangelium nach Thomas* (Berlin, 1967) 10; B. Layton, *HTR*
67 (1974) 363 and 373 f.; 69 (1976) 44 ff. (passim). See particularly *Eugnostos the Blessed*
(CG III,*3* and V,*1*) and the *Sophia of Jesus Christ* (CG III,*4* and BG 8502,*3*; cf. now
D. M. Parrot's brief introduction to his translation of both of these writings in *NHLibEng*
206 ff.), further the *Exegesis on the Soul* (CG II,*6*; cf. W. C. Robinson, Jr., *NovT* 12
(1970) 110 ff., and *NHLibEng* 180). It is significant that a fragment of Plato's *Republic*
and a part of the *Sentences of Sextus* have been found in the Nag Hammadi library
(F. Wisse, *Zum Hellenismus* [see above under Böhlig] 55 ff.).

[9] *ICS* 3 (1978) 164 ff.

baptismal rites of the community in which he lived and which he wanted to reform fits the situation precisely; if he did not use such words, they are very much what he should have said. But the chances are that we read what Mani himself later recalled of his words and of the situation, and which he then reported to his pupils. [10]

In his speech, Mani concludes from the fact of continuous digestion that the body can never become clean and that, in consequence, the daily rites of baptism do not effect cleanliness of the body. If this is so, Mani continues, the references in Scripture to baptism must speak of *gnosis*, not the purification of the body. The passage reads as follows (CMC 83.20-85.1):

(20) τοὐντεῦθεν ⟨δ⟩ὲ[11] [τί ἐστιν] | ὑμῶν ἡ καθα[ρότης, ἐξ] | ἑαυτῶν κατ[ασκέψα]|σθε. ἀδύν[ατον γὰρ] | (84.1) τὰ σώματα ὑμῶν παν|τελῶς καθαρίσαι· καθ᾽ ἑ|κάστην γὰρ ἡμέραν | (4) κινεῖται καὶ ἵσταται τὸ | σῶμα διὰ τὰς ἐκκρίσεις | τῆς ὑποστάθμης τὰς | [ἐ]ξ αὐτοῦ ὡς καὶ γενέσ-θαι | (8) τὸ πρᾶγμα δίχα ἐντολῆς | τῆς τοῦ σωτῆρος. ἡ τοίνυν | καθαρότης περὶ ἧς ἐλέ|χθη αὕτη τυγχάνει ἡ διὰ | (12) τῆς γνώσεως, χωρισμὸς | φωτὸς ἀπὸ σκότους καὶ | τοῦ θανάτου τῆς ζωῆς | [κα]ὶ τῶν ζώντων ὑδά|(16)[τω]ν ἐκ τῶν τεθαμβω|[μέ]νων·[12] καὶ ἵνα γνοῖ|[τε ὅ]τι ἑκάτερον τυγχά|[νει ...]ον[13] ἀλλήλων καὶ κα|(20)[τ.....][14] τὰς τοῦ

---

[10] Reasons for the authenticity and accuracy of Mani's autobiographical accounts and other parts of the CMC are discussed in *ZPE* 5 (1970) 114ff.; 8 (1971) 249 n. 2 (cf. 19 [1975] 77); *ICS* 3 (1973) 181 ff., 187f. and n. 107a. See also below, n. 45, and now *ZPE* 32 (1978) 181.

[11] τε[or το[ι cod. On the text and its problems cf. commentary, n. 204 (in addition to nn. 13-16 below).

[12] This is an Aramaism; see n. 43 and, for more details, our commentary ad loc. (n. 208) and A. Henrichs in a forthcoming article in *HSCP* 83 (1979).

[13] Probably τυγχά|[νει ἄνισ]ον. Cf. Augustine, *C. Fort.* 14, CSEL 25. 91.5ff., "... nihil simile tenebrae et lux, nihil simile veritas et mendacium, nihil simile mors et vita, nihil simile anima et corpus et cetera istis similia." Alexander of Lycopolis, *Man.*, p. 6.1ff. Brinkmann, μεμῖχθαι τὴν ψυχὴν τῇ ὕλῃ, ἀνόμοιόν τι πρᾶγμα ἀνομοίῳ.

[14] κα|[τέχοιτε] or κα|[τέχετε]. If this is correct, κατέχειν is used in the meaning which in the NT is expressed by τηρεῖν (cf. below on 1 John 2:3) and φυλάττειν. Cf. phrases like παραδόσεις, πίστιν, or διδασκαλίαν κατέχειν; John Chrysostom *Hom.* 59.2 on Matthew (PG 58. 575), καὶ μίας μὴ κατασχεῖν ἐντολῆς (if the genitive is correct). The CMC uses the phrases κατέχειν τὴν ἀνάπαυσιν (5.5f. [cf. n. 9 ad loc.]; 102.14ff. περὶ - - - κατοχῆς ἀνα[πα]ύσεως) and κατέσχατε τὴν τοῦ σώματος κάθαρσιν (85,6ff.), which both refer to keeping ritual regulations (the latter to observance of baptism, just as in the passage under discussion). The κατέχειν of the CMC is, in fact, a literal translation of Aram. *nṭr* (cf. A. Henrichs, *HSCP* 77 [1973] 49 n. 95). In the CMC, biblical allusions and the use of biblical language are frequently obscured by the fact that (1) Mani and the Manichaeans read the Bible in translation and (2) the CMC is translated from Aramaic (see n. 12). The wording depended on whether or not the translator recognized the allusion and took care to use the original words of the Greek Bible.

σωτῆρος ἐντο|[λὰς ὅπω]ς ἀπολυτρώσῃ | [......].¹⁵ τὴν ψυχὴν ἐκ | [τοῦ ὀλέθρ]ου¹⁶ καὶ τῆς ἀ|(85. 1)πωλείας.

"Therefore inspect yourself and find out what your purity means. For it is impossible to make your bodies entirely clean. Every day the body is set in motion and (again) stands still, because it discharges the waste of digestion. Accordingly, your rite (sc. baptism) is performed without a commandment of the Savior. Hence, the purification mentioned in the Scriptures is the purification through *gnosis*, i.e., the separation of Light from Darkness, of Death from Life, of Living Waters from Turbid Waters.¹² You should recognize that the one is [different] from the other (i.e., Light from Darkness, etc.);¹³ and [you should keep] the commandments¹⁴ of the Savior in order that he may redeem [your] soul [too]¹⁵ from [ruin] and destruction."¹⁶

Unfortunately, the decisive sentence is damaged by three lacunae and the supplements seem doubtful. It may, however, be reconstructed on the basis of a *logion* which is quoted in a Parthian Manichaean fragment. There it runs: "... in order that I redeem you from death and destruction."¹⁷ Hence the general sense seems clear: exercise *gnosis*

---

¹⁵ E.g., [καὶ ὑμῶ]ν, or ἀπολυτρώσῃ[ται ὑμῶ]ν, or, referring to the *logion* discussed below (see nn. 16 and 17), [καθὰ ἔφ]η (sc. ὁ σωτήρ; there is, however, in the CMC no parallel for the latter expression): "in order that he, [as he has said,] may redeem your soul, etc." In *ŻPE* 5 (1970) 137f. n. 103 this part of the sentence was restored differently: καὶ κα|[τ᾽ αὐτὰς] τὰς τοῦ σωτῆρος ἐντο|[λὰς ὅπω]ς ἀπολυτρώσῃ | [ἡ γνῶσι]ς τὴν ψυχὴν ἐκ | [τοῦ θανάτ]ου κτἑ.: "and in order that, according to the commandments (= teachings) of the Savior, *gnosis* might redeem the soul from death and destruction." In this case, *gnosis* itself would redeem men, without the intervention of the Savior and the obedience to the commandments being mentioned. Regarding the Valentinians, H. Jonas indeed thought that *gnosis* itself works redemption (*gnosis* is "als Ontologie der Erlösung selber Vollzug der Erlösung," *Gnosis*, 374). Cf. also *ZPE* 19 (1975) 18 n. 35 and H.-Ch. Puech, *ErJb* 4 (1936) 187f. (English tr. in *The Mystic Vision* [Bollingen Series 30/6; Princeton, 1968] 249ff.). But our earlier reconstruction of the passage does not correspond closely enough to the *logion* in which Jesus talks of himself as redeemer; and, in addition, the trace of ink after the lacuna seems to belong to a vertical stroke and does not easily suit γνῶσι]ς.

¹⁶ ὀλέθρ]ου, according to 1 Tim 6:9 εἰς ὄλεθρον καὶ ἀπώλειαν. But the Parthian Manichaean *logion* M 789 = 551 (the entire text is quoted in n. 17) reads: "from death (*mrn*) and destruction." ὄλεθρος means both "ruin" and "death"; cf. Syr. *saupānā*, "mors" and "pernicies" (Brockelmann, *Lexicon Syriacum*, 465a). It cannot be determined whether it was the translator of the Parthian version who restricted the meaning to "death," or whether this happened earlier in the Manichaean tradition of the *logion*. But even if we could be sure that the Aramaic original of the CMC read "death," the actual reading of the CMC would remain doubtful.

¹⁷ From a series of *logia* (M 789 = 551; F. W. K. Müller, *Handschriftenreste in Estrangelo-Schrift aus Turfan* 2 (*AbhAkBerlin*, 1904) 67f.; H.-Ch. Puech in Hennecke-Schneemelcher⁴, 1. 263 and 217): "] damit ich euch erlöse von dem Tode und der Vernichtung (cf. 1 Tim 6:9). Ich will euch geben, was ihr mit dem Auge nicht gesehen, den Ohren nicht gehört und nicht ergriffen mit der Hand (*GTh* 17. CG II 36: 5ff. [*NHLibEng* 120 (tr T.O. Lambdin)]; *Apocalypse of Elias*, in Origen, *Comm. ser. in Mt.* 27:3-10, GCS 11.250.5f., cf. B. Krebber [now Kramer], *Didymos der Blinde, Kommentar*

and keep the commandments of the Savior so that he may redeem your soul. This sense is confirmed by 1 John 2:2f., where the idea that Christ is the propitiation for men's and the world's sins is connected with the sentence "Hereby do we know that we know him, if we keep his commandments" (– – – ἐγνώκαμεν αὐτόν, ἐὰν τὰς ἐντολὰς αὐτοῦ τηρῶμεν).[17a] In general terms, the Letter of John and the CMC express the same idea; moreover, in the same context, both authors refer to light and darkness (1 John 2:8). The specific meaning, however, differs, as will soon be discussed in the course of our consideration.

1. Interpretation of the Text:
Gnosis, Obedience, Faith, and Redemption

In the CMC, the passage is directed against the baptists. Mani rejects their rite of daily baptism on the ground that it is not in accordance with the commandments of the Savior. Mani agreed with the baptists that the commandments must be obeyed and obedience would lead to redemption by the Savior. He differed, however, in the interpretation of the rite of purification. For him this lay in the use of *gnosis*. This *gnosis* is part of a larger concept of salvation. Thereby three successive steps are distinguished: (1) *gnosis*, i.e., recognition of the truth that, in the present world, Light and Darkness are mingled with each other and have to be separated again; (2) obedience to the commandments of the Savior; (3) redemption by the Savior.

Already in Jewish apocalyptic literature the knowledge of God meant salvation and vice versa. They were different aspects of the same religious experience. In gnosticism, however, salvation was clearly differentiated from knowledge and followed it.[17b] For Mani both *gnosis* and redemption were tied up with the observance of the commandments. The same general idea is already expressed in 1 John 2:2ff. (see above). But there *gnosis* and obedience to the commandments are again almost the same; they are different aspects of the same response to Christ. A person who does not keep the commandments does not

---

zum *Eccl.* 4 [Bonn, 1972] 160; 1 Cor 2:9; *Agraphon* 4 Resch; cf. CMC 43.7f.). Der, welcher über die Sünder [".

[17a] Cf. also *1 Clem.* 40.1: προδήλων οὖν ἡμῖν ὄντων τούτων καὶ ἐγκεκυφότες εἰς τὰ βάθη τῆς θείας γνώσεως πάντα τάξει ποιεῖν ὀφείλομεν ὅσα ὁ δεσπότης ἐπιτελεῖν ἐκέλευσεν κατὰ καιροὺς τεταγμένους. In this passage the commandments of the Lord refer to the orderly celebration of the liturgy.

[17b] For the concept of Jewish apocalyptic literature see I. Gruenwald, *Israel Oriental Studies* 3 (1973) 63 ff.

have *gnosis* of Christ (3:6). Mani interpreted the relationship between *gnosis* and obedience differently. Keeping the commandments of the Savior is the result of *gnosis* and leads to salvation.[18]

The same relationship is expressed by the notions of *gnosis* and faith. Later the Manichaean Photinus would use the formula "The Manichaeans are rescued by *gnosis* and faith."[19] This idea is peculiar. Generally in gnosticism, *gnosis* is separated from faith, and the gnostic is not restricted by faith.[20] If, however, faith is understood as accepting the whole body of beliefs and their moral implications, the Manichaean *gnosis* was indeed inseparable from faith. For the notions of faith and observance of the commandments are almost synonymous. Christian authors used the term "commandments of the Savior" and similar expressions not only in reference to specific commandments, but also to the entirety and unity of religious convictions.[21] In the case of

---

[18] F. C. Andreas and W. Henning, "Mitteliranische Manichaica aus Chinesisch Turkestan 2" (*SitzungsberAkBerlin*, 1933) 298: M 9 I r. 12-17 "Und wenn man in der Welt das begrenzte und vergängliche Gut- und Bösesein und die Vermischung des einen mit dem anderen nicht sähe, (dann) könnte der Befehl zum Fernbleiben vom Bösesein und zum Hingelangen zum Gutsein nicht zum Denken jemandes gelangen." Cf. *Psalm-Book*, p. 59.29 ff. Alberry: "Thou art the way, thou art the door of life eternal, in truth the son of God, my Saviour, who has taught me to wear his holy commandments. ... Thou also art he who shall give the victory to the soul of Mary." See also 83.8 and 88.31; cf. H.-Ch. Puech, *ErJb* 4, 209 (*Mystic Vision*, 263 ff.). Mani's sequence is almost anticipated in *1 Clem.* 40.1 (see n. 17a). The importance of obedience to the law he learned directly from the community of baptists in which he grew up; they regarded themselves as Elchasaites (cf. our commentary, n. 272), who stressed obedience to the book of Elchasaeus and faith as a precondition for the remission of sins through baptism (Hippolytus, *Haer.* 9.13.4 and 15.3, GCS 3. 252.2 ff. and 253.23 ff.; Theodoret of Cyrus, *Haer.* 2.7, PG 83. 393B; Timothy of Constantinople, *Haer.* [Περὶ Ἑλκεσαϊτῶν] PG 86. 32B; A. F. J. Klijn and G. J. Reinink, *Patristic Evidence for Jewish-Christian Sects* [NovTSup 36; Leiden, 1973] test. 114 ff.; 250; 258).

[19] Paulus Christianus, *Disputatio cum Photino Manichaeo* 43, PG 88. 572C, – – – γνώσει καὶ πίστει διασώζονται οἱ Μανιχαῖοι, – – – σωθῆναι – – – μετὰ γνώσεως καὶ πίστεως. Cf. n. 18.

[20] Cf. Clement of Alexandria, *Str.* 2.10.1, GCS 2. 118.11 ff., referring to Basilides and Valentinians. According to the latter, faith is for the simpleminded, *gnosis* for the gnostics who will be redeemed through the advantage of their germ of superior excellence. Orthodox Christians, on the contrary, insisted upon the unity of faith and *gnosis*; cf., for example, Clement, *Str.* 6.31.3, GCS 2. 129.28 ff.; Origen, *Jo.* 10.241, GCS 4. 211.24 f.; *LPGL* s.v. γνῶσις B 5a, and below, n. 25.

[21] E.g., ἐντολή τοῦ θεοῦ (Matt 15:3, etc.); ἐντολαὶ τοῦ κυρίου (*2 Clem.* 8.4; 17.3, etc.) or Ἰησοῦ Χριστοῦ (*2 Clem.* 17.6; Ignatius, *Eph.* 9.2, etc.); ἡ τῶν ἀποστόλων ὑμῶν ἐντολὴ τοῦ κυρίου καὶ σωτῆρος (*2 Pet* 3:2); τοῦ σωτῆρος αἱ ἐντολαί (as opposed to the "law"; Severianus on 1 Tim 1:8-9, p. 336.14 Staab). For the notion of ἐντολαί as embracing the entire Christian religion, see Bauer, *Wörterbuch* (Berlin, ⁵1958) s.v. ἐντολή f.; on the different meanings and, particularly, the Jewish background in the use of this term, see Schrenk, *TWNT* s.v. (2. 542).

the baptists the commandments of the Savior referred to the entirety of their beliefs and, particularly, to their rites of purification, the keeping of the Sabbath (see n. 14), and their abstention from certain kinds of food. For the Manichaeans, of course, the content of the commandments of the Savior changed so that the term then would comprehend Mani's teaching in addition to what he approved as the true teachings of Jesus and other religious authorities.[22] For, as was already said, Mani himself was regarded as an embodiment of the Savior, in the same way as Jesus was.[23] In the context of the passage from the CMC, however, and in the context of the *logion*, it was predominantly Jesus who was meant by the term "Savior."

Men have to obey the commandments of the Savior, i.e., believe in the Savior, and—as the wording itself suggests—act correspondingly. The Manichaeans stressed the necessity of good deeds.[24] But before

---

[22] CMC 80.11; 91.20; parallels from other Manichaean writings are collected in n. 179 of the commentary on CMC 79.21. For the use of the term by the community of baptists see CMC 79.21 and 91.10f.

[23] CMC 107.8ff.; for Mani as Savior cf. n. 24 below; moreover, for example, T II D 123 r. 1ff. (W. Henning, *Ein Manichäisches Bet- und Beichtbuch* [*AbhAkBerlin*, 1936; Berlin, 1937] 45): "... Wenn du gehst, o Herr, so erlöse auch uns vom Geburtstod. Du gehst, Mani, erlöse mich ..."; 26ff. (p. 46): "Mar Mani, ... erlass meine Sünden. ... O Mani, ... rette mich, rette, erlass meine Sünden"; M 114.15f. (ibid., 47): "Mar Mani, erlass meine Sünden. Du, Mar Mani, erlöse meine Seele"; M 42.92ff., in a dialogue between Jesus the Splendor and Jesus the Child (Andreas and Henning, "Mitteliranische Manichaica 3" [*SitzungsberAkBerlin*, 1934] 881 = H. H. Schaeder, *Morgenland* 28 [Leipzig, 1930] 107 = H.-Ch. Puech, *ErJb* 4, 269): "Und sie sandten Mar Mani den Erlöser zu mir, der mich führte aus der Haft, da ich den Feinden diente wider Willen und Angst"; see also above p. 735. The redeeming power was brought to Mani by his *syzygos* (CMC 20.1ff.; cf. 69.13ff.; G. Quispel, *ErJb* 36 [1967] 27; below, pp. 741 and 742f., and n. 26). In this context the Manichaean interpretation of the term "crucifixion" is relevant. It conveys the *gnosis* that the divine power is crucified in matter (Alexander of Lycopolis, *Man.*, p. 7.14 Brinkmann). In this sense, the term "crucifixion" could also be used for Mani's death (cf. *ICS* 3 [1978] 191f.). Thus understood, crucifixion creates redemption. For the Manichaean concept of crucifixion see now H. J. Klimkeit, *Zeitschrift für Religions- und Geistesgeschichte* 31 (1979) 99ff.

[24] For example, T II D 126 I r. 16 (Andreas and Henning, "Mitteliranische Manichaica 2," 295): "Gebote und Werke"; ibid., v. 3f. (p. 296) "Weisheit (i.e., *gnosis*) und Werke"; T II D II 134 I 97ff. ("Mitteliranische Manichaica 3," 856ff.): "Denn in diesem Geburt-Tod gibt es ja nichts Schönes ausser allein dem Verdienst und den frommen Taten, die die wissenden Menschen [i.e., the gnostics] tun. Diejenigen, die mir, Mar Mani, Gefolgschaft leisten und die auf Gott Ohrmizd vertrauen [i.e., those who keep the commandments and have faith in God] und die die reinen und gerechten Denawars als Führer wünschen, die sind es, welche befreit werden und die Erlösung von diesem Geburt-Tod finden und die ewige Erlösung erlangen." Augustine, *C. Faust.* 5.1, CSEL 25. 271.8ff.: "Faustus dixit: 'accipis evangelium,' tu me interrogas. utrum accipiam, in quo id ipsum accipere adparet, quia quae iubet observo. ... ego patrem

men can keep the commandments, they have to have *gnosis*. According to Mani, *gnosis* leads to faith, and not faith to *gnosis*, as Clement of Alexandria had maintained.[25] In the literary structure of the CMC the sequence *gnosis*-obedience-redemption corresponds to the narration of Mani's life. He first received the revelation which was brought to him by his heavenly twin or *syzygos*. The twin was Mani's alter ego. He acted as Mani's Savior. Mani kept the revelation secret until the age of twenty-four. Then he started his teaching, which, on the part of his followers, led to repentance and remission of sins and, on the part of Mani himself, made him the redeemer and Savior.[26] Again, the same sequence is implied: first, acceptance of the revelation and *gnosis*; second, repentance, obedience and deeds; and, third, remission of sins and redemption through the Savior.

Mention of the commandments of the Savior in connection with *gnosis* is remarkable and, in comparison with other gnostics, seems to give the passage a particular Manichaean ring.[26a] In combination with the hierarchical structure of the later Manichaean church, it

---

dimisi et matrem, uxorem, filios et cetera quae evangelium iubet [Matt 19:29], et interrogas, utrum accipiam evangelium? nisi adhuc nescis, quid sit quod evangelium nuncupatur. est enim nihil aliud quam praedicatio et mandatum Christi. ego aurum argentumque reieci et aes in zonis habere destiti cotidiano contentus cibo [Matt 10:9f.] nec de crastino curans nec unde venter inpleatur aut corpus operiatur sollicitudinem gerens [Matt 6:25ff.], et quaeris a me, utrum accipiam evangelium?" Nevertheless, there is no salvation but by grace; Augustine, ibid., 33.1, p. 785.25ff.: "consentiamus, inquam, hactenus in caelum reductos eos, non quia mererentur, sed quia vincat divina clementia vim peccatorum." The Manichaean elect had to confess his sins in a rite which was performed weekly.

[25] Clement of Alexandria, *Str.* 7.55.1ff., GCS 3. 40.21ff.; 6.165.1, GCS 2. 517.3f.; cf. Didymus of Alexandria, *Comm. in Zach.* (*ZachT*), vol. 3, 279.15ff. Doutreleau. In this context, however, both authors stress the necessity of a moral life, just as Mani does. Cf. R. Bultmann, *TWNT* 1. 712ff. (*TDNT* 1. 708ff.). When Marcus the Eremite states, ἡ γὰρ γνῶσις κατὰ φύσιν προηγεῖται τῆς πίστεως (PG 65. 920A), γνῶσις has a different meaning.

[26] For Mani's twin and *syzygos* (cf. n. 23) as his alter ego see *ZPE* 5 (1970) 161ff.; *ICS* 3 (1978) 167ff.; for the concept of salvation in Manichaeism cf., for example, T II D 126, I v. in Andreas and Henning, "Mitteliranische Manichaica 2," 296: the Manichaean religion is the "gate of salvation." According to M 9, I v. (ibid., 298) "ist ihr [sc. for the soul] ein Führer und Wegweiser nötig, der ihr Weg und Pfad weist, die zum Erlöstwerden vom Bösesein und zum Hingelangen der Seele, d. h. zum ewigen, unvermischten und unvergänglichen Gutsein (führen)." Cf. also n. 18 above. Such ideas were modelled on Christ who is the gate (John 10:7, 9) and the redemption (ἀπολύτρωσις, 1 Cor 1:30; cf. Rom 3:24ff.; Eph 1:7; Col 1:14; Heb 9:15; cf. Büchsel, *TWNT* 4. 354ff.). For the significance of Mani's death (= crucifixion) see n. 23. Final redemption comes with death; cf. Mani's last prayer in *Hom.* 53.6ff. Polotsky; p. 749 below (on the "baptism of the gods"); and n. 24 above.

[26a] But cf. below, n. 71.

became a strong ecclesiastical element which restricted and disciplined
gnosis. But this was still in the future at the time when Mani talked
to his baptists. At that time, however, the other aspect of the obedience
to the commandments was already important. Obedience to the
commandments must complement knowledge and theoretical beliefs.
Gnosis may necessarily lead to redemption, as, for Socrates, virtue
follows knowledge; but according to Mani fulfillment of the commandments is a notion distinguished clearly from *gnosis*. Ethics and ontology
are distinct, but inseparable.[27]

If we now return to our comparison of Mani's arguments in the
CMC with the First Letter of John, we may briefly consider the
difference in what is meant by the term *gnosis*. In the letter, *gnosis*
is—as we already said—almost the same as obedience to the commandments. In the CMC, however, *gnosis* is a term in its own right. It is the
recognition of the mixture of the two opposite principles in this world.
The principles are described by pairs of opposites: light and darkness,
death and life, living waters and turbid waters. This concept of the
separation of opposites is well known from other Manichaean sources.
Here it should suffice to refer to one parallel. According to Augustine,
Fortunatus stated that there is no similarity between darkness and
light, truth and lie, death and life, soul and body.[28] In other
passages of the CMC the revelation given to Mani is described
differently; it is the recognition of Mani's and man's provenance
(past), of their presence in this world (present), and of their goal of
returning to heaven (future). These are the basic questions for all
gnostics.[29] As I mentioned before, the revelation was brought to Mani
by his twin or *syzygos*, i.e., Mani acquired his *gnosis* by looking at

---

[27] Cf. C. Colpe, *Ex Orbe Religionum* (Festschrift Widengren; Supplements to *Numen*
21; Leiden, 1972) 401.

[28] See n. 13 and cf. M 9 (see n. 18); T II D 126, I v. (Andreas and Henning, "Mitteliran.
Manichaica 2," 296); Chinese MS Stein (G. Haloun and W. B. Henning, *Asia Major*
N. S. 3 [1952] 193 f.): "The teaching expounds the principle of light, thus removing the
delusion of darkness; the doctrine explains the two Natures, taking discrimination
[between them] for its particular method. ... [When] the Nature will be separated from
the Lightless, its name will be homomorphic." For further parallels see n. 207 of the
commentary on CMC 84.13; *ZPE* 5 (1970) 137 n. 101; and H.-Ch. Puech, *ErJb* 4,
201 ff.; idem, *Le Manichéisme* (Paris, 1949) 74.

[29] CMC 14.4 ff.; 21.2 ff.; 26.1 ff.; 33.2 ff. (transmission of the revelation in teaching);
cf. *ZPE* 19 (1975) 19 n. 36 and 23 n. 52; K. Koschorke, *Hippolyt's Ketzerbekämpfung*,
43, on *Exc. Thdot.* 78.2 in Clement of Alexandria, GCS 3. 131.16 ff. (see below, n. 78)
and *ThCont* CG II 138: 7 ff., *NHLibEng* 189 (tr. J. D. Turner); *GTr* CG I 22: 12 ff.,
NHLibEng 40 (tr. G. W. MacRae); *GTh* 50, CG II 41: 31 ff., *NHLibEng* 123 (tr. T. O.
Lambdin); cf. H.-Ch. Puech, *ErJb* 4, 191 ff. (*Mystic Vision*, 252 f.).

the better part of himself.[30] *Gnosis* means self-recognition, just as, in our passage, Mani advises the baptists to look at themselves and find out that their baptismal rites are futile. Manichaean self-recognition, however, results in the recognition of the mixture of the principles and their separation. The myth of creation explains how the present mixture came about (past); and its separation by *gnosis* will finally result in the return of almost all divine parts to heaven (future). By *gnosis* man participates in the separation of the mixture which has been created in mythical time. Thus *gnosis* is that which works salvation. But, as I said already, this *gnosis* needs (1) the presence of the redeemer who brings the revelation and (2) the acceptance of the religion by the follower who obeys the commandments.

The elements of these thoughts are traditional. Self-recognition, the well-known postulate of the Delphic Apollo, is a common idea in gnosticism[31] as well as in the Platonic tradition. With the Naassenes, *gnosis* had to begin with the recognition of man, i.e., Adamas, the mythical archetype of men. This reveals three parts: the earthly (χοϊκόν), the psychic (ψυχικόν), and the intellectual (νοερόν). From this knowledge man can proceed to the *gnosis* of god, which is the perfection of man.[32] Moreover, in the Manichaean *gnosis* of opposites one recognizes easily the widespread habit of combining opposite terms into syzygies. One may particularly think of the syzygy of male and female which seems to have caused at least a late community of Elchasaites (see n. 18) to base their abstention from certain vegetables on botanical dualism.[32a] In the *Ps.-Clementines*, which reflect ideas of Judaeo-

---

[30] For the *syzygos* see n. 26 above; for *gnosis* as self-recognition cf., for example, Henning, *Manichäisches Beichtbuch* 548 ff., p. 34: "Wer sich selbst nur aussen sieht, nicht innen sieht, der wird selbst gering und macht andre gering"; H.-Ch. Puech, *Manichéisme*, 71; J. E. Ménard in *Christentum und Gnosis* (BZNW 37) 58 ff., on the *Gospel of Truth* and other gnostic texts.

[31] Cf., e.g., the *Testimony of Truth* (CG IX 45: 1 ff.; *NHLibEng* 411 [tr. S. Giversen and B. A. Pearson]: "When man knows himself and God [cf. n. 34 below], he will be saved, and he will be crowned with the crown unfading." See also below, p. 750f.

[32] Hippolytus, *Haer.* 5.6.6, GCS 3. 78.11 ff. (W. Foerster, *Die Gnosis* 1 [Zürich and Stuttgart, 1969] 399 f.; English tr. *Gnosis* [tr. R. McL. Wilson; Oxford, 1972] 264): – – – καὶ νομίζουσιν εἶναι τὴν γνῶσιν αὐτοῦ [of Adamas, consisting of the three parts mentioned] ἀρχὴν τοῦ δύνασθαι γνῶναι τὸν θεὸν λέγοντες οὕτως· ἀρχὴ τελειώσεως γνῶσις ἀ[νθρώπου, θεοῦ δὲ] γνῶσις ἀπηρτισμένη τελείωσις. In our present context we may neglect the fact that the Naassenes, contrary to the Manichaeans, assumed three principles. Cf. also n. 65.

[32a] Al-Nadim, *Fihrist* (tr. B. Dodge, *The Fihrist of al-Nadim* [New York and London, 1970] 2. 811); "They assert that the two existences are male and female and that the herbs are from the likeness of the male, whereas the parasite plants are from the likeness of the female, the trees being veins (roots)." For the syzygy of male and female

Christian baptists that were also shared by Mani's baptists and the Elchasaites, we read not only about the syzygy of male and female, but also about such syzygies as day and night, life and death, and so on.[33] Day and night, life and death are also mentioned in the *Gospel of Philip*.[34]

The separation by *gnosis* had consequences for the life of Manichaeans. In the CMC it resulted, on the biographical level, in Mani's election by the divine Father and his growing alienation and final physical separation from the community of baptists,[35] whose leading presbyter did not belong to Mani's chosen *ekloge*, as the narrative makes perfectly clear.[36] Mani's paradigm was the Jesus of the canonical Gospel who came to separate mankind and to elect his own (John).[37] The *Gospel of Philip* is even closer to Manichaean thought and can almost be understood in the light of Manichaean myth. For it states that Christ came to set apart those who belonged to him. They are his life which "he laid down from the very day the world came into being," and

---

see, e.g., *Ps.-Clem.*, *Hom.* 2.15; Philo, *Heres* 139; Aristotle, *Metaph.* 1.5, 986a24f. [Pythag.]; cf. our commentary, n. 231.

[33] *Hom.* 2.15 (cf. G. Strecker, *Das Judenchristentum in den Pseudo-Klementinen* [TU 70; Berlin, 1958] 188 f.); 2.16 δεξιά καὶ ἀριστερά; cf. Philo, *Heres* 207 ff.: among others σκότος—φῶς, νύξ—ἡμέρα, ὕδατος τὸ γλυκύ—(ὕδατος) τὸ πικρόν, ζωή—θάνατος, δεξιά—εὐώνυμα. The λόγος τομεύς creates the world by dichotomic diaeresis, which first takes place in the intelligible world and creates the ideas, and accordingly is realized in matter (cf. W. Theiler, *Die Vorbereitung des Neuplatonismus* [Berlin and Zürich, 1964] 3 ff.; H. J. Krämer, *Ursprung*, 269 ff.; J. Dillon, *Middle Platonists*, 160). See also Porphyry, *Antr.* 29 (ἀριστερά—δεξιά, νύξ—ἡμέρα, et al.). The Platonic tradition is, of course, closely connected with the Pythagorean opposites (Aristotle, *Metaph.* 1.5, 986a22 ff. = *Vorsokr.* 58 B 5 δεξιόν—ἀριστερόν, φῶς—σκότος ἀγαθόν—κακόν; cf. W. Burkert, *Weisheit und Wissenschaft* [Nuremberg, 1962] 45 [= *Lore and Science* (tr. E. L. Minar, Jr.; Cambridge, Mass., 1972) 51]) and with Heraclitus (fr. 77 Marcovich = *Vorsokr.* 22 B 67: ἡμέρη—εὐφρόνη).

[34] Logion 10, CG II 53: 14 ff., *NHLibEng* 132 (tr. W. W. Isenberg). In addition, the syzygy of right and left (cf. n. 33; *HypArch* CG II 95: 35 ff., *NHLibEng* 159 [tr. B. Layton]) is listed. The *logion* describes the mixture in this world. The goddess who reveals herself in the *Thunder* (CG VI 13 ff.) describes her absolute transcendence in terms of endless series of opposites (cf. D. M. Parrott's introduction, *NHLibEng* 271); p. 16: 11 ff. (*NHLibEng* 274: "I am the one whom they call Life and you have called Death"; cf. G. W. MacRae, "Discourses of the Gnostic Revealer," *Proceedings of the International Colloquium on Gnosticism* (Kungl. Vitterhets Historie och Antikvitets Akademiens, Handlinger, Filol.-filos. serien 17; Stockholm, 1977) 111 ff.

[35] CMC 20.7 ff.; 30.3 ff.; 44.2 ff.; 72.17 ff.; 100.4 ff.; 102.1 ff.; A. Henrichs, *HSCP* 77 (1973) 33 ff.

[36] Cf. Henrichs, "Literary Criticism," p. 732.

[37] Cf., particularly, CMC 107.14 ff. (*ICS* 3 [1978] 193 f.). On John, cf. R. Bultmann, *ZNW* 24 (1925) 100 ff. = *Johannes und sein Evangelium* (ed. K. H. Rengstorf; WF 82; Darmstadt, 1973) 402 ff., particularly 426 ff.

they were taken back by him after they had fallen into the hands of robbers.[38]

On the literary level of the CMC the correspondence between *gnosis* as separation of the principles and Mani's life is evident. Moreover, on the theological level, this correspondence transcends the limits of Mani's own life. It anticipates the life of the future elect and his obligation to separate the divine particles imprisoned in food and to liberate them by eating.[39]

2. THE MANICHAEAN REPLACEMENT OF BAPTISM BY GNOSIS; THE LIVING WATER AND THE TURBID WATER

Gnosis as separation is, indeed, the center of the Manichaean religion. It is by this *gnosis* that, according to our passage from the CMC, Mani wanted to replace the baptismal rites of the baptists (see p. 738 above). In this context, he mentioned as one of the manifestations of the opposite principles the "living waters" and the "turbid waters." In the myth of creation, the two kinds of waters correspond respectively to the heavenly water, which is one of the five elements of the First Man, and to the earthly water, which is one of the five elements of the Darkness. Since, according to the Gospel of John (4:10), Jesus had interpreted the "living water" as the water which gives men eternal life and since Christ was regarded as the "living water" (*Agraphon* 119 Resch), the living water was commonly understood as the water of salvation, by church fathers as well as by gnostics.[40] According to the Sethians, a ray from the Perfect Light, which is an equivalent of the "living water," had been captured by the dark, dreadful, bitter, and filthy water; and it was to be redeemed by the Perfect Man, the *Logos*, who would descend and drink "the cup of living ... water which by all means he must drink who is to take off the form of the servant (Phil 2:7) and put on the heavenly robe."[41]

---

[38] Logion 9, CG II 52: 35 ff., *NHLibEng* 132 (tr. W. W. Isenberg).

[39] Cf. *ICS* 3 (1978) 176 ff.

[40] Cf. *ZPE* 5 (1970) 137 n. 102; *LPGL* s.v. ὕδωρ Koenen, *APF* 17 (1960) 70f.; A. Kehl, *Der Psalmenkommentar von Tura, Quaternio IX* (Cologne and Opladen, 1964) 127 f.; cf. also Yesseus Mazareus Yessedekeus as "Living Water" (below p. 751 f.); *Odes of Solomon* 11.6 ff. (Hennecke-Schneemelcher³ 2. 591) and 30.1 ff. (ibid., 611).

[41] Hippolytus, *Haer.* 5.19.16-21 (Foerster, *Die Gnosis*, 1. 386f., *Gnosis*, 302 f.). According to the *Acts of Philip* 141 and 144 (p. 76 ff. Bonnet), the dead on his way to heaven follows the Cross of Light (cf. *ICS* 3 [1978] 185 n. 122) and passes through the regions of the demons: the dark air, the waters of fire, and the abyss (or the smoke, and the waters of the abyss). These *Acts*, however, are late.

The distinction between the two kinds of water was derived from interpretation and elaboration of the creation account of Genesis. The *pneuma* of God was above the water (1:1); and, in the middle of the water, God created the firmament which separated water from water (1:6).[42] It is therefore not astonishing that the closest parallel for Mani's distinction between the two waters is provided by the Mandaeans. They thought that the savior *Mandā dHaiyê*, i.e., "The *Gnosis* of Life," drew down a small draught of living water into the turbid water in order to render it tasty and to make men, when they drink it, similar to the Great Life.[43] The living water being mingled with the other water suffers pain and loses its power.[44] Precisely such ideas are illustrated by two stories in the Cologne Mani Codex. They report that Elchasaeus, who was regarded as the founder of the group of Mani's baptists, was addressed by the water in which he wanted to wash himself. The water told him that it would be harmed by the dirt; thus he refrained from washing himself.[45] Mandaeans and

[42] γενηθήτω στερέωμα ἐν μέσῳ τοῦ ὕδατος καὶ ἔστω διαχωρίζον ἀνὰ μέσον ὕδατος καὶ ὕδατος. Cf. n. 80. Water as a negative force is, of course, also related to water as a philosophical symbol for matter.

[43] E.g., *Ginza* R 11, p. 266.33ff. Lidzbarski; W. Foerster, *Die Gnosis*, 2 (tr. K. Rudolph; Zurich and Stuttgart, 1971) 250, *Gnosis* 2 (Oxford, 1974) 185f. Cf. K. Rudolph, *Theogonie, Kosmogonie und Anthropogonie in den mandäischen Schriften* (Göttingen, 1965) 205f.; idem, *Die Mandäer* 2 (Gottingen, 1961) 62ff. It is significant that the Greek word used for turbid waters (τὰ τεθαμβωμένα, sc. ὕδατα) is a mistranslation of *mia tahmia*, the turbid waters of the Mandaeans (cf. n. 12). Compare also the dark and the clear waters of the vision in *2 Apocalypse of Baruch* (i.e., Syriac), visio 6, tr. B. Violet, GCS 281ff. (P. Riessler, *Altjüdisches Schrifttum ausserhalb der Bibel* [Heidelberg, 1928] 89ff. [chaps. 53ff.]), where the dark and the clear waters are explained as representing the deeds of the sinners and pious throughout Jewish history.

[44] *Ginza* R 15.3, p. 307ff. Lidzbarski; Foerster, *Die Gnosis*, 2. 355ff., *Gnosis*, 2. 277f. Guardians were put in charge of the living water which had been drawn down. Similar guardians occur in the *Apocalypse of Adam* (see below).

[45] CMC 94.2ff.; also *ICS* 3 (1978) 188f. n. 129 and 130. These and other stories on miraculous experiences of Elchasaeus—his name occurs in the CMC only in this context—and other authorities are the final part of an apology in which Mani answered to accusations of a synod of the baptists and argued that his religious convictions and manners would conform to the actual teaching of their religious authorities. The accusations and the first part of Mani's answer are quoted from Baraies, the second part from an authority whose name could be restored as Za[cheas] and, perhaps, identified with the well-known Manichaean "Teacher" Mar Zaqū (commentary, n. 269). Even if the stories should not be authentic in the sense that they were actually used by Mani in his apology, they still ought to represent the beliefs of Mani's baptists (commentary, loc. cit.). The reference to Elchasaeus seems to indicate that they were told to baptists who accepted the authority of the book of Elchasaeus. Some of the details in the stories indeed fit better what we know about the Elchasaites and learn about Mani's baptists than the Manichaeans (commentary, nn. 284, 289, 296, cf. 273,

Mani's baptists have common ancestors.[46] Both of them developed from Jewish baptists. In their thought, the notion of two different natures of water had been amalgamated with the notion of a world created and consisting of opposites (or "syzygies" in the late Jewish tradition).[47] Already Philo—and with him this is a basically Platonic tradition which had not yet been developed into gnosticism—mentioned the two opposite waters, the sweet water and the salt water (ὕδατος τὸ γλυκὺ τῷ πικρῷ), in his list of opposites created by the *logos tomeus*, the Demiurge, in order to create the world (cf. n. 33).

It was only a small draught of living water which was mingled with other water. This situation called for extreme care in handling water. According to the two stories of the CMC referred to above, Elchasaeus was forbidden and consequently forbade his followers to use the water for profane purposes. It would hurt the water. Therefore the use of water had to be protected by a ritual. It is the essential function of ritual to enable men to do what is needed and yet not permitted in normal life. Rites made it permissible to kill animals for food.[48] Rites licensed even the killing of men in war. Rites regulated and restricted sexual intercourse. In a similar sense, rites were needed for permitting men the use of water. For rites would insure that the water does not object to cleaning the sinner and taking his sins upon itself.[49] For this purpose the water might offer itself, as, in other

---

280, and 288). But on the other hand, Mani or the Manichaeans manipulated the stories (commentary, n. 269) so that they also expressed Manichaean beliefs. Cf. *ICS* 3 (1978) 181ff., 187ff., and ibid. n. 107a; commentary nn. 272; A. Henrichs in a forthcoming article in *HSCP* (1979).

[46] *ZPE* 5 (1970) 140; K. Rudoph, *Mélanges Puech*, 482; idem, *Die Mandäer* 1 (Göttingen, 1960) 233ff., particularly 238; 2, index s.v. Elchasaiten; idem in *Gnosis und Neues Testament* (ed. K. W. Tröger; Berlin, 1973) 138.

[47] Cf. p. 743f. on the *Ps.-Clementines*.

[48] Cf. K. Meuli, *Phyllobolia* (Festschrift P. Von der Mühll; Basel, 1946) 185ff.; W. Burkert, *Homo Necans* (RGVV 32; Berlin and New York, 1972) passim; idem, *Griechische Religion der archaischen und klassischen Epoche* (Berlin, Cologne and Mainz, 1977) 101ff.; M. Eliade, *Traité d'histoire des religions* (Paris, ²1964) 26ff. = *Patterns in Comparative Religion* (tr. R. Sheed; London and New York, 1958) 14ff.

[49] The phrasing is illuminating. In the first of the two stories, Elchasaeus defends himself (CMC 95.1ff.): [ἡ] πορνεία καὶ ἡ μιαρότης καὶ ἡ ἀκαθαρσία τοῦ κόσμου ἐπιρίπτεταί σοι καὶ οὐκ ἀπαυδᾷς, ἐπ᾽ ἐμοὶ δὲ λυπῇ, The water takes upon itself the adultery, foulness, and impurity of those who do not recognize the divine nature of the water; it objects only to being used by Elchasaeus, the righteous baptist, who ought to know better (cf. commentary, n. 277). Elchasaeus wanted to use the water for the profane purpose of washing himself physically. Had he needed the water for the purpose of the ritual, it would have been a different situation. Certain restrictions which the Elchasaites obeyed in their rite of baptism are known. In particular, the person to be baptized for the remission of his or her adultery or other sins had to

cultures, the animal offered itself to be slaughtered. More to the specific point, one might recall that also in ancient Persia we find a combination of the use of water for ritual purifications with a prohibition of defiling the water.[49a] Regarding Mani's baptists, we do not know the details, but the general purpose of the two stories seems clear: do not misuse water for washing yourself. Significantly, the complementary stories were not reported by Mani. They must have taught the baptists under what precautions and rites the cleansing of the body became a holy act which takes away even sins and, therefore, ought to be performed whenever needed.[50] At this point, it is, once more, illuminating to compare the Mandaean baptists. Their priests have to cover their mouths with liturgical bandages in order to protect the water from their breath.[51]

Mani selected the stories to suit his purpose. The baptists could not deny them; they were true, according to their belief. They became angry and almost killed Mani. But the stories were only half of the truth. And it was from this half of their beliefs that Mani drew his conclusions. The baptists thought that, under the necessary ritual precautions, the component of heavenly water would make the water useful for baptism. Mani, however, concluded from the same assumption that (a) on earth no water exists clean enough to be used for purification[52] and that, on the other hand, (b) the particles of good water mingled with the other water would suffer unnecessarily and become even more solidly fettered in matter if, in addition, they would have

---

recite a formula by which seven elements were called upon as witnesses and promise not to commit such sins again. The water was one of the witnesses. See Hippolytus, *Haer.* 9.15.1, 6, GCS 253.11 ff.; Epiphanius, *Haer.* 19.1.6, GCS 1. 218.10 ff.: 19.6.4, p. 223. 26 ff.; cf. W. Brandt, *Elchasai* (Leipzig, 1912) 25 ff.; K. Rudolph, *Mandäer*, 1. 234; *ICS* 3 (1978) 189 f. n. 134.

[49a] R. Reitzenstein, *Die Vorgeschichte der christlichen Taufe* (Leipzig and Berlin, 1929) 44 f.; cf. also commentary, n. 273.

[50] This explanation of the two stories differs from the one I have given in *ICS* 3 (1978) 188. There I thought that the stories were circulated in a small group of baptists which, under gnostic influence, had given up even the practice of baptism. Though this is possible, I admit that the idea of antibaptistic baptists is hard to believe, a fact which A. Henrichs has repeatedly pointed out to me. Cf. commentary, nn. 273 and 280.

[51] K. Rudoph, *Mandäer*, 2. 65. For ritual precautions accompanying baptism see ibid., 81 ff.

[52] Therefore the water would wound man's soul; *Act. Archel.* 10.4, p. 16.10 Beeson: εἴ τις λούεται εἰς τὸ ὕδωρ, τὴν ἑαυτοῦ ψυχὴν π⟨λ⟩ήσσει (si quis laverit se in aqua, animam suam vulnerat). In the two stories preventing Elchasaeus from washing himself, it is, on the contrary, the water that is wounded by animals and men; CMC 94.17 ff.: οὐκ αὐ[τάρ]κως ἔχει τὰ ζῷά σου [πλή]ττειν με; 96.8 ff. ἦλθες οὖν καὶ ἐνταῦθα ἁμαρτῆσαι καὶ πλῆξαι ἡμᾶς (sc. ὕδατα); for more parallels see commentary, n. 275.

to carry man's dirt.[53] Hence, baptism was to be eliminated on earth
and to be postponed until, after death, the soul ascends to the moon,
which is called the ship of the Water of Life (navis vitalium aquarum).
It is made of good water (ex bona aqua) or, according to a Parthian
fragment, of wind and immortal water.[54] There, or just below the
moon in the Milky Way, which was regarded as the Column of Glory
or the Perfect Man, the soul was to receive the "baptism of the gods."[55]
The Column of Glory was closely related to Jesus.[56] Therefore this
baptism which was opposed to baptism by water on earth could
easily be regarded as baptism of Jesus (Matt 3:11 par.). The old
affinity between water and moon was reinterpreted by the Manichaeans in language which was derived from, and literally suited,
baptism.[57]

3. THE GNOSTIC TRADITION OF REPLACING PHYSICAL BAPTISM

Replacement and sublimation of baptism was common among
gnostics and is frequently attested in the Nag Hammadi texts. I referred
already to the dark and filthy water of Hippolytus's Sethians. In the
Paraphrase of Shem, the water is similarly regarded as frightful, dark,
feeble, idle, and destructive. Baptism with the uncleanness of water is a
deceit by the demons. In the water is bondage, error, unchastity, envy,
murder, adultery, etc., and, consequently, baptism is an impure

---

[53] *ICS* 3 (1978) 190 n. 136.

[54] *Thesaurus* in Augustine, *Nat. bon.* 44, CSEL 25. 883.17f. (A. Adam, *Texte zum
Manichäismus* [Berlin, 1969] no. 2.50, p. 3); Augustine, *Haer.* 46, PL 42. 35 (Adam,
Texte, no. 49.54, p. 67); M 183.1215ff. (W. Sundermann, *Mittelpersische und parthische
kosmogonische und Parabeltexte der Manichäer* [Berliner Turfantexte 4; Berlin, 1973]
63f.; cf. also *Keph.* 37.11. Similarly the moon is one of the two "lucidae naves"
(*Thesaurus* loc. cit., CSEL 25.881.24 [see *ICS* 3 (1978) 176f. n. 88] and 883.5) which
have been made "de substantia dei pura" (Augustine, *Haer.* 46, PL 42. 35 [Adam,
Texte, 49.35f., p. 66]; Alexander of Lycopolis, *Man.* 20, p. 28 Brinkmann).

[55] *Psalm-Book* 22.13f.; cf. particularly 58.27f.; 99.9ff.; 103.34f.; 137.32f.; 139.19ff.;
M 564 in Andreas and Henning, "Mitteliranische Manichaica 2," 231.

[56] The moon too was regarded as the seat of the wisdom of Christ (Augustine,
C. Faust. 20.2, CSEL 25. 536.9ff.; cf. *Act. Archel.* 13.2, p. 21.10 Beeson).

[57] F. C. Baur, *Das manichäische Religionssystem* (Tübingen, 1831) 226ff. and 311f.
One may compare particularly Mandaean beliefs in a baptism of the soul after death
in the heavenly Jordan (K. Rudolph, *Mandäer*, 2. 93). This baptism in heaven
corresponds to the rite of baptism of the dying (Rudolph, *Mandäer*, 2. 262f.; 269ff.;
cf. below, n. 81). More generally, one is also reminded of the myth at the end of
Plutarch's *De facie in orbe lunae* in which the minds of good men ascend to the moon
and then from the moon to the sun. They are cleansed in the air below the moon by
the elements (942ff.; cf. above, n. 8).

practice.[58] All this sounds very much like the Manichaean turbid waters and the belief that the water endangers the soul. Moreover, one is reminded of the Elchasaite stories I mentioned earlier according to which the water is afraid of taking all the adultery, foulness, and impurity of the world upon itself. Also in the *Testimony of the Truth* the Jordan river, i.e., baptism, became equated with the "power of the body, that is, the senses of pleasures." Its water "is the desire for sexual intercourse."[59] "But the baptism of truth is something else; it is by renunciation of the world that it is found."[60] Therefore "the Son of Man did not baptize any of his disciples." "And the fathers of baptism were defiled."[61] Here baptism with water is replaced by a spiritual baptism of renunciation.

In the *Exegesis on the Soul*, similarly, the biblical baptism for repentance is understood metaphorically. Baptism takes place when the womb of the soul, that is, allegorically, the mind of the soul[62] "turns inward" upon itself.[63] In other words, the soul recognizes its present state, the pollution it is in, and remembers its father's house whence it fell.[64] By this recognition the soul is cleansed of external pollution. It becomes ready for its bridegroom and brother, an equivalent of what Mani called his *twin* or *syzygos*. The soul gradually continues its *gnosis* of its former pure nature by recognizing this brother, who comes to the soul by the will of the Father.[65] Similarly Mani recognized

---

[58] CG VII 37: 19 ff., *NHLibEng* 324 (tr. F. Wisse; for the translation "destructive" water ["disturbing," Wisse in *NHLibEng*] see Wisse, *NovT* 12 [1970] 137; cf. E. M. Yamauchi, *Textes et Memoires*, 4, *Etudes Mithraïques* [*Acta Iranica*, 1978] 542; and A. Henrichs in his forthcoming article in *HSCP*); cf. also 30: 21 ff. (*NHLibEng* 321): "For at that time the demon will also appear upon the river to baptize with an imperfect baptism and to trouble the world with a bondage of water."

[59] CG IX 30: 28 ff., *NHLibEng* 407 (tr. S. Giversen and B. A. Pearson); cf. H. Jonas, *Gnosis* 1, 391; H. Chadwick, "The Domestication of Gnosis," above, vol. 1, pp. 3-16.

[60] CG IX 69: 23 ff., *NHLibEng* 414.

[61] CG IX 69: 15 ff., *NHLibEng* ibid.

[62] Cf. Philo, *Sacr.* 102; A. Kehl, *Psalmenkommentar*, 189 f. and 196 (on *PsT* 142 = IX 14 and 143 = IX 15; M. Gronewald, *Didymos der Blinde, Psalmenkommentar III* [Bonn, 1969]).

[63] CG II 131: 19 ff., *NHLibEng* 183 (tr. W. C. Robinson, Jr.). Use of the term "baptism" for recognition of one's self is a step which logically follows the interpretation of the baptismal rite and anointment as the washing off of error (πλάνη), cf. *A. Thom.* 25, Lipsius-Bonnet 2. 140.10 ff.

[64] For the soul's home and nature see CG II 127: 22 ff.; 128: 34 ff.; 134: 6 ff., 13 ff., and 25 ff., *NHLibEng* 180 ff.

[65] CG II 133: 10 ff.; 131: 16 ff. and 27 f.; 132: 7 f., 21 f., and 23 f., *NHLibEng* ibid. In the bridal chamber, the soul cleanses itself again: CG II 132: 13, *NHLibEng* ibid. For the recognition of man's self cf. nn. 31 and 32.

himself by looking at his *twin* (cf. n. 30). In the *Exegesis on the Soul*, the "light of salvation" follows by the grace of the Father upon repentance.[66] Thus the "turning inward"—a phrase in the Platonic tradition[67]—replaces, and is regarded as, the baptism of repentance, i.e., the baptism of John;[68] it is followed by salvation, just as, with the Manichaeans, *gnosis*, i.e., the recognition of the present mixture of the two principles, is regarded as true purification which leads to obeying the "commandments of the Savior" and finally to salvation (see pp. 737 ff. above). In the *Exegesis*, repentance and turning inward follow the will of the Father. The Father has mercy on the soul, when it "perceives the straits" it is in,[69] and the brother/bridegroom rescues the soul.[70] In short, *gnosis* and redemption by the Savior are two different stages of the process of salvation, in Manichaeism as in the gnosticism of the *Exegesis*. The latter, however, does not stress the obedience of the "commandments of the Savior" in the same way as Manichaeism did, though, of course, the soul has to be faithful to its bridegroom and his requirements and is bound by the Bible.[71] What differs is not the basic triad of *gnosis*, obedience, and Savior, but the concept of the Manichaean church which was to become connected with Mani's definition.

At this point, also the *Apocalypse of Adam* with its particularly strong Jewish background deserves consideration. There the living water is under the authority of Micheu, Michar, and Mnesinous, who have a function similar to the guardians of the living water according to the Mandaeans. In the *Apocalypse of Adam*, however, the three guardians are said to have given the living water into the hands of the evil powers whom they themselves serve.[72] Shortly afterwards, at the end of the *Apocalypse*, the implications become clear. The present revelation given by Adam to Seth, the "hidden knowledge of Adam," that is his *gnosis*, is called the "holy baptism of those who

---

[66] CG II 135: 26 ff., cf. 134: 32 ff., *NHLibEng* ibid.

[67] Cf. also the allegorical interpretation of the *Odyssey* in the *Exegesis* (CG II 136: 27 ff.), and, in general, cf. n. 8 above.

[68] Acts 13:24 is quoted in CG II 135: 21 ff., *NHLibEng* ibid.

[69] CG II 131: 16 f., *NHLibEng* ibid.

[70] CG II 134: 25 ff., *NHLibEng* ibid.

[71] CG II 133: 20 ff., *NHLibEng* ibid.; cf. *GTr* (CG I,3) 22: 9 ff., *NHLibEng* 40 (tr. G. W. MacRae), "Having knowledge, he does the will of the one who called him."

[72] CG V 84: 4 ff., *NHLibEng* 263 (tr. D. M. Parrott). Elsewhere the three guardians have a positive function; cf. A. Böhlig and Pahor Labib, *Koptisch-Gnostische Apokalypsen* (Halle/Saale, 1963) 94; A. Böhlig, *Mysterion und Wahrheit* (Leiden, 1968) 152.

know the eternal *gnosis* through those born of the *Logos* and the imperishable *Phosteres*... Yesseus, Mazareus, [Yesse]dekeus, [the Living] Water."[73] In this passage, and similarly in the *Gospel of the Egyptians*, Jesus is identified through three variations of his name and, finally, called the Living Water;[74] and the *gnosis* which is revealed in the *Apocalypse of Adam* becomes the true baptism of Jesus, whereas baptism with water is regarded as the work of evil powers.

These examples may be sufficient. They should illustrate that such ideas are not far from Manichaean gnosticism. They illuminate the complex background from which the Manichaean rejection of baptism arose.

Nevertheless, the vitality of baptismal rites was very strong, even among gnostics.[75] In later Manichaeism, Felix, the opponent of Augustine, was baptized, either by Manichaeans or by orthodox Christians.[76] Some of the Valentinians continued the practice of baptism.[77] According to the *Excerpta ex Theodoto*, it is not baptism

---

[73] CG V 85: 19ff., *NHLibEng* 264. The difficult passage seems to record how the revelation of Adam, i.e., *gnosis* and true baptism, was transmitted, in the realm of God, from (1) the sons of Logos to (2) the three Phosteres who are said to come from the holy seed (85: 28f.). The Phosteres then brought the *gnosis* down to (3) Adam (cf. the three men who appeared before Adam [65: 26ff.] and revealed it to him [67: 14ff.]); Adam instructed (4) Seth. Thereafter the *gnosis* is transmitted (5) among the descendants of Seth (85: 20ff.). The three Phosteres represent aspects of Jesus (see above and n. 74 below); correspondingly the chain of transmission begins with the sons of Logos. This alludes to, and changes, the orthodox belief in Jesus as the embodiment of the Logos. (For different opinions on the details of the chain of transmission see A. Böhlig and P. Labib, *Apokalypsen*, 95; K. Rudolph, *Die Gnosis*, 148). Such chains of transmission were thought of as providing the authenticity of the revelation, and they are part of the Jewish heritage (see n. 224 of our commentary). In the *Apocalypse of Adam*, it is made clear that this text is only the beginning of the revelation of *gnosis*.

[74] Ibid., and CG III 64: 9ff. = IV 75: 24ff. and III 66: 8 = IV 78: 10ff., *NHLibEng* 203f. (tr. A. Böhlig and F. Wisse). For Christ as the Living Water see above, p. 755; on the practice of hiding the true name of a god behind a multiplicity of names cf., for example, *GPh* logion 11f. (CG II 53: 23ff., *NHLibEng* 132 f. [tr. W. W. Isenberg]; cf. *A. Jo.* 98, p. 200.5 Bonnet 2, and *ICS* 3 [1978] n. 123), particularly logion 12 (CG II 54: 5ff.): "One single name is not uttered in the world, the name which the father gave to the Son, the name above all things," etc.; logion 19 (CG II 56:3ff., *NHLibEng* 134): "'Jesus' is a hidden name, 'Christ' is a revealed name. ... 'The Nazarene' is he who reveals what is hidden"; E. Norden, *Agnostos Theos* (Darmstadt, ⁴1956) 216ff.; Koenen, *ICS* 1 (1976) 141f. Also cf. the name of the Nazoraeans, a sect of baptists. The *Apocalypse of Adam* is commonly regarded as non-Christian, but see now E. M. Yamauchi, *Textes et Mémoires* 4. 542ff.

[75] Cf. K. Rudolph, *Die Gnosis*, 242f.

[76] According to al-Nadim, the Manichaeans washed themselves with running or other water before they prayed (2. 790 B. Dodge; 333 Flügel; Adam, *Texte*, 126f.).

[77] *GPh* logion 59 (CG II 64:22ff., *NHLibEng* 139 [tr. W. W. Isenberg]); 68 (67:27ff., *NHLibEng* 140); 90 (73: 1ff., *NHLibEng* 144); 109 (77: 7ff., *NHLibEng* 146). The

alone that frees men, but also *gnosis*.[78] Correspondingly, Irenaeus reports that the school of Marcus differentiated between the baptism of the visible Jesus proclaimed by John the Baptist, which is psychic and results in remission of sins, and the redemption (ἀπολύτρωσις) of Christ, which is pneumatic and leads to perfection. The latter is the baptism that Christ referred to as the baptism he was to undergo (Luke 12:50); and this redemption is needed by those "who have received the perfect *gnosis* in order to be reborn in the power which is above all."[79] A similar distinction is drawn by Justin the Gnostic. He tells us that earthly,and psychic men were baptized in the water of this world, whereas pneumatic and living men had heavenly water.[80] This is again the distinction between the two waters found in Manichaeism, Mandaeism, and some of the Nag Hammadi texts.

To return to Irenaeus, he reports that the Marcosians performed the redemption of Christ in different ways. One of them, the spiritual wedding, we have already met in the *Exegesis on the Soul*. This redemption imitated the wedding of the syzygies in heaven. Other Marcosians conducted the redemption by baptizing in a river, others by baptizing with a solution of oil and water. Or they used balsam for anointment. Others, again, baptized the dying or recently deceased, like the Mandaeans.[81] It is not difficult to see here the same tendencies

anointment, however, is the superior sacrament: 95 (74: 12 ff., *NHLibEng* 144); 76 (69: 14 ff., *NHLibEng* 142). Cf. K. Rudolph, *Mandäer*, 2. 384 ff.

[78] Clement of Alexandria, *Exc. Thdot.* 78.2, GCS 3. 131.16 ff.: ἔστιν δὲ οὐ τὸ λουτρὸν μόνον τὸ ἐλευθεροῦν, ἀλλὰ καὶ ἡ γνῶσις, τίνες ἦμεν, τί γεγόναμεν, ποῦ ἦμεν, {ἢ} ποῦ ἐνεβλήθημεν, ποῦ σπεύδομεν, τόθεν λυτρούμεθα, τί γέννησις, τί ἀναγέννησις. Cf. *LPGL* s.v. ἐλευθερόω.

[79] *Haer.* 1.21.2 = Epiphanius, *Haer.* 34.19.3 f., GCS 2. 35.9 ff. (Foerster, *Die Gnosis*, 1. 283, *Gnosis*, 1. 218); cf. K. Rudolph, *Mandäer*, 2. 387 f.; H.-Ch. Puech, *ErJb* 4, 189 (*Mystic Vision* 250 f.); A. Orbe, *La Teologia del Espiritu Santo* (AnGreg 158; Rome, 1966) 603 ff.; E. H. Pagels, *HTR* 65 (1972) 153 ff., where the author combines Hippolytus's report with information on Heracleon gathered from Origen's *Commentary on John*: John the Baptist offers baptism on the somatic and pneumatic levels, Christ on these levels as well as on the third level of pneumatic redemption.

[80] Hippolytus, *Haer.* 5.27.3, GCS 3. 133.7 ff.: διακεχώρισται γάρ, φησίν, ἀνὰ μέσον ὕδατος καὶ ὕδατος, καὶ ἔστιν ὕδωρ τὸ ὑποκάτω τοῦ στερεώματος τῆς πονηρᾶς κτίσεως, ἐν ᾧ λούονται οἱ χοϊκοὶ καὶ ψυχικοὶ ἄνθρωποι, καὶ ὕδωρ ἐστὶν ὑπεράνω τοῦ στερεώματος τοῦ ἀγαθοῦ ζῶν, ἐν ᾧ λούονται οἱ πνευματικοὶ ζῶντες ἄνθρωποι ...; cf. n. 42. The Naassenes practiced baptism with what they called living water. This water, in turn, was regarded as Euphrates, i.e., as the river that is the water above the firmament and the mouth through which prayer goes forth and nourishment comes in and which nourishes the spiritual and perfect man (Hippolytus, *Haer.* 5.7.19, GCS 3. 83.5 ff., and 9.18, p. 101.19 ff.; Foerster, *Die Gnosis*, 1. 343 and 360 f., *Gnosis*, 1. 266 f. and 281; cf. K. Rudolph, *Mandäer*, 2. 387.

[81] The Latin has *mortuos* (Irenaeus, *Haer.* 1.21.5); Epiphanius ends his report on Marcus just before this sentence. In his report on the Heracleonites (*Haer.* 36.2.4 f.,

which led to the Manichaean belief in the "baptism of the gods" which the deceased received on his or her journey to heaven, though —and this is the difference—the Manichaeans did not connect this belief with any rites.

Precisely this decisive step was also taken by another group of Marcosians. They rejected all rituals of baptism and thought that perfect redemption is the "*gnosis* of the unutterable Greatness" (ἐπίγνωσις τοῦ ἀρρήτου Μεγέθους).[82] Deficiency and passion stem from ignorance, they said; but *gnosis* disposes of this state of ignorance. "Therefore," they continued, "the *gnosis* is redemption of the inner man. The redemption is not bodily—for the body is mortal—nor psychic. For the soul derives from deficiency too, as, so to speak, a house of the *Pneuma*. Hence the redemption also must be spiritual, for the inner, spiritual man is redeemed through *gnosis*. They are content with the *gnosis* of the All; and this *gnosis* is the true redemption."[83]

Within Valentinian communities discussions of the same sort were going on as those between Mani and the baptists. Once the human body was considered to be part of a bad creation and consequently precluded from salvation, the value of ritual practices involving the body became questionable. The general discussions influenced the thoughts even of orthodox Christians. They could not reject baptism, but they could expand its meanings so that it would comprehend *gnosis* as well. Justin, for instance, regarded baptism as "the bath of repentance and of the knowledge (*gnosis*) of God."[84]

GCS 2. 45.19 ff.), however, he offers the corresponding Greek text: τοὺς τελευτῶντας. Cf. K. Rudolph, *Mandäer*, 2. 421 and n. 57 above.

[82] Irenaeus, *Haer.* 1.21.4 = Epiphanius, *Haer.* 34.20.10, GCS 2. 37.12 f. (Foerster, *Die Gnosis*, 1. 285, *Gnosis*, 1. 220); cf. n. 84. Irenaeus mentions yet other differences.

[83] Ibid.: ὥστε εἶναι τὴν γνῶσιν ἀπολύτρωσιν τοῦ ἔνδον ἀνθρώπου. καὶ μήτε σωματικὴν ὑπάρχειν αὐτήν—φθαρτὸν γὰρ τὸ σῶμα—μήτε ψυχικήν, ἐπεὶ καὶ ἡ ψυχὴ ἐξ ὑστερήματός ἐστι τοῦ ⟨πνεύματος⟩ ὥσπερ οἰκητήριον (*scripsi sec. Lat.* [quoniam et anima de labe est spiritus velut habitaculum]: καὶ ἔστι τοῦ πατρὸς ᾧ. οἰκ. *mss.*: ἐστι, καὶ τοῦ ⟨πνεύματος⟩ ᾧ. οἰκ. Harvey: ⟨ἐστι⟩ καὶ ἔστι τοῦ ⟨πνεύματος⟩ ᾧ. οἰκ. Holl). πνευματικὴν οὖν δεῖν καὶ τὴν λύτρωσιν ὑπάρχειν. λυτροῦσθαι γὰρ διὰ γνώσεως τὸν ἔσω ἄνθρωπον τὸν πνευματικόν· καὶ ἀρκεῖσθαι αὐτοὺς τῇ τῶν ὅλων ἐπιγνώσει. καὶ ταύτην εἶναι λύτρωσιν ἀληθῆ. (For the emendation, note that πνεύματος and πατρός are easily confused when written in abbreviated form.) The thought that the soul is the house of the spirit is a Valentinian adaptation of the Middle Platonic idea that the soul, in itself a body of light matter, is the vehicle (ὄχημα) or—with Christian authors, in interpretation of 2 Cor 5:1 and Wis 9:15—the tent of the mind (cf. *ZPE* 19 [1975] 73 f.; regarding Didymus of Alexandria on 2 Cor 5:1, p. 27.14 Staab, cf. now Didymus, *Sur la Genèse* 1. 107.10 ff. Nautin-Doutreleau; cf. also Philo's ψυχὴ ψυχῆς in *Heres* 55.

[84] *Dial.* 14: τὸ λουτρὸν τῆς μετανοίας καὶ τῆς γνώσεως τοῦ θεοῦ (cf. R. Reitzenstein, *Vorgeschichte*, 101). According to Clement of Alexandria, baptism results in φωτισμός

4. OPPOSITION TO EXTERNAL PURIFICATION IN THE NEW TESTAMENT

The Valentinian rejection of baptism was based on the interpretation of the New Testament.[85] Similarly, the Mani of the CMC tells the baptists that for baptism they should not appeal to the Scriptures and the Savior. This implies that Mani did not accept the baptism of Jesus as a historical event, a denial which is attested in the *Acta Archelai* and by Augustine.[86] Mani could indeed think of several passages in the New Testament which could be understood as opposing the ritual of baptism. First of all, in Matthew, Luke, and Acts, Jesus brings baptism in the Holy Spirit, as opposed to John's baptism with water. According to a famous passage in Josephus, John himself understood his baptism as if, after the purification of the soul by righteousness, a consecration of the body through water would be acceptable to God (*Ant.* 18.5.2 § 117). This sentence hardly reflects what baptists thought of the effectiveness of their rites. It reduces the theological significance to a minimum.

In the New Testament itself and in its tradition, Mani could find other passages suggesting to him rejection of baptism and physical purifications. For example, in Marcion's version of the Lord's Prayer the first request ("Father, hallowed be thy name") has been changed to "Father, may the Holy Spirit come to us and purify us."[87] Because in the biblical context the Lord's Prayer was regarded as an analogy to the prayers taught by John the Baptist,[88] Marcion's version was easily understood as a prayer for spiritual baptism as opposed to John's baptism. Or Mani could have thought of the Pauline letters, since he found them extremely attractive and congenial. In Eph 5:2 it is said that Christ gave his life for the church "in order to sanctify the church and purify it with the bath of water by the word." This could easily be understood as if "the word" were the true "bath of water," the true baptism. And in Heb 9:13f. the Jewish sacrificial

---

and γνῶσις (*Paed.* 1.30.1, GCS 1. 108.3 ff.); the illumination through baptism is defineu as ἐπιγνῶναι τὸν θεόν (*Paed.* 1.25.1, p. 104.28 ff.; cf. A. Wlosok, *Laktanz und die philosophische Gnosis* [*AbhAkHeid*, 1960/2] 164 ff.). Sarapion of Thmuis in Socrates, *H.E.* 4.23: ὁ νοῦς μὲν πεπωκὼς πνευματικὴν γνῶσιν τελείως καθαίρεται.

[85] Matt 3:11 f. par.; 20:22; Luke 12:50.

[86] *Act. Archel.* 60.11, p. 88 f. Beeson; Augustine, *C. Faust.* 23.3 and 32.7, CSEL 25. 709.12 ff. and 766.15 ff.

[87] A. von Harnack, *Marcion* (Leipzig, ²1924) 207* (Luke 11:2).

[88] κύριε, δίδαξον ἡμᾶς προσεύχεσθαι καθὼς καὶ Ἰωάννης ἐδίδαξεν τοὺς μαθητὰς αὐτοῦ (Luke 11:1).

rites aim at purifying the body; Christ's sacrifice, however, purges the conscience from dead works and leads men to serve the living God.[89]

In this context, the discussions the biblical Jesus had with the Pharisees are of particular importance. In Luke 11:38 and Matt 23:25 f., he uses the example of cleansing cup and plate in order to object to the Pharisaic practices of physical purification (cf. also Mark 7:14 ff.). This *logion* is taken up in the *Gospel of Thomas* where it becomes a plain, literally understood rejection of Pharisaic precepts.[90] Hence, Mani could indeed model his own attacks against the baptists of his time and their rites of physical purification on Jesus attacking the Pharisees (cf. p. 734). It is indeed part of the message of the New Testament that—in spite of acceptance of rites—the purity of the inner man is much more essential than physical purification by external rites. In this respect, the Sethian, Valentinian and finally Manichaean discussions continued rigidly and in a biased fashion what had begun in the New Testament.

We started with Mani's sublimation of baptism into *gnosis*, which was in itself a reaction to the Jewish and Judaeo-Christian rites and beliefs of the baptists who had educated Mani. But their disputes had their roots in Jewish developments dating back to the time of Jesus. Moreover Mani's reaction was anticipated by, and is in line with, the controversies of gnostics leading to the elimination of baptism with water and its replacement by *gnosis*. The emerging picture is extremely complex, and we could easily complicate it further. And the irony is that the more complicated the picture becomes, the more closely it seems to resemble the truth.

---

[89] One should keep in mind that early gnostics could derive their understanding of baptism as resurrection partly from the Greek mysteries, partly, however, from Paul; cf. H. Fr. Weiss in *Christentum und Gnosis* (BZNW 37) 122 ff.

[90] Logion 89 (CG II 48: 13 ff., *NHLibEng* 127 [tr. T. O. Lambdin]); cf. J. Leipoldt, *Das Evangelium nach Thomas*, 19 and 72. In addition to rejecting baptism and ritual cleansings, Mani did not observe the abstention of the baptists from wheat bread and certain vegetables. This may be compared with 1 Tim 4:3.

GNOSTIC INSTRUCTIONS ON THE ORGANIZATION OF THE CONGREGATION:

The Tractate Interpretation of Knowledge from CG XI*

BY

KLAUS KOSCHORKE

THIS paper has a double aim. The first part introduces a recently discovered Gnostic tractate which demonstrates how the organization of the congregation is constituted on the basis of Gnostic premises. The second part raises the question of the attitude of the Gnostics towards ecclesiastical office. Both parts seek to provide a contribution to the issue of "Spirit and office in early Christianity" as seen from a Gnostic perspective.

I. THE TRACTATE INTERPRETATION OF KNOWLEDGE (CG XI,1)

1. The significance of the tractate. Gnostics are generally not known for their community spirit. Rather, they are reputed to be pneumatic individuals who boast about their possession of the spirit and immediacy to God and who consequently feel no real need for human fellowship. Where they gain the upper hand the Christian congregation has been thought to run the risk of "disintegrating, whereby each member appeals to his private understanding and goes his own way."[1] So the Gnostics would appear to be representatives of a religiosity which avoids the world and human fellowship, or anarchic enthusiasts who endanger the existence of the Christian community.

In the light of such an evaluation of the Gnostics the discovery of a Gnostic *Gemeindeordnung* does come as a surprise. The tractate in question is *The Interpretation of Knowledge* (*InterpKn*) from Nag Hammadi Codex XI, which presents instructions on the organization of the congregation. *InterpKn*, which until recently was only available in the

---

* I should like to thank John Turner and Elaine Pagels, who kindly provided me with the manuscript of their text edition of the *Interpretation of Knowledge*. Thanks are also due to W.-P. Funk, A. M. Ritter, A. Schindler and F. Wisse for their critical suggestions and comments.
[1] E. Schweizer, *Gemeinde und Gemeindeordnung im Neuen Testament* (1959) 77, with reference to the Pastoral Epistles.

Facsimile Edition of the Nag Hammadi Codices, can now be consulted in the translation of John D. Turner in *The Nag Hammadi Library in English*; the complete edition by Turner and Elaine H. Pagels is expected in the near future.[2]

In the brief outline of the tractate that follows, we are especially interested in pursuing the questions of how a congregation is to be organized on Gnostic premises and how conflicts within such a community are to be resolved: *InterpKn* offers a unique opportunity to answer these questions. In the process of our investigation the contrast with the early catholic concept of community and church order will become clear. For *InterpKn* does not refer to ecclesiastical offices, how they are defined with reference to each other and how they are ranked, but speaks of the manifold "charismata," "gifts," and "graces" which constitute the Christian congregation as a spiritual organism. Thus *InterpKn* is documentation of a pneumatic-charismatic congregational organization. The close connection with the Pauline tradition is obvious, though *InterpKn* appears to develop and interpret it in its own way. The following passages in the Pauline corpus are of basic importance for *InterpKn*: 1) 1 Corinthians 12 and Romans 12 (Ephesians 4): the manifold "charismata" presented in the imagery of the different "members" of the "one body"; 2) Colossians and Ephesians: the "ecclesia" as the "body" with Christ as its "head"; 3) other Pauline passages—such as the hymn in Philippians 2—whose ecclesiastical relevance is demonstrated in *InterpKn*.

For our question the third (and last) section of the tractate is of primary interest. After our author has shown (*InterpKn* 9-15) how Christ (as "head") has saved the ecclesia (his "body"),[3] he deals (15-21)

---

[2] *Nag Hammadi Codices XI-XIII* in the series Nag Hammadi Studies (Brill: Leiden). This volume is part of the text edition of all the Nag Hammadi tractates prepared by the Claremont team. As of now the text of *InterpKn* is available in *The Facsimile Edition of the Nag Hammadi Codices, Codex XI-XIII* (Leiden, 1973) and in translation in *NHLibEng*, 427-34. Literature: Elaine Pagels's commentary in the edition mentioned above; K. Koschorke, *Die Polemik der Gnostiker gegen das kirchliche Christentum, unter besonderer Berücksichtigung der Nag-Hammadi-Traktate "Apokalypse des Petrus" (NHC VII,3) und "Testimonium Veritatis" (NHC IX,3)* (Nag Hammadi Studies 12; Leiden, 1978) 69-71; K.-W. Tröger, *Die Passion Jesu Christi in der Gnosis nach den Schriften von Nag Hammadi* (Hab. theol. Berlin [DDR], 1978) 18-24. I have discussed *InterpKn* more completely in "Eine neugefundene gnostische Gemeindeordnung. Zum Thema Geist und Amt im frühen Christentum," ZTK 76 (1979) 30-60.

[3] Pages 9-15 treat the ecclesia as it stands in need of salvation. The ecclesia is seen here as the total of the pneumatic souls (or "members" of Christ) who, like the savior, have their origin in the realm of light, but have now "fallen" into the "depth" of worldly existence and consequently need salvation. This salvation is brought by

with relationships among the "members" of the ecclesia. We shall concentrate on this third section.[4]

2. The background situation. InterpKn is directed to a community whose unity is threatened by "hate" and "strife" between its members. It is especially envy which threatens to tear the community apart,[5] that is to say, envy of two types: on the one hand the jealous ill will of those who withhold their spiritual gifts from others, and on the other hand the envy of those who are less endowed. The directives of *InterpKn* thus cut two ways. On the one side *InterpKn* addresses the pneumatics who consider other members of the congregation to be "ignorant"[6] or treat them as "strangers,"[7] and consequently deny them participation in their own spiritual gifts. These pneumatics are reminded, "How do you know [that someone] is more ignorant of the [brethren]? For [you] yourself are ignorant when you [hate them] and are jealous (φθονεῖν) of them."[8] Over against these are the less richly endowed members who, "full of envy," approach the one who "has a prophetic gift"[9] or who are "offended" when another "makes progress in the Word."[10] They are not only jealous of the higher gift of the brother but also murmur against Christ as the "head" from whom all charismata proceed. Therefore *InterpKn* warns (adapting the Pauline imagery), "Do not accuse (ἐγκαλεῖν) your Head because it has not appointed you as an eye but rather as a finger. And do not be jealous (φθονεῖν) of that (member) which has been made as an eye or a hand or a foot.... Why do you despise [him]?"[11] *InterpKn* makes

---

Christ by his "reminding" the ecclesia of her heavenly origin. "He spoke with the ecclesia; he became for her the teacher of immortality" (9: 17-19; cf. the following speeches to the ecclesia: 9: 27 ff.; 10: 17 ff.; probably also 20: 12 ff.). Thus Christ brings the ecclesia saving gnosis, i.e., the knowledge of her heavenly destination. By preceding them into the realm of light he also opened the way for his "members." "Thus, as the Head looked from on high to his members, the members hurried upwards to the place where the Head was" (13: 33-36). That is the "ascent" of the "ecclesia" (13: 24 f.). Thus pages 9-15 treat the salvation of the ecclesia. This is the precondition of the following admonitions to the "members" (pp. 16-21).

[4] The manuscript containing *InterpKn* is in part badly damaged; consequently the interpretation is encumbered by uncertainties. Yet of the three main sections the third is the best preserved.

[5] "Envy": 15: 29, 30, 38; 17: 28, 38; 18: 31; cf. 15: 21; 17: 35 f.

[6] 21: 25 f.

[7] 16: 24 f.

[8] 17: 25-28.

[9] 15: 35-38.

[10] 16: 31-33.

[11] 18: 28-32, 38 f.

clear to both groups what it means to be members of the body of
Christ.

What kind of groups are these? Is the conflict between groups of
Gnostics who have, respectively, more or less "progressed,"[12] or is
it between Gnostic pneumatics and ordinary, "simple" members of the
congregation? There are many reasons to consider the latter more
probable. *InterpKn*, in significant contrast to Paul, leaves no doubt
about the different ranks of the various "members" and "charismata."
The less richly endowed members of the congregation should be happy
that they may belong at all. They should be humble and "thankful
that they do not exist outside the body."[13]

3. The charismata in question. Which charismata are the bone of
contention? Unfortunately, the fragmentary state of the text leaves
only an incomplete picture. Yet it is clear that the conflict is primarily
about the gift of "prophecy" and spiritual "speech." These two charismata are also not absent in the list of charismata mentioned by Paul.
"Someone has a *prophetic* gift (*hmat*, προφητικόν). Participate in it
without hesitation. Do not approach your brother full of envy
(φθόνος)...."[14] He who does not possess the charisma of prophecy
thus should not be envious of this gift in his brother. On the contrary,
he should seek to "participate" in it.

A similar conflict has arisen about the gift of spiritual *speech*.
"But someone is making progress (προκόπτειν) in the Word (λόγος).
Do not be offended by this. Do not say, 'Why does this one speak
while I do not?'"[15] Here *InterpKn* responds that it is just as much
the working of the spirit to be able to "understand" such spiritual
speech. Thus the ability to *understand* is also a charisma; for "he
who understands (νοεῖν) the Word and he who speaks—it is the same
power (that is at work in both)."[16] Other charismata may be those
of "*knowledge*" or the inspired *interpretation of Scripture* (of which
InterpKn itself supplies many examples). A list of various activities
of the Spirit "in the ecclesia" appears to be present on p. 19 of the
tractate; there is, for example, a reference to those who "proclaim
[the knowledge] of the Pleroma." Still other charismata mentioned in
InterpKn are typical for the lower members of the congregation; but

---

[12] Cf. 16: 32.
[13] 18: 33 f.
[14] 15: 35-38.
[15] 16: 31-35.
[16] 16: 37 f.

it is not possible to define them more precisely.[17] Thus a variety of spiritual gifts is present in the congregation to which *InterpKn* addresses itself.

4. The concept of community in InterpKn. How does *InterpKn* counter the centrifugal forces within this community? What standards and principles does it apply? First of all, *InterpKn* calls to mind that all belong to the *one body of Christ.* It is to the "one body" that the various members belong; it is "one power" that is at work in the manifold gifts and charismata; and it is to "one Head" that the honorable and less honorable members owe their existence. Only in this "one body" do the various members that would want to be independent of one another have "life." Apart from this body they are "dead." This applies first of all to the pneumatic who withdraws from the fellowship of those members whom he despises for their ignorance and from whom he wants to withhold his spiritual gifts. He is told: whoever wants to be a "member" for himself "alone" is "dead." Whoever seeks to keep "the gift that he has received" to himself "destroys himself with his gift."[18] In a similar vein the tractate addresses the less richly endowed member of the congregation who is "envious" of the higher gift of his "brother" and who "complains" that he has been made only a "finger" and not the "eye." He is reminded that he has "the same Head" as the "eye" and that "the same power" is working in him if he can "understand" the spiritual speech of someone else. Therefore he should be content and "be thankful" that he does not exist "outside the body."[19]

Thus the Christian congregation is pictured in *InterpKn* as a spiritual organism, whose members with their various and contrasting gifts stand in a relationship of *reciprocal giving and taking.* On this basis *InterpKn* tries to confront the conflicts which have arisen within the congregation. The ordinary Christians who are "envious" of the higher gifts of the Gnostic pneumatics, and who are "offended" by their "advancements," are admonished to be content and rather to "participate" in the gift of the more richly endowed members of the congregation. For "what that one says belongs (also) to you." On the

---

[17] 16: 23f.; 17: 29, 34. One of these gifts typical for the more ordinary members of the congregation is certainly the ability to "understand" the spiritual "speech" of another (16: 37f.; see below). Yet *InterpKn* must have also other similar charismata in mind; cf. 17: 32-34; 16: 22-24.

[18] 15: 26-32.

[19] 18: 33f., 28ff.

other hand, the pneumatics, who out of ill will want to withhold
their gifts from those fellow Christians who are classified as "ignorant"
and treated as "strangers," are reminded that these gifts are not their
exclusive possession. Rather, they are the "gifts" of the "Head" and
thus belong to all the "members" of the "body." "That which belongs
to you is (at the same time) that which each of your fellow members
(within the body) has received."[20] Therefore the Gnostic pneumatics
should share their "gifts" with the members they despise. In addition,
the latter should seek to participate in the specific gifts that were
entrusted to the former.[21] Thus no member can exist alone; no one
can out of envy or ill will close himself off from others, for to be "alone"
is to be "dead." The "members" of the "body"—with all their differences in ability and spiritual level—must give to one another and
take from one another, and enjoy together the gifts that they have
received from the Father.

In the conflict over spiritual gifts *InterpKn* points with great emphasis
to the *example of Christ*, the origin of all charismata. He sets the
standards for the way the spiritual gifts should be employed. "For
the Logos is rich, *without envy* (-φθονεῖν) and kind (χρηστός). He
presents gifts to his people in this world without jealousy (φθονεῖν)."[22]
Just as Christ as the head distributes his gifts generously and without
envy so also must the Gnostic pneumatic conduct himself and share
selflessly and without envy with others the gifts that he has received.
In *InterpKn* the generosity of Christ stands in close relationship to
his incarnation and voluntary humiliation. On page 15, *InterpKn*
programmatically refers first to the example of Christ, who out of love
for his members and without jealousy separated himself from "all"
his heavenly glory and descended into the lowness of human existence,
and treats only second the relationship of the "members" to each other.
InterpKn describes this loving self-humiliation of Christ with the word
ταπεινοφροσύνη (ⲑⲃⲉⲓⲟ) used in Philippians 2.[23] This *humilitas Christi*
is the orientation point for the Gnostic pneumatic, who has to practise
the same kind of humility towards the ordinary Christian.

5. *The relationship to catholic church orders.* *InterpKn* does not
confront the conflict within the community in question by referring
to authoritative functionaries, but by bringing to mind the common

---

[20] 16: 25-27.
[21] 16: 22-24; 17: 28-34.
[22] 17: 35 ff.
[23] 10: 28.

origin of the various "charismata" which are present in the congregation. And according to *InterpKn* it is not an ecclesiastical office that can safeguard the threatened unity of the congregation, or embody it; rather, this unity exists only as the unity of the "one body" through which each "member" participates in the gift of the other. Thus *InterpKn* serves as documentation of a pneumatic-charismatic organization of a congregation. In this, it stands unambiguously and consciously within the Pauline tradition. The Pauline teaching on the charismata and the *soma Christou* ecclesiology play a decisive role.

With this retention of the "Pauline concept of organization of the congregation on the basis of the charismata" (Käsemann)[24] the most prominent difference from the church orders of the catholic sphere has already been mentioned. For in the latter the Pauline tradition has been discontinued, to a large extent. Von Campenhausen has studied the first letter of Clement, the Ignatian corpus and the Pastoral Epistles as three typical representatives of the early catholic concept of office. He has come to the conclusion that they—in spite of all differences among them and precisely in view of their diverse origins—witness to a "common line of development." "In the three areas they represent, the patriarchal system of elders forms the starting point and sustaining framework of the 'catholic' church order. *Pauline traditions in them function at best as a kind of spiritual corrective.*"[25] "No one attempts any more [i.e., in the second century] to found the life and organization of the church, as Paul had tried, solely on the Spirit and its gifts. The firm framework of the presbyterian-episcopal structure has become a matter of course in the orthodox congregations."[26] *InterpKn* proves that the opposite is true for the Gnostic realm. The Pauline tradition, which in the catholic realm survived only in part or in hierarchical transformation,[27] is here continued and has been made, in Gnostic modification, the foundation of communal life.

The discontinuity of the Pauline tradition is especially apparent in those places where otherwise the Pauline inheritance has obviously

---

[24] E. Käsemann, "Amt und Gemeinde im Neuen Testament," (*Exeg. Versuche und Besinnungen* 2 [1964] 109-34), at 129.

[25] H. Frh. v. Campenhausen, *Kirchliches Amt und geistliche Vollmacht in den ersten drei Jahrhunderten* (2d ed.; 1963) 131; cf. 328, 80-81.

[26] Ibid., 195f.

[27] The latter is illustrated by *1 Clement*, which in chap. 37f. takes up the imagery of the body and its members from 1 Corinthians 12 in order to establish a regular gradation and "subordination" in analogy to the Roman army.

been preserved and cultivated. This happens to be the case in the
Pastoral Epistles. Paul is here the sole apostolic authority, and his
teaching is cited as a binding entity and is interpreted with reference
to the pressing controversies of the moment. Yet the "ecclesiastical
office in the Pastoral Epistles" does, as von Campenhausen has shown,
"in its essence not come forth from the Pauline tradition.... It originates
from the soil of the originally Jewish system of elders, which was
first taken over in a patriarchal sense."[28] This discontinuity of tradition
is, as has often been maintained, related to the anti-Gnostic struggle
evident in the Pastoral Epistles. Thus also from this side it is clear
that the retaining of the Pauline tradition in *InterpKn* involves not an
accidental but an essential difference from the organizational concepts
in the catholic camp.

Does this mean that the retention of the Pauline charismatic concept
of the congregation in *InterpKn* is in turn a deliberate opposition and
alternative to the episcopal-presbyterian structure of the catholic congregations? That would certainly be an exaggeration. *InterpKn* is only
interested in those functions within the congregation that constitute
the Christian community as a spiritual organism. Not a word is said
about such matters as technical functions and practical duties. It can
only be concluded that *InterpKn* shows little interest in the Christian
community's external organization, which stands in the foreground
of the catholic concept of office. Beyond this, further conclusions
cannot be drawn.

II. The Attitude of the Gnostics to Ecclesiastical Offices

1. Indifference towards the offices of that time. We cannot speak
of fundamental opposition by the Gnostics to the ecclesiastical offices
of that time. This is demonstrated by the fact that there were Gnostics
who filled such offices. For example the Valentinian Florinus, who
conducted a lively propaganda as far as Gaul, was a presbyter of
the Roman congregation under Bishop Victor; it was only at the urging
of Irenaeus that he was removed from office.[29] Similarly the Gnostic
Peter, a contemporary of Epiphanius and the alleged founder of the
sect of the Archontics, was active as presbyter of a Palestinian
congregation during the episcopate of Aëtius until he was deposed.[30]

---

[28] Von Campenhausen, *Kirchliches Amt*, 127.

[29] Iren. frg. syr. 28 (Harvey 2. 457); Eus., *H.E.* 5.20.15; cf. K. Koschorke, *Polemik*,
67-69.

[30] Epiph. *Haer.* 40.1.5.

Tertullian reports the great success of Gnostic propaganda among ecclesiastical functionaries; from bishop and deacon to martyr, they all were subject to the Gnostic temptation.[31] This agrees with the complaint heard in orthodox circles that the offices were in the hands of heretics.[32]

Examples like these show that the Gnostic Christians did not reject such ecclesiastical offices as might be found in Christian congregations. Rather, their attitude towards the offices of that time was characterized by indifference. In those places where they lived in fellowship with catholic Christians—and that was much more frequent and lasting than is generally assumed—they appear to have participated in the existing structure of the congregation, just as when they lived in their own communities they could perpetuate precatholic structures or organize themselves analogously to the philosophical schools (and at times also to the mystery cults). It should also be remembered that the proportionate relationship between orthodox and Gnostic Christianity could change. That is already enough reason not to equate too easily the organizational structure of the congregation with the party that was dominant at the time.

The difference therefore between Gnostic and catholic Christianity does not lie in the insistence on a certain congregational structure. Rather, it rests in the opposite evaluations of ecclesiastical office made by either side. What, according to a Gnostic, the office could accomplish in a positive way—such as an auxiliary function in the appropriation of salvation—is not something reserved for the office bearer to the exclusion of others.[33] Therefore, the Gnostics raised objections to any attempt at attributing constitutive importance to the ecclesiastical office—as, for example, seeing in it a mediating agency between God and man without which there can be no fellowship with God. They counter such views with a vehement polemic.

Two questions are to be distinguished here. First of all, how did Gnostic Christians in principle evaluate the effort to acquire the salvation brought by Christ through the mediation of an outside agency? Secondly and more concretely, what position did they take with reference to the claims raised in behalf of the ecclesiastical office?

2. *Outside mediation as a lesser participation in salvation.* According

---

[31] Tert., *Praescr.* 3.5.2.
[32] See, for example, *Asc. Isa.* 3.23f.
[33] A very similar attitude is evident in Clement of Alexandria (*Str.* 7.3.3f.).

to the Gnostics the psychics, i.e., the mass of ordinary Christians,
are *dependent* on outside instruction. This distinguishes them from
the Gnostic pneumatics. This does not mean that the latter deny
the importance of human mediation. They themselves have been
actively involved in missionary activities and thus have tried to transmit
the "knowledge" of the Christian truth to others. Yet they saw this
activity only as a preparatory stage. For them only the direct confrontation with the truth itself was decisive (Heracleon frg. 39). The
situation is different in the case of the psychics. In the Gnostic view
they stand in need of outside instruction; there is for them no other
way to participate in salvation. This is made clear for example in the
Valentinian *Tripartite Tractate* (CG I). Here pneumatics and psychics
are contrasted and compared with one another. "The spiritual kind
is like light from light and like a spirit from a spirit. When its head
(i.e., Christ) was revealed, it rushed to it immediately (and) became
a body immediately for its head, and it received immediately the
knowledge of the revelation."[34] Thus the pneumatics are like light
from light, having the same essence and the same origin as the savior,
and therefore are able to recognize him directly without a roundabout
way via mediating agencies. This is not possible for the psychics. "But
the psychic kind is like light from a fire. It hesitated to receive the
knowledge of the (head) which was revealed to it, rather than rush to
it in faith. Rather, they ⟨were⟩ taught through a voice ..."[35] Thus in
contrast to the pneumatics the psychics are not like light from light
but only like light from fire. They do not have the same origin and
the same essence as the savior and therefore can recognize him only
dimly. This is evident in that they gain knowledge of him only
"hesitantly" and stand in need of "teaching" about him. The need
for such "teaching" is, however, a sign of deficiency. They do participate
in the savior but not completely or with pneumatic immediacy, but
only through outside mediation. They cannot cope without outside
support and sensory aids to gain knowledge.

This is apparent in many things, as, for example, in the sacraments.
While, according to the views of at least a part of the Valentinians,
only the "baptism of the Spirit" is truly valid in that it brings
"salvation" and is, in accordance with its spiritual character, carried
out only purely "spiritually"—without the help of any "material

---

[34] *TriTrac* (CG I,5) 118: 28-36.
[35] *TriTrac* 118: 37-119: 3.

objects"—the psychic Christians are satisfied with the water baptism
which makes use of something material (water). But this water baptism
secures, in accordance with its psychic character, only a lower level of
salvation—only "forgiveness of sins" instead of "perfection" (Iren.,
Haer. 1.21.4.2).

Thus the psychics remain dependent on the external mediation of
salvation as it is found in the catholic congregation. When von Campenhausen concludes with reference to Clement of Alexandria that he sees
the ecclesiastical office "only as a pedagogical aid to a Christianity
that is not yet spiritually free and truly alive,"[36] this would characterize
also, mutatis mutendis, the attitude of the Valentinian gnostics to the
ecclesiastical office. It fits the lower level of faith of the psychic
Christians, who are dependent on the outside mediation of salvation.
The *limited* legitimacy of this is, therefore, not denied.

3. Polemic against the exclusive claims of the church. Thus the
polemic of Gnostics is not directed against ecclesiastical office as such.
To the contrary, the Gnostic attitude towards the congregational
structures of that time was characterized more by indifference; in view
of the lower level of faith of the psychic Christians, who could not
manage without outside support, they did not deny a relative legitimacy
to the catholic offices. Rather, the polemic of the Gnostics was directed
against the exclusive claims made in behalf of ecclesiastical office.
After Ignatius "one can no longer speak of a church" if there is no
bishop, presbyter, and deacon.[37] For the Syrian *Didascalia* the bishops
are "mediators between God and his faithful."[38] One is not supposed
to do anything without the bishop, for "if someone does something
without the bishop he does it in vain."[39] A Gnostic could see in such
remarks only evidence of the greatest deception caused by the archons.
They add up to a position in which salvation is integrally tied to
something purely external, to an agency that stands over against man,
while the essential thing must take place within man. The ecclesiastical
mediation of salvation can in itself be understood as a first stage
which points beyond itself and can as such be evaluated positively
without difficulty. Yet the opposite is true when exclusive claims are
made. For these claims are baseless and therefore laughable. But above
all, they are dangerous. They lull the people into false security, prevent

---

[36] Von Campenhausen, *Kirchliches Amt*, 231.
[37] Ign., *Trall.* 3.1.
[38] Syr. *Didasc.* 7 (Achelis-Flemming 40.28f.).
[39] Syr. *Didasc.* 9 (Achelis-Flemming 45.29f.).

them from advancing to real salvation, and therefore play de facto into the hands of the archons, who want to hold back mankind in the prison of this creation. According to the Gnostics such statements of the church are inspired by the archons. Time and time again this becomes evident. Archontic inspiration accounts for the futile claim of the church leaders that they "alone" can provide access to God. Archontic inspiration is also visible in the presumptuous belief of the catholics that they "alone" are in possession of the "mystery of the truth".[40] It is also due to archontic inspiration that people apply the "name" of the "church" to the worldly assembly of the catholics instead of to the heavenly ecclesia.[41] Similarly, archontic influence is present when catholic Christians make the fatal mistake of thinking that the administration of the sacrament is in itself sufficient for salvation (and do not recognize that the gift of the sacrament is useless without the actualization through Gnosis).[42] Each time, the error of the catholic Christians is that they mistake the outward appearance for the thing itself, and each time this error is to be attributed to the influence of the archons. That is why the Gnostic Christians direct their polemics against the exclusive claims made in behalf of the ecclesiastical mediation of salvation that threatens to imprison man in the creation of the archons.

III. CONCLUDING REMARKS

Gnostic Christianity and ecclesiastical office are generally considered to lie at opposite poles. This is due to the fact that ecclesiastical office gained its importance especially in the struggle against Gnosticism; the Pastoral Epistles furnish a clear example of this. Therefore, with reference to the Pastorals, von Campenhausen speaks of the ecclesiastical office as an "office against the Gnostics." However, it is not possible simply to reverse this relationship and to speak in the same way of a Gnostic opposition to ecclesiastical office. Our sources furnish no basis for this. It is true that the Gnostic concept of the congregation is clearly different from that of the catholic camp, as the example of *InterpKn* shows. Here, in significant contrast to the organizational structures of the catholic sphere, the Pauline tradition (with its charis-

---

[40] *ApocPet* (CG VII,3) 77: 12f.
[41] *GPh* (CG II,3) §§ 11 (53:23-54: 5), 13 (54: 18-31).
[42] *GPh* §§ 105 (76: 17-22), 67 (67: 9-27), 59 (64: 22-29).

matic concept of the congregation and *soma Christou* ecclesiology) is made the basis of communal life. No mention is made of any kind of ecclesiastical office. This does not, however, mean that the Gnostics rejected ecclesiastical office as such. Rather their attitude to such ecclesiastical offices as might be found in Christian congregations is marked by indifference. As a rule the Gnostic polemic was not directed against ecclesiastical office as such but against the exclusive claims which were made by its proponents.

THE NAASSENE PSALM IN HIPPOLYTUS (*HAER.* 5.10.2)

BY

M. MARCOVICH

TEXT

Νόμος ἦν γενικὸς τοῦ παντὸς ὁ πρωτό⟨τοκο⟩ς Νόος,
ὁ δὲ δεύτερος ἦν τοῦ πρωτοτόκου τὸ χυθὲν Χάος,
τριτάτη⟨ν⟩ Ψυχὴ δ᾽ ἔλαβ᾽ ⟨ἐξ⟩εργαζομένη νόμον·
  διὰ τοῦτ᾽ ἐλάφου μορφὴν περικειμένη
  κοπιᾷ, θανάτῳ μελέτημα, κρατουμένη·
  ποτὲ ⟨μὲν⟩ βασίλ(ειον) ἔχουσα βλέπει τὸ φῶς,
7 ποτὲ δ᾽ εἰς ⟨σπ⟩ήλαιον ἐκρι⟨πτο⟩μένη κλάει.
  7a { ⟨ποτὲ μὲν⟩ χαίρει, ποτὲ δὲ κλαίεται,
  7b ⟨ποτὲ μὲν⟩ κρίνει, ποτὲ δὲ κρίνεται,
  7c ποτὲ μὲν θνῄσκει, ποτὲ δὲ γίνεται. }
  ⟨κ⟩ἀνέξοδον ἡ μελέα κακῶ⟨ν⟩
  λαβύρινθον ἐσῆλθε, πλανωμένη.
  εἶπεν δ᾽ Ἰησοῦς· ἐσόρ⟨α⟩, πάτερ·
  ζήτημα κακῶν ⟨τόδ᾽⟩ ἐπὶ χθόνα
  ἀπὸ σῆς πνο⟨ι⟩ῆς ἀποπλάζεται·
  ζητεῖ δὲ φυγεῖν τὸ πικρὸν Χάος
14 κοὐκ οἶδε⟨ν ὅ⟩πως διελεύσεται.

  τούτου με χάριν πέμψον, πάτερ·

---

1 πρωτό⟨τοκο⟩ς H. Usener (1887) : πρῶτος P 3 τριτάτη⟨ν⟩ (sc. μοῖραν seu τάξιν) scripsi : τριτάτη P ἔλαβ᾽ E. Miller (1851) : ἔλαβεν P : ἔλαχεν P. Cruice (1860), at cf. *Il.* 23.275 ⟨ἐξ⟩εργαζομένη scripsi : ἐργαζομένη P : ἔν⟨θ᾽⟩ ἐργαζομένη Miller 4 τοῦτο P ἐλάφου Miller : ἔλαφον P : ἐλαφρὰν Gu. Harvey (1857), ἐλαφρὸν Gu. Christ (1871) 6 ⟨μὲν⟩ add. Miller βασίλειον A. Swoboda (1905) : βασι̅ P : βασιλείαν Miller 7 ⟨σπ⟩ήλαιον ci. Th. Wolbergs (1971) : ἔλαιον P : ἔλεον Miller : ἐλεείν᾽ Cruice ἐκρι⟨πτο⟩μένη Cruice : ἐρριμένη P, ἐρριμμένη Miller κλάει Christ : κλαίει P 7abc del. Cruice (1860) et A. ab Harnack (1902) 7abc scripsi : ποτὲ δὲ κλαίεται χαίρει, ποτὲ δὲ κλαίει κρίνεται, ποτὲ δὲ κρίνεται θνῄσκει, ποτὲ δὲ γίνεται P 8 ⟨κ⟩ add. Cruice et ἀνέξοδον scr. Christ : ἀνέξοδος P κακῶ⟨ν⟩ Miller : κακῶ P 9 εἰσῆλθε P, corr. Miller 10 διησοῦς P, corr. Miller ἐσὸρ P, corr. Miller 11 ⟨τόδ᾽⟩ add. Miller, ⟨ἔτ᾽⟩ add. Cruice 12 πνοῆς P, corr. Cruice ἀποπλάζεται Cruice : ἐπιπλάζεται P 14 καὶ οὐκ οἶδε πῶς P, corr. Miller

σφραγῖδας ἔχων καταβήσομαι,
   Αἰῶνας ὅλους διοδεύσω,
   μυστήρια πάντα δ' ἀνοίξω
   μορφάς τε θεῶν ἐπιδείξω·
   {καὶ} τὰ κεκρυμμένα τῆς ἁγίας ὁδοῦ,
21   γνῶσιν καλέσας, παραδώσω.

---

18 διανοίξω P, corr. Miller   19 τε Harvey (1857) et R. Lipsius (1860) : δὲ P
20 καὶ del. Lipsius

TRANSLATION

THE universal law of the All was the First-born Mind;
the second one after the First-born was the outpoured Chaos;
while the Soul got the third rank, with the duty to fulfil the law.

For that reason she put on the form of a hind
and started toiling as a captive, being a game (spoil) for Death.
Sometimes she would live in a royal palace and look at the light;
7 but sometimes she is being thrown in a den, and there she weeps.

7a [Sometimes she rejoices, sometimes she weeps aloud;
7b   sometimes she is a judge, sometimes she is being judged;
7c   sometimes she dies, sometimes she is being born.]

Finally, she—wretched in her sorrows—
in her wanderings entered the exitless Labyrinth.
Then Jesus said: "Look, Father:
this prey to evils is wandering away to earth,
far from thy spirit (breath).
And she seeks to escape the bitter Chaos,
14 but knows not how to win through.

For that reason send me, Father.
Bearing the seals I will descend;
I will pass through all the Aeons;
I will reveal all the mysteries
and show the forms of the gods:
I will transmit (deliver) the secrets of the holy way,
21 calling them Gnosis (Knowledge)."

COMMENTARY

1 νόμος γενικός = ὁ κοινὸς νόμος, "the universal law" (A. Hilgenfeld). Compare Heraclitus fr. 23 Marcovich (= 114 *Vorsokr.*); D. L. 7.88; Diodorus Tarsensis fr. 20 *In Deut.* (*PG* 33. 1583c) γενικὴ (opp. μερικὴ) νομοθεσία. — νόμος ~ νόος : Cic. *Leg.* 2.8 ita principem legem ... mentem esse ... dei. *PGM* 5.465 ὁ μέγας Νοῦς ἐννόμως τὸ πᾶν διοικῶν. — ὁ πρωτότοκος Νόος : cf. Thdt. *Haer.* 1.4 πρωτόγονος Νοῦς; Iren. *Haer.* 1.24.3-4 (Basilides) innatum ... Patrem ... misisse primogenitum Nun suum. 1.1.1 (Ptolemaeus) τὸν δὲ Νοῦν τοῦτον καὶ Μονογενῆ καλοῦσι καὶ Πατέρα καὶ Ἀρχὴν τῶν πάντων. NHC I,*1* A : 38; V,*1* 9 : 7 (*NHLibEng*).

2 τὸ χυθὲν Χάος = Hippol. 5.7.9 τὸ ἐκκεχυμένον Χάος, "the out-poured (= boundless) Chaos." Cf. NHC II,*5* 99 : 27f. "all of that (Chaos) is a boundless darkness and water of unfathomable depth"; 98 : 31 "the limitless Chaos"; I,*5* 89 : 26f. "the Outer Darkness and Chaos and Hades and the Abyss." Iren. 1.30.1 (Ophites) ὕδωρ, σκότος, ἄβυσσος, χάος. Hippol. 10.32.1 χάος ἄπειρον. Zeno (*SVF* 1 no. 103) aquam χάος appellatum ἀπὸ τοῦ χέεσθαι.

3 ἐξεργαζομένη νόμον, "fulfilling the law" : cf. Ps 14:2 = Acts 10:35 ἐργαζόμενος δικαιοσύνην, "bringing about justice." Ptol. *Ep.* 4.5 = Rom 7:12 ὥστε ὁ μὲν νόμος ἅγιος, καὶ ἡ ἐντολὴ ἁγία καὶ δικαία καὶ ἀγαθή.

4 ἐλάφου μορφὴν περικειμένη : cf. Ps 41:2 ὃν τρόπον ἐπιποθεῖ ἡ ἔλαφος ἐπὶ τὰς πηγὰς τῶν ὑδάτων, οὕτως ἐπιποθεῖ ἡ ψυχή μου πρὸς σέ, ὁ θεός. Hence the image of a hind standing by Jesus at the baptism in an early Christian fresco (J. Wilpert, *Die Malereien der Katakomben Roms* [1903] pl. 259; cf. 150). (A more remote possibility is the influence of the myth of Actaeon changed into a stag.) Cf. Thielko Wolbergs, *Psalmen und Hymnen der Gnosis* (Beiträge zur klass. Philologie 40; Meisenheim am Glan, 1971) 45f. The reading ἐλάφου is strongly supported by 5 θανάτῳ μελέτημα, "a spoil or game for the hunting Death" : cf. X. *Cyn.* 13.15 (ἡ μελέτη τῶν κυνηγετῶν).

5 κοπιᾷ (διὰ τοῦτο, i.e., ἐξεργαζομένη νόμον), "the Soul works hard, toils (while bringing life to the creation)" : cf. NHC II,*1* 20:19

"And she (the luminary Epinoia) assists the whole creature, by toiling with him …;" Hippol. 5.7.25 Λέγουσιν οὖν περὶ τῆς τοῦ πνεύματος οὐσίας, ἥτις ἐστὶ πάντων τῶν γινομένων αἰτία, ὅτι τούτων ἐστὶν οὐδέν, γεννᾷ δὲ καὶ ποιεῖ πάντα τὰ γινόμενα. — θανάτῳ μελέτημα : cf. perhaps NHC II,*3* 60:12 "Echmoth is the Wisdom of death, which is the one which knows death" = Ψυχή, Hippol. 6.32.8-9.

6-7 ποτὲ μὲν … ποτὲ δὲ : cf. Iren. 1.4.2 (Ptolemaeus) Ποτὲ μὲν γὰρ ἔκλαιε (sc. Ἀχαμὼθ ἡ ἐκτὸς τοῦ πληρώματος) καὶ ἐλυπεῖτο, ὡς λέγουσι, διὰ τὸ καταλελείφθαι μόνην ἐν τῷ σκότει καὶ τῷ κενώματι· ποτὲ δὲ εἰς ἔννοιαν ἤκουσα τοῦ καταλιπόντος αὐτὴν φωτὸς διεχεῖτο καὶ ἐγέλα … (A. von Harnack, *SitzungsberAkBerlin* 1902, 544 n. 1). — βασίλειον, "royal palace (open to sunshine)," cf. X. *Cyr.* 2.4.3. — ἔχουσα = ἐνοικοῦσα, "dwelling in," cf. S. *El.* 181. — τὸ φῶς = 1 Νόος = 12 πνοιή (πνεῦμα) : cf. Ptol. *Ep.* 5.7 (πατήρ = φῶς); Hippol. 5.19.2 (the Sethians) φῶς καὶ σκότος, τούτων δέ ἐστιν ἐν μέσῳ πνεῦμα ἀκέραιον (and Wolbergs 48 f.).

7 σπήλαιον : cf. Plot. 2.9.6,8 ἀναβάσεις ἐκ τοῦ σπηλαίου (Wolbergs 49 f.); Pl. *R.* 514a, 5 τὸ σπήλαιον; Iren. 1.4.2 ἐν τῷ σκότει καὶ τῷ κενώματι. — Matt 21:13 = Jer 7:11 σπήλαιον λῃστῶν, "den of the robbers"; NHC II,*3* 53:11 "It (the soul of Christ) fell into the hands of robbers and was taken captive, but he (Christ) saved it." Hippol. 5.6.7 καὶ τρεῖς ἐκκλησίαι, ἀγγελική, ψυχική, χοϊκή· ὀνόματα δὲ αὐταῖς ἐκλεκτή, κλητή, αἰχμάλωτος.

6-7 βασίλειον : σπήλαιον = φῶς : σκότος : Hippol. 5.7.9 τὰς δὲ ἐξαλλαγὰς ταύτας (sc. τῆς ψυχῆς) τὰς ποικίλας ἐν τῷ ἐπιγραφομένῳ κατ' Αἰγυπτίους εὐαγγελίῳ κειμένας ἔχουσιν (sc. the Naassenes). *Corp. Herm.* 10.7 τούτων τοίνυν τῶν ψυχῶν πολλαὶ αἱ μεταβολαί, τῶν μὲν ἐπὶ τὸ εὐτυχέστερον, τῶν δὲ ἐπὶ τὸ ἐναντίον (and A.-J. Festugière ad loc.). Clem. *Exc. Thdot.* 56.3 τὸ μὲν οὖν πνευματικὸν φύσει σῳζόμενον, τὸ δὲ ψυχικὸν αὐτεξούσιον ὂν ἐπιτηδειότητα ἔχει πρός τε πίστιν καὶ ἀφθαρσίαν καὶ πρὸς ἀπιστίαν καὶ φθορὰν κατὰ τὴν οἰκείαν αἵρεσιν· τὸ δὲ ὑλικὸν φύσει ἀπόλλυται. Iren. 1.6.1 (p. 51 f. Harvey).

7 κλάει : Iren. 1.4.1-2 ἀπὸ γὰρ τῶν δακρύων αὐτῆς (sc. Achamoth) γεγονέναι πᾶσαν ἔνυγρον οὐσίαν, ἀπὸ δὲ τοῦ γέλωτος τὴν φωτεινήν …;

NHC II,*1* 31 : 6 Pronoia in the realm of darkness (prison, Chaos, Hades) "wept and shed tears, bitter tears ..." (cf. Wolbergs 50f.).

7abc The intrusion of three *dochmiacs* into the anapaestic system delates the lines as being a later expansion inspired by 7 κλάει (so Harnack), probably by somebody who wanted to have a psalm consisting of 24 (instead of 21) lines (or by somebody who wanted to elaborate on the destiny of Soul). — 7b ποτὲ μὲν κρίνει (?), ποτὲ δὲ κρίνεται: cf. Matt 7:1-2; Luke 6:37; *S.Sext.* 183; BG 15: 16 And the Soul said, "Why do you judge me, although I have not judged?"

8 ἀνέξοδον ... λαβύρινθον: λαβύρινθος ἀνέξοδος *A.Pl.* 12.93.1 (Rhianus); ἀνέξοδον εἰς Ἀχέροντα Theoc. 12.19 (and A. S. F. Gow ad loc.). — ἡ μελέα κακῶν: E. *Med.* 96 δύστανος ἐγὼ μελέα τε πόνων.

10 = 15 πάτερ: i.e., 1 Νόος. The father of Jesus, Son of Man, is Man.

11 ζήτημα κακῶν = 5 θανάτῳ μελέτημα, i.e., "a prey to evils" (Harnack); (cf. Hp. *VM* 3 ζήτημα ... εὕρημα, "thing sought and thing found").

12 ἀπὸ σῆς πνοιῆς ἀποπλάζεται, "is wandering away *far* from thy spirit (breath): "cf. Il. 13.591f.; Od. 1.75. — πνοιῆς = πνεύματος: cf. πνοὴ θεοῦ *1 Clem.* 21.9; Gen 2:7; 7:22; *Ps.-Clem. Hom.* 16.16 ψυχὰς ... τὴν τοῦ θεοῦ πνοὴν ἠμφιεσμένας.

13 τὸ πικρὸν Χάος: πικρὸς Ἅιδης W. Peek, *Griechische. Vers-Inschriften* no. 567.4; *A. Pl.* 7.303.6.

14 οὐκ οἶδεν ὅπως διελεύσεται: the opposite is 21: γνῶσις as the γνῶσις τῆς ἁγίας (ἀν)όδου (R. Reitzenstein, *Hellenistische Mysterien-religionen* [1927] 295).

16 σφραγῖδας ἔχων: probably "passes," magic formulas each one different for each Aeon, for both the descending Redeemer and the ascending Soul and the gnostics. Cf. *1 Jeu* 33-38 Schmidt-Till (seven seals); *2 Jeu* 45-48 (eight seals); Fr. J. Dölger, *Sphragis* [1919] 160ff.; BAG, s.v., 1d; G. Fitzer in Kittel, *TWNT* 7 [1964] 953; Wolbergs 56. BG 16: 14-17: 6.

17 Αἰῶνας ὅλους: probably either seven or thirteen of them; cf. Hippol. 5.7.20; 5.6.5; 5.8.45; 5.9.5. According to the Naassenes, Jesus himself is μακάριος Αἰὼν Αἰώνων (Hippol. 5.8.45). Cf. *PGM* 4.2198 ὁ Αἰὼν τῶν Αἰώνων (and, e.g., A. D. Nock, *Essays on Religion* ... [1972] 1.383 and 388).

18 μυστήρια πάντα: probably a concrete thing: a secret password, sign or symbol, different for each one of the archons (aeons). Cf. Or. *Cels.* 6.31; BG 16: 5; Rev 1:20; Hippol. 5.9.22 (and Harnack 545; Nock 2. 798 n. 28; 889 and n. 43).

19 μορφὰς ... θεῶν: "the shape (form) of each one of the aeons," such as lion, bull, serpent, eagle, bear, dog, ass: Or. *Cels.* 6.30 and 33 (Wolbergs 56 n. 95). — θεοί = αἰῶνες, ἀστέρες: *PGM* 13.997; Hippol. 5.16.6.

20 τὰ κεκρυμμένα ("the secrets") = σφραγῖδες + μυστήρια + μορφαὶ θεῶν? — ἡ ἁγία ὁδός = ἡ τῆς Ψυχῆς καὶ τῶν πνευματικῶν ἄνοδος.

21 ἀνοίξω ... ἐπιδείξω ... παραδώσω, sc. τοῖς πνευματικοῖς (νοεροῖς, ἐκλεκτοῖς, ἀγγελικοῖς) μόνοις: Hippol. 5.6.7.

Some Conclusions

(1) The Naassene psalm is a complete creed of a three-principle Gnostic system: in twenty-one brief lines it comprises no less than thirty Gnostic key-words. In addition, the psalm is a gem of the Christian Gnosticism: compare Jesus in line 10 and Hippol. 5.9.21-22: "for we [the Naassenes] enter in through the true gate, which is Jesus the Blessed one [cf. John 10:9; Ps 117:20]. And out of all men we are the only true Christians, who perform the mystery at the third gate [cf. 2 Cor 12:2; Gen 28:17; Hippol. 5.8.31]."

(2) The psalm consists of three hebdomads (21 lines). (Incidentally, the cosmic hebdomad of seven planets is mentioned at Hippol. 5.7.23-24; and Jesus reveals himself in the fourteenth aeon, Hippol. 5.7.20; cf. 2 Cor 12:2 and M. Marcovich, *JTS* 20 [1969] 60-64). First hebdomad (1-7), written in six (1-3) and five (4-7) catalectic anapaests each line, states three basic principles of the system (1-3; notice three past

tenses, ἦν, ἦν, ἔλαβ᾽) and succinctly describes the mission of the Soul in this world (4-7; notice three present tenses, κοπιᾷ, βλέπει, κλάει). Second hebdomad (8-14), written in four catalectic anapaests each line, reveals that the time for the Apocatastasis has come. Third hebdomad (15-21), with paroemiacs in lines 17-19 and 21, speaks of the Redemption itself: it is separated from the second hebdomad by no less than five future tenses, all placed at the line end. As a whole, the psalm shows the figure of an inverted pyramid, with the line containing the word Gnosis (21) at its top. The intention seems to be clear: the salvation comes from above. But maybe the psalm itself was devised as a *mysterion* (magical formula) for the pneumatics enabling them to achieve salvation? (As for the figure, compare, e.g., *Securis* in E. Diehl, *Anth. Lyr.*, 2. 260.)

(3) The three principles of the psalm (Nous, Chaos, Psyche, 1-3) seem to be genuinely Naassene: compare Cau-lacau, Sau-lasau, Ζεησάρ (Ze'er Sham) at Hippol. 5.8.4 (Isa 28:10; Iren. 1.24.5); or ὁ Προών, τὸ ἐκκεχυμένον Χάος, ὁ Αὐτογενής at Hippol. 5.7.9; or else (Ἀρχ)άνθρωπος, ἡ θνητὴ φύσις ἡ κάτω, Υἱὸς Ἀνθρώπου at Hippol. 5.8.2; 10.9.1. "He who says that the All is composed of three (principles), speaks the truth and will be able to give the proof about the universe" (5.8.1). The conclusion of B. Herzhoff (*Zwei gnostische Psalmen* [Diss. Bonn; 1973] 135), that Valentinus himself is author of the Naassene psalm, cannot stand criticism: the psalm can be explained in terms of the Naassene system (involving three principles) as preserved in Hippol. 5.6.3-5.10.2 and 10.9.

(4) The lion's share belongs to the mission of the third (middle) principle, the Soul (11 lines), and to her salvation (along with the salvation of all the pneumatics; 8 lines). The Soul "fulfills the law" of the All (i.e., of Nous) by bringing life to the κτίσις: "For the Soul is the cause of everything that comes into being" (Hippol. 5.7.10). For that reason (διὰ τοῦτ᾽, 4) she puts on the form of a hind (probably under the influence of Ps 41:2) and descends to earth to fulfil her mission (4-7).

In other words, I think that νόμος in line 3 has the same meaning as νόμος in line 1 (a kind of ring composition): "the law of the All," and not the derogatory sense of ὁ νόμος τῆς κτίσεως (contra, e.g., R. Reitzenstein, *SitzungsberAkHeid* 10 [1917] 49; Wolbergs 44f.). The very fact that the Soul "puts on a form" (μορφὴν περικειμένη) attests to a special mission of a divine principle. That this mission is by no means limited to the creation only becomes clear from Hippol. 5.7.11-13:

πᾶσα οὖν φύσις ἐπουρανίων, φησί, καὶ ἐπιγείων καὶ καταχθονίων (Phil 2:10) ψυχῆς ὀρέγεται, including ἡ τῶν ὑπερκοσμίων καὶ αἰωνίων ἄνω μακαρία φύσις.

(5) Accordingly, there is no disagreement between the first and the second hebdomad of the psalm: the former deals with Cosmogony, the latter with Apocatastasis. In part one, κοπιᾷ ("works hard, toils") was to be expected as part of the Soul's mission (and was authorized by the universal law of the All, Nous). But the Soul's perishing in the Labyrinth (Chaos) was not expected. As soon as she reaches this point (in part two of the psalm), the time for redemption has come and the Redeemer acts: "Then Jesus said: Look, Father, this prey to evils … . For that reason send me, Father." This point of mortal danger for the Soul is stressed by the phrase 12 ἀπὸ σῆς πνοιῆς (implying "too far from thy protecting spirit"), sandwiched between two words expressing "hopelessness," placed at the beginning and end of the second hebdomad (8 ἀνέξοδον ... λαβύρινθον and 14 οὐ διελεύσεται τὸ πικρὸν Χάος).

(6) The Redeemer Jesus (Son of Man, Adamas) is a doublet of the Soul: both are bisexual (Hippol. 5.6.5 vs. 5.7.13). The Father to whom Jesus, Son of Man, speaks (in lines 10 and 15) is Man (Archanthropos, Nous): here Harnack (*SitzungsberAkBerlin* 1902, 544) is correct, contra Herzhoff 110 (Jesus' father is "the unborn Father" of Basilides). Again, there are only three principles in the Naassene system: the only apparent "fourth principle" there is the Demiurge Esaldaeus, "the fiery god, the fourth in number" (Hippol. 5.7.30); but he is equated with Chaos (5.8.5).

When descending to this world, the Soul takes the form of a hind: the descending Jesus apparently takes the form of Man. While Psyche is predominantly psychic, the affinity between Psyche and Jesus may well consist in the fact that both share in the πνεῦμα. Jesus is pneumatic par excellence, while Psyche is pneuma qua Life: λέγουσιν οὖν περὶ τῆς τοῦ πνεύματος οὐσίας, ἥτις ἐστὶ πάντων τῶν γινομένων αἰτία, ὅτι τούτων ἐστὶν οὐδέν, γεννᾷ δὲ καὶ ποιεῖ πάντα τὰ γινόμενα (Hippol. 5.7.25).

Incidentally, Psyche (and the psychics) is αὐτεξούσιος and can choose between salvation and perdition (Clem. *Exc. Thdot.* 56.3); hence the Naassene ἡ ψυχικὴ = ἡ κλητὴ ἐκκλησία (Hippol. 5.6.7; cf. Matt 22:14; *Exc. Thdot.* 58.1). On the other hand, Jesus, like the three-bodied giant Geryon (Hippol. 5.6.6; 5.8.4), comprises all three "men" (pneumatic, psychic, choic, 5.6.7).

(7) Finally, the presence in the psalm of a preexistent Jesus (for the expected Christ) does not prove Valentinian authorship of the psalm. It may be explained by strong Christian feelings of the Naassenes: compare, e.g., Hippol. 5.9.21-22 (quoted above, under Conclusions, 1), or 5.8.45 (Jesus as ὁ μακάριος Αἰὼν Αἰώνων), or else 5.8.20-21 (Jesus, the true gate, equated with the perfect Man, fully "characterized" from the Uncharacterized One above).

But pre-existent Jesuses are known from other Gnostic systems as well: compare, e.g., NHC III,2 64: 1 and 65: 16 (and Böhlig-Wisse, p. 193); VII,2 66: 8; II,5 105: 26; Pistis Sophia 81 (p. 114f. Schmidt-Till).

Valentinian flavor may be detected in 7 κλάει (cf. Iren. 1.4.2), as Harnack had suggested (544 n. 1). But compare also, e.g., NHC II,1 31: 6f., "And he (the spirit in the chains of prison) wept and shed tears. Bitter tears he wiped from himself ..."

In conclusion, the content of the fascinating Naassene psalm is Naassene, not Valentinian.

LE CADRE SCOLAIRE DES TRAITES DE L'AME ET LE
DEUXIEME TRAITE DU GRAND SETH (CG VII,2)

PAR

LOUIS PAINCHAUD

LE rédacteur du *Deuxième Traité du Grand Seth (GrSeth)* a utilisé des sources fort disparates au plan de la doctrine comme au plan de la forme, et aucun de ceux qui en ont étudié le texte n'a manqué de le souligner.[1] La critique des sources laisse clairement apparaître ce fait que Gibbons a d'ailleurs bien mis en évidence,[2] et même pour un lecteur non averti, il est facile de repérer dans le *GrSeth* plusieurs sources ou fragments qui se distinguent tantôt par leur doctrine, tantôt par leur forme ou leur vocabulaire, et que l'on peut, dans certains cas, rattacher à un courant gnostique particulier.

Cependant, quelle que soit la maladresse apparente du rédacteur à harmoniser ses sources, cette diversité ne devrait pas obnubiler le chercheur au point qu'il néglige de chercher la cohérence interne du texte. Le rédacteur, en construisant ce traité, avait certainement une intention qui le guidait et qui a dû se refléter dans la façon dont il a organisé son matériel. Si nous arrivons à trouver son mode de composition, nous serons alors en mesure d'apprécier plus justement son travail et de mieux comprendre la doctrine du traité.

Dans cette étude, nous voulons montrer que notre rédacteur a utilisé le cadre scolaire des traités de l'Ame pour composer son texte. A cette fin, nous prendrons comme point de comparaison le *De Anima* de Tertullien et le *Poimandrès* du Corpus Hermeticum et, pour la bibliothèque de Nag Hammadi, l'*Authentikos Logos (AuthLog [AuthTeach])* du codex VI.[3]

---

[1] Cf. F. Wisse, «The Nag Hammadi Library and the Heresiologists», *VC* 25 (1971) 219-20 ; J. A. Gibbons, *A Commentary on the Second Logos of the Great Seth*, Ph. D. Dissertation, Yale University, 1972, 39, et «The Second Logos of the Great Seth, Considerations and Questions», *MacRae Seminar Papers* 2, Society of Biblical Literature, Cambridge, 1973, 246-52 ; Berliner Arbeitskreis für koptisch-gnostische Schriften, «NHC VII,2/p. 49-70 : Der zweite Logos des grossen Seth» in *Gnosis und Neues Testament*, éd. K. W. Tröger, Berlin, 1973, 60-61 ; H.-G. Bethge, «Zweiter Logos des grossen Seth. Die zweite Schrift aus Nag-Hammadi-Codex VII (eingeleitet und übersetzt vom Berliner Arbeitskreis für koptisch-gnostische Schriften)» *TLZ* 100 (1975) 98-100.

[2] J. A. Gibbons, *A Commentary...*, 29-38.

[3] Pour les relations entre l'*AuthLog* et les traités de l'âme, cf. G. W. MacRae,

1. LE CADRE SCOLAIRE DES TRAITES DE L'AME

Nous ne voulons pas ici retracer les origines ni les développements de ce cadre littéraire, mais rappeler seulement qu'à l'époque où, vraisemblablement, notre texte a été composé, soit entre 235 et 345,[4] le cadre de composition des traités de l'Ame appartenait «à cette sorte de koinè philosophique dont usait en ce temps un homme de moyenne culture».[5] Et il est plausible que notre traité, comme bien d'autres de la bibliothèque de Nag Hammadi, porte les traces de cette culture commune.[6]

Selon Festugière qui l'a étudié à partir du *De Anima* de Tertullien, du *Peri Psuchès* de Jamblique et du *Poimandrès* du Corpus Hermeticum (*Corp. Herm.* 1), ce cadre de composition comporte quatre parties : Nature de l'Ame; Origine, temps et mode d'incarnation de l'Ame; Sort de l'Ame incarnée et Eschatologie.[7] Voici ce cadre tel qu'il le dégage du *De Anima* et du *Poimandrès* :

		De Anima	*Poimandrès*
I	Nature de l'Ame	Les qualités de l'Ame (ch. 4-22)	Origine céleste de l'Ame (*Corp. Herm.* 1, 12)
II	Origine, temps et mode de l'incarnation de l'Ame	1. Théories fausses dérivant de l'*anamnèsis* platonicienne (ch. 23-24)	1. Péché originel de l'Ame (13)
		2. Vraie doctrine (ch. 25-27), digression sur la métempsychose (ch. 28-35)	2. Descente à travers les sphères (14-15)
			3. Union de l'Ame avec la nature et début de la génération (16-20)
	Résumé[8]	Retour sur la vraie doctrine (ch. 36)	Reprise des thèmes de l'introduction (21)

«A Nag Hammadi Tractate on the Soul» in *Ex Orbe Religionum, Studia Geo. Widengren Oblata* (Supplements to *Numen*, 21, Leiden, 1972) 1. 471-79.

[4] Cf. F. Wisse, «The Nag Hammadi Library...» 217, n. 8 ; H.-Ch. Puech, «Les nouveaux écrits gnostiques découverts en haute Egypte», in *Coptic Studies in Honor of Walter Ewing Crum*, Boston, Byzantine Institute of America, 1950, 105 ; R. Kasser, «Fragments du livre biblique de la Genèse cachés dans la reliure d'un codex gnostique», *Muséon* 85 (1972) 68.

[5] A.-J. Festugière, *La révélation d'Hermès Trismégiste* 3, *Les doctrines de l'âme*, Paris, 1953, 2.

[6] A. Böhlig, «Die griechische Schule und die Bibliothek von Nag Hammadi» in *Les textes de Nag Hammadi*, éd. J. E. Ménard (NHS 7), Leiden, 1975, 41-44.

[7] A.-J. Festugière, *La révélation...* 3, 3-26.

[8] Nous avons ajouté ce point au plan de Festugière. Il nous semble caractéristique des œuvres étudiées.

III Sort de l'Ame incarnée   1. Croissance et puberté de   1. Choix de vie (22-23 et
                              l'être vivant : choix de vie   27-29)
                              (ch. 37-41)

                              2. Mort du vivant (ch. 42-   2. Mort du vivant (24-25)
                              53)

IV   Eschatologie   (ch. 54-58)   (26)

Outre le parallélisme évident du cadre de composition de ces deux
traités, nous voulons en souligner deux aspects qui revêtent à nos
yeux une importance capitale. D'une part, ils présentent tous deux
une sorte de résumé ou reprise entre les parties II et III. Dans le
De Anima, Tertullien reprend au ch. 36 la discussion sur l'origine
simultanée du corps et de l'âme. Quant à l'auteur hermétiste, il revient,
dans le paragraphe 21, aux thèmes de l'introduction (12). D'autre part,
les thèmes évoqués en introduction et en conclusion de chacun des
traités se rejoignent, comme l'avait déjà noté Waszink pour le *De
Anima* :[9]

> Or le Noûs, Père de tous les êtres, étant vie et lumière, enfanta un
> Homme semblable à lui, dont il s'éprit comme de son propre enfant.
> (*Corp. Herm.* 1, 12)

> Oui, j'ai la foi et je rends témoignage : je vais à la vie et à la lumière.
> Tu es béni, Père : celui qui est ton homme veut te prêter aide dans l'œuvre
> de sanctification, selon que tu lui as transmis toute la puissance. (*Corp.
> Herm.* 1, 32)[10]

> De solo censu animae congressus Hermogeni ... (*Anim.* 1, 1)

> Ad omnem ... humanam super anima opinionem ... congressi ... (*Anim.*
> 58, 9)[11]

Au sujet de cette reprise, Waszink fait remarquer qu'il s'agit d'une
habitude de composition de Tertullien,[12] mais le fait que cette répétition
se trouve aussi dans le *Poimandrès*, et placée au même endroit, indiquerait
plutôt, dans ce cas-ci, qu'il s'agit bien d'une règle du genre.

Nous nous trouvons donc devant deux textes qui présentent un plan
commun composé de quatre parties et qui, tous deux, reprennent des
éléments des premières parties entre les sections II et III, et répètent
en conclusion les thèmes de l'introduction.

---

[9] Tertullien, *De Anima*, éd. J. H. Waszink, Amsterdam, 1974, 593.
[10] A. D. Nock et A.-J. Festugière, *Corpus Hermeticum* 1, Paris, 1945, 10 et 19.
[11] Tertullien, *De Anima*, 1 et 80.
[12] Tertullien, *De Anima*, 320 et 593.

2. LE PLAN DE L'AUTHENTIKOS LOGOS[13] ET DU DEUXIEME TRAITE DU GRAND SETH[14]

Nos deux traités gnostiques, quoique présentant une doctrine différente, sont tous deux composés sur le même plan que le *De Anima* et le *Poimandrès*. Voici ce plan :

		GrSeth	*AuthLog*
I	Nature de l'Ame	Nature et origine du Sauveur (49, 10-20). Rôle du S. auprès des siens (49, 20-25). Communion du S. et des siens (49, 25-50, 1)	Origine de l'Ame (22, 1-20). Rôle·du Logos et anticipation du salut final (22, 20-34)
II	Origine, temps et mode de l'incarnation de l'Ame	Envoi en mission du Sauveur (50, 1-24). Chute des âmes (50, 25-51, 20). Descente du S. et effroi des Archontes (51, 20-54, 14)	1° métaphore : l'homme ayant une femme qui a des enfants (23, 4-24, 4) 2° métaphore : l'Ame insensée et le fils réfléchi (24, 4-25, 10) 3° métaphore : la paille et le bon grain (25, 11-25)
	Récapitulation	Origine et descente Sauveur (54, 14-27)	Retour sur la première partie (25, 25-26, 6)
III	Sort de l'Ame incarnée	1. *Le Sauveur* (54, 27-59, 19). Combat et triomphe du S. contre les archontes : récit docétique de la Passion (54, 27-57, 7). La remontée du S. avec les Fils de la Grandeur (57, 7-27). ... modèle de la remontée de l'Ame (57, 27-58, 13). La Passion assure la libération des âmes (58, 13-59, 19)	
		2. *Les âmes* (59, 19-65, 33). Persécution des gnostiques par les archontes et leurs créatures (59, 19-32). Description des archontes et de leurs créatures (59, 33-61, 27). Assurance du	Le combat est voulu par le Père afin que se révèlent les lutteurs (26, 7-27, 13). L'Ame en exil est dans la misère, mais le Logos lui apporte le salut (27, 14-28, 27). Les adversaires,

---

[13] Pour le texte de l'*AuthLog* cf. J. E. Ménard, *L'Authentikos Logos* (BCNH 2), Québec, 1977.

[14] Pour le texte du *GrSeth*, nous utilisons notre propre traduction faite à partir de l'édition fac-similé du codex VII et de la collation du manuscrit par M. Roberge.

triomphe final (61, 27-62, 7). Tout l'Ancien Testament illustre cet affrontement (62, 7-65, 2). Les adversaires sont insensés (65, 17-33)

comme des pêcheurs, veulent se saisir de l'Ame (28, 27-31, 24)

IV Eschatologie

Le mariage céleste primordial (65, 34-67, 11). ... modèle du salut final (67, 12-68, 25)

L'Ame triomphe (31, 24-32, 28)

Les adversaires sont confondus (68, 25-69, 19). Invitation au repos final (69, 20-70, 10)

... et ses adversaires sont confondus (32, 28-34, 32). L'Ame qui détient le Logos obtient le repos (34, 32-35, 22)

Nous devons maintenant établir la pertinence de l'application de ce plan à nos traités. Pour ce faire, nous allons procéder à une triple vérification au niveau de la rédaction, de l'emploi des pronoms et du vocabulaire.

Au niveau de la rédaction, deux caractéristiques de ces textes justifient notre hypothèse : la reprise des thèmes de l'introduction en conclusion et le rappel des thèmes du début entre les sections II et III.

Dans le *GrSeth*, les thèmes du repos, de l'habitation du Sauveur avec le Père et de l'unité du Sauveur et des siens apparaissent dans la première partie (49, 10-20) et sont repris en conclusion (70, 4-10). Dans l'*AuthLog*, c'est le thème du repos sur lequel s'ouvre le traité (22, 4-7) qui est repris en conclusion (35, 8-21).

Quant à la reprise des éléments des premières parties entre les sections II et III, elle se présente dans le *GrSeth* comme un rappel de l'origine céleste du Sauveur et de la descente de son Ennoia (54, 14-27), alors que dans l'*AuthLog* (25, 26-26, 6), elle prend la forme d'un rappel du temps primordial qui est évoqué au début du texte (22, 7-12).

Ainsi, nos deux traités présentent bien au niveau de la rédaction les mêmes caractéristiques que le *De Anima* et le *Poimandrès*. Dans les traités scolaires sur l'Ame, cette reprise des thèmes de l'introduction ou de la première partie entre les parties II et III correspondait sans doute à une intention pédagogique. Son maintien dans des traités qui n'émanent plus d'un milieu scolaire indique qu'il s'agit bien d'un cadre devenu fixe et réutilisé sans changement.

Au niveau de l'utilisation des pronoms, nous retrouvons sinon les

mêmes variations de pronoms, du moins un parallélisme remarquable
dans l'apparition de ces variations dans le *Poimandrès*, le *Deuxième
Traité du Grand Seth* et l'*Authentikos Logos* :

I	Il (l'Homme)	Je (le Sauveur)	Elle (l'Ame)
II	Il (l'Homme)	Je (le Sauveur)	Elle (l'Ame)
III	Eux—vous (les hommes)	1. Je (le Sauveur)	1. Nous—eux (les Ames)
		2. Nous—eux (les hommes)	2. Elle (l'Ame)
IV	Il (l'Homme)	Nous—eux	Elle (l'Ame)

Ainsi, dans les trois textes, on passe d'un pronom singulier qui renvoie
à un acteur mythique[15] (l'Homme, le Sauveur ou l'Ame) à des pronoms
pluriels qui renvoient à des acteurs réels (les hommes, les gnostiques
ou leurs âmes et leurs adversaires) et dans les trois cas, ce passage
se fait dans la troisième partie des textes.

Au niveau du vocabulaire enfin, on trouve concentrée dans la
troisième partie de nos deux traités gnostiques une série de substantifs
et de verbes qui ont un sens d'affrontement, de combat, alors qu'ils
sont absents des autres parties des mêmes traités. Il est donc clair
que ces divisions que nous avons repérées par comparaison de nos
traités avec d'autres textes de l'époque correspondent bien dans nos
textes à des unités littéraires, au moins pour ce qui concerne la troisième
section.[16]

Cette triple vérification nous permet donc de constater que les
caractéristiques formelles du cadre de composition des traités de
l'Ame se retrouvent dans notre texte et que les divisions de notre plan

---

[15] Nous préparons une analyse de ces acteurs et de leur fonctionnement à l'intérieur
du *GrSeth* envisagé comme récit du point de vue de l'analyse structurale.

[16] En voici la liste pour l'*AuthLog* : ἀγων 26, 11 ; ἀγωνιστής 26, 13 ; ἀντικείμενος
26, 21 ; 30, 6 ; 31, 9 ; βία 29, 31 ; 31, 15 ; ἐνεργεῖν 33, 19 ; κατέχειν 26, 29 ; κράτος
28, 21 ; πολέμιος 28, 14 corr.; ⲁⲙⲁ2ⲧⲉ 28,28 ; 29, 33 ; ⲙⲟⲩⲕ2 29, 2 ; ⲙⲟⲕ2 27, 23 ;
35, 3 ; ⲙⲕⲁ2 ⲛ2ⲏⲧ⸗ 30, 30 ; ⲡⲱⲧ ⲛⲥⲁ- 27, 30 ; 29, 26 ; 31, 20 ; ⲣⲱ2ⲧ 29, 6.7;
30, 20 ; † ⲟⲩⲃⲏ 28, 32 ; † ⲉ2ⲣⲁⲓ 29, 10 ; ⲟⲩⲁⲙ ⲣⲱⲙⲉ 29, 18 ; ⲱⲧⲡ ⲉ2ⲟⲩⲛ 28, 17 ;
ⲱⲁⲭⲉ ⲛⲥⲁ- 27, 8 ; ⲱⲁⲭⲉ (ⲙⲛ-) 26, 14.20.22 ; ⲱⲱⲱⲃⲉ 27, 28 ; 2ⲟⲟⲅⲱ 27, 9 ;
ⲭⲣⲟ ⲉ- 26, 22 ; ⲙⲛⲧⲭⲱⲱⲣⲉ 27, 24 ; ϭⲱⲡⲉ 29, 18.23 ; 30, 9.16.32 ; ϭⲱⲣⲃ 29, 6 ;
30, 7.27 ; et pour le *GrSeth* : ἀντικείμενος 62, 13 ; ἀπειλή 61, 26 ; βία 61, 26 ;
κολάζειν 55, 16 ; 56, 5 ; κόλασις 52, 29 ; πόλεμος 60, 5 ; ⲁⲙⲁ2ⲧⲉ 58, 29 ; 64, 35 ;
66, 9 ; ⲃⲱⲗ ⲉⲃⲟⲗ 54, 35 ; 55, 12 ; 58, 30 ; 59, 16 ; ⲙⲟⲩⲕ2 55, 16 ; ⲙⲗⲟⲟ2 60, 5 ;
ⲙⲟⲥⲧⲉ 58, 5 ; 59, 22.32 ; 60, 33 ; ⲛⲁⲱⲧ 57, 1 ; ⲡⲱⲧ ⲛⲥⲁ- 59, 23.31 ; ⲡⲱⲧ
ⲛⲥⲁⲃⲟⲗ 58, 17 ; † ⲉ2ⲟⲩⲛ ⲉⲭⲛ- 55, 14 ; † 54, 33 ; ⲧⲱⲱⲛ ⲉⲭⲛ- 64, 15 ;
65, 11 ; 2ⲱⲙ ⲉⲭⲛ- 56, 35 ; 2ⲓⲟⲅⲉ ⲛⲥⲁ- 56, 8 ; 2ⲟⲭ2ⲉⲭ 2ⲛ- 58, 23 ; ⲭⲣⲟ 60, 3 ;

correspondent, au niveau du contenu, soit à des changements de pronoms ou d'acteurs, soit à des unités littéraires (thème de la lutte pour la troisième section).

3. LE CADRE DES TRAITES DE L'AME DANS LE GRSETH ET L'AUTHLOG

Ces similitudes formelles entre les deux traités de Nag Hammadi indiquent clairement que leurs rédacteurs ont utilisé une même cadre littéraire. Pourtant, les deux œuvres, à première vue, présentent peu de caractères communs. Comme le souligne Ménard, le genre littéraire de l'*AuthLog* tient à la fois de l'homélie et de l'écrit didactique,[17] ce qui est aussi le cas pour le *GrSeth* sauf que ce dernier se présente en partie comme un discours de révélation. En effet, dans près de la moitié du texte, c'est le Sauveur lui-même qui fait le récit de sa descente à travers les sphères, de sa Passion et de sa remontée au ciel. De plus, l'*AuthLog* ne porte aucune trace de gnose chrétienne[18] alors que le *GrSeth* est manifestement un écrit gnostique chrétien.

Quel est donc le motif qui a amené ces deux rédacteurs à utiliser un même cadre littéraire pour mouler leur enseignement?

Pour répondre à cette question, il faut revenir au *Poimandrès* et aux traités de l'Ame. Au terme de la révélation de l'Anthropos, Hermès se met à prêcher et le thème de sa prédication est le choix de vie (*Corp. Herm.* 1, 27). Cette notion, comme le constate Festugière, constitue l'un des chapitres de la troisième section des traités scolaires sur l'Ame.[19] C'est là le motif qui réunit nos deux traités et qui les apparente aux traités de l'Ame, à ceci près cependant que ce qui était un choix moral entre deux genres de vie chez les philosophes païens[20] devient, aussi bien chez Tertullien et chez l'hermétiste que chez les gnostiques, un choix entre la vie et la mort. "En effet, la mort et la vie s'offrent à chacun; et ce que l'on désire de ces deux choses on le choisira pour soi».[21] Chez le gnostique et l'hermétiste, ce choix se fera grâce à la connaissance. Cette option, pour l'auteur de l'*AuthLog*, est dans le plan du Père qui

> institua ce grand combat en ce monde, désirant que les lutteurs se révèlent et que tous ceux qui combattent abandonnent les choses qui sont venues à

65, 9 ; ⲭⲣⲟ ⲉⲝⲛ- 62, 31 ; 63, 1.8.15.23 ; 64, 27 ; ⲡ ⲭⲟⲉⲓⲥ 64, 30 ; ⲡ ⲭⲁⲝⲉ 62, 18 ; ⲙⲛⲧⲭⲁⲝⲉ 62, 9 ; 67, 35.

[17] J. E. Ménard, *Authentikos Logos*, 2.
[18] Du moins est-ce l'avis de J. E. Ménard, *Authentikos Logos*, 3.
[19] A.-J. Festugière, *La révélation...* 3, 13-18.
[20] A.-J. Festugière, *La révélation...* 3, 98-99.
[21] J. E. Ménard, *Authentikos Logos*, 13.

l'être et qu'ils les méprisent grâce à une connaissance supérieure (et) inaccessible et qu'ils s'empressent vers celui qui est ; quand à ceux qui nous combattent, étant nos adversaires, il (veut que) dans ce combat qu'ils nous livrent nous vainquions leur ingorance par notre connaissance, parce que nous avons connu à l'avance l'Inaccessible d'où nous sommes émanés.[22]

De même dans le *GrSeth*, c'est le choix de vie qui occupe toute la troisième partie, choix qui concerne cette fois, une Eglise et une doctrine. Ceux à qui s'adresse le traité ont à choisir entre l'assemblée des archontes, contrefaçon de l'Assemblée parfaite (60, 25), et la véritable Assemblée, «communauté fraternelle» de tous ceux qui ne «connaissent nulle hostilité ni malice» et qui sont réunis par la connaissance du Sauveur (67, 32-68, 1). Ils doivent choisir entre l'enseignement d'un mortel, les mensonges proférés par les archontes et leurs créatures (60, 21-23), et la Vérité transmise par le Sauveur lui-même (69, 20-25).

C'est ce choix, aussi bien dans l'*AuthLog* et dans le *GrSeth* que dans le *Poimandrès*, qui départage ceux qui sont «saints, bons et purs, miséricordieux et pieux» et ceux qui sont «mauvais, vicieux, envieux, cupides, meurtriers et impies» (*Corp. Herm.* 1, 22-23).[23]

4. CONCLUSION

Notre traité, malgré la diversité des sources qu'il utilise, suit un plan rigoureux, celui des traités de l'Ame qui, à cause de la place qu'il accorde au choix de vie, est bien fait pour servir les intentions polémiques de notre rédacteur.[24] Il faut ici ouvrir une parenthèse pour noter le caractère polyvalent de ce cadre scolaire des traités de l'Ame. Il est utilisé par Tertullien dans une perspective polémique, par l'auteur du *Poimandrès* pour couler un discours de révélation, et le rédacteur de l'*AuthLog* l'utilise dans un écrit didactique. Quand au rédacteur du *GrSeth*, il l'utilise dans un écrit à la fois polémique et didactique, qui se présente en partie comme un discours de révélation. La présence de ce cadre dans le *Corpus Hermeticum*, dans la bibliothèque de Nag Hammadi et chez un théologien chrétien

---

[22] J. E. Ménard, *Authentikos Logos*, 17.

[23] A. D. Nock et A.-J. Festugière, *Hermès Trismégiste* 1, 14.

[24] Cf. K. Koschorke, *Die Polemik der Gnostiker gegen das Kirchliche Christentum unter besonderer Berücksichtigung der Nag Hammadi Traktate «Apokalypse des Petrus» (NHC VII,3) und «Testimonium Veritatis» (NHC IX,3)*, Dissertation, Universität Heidelberg, 1976, 41-46 et J. A. Gibbons, *A Commentary...*, 27 et 41-42.

illustre bien sa large diffusion à une époque où la nature et la
destinée de l'âme étaient une préoccupation universelle.

De plus, le fait que nous retrouvions ce cadre dans deux traités
de la bibliothèque de Nag Hammadi devrait nous inciter à faire porter
nos recherches du côté des procédés de composition des gnostiques
et de la structure littéraire des textes de la bibliothèque copte.

Enfin, il faudrait s'interroger sur les avenues nouvelles que la
découverte de ce cadre de composition ouvre à la recherche pour la
compréhension du *GrSeth*. Nous n'avons pas ici la possibilité de les
explorer, aussi nous contentons-nous d'émettre une hypothèse quant
à une éventuelle forme antérieure du texte. On aura sans doute
remarqué que la première partie de la troisième section du *GrSeth*
n'a pas son pendant dans l'*AuthLog* et qu'elle ne suit pas les variations
de pronoms que nous retrouvons dans le *Poimandrès* et l'*AuthLog*.
Cette section qui concerne le sort du Sauveur ici-bas (54, 27-59, 19)
a peut-être été ajoutée à un texte initial qui ne comprenait pas ou peu
de références à la Passion, pour renforcer l'opposition doctrinale entre
le groupe des gnostiques chrétiens et celui de ses opposants ortho-
doxes. Pourrions-nous aller jusqu'à retracer un état pré ou non-chrétien
du texte ? Nous ne saurions l'affirmer pour le moment. Quoi qu'il
en soit, cette nouvelle hypothèse nécessitera un examen minutieux
de notre traité.

THE BARBELO AEON AS SOPHIA IN
ZOSTRIANOS AND RELATED TRACTATES

BY

JOHN H. SIEBER

THE heavenly world visited by Zostrianos, in the tractate of that name
(CG VIII,*1*), is dominated by the Invisible Spirit as the true god.
Below the Spirit range four aeons: Barbelo, Kalyptos, Protophanes,
and Autogenes. The latter three are in turn identified with the more
philosophical terms of Existence, Mind, and Life. Previous studies
by John Turner and James M. Robinson have demonstrated that this
heavenly world is shared by the tractates *Allogenes* (CG XI,*3*) and
the *Three Steles of Seth* (CG VII,*5*), and that the philosophical triad
is related to Neoplatonic philosophy.[1] In Plotinus's system the cosmos
has three levels: the first is occupied by the One; in the second is the
hypostasis Intellect; the third level comprises the physical or material
world. In our Sethian gnostic documents Spirit represents the One
of Plotinus. His Intellect, which is sometimes tripartite, is represented
by the Barbelo aeons.[2]

The present paper attempts to advance this line of research in two
ways. First, it provides a more detailed analysis of the cosmology in
Zostrianos, using the model suggested by Robinson and Turner and
showing how the Barbelo aeon of *Zostrianos* contains within herself
the other three aeons. Second, it explores the ways in which the role
of this Barbelo aeon may be related to the figure of Sophia who plays
a prominent role in other types of gnostic systems.

---

[1] James M. Robinson, "The Three Steles of Seth and the Gnostics of Plotinus,"
in G. Widengren, ed., *Proceedings of the International Colloquium on Gnosticism* (Leiden:
Brill, 1977) 132-42. John Turner, "The Gnostic Threefold Path to Enlightenment,"
unpublished paper, 1975. Turner's list correctly includes also the *Apocryphon of John*
from codex II, and the *Trimorphic Protennoia* from codex XIII. The *Gospel of the
Egyptians* should be added to this list also. Cf. Hans-Martin Schenke, "Das sethianische
System nach Nag Hammadi Handschriften," *Studia Coptica* (1974) 165-72.

[2] Turner, "Gnostic Path," 6-8, 12-21. See also Pierre Hadot, "La métaphysique
de Porphyre," *Les sources de Plotin* (Fondation Hardt, Entretiens 12; Geneva: Fondation Hardt, 1966) 127-63. Pierre Hadot, "Etre, Vie, Pensée chez Plotin et avant Plotin,"
Les sources de Plotin (Fondation Hardt, Entretiens 5; Geneva: Fondation Hardt,
1966) 159-90. Michael Tardieu, "Les Trois Stèles de Seth," *RSPT* 57 (1973) 545-75.

In the *Three Steles of Seth* and *Allogenes* Barbelo is the name given to the first aeon of the Invisible Spirit. Other epithets ascribed to her include triple-power (thrice-power), first thought, the male-virgin, perfect, shadow of the holy Father. As the first aeon, she is derived from the one Spirit and retains the quality of oneness.[3] Although references to Barbelo are not numerous in the extant text of *Zostrianos*, her position and importance in the cosmos are the same as that reported for the other two tractates. She is regularly called the Virgin Barbelo or the Male-Virgin Barbelo.[4] Two passages near the end of the tractate identify her as the first emanation of the Spirit. In the first she is named as the gnosis of the Spirit (118: 9-13): "when she strengthened the one who knew her, Barbelo the aeon, the knowledge of the Invisible Triple-Power Perfect Spirit, gave [...] to her saying [...]." The second text, which is part of a description of Zostrianos's descent to leave his gnosis for the elect of Seth, occurs in a blessings formula (129: 8-12): "I joined with all of them and blessed the Kalyptos Aeon and the Virgin Barbelo and the Invisible Spirit." Similar passages can be found elsewhere.[5]

The most important characteristic of the Barbelo aeon in *Zostrianos* is that she is the source of the three aeons of the Neoplatonic triad. A key passage occurs early in the account of Zostrianos's ascent (14: 1-6): "He (Ephesech) said, Zostrianos, listen about these [...], for the first [...] origins are three because they appeared from a single origin, the aeon Barbelo." The order of the emanation can be determined both from the accounts of the ascent and descent and from the various liturgical blessings that occur throughout the text.[6] Her first aeon is Kalyptos, or the Hidden One, who is in turn the source of Protophanes, or the First-Appearing One, and Autogenes, or the Self-Begotten One.[7] It is these three who are identified in turn with the philosophical triad from Neoplatonic thought, Kalyptos with Existence, Protophanes with Mind (often also called Blessedness), and Autogenes with Life (15: 4-17):[8]

[3] Robinson, "Three Steles," 132-34.

[4] The meaning of the name Barbelo is not known. See the discussion in Alexander Böhlig and Frederik Wisse, *Nag Hammadi Codices III,2 and IV,2: The Gospel of the Egyptians (The Holy Book of the Invisible Spirit)* (NHS 4; Leiden: Brill, 1975) 40-41.

[5] See also VIII 63: 6-9; 87: 10-16; et al.

[6] A fuller account of this evidence is given in my unpublished paper "What's in a Name? A Study of the Names of Some Heavenly Beings in *Zostrianos* and Related Writings from Nag Hammadi," 1-18.

[7] VIII 20: 5-18.

[8] See also Robinson, "Three Steles," 135-38.

It is the water of Life which belongs to Vitality in which you have now been baptised in the Autogenes. It is the water of Blessedness which belongs to Knowledge in which you will be baptized in the Protophanes. It is the water of Existence which belongs to Divinity and the Hidden One.

This identification of Barbelo as the source of the other three compares favorably with her epithet as "aeon-giver" in the *Three Steles*, where she is portrayed as the one who has become numerable. She is threefold, yet still one.[9] Likewise in *Allogenes* the Triple-Power should probably be understood as a title for Barbelo, for he becomes in turn Kalyptos (XI 45: 31), Protophanes (XI 45: 34-35) and contains Autogenes (XI 46: 10-11).[10]

The fact that Barbelo stands as a collective name for the entire system of aeons represented by the triad permits the individual members of the system also to be labeled as "Barbelos," for example, the Kalyptos Aeon "comes into existence as a Barbelo" (*Zost* 122: 1). It also aids in understanding a fragmentary passage near the center of the codex where Zostrianos calls upon the Lights of the Aeon Barbelo for help in further revelations.[11] These Lights are three in number but do not bear the more familiar aeon names. Only two names are extant: Salamex and Selmen; the name of the third begins Ar[...] and should be completed by two or three letters. These names appear only in *Zostrianos* and ought to be understood as still other names for the triad.[12] One reference places Selmen in apposition to Protophanes (54: 15-21): "The self-controlled glory, the mother [...] the glories, Youel, and the four perfect Lights, the Protophanes of the Great Mind, Selmen and those who are with him." Since Salamex is named first in the references of this section, it should be understood as another designation for Kalyptos.

Because she is the origin of the three aeons, Barbelo is in fact

---

[9] See especially VII 122: 4-18. The entire *Second Stele* is addressed to Barbelo. In it she is specifically identified with Kalyptos (VII 122: 14) and Protophanes (VII 123: 4-5). If the "unconceived" mentioned later in the *Stele* (VII 123: 25-27) refer to the Autogenes aeons of the *First Stele*, the role of Barbelo would be almost exactly the same in this tractate as in *Zostrianos*.

[10] Turner, "Gnostic Path," 6-8, argues that the Triple-Power is a mediating principle between the Spirit and Barbelo in *Allogenes*. On the basis of the identification of the aeons and the philosophical modalities in *Zostrianos*, I would interpret the Triple-Power as one of the epithets for Barbelo.

[11] VIII 62: 11-63: 20.

[12] The terms aeon and light are interchangeable. Cf. VIII 119: 3-12, where Armedon, etc., are called Lights.

the source of the entire cosmos. Each of her three major aeons contains within himself four other aeons together with numerous other celestial beings called glories, powers, angels, and the like.[13] The aeons in Kalyptos are named Harmedon, Diphanes, Malsedon and Solmis.[14] The Protophanes contains Solmis, Akremon, Ambrosios, and a fourth whose name is not extant but who is titled "the blesser."[15] The more familiar names of Harmozel, Oraiael, Daveithe, and Eleleth appear as the titles of the Autogenes aeons.[16]

As the aeon closest to the material world, the Autogenes system is the one responsible for its creation. In order to understand the role of the Sophia myth in *Zostrianos*, then, we must look more closely at the Autogenes. From a Sethian point of view the most important members of Autogenes must have been the heavenly Adam and his son Seth, the father of the chosen race. They are mentioned in conjunction with Autogenes aeons, as the following passage shows (*Zost* 30: 4-14):[17]

> Adam is the perfect man because he is the eye of the Autogenes, an ascending knowledge of his, because the Autogenes is a word of the perfect Mind of the Truth. The son of Adam, Seth, comes to each of the souls, because he is knowledge sufficient for them. Therefore, a living seed came from him.

In the same way, one of the benedictions addressed to all three Barbelo aeons can include also a word of praise for Geradamas. Geradamas,[18] which means "the old Adam," appears to be another name for Adam, as he too is known as the eye of the Autogenes, who is called the Perfect Child here (13: 1-7): "[I] bless the god who is above the great aeons, and the unborn Kalyptos, and the Great Male Protophanes, and that Perfect Child and his eye, Geradamas."

Along with the references to Adam and Seth as members of Autogenes come several very fragmentary references to the name Mirothea and

---

[13] A fuller discussion of each aeon is available in Sieber, "What's in a Name?", 8-11. Cf. Turner, "Gnostic Path," 22-23.

[14] VIII 119: 1-121: 24. Cf. VIII 86: 12-20; 125: 11-16.

[15] VIII 126: 1-21; cf. VIII 54: 19-25. Akremon has a second Light called Zachthos and Yachthos. Ambrosios has Setheus and Antiphantes as Lights. The Lights of the fourth aeon are Seldao and Elenos. The name of the fourth may end in *-genos* (VIII 124: 18), but there is not a stroke above these letters.

[16] VIII 127: 15-128: 6. Cf. VIII 29: 1-15; 51: 17-18. These names also appear in the *Apocryphon of John* (e.g., II 8: 4-20) and the *Gospel of the Egyptians* (e.g., III 51: 17-20).

[17] Cf. VIII 6: 21-28; 51: 14-19.

[18] The name appears as Pigeradamas with a stroke over all letters.

the title "mother."[19] In the *Three Steles of Seth* Mirotheos is used as
one of the designations for Autogenes (VII 119: 11-18): "Thou art
Mirotheas; thou art my Mirotheos. I bless thee as God; I bless thy
divinity. Great is the good Self-Begotten who stood, and the God who
was first to stand." The same figure appears in the *Gospel of the
Egyptians* where she is named as the mother of Adam (IV 60: 30-61:
8-11 and III 49: 1-10):

> Then there came forth at [or from] that place the cloud of the great
> light, the living power, the mother of the holy, incorruptible ones, the great
> power, Mirothoe. And she gave birth to him whose name I name, saying,
> ien ien ea ea ea, three times. For this one, Adamas, is a light which
> radiated from the light; he is the eye of the light.

From these and like references we can infer that Mirothea may also
have appeared in *Zostrianos* as the mother of Adam and as part of the
Autogenes.

One other figure of note, Sophia or Wisdom, appears also among
the members of the Autogenes aeon. Her role in the system is also
somewhat unclear from the extant references in *Zostrianos*. She is not
mentioned at all in *Allogenes*[20] and only, if at all, through the use of
the term "wisdom" in the *Three Steles of Seth*. From a reference in
Epiphanius's "Against the Simonians" we might expect to be able
to equate Sophia with Barbelo, for he writes (*Haer.* 21.2.5): "the
Simonians say that she is Prunicus, but she is called Barbero or Barbelo
by other sects."[21] Since Barbelo is clearly the source of the cosmos,
the first emanation from which all the rest finally proceed, she would
at least to that degree be responsible for the dualism that exists in the
present world and from which Zostrianos's gnosis can save.[22] Nevertheless, the equation of Barbelo and Sophia does not work. The
references to Sophia in *Zostrianos* and the parallels from other documents point us away from a direct identification of Barbelo and Sophia
and towards an understanding which sees Sophia as a part of the
Autogenes system and in that way also a Barbelo.

The longest and clearest passage comes during Zostrianos's initial
ascent through the four aeons of the Autogenes. At each level he is

---

[19] VIII 6: 30; 30: 14.

[20] Cf. Turner, "Gnostic Path," 24.

[21] See also Ireneus, *Haer.* (1.29.1-4). Cf. Hans Jonas, *The Gnostic Religion* (2d ed.;
Boston; Beacon, 1963) 135 n. 5.

[22] For the relationship of Thought to Sophia in Syrian-Egyptian gnosis see Jonas,
Gnostic Religion, 105-108.

baptised in the name or names of the powers of that place. After being baptised for the fourth time and becoming a perfect angel, he asks a set of questions, all of which deal with the origins of the heavenly world through which he has now begun to pass. The answers to his questions form the content of the gnosis which he is passing on to future generations. This question and answer device is used throughout the entire discourse, though the heavenly interlocutors change as he ascends higher and higher. Authrounios, who is called "the ruler of the height," begins his answer to this first set of questions with a brief form of the myth of Sophia and her offspring the creator Archon (9: 16-10: 17):

> But when Sophia looked at these same ones, she produced the darkness, [...] he saw a reflection and with the reflection which he saw in it he created the world. With a reflection of a reflection he worked on the world, and the reflection of the appearance was taken from him. But a place of rest was given to Sophia in exchange for her repentance. Thus there was within her no prior reflection, pure in itself, beforehand.
> After they had already come into being through him, he appeared and worked on the remainder also, for the image of Sophia was [lost] every time because her countenance was deceiving.

After this answer, which is aimed chiefly at explaining the different kinds of souls within men, another revealer by the name of Ephesech, who is called the angel of god, is called upon to give the gnosis concerning the Barbelo aeons. It is who introduces the Life-Existence-Mind material into the gnosis. As a part of his revelation, a second reference to the Sophia story is made (almost in passing) within his commentary on the reasons for the differences in souls (27: 9-12): "Other immortal souls are companions with all these souls because of Sophia who looked down." Thus, the Sophia myth appears in *Zostrianos* primarily as an explanation for gnostic anthropology. In each case this explanation occurs as part of the gnosis concerning the Autogenes aeon.

There is one other section of *Zostrianos* which may contain an allusion to Sophia, though her name does not appear in the extant text.[23] In a very damaged section near the center of the codex we find a fairly long passage dominated by a female personage. The context is clearly that of further descriptions of the three Barbelo aeons as Existence, Life, and Blessedness. It may be that the "she" of this section should be identified directly with Barbelo herself. It is said that she is "the introspection of the preexisting God" (82: 23-83: 1),

---

[23] VIII 76: 17-83: 24.

and that "she was named a Barbelo through Thought" (83 : 7-10). But we also read of her that "she was darkened through the greatness of the [...] of his" (78 : 17-19), that "she became ignorant" (81 : 1), and that something has happened "in order that she may not depart any more and come into being apart from perfection" (81 : 8-10).

Although this last passage can be interpreted as referring to the entire Barbelo aeon, it is much more likely that Sophia was thought of as a Barbelo aeon because she was contained within the lower levels of Autogenes. Since all of the members of the system can be named as "Barbelos" as shown above, Sophia could be called "a Barbelo." The reference to Barbelo as "wisdom" in the *Three Steles of Seth* should be understood as the reverse of that process, Barbelo taking on the aspects of her many parts (VII 123: 15-17): "Salvation has come to us; from thee is salvation. Thou art wisdom, thou knowledge; thou art truthfulness."

The use of the Sophia material in the *Apocryphon of John* supports the above conclusion. Though the *Apocryphon* is an example of Christian Sethian gnosis and is not as closely related to *Zostrianos* as the *Three Steles of Seth* and *Allogenes*, it does share much of the same cosmology, especially for the Autogenes aeon. One passage specifically names Sophia as a lowest aeon of Autogenes (II 8: 16-20): "The fourth aeon was placed on the fourth light, Eleleth. There are three other aeons with him: Perfection, Peace, and Sophia. These are the four lights which stand by the divine Autogenes..." It is this Sophia who a few lines later brings forth from herself alone the creator Archon Ialdabaoth.[24] In spite of the considerable differences between this account and that of *Zostrianos*, their agreement about the names of the four aeon-lights as well as that about Spirit, Barbelo, and Autogenes, indicate that both belong to the same general thought world and that the *Apocryphon* may be used to help understand the cosmology of Zostrianos.[25]

Thus, we conclude that the Barbelo aeon in *Zostrianos* is the name given to the intermediate level of the cosmos. She is a cosmic entity which contains the entire heavenly world apart from the Invisible Spirit. Her aeon constituents are identified with the Neoplatonic triad

---

[24] II 9: 25-10: 19. Sophia is also a part of the Eleleth aeon according to the *Gospel of the Egyptians* (III 56: 22-57: 5).

[25] Cf. Turner, "Gnostic Path," 1-11, and Schenke, "Das sethianische System," 165-67.

of Existence, Mind, and Life. It was through the ignorance and error of her lowest level, the Sophia aeon of the Autogenes, that the material world or nature, the third Neoplatonic level of reality, was brought into existence.

THE HISTORY OF THE TERM GNOSTIKOS

BY

MORTON SMITH

THIS article continues a discussion with Prof. Bianchi which began with my review of the papers of the Messina conference,[1] when I pointed out, inter alia:

1. That the "working hypothesis" proposed by the "final document" of the conference would not work—the "coherent series of characteristics" it tried to find in second-century gnosticism was not coherent; each of its elements was absent from one or more of what are commonly called "the gnostic systems," and some of them contradicted major points of major systems.

2. That Prof. Jonas's attempt, in his paper at the Messina conference, to describe an "ideal type" of gnosticism, was a failure—the resultant miscarriage had few traits that were common to all systems and itself corresponded to none.

3. That none of the conference's speakers who had attempted to define gnosticism had thought of asking which groups actually called themselves "gnostics" or were called so by their neighbors.

To these objections Prof. Bianchi replied in his paper at the Stockholm conference.[2] First he mixed up my criticisms of Jonas's paper with my remarks on the conference's document, and took me to task for accusing the conference of trying to establish an "ideal type" of gnosticism[3] (which I had not done), then he reiterated his notion of trying "d'établir une série cohérente (d'une cohérence objective) de traits qui soit indubitablement gnostique" (ibid.)—this in spite of the

---

[1] In *JBL* 89 (1970) 82 ff.

[2] U. Bianchi, "A propos de quelques discussions récentes sur la terminologie, la définition et la méthode de l'étude du gnosticisme," *Proceedings of the International Colloquium on Gnosticism, Stockholm, Aug. 20-25, 1973* (G. Widengren and D. Hellholm, eds.; Kungl. Vitterhets Historie och Antikvitets Akademiens, *Handlingar*, Filol.-Filos. Ser. 17; Stockholm, 1977) 16 ff.

[3] Ibid., 18. Jonas, whose paper I had criticized for this attempt, not only made it, but dogmatically declared "the 'ideal type' construct" a thing "which the historian, at least for heuristic purposes, cannot do without"—an interesting specimen of unusually pure poppycock: H. Jonas, "Delimitation of the Gnostic Phenomenon—Typological and Historical," in *The Origins of Gnosticism, Colloquium of Messina* (ed. U. Bianchi; Leiden, 1967) 90.

fact that not only I but also Prof. Drijvers had pointed out that the elements of his "coherent series" did not cohere, but were found in different "systems" most of which lacked or even contradicted one or more of them.[4]

To meet these criticisms he fell back on the claim that if even one of his proposed traits—for example, the creation of the world as the consequence of a divine *crise*—was found "dans les contextes respectifs" (by which I suppose he means, "in several systems commonly called 'gnostic'") it would necessarily be "une idée typiquement gnostique."[5] Hence, I suppose, he thought we could collect a set of the typical ideas of "gnosticism."

However, this notion overlooks the problem indicated by my third objection, that none of the writers of the Messina conference had considered the question, "Which groups in antiquity did call themselves 'gnostics' or were so called by their neighbors?" Here I may have led Prof. Bianchi into error. I pointed out that if ancient usage had been considered, "Someone might have noticed that the most insistently self-styled 'gnostic' whose works have come down to us is Clement of Alexandria. As things were, orthodox Christian gnosticism was wholly ignored."[6] By "orthodox Christian gnosticism" I meant, of course, that gnosticism which eventually, thanks to the victory of the "catholic" Christians, came to be thought "orthodox." But Prof. Bianchi commented, "Il nous semble que cette phrase contienne la source de confusions remarquables, car elle juxtapose dans une même proposition herméneutique [whatever that means] les groupes qui s'appelaient 'gnostiques', comme dénomination d'une 'secte', et l'appellation de 'gnostique', voire de 'vrai gnostique' que Clément s'attribue dans le contexte d'une école, mieux dans le contexte de la révendication des profondités (et de l'orthodoxie) d'une théologie."[7]

For my part, I think Prof. Bianchi's comment not the source, but the result of profound misunderstandings, viz., the notions: (1) that the gnostic groups considered themselves "sects" (in the modern sense, viz., as opposed to the Church, which I take to be the sense Prof. Bianchi had in mind); (2) that none of the gnostic groups could have thought themselves schools within the Church; and (3) that their use of

---

[4] Drijvers's criticisms are cited by Bianchi, "Quelques discussions," 21.

[5] Ibid., 18.

[6] *JBL* 89 (1970) 83.

[7] "Quelques discussions," 20 f.

gnostikos did not indicate the claim to a profound and orthodox theology. Yet worse is (4) the notion that words must have had in antiquity, as *distinct* meanings, the different senses assigned to them by modern dictionaries. (Sometimes they did, but more often they had one meaning which the ancients perceived as appropriate for matters we feel it necessary to describe by various terms.) Worst of all is (5) the notion that to investigate the ancient usage of a word will be a "source of remarkable confusions" if it reveals that the usage does not accord with modern terminology. Here the problem, for Prof. Bianchi, becomes acute because he is trying to find the "idées typiquement gnostiques" of "les systèmes du IIe siècle que tout le monde s'accorde à dénommer gnostiques."[8] But which world? Not, it seems, the ancient world of the gnostics themselves, but rather the *beau monde* of contemporary scholarship. To paraphrase Louis XIV, "Le monde, c'est nous." By our academic prerogative, without considering ancient usage, we recognize certain schools as "gnostic"; hence the ideas held by those schools become "typically gnostic"; hence "gnosticism" will be defined; and the resultant definition of "gnosticism" will prove the "gnostic" character of these schools. Since Plato said "the most perfect of forms" was that most completely circular (*Ti.* 33b), we may describe this research program as Platonically perfect.

I propose, however, to break the magic circle and descend from the neatly constructed pleroma of Platonic ideas into the chaos of material, historical facts. Like Sophia, I want to know:

1. What was the original meaning of *gnostikos*, and how did it develop, down to early Christian times?

2. What Christians, individually or in groups, claimed to be *gnostikoi*, and when, and why?

3. What, if any, non-Christians made the same claim, and when, and why?

4. What Christians and non-Christians came to use the word as a term of abuse, and when, and why, and for whom?

In proposing these questions I do not have the answers up my sleeves. All will require long research; for some, no doubt, the lack of evidence will prevent us from reaching answers better than conjectural. However, I have made some preliminary investigations with the indices verborum available to me, and the results have surprised me. They are as follows.

Gnostikos was not a common word. Perhaps it was coined by Plato.

---

[8] Ibid., 18 f.

At all events, in preserved material it seems to have been first used by Plato[9] in the *Politicus* 258e-267a, where the *gnostike techne*—the art of knowing—is opposed to the *praktike*, and where the ideal politician is defined as the master of the gnostic art; if such a being were to appear he would be a god come down to rule mankind. From Plato's time to the second century A.D. I have found *gnostikos* used only by Aristotle,[10] the Aristotelian Strato of Lampsacus,[11] a series "Pythagoreans" (Archytas,[12] Clinias,[13] Ocellus Lucanus,[14] and perhaps Ecphantus[15]), Philo Judaeus,[16] Plutarch (only in the *Moralia*),[17] and Pseudo-Plutarch.[18] The meanings are, roughly, "leading to knowledge,

[9] Its appearance in Psellus's description of Anaxagoras's teachings (*De omnifaria doctrina*, ed. Westerink, 46, end) is probably due to Psellus's rephrasing. This seems to have been the opinion of Diels, who put the description in the *testimonia*, not in the *fragmenta*: *Vorsokr.*, 7th ed., 2. 30 (101a).

[10] *A.Po.*, end (100a11): general concepts, being *hexeis* (states/conditions) arise from experience, not from other, more "gnostic" *hexeis*. Ross translates "more cognitive."

[11] On the origin of dreams: they arise in the irrational element of the mind, which becomes more capable of sensation in sleep and is therefore moved by the "gnostic" (cognitive) element. Quoted as Strato's by Pseudo-Plutarch, *De placitis philosophorum* (*Moralia* 904, end). Diels, *Doxographi Graeci* 416, thinks this drawn from Aëtius, *Placita philosophorum*, of the first or second century A.D.

[12] *Peri nou*, Stobaeus, *Anth.* 1.48.6, end (Wachsmuth-Hense, p. 317) = Iamblichus, *Comm. Math.* 8 (Festa, p. 36): like is always "gnostic" (capable of the knowledge) of like, etc. *Peri andros agathou*, Stobaeus, *Anth.* 3.3.65 (Wachs.-He., 218): prudence arises from two practices, one, that to acquire a scientific and "gnostic" *hexis*, the other, to see much and have much practical experience. *On the Categories*, ed. Thesleff, *Pythagorean Texts*, p. 32: science, beginning with finite matters, becomes "gnostic" (capable of knowing) infinite ones.

[13] Stobaeus, *Anth.* 3.1.75 (Wachs.-He., 31): those who have the noetic and "gnostic" element of *arete* are called subtle (*deinoi*) and intelligent.

[14] *De universi natura* 25, end (ed. Harder, p. 17 = Thesleff, p. 131): touch is "gnostic" and "critical" (that by which we know and judge) of the distinguishing qualities of physical objects (heat, cold, etc.).

[15] L. Delatte, *Les traités de la royauté d'Ecphante, Diotogène et Sthénidas* (*Bibliothèque de la Faculté de Philosophie ... de l'U. de Liège* 97; Liège, 1942) 183 f., on Ecphantus, *Peri basileias*, in Stobaeus, *Anth.* 4.7.64 (Wachs.-He., 272, 15), where the text is corrupt. Many conjectures have been proposed. Delatte suggested *gnostikon* in his notes (*loc. cit.*), but printed *ennoetikon* in his text (p. 28).

[16] *Op.* 154, end, according to all MSS except M (Laurentianus plut. X cod. 20), which reads *horistikou*. Wendland needlessly conjectured *gnoristikou*, but *gnostikou* makes perfect sense: "By 'the ⟨power⟩ capable of knowing good and evil ⟨things' Genesis refers to⟩ prudence."

[17] *Gryllus* 7 (990a): taste occurs in the tongue when the juices of food are mingled with the "gnostic" (organ, i.e., that capable of discerning them). *An. proc.* 23 (1023e): the souls of mortals have a power "gnostic" (capable of the knowledge) of what is sensibly perceptible.

[18] For *De placitis* (904f.) see above, note 11, on Strato. Again in *De musica* 33 (1142f): each science studies some special object, thus harmonics is "gnostic" (takes cognizance) of the relations of sounds.

resulting in knowledge, capable of knowing, cognizant of." The term describes types of study, powers or elements of the personality, and thence, if Delatte's conjecture for Ecphantus's text is correct, an individual possessed of such powers. As in Plato (and the coincidence strengthens Delatte's case) this individual would be the ideal king, the only man capable of knowing God, who would therefore act as the mediator between God and man; he would be, in effect, the *nous* of his subjects, in whom he would restore their lost contact with the heavenly world from which he came.[19]

This picture of the usage is derived from incomplete indices verborum; it will have to be tested by the *Thesaurus*. If it prove correct, some conclusions will follow.

First: the claim to be a *gnostikos* must be a claim to be a figure defined by the Platonic-Pythagorean philosophic tradition. The term is not Stoic; the only uses in *Stoicorum Veterum Fragmenta* occur in passages cited from Clement of Alexandria; Epictetus and Marcus Aurelius did not use it.[20] I have not found it in Greco-Roman religious texts or inscriptions, nor in texts marginal to the official religion (Orphica, Hermetica,[21] magical texts). It was not common in Judaism: it is not in the Septuagint, the Greek pseudepigrapha to which I have indices,[22] the *Corpus Papyrorum Iudaicarum*,[23] or Frey, *Corpus Inscriptionum Iudaicarum* 1; the one (dubious) usage in Philo (above, n. 16) is probably Platonic. Its rarity in Greek literature is surpassed by its apparently total absence from Greek popular usage.[24] Consequently I think we may conclude that the *gnostikoi* probably got their claim to be *gnostikoi* from the Platonic-Pythagorean tradition. This does not settle the question whence they got their doctrines, but it does

---

[19] Delatte, *Traités*, 183 f., where the similarity of this doctrine to "gnosticism" is noticed.

[20] At least, it was not one of those words in Marcus's text that Farquharson saw fit to index.

[21] The reference in the index graecitatis of Scott's *Hermetica* (4. 156) is to an attack on heretics attributed to Anthimus of Nicomedia, about 300 A.D.

[22] *Greek Enoch, Testaments of the Twelve Patriarchs, Joseph and Asenath, Testament of Solomon, Prophetarum Vitae, Greek Apocalypse of Baruch, Sibylline Oracles III, Letter of Aristeas.* It does not occur in any of the brief indices made by James for the texts he published.

[23] The relevant indices are headed "Technical Terms," but are fairly full.

[24] It is not in the indices to *Inscriptiones Graecae, Supplementum Epigraphicum Graecum, Sylloge Inscriptionum Graecarum, Orientis Graeci Inscriptiones Selectae*, Robert's *Bulletin Epigraphique*, the dictionaries of the papyri by Preisigke and Kiessling, the *Sammelbuch griechischer Urkunden aus Ägypten*.

establish a strong presumption in favor of Platonic and Pythagorean origins.

Second: the claim to be a *gnostikos* was rather *to be capable of knowing* than to possess particular items of information. The second meaning is not excluded, but, if the word were used in its customary sense, it would be at best subordinate. Thus being gnostic would seem to have been the essential claim, and having gnosis merely a consequence. However, if gnosis was the means and sine qua non for salvation, its importance in the thought of a group pursuing salvation may have become so great as to cause a shift in the meaning of *gnostikos*.

So much for the term; now when, how, and why did Christians come to use it? It is not in the New Testament, Apostolic Fathers, or second-century Apologists. As far as I know, the first record of Christian usage is the report of Celsus that among the many different sorts of Christians there are some who call themselves "gnostics."[25] These Celsus distinguishes from the Catholics and also from the Sibyllistai, Simonians, Marcellians who follow Marcellina, Harpocratians who follow Salome, others who follow Mariamme, others Martha, others Marcion, and yet other groups whom Origen identifies, on the basis of characteristics given by Celsus, as Valentinians and Ebionites. Clearly if one group can be distinguished as "those who call themselves 'gnostics' from all these others, then none of the other groups called itself, as a group, "gnostics," and their members did not, as individuals, make the claim in such a striking fashion that their groups could be distinguished by this trait. However, some individuals in these other groups may have claimed to be gnostics; Clement, a Catholic, did. Against Prof. Bianchi, I see no reason to suppose that the claim made by a group or all its members must have been essentially different from that made by an isolated individual. Finally, Celsus may have been misinformed, confused, dishonest, or all three, and may have reported different characteristics of Christians in such a way as to suggest that each one defined a different group; his objective, after all, was to show up Christian divisions and self-contradictions. Some of the characteristics he listed may have been shared by several groups; etc. Granting such possibilities, we must also grant that Celsus's report does seem, in the main, probably true. We should expect that by his time some Christian groups were beginning to have philosophic pretensions, and one may have distinguished itself

---

[25] Origen, *Cels.* 5.61f.

by claiming to be *the gnostikoi*—the group of those able to know the things that mattered.

In fact our next evidence from Alexandria shows approximately this state of affairs. Clement himself claims to be a gnostic and his account of the meaning of the term is our fullest explanation of why an early Christian should have claimed it. To this one of my questions the answer is therefore so extensive that I pass over it, with the hope that much of the answer will appear in the paper by Prof. Méhat (published in volume 1 of these proceedings). Besides Clement, other Christians claimed the term for other reasons and understood it to have other meanings. Clement knows some of these who seem to be members of his own church.[26] He is also given to attacking all "self-loving and notoriety-loving heresies" as "not having learned or received tradition correctly, but having acquired a false opinion of ⟨their own⟩ knowledge (*gnosis*)"—GCS 3.64.21 ff. Such attacks do not indicate that all these heretics were, or claimed to be, "gnostics" (2.35.5-15; 138.15 ff.). He does know one group, the followers of Prodicus, whom he stigmatizes as "falsely calling themselves gnostics" (2.209.30; cf. 3.31. 2 ff.), and he distinguishes them clearly from other groups, such as the Antitactites, who apparently made no such claim (2.208-211). In his many attacks on the Carpocratians he never calls them "gnostics" nor says directly that they claimed to be so, but he comes very near it when he says that Epiphanes, the son of Carpocrates, "was taught by his father the ⟨subjects proper to a⟩ liberal education and also the ⟨teachings⟩ of Plato, and himself was the first to teach the monadic gnosis, and from him ⟨comes⟩ the heresy of the Carpocratians" (2. 197.25 ff.). At the end of book 3 of the *Stromateis*, in which Clement reviewed the whole range of heresies (many certainly not "gnostic") and particularly the libertine sects, he concluded with a general denunciation of those "who teach others to give up self-restraint for dissolute living" and "choose for themselves, under the false name of knowledge [*gnosis*], the road into outer darkness" (2.246.26 ff.). It is hard to decide here whether to write "knowledge" or "gnosis," but probably "knowledge" is right, since I know of no other passage in which Clement even seems to refer to all the libertine groups as "gnostics," and I cannot believe he would have passed over the claim in silence if most of them had made it. His specification of the followers of Prodicus, and

---

[26] Clemens Alexandrinus, ed. O. Stählin and L. Früchtel (3 vols.; 2d-3d eds.; GCS; Leipzig, 1936-70). I cite GCS vol., page, and line. Here 1.104.23 ff.; 2.298.23 ff. (perhaps).

perhaps of the Carpocratians, would be surprising if the claim were general.

The specification of Prodicus only is found also in Tertullian. In his *Scorpiace* he begins with the observation that, as scorpions come out in summer, so when faith grows fervid "tunc Gnostici erumpunt, tunc Valentiniani proserpunt" (1.5). This looks like a distinction of Gnostics from Valentinians; it is proved to be so by the end of the tractate, where he comes back to the antithesis, but makes the contrast between Prodicus and Valentinus (15.6). So the "Gnostici" of the beginning are presumably the followers of Prodicus, as Clement said they were. Elsewhere Tertullian says little of them. In *De praescriptione haereticorum* he attacks Hermogenes, Phygelus, Philetus, Hymenaeus, Apelles, Valentinus, Marcion, Ebion (whom he thinks a heresiarch), Simon, Nigidius ("nescio qui"), the Nicolaitans and the Cainites, but never mentions gnostics. Similarly Hippolytus refers to only a few groups as "calling themselves gnostics"—the Naassenes/Ophites and their subspecies, the followers of Justin.[27] The presumption, again, is that if these groups could be distinguished by the fact that they claimed to be gnostics, the other groups, at least as groups, did not make this claim. Accordingly Lampe's *Patristic Greek Lexicon* (the first Greek lexicon I know to give even a roughly correct account of the Christian use of *gnostikos*) states that "modern use of the term for a variety of second-century dualistic heresies is probably of eighteenth-century origin." (Here "dualistic" shows the continuing influence of Jonas's early errors; contrast Clement's reference to "the monadic gnosis," cited above. As an authority on gnosticism, Clement has one great advantage over Jonas—he knew what he was talking about.)

Not all the blame, however, can be put on eighteenth-century scholars. They were following Irenaeus, in whose works we find a change of terminology. He says Valentinus "was the first who from the so-called gnostic heresy reshaped the principles into a teaching of his own with a peculiar character."[28] This seems an attempt to suggest that the Valentinians were gnostics, without quite saying so.

---

[27] *Haer.* 5.2; 5.6.4; 5.8.1.29; 5.11.1; 5.23.3. His statement in 7.36.2ff. that the different sorts of gnostics were (all?) misled by the Nicholas of Rev 2:6 is presumably false. N. was a notorious libertine, so this is a reference of libertine sects to a common ancestor. However, it does indicate that the "gnostics" were seen as a single set of heretics, distinguished sharply from the many others. Hippolytus accuses Theodotus of Byzantium (7.35; 10.23) and Elchasai (9.4) of borrowing ideas from the gnostics, but not of being gnostics themselves, still less of claiming to be so.

[28] Ed. Harvey, 1.5.1; I follow the Greek here, as Harvey advises.

A little later (1.5.3) he mentions other Valentinians who claim that there are powers prior to Bythos and Sige, and pretend to knew them, "in order that they may seem more fully initiated than the full initiates and more gnostic than the gnostics." Again the implication that the Valentinians are gnostics, even when he distinguishes them from the gnostics! Similar hints abound in his description of Marcus's doctrines (1.7.5 f.; 8.13; 14.3 f.). Next he says Simon Magus's followers were the source of "pseudonymous gnosis" (1.16.3) and the role of knowledge and knowing is heavily emphasized in the account of Basilides' teaching (1.19.2 ff.). It is bluntly said that the Carpocratians "call themselves gnostics" (1.20.4), although it is also said that they teach, "We are saved by faith and love, all else is indifferent" (20.3) —an odd teaching for gnostics. Next "all who in whatever way adulterate the truth and harm the image of the Church are disciples and successors of Simon the Samaritan magician, *although they do not admit the name of their teacher*" (1.25.2, my italics; cf. 1.15, end). Here the polemic nature of these charges is clear. We go on to learn that the Barbelognostics, too, arose from Simon (1.27.1 ff.). The Cainites say only Judas, of all the disciples, had the true gnosis (1.28.9). Finally Irenaeus explains, "It has been necessary to prove clearly that those who come from Valentinus ⟨are derived⟩ from such mothers, fathers, and ancestors [i.e., from Simon, the Carpocratians and the Barbelognostics] as their own teachings and rules show them ⟨to be⟩" (1.29). Clear polemic supported by inferential argument, presumably to contradict denials by the parties attacked. More of the same recurs at the beginning of book 2: we have exposed Simon and "the multitude of those gnostics who descended from him" (including the Valentinians and the Marcosians) and "have demonstrated that all heretics deriving their origin from Simon have introduced impious and irreligious teachings."

To understand such stuff we should imagine what the history of our own time would look like, fifteen hundred years from now, if the Communists should win their present struggle for control of the world. The surviving documents would then report that, in spite of the outcome of the Second World War, western Europe and the Americas, except for Cuba, continued to be ruled by "Fascists" and "Nazis" throughout the rest of the twentieth century. Scholars of the fourth millennium would be divided between those who held that "Fascists" and "Nazis" were identical, and those who tried in various ways to distinguish them. Both sides would search the surviving works of the holy Fathers of the Party for evidence from which they could construct an "ideal type" of Fascism, or put together a set of "typical Nazi ideas" from the fragments quoted by Communist writers from Hitler, Mussolini, Churchill, Truman, de Gaulle, Nixon, Golda Meir, and other figures "que tout le monde s'accorde à dénommer" Nazi.

By analogy, I think it fairly easy to see what Saint Irenaeus did. With characteristic concern for veracity, he picked a few outstandingly unpopular heretics—Simon Magus and the notoriously libertine "gnostics" and Carpocratians—and he set out to represent all other heretics as descendants and secret followers of these loathsome ancestors. Since he had to argue by inference and innuendo, we can be fairly sure his arguments were false. However, they were popular, and he was a bishop and became a martyr and a hero of the party that ultimately won. Later Christian usage is shaped by his polemic, though not entirely. In the East, for instance, the influence of Clement continued to be felt and "gnostic" remained a term of praise to which writers of the victorious "catholic" party continued to lay claim. In polemics against the sects attacked by Irenaeus, however, his usage was followed. We may conjecture that it was particularly successful at Rome, where he had worked.

Perhaps its success there decided Porphyry, when editing Plotinus's tractates, to make up the title, "Against the Gnostics" for one that had been written to refute some schismatic Platonists. On the other hand, it is possible and not unlikely that these groups may have called themselves "gnostics." As we have seen, the term comes from the Platonic tradition and some small schools claiming it had been active in Alexandria for half a century. That Roman Platonists should imitate Alexandrian ones after such an interval is not surprising. Porphyry describes Plotinus's opponents as "members of the sects derived from the old philosophy, the followers of Adelphius and Aquilinus, who had got hold of many works of Alexander the Libyan and Philocomus and Demonstratus and Lydus and, trotting out apocalypses of Zoroaster and Zostrianus and Nicotheus and Allogenes and Messus and suchlike others, were deceiving many and themselves deceived, ⟨pretending that Plato had not penetrated into the depth of noetic being."[29] These Porphyry distinguishes from the "many Christians of many sorts" who also buzzed about Plotinus. Whether Plotinus's

---

[29] *Plot.* 16.

refutation (*Enn.* 2.9) was intended to refute the Christians, too, is not clear, either from its text or from Porphyry's report. Two books with titles Porphyry mentions—*Zostrianos* (perhaps subtitled "Zoroaster"), and *Allogenes* (to Messus)—have turned up at Nag Hammadi (VIII,*1* and XI,*3*). Neither contains any Christian trait, and of course appearance at Nag Hammadi does not prove them Christian. Portions of Plato's *Republic* and the Hermetic *Asclepius* were also included in the Nag Hammadi library. Nor does the use of these books by Porphyry's groups prove that those groups wrote them; in fact, Porphyry speaks as if they had "got hold of" them from others. Thus even if Porphyry's groups called themselves "gnostics" it would not be certain that the authors of these books did so; on the other hand, if the books were known to be gnostic, the groups' use of them may have led Porphyry to extend the term to the users. Of such various possible relations we simply do not know which actually pertained.

At least it is not improbable that we should add the followers of Adelphius and Aquilinus to those of Prodicus and Carpocrates and the Naassenes/Ophites in the list of those ancients who actually claimed to be "gnostics." They show us that the claim was not limited to Christians, and they confirm our conclusion that it was primarily a phenomenon of later Platonism. It seems to have been made by a few small circles characterized by wild proliferation of Platonic mythology; also those mentioned by the Christian heresiologists had practices so scandalous that Irenaeus chose to make them and Simon Magus the spiritual ancestors of the many Christian schools he wished to discredit. (The opponents of Plotinus, too, practiced magic—2.9.14.) This is not to say that the true gnostics may not have had many traits in common with the victims of Irenaeus's attack. True Nazis, Fascists and Communists held many opinions also held by persons to whom those terms are unjustly applied, but in talking of them most educated people know enough to distinguish between ideas generally current and those peculiar to these particular parties. In talking of gnostics we should try to achieve similar precision. When lack of information makes precision impossible, we should at least try not to know too much.

I am sure that this recommendation will not be widely followed. Not only is it psychologically repulsive, but it neglects a much neglected subject—the influence of modern economics on ancient history. The term "gnosticism" has become in effect a brand name with a secure market. "Gnosticism" is salable, therefore it will continue to be produced. Indeed, our lack of information about true, ancient gnosticism will probably prove a great advantage to manufacturers of the modern, synthetic substitute. They need no longer be distracted by consideration of ancient data, since those prove to be mostly unreliable. Now they can turn without restraint to the important question, the philo-sophic definition of the concept. As gnostics themselves, they can follow the gnostic saviour, escape from the lower world of historical facts, and ascend to the pleroma of perfect words that emanate forever from the primaeval void.

AHER: A GNOSTIC

BY

GEDALIAHU G. STROUMSA

A̲ḤER is one of the four rabbis who ventured into "paradise," according
to the well-known—yet still hardly clear—story told in *t. Ḥag.* 2.3
and in parallel passages.[1] As the result of his unsuccessful incursion,
he "cut down the saplings" (קצץ בנטיעות). Aḥer is in fact the byname
of Elisha' ben Abuya, a famous Palestinian Tanna from the early
second century. He was called Aḥer (a word rendered by Jastrow,
for instance, as "another, the other, stranger ...")[2] after his alleged
apostasy.

Much has already been written on this topic, and I would not have
dared to enter the "pardes" of talmudic scholarship had I not stumbled
upon one fact that has hitherto escaped the sagacity of scholars.[3] I shall
here offer a new interpretation for the name Aḥer, as well as some
indication of the possible nature of Elisha''s apostasy. In addition
I shall show that the same use of the term *aḥer* is found in Rabbinic
literature in regard to at least one other figure.

Early Palestinian sources are quite parsimonious in their account
of the nature of Elisha''s heresy. What we have are rather descriptions
of the horrible deeds which the heretic is said to have performed.
He is said to have been found of killing promising students of the Torah,
or to have tried to persuade them (during or in the aftermath of
the Hadrianic persecution) to abandon their study.[4]

---

[1] In Saul Liebermann, ed., *Tosepta kipshutah, Mo'ed, Ḥag.* 2, p. 381, as well as
y. Ḥag. 2.1, 77b and *b. Ḥag.* 14b. My warm thanks to go to Rabbi W.G. Braude, who
reviewed the Rabbinic texts with me, and to Profs. A. Altmann and J. Strugnell, for
their many valuable suggestions.

[2] Marcus Jastrow, *A Dictionary of the Targumim, the Talmud Babli and Yerushalmi,
and the Midrashic Literature,* 1 (New York: Putnam, 1895) 41.

[3] For bibliography on Elisha', see Shmuel Safrai's article "Elisha ben Avuyah,"
EncJud 6, 670, as well as Henry A. Fischel, *Rabbinic Literature and Greco-Roman
Philosophy: A Study of Epicurea and Rhetorica in Early Midrashic Writings* (SPB;
Leiden: Brill, 1973) 112 nn. 93, 94.

[4] *y. Ḥag.* 2.1, 77b. Other sources interpret this killing as having been done through
the means of magical incantations: *Song of Songs Rabbah,* on 1:4; see *Qorban ha'Edah*
on *y. Ḥag.* 2.6.

What led Elisha' to apostasy was the discovery of the injustice of the human condition. Elisha' once saw a man die while accomplishing a commandment of the Torah (stated in Deut 22:6-7), while another man, who disregarded the same commandment, lived. Elisha' then supposedly exclaimed, "Where is the 'good' of this one, his 'length of days'?"[5]

Similarly, the vision of the still bloody tongue of a martyred sage in the mouth of a dog made him cry in revolt, "Are these the wages of Torah [learning]?"[6]

As if apostasy on the part of a Tanna were so incomprehensible as to require a supernatural explanation, the Jerusalem Talmud gives two additional explanations of Elisha''s heresy.[7] According to one, Elisha''s father had vowed, when the child was circumcised, to dedicate him to the study of Torah, but had done so for the sake of honor, and not out of a pure heart. According to the other, his mother is said to have walked in front of a pagan temple when she was pregnant with Elisha', and to have inhaled its venomous incense.

We are thus provided with a variety of statements; it seems that the historical traditions had been blurred and surrounded with legendary material before the redaction of the Jerusalem Talmud.

The Babylonian tradition is slightly more prolix. The Babylonian Talmud tells us that Elisha' once saw Meṭaṭron seated in heaven, writing down the merits of Israel. He was thus brought to believe that there were two powers in heaven.[8]

This passage of the Talmud is developed, a few centuries later, by the Babylonian R. Hai Gaon: "Aḥer thought that there are two powers, like the Magi, who speak about Ohrmuz and Ahriman, the source of good and the source of evil, the abode of light and the abode of darkness."[9]

---

[5] y. Ḥag. 2.1, 77b.

[6] Ibid. The sage is R. Yehuda the Baker. In the parallel passage of b. Qidd. 39b, it is Ḥuspit the Interpreter whose tongue is dragged around by a pig.

[7] Ibid.

[8] b. Ḥag. 15a. See Maimonides' Commentary on the Mishna Sanhedrin 10.3 (ed. Kapaḥ, 141). Maimonides emphasizes the polytheistic implications of Elisha''s words. On the important question of the "two powers" (רשויות), see now A. F. Segal, Two Powers in Heaven: Early Rabbinic Reports about Christianity and Gnosticism (SJLA 25; Leiden: Brill, 1977). From his standpoint, Segal deals with the Talmud's denunciation of Aḥer's belief in two powers (60-63). Segal sees the Talmudic story as an "etiology of heresy," and adds, "Aher functions as the heretic par excellence, as Simon Magus does in Christian antiheresiological [sic] tracts" (62). Segal's study does not investigate Elisha''s byname.

[9] Oṣar haGeonim (ed. B. M. Levin; Jerusalem: Hebrew University, 1932) 4 (on Ḥagiga), 15.

The granting of the byname Aḥer to Elisha´, and its meaning, is
also explained in various ways by the Rabbinic tradition. One (geonic)
source calls him Aḥor, i.e., "backward," since he turned away (from
· the Torah),[10] while the *Tosafot*, basing themselves on Job 42:12,
"And God blessed the end (*aharyt*) of Job more than his beginning,"
interpret the name Aḥer as stemming from the alleged repentance
of Elisha´ ben Abuya on his deathbed.[11]

Modern scholars, in their turn, have also attempted to solve the riddle
of Elisha´'s apostasy and of his byname. Grätz was the first to claim
that Elisha´ had become a Gnostic.[12] In this he was followed by
Friedländer.[13] Bacher, who cites the texts about the teachings of
Elisha´,[14] does not commit himself on the problem of his byname,
while Ginzberg, with rather weak arguments, tries to prove that
Elisha´ had become a Sadducee.[15]

Ginzberg denies any historical value to the statement of *b. Ḥag.* 15a
about Elisha´'s belief in "two powers," on the grounds that the figure
of Meṭaṭron was unknown in second-century Palestine. Even if this
were the case,[16] it could also be that an early tradition about the nature

---

[10] *Sefer haMafteaḥ*, fragments ed. S. Abramson, *Tarbiz* 26 (1956) 61 and n. 6.
Cf. Liebermann, *Tosepta kipshutah*, commentary on *Ḥagiga*, 1289 n. 16. Cf. Henoch
Yalon, "Midrashot u-Miqra'ot," *Leshonenu* 29 (1964) 215, who quotes *Oṣar haGeonim*,
4. 13 n. 3, and *Sefer haMafteaḥ*, ed. J. N. Epstein, *Tarbiz* 2 (1930) 11. These two
fragments attest the same tradition.
[11] On *b. Ḥag.* 14a. (Job 42:12 is already quoted in *y. Ḥag.* 2.1, 77b.)
[12] Hirsch (Heinrich) Grätz, *Gnostizismus und Judenthum* (Krotoschin: Monasch, 1846)
62-71. Without completely committing himself, Grätz proposed to see a connection
between some of the stories about Elisha´ and the antinomian tenets of Carpocratian
Gnosticism.
[13] Israel Friedländer, *Der vorchristliche jüdische Gnostizismus* (Göttingen: Vandenhoeck & Ruprecht, 1898) 101-103. For him Aḥer, like other Gnostic Jews of the late
first and early second century, belonged to the sect of the Ophites (100); the accusation
that he "cut the saplings" indicated antinomianism (102).
[14] Wilhelm Bacher, *Die Agada der Tannaiten*, 1 (Strassburg: Trübner, 1884) 432-436.
[15] "Elisha ben Abuyah," *Jewish Encyclopedia* 5. 138-139. Ginzberg says, for instance,
that had Elisha´ been a "Min" and not a Sadducee R. Meir's constant friendship to
him would not have been possible. But is this friendship more understandable when
extended to an informer in times of persecution (Ginzberg accepts as historically valid
the accusation of treason mentioned in *y. Ḥag.* 2.1, 77b)? Moreover, would a mere
Sadducee have been punished so fiercely that a fire would burn upon his grave?
On this topic, see A. Büchler, "Die Erlösung Eliša b. Abujahs aus dem Höllenfeuer,"
MGWJ 76 (1932) 412-456.
[16] On Meṭaṭron, see Gershom Scholem, *Major Trends in Jewish Mysticism* (New York:
Schocken, ²1965) 68, 69, 358. Cf. P. S. Alexander, "The Historical Setting of the Hebrew
Book of Enoch," *JJS* 28 (1977) 156-180, esp. 162-167 and 177-178 (on *b. Ḥag.* 15a).

of Elisha'ʼs heresy, originally without the name Meṭaṭron, has been preserved here, but put into a new frame by the Babylonian Amoraim. The fact that this tradition appears only in the Babylonian Talmud should not surprise us: Elisha'ʼs apostasy, conceivably, had left many scars and painful memories amongst the Palestinian sages; it is understandable that they decided, in their redaction of the Jerusalem Talmud, not to record his views completely. In Babylonia, on the other hand, the episode being more distant, these views could have somehow been recorded.

In his rich Hebrew article (still the most condensed organization of all the evidence), Bin Gorion expressed the view that Elisha' was anathematized not merely on the grounds of his revolt, which was not mainly of a theological nature, but rather because he had become a type, a symbol of religious opposition to the Rabbis.[17]

A linguistic analysis of the meaning of the word *aḥer* in Rabbinic literature has been put forward by Henoch Yalon in two articles.[18] From evidence in various contexts he reached the conclusion that the word was used as an epithet for someone involved in prostitution, or, more generally, indicated depravity of sexual mores. Yalon clearly shows the pejorative connotations of the word in Rabbinic literature. As to its application to Elisha', it has its origin, according to Yalon, in a story connecting Elisha' with a whore. We shall not discuss this story here: suffice it to say that Yalon understands the text in question in an overly literal fashion. Moreover, the choice of this story as the single source for this epithet is arbitrary—one could as well explain the story as playing on the derogatory meaning of *aḥer* after this name had already been given to Elisha'.[19]

---

[17] "Erekh: Aḥer", *HaGoren* 8 (1912) 76-83.

[18] His article quoted in n. 10 is a revised Hebrew version of "אחר im Talmudisch-Hebräischen," *MGWJ* 79 (1935) 238-240.

[19] The story appears in *b. Ḥag.* 15a, where it is said that Elisha' once approached a harlot. She recognized him and exclaimed, "But arenʼt you Elisha' ben Abuyah?" Upon this, "he plucked (*'aqar*) a radish from its bed on a Sabbath" and gave it to her. She then said, "אחר הוא" (he is *aḥer*), which has usually been interpreted either as "he is someone else" or "he has become a different man." For Yalon ("Midrashot," 215) this story alludes to an actual encounter, and should be seen as the origin of Elisha'ʼs byname: the whore, seeing Elisha'ʼs typical antinomian violation of the Sabbath (see Matt 12:1-9; Mark 2:23; Luke 6:1-5), concluded that she had been mistaken in her initial identification of her client. Thereafter the byname, with its connotations of association with prostitutes, would have stuck to Elisha'. However, a less candid reading of the passage is also possible. On the one hand, the figure of the prostitute is widely used as a metaphor for idolatry, "turning to other gods." See for instance Jer 2:20; 3:3; 5:7; Ezekiel 16; or 4Q184, in J. M. Allegro, *Qumrân Cave 4* (DJD 5;

Scholem, in his study of "the four who entered paradise," does not commit himself on Elisah''s byname, beliefs, or deeds: "Elisha Aḥer, who became a heretic, or *min*, cut down the saplings—whatever this metaphor may signify."[20] Safrai simply says that the cutting down of the saplings refers to "one of the several forms of sectarianism then rife in Ereẓ Israel."[21]

An interesting attempt was recently made by Henry A. Fischel to present the story about "the four who entered paradise" as an anti-Epicurean parody.[22] In his account, Aḥer would have shown some Epicurean tendencies; "cutting down the saplings", for instance, would mean corrupting the youth, endeavoring to have them relinquish their studies—which Epicurus and his followers are accused, in ancient literature, of having done. Fischel's overly systematic attempt, which convinces me on some other points,[23] fails to do so here. It falls short of explaining Elisha''s byname, or his strongly negative image in Rabbinic literature, which does not have much in common with those of Ben Azzai or Ben Zoma, other convinced Epicureans according to Fischel.

No one, however, seems to have remarked until now the simple

Oxford: Clarendon, 1968) 82-86, and the critical remarks of J. Strugnell, *RevQ* 7 (1970) 263-268. On the other hand, the expression "on the Sabbath" (or, even more strongly, "on the Day of Atonement which fell upon a Sabbath") functions in Jewish literature as a *topos* which intends to convey the horror of certain grave sins. See Josephus, *Ant.* 14.66 (and note there in the Loeb edition), or *Pesiq. Rab Kah.* 15.7 (see B. Mandelbaum, ed., *Pesiqta de-Rab-Kahana* [New York: Jewish Theological Seminary, 1962] 258). It may be that this *topos* is used here in connection with Elisha'; cf. *y. Ḥag.* 2.1, 77b, where it is reported that Elisha' once rode in front of the Temple on a "Yom Hakippurim which fell on a Sabbath." The encounter with the prostitute on a Sabbath, therefore, might be only a frame story for the evil deed of Aḥer, who "plucked a radish from its bed" (עקר פוגלא ממישרא). This expression also appears in *b. 'Abod Zar.* 10a, where it clearly signifies "to kill."

[20] *Jewish Gnosticism, Merkabah Mysticism and Talmudic Tradition* (New York: Jewish Theological Seminary, ²1965) 16 and n. 16. In a later study, Scholem specifies that Elisha' "surely was not the first *Gnostic* sectarian (Hebrew: min) but only the most widely known" (italics mine). He suggests that the name Yaldabaoth may have been coined by "someone like him" ("Jaldabaoth Reconsidered," *Mélanges d'histoire des religions offerts à H.-C. Puech* [Paris: Presses Universitaires, 1974] 418-419).

[21] "Elisha ben Avuyah," 669. In this line, André Néher, by rather unconvincing arguments, tries to make a Jewish-Christian out of Elisha'. Cf. "Le voyage mystique des Quatre," *RHR* 140 (1951) 59-82.

[22] *Rabbinic Literature*, 1. 1-34.

[23] See E. Rivkin's review, *JBL* 96 (1977) 135-136, and Anthony J. Saldarini, "Form Criticism of Rabbinic Literature," *JBL* 96 (1977) 261-262.

fact that *aḥer* could well be the equivalent of the Greek ἀλλογενής, or of the Syriac *nukrayā* which translates ἀλλογενής in Syriac sources.

We know from Epiphanius's *Panarion* (chaps 39 and 40) that the Sethian Gnostics as well as the closely related Archontics considered themselves as alien to this world[24] on the basis of their exegesis of Gen 4:25, since their mythical forefather, Seth,[25] had come from "another seed" (σπέρμα ἕτερον, *zera' aḥer*). The Sethians saw this "other seed" as coming from the heavenly world, from the "power on high,"[26] while Cain and Abel, on the other hand, were seen, according to various forms of the myth, as sons of the Demiurge or of some of the archons. Indeed, the Sethians, as well as other groups related to them, possessed books, or apocalypses, attributed to the Allogenes *par excellence*, Seth, or to the Allogeneis, his mythical seven sons.[27] Apart from Epiphanius, writers as distant in time as Porphyry and Theodore bar Konai provide us either with mention of,[28] or even with actual quotations from,[29] these books. One of the treatises found in a Coptic translation in the Gnostic library at Nag Hammadi is in fact

---

[24] Epiphanius, *Haer.* 39.2.6 (ed. Holl 2. 73): καὶ τὸ γένος τοῦ Σὴθ ἀφορισθὲν ἐντεῦθεν κατάγεται, ἐκλογῆς ὂν καὶ διακεκριμένον τοῦ ἄλλου γένους. For a phenomenological analysis of the whole notion of "strangeness" in Gnostic thought, see H.-Ch. Puech, *En quête de la gnose* (Paris: Gallimard, 1978) 1. 207-13.

[25] Ibid., 39.2.3 (Holl 2. 72).

[26] Ibid., 39.2.4 (Holl 2. 73); cf. 40.7.1 (2. 87); καταλαβοῦσα ἐν αὐτῷ (sc. Σὴθ) σπέρμα τῆς ἄνωθεν δυνάμεως καὶ τὸν σπινθῆρα τὸν ἄνωθεν πεμφθέντα εἰς πρώτην καταβολὴν τοῦ σπέρματος καὶ συστάσεως.

[27] Ibid., 39.5.1 (Holl 2. 75); 40.7.4-5 (Holl 2. 78). In the myth these seven sons stand in opposition to the seven sons of Yaldabaoth, the archons who rule the world. See the first chapter of Wilhelm Bousset's *Hauptprobleme der Gnosis* (Göttingen: Vandenhoeck & Ruprecht, 1907), Die Sieben und die Μήτηρ, as well as Irenaeus, *Haer.* 1.30.5; Epiphanius, *Haer.* 26.10.1-3; Origen, *Cels.* 6.30-33, and *OnOrgWld*, CG II 101 : 9-26.

[28] Porphyry, *V.P.*, chap. 16.

[29] Theodore bar Konai, *Liber Scholiorum* 9, ed. and tr. Henri Pognon, *Les inscriptions mandaites des coupes de Khouabir* 2 (Paris: Welter, 1899); or cf. the better edition (but without translation) of Msgr. Addai Scher (CSCO 55, 69; Paris, 1910). A new edition of this precious text is in preparation at Louvain. On these quotations by Theodore of the "gelyōnā denukrāyē," see Henri-Charles Puech, "Fragments retrouvés de l'"Apocalypse d'Allogène'," *Mélanges Franz Cumont* (Annuaire de l'Institut de Philologie et d'Histoire Orientales et Slaves 4; Brussells, 1936) 935-962. In this article, Puech was the first to identify the "*Apocalypse of the Strangers*," still used, as Theodore attests, by the eighth-century Audians, with the book of the same name read by Plotinus's Gnostic auditors in Rome. (Ἀποκαλύψεις τε προφέροντες ... Ἀλλογενοῦς, Porphyry, *V.P.* 16). See also H.-Ch. Puech, "Les nouveaux écrits gnostiques découverts en Haute-Egypte (Premier inventaire et essai d'identification)," *Coptic Studies in Honor of Walter Erwing Crum* (Boston: Byzantine Institute, 1950), esp. 126-130.

called "The Allogenes."[30] In the second century itself, Irenaeus mentions that according to these Gnostics Seth and his sister Norea were born "from the providence of Prunicus."[31]

Since this theologoumenon about the "otherness" of Seth and his offspring is obviously at the core of Sethian Gnosticism,[32] we can be sure that it played a central role in the theology of the earliest Sethians.

We, of course, know next to nothing about these early Gnostics,[33] but it is more than probable that, in the early second century, there indeed existed some group, or groups, who identified themselves as the offspring of the "supreme Allogenes," and as a race of "strangers." Actually, such a self-description of the Gnostics as "strangers," or "aliens," is by no means limited to the Sethians. For example, in his phenomenological analysis of this central aspect of the Gnostic attitude, Hans Jonas was able to quote many parallel texts from the Mandaean hymns.[34]

As we know that some of these Gnostic "strangers" (the Archontics) were actually present in Palestine,[35] it is likely that the Rabbis were aware of their existence. They probably knew—even if vaguely—some of the central concepts of their theology (or at least the outlines of their basic myths). They therefore could not ignore the fact that these

---

[30] CG XI,3, still unedited, but translated in *NHLibEng*.

[31] *Haer.* 1.30.9 (269-270 Stieren; 1. 236 Harvey): "Post quos secundum providentiam Prunici dicunt generatum Seth, post Noream." Irenaeus simply refers to these Gnostics as "others" (*alii*), but according to Theodoret (fifth century) these are "Sethians whom some call Ophians, or Ophites" (*Haer.* 1.14; PG 83, 364C).

[32] In "Les nouveaux écrits," 127, Puech writes "La race de Seth, de ses fils et de leur descendance est une 'autre' race, une race 'étrangère' au sens fort du terme," or "la naissance de Seth, principe des 'pneumatiques', est entièrement différente de la leur [the races of Cain and Abel], singulière, 'autre' en un mot."

[33] For an attempt to organize our scant sociological knowledge of Gnosticism, see Henry A. Green, "Gnosis and Gnosticism: A Study in Methodology," *Numen* 24 (1977) 95-134, and K. Rudolph, "Das Problem einen Soziologie und 'sozialen Verortung' der Gnosis," *Kairos* 19 (1977) 35-44. For the intricate problem of what can be said about the early Sethians, see H.M. Schenke, "Das sethianische System nach Nag-Hammadi-Handschriften," *Studia Coptica* (ed. P. Nagel; *BBA* 45; Berlin: Akademie, 1974) 165-172, as well as the critical remarks of Michel Tardieu, "Les livres mis sous le nom de Seth et les Séthiens de l'Hérésiologie," *Gnosis and Gnosticism* (ed. Martin Krause; NHS 8; Leiden: Brill, 1977) 210. I tend to disagree with Tardieu's scepticism about the early strata of Sethian Gnosticism, and hope to dwell on that problem elsewhere.

[34] *Gnosis und spätantiker Geist* 1 (FRLANT 51; Göttingen: Vandenhoeck & Ruprecht, 1934) 96-97. Cf. *The Gnostic Religion* (Boston: Beacon, 1958) 49-51, 75-80.

[35] Epiphanius devotes a chapter of his *Panarion* to the Archontics "who can be found only in Palestine." Cf. *Haer.* 40.1.3 (Holl 2. 80).

people, whoever they were, looked upon themselves as "sons of the Stranger," who had come from a "*zeraʿ aḥer*."

Now this very "strangeness," of which the Gnostics were so proud, could easily be—and probably was—given quite a different meaning by anyone who despised them. As Yalon showed, the word *aḥer* has in some cases a deprecatory meaning in Rabbinic Hebrew, which could very easily have been exploited by the Rabbis in their use of the Sethians' Hebrew name.[36]

We do not have a positive proof that Elishaʿ actually became a Sethian Gnostic. Nevertheless, we can say with confidence that when this respected Tanna rejected the yoke of Torah, he turned himself to some kind of Gnostic teaching. For the contemporary Palestinian Rabbis, in any case, the nature of his heresy was clear enough to let them identify him with the "sons of the Stranger," the "other ones," and thus Elishaʿ became known, after his apostasy, as Aḥer, i.e., the Gnostic.

We are left by our sources without any indication about the Gnostic works that Elishaʿ might have known, though the Babylonian Talmud recalls that he knew—and appreciated—Greek[37] and that, when he came to the house of study, he used to hide some heterodox (possibly Gnostic) books under his cloak.[38]

---

[36] See also N. Krochmal's interpretation of "*derek aḥeret*" (*y. Ber.* 9.1) in his *Moreh Nebukei haZeman* (*Kitvei R. Nahman Krochmal* [ed. S. Rawidowicz; Waltham, Mass., and Leiden: Ararat, ^{2}1961] 277): "the other way" signifies, according to this interpretation, the Gnostic belief in the utter remoteness of the supreme God. Krochmal adds that this was Elishaʿ's heresy. Krochmal is correct in his interpretation, but he does not give an explanation of the epithet Aḥer, *aḥeret*.

The tide of the late nineteenth century's *Wissenschaft des Judenthums* had brought some more interesting intuitions about our problem. M. D. Hoffmann, *Toledot Elisa ben Abuyah* (Vienna 1880) states that "Aḥer" was a self-given pseudonym, which Elishaʿ was bearing proudly. Only when used by his opponents did it become a title of shame. Unfortunately, other developments of Hoffmann's argument are rather farfetched. Adolph Hönig, on his side (*Die Ophiten: Ein Beitrag zur Geschichte des jüdischen Gnosticismus* [Berlin: Menner & Mueller, 1889] 96 n. 1), suggested that the name Aḥer could come from *Zeraʿ aḥer* (Gen 4:25) and thus have been used by Hebrew-speaking Sethians as their name. The word would then have been picked up by their Rabbinic opponents. Despite the fact that this last assumption remains unproven, and that Hönig was not aware of the actual figures of the Ἀλλογενεῖς in Sethian theology, his intuition is remarkable. Yet I did not find any mention of it in later scholarship.

[37] *b. Hag.* 15b: אחר מאי? זמר יוני לא פסק מפומי ("Why was he called Aḥer? [Because] Greek songs were always on his lips"). His hellenophilia is thus presented as an explanation of his name: Aḥer would mean "the foreigner."

[38] Ibid.

What was the cause of Elisha''s revolt[39] we do not know for sure. But it may have been a meditation upon the problem—the scandal—of evil, or more specifically, the contemplation of the atrocious sufferings of the martyrs of the Roman persecution.[40] It has been, after all, common knowledge since late antiquity that Gnostic attitudes grew out of a relentless anguish over the question *unde malum et quare*.[41]

What does appear clearly from the Palestinian sources themselves, however, is that Elisha' did not remain aloof when he turned to to Gnosticism: rather, he became actively involved in proselytizing among the students of the Rabbis on behalf of his newly acquired wisdom. This is, at least, how the Talmud understands "cutting down the saplings." According to its testimony, Aḥer "used to kill promising students (of the Torah)," i.e., "to kill them by his words."[42] A modern interpreter such as Leo Baeck can therefore read the formula as meaning that "he caused entanglement and apostasy among youth."[43]

The vehemence of the accusations of "murder" in the Palestinian sources[44] leads us to think that he actually succeeded, at least partly, in his proselytizing endeavors. In any case, this heterodox propaganda was considered by the Palestinian Rabbis as a serious threat to Judaism.[45]

---

[39] In *y. Ḥag.* 2.1, 77b a voice from the Holy of Holies says about Aḥer: ידע כוחי ומרד בי, "He knew my power and (nevertheless) revolted against me."

[40] See nn. 5 and 6.

[41] Cf. Ps.-Tertullian, *Haer.* 7 (F. Oehler, ed., *Tertulliani Opera* 2 [Leipzig: Weigel, 1854] 9). On the problem of evil in Gnostic thought, see Puech, *En quête de la gnose* 1. 190-206.

[42] *y. Ḥag.* 2.1, 77b. Diametrically opposed to this image of "uprooting" or "cutting the saplings" is that of planting, which is connected to life. See A. Altmann, "Gnostische Motive in rabbinischen Schrifttum," *MGWJ* 83 (1939), esp. 379-383.

[43] "Jewish Mysticism," *JJS* 2 (1950) 9.

[44] See n. 4 above.

[45] Of all the former students and colleagues of Elisha', R. Meir is the only one who kept respect and love for Aḥer after his apostasy. Moving stories are related in talmudic literature about R. Meir's behavior towards Aḥer, as well his repeated attempts (deemed finally successful) to have him repent (see *y. Ḥag.* 2.1, 77c). Whatever the reasons for R. Meir's continued love for his former teacher may have been, his attitude could well have been felt by other Rabbis as dangerously close to sympathy to Aḥer. After a clash that R. Meir and R. Nathan had with Simeon ben Gamaliel, the head of the Sanhedrin, the Rabbis decided to record the former's opinions under the anonymous "*aḥerim*," i.e., "others (say)": (*b. Hor.* 13b: אסיקו לר' מאיר אחרים ולר' נתן יש אומרים). The *Tosafot* report—though without agreeing with it—the view of a "*Quntres Ṣarfat*" according to which R. Meir's opinion is quoted under *aḥerim* whenever he cites an opinion that he learned from Elisha' (*Tosafot* on *b. Sota* 12a: שמועות שקיבל מאלישע בן אבויה קבלום בשם אחרים). See, however, Wilhelm Bacher, *Agada der Tannaiten*, 2. 9-10. Even if the Rabbis' decision had originally been made

This paper focuses upon the name Aḥer itself; however, I cannot refrain from mentioning here one strikingly suggestive theme which might strengthen our Sethian conjecture.

The *Tosepta* of *Ḥagiga* with which we began mentions the cryptic warning of R. 'Aqiba to his colleagues when they entered the *pardes*: "When you reach the place of pure marble stones, do not say, 'Water! Water!'" Various attempts have been made to explain these words. However, a new light may be shed upon them by some of the Gnostic documents.

The Gnostic Justin, in his book *Baruch*, spoke of waters from above, corresponding to the waters from below.[46] These "waters that are above" are also mentioned in the treatise *Melchizedek* (CG IX 8: 1), a work which shows some very distinctive Sethian features. The same Sethian features appear in *Zostrianos* (CG VIII 18: 5-9), which mentions the presence of water at the end of the ecstatic trip: "The great male invisible perfect Mind, the First-Appearing One, has his own water, as you [will see] when you arrive at his place" (tr. J. Sieber, *NHLibEng*).

Since the image of water appears to be so central in Gnostic visions of ecstasy, it is a most interesting possibility that when R. 'Aqiba warns his colleagues, he warns them against behavior similar to that of the Gnostics.

Finally, I would like to offer a suggestion on a parallel use of the word *aḥer* as a *terminus technicus* for Gnostic in Rabbinic literature. In *Gen. Rab.* 23.3 (on Gen 4:22) we read:

> And the sister of Tubal-Cain was Na'amah. R. Abba bar Kahana said: Na'amah was Noah's wife. And why was she called Na'amah? Because her deeds were pleasing [ne'imim]. The Rabbis said: Na'amah was *aḥeret*, since she was singing [man'emet] to the timbrel for idolatry.[47]

In his translation, Freedman renders *aḥeret* by "a woman of a different stamp."[48]

Now, Birger A. Pearson has convincingly shown, in a recently

---

without any reference to Meir's teacher, it is inconceivable that, once his opinion was reported in this anonymous way, "aḥerim" did not ring the familiar bell of "aḥer."

[46] Hippolytus, *Haer.* 5.26 and 5.27.3. Cf. the מים עליונים and the מים תחתונים in *y. Ḥag.* 2.1, 77b.

[47] 224 Theodor (Berlin: Issowzky, 1903).

[48] *Midrash Rabbah* 1 (London: Soncino, 1939).

published article, that the important Gnostic figure Norea is in fact the Gnostic avatar of the Jewish Na'amah.[49] I suggest here that the Rabbis were aware of Na'amah's central place in Gnostic myth (where she plays a crucial role in the salvation of Gnostic mankind), and that when they called her *aḥeret* they meant exactly what they meant when they called Elisha' "Aḥer": a Gnostic.

Elisha' ben Abuya has remained, in some sense, a fascinating figure to Jewish intellectuals of the modern age. When Meir Letteris, a man of letters of the nineteenth-century Haskalah, rendered Goethe's *Faust I* into Hebrew, he could think of no better title for it than "Ben Abuya".[50] He did not know how right he was. Gilles Quispel, indeed, has been able to trace the roots of Faust to the legends surrounding Simon Magus, the traditional first proponent of Gnosticism in Palestine of the first century C.E.[51] And so, characters so distant as the Rabbi-turned-rebel and the mythical figure of modern Western consciousness are both linked, in some way, to the widespread and dangerous movement which the Church Fathers called "a hydra."[52]

---

[49] B. A. Pearson, "The Figure of Norea in Gnostic Literature," *Proceedings of the International Colloquium on Gnosticism, Stockholm, August 20-25, 1973* (Filologisk-filosofiska serien 17; Stockholm: Almqvist & Wicksell, 1977) 143-152.

[50] Vienna, 1895.

[51] "Faust: Symbol of Western Man" (tr. John B. Carman), *ErJb* 35 (1966) 241-265.

[52] At the time of going to press, my colleague Yehuda Liebes refers me to his Hebrew article "Tsaddiq Yesod Olam—A Sabbatian Myth," *Daat* 1 (1978) 73-120. In appendix A (p. 115) Liebes suggests that "Aḥer" might have been Elisha's self-chosen epithet, pointing to the Gnostic concept of the "otherness" of the Good God. This suggestion is fully supported by my whole argument.

STABILITY AS A SOTERIOLOGICAL THEME
IN GNOSTICISM

BY

MICHAEL A. WILLIAMS

In the Nag Hammadi tractate *Allogenes*, there occurs an intriguing account of the withdrawal (ἀναχώρησις) of the figure called Allogenes through a succession of levels or conditions, culminating in a level referred to as "Existence" (ὕπαρξις).[1] This process of withdrawal is actually described twice: first in the form of instructions given to Allogenes by certain holy powers, and then in a narrative in the first person in which Allogenes tells of his experience of this retreat. The withdrawal constitutes the climatic revelatory moment in this document, and one of its most interesting features is the prominence which is given to the theme of stability:

> "Allogenes, behold the bliss which belongs to you, how it exists in silence; by it know yourself as you really are. And, in search of yourself, withdraw (ἀναχωρεῖν) into Life, which you will see moving (ⲉⲥⲕⲓⲙ). And though you are unable to *stand* (ⲉⲙⲛ6ⲁⲙ ⲛⲅⲁ2ⲉⲣⲁⲧⲕ), have no fear; but rather, if you desire to *stand*, withdraw into Existence and you will find that it *stands* and is still (ⲉⲥ2ⲟⲣⲕ ⲙⲙⲟⲥ), after the image of the One who is truly still and embraces all of these silently and without any activity. And if you receive a revelation from this one by means of a primary revelation of the Unknown One—whom, if you know him, be ignorant of him—and if (because of this) you are afraid in that place, withdraw behind[2] because of the activities; and when you become perfect in that place, be still. And, in accordance with the pattern within you, know that it is likewise among all these, after the same pattern. And [do not] further dissipate, [so that] you may be able to *stand*; neither desire to [be active],[3] lest in any way you fall away [from] the inactivity of the Unknown One which is within you. Do not [know] him, for that is impossible. But if, through an enlightened thought you should know him, be ignorant of him."

---

[1] The author gratefully acknowledges the travel grant awarded him by the Graduate School of Arts and Sciences of the University of Washington, which made possible the presentation of this paper.

[2] ⲁⲣⲓⲁⲛⲁⲝⲱⲣⲓ ⲉⲡⲁ2ⲟⲩ. The idea seems to be that Allogenes is to withdraw further, to a tranquil mode transcending the "activities" produced by the fear. See below, n. 15.

[3] I think that there is room to reconstruct ⲉⲣ ⲉⲛ[ⲉⲣⲅⲓ]; this would go well with the sense of the passage, although admittedly it is a tight fit.

820 MICHAEL A. WILLIAMS

Now I was listening to these things as they were speaking them; within me there was a silent stillness; I heard the bliss by which I knew myself as ⟨I am⟩,[4] and in search of ⟨myself⟩[4] I withdrew into Life; and I entered into harmony with it. I did not *stand* firmly (ϩⲛ ⲟⲩⲧⲁϫⲣⲟ), but tranquilly (ϩⲛ ⲟⲩϩⲣⲟⲕ). And I saw an eternal, intellective, undivided movement belonging to all the formless powers which do not limit it (the movement?) with limitation. And when I desired to *stand* firmly, I withdrew into Existence, which I found *standing* and still, in the image and likeness of that which was put upon me through revelation of the Undivided One and Him who is still. And I was filled with revelation by means of a primary revelation of the Unknown One. [As if] I were ignorant of him, I [knew] him, and I received power from him, becoming eternally strengthened through him. I knew that which exists within me and the Triple-Power and the revelation of his uncontainableness. By means of primary revelation of the First who is unknown to all, the God who is beyond perfection, I saw him and the Triple-Power within them all. I was searching after the ineffable, unknown God, the One of whom a person is altogether ignorant if he knows him, the mediator of the Triple-Power, who is in stillness and silence and is unknown. (*Allog* 59: 9-61: 22)

There are indications elsewhere in the text of *Allogenes*[5] that the two levels which are mentioned here, Life (ⲧⲙⲛⲧⲱⲛϩ) and Existence, are part of a triad: Intellection, Life, and Existence—a triad of which there are well-known variations in Neoplatonic material.[6] It may be that Allogenes is presumed already to have arrived at the first level of the triad, Intellection, since immediately preceding the passage in question he is said to have been taken up to a holy place where he was able to behold realities about which he previously had received only auditory revelation (58: 30-37). The withdrawal to Life is a transitional stage between a vision of reality which involves noetic apprehension or conceptualization and an absolutely direct apprehension which in *Allogenes* is called "primary revelation" (ⲟⲩⲙⲛⲧϣⲟⲣⲡ ⲛⲟⲩⲱⲛϩ ⲉⲃⲟⲗ 59: 28f.; 60: 39f.; 61: 9f., 30f.; 63: 14f.), or the "ignorance which sees Him" (ⲧⲙⲛⲧⲁⲧⲥⲟⲩⲱⲛⲥ ⲉⲧⲛⲁⲩ ⲉⲣⲟϥ 64: 13f.), and which is achieved when Allogenes withdraws to Existence. The level called "Life" seems to be a continuous stream or fountain of formless,

---

[4] The text has ⲕⲁⲧⲁⲣⲟⲥ and ⲛⲥⲱⲥ, respectively. The emendations ⲕⲁⲧⲁⲣⲟⲓ and ⲛⲥⲱⲓ are based on 59: 10ff.

[5] *Allog* 49: 26-38; cf. 61: 36-38.

[6] E.g., Proclus, *Elem. theol.*, prop. 103, which is remarkably close to *Allog* 49: 26-38. See Pierre Hadot, "Etre, Vie, Pensée chez Plotin et avant Plotin," in *Les sources de Plotin* (Fondation Hardt, Entretiens 5; Geneva: Fondation Hardt, 1960), 105-41.

intellective power proceeding from reality as sheer Existence to reality as conceptualized in Intellection.[7]

As Allogenes withdraws to Life, he is unable to "stand firmly," since Life is characterized by continuous movement. The Coptic term here for "to stand," ⲁ2ⲉⲣⲁⲧ⸗, is almost certainly translating forms of the Greek ἑστάναι. The condition of "standing at rest" is portrayed in this passage as the apex of the revelatory experience, and it is attained only when Allogenes withdraws finally to Existence, since Existence "stands and is still" (59: 21 f.; 60: 32).[8] There follows in the tractate an extensive revelation of attributes which the Unknown God does *not* possess and superlatives which he transcends. Therefore, it would seem that this Existence in which Allogenes is ultimately able to achieve stability is a mode of awareness in which every effort to conceptualize the Unknown God in terms of quality or quantity is abandoned absolutely, and simply his existence is experienced. Allogenes "stands at rest," participating in the stability of the Unknown God, who is described later in the tractate as "standing eternally" (66: 31 f.).

This description in *Allogenes* of the decisive revelatory experience as the attainment to stability, the participation in that which is truly stable, is not unique in Gnostic literature as far as the concept is concerned, and even the technical expression which is so visible here, "to stand at rest," is now well-attested in several other Gnostic texts as a technical term for the stability to which the Gnostic returns through reception of gnosis.[9] The opposite condition, instability, crops up

---

[7] Cf. Plot. 6.7.17,9-26, where Plotinus speaks of Life given forth as a kind of trace (ἴχνος) of the One, which is itself prior to any life or activity; Life comes forth unlimited or infinite (ἀόριστος), but by looking toward the One it receives definition (ὁρίζεται); Life so defined is Intellect (ὁρισθεῖσα γὰρ ζωὴ νοῦς).

[8] A similar association of ἑστάναι with ὕπαρξις, where ὕπαρξις is at the same time a part of the triad ὕπαρξις, ζωή, νόησις, is to be found in the anonymous commentary on the *Parmenides*, now edited by Pierre Hadot, *Porphyre et Victorinus* (Paris: Études Augustiniennes, 1968), vol. 2. In 12.16-27 (Hadot 2. 110-12) the unfolding of reality is said to consist of three moments: (1) in the first, Existence (ὕπαρξις), knower (τὸ νοοῦν) and known are the same; (2) in the second, Life (ζωή), the knower proceeds from Existence into the act of knowing; (3) in the third, Intellection (νόησις), the knower turns to itself to know itself. All three moments can be described as "activities" (ἐνέργειαι): "The activity with respect to Existence would be *standing at rest* (ἑστῶσα); the activity with respect to Intellection, turned toward itself; the activity with respect to Life, having moved out of Existence" (12.22-27).

[9] On the theme of stability in Gnosticism, see my recent dissertation, "The Nature and Origin of the Gnostic Concept of Stability" (Ph. D. diss., Harvard University, 1977), where I have examined the usage of several recurring expressions in Gnostic literature, such as ⲥⲙⲓⲛⲉ, "to establish/be established" (e.g., *TriTrac* 92: 22-93: 13; *GPhil* 53: 23-35), ἡ ἀσάλευτος γενεά, "the immovable race" (e.g., *ApocryJn* BG 22: 10-17 et

frequently in Gnostic literature as the hallmark of ignorance. In the *Apocryphon of John*, for example, Sophia paces restlessly to and fro in the darkness of forgetfulness (BG 44: 19-45: 14). The counterpart of Sophia in the *Tripartite Tractate*, the Logos, is stunned to discover that as the fruit of his attempt to grasp the essence of the Father, he has succeeded only in unleashing a bewildering menagerie of inferior beings which clash and struggle with one another, producing a ceaseless and nightmarish clamor (*TriTrac* 78: 29-81: 7). In *Allogenes*, this obstructive instability arises from the itch to find predicates for the Unknown God, which, having been discovered and taken for appropriate definitions, turn out simply to be guarantees that the discoverer is still stumbling in darkness (*Allogenes* 61: 17-19). Allogenes is admonished by the holy powers to cease dissipating the inactivity (ⲡⲓⲁⲧⲉⲛⲉⲣⲅⲓⲁ) within him by chasing after things which are incomprehensible (*Allog* 61: 25-28; cf. 67: 33-35). This same message—that the stability to which the Gnostic aspires is jeopardized by the futile (one might almost say blasphemous) effort to pin down the Unknown God through definition—is also being expressed in the important Sophia/Logos mythology mentioned above.

Outside of Gnostic literature there are two particularly striking parallels to this account of Allogenes' withdrawal to a condition of "standing at rest," and these two parallels offer inviting clues as to the matrix from which stability as a soteriological theme in Gnosticism arises. The first parallel is to be found in Plotinus's references to the experience of "standing at rest" in contemplation of, or in mystical union with, the One. The mystical ascent according to Plotinus involves the retreat of the self from the unstable realm of sense perception, the realm of opinion, in which the self falls prey to deceptive fantasies that give rise to turbulent passions.[10] The self withdraws alone unto itself in contemplation, waiting in tranquillity for the vision of the One:

> Therefore, it is necessary not to chase after it, but rather to remain in stillness until it appears, preparing oneself to be a spectator, just as an eye waits

---

passim; *3StSeth* 118: 10-13), etc. Some of the results of that research are summarized in portions of this paper. As examples of the widespread use of the expression "to stand at rest" in this connection, cf. *3StSeth* 119: 4, 15-18; 121: 9f.; *Mar* 15: 4; *Zost* 78: 15f.; 81: 10-14; 114: 14f.; 116: 6-8; 127: 15-17; *OnOrgWld* 104: 20ff.; *ApocAd* 83: 14-24; *DialSav* 120: 5-8; 127: 5f.; 128: 13f.; 133: 23f.; 142: 19f.; *GrPow* 43: 9-11; *OnRes* 48: 30-33.

[10] Plot. 1.1.9,5-9; 3.6.4,8-27.

for the rising of the sun. The sun, appearing above the horizon—"out of Oceanus," as the poets say—gives itself to the eyes to be beheld. But from whence does that which the sun imitates rise and what is it that it must rise above in order to appear? It rises above the mind which is in contemplation. For the mind will stand still (ἑστήξεται) toward the vision, looking to nothing else but the Beautiful, turning and giving itself completely to That; and having stood (στάς) and, as it were, having been filled with strength,[11] it first sees itself to have become more beautiful and brilliant, since That One is near. (Plot. 5.5.8,5-15)

Such a description is an interesting parallel to the text from *Allogenes* discussed above not only because of their thematic similarities, but also because they use the same technical term to describe the stability which the self experiences in the vision: ἑστάναι.[12] A quotation from perhaps the most famous tractate in which Plotinus attempts to convey what it is to know union with the One, *Ennead* 6.9, will further illustrate this usage:

Now since there were not two things, but the beholder himself was one with the beheld—as though it were not something beheld but united with—if he would remember what he became when he was mingled with That One, he would have within himself an image of That One. He was one, and he had within himself no difference with regard to himself or to other things. Nothing in him moved: no emotion, no desire was in him when he ascended, not even reasoning, not even any intellection—not even his very self, if one could say that! But as though caught up or raptured in stillness (ἡσυχῇ), he had attained a solitary steadiness (καταστάσει) in the calm (ἀτρεμεῖ) essence of That One, not turning away in any direction, nor even turning toward himself, standing completely at rest (ἑστὼς πάντη), and, as it were, having become Rest (στάσις) itself. (Plot. 6.9.11,4-16)

The mere fact that ἑστάναι and its cognates are employed as technical terms for Rest vis-à-vis Movement is not at all surprising, since this usage had a very long history, especially in the Platonic tradition.[13] But what is more interesting is that in both *Allogenes* and Plotinus "standing" is a condition attained by the *individual* who engages in a mystical withdrawal to the Transcendent. If it were

---

[11] Cf. above in the quotation from *Allog* 59: 9-61 : 22, where Allogenes, when he achieves the condition of "standing," is also said to be "eternally strengthened" (ελειχι noyχρο ... [n]ωλ ενεϩ 61: 4f.).

[12] For convenience, I am using the infinitive of the second perfect to refer to this term. The future perfect and second aorist forms of this verb, found in the quotation just given from Plotinus, have, like the second perfect, an intransitive meaning; while the present active forms, for example, have a transitive sense ("set, make to stand," etc.).

[13] E.g., Plato, *Prm.* 138b-c; 145e-146a, etc.; *Sph.* 255b ff.

only *Allogenes* and the writings of Plotinus which came into consideration, then the possibility of a literary borrowing might be a likely
hypothesis as to the reason for this similarity, especially since Porphyry
(*Plot.* 16) claims that an apocalypse in the name of "Allogenes" was
among the writings produced by certain opponents of Plotinus.[14] And,
in fact, such a literary connection between *Allogenes* and Plotinus is
attractive on a number of grounds.[15] However, whatever the verdict
is on that question, the motif of the mystical retreat to stability is not
confined to these two sources. It is impossible that all the other
Gnostic works in which this concept appears are dependent on Plotinus.
It would be much more likely that Plotinus himself is dependent on
Gnostic sources at this point. And yet I think that the most probable
explanation is that *both* are dependent on a model of mystical contemplation which had been around for some time.

   This brings me to the second parallel to the account of Allogenes'
attainment to stability: that is, the description offered by Philo of
Alexandria of how wise men achieve stability when they draw near
to the stability of God. In good Platonic style, Philo distinguishes
between on the one hand the instability of the sense realm, and on
the other hand the stability of Being, ὁ ὤν, which in Philo is often just
another name for God.[16] Philo assures us that God alone eternally
and truly "stands at rest."[17] Yet Philo is impressed by two Biblical
passages which seem to ascribe the same condition of stability to two
patriarchs. One passage is Gen 18:22, where Abraham is said to have

---

   [14] Cf. Henri-Charles Puech, "Plotin et les Gnostiques," in *Les sources de Plotin*,
159-74.
   [15] Plot. 3.8.9,13-40 merits close comparison with the lengthy passage I have quoted
from *Allog* 59: 9-61 : 22. As one example of the points of contact between these two
texts, I would call attention to the fact that—like the author of the *Allogenes* passage—
Plotinus refers to the "withdrawing" of the Nous "behind" (εἰς τοὐπίσω ἀναχωρεῖν)
so that it reaches a mode prior to its role as "first life" (ζωὴ πρώτη), and is therefore
no longer engaged in "activity" (ἐνέργεια). It must do this, says Plotinus, if it is to
give itself up to the One. This seems to be essentially the same thing being said in the
Allogenes text, and the phrase in *Allog* 59: 34, ⲁⲣⲓⲁⲛⲁⲭⲱⲣⲓ ⲉⲡⲁϩⲟⲩ, "withdraw
behind," seems to correspond to Plotinus' wording almost exactly. *Enn.* 3.8 is the first
of four parts of a larger writing, the last part of which is *Enn.* 2.9; this latter tractate has
been titled by Porphyry "Against the Gnostics," but it may be that portions of the
preceding three tractates (3.8; 5.8; 5.5) also reflect discussion between Plotinus and
Gnostic opponents. On the four-part writing, see Richard Harder, "Eine neue Schrift
Plotins," *Hermes* 71 (1936) 1-10; Dietrich Roloff, *Plotin: Die Grossschrift III,8—V,8—V,
5—II,9* (UALG 8; Berlin: de Gruyter, 1970).
   [16] E.g., Philo, *Post.* 19ff.; *Leg. All.* 2.83; *Mut.* 57.
   [17] *Mut.* 57; *Post.* 49; *Gig.* 49; *Conf.* 30.

been "standing before the Lord" (LXX: ἑστηκὼς ἐναντίον κυρίου). The other is Deut 5:31, where God tells Moses to "stand" (LXX: στῆθι) with him while he gives Moses the Torah. These two passages are mentioned several times in Philo's works,[18] but one of the most important instances is in *Post.* 27-28. In the preceding discussion, Philo has meandered into the topic of God's stability as contrasted with the instability of creation. This, characteristically, brings to Philo's mind a related subject: the contrast between the stable person and the unstable person. The paradigm for the unstable person in this instance is Cain, who has gone off into the land of Nod (נוד), which Philo understands to mean the land of "Tossing" (cf. נוד, "to shake, toss, etc."):

> It is worth noticing the region into which he departs when he had left the presence of God. It is the land called "Tossing" (σάλος), and by this the lawgiver indicates that the foolish man, being characterized by unstable and unsettled impulses, submits to tossing and violent motion, like a swelling sea against contrary winds in winter; ... the worthless man, having a mind which is reeling and driven by storm, unable to steer his course correctly and without deviation, constantly tosses about, and is ready for his life to end in shipwreck. The perfect sequence in this series of things astonishes me in no small measure! What happens is that that which draws near to that which stands at rest (τῷ ἑστῶτι) desires rest (ἡρεμίας) out of a longing to be like it. Now that which stands unwaveringly at rest is God (τὸ μὲν οὖν ἀκλινῶς ἑστὼς ὁ θεός ἐστι), and that which is moved is creation; so that one who approaches God desires stability, whereas he who departs from God, since he approaches changing creation, is naturally carried about. (*Post.* 22-23)

The nature of the fool, continues Philo, is hostile to the stillness and rest which belong to the wise man, and the fool never "stands firmly at rest" (ἑστάναι παγίως *Post.* 24). In this connection, Philo stresses the tendency for this instability to manifest itself in constantly changing opinions (*Post.* 25).

By contrast, the wise man is not susceptible to this ceaseless change, but rather has come to partake in the stability of Being. And here Philo brings forward his favorite examples:

---

[18] *Cher.* 18 f.; *Somn.* 2.226 f.; *Gig.* 49; *Conf.* 31 f.; *Sacr.* 8. Philo's notion of "standing firm in God" has been treated by Joseph Pascher, Η ΒΑΣΙΛΙΚΗ ΟΔΟΣ: Der *Königsweg zu Wiedergeburt und Vergottung bei Philo von Alexandreia* (SGKA 17/3-4; Paderborn: Schöningh, 1931) 228-38; cf. Antonie Wlosok, *Laktanz und die philosophische Gnosis* (*AbhAkHeid* 1960/2) 73 f.

> Abraham the wise man, since he stands (ἕστηκε), draws near to the standing God (ἑστῶτι θεῷ), for it says, "He was standing before the Lord and he drew near and said ..." (Gen 18:22f.). For approach to the immutable God is granted only to a soul which is truly immutable (ἀτρέπτῳ), and a soul which is in this state does truly stand near divine power. But that which most clearly reveals the firm steadfastness of the man of excellence is the oracle given to the all-wise Moses: "Stand here by me" (Deut 5:31). Two things follow from this: first, that the Being who moves and turns everything is himself immovable and immutable; secondly, that he shares with the man of excellence his own nature, which is rest. (*Post.* 27-28)

For Philo, the mention of Moses' achievement of stability is especially pregnant with significance, because Moses' ascent to Sinai is interpreted by Philo allegorically to mean the ascent to the noetic realm of Platonic Forms.[19] It is the symbol par excellence of contemplation. While this is not precisely equivalent to the mystical union with the One encountered in Plotinus, nevertheless the family resemblence is remarkable—particularly the conspicuous use of ἑστάναι to describe the stability experienced by the mind in contemplation.

Together with the examples from Plotinus and *Allogenes*, the evidence from Philo points to the existence of an underlying model for the retreat of the wise man to a condition of participation in the stability of the Transcendent—a condition in which knowledge of the Transcendent is received. In the examples discussed here, Platonic tradition is an important common denominator; and I believe, in fact, that the origins of the conception are to be sought within that tradition. One can find in the second-century C.E. Middle Platonist Albinus, for example, a comparable description of this achievement of stability:

> Therefore, the soul, when it is directed toward the sensible by means of the body, becomes dizzy and confused as though it were drunk; but when, alone unto itself, it is directed toward the noetic, it is established and is at rest (καθίσταται καὶ ἠρεμεῖ). (*Didasc.* 25.1)

And of course Albinus is only paraphrasing here a passage from Plato himself (*Phd.* 79c-d).[20]

But Philo's portrayal of the stability in which the wise man participates not only represents evidence for the Platonic ancestry of the later Gnostic formulations of this motif, it also provides an example of the cross-fertilization of Jewish wisdom tradition with this Platonic

---

[19] See *Vita Mos.* 1.157f.
[20] Cf. also Maximus of Tyre, *Or.* 10.3a-b.

theme. The stability of the ·wise man and the instability of the fool is not an uncommon refrain in Jewish wisdom literature.[21] When this refrain is translated in accordance with Platonic presuppositions, one gets the kind of interpretation of the wise man's stability we see in Philo's discussion, where the metaphysical dimensions are heavily underscored.

This link with Jewish wisdom tradition seems to me to be very suggestive, given the continuity which can be traced in several other areas between Jewish wisdom speculation and Gnostic thought.[22] Indeed, there are certain features of the theme of stability/instability in Gnostic literature which may be best explained as developments from Jewish wisdom. One example of this is the association of the instability of the passions with inadequate or conflicting opinions about the Transcendent. In the *Tripartite Tractate* (109: 24-110: 22) one finds a polemic against the contradictory opinions of competing philosophical schools. This competition of viewpoints is, according to this tractate, the historical manifestation of what had been mythologically depicted earlier in the document in the attempt of the Logos to define the Father in terms of only one of his properties (*TriTrac* 75: 17ff.). In the *Tripartite Tractate* this mistake of the Logos is the paradigmatic error resulting in the loss of stability and the onslaught of passions. This connection of inadequate conceptions of the Transcendent with an instability which expresses itself in passions is reminiscent of the famous passage in Wis 13:1 ff., in which inadequate conceptions of God are criticized, and idolatry is directly linked to immoral passions (Wis 14:12). The stupidity of idolatry which the Wisdom of Solomon ridicules corresponds in a document like the *Tripartite Tractate* to the stupidity and arrogance of philosophers who think themselves to have discovered a definition of the Father. In Jewish wisdom literature, the prototype of the later Gnostic who is rescued from such errors and is restored to stability through reception of gnosis is the wise man who takes on wisdom's yoke and finds rest.

I see no reason to assume that the Platonized version of this theme is original with Philo in the early first century c.e. I think that it is more likely that Philo himself, in his portrait of Moses "standing at rest," is drawing upon an already existing motif which then appears fully

---

[21] E.g., Wis 4:3-7; 5:1-2; Sir 22:16ff.; 28:16; 51:27.

[22] See, for example, George MacRae, "The Jewish Background of the Gnostic Sophia Myth," *NovT* 12 (1970) 86-101.

developed in later Gnostic literature, where "to rest," "to stand at rest," "to be established," to belong to the "immovable race," have become central symbols of redemption.[23] If Philo can find in Cain the protótype of instability, perhaps others were already seeing Seth as the father of the "immovable race."[24] This might also explain the similarities between Moses' ascent to Being, where he "stands at rest" like "Him who stands eternally," and Allogenes' withdrawal to Existence, where he also is able to "stand at rest" like "Him who stands eternally." If "Allogenes" is indeed a pseudonym for Seth,[25] perhaps earlier versions of this myth of Seth's retreat to participation in stability were already around in Philo's day.

I might add here, parenthetically, that the period between Philo and second-century Gnosticism is not entirely devoid of evidence for the influence of stability as a soteriological theme. In early Christianity, the achievement of stability seems already to have been something of a rival of other soteriological motifs, such as resurrection. I have in mind in particular the soteriology of Paul's opponents in 1 Corinthians, which I think includes a usage of the theme of stability resembling Philo's in many ways, with some of the same mixture of Jewish wisdom tradition and mystical Platonism, and perhaps even employing the technical term ἑστάναι in the same way.[26] This would be a further piece of evidence[27] for the continuity between Jewish wisdom traditions, the interest in wisdom in an early Christian community like that at Corinth, and further stages in the development of these traditions which can be seen in Gnostic texts such as the *Gospel of Thomas*.[28]

The theme of stability could be added to the catalogue presented by Hans Jonas[29] of images and symbols (such as "the alien," "mixture,"

---

[23] See above, n. 9.

[24] He is called this in, among other places, *3StSeth* 118: 12 f.

[25] Cf. Epiphanius, *Haer.* 40.7.2, where Seth is said to have been called "Allogenes" by the Archontics.

[26] I have attempted in another study, which I hope to publish in the future, to demonstrate the importance of the theme of stability in the controversy in 1 Corinthians.

[27] See James M. Robinson and Helmut Koester, *Trajectories through Eearly Christianity* (Philadelphia: Fortress, 1971) 30-46, 71-113, 166-87, 219-23; and James M. Robinson, "Jesus as Sophos and Sophia: Wisdom Tradition and the Gospels," in Robert L. Wilken, ed., *Aspects of Wisdom in Judaism and Early Christianity* (Notre Dame: University of Notre Dame, 1975) 1-16, esp. 11-15.

[28] In the *Gospel of Thomas*, "to stand at rest" is a technical term designating the stability of the μοναχοί, the "single ones" (logion 16; cf. 18; 23).

[29] Hans Jonas, *Gnosis und spätantiker Geist*, vol. 1 (3d ed.; Göttingen: Vandenhoeck & Ruprecht, 1964), 94-140; idem, *The Gnostic Religion* (2d ed.; Boston: Beacon, 1963), 48-97.

"dispersal," "sleep," "intoxication," etc.) which repeatedly articulate Gnostic experience. The popularity of stability as a soteriological theme in Gnostic literature arises from concerns which lie at the very heart of this religious current in antiquity. In Gnosticism, this theme is able to express the acute frustration with conflicting theological/philosophical opinions; the acute awareness of the unpredictable, undulating passions which jerk the strings of life; the consciousness of a kinship with a level of reality transcending the world of change; and the experience of having been restored to this level, and of having been mixed again with the Unchangeable.

PARTICIPANTS OF THE CONFERENCE

Abramowski, Luise
  (University of Tubingen)
  Brunsstr. 18
  D-7400 Tubingen
  West Germany
Adler, William
  (University of Pennsylvania)
  1335 Ellsworth Street
  Philadelphia, PA. 19147
Ahlstrom, Sydney
  (Yale University)
  99 Armory Street
  Hamden, CT. 06517
Alan, Hank
  (Christ Brotherhood)
  P. O. Box 419
  Santa Fe, N.M. 87501
Aland, Barbara
  (University of Munster)
  Roxelerstr. 12
  44 Munster
  West Germany
Andrews, Susan L.
  (Yale University)
  19 Spring Rock Road
  Branford, CT. 06405
Aronson, Shirley
  (Nassau Community College)
  159 Kings Point Road
  Great Neck, N.Y. 11024
Attridge, Harold W.
  (Perkins School of Theology)
  Southern Methodist University
  Dallas, TX. 75225
Baker, George
  (Graduate Theological Union)
  2465 Le Conte
  Berkeley, CA. 94709
Baltzer, Klaus
  (University of Munich)
  21 Bannzaunweg
  D-8024 Deisenhofen
  West Germany
Balukas, Laima
  102 Emerson Street
  New Haven, CT.

Bamford, Christopher
  (Lindisfarne Association)
  RFD. 1, Box 421E
  Craryville, N.Y.
Barroll, J. Leeds, III
  (National Endowment for the
    Humanities)
  806 15th Street, N.W.
  Washington, D.C. 20506
Bassler, Jouette M.
  (Yale University)
  277 Davis Street
  Hamden, CT.
Bechtel, Daniel R.
  (Dickinson College)
  Carlisle, PA. 17013
Beckwith, Tom
  (Lindisfarne Association)
  61 W. 37th Street, Apt. 2B
  New York, N.Y. 10018
Belcastro, David
  (University of St. Andrews)
  1536 Meadowlawn Drive
  Macedonia, OH.
Bellet, Paulinus
  (Catholic University of America)
  Washington, D.C. 20064
Bergeron, Richard
  (University of Montreal)
  1181 Dorion Street
  Montreal, P.Q.
  Canada H2K 3Z9
Berman, Lawrence M.
  (Yale University)
  84 Howe Street, 503
  New Haven, CT.
Berry, Donald L.
  (Colgate University)
  Department of Philosophy and Religion
  Hamilton, N.Y. 13346
Bianchi, Ugo (*in absentia*)
  (University of Rome)
  Via Principe Amedeo 75
  00185 Rome
  Italy

Bisbee, Gary A.
(Harvard Divinity School)
Cambridge, MA. 02138
Bishirjian, R. J.
(College of New Rochelle)
87 Barnes Road
Tarrytown, N.Y. 10591
Bloom, Harold
(Yale University)
179 Linden Street
New Haven, CT. 06511
Blumenfeld, Bruno
(Brown University)
P. O. Box 1927
Providence, R.I. 02912
Blumenfeld, Rodica Laelia
(Brown University)
P. O. Box 1927 RS
Providence, R.I. 02912
Böhlig, Alexander
(University of Tubingen)
24 Wolfgang-Stock-Str. 24
Tubingen
West Germany
Böhlig, Gertrude
(University of Tubingen)
24 Wolfgang-Stock-Str. 24
Tubingen
West Germany
Bovon, François
(University of Geneva)
Sous-la-Ville
CH 1261 Genolier
Switzerland
Bram, Jean Rhys
(Hunter College)
4 Prospect Street
Baldwin, N.Y. 11810
Bregman, Jay
(University of Maine)
211 E. Annex
Orono, ME. 04473
Brennan, Virginia
(Yale University)
1685 Yale Station
New Haven, CT. 06520
Bryce, Jackson
(Carleton College)
410 Nevada Street
Northfield, MN. 55057
Buchanan, James
(Yale University)
61 Foster Street
New Haven, CT. 06511

Bursey, Ernest
(Yale University)
386 Prospect Street,
D-8
New Haven, CT. 06511
Cahill, Joseph
(University of Alberta)
10701 University Avenue
Edmonton,
Alberta
Canada
Cameron, Ron
(Harvard University)
4 Carver Street
Cambridge, MA. 02138
Cardman, Francine
(Wesley Theological Seminary)
4520 Sargent Road, N.E.
Washington, D.C. 20017
Cartlidge, David R.
(Maryville College)
Maryville, TN. 37801
Chadwick, Henry
(University of Cambridge)
Magdalene College
Cambridge
England
Chagnon, Lionel
(Laval University)
733, Ave. de l'Alverne
Quebec, P.Q.
Canada
Chandler, Karen
(Brown University)
P. O. Box 1927, Dept. RS
Providence, R.I. 02912
Charet, F. X.
(McGill University)
4316 Melrose
Montreal
Canada
Clark, Elizabeth
(Mary Washington College)
1104 William Street,
Apt. 812
Fredericksburg, VA. 22401
Colpe, Carsten
(Free University of Berlin)
Schuetzallee 112
D-1000 Berlin 37
West Germany
Conroy, J. Peter
(Fordham University)
Bronx, N.Y. 10458

Cummings, Mark
(Yale University)
1928 Chapel Street
New Haven, CT. 06515
Dahl, Nils A.
(Yale University)
38 Broadfield Road
Hamden, CT. 06517
D'Angelo, Mary R.
(Iliff School of Theology)
865 South Corona
Denver, CO. 80204
Darrow, William
(Harvard University)
42 Francis Avenue, No. 11
Cambridge, MA. 02138
de Boer, Martinus C.
(Union Theological Seminary)
99 Claremont Avenue, No. 414
New York, N.Y. 10027
Delp, George J.
(Harvard Divinity School)
21 W. Elm Avenue
Wollaston, MA. 02170
Dewey, Arthur
(Harvard University)
37 Magnolia Street
Malden, MA.
Dillon, John
(University of California, Berkeley)
1584 Leroy Avenue
Berkeley, CA. 94708
Dittes, James E.
(Yale University)
Department of Religious Studies
320 Temple Street
New Haven, CT. 06520
Donovan, Mary Ann
(Jesuit School of Theology)
1735 Leroy Avenue
Berkeley, CA.
Drijvers, Han J. W.
(University of Groningen)
Acacialaan 54
9741 KZ Groningen
Netherlands
Duntley, Stephen P.
(Yale University)
5756 Yale Station
New Haven, CT. 06520
Eames, Charles J.
(Fordham University)
1815 Bay Ridge Parkway
Brooklyn, N.Y. 11204

Ellery, Mary Ann C.
(Catholic University of America)
110 D Street, S.E., Apt. 404
Washington, D.C. 20003
Ellis-Killian, D.
P. O. Box 541
Valley Forge, PA. 19481
Ellwood, Robert S., Jr.
(University of Southern California)
2011 Rose Villa Street
Pasadena, CA. 91107
Emmel, Stephen
(Yale University)
320 Temple Street
New Haven, CT. 06520
Fallon, Francis T.
(University of Kansas)
Department of Religious Studies
Lawrence, KS. 66045
Farmer, Chris
(Cal Tech/Humanities)
P. O. Box 8731
San Marino, CA. 91108
Ferguson, Everett
(Abilene Christian University)
609 E. N. 16th
Abilene, TX. 79601
Filoramo, Giovanni
(University of Turin)
Via Saliceto 10
Torino
Italy
Finch, Henry L.
(Hunter College)
106 Liberty Avenue
New Rochelle, N.Y. 10805
Fineman, Joel
(University of California, Berkeley)
English Department
Berkeley, CA. 94720
Finney, P. C.
(University of Missouri)
Department of History
8001 Natural Bridge Road
St. Louis, MO. 63121
Fiore, Benjamin
(Yale University)
682 Prospect Street
New Haven, CT. 06511
Fitzgerald, John
(Yale University)
307-J Mansfield Street
New Haven, CT. 06511

Fossum, Jarl
(University of Utrecht)
Ridderspoor 11
3434 ED Nieuwegein
Netherlands
Frei, Hans
(Yale University)
Ezra Stiles College
New Haven, CT. 06520
Gager, John A.
(Princeton University)
Department of Religious Studies
Princeton, N.J. 08540
Galbreath, Robert
(University of Wisconsin, Milwaukee)
4217 N. Woodburn Street
Shorewood, WI. 53211
Gallant, Robert
(Yale University)
165 Norton Street
New Haven, CT. 06520
Geanakoplos, Deno
(Yale University)
2 Marion Court
North Haven, CT. 06473
Gero, Stephen
(Brown University)
Department of Religious Studies
Providence, R.I. 02912

Gianotto, Claudio
(University of Turin)
74, Corso Vercelli
10015 Ivrea
Italy
Giebisch, Tina
(Yale University)
12 Lincoln Street
New Haven, CT.

Godron, Gérard
(Centre National de la Recherche
  Scientifique)
14, Ancien Chemin de l'Empereur
92420 Vaucresson (Hauts-de-Seine)
France
Good, Deirdre
(Harvard University)
45 Francis Avenue
Cambridge, MA. 02138
Goodchild, Linda S. B.
(Yale University)
3530 Yale Station
New Haven, CT. 06520

Green, Henry
(University of St. Andrews)
St. Mary's College
St. Andrews, Fife
Scotland KY16 9JU
Green, Tamara M.
(Hunter College)
695 Park Avenue
New York, N.Y. 10021
Greer, Rowan A.
(Yale Divinity School)
409 Prospect Street
New Haven, CT. 06520
Greten, Barbara Jean
(Yale University)
1266 Townsend Avenue
New Haven, CT. 06513
Grewe, Christa
(Yale University)
420 Temple Street, Box 182
New Haven, CT. 06511
Griggs, C. W.
(Brigham Young University)
427 E. 500th, S.
Orem, UT. 84057
Groh, Dennis E.
(Garrett-Evangelical Theological
  Seminary)
715 South Boulevard
Evanston, IL. 60202
Gruenwald, Ithamar
(University of Tel Aviv)
3 Divrei Yerucham Street
Bayit Vagan
Jerusalem
Israel
Gunn, Roland D.
(Villanova University)
RFD 5, Box 423
Blountville, TN. 37617
Guttman, Fred
(Hebrew Union College)
50 W. 72nd Street
New York, N.Y.
Hallo, William
(Yale University)
245 Blake Road
Hamden, CT.
Harl, Marguérite
(University of Paris-Sorbonne)
3, av. Constant Coquelin
75007 Paris
France

Harries, Karsten
(Yale University)
16 Morris Street
Hamden, CT.
Hawthorne, Barbara
(University of California)
Helderman, J.
(University of Amsterdam)
Ampèrestr. 46
1171 BV Badhoevedorp
Netherlands
Helmbold, Andrew
(Tidewater Community College)
3512 Pine Road
Portsmouth, VA. 23703
Hendrix, Holland L.
(Harvard Divinity School)
114 Western Avenue,
No. 3
Cambridge, MA. 02139
Henrichs, Albert
(Harvard University)
144 Longwood Avenue
Brookline, MA.
Herington, John
(Yale University)
68 Morris Street
Hamden, CT.
Higgins, William E.
(Center for Hellenic Studies)
3100 Whitehaven Street, N.W.
Washington, D.C. 20008
Hillmer, Melvyn R.
(McMaster Divinity College)
Hamilton, Ontario
Canada L7T 3V5
Himmelfarb, Martha
(University of Pennsylvania)
4537 Osage Avenue
Philadelphia, PA. 19143
Hogenson, George B.
(Yale University)
111 Park Street,
Apt. 14-O
New Haven, CT. 06511
Holladay, Carl R.
(Yale University)
SDQ 226
New Haven, CT. 06520
Hollar, John A.
(Fortress Press)
2900 Queen Lane
Philadelphia, PA. 19129

Hotchkiss, Robert V.
(Philadelphia Seminar on
Christian Origins)
214 E. Wyoming Avenue
Philadelphia, PA. 19120
Hume, W. Snow
(Yale University)
895 Yale Station
New Haven, CT. 06520
Hutaff, Peggy
(Harvard Divinity School)
137 Oxford Street
Cambridge, MA. 02140
Hutchison, Norman
(Knox Presbyterian Church)
335 Fitch Street
Welland,
Ontario
Canada
Jacobsen, Jorunn
(University of Chicago)
5458 S. Harper
Chicago, IL. 60615
Johnson, Beth
(Yale University)
80 Sherman Avenue,
No. 31
New Haven, CT. 06511
Johnson, Kathryn
(Yale University)
97 Canner Street
New Haven, CT. 06511
Johnson, Luke T.
(Yale Divinity School)
271 Stevenson Road
New Haven, CT. 06515
Jonas, Hans
9 Meadow Lane
New Rochelle, N.Y. 10805
Kaestli, Jean-Daniel
(University of Lausanne)
14, ch. des Fauconnières
1012 Lausanne
Switzerland
Kee, Howard C.
(Boston University)
121 Pinckney Street
Boston, MA. 02114
Kenyon, M. J.
(Yale University)
280 Yale Station
New Haven, CT. 06520

Kimelman, Reuven
 (Brandeis University)
 31 Evans Road
 Brookline, MA. 02164
Kipgen, Kaikhohen
 (University of Oxford)
 1 Telford Court
 Alma Road
 St. Albans, Herts.
 England
Kitchen, Robert A.
 (Springfield College)
 Department of Religion and Philosophy
 Springfield, MA. 01109
Knight, John R.
 (Harvard University)
 RFD 1, Box 218
 Hubbardston, MA. 01452
Koenen, Ludwig
 (University of Michigan)
 1312 Culver
 Ann Arbor, MI. 48103
Koenen, Margret
 1312 Culver
 Ann Arbor, MI. 48103
Koester, Gisela
 (Harvard University)
 12 Flintlock Road
 Lexington, MA. 02173
Koester, Helmut
 (Harvard University)
 12 Flintlock Road
 Lexington, MA. 02173
Kolenkow, Anitra Bingham
 (Graduate Theological Union)
 2435 Virginia
 Berkeley, CA. 94709
Koschorke, Klaus
 (University of Heidelberg)
 Merianstr. 16
 6903 Neckargemund
 West Germany
Kraft, Robert
 (University of Pennsylvania)
 11 Conwell Drive
 Maple Glen, PA. 19002
LaBarge, David E.
 (Yale University)
 100 York Street
 New Haven, CT. 06511
Lagzdins, Lauma
 (Yale University)
 10 Livingston Street, Apt. B2
 New Haven, CT. 06511

Lattke, Michael
 (University of Augsburg)
 24 Kriemhildstr.
 D-8901 Neusaess
 West Germany
Layton, Bentley
 (Yale University)
 Department of Religious Studies
 320 Temple Street
 New Haven, CT. 06520
Lease, Gary
 (University of California, Santa Cruz)
 333 Alamo Avenue
 Santa Cruz, CA. 95060
Levenson, David
 (Florida State University)
 Religion Department
 Tallahassee, FL. 32306
Lewis, Lloyd A.
 (Yale University)
 Department of Religious Studies
 320 Temple Street
 New Haven, CT. 06520
Lewis, LeMoine G.
 (Abilene Christian University)
 902 E. N. 12th
 Abilene, TX. 79601
Litt, John
 (Yale University)
 2267 Yale Station
 New Haven, CT.
Loge, John P., Jr.
 (Independent Study Center)
 112 Livingston Street
 New Haven, CT. 06511
Long, William
 (Brown University)
 72 Rutland Street
 Boston, MA. 02118
Loudon, John
 (Harper & Row)
 10 E. 53rd Street
 New York, N.Y. 10022
Lucas, Jack A.
 (Central Connecticut State College)
 Department of Sociology and
  Anthropology
 New Britain, CT. 06050
Lüdemann, Gerd
 (McMaster University)
 1260 Main Street, W.
 Hamilton, Ontario
 Canada L8J 4K1

Lund, Shirley
(Boston University)
Department of Religion
745 Commonwealth Avenue
Boston, MA. 02215

Lyman, J. Rebecca
(Catholic University of America)
613 Hamlin, N.E., No. 2
Washington, D.C. 20017

McArthur, H. K.
(Hartford Seminary Foundation)
55 Elizabeth Street
Hartford, CT. 06105

McCue, James F.
(University of Iowa)
School of Religion
Iowa City, IO. 52242

MacDermot, Violet
(University College, London)
43 High Street
Ditching, Sussex
England BN6 8SY

McGuire, Anne M.
(Yale University)
36 Derby Avenue
New Haven, CT. 06511

McKnight, Stephen A.
(University of Florida)
419 Little Hall
Gainesville, FL. 32611

MacMullen, Ramsay
(Yale University)
25 Long Hill Road
Clinton, CT.

McNamara, David Alan
56 Prescott Avenue
Bronxville, N.Y.

MacRae, George
(Harvard University)
45 Francis Avenue
Cambridge, MA. 02138

McVey, Elizabeth A.
(Catholic University of America)
4014 Ninth Street, N.E.,
No. 3
Washington, D.C. 20017

McVey, Kathleen
(Dumbarton Oaks)
4447 McPherson
St. Louis, MO. 63108

McWilliams, Linda K.
(Library of Congress)
2603 Ridge Road Drive
Alexandria, VA. 22302

Magliocco, Joseph J.
(Yale University)
4252 Yale Station
New Haven, CT. 06520

Magne, Jean
(College de France, Institut
d'Etudes Sémitiques)
23, rue Lacharrière
75011 Paris
France

Malherbe, Abraham
(Yale University)
71 Spring Garden Street
Hamden, CT.

Mallon, George Barry
(State University of New York
at Buffalo)
128 Pleasant Avenue
Hamburg, N.Y. 14075

Maloney, Scott
(Yale University)
39 Lambert Rd.
New Canaan, CT.

Mansoor, Menahem
(University of Wisconsin)
1225 Sweet Briar
Madison, WI. 53705

Marcovich, Miroslav
(University of Illinois)
2509 Cottage Grove
Urbana, IL. 61801

Martin, Luther H.
(University of Vermont)
Underhill Center, VT. 05490

Martz, Louis
(Yale University)
46 Swarthmore Street
Hamden, CT.

Matter, Ann
(University of Pennsylvania)
Department of Religious Studies
Philadelphia, PA. 19104

Maurer, Dennis M.
(St. Mary's-University of St. Andrews)
1619 St. Anthony Road
Coldwater, OH.

Mayer, Marc
(Yale University)
333 Sherman Avenue
New Haven, CT. 06511

Meeks, Wayne A.
(Yale University)
43 Allene Drive
Hamden, CT.

Méhat, André
(University of Nancy II)
9, chemin du Janicule
78000 Versailles
France
Merdinger, Jane E.
(Yale University)
Jonathan Edwards College
New Haven, CT. 06520
Michaels, J. Ramsey
(Gordon-Conwell Theological Seminary)
14 Daniels Road
Wenham, MA. 01984
Moon, Beverly
(Columbia University)
527 Riverside Drive
Apt. 6H
New York, N.Y. 10027
Moore, Lewis Tanner, Jr.
(Hampshire College)
P. O. Box 225
Sunderland, MA. 01375
Mortley, Raoul
(Macquarie University, Sydney)
School of History
North Ryde
N.S.W. 2113
Australia
Nelson, Edwin S.
(Milligan College)
1809 Oakland
Johnson City, TN.
Newman, Barbara
(Yale University)
790 Orange Street
New Haven, CT. 06511
Nickelsburg, George
(University of Iowa)
1713 E. Court Street
Iowa City, IA. 52242
Noda, Motoko
(Yale University)
406 Prospect Street
New Haven, CT.
O'Cleirigh, Padraig
(McMaster University)
131 James Street, N.
Hamilton,
Ontario
Canada
O'Meara, D. J.
(Catholic University of America)
8 Woodmoor Drive
Silver Spring, MD. 20901

Orlandi, Tito
(University of Rome)
Via Civinini, 24
00197 Rome
Italy
Osiek, Carolyn
(Catholic Theological Union)
5401 S. Cornell
Chicago, IL. 60615
Ozment, Steven
(Yale University)
Timothy Dwight College
New Haven, CT. 06520
Pagels, Elaine
(Barnard College)
27 West 87th Street
New York, N.Y. 10024
Painchaud, Louis
(Laval University)
923 Place Belœil,
No. 7
Sainte-Foy,
P.Q.
Canada
Parrott, Douglas M.
(University of California, Riverside)
Department of Religious Studies
Riverside, CA. 92521
Pearson, Birger A.
The University of California
Scandinavian Study Center of Lund
University
Skomakaregatan 8
223 50 Lund, Sweden
Peel, Malcolm L.
(Coe College)
Box 26,
Hickok Hall
Cedar Rapids, IA. 52402
Pelikan, Jaroslav
(Yale University)
156 Chestnut Lane
Hamden, CT.
Perry, Matthew
(Yale Divinity School)
409 Prospect Street
New Haven, CT. 06510
Pfaff, Susan R.
(Yale University)
1502 Yale Station
New Haven, CT. 06520
Poehlmann, William R.
(St. Olaf College)
Northfield, MN. 55057

Poirier, Paul Hubert
(Laval University)
170 Bld. Montparnasse
75014 Paris
France
Pope, Marvin H.
(Yale University)
250 West Rock Avenue
New Haven, CT.
Post, Stephen
(Unification Theological Seminary)
10 Dock Road
Barrytown, N.Y. 12507
Price, William W.
(Yale University)
388 Whitney Avenue
New Haven, CT. 06511
Prochaska, Harry
(C. G. Jung Institute, San Francisco)
905 Menlo Avenue, No. C
Menlo Park, CA.
Quispel, Gilles
(University of Utrecht)
Noordhoudringelaan 32
Bilthoven
Netherlands
Rensberger, David
(Yale University)
517 Prospect Street, Apt. 1
New Haven, CT. 06511
Rewolinski, Edward T.
(Harvard University)
99 Brattle Street
Cambridge, MA. 02138
Roberts, Janet
(Memorial University of Newfoundland)
Spruce Hill Road
Topsail, Newfoundland
Canada
Robillard, Edmond
(University of Montreal)
2715 Ch. de la Côte Ste. Catherine
Montreal
Canada H3T 1B6
Robinson, James M.
(Institute for Antiquity and Christianity)
Claremont Graduate School
Claremont, CA. 91711
Robinson, Thomas
(Harvard University)
191 Raymond Street
Cambridge, MA. 02140
Robinson, W. C.
(Andover Newton)

210 Herrick Road
Newton, MA. 02159
Rogow, Margarett
(Yale University)
281 Edwards Street, Apt. 5
New Haven, CT. 06511
Rudolph, Kurt (*in absentia*)
(Karl Marx University)
Religionsgeschichtliche Institut
Peterssteinweg 8
701-Leipzig
German Democratic Republic
Ruhter, Cindy Gruhzit
(Catholic University of America)
1603 16th Street, N.W., Apt. 2
Washington, D.C. 20009
Saso, Michael
(University of Hawaii)
656 Apuwai Place
Honolulu, Hawaii 96816
Schenke, Hans-Martin (*in absentia*)
(Humboldt University)
Hans-Beimler Str. 29
102-Berlin
German Democratic Republic
Schoedel, William R.
(University of Illinois)
1207 S. Race
Urbana, IL. 61801
Scholer, David M.
(Gordon-Conwell Theological Seminary)
12 Arlington Avenue
Beverly, MA. 01915
Schwartz, James
(Columbia University)
New York, N.Y.
Scopello, Madeleine
(Faculté de Théologie Protestante)
12, rue P. Janet
67 Strasbourg
France
Scott, Gerry
(Yale University)
3096 Yale Station
New Haven, CT. 06520
Scott, Rachel
(Yale University)
1537 Yale Station
New Haven, CT. 06520
Seal, Welton O., Jr.
(Union Theological Seminary)
527 Riverside Drive-8G
New York, N.Y. 10027

Segal, Alan F.
(University of Toronto)
14337 Roberts Library
Toronto, Ontario
Canada M5S 1A1
Segal, Robert A.
(Reed College)
Religion Department
Portland, OR. 97202
Sellew, Philip
(Harvard Divinity School)
2 Soldiers Field Park, Apt. 409
Boston, MA. 02163
Septimus, Bernard
(Yale University)
173 Ellsworth Avenue
New Haven, CT.
Shapiro, Jane S.
(Columbia University)
60 Haven Avenue
New York, N.Y.
Shephard, Donna M.
(Yale University)
5953 Yale Station
New Haven, CT. 06520
Sieber, John H.
(Luther College)
401 Leif Erikson
Decorah, IA. 52101
Simpson, William K.
(Yale University)
Katonah Woods Road
Katonah, N.Y.
Skwerer, Lory
(Yale Divinity School)
219 Bradley Street
New Haven, CT. 06511
Smith, Dennis E.
(Harvard Divinity School)
72 Broadway, Apt. 1
Arlington, MA. 02174
Smith, James David, III
(Harvard University)
107 Hobart Street
Wollaston, MA. 02170
Smith, Jonathan Z.
(University of Chicago)
5638 S. Blackstone
Chicago, IL. 60637
Smith, Morton
(Columbia University)
Department of History
New York, N.Y. 10027

Smith, Richard
289 Wallis Street
Pasadena, CA. 91106
Smith, Terence Vaughan
(Kings College, London)
19 Saltash Road
Welling, Kent,
England
Snipes, James C.
(Yale Law School)
4468 Yale Station
New Haven, CT. 06520
Soleau, Jeffrey
(Yale University)
42 Waverly Road
Branford, CT.
Spencer, Mary Jo
(C. G. Jung Institute, San Francisco)
901 Cambridge
Menlo Park, CA.
Stead, G. C.
(University of Cambridge)
The Black Hostelry
The College,
Ely, Cambs.
England
Stendahl, Krister
(Harvard Divinity School)
45 Francis Avenue
Cambridge, MA. 02138
Stephens, Joseph J.
(Harvard University)
51 Esmond Street
Boston, MA. 02121
Stephens, Susan
(Yale University)
133 Bishop Street
New Haven, CT.
Stone, M. E.
(Hebrew University)
74 Shmar Yahu Levin
Kiryat Hayyovel
Jerusalem
Israel
Stoops, Robert F., Jr.
(Harvard University)
303-C Holden Green
Cambridge, MA. 02138
Story, G. L.
(Illinois Wesleyan University)
Bloomington, IL. 61701
Stowers, Stan
(Yale University)

375 Canner Street,
No. 1
New Haven, CT. 06511
Stroumsa, G.
    Comparative Religion
    Hebrew University
    Jerusalem
    Israel
Strugnell, John
    (Harvard Divinity School)
    45 Francis Avenue
    Cambridge, MA. 02138
Swogger, John H.
    Burnside
    Reservoir Road
    Hanover, N.H. 03755
Tanner, Kathryn E.
    (Yale University)
    3678 Yale Station
    New Haven, CT. 06520
Tardieu, Michel
    (Ecole Pratique des Hautes Etudes)
    50, rue de Clichy
    75009 Paris
    France
Teeple, Howard M.
    (Religion and Ethics Institute)
    400 Main Street
    Evanston, IL.
Thiel, John
    (Fairfield University)
    167 Bradley Street
    Bridgeport, CT. 06610
Timbie, Janet
    (University of Pennsylvania)
    4622 Bayard Boulevard
    Washington, D.C. 20016
Tobin, Thomas
    (Harvard University)
    6 Sumner Road
    Cambridge, MA. 02138
Valesio, Paolo
    (Yale University)
    Italian Department
    80 Wall Street
    New Haven, CT. 06520
Vallée, G.
    (McMaster University)
    9 Forsyth, S.
    Hamilton, Ontario
    Canada
Van Dooren, Virginia
    (Yale University)

294 Ridgewood Avenue
Hamden, CT. 06517
Van Elderen, Bastiaan
    (Calvin Theological Seminary)
    1225 Bates Street, S.E.
    Grand Rapids, MI. 49506
Virginia, Anne
    (Christ Brotherhood)
    220 W. Manhattan
    Santa Fe, N.M.
Von Staden, Heinrich
    (Yale University)
    Ansonia Road
    Woodbridge, CT.
Walls, A. F.
    (University of Aberdeen)
    Department of Religious Studies
    Aberdeen
    Scotland AB9 2JB
Weber, Michael
    (Yale Divinity School)
    350 Canner Street
    New Haven, CT.
Weisbrod, Carol
    (University of Connecticut)
    100 York Street
    New Haven, CT.
Wells, John
    (Unification Theological Seminary)
    10 Dock Road
    Barrytown, N.Y. 12507
Werblowsky, R. J. Zwi
    (Hebrew University)
    Jerusalem
    Israel
Wesselschmidt, Quentin F.
    (Concordia Seminary, St. Louis)
    801 De Mun Avenue
    St. Louis, MO. 63105
White, L. Michael
    (Yale University)
    80 Cold Spring Street
    New Haven, CT. 06511
Whitehouse, David J. M.
    (Harvard Divinity School)
    6 Soldiers Field Park, Apt. 211
    Boston,
    MA. 02163

Whittaker, John
    (Memorial University of Newfoundland)
    Department of Classics
    St. John's, Newfoundland
    Canada A1C 5S7

Williams, Frank
(University of Texas, El Paso)
1006 Madeline
El Paso, TX. 79902
Williams, Mary E.
(AMC)
581 George Street
New Haven, CT.
Williams, Michael A.
(University of Washington)
School of International Studies
Seattle, WA. 98195
Wilson, Andrew
(Unification Theological Seminary)
10 Dock Road
Barrytown, N.Y. 12507
Wilson, R. McL.
(University of St. Andrews)
St. Mary's College
St. Andrews, Fife
Scotland KY16 9JU
Wilson, Robert R.
(Yale University)
1199 Whitney Avenue
Hamden, CT.
Wilson, Sharyn B.
(Yale University)
1199 Whitney Avenue
Hamden, CT.
Wire, Antoinette
(San Francisco Theological Seminary)
10 Kensington Court
San Anselmo, CA.
Wisse, Frederik
(McMaster University)
Religious Studies Department
1280 Main Street, W.
Hamilton, Ontario
Canada L85 4K1

Wlosok, Antonie
(University of Mainz)
19 E. Brändströmstr.
D-6500 Mainz
West Germany
Wood, Robert E.
(Villanova University)
400 Easton Road,
No. 4
Horsham, PA. 19044
Worley, David
(Yale University)
157 Haverford
Hamden, CT. 06517
Yamauchi, Edwin
(Miami University)
807 Erin Drive
Oxford, OH. 45056
Yarbrough, Larry
(Yale University)
393 Mansfield Street,
Apt. 10
New Haven, CT. 06511
Yohe, Ginny
(Yale University)
4124 Yale Station
New Haven, CT. 06520
Young, Dwight W.
(Brandeis University)
Beacon Hill
Gloucester, MA. 01930
Young, William
(Institut Catholique, Paris)
Box 2342
Davidson, N.C. 28036
Zaremba, Hillel
(Yale University)
19 Compton Street
New Haven, CT. 06511

INDEXES TO VOLUMES 1 AND 2

NOTE: n = footnote(s). Pseudonymous works are filed under the supposed author; e.g., for Pseudo-Justin, *see* Justin. Mandaean, Samaritan, and most Manichaean works are under Mandaean, Samaritan, and Manichaean. The index of modern scholars is selective, being mostly limited to author entries and substantive discussion of views. The indexes were prepared with the assistance of John Fitzgerald.

I. ANCIENT TEXTS AND AUTHORS

A. OLD TESTAMENT (WITHOUT APOCRYPHA)

B. APOCRYPHA AND PSEUDEPIGRAPHA OF THE OLD TESTAMENT

C. NEW TESTAMENT

D. DEAD SEA SCROLLS AND RABBINICA

E. Vedic Literature

F. Coptic Gnostic Library

G. OTHER ANCIENT TEXTS AND AUTHORS

II. MODERN SCHOLARS

Benjamin, W., 71, 72
Benoît, A., 155n, 165n
Bergson, H., 27
Berliner Arbeitskreis für koptisch-gnostische Schriften, 654
Bertrand, D.A., 394n
Betz, H.D., 255n
Betz, O., 641
Bianchi, U., 36n, 74, 103-111, 115-117, 328n, 332, 796, 801
Bignone, E., 367n
Bloch, E., 45
Bloom, H., 57-72
Böhlig, A., 476n, 501, 504-514, 538, 540, 552-562, 578-587, 590, 594n, 607, 617-642, 662-685, 697n
Bolgiani, F., 428n
Bollack, J., 37n
Bonner, C., 439, 451n
Boullan, J.-A., 5
Bousset, W., 494n
Bouyer, L., 432
Bovon, F., xiv
Bowman, J., 593
Boyancé, P., 81n, 108n
Brashler, J., 274n
Brisson, L., 365n
Bruun, P., 440n
Buchheit, V., 445n
Bullard, R.A., 702
Bultmann, R., 53, 239n, 244n
Buresch, K., 187n
Bursey, E., 456, 504n

Cameron, A., 187n
Campanella, T., 45
Carcopino, J., 443n, 445n, 447n, 449n
Cardona, G.R., 469
Casey, R.P., 435n
Cassirer, E., 27, 35
Cecchelli, C., 442n, 449n
Chadwick, H., 3-16, 6n, 435n, 504-514, 552-562, 578-587, 634-642, 662-685
Cherniss, H., 366n, 367n
Chiflet, J., 442n
Cilento, V., 376n
Colpe, C., 32-56, 390n, 504-514, 540-562, 578-587, 634-642, 655, 659, 662-685
Conzelmann, H., 240n, 241n
Couchond, P.-L., 449n
Cumont, F., 195

Dacqué, E., 34, 52, 53

Dahl, N.A., 689-712
Daniélou, J., 83n, 181n, 440n
Datta, Narendra Nath (Vivekananda), 42
Delbrueck, R., 441n
Des Places, E., 232
Deussen, P., 42
Dibelius, O., 406n
Dietrich, A., 21
Dillon, J., 357-364
Dittes, J.E., xv
Dölger, F.J., 437n, 449n
Dörrie, H., 368n
Donovan, M.A., xiv
Doresse, J., 17, 18, 441n, 475, 563n, 570n, 605n, 613n, 620n, 634
Drijvers, H.J.W., xv, 641, 797
Drioton, E., 18
Drower, E.S., 435n

Ebreo, L., 27
Eddy, S.K., 552
Effe, B., 366n
Eitrem, S., 451n
Eliade, M., 45
Ellwood, R.S., Jr., xv
Elsas, C., 372n, 613, 614

Fallon, F.T., xiv
Fauth, W., 453n, 510
Faye, E. de, 75, 95, 99
Ferrua, A., 439n, 442n
Festugière, A.J., 79n, 195, 219
Février, P.-A., 443n
Ficino, M., xi
Fineman, J., 74, 95-102, 111-115, 128-132, 141-145, 171-175, 189-193, 232-237, 256-261, 289-312
Finney, P.C., 434-454
Fletcher, A., 65
Fludd, R., 28
Förster, W., 82, 175
Fossum, J., xvi, 702n
Frazer, J.G., 38
Frei, H.W., xvii
Frend, W.H.C., 266n, 271n
Freud, S., 26, 63, 289-318 passim
Frey, J.B., 467n
Furley, S.J., 369n

Gaffron, H.G., 435n
Gager, J., xiii
Galbreath, R., xvi
Garrucci, R.P., 434n, 439n